M000095948

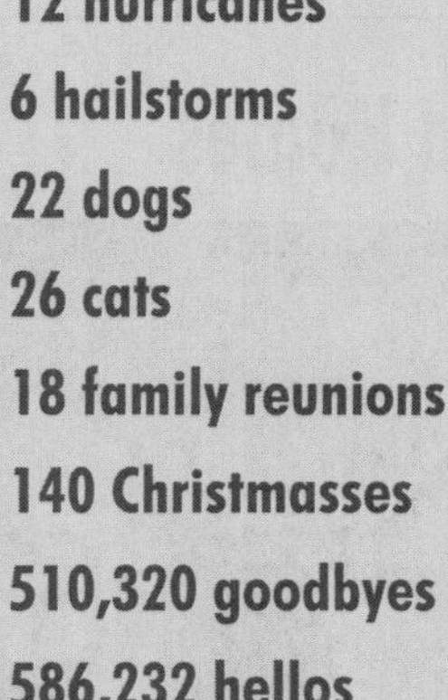

Contents

Featured Homes

Plan L-363-MSB page 11

Plan HDS-99-179 page 94

Sections

Home-Plan Chapters

Ordering Your Plans

The Family Handyman® magazine and Homestore™ Plans and Publications are pleased to join together to bring you this outstanding collection of home designs. Through our combined efforts, we have compiled the finest work from 35 of North America's leading home-design firms.

This issue features our top one-story designs, in chapters highlighting some of today's most popular living spaces, to make it easy to find the home that meets your needs.

With an inventory of thousands of plans, Homestore Plans and Publications has supplied blueprints for more than 250,000 new homes. We look forward to helping you find your dream home.

On the Cover

Plan E-2004 page 207

MAIN FLOOR

All photos on this page and on the cover are by Mark Englund/Homestore™ Plans and Publications.

Handyman **HomePlans**

Publisher
Jim Schiekofer
The Family Handyman®

Editor
Eric Englund
Homestore™
Plans and Publications

Marketing Manager
Andrea Vecchio
The Family Handyman

Production Manager
Judy Rodriguez
The Family Handyman

Production Associate
Lynn Colbjornsen
Homestore
Plans and Publications

Graphic Designer
Jeff Harrison
Homestore
Plans and Publications

The homes pictured here and on the cover may have been modified by the homeowners. Please refer to the floor plan and/or the drawn elevation for actual blueprint details.

Angled Solar Design

- This passive-solar design with a six-sided core is angled to capture as much sunlight as possible.
- Finished in natural vertical cedar planks and stone veneer, this contemporary three-bedroom requires a minimum of maintenance.
- Double doors at the entry open into the spacious living and dining areas.
- The formal area features a domed ceiling with skylights, a freestanding fireplace and three sets of sliding glass doors. The central sliding doors lead to a glass-enclosed sun room.
- The bright eat-in kitchen merges with the den, where sliding glass doors lead to one of three backyard terraces.
- The master bedroom, in the quiet sleeping wing, boasts ample closets, a private terrace and a luxurious bath, complete with a whirlpool tub.
- The two secondary bedrooms share a convenient hall bath.

Plan K-534-L

Bedrooms: 3	**Baths:** 2
Living Area:	
Main floor	1,647 sq. ft.
Sun room	109 sq. ft.
Total Living Area:	**1,756 sq. ft.**
Standard basement	1,505 sq. ft.
Garage and storage	417 sq. ft.
Exterior Wall Framing:	2x4 or 2x6
Foundation Options:	
Standard basement	
Slab	

(All plans can be built with your choice of foundation and framing. A generic conversion diagram is available. See order form.)

BLUEPRINT PRICE CODE: B

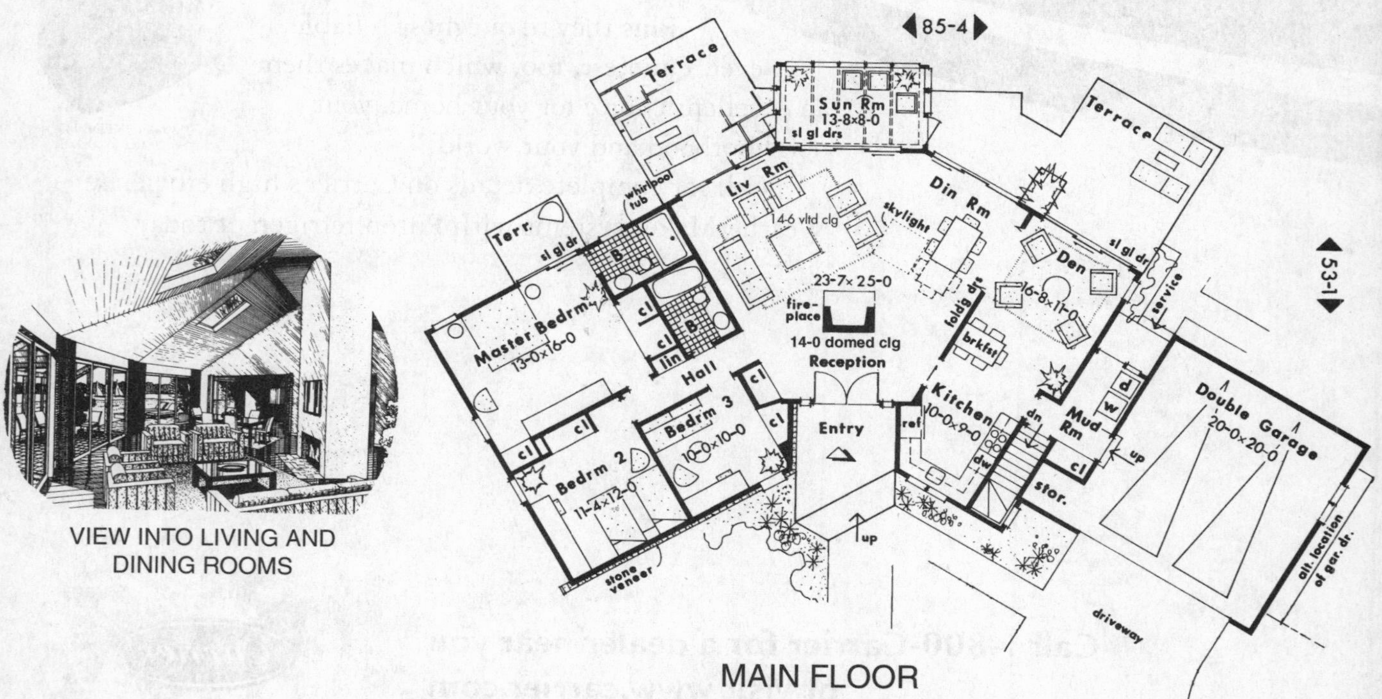

VIEW INTO LIVING AND DINING ROOMS

MAIN FLOOR

Plan K-534-L

SEE ORDER INFO ON PAGES 12-15

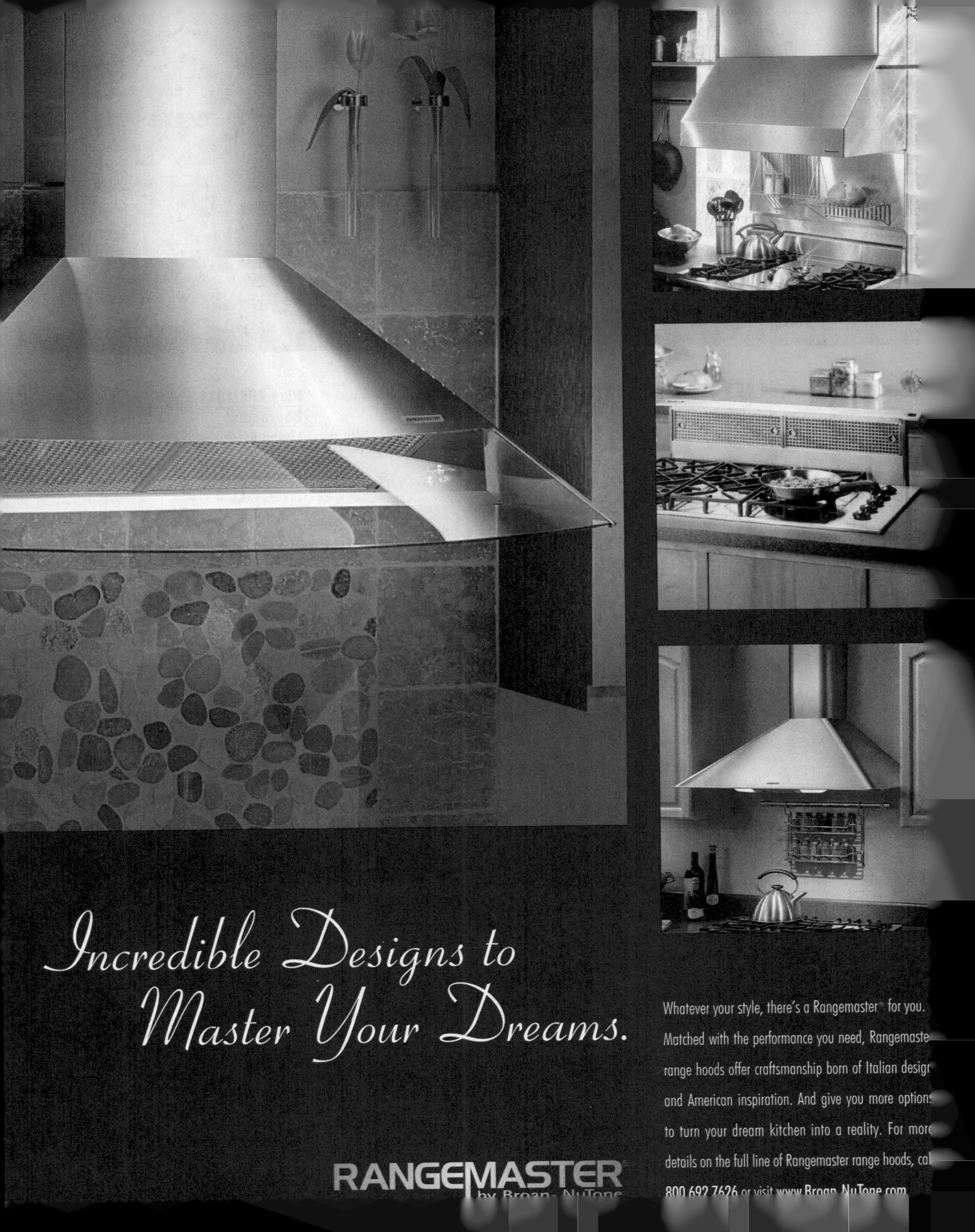

Incredible Designs to
Master Your Dreams.

Classic Combo

- This snappy home combines classic touches with thoughtful design.
- Eye-catching arches frame the front porch. Inside, you'll be stunned by the expansive family room, where a vaulted ceiling and a majestic fireplace enhance the space.
- Double doors lead into the living room, where a vaulted ceiling and a Palladian window create an ideal spot for entertaining visitors.
- Through a graceful archway, the efficient kitchen includes a handy pantry and a serving bar overlooking the bayed breakfast nook.
- A screened porch with a vaulted ceiling opens to a deck for alfresco meals and relaxation.
- The dining room showcases a pair of tall windows and a tray ceiling.
- In the master suite, a vaulted ceiling, a separate sitting area, a lavish private bath and access to the deck create a wonderful retreat.
- Two more bedrooms share a bath on the other side of the home.
- The blueprints offer the choice of a two- or three-car garage.

Plan APS-1911

Bedrooms: 3	**Baths:** 2½
Living Area:	
Main floor	1,992 sq. ft.
Total Living Area:	**1,992 sq. ft.**
Screened porch	192 sq. ft.
Standard basement	1,992 sq. ft.
Garage	649 sq. ft.
Exterior Wall Framing:	2x4

Foundation Options:
Standard basement
Crawlspace
Slab
(All plans can be built with your choice of foundation and framing. A generic conversion diagram is available. See order form.)

BLUEPRINT PRICE CODE: B

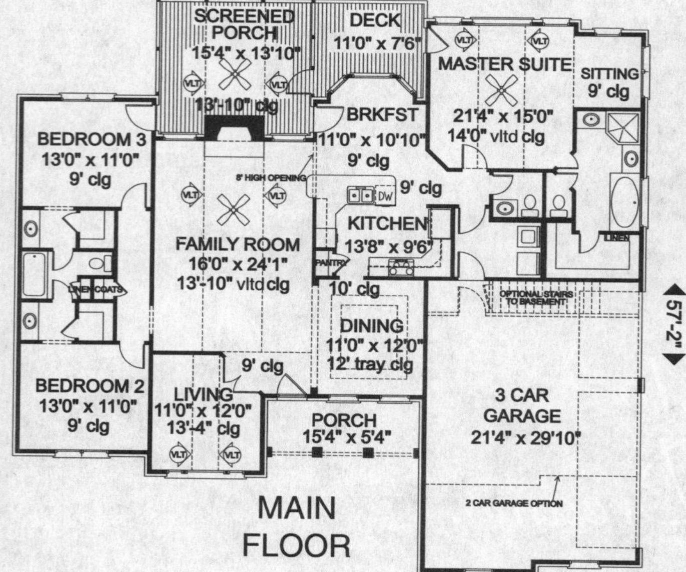

MAIN FLOOR

REAR VIEW

VIEW INTO FAMILY ROOM

ORDER BLUEPRINTS ANYTIME! CALL TOLL-FREE 1-800-820-1296

Plan APS-1911

Plan copyright held by home designer/architect

SEE ORDER INFO ON PAGES 12-15 familyhandyman.com/homeplans

Versatile Sun Room

- This cozy country-style home offers an inviting front porch and an interior just as welcoming.
- The spacious living room features a warming fireplace and windows that overlook the porch.
- The living room opens to a dining area, where French doors access a covered porch and a sunny patio.
- The island kitchen has a sink view, plenty of counter space, and a handy pass-through to the adjoining sun room. The bright sun room is large enough to serve as a formal dining room, a family room or a hobby room.
- The private master suite is secluded to the rear. A garden spa tub, dual walk-in closets and separate dressing areas are nice features found in the master bath.

Plan J-90014	
Bedrooms: 3	**Baths:** 2½
Living Area:	
Main floor	2,190 sq. ft.
Total Living Area:	**2,190 sq. ft.**
Standard basement	2,190 sq. ft.
Garage	465 sq. ft.
Storage	34 sq. ft.
Exterior Wall Framing:	2x6
Foundation Options:	
Standard basement	
Crawlspace	
Slab	

(All plans can be built with your choice of foundation and framing. A generic conversion diagram is available. See order form.)

BLUEPRINT PRICE CODE:	**C**

VIEW INTO KITCHEN AND LIVING ROOM

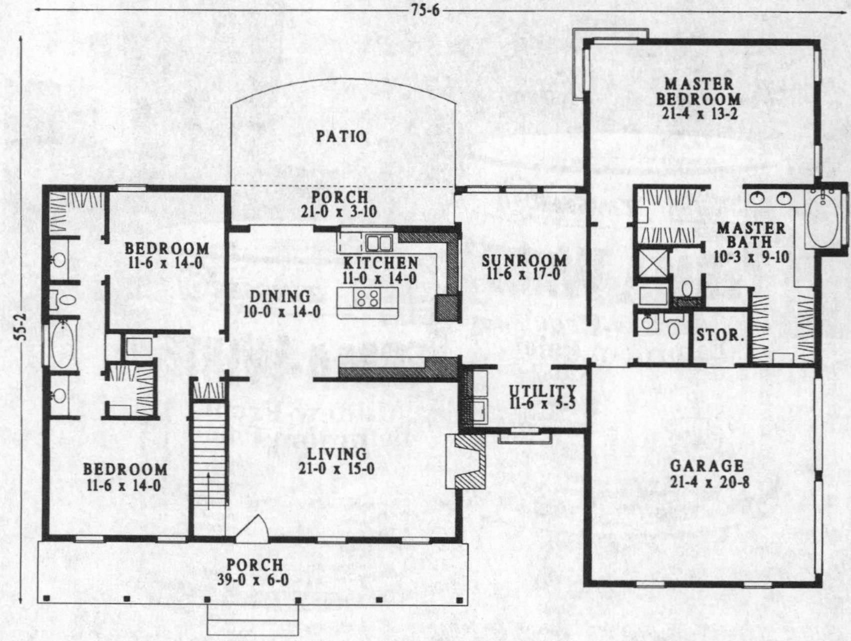

MAIN FLOOR

Grip-Rite® Hand Drive Fasteners ▪ Grip-Rite® Collated Fasteners ▪ Grip-Rite® PrimeGuard Plus™

Use anything else, and you've got a screw loose.

For the most demanding outdoor conditions, PrimeGuard Plus fasteners hold everything together – from fences and gazebos to spas and decks.

When you use woods like cedar and redwood to weather tough conditions, make sure your fasteners are also up to the task. Always use PrimeGuard Plus.

Because all PrimeGuard Plus fasteners are built to last, everything you build will also stand the tests of time.

And that's because nothing is more reliable than Grip-Rite® PrimeGuard Plus™ premium exterior fasteners. With PrimeGuard Plus aluminum, stainless steel, and coated fasteners, when it rains — well, it just doesn't matter. And with a lifetime guarantee against rust and corrosion, why trust anything else? For your nearest Grip-Rite dealer, call **1-800-676-7777** today.

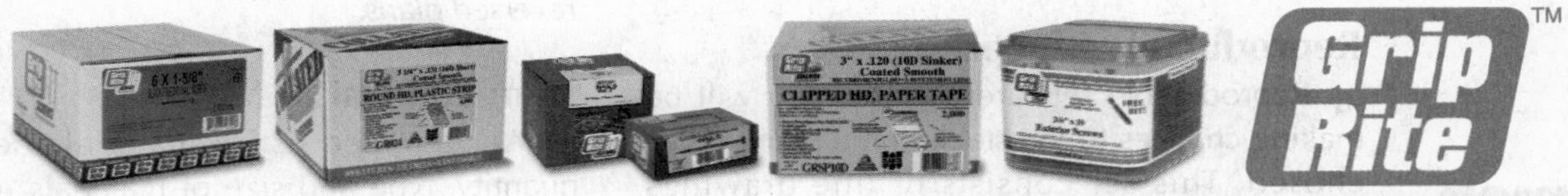

Grip Rite™

Built better so that you can build better.

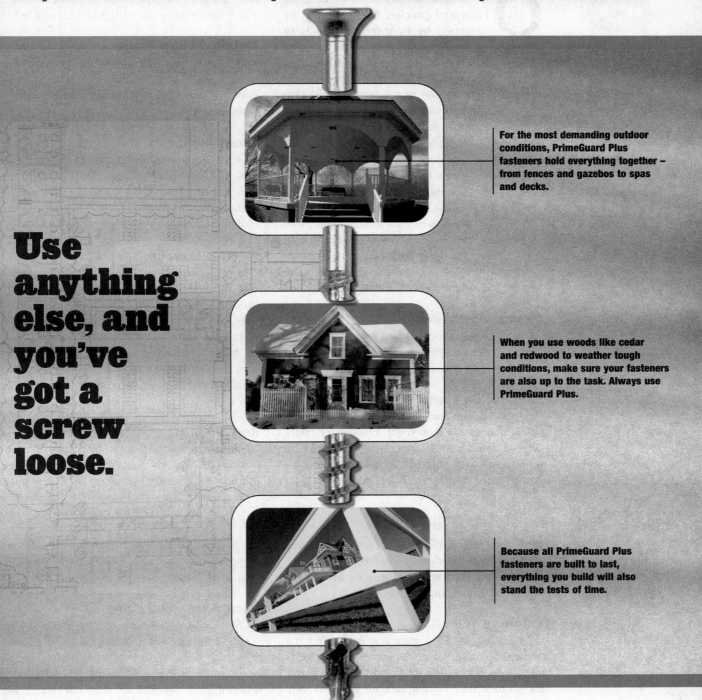

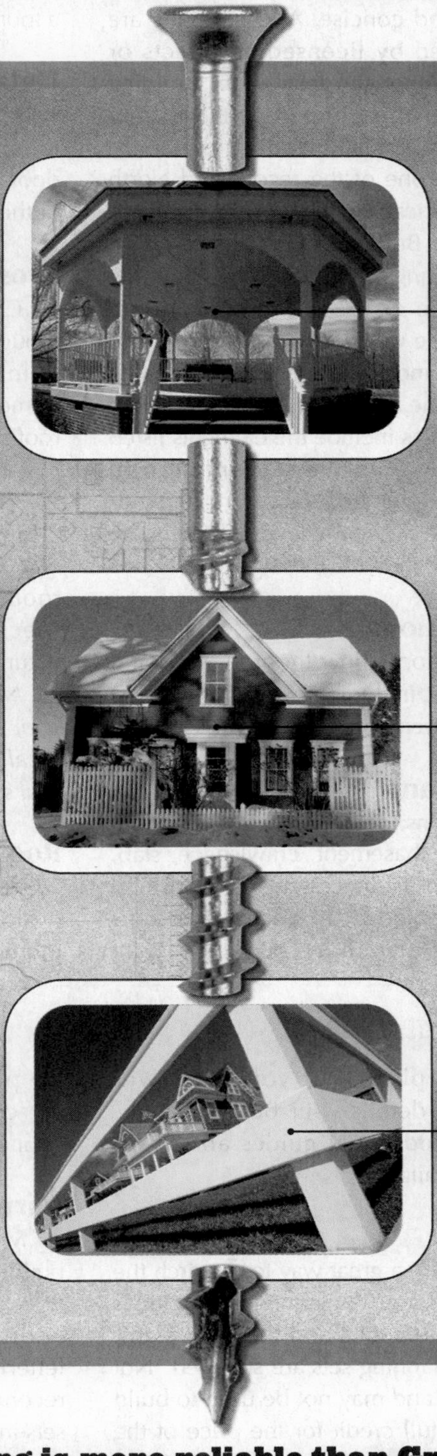

The Package

what our plans include

Our construction blueprints are detailed, clear and concise. All blueprints are designed by licensed architects or members of the American Institute of Building Design (AIBD) or the Council of Publishing Home Designers (CPHD), and all plans are designed to meet one of the recognized North American building codes (the Uniform Building Code, the Standard Building Code, the Basic Building Code or the National Building Code of Canada) in effect at the time and place they are drawn.

The blueprints for most home designs include the elements listed below, but the presentation of these elements may vary depending on the size and complexity of the home and the style of the individual designer.

Exterior Elevations

Exterior elevations show the front, rear and sides of the house, including exterior materials, details and measurements.

Foundation Plans

Foundation plans include drawings for a full, daylight or partial basement, crawlspace, slab, or pole foundation. All necessary notations and dimensions are included. (Foundation options will vary for each plan. If the home you want does not have the type of foundation you desire, a foundation conversion diagram is available.)

Detailed Floor Plans

Detailed floor plans show the placement of interior walls and the dimensions for rooms, doors, windows, stairways, etc., of each level of the house.

Cross Sections

Cross sections show details of the house as though it were cut in slices from the roof to the foundation. The cross sections specify the home's construction, insulation, flooring and roofing details.

Interior Elevations

Interior elevations show the specific details of cabinets (kitchen, bathroom and utility room), fireplaces, built-in units, and other special interior features, depending on the nature and complexity of the item.

Note: To save money and to accommodate your own style and taste, we suggest contacting local cabinet and fireplace distributors for sizes and styles.

Roof Details

Roof details show slope, pitch and location of dormers, gables and other roof elements, including clerestory windows and skylights.

Other Helpful Building Aids

Every set of plans that you order will contain the details your builder needs. However, additional guides and information are also available:

Planning Sets

Planning sets are a great way to research the home that interests you. A planning set includes all four exterior elevations and the floor plans, shown to scale. Planning sets are stamped "Not for Construction," and may not be used to build a home. Receive full credit for the price of the planning set when you purchase a 5-, 9- or reproducible-set package of blueprints for that home within 60 days of your planning set purchase. See the chart on page 14 to see if a planning set is available for your design.

Reproducible Blueprint Set

Reproducible sets are useful if you will be making changes to the stock home plan you've chosen. This set consists of line drawings produced on erasable, reproducible paper for the purpose of modification. When alterations are complete, working copies can be made.
*Bonus: Includes free working set

Mirror-Reversed Plans

Mirror-reversed plans are used when building the home in reverse of the illustrated floor plan. Reversed plans are available for an additional one-time surcharge. Since the lettering and dimensions read backward, we recommend ordering only one or two reversed sets in addition to the regular-reading sets.

Note: Full-reverse blueprints are available for a limited number of plans. Because lettering and dimensions read normally, all sets in your order will be reversed if your plan is available in full reverse. There is a $50 one-time surcharge for all reversed plans.

Itemized List of Materials

An itemized list of materials details the quantity, type and size of materials needed to build your home. This list is helpful in acquiring

These details may be shown on the elevation sheet or on a separate diagram.

Note: If trusses are used, we suggest using a local truss manufacturer to design your trusses to comply with local codes and regulations.

Electrical Layouts

Schematic electrical layouts show the suggested locations for switches, fixtures and outlets. These details may be shown on the floor plan or on a separate diagram.

General Specifications

General specifications provide general instructions and information regarding structure, excavating and grading, masonry and concrete work, carpentry and wood, thermal and moisture protection, and specifications about drywall, tile, flooring, glazing, caulking and sealants.

Note: Due to regional variations, local availability of materials, local codes, methods of installation, and individual preferences, it is impossible to include much detail on heating, plumbing and electrical work on your plans. The duct work, venting and other details will vary depending on the type of heating and cooling system (forced air, hot water, electric, solar) and the type of energy (gas, oil, electricity, solar) that you use. These details and specifications are easily obtained from your builder, contractor and/or local suppliers.

an accurate construction estimate. An expanded material workbook is available for some plans. Call for details.

Description of Materials

A description of materials may be required by your bank in order to secure a loan through the Federal Housing Administration or the Department of Veterans Affairs. The list specifies the minimum grade of building materials required to meet FHA or VA standards.

Generic "How-To" Diagrams

Plumbing, wiring, solar heating, and framing and foundation conversion diagrams are available. These diagrams detail the basic tools and techniques needed to plumb; wire; install a solar-heating system; convert plans with 2x4 exterior walls to 2x6 (or vice versa); or adapt a plan for a basement, crawlspace or slab foundation.

Note: These diagrams are general and not specific to any one plan.

Ordering Information

read before you buy

Blueprint Prices

Our pricing schedule is based on total heated living space. Garages, porches, decks and unfinished basements are not included in the total square footage.

Architectural and Engineering Seals

The increased concern over energy costs and safety has prompted many cities and states to require an architect or engineer to review and "seal" a blueprint prior to construction. There may be a fee for this service. Contact your local lumberyard, municipal building department, builders association, or local chapter of the AIBD or the American Institute of Architects (AIA).

Note: Plans for homes to be built in Nevada, Delaware, New Jersey or New York may have to be re-drawn and sealed by a design professional licensed in the state in which they are to be built.

Foundation Options and Exterior Construction

Depending on your location and climate, your home will normally be built with a slab, crawlspace or basement foundation; the exterior walls will usually be of 2x4 or 2x6 framing. Most professional contractors and builders can easily adapt a home to meet the foundation and exterior wall requirements that you desire.

If the home you select does not offer your preferred type of foundation or exterior walls, you may wish to purchase a generic foundation and framing conversion diagram.

Note: These diagrams are not specific to any one plan.

Exchange Information

We want you to be happy with your home plans. If, for some reason, the blueprints that you ordered cannot be used, we will be pleased to exchange them within 30 days of the purchase date. A handling fee will be assessed for all exchanges. For more information, call toll-free.

Note: Reproducible sets may not be exchanged for any reason.

Estimating Building Costs

Building costs vary widely with the style and size of the home, the finishing materials you select and the local rates for labor and materials. A local average cost per square foot can give you a rough estimate. Contact a local contractor, your state or local builders association, the National Association of Home Builders (NAHB), or the AIBD. A more accurate estimate will require a professional review of the working blueprints and the materials you will be using.

How Many Blueprints Do You Need?

A single planning set is sufficient to study and review a home in greater detail (see page 12). However, to get cost estimates or to build, you will need at least four sets (see the checklist on page 15). If you plan to modify your home plan, we recommend ordering a reproducible set.

Customization and Modifications

The designers at Homestore™ Plans & Publications Design Services can make your dream home uniquely yours. They'll customize virtually any plan to better suit your budget, lifestyle and design preferences.

Call toll-free 1-888-266-3439 or e-mail customize@homeplans.com describing the changes you'd like. Tell us the state in which you are building and the foundation type and exterior wall framing you desire. Be sure to include a daytime phone number so our consultants can reach you with any questions they may have. A Design Services associate will prepare an estimate for the cost and turnaround time of customizing your plan—FREE! Then, with your approval, Design Services will go to work and make that plan uniquely yours.

Compliance with Codes

Every state, county and municipality has its own codes, zoning requirements, ordinances and building regulations. Modifications may be needed to comply with your specific requirements—snow loads, energy codes, seismic zones, etc. All of our plans are designed to meet the specifications of seismic zones I or II. We authorize the use of our blueprints expressly conditioned upon your obligation and agreement to strictly comply with all local building codes, ordinances, regulations and requirements, including permits and inspections at the time of construction.

License Agreement and Copyright

When you purchase a blueprint or reproducible set, we grant you a license to use it to construct a single unit. Our plans are protected under the Federal Copyright Act, Title XVII of the United States Code and Chapter 37 of the Code of Federal Regulations. Each designer retains title and ownership of the original documents. The blueprints licensed to you may not be resold to or used by any other person, copied or reproduced by any means. When you purchase a reproducible set, you reserve the right to modify and reproduce the plan. Reproducible sets may not be resold or used by any other person. For more details, see page 16.

Order Form

three ways to order

1.
Call toll-free anytime: 1-800-820-1296.

2.
Fax order form to (651) 602-5002.

3.
Mail your order to the address at the bottom of the form.

AVAILABILITY

plan prefix	planning set	reproducible set	itemized list of materials	description of materials	next-day delivery
AHP	●	●	●	●	●
APS	●	●	C		●
AX	C	●	C		●
B	●	●	C		●
BOD		●	C		●
BRF	●	●			●
C	●	●	●		●
CHD		●			●
CHP	●	●			●
DBI		●	●		●
DD	●	●	C		●
DHI	●	●			●
DP	C	●			●
DW	●	●	●		●
E	C	●	C		●
EOF		●	C		●
HDC	●	●			●
HDS	●	●	C		●
HFL	C	●	●		●
HOM	●	●	●		●
J	●	●	C		●
K	●	●	●	●	●
KD	●	●			●
KLF	●	●			●
L	●	●	C		●
LS	●	●			●
NW	●	●	C		●
P	●		●	●	●
PH	●	●	●	●	●
PI	●	●			●
PSC	●	●			●
RD	●	●			●
S	●	●	C		●
SDG	●	●			●
SUN	●	●	●		●
TS	●	●			●
UD		●	C		●
VL		●	●	●	●

Legend

● Available
C Call for availability.

PRICING

Blueprints & Accessories

Price Code	Planning Set	5 Sets	9 Sets	Additional Sets*	Reproducible Set**
AAA	$99	$369	$449	$25	$533
AA	$99	$413	$493	$25	$578
A	$99	$462	$542	$25	$649
B	$99	$506	$586	$25	$693
C	$99	$550	$630	$25	$737
D	$99	$649	$729	$25	$776
E	$99	$710	$790	$25	$891
F	$99	$754	$834	$25	$942
G	$99	$803	$883	$25	$996
H	$99	$847	$927	$25	$1,046
I	$99	$898	$978	$25	$1,085

Prices subject to change

*When purchased together with a minimum 5-set order. Additional sets purchased within 12 months of original order are $50 each; limit of 4. **Printed on erasable vellum to allow modification. Includes one free blueprint. See p. 14 for availability.

Itemized List of Materials

Price Code	1 Set*	Price Code	1 Set*	Price Code	1 Set*
AAA	$60	C	$65	G	$75
AA	$60	D	$65	H	$75
A	$60	E	$70	I	$80
B	$60	F	$70		

See page 14 for availability. *Additional sets are available for $15 each.

Generic How-To Diagrams

Quantity	Any 1	All 4
Price	$20	$50

Shipping & Handling

	Planning Set	Reproducible Set	5 Sets	6+ Sets
U.S. Next Day* (1 WORKING DAY*)	$19.95	$45.00	$47.50	$50.00
U.S. Express (2-3 WORKING DAYS)	$14.95	$30.00	$32.50	$35.00
U.S. Regular (5-7 WORKING DAYS)	$9.95	$15.00	$17.50	$20.00
Canada Express (2-4 WORKING DAYS)	$34.95	$50.00	$55.00	$60.00
Canada Regular (5-7 WORKING DAYS)	$24.95	$35.00	$40.00	$45.00
International (7-10 WORKING DAYS)	$49.95	$60.00	$70.00	$80.00

*Order before noon Central Time for next-day delivery to most locations.

BLUEPRINT CHECKLIST

_____ YOUR SETS *(We suggest 2-3)*

_____ GENERAL CONTRACTOR *(We suggest 2)*

_____ PLUMBING CONTRACTOR *(We suggest 1)*

_____ ELECTRICAL CONTRACTOR *(We suggest 1)*

_____ HEATING CONTRACTOR *(We suggest 1)*

_____ COLLECTING BIDS *(We suggest 2-4)*

_____ LOCAL BUILDING DEPT. *(We suggest 1)*

_____ LENDER *(We suggest 1)*

_____ TOTAL NUMBER OF SETS

BLUEPRINT ORDER FORM

Your Order

Plan Number: FHTR174-__________ **Price Code:** __________

Foundation: __________

(Carefully review the foundation option(s) available for your plan—basement, crawlspace, pole, pier or slab. If several options are offered, choose only one.)

Blueprints

❑ **Planning Set** See page 14 for availability. Recommended for review/study. Stamped "Not for Construction." $ ______ (see left)

❑ **Minimum Order: 5-Set Package** $ ______ (see left)

❑ **9-Set Package (Best Value)** $ ______ (see left)

❑ **Additional Sets** QTY: ______ Consult the **BLUEPRINT CHECKLIST** at left to calculate your needs. Available on all plans. With 5-set or 9-set order only. $ ______ (see left)

❑ **Reproducible Set** See page 14 for availability. Recommended for construction/modification. Includes one free blueprint.

Reversed Sets

QTY: ______ $ ______ ($50 surcharge)

If you wish your home to be the mirror image of the illustrated floor plan, please specify how many of your sets should be reversed. (Because the lettering on reversed plans reads backward, we recommend reversing only one or two of your sets.) There is a $50 one-time charge for any number of reversed sets.

Itemized List of Materials

QTY: ______ $ ______ (see left)

See pricing at left. See page 14 for availability.

Description of Materials

$ ______ ($60 for set of two)

Sold only in sets of two for $60. See page 14 for availability.

Generic How-To Diagrams

$ ______ (see left)

General guides on plumbing, wiring and solar heating, plus information on how to convert from one foundation or exterior framing to another. See pricing at left.

Note: These diagrams are not specific to any one plan.

❑ PLUMBING ❑ WIRING ❑ SOLAR HEATING ❑ FRAMING & FOUNDATION CONVERSION

Order Total

Subtotal $ ______

Sales Tax $ ______

All U.S. residents add appropriate sales tax.
Attention Canadian customers: All sales are final, FOB St. Paul, Minnesota.

Shipping/Handling $ ______

See chart at left.

Total $ ______

Payment Information

❑ CHECK OR MONEY ORDER ENCLOSED (IN U.S. FUNDS)
❑ VISA ❑ MASTERCARD ❑ AMEX ❑ DISCOVER

CARD NUMBER __________ EXP. DATE ______

NAME __________

ADDRESS __________

CITY __________ STATE ______ COUNTRY ______

ZIP CODE __________ DAYTIME PHONE (______) ______

❑ CHECK HERE IF YOU ARE A BUILDER HOME PHONE (______) ______

MAIL TO Homestore, Dept. FHTR174
P.O. Box 75488
St. Paul, MN 55175-0488

OR FAX TO (651) 602-5002

SOURCE CODE: FHTR174

Copyright

Just like books, movies and songs, our plans are copyrighted. Federal copyright laws protect the intellectual property of architects and home designers. These laws allow for statutory penalties of up to $100,000 per incident, plus legal fees and actual damages, for copyright infringement involving any of the plans found in this publication or on our Web site. These laws stipulate the following:

Construction blueprints may not be duplicated.

If additional sets are required, they may be purchased at a nominal cost. With the purchase of a reproducible set, a license and copyright release are also provided, allowing you to make up to 12 copies of the design. But these copies may only be used for the construction of a single home.

Blueprints may be used for the construction of only one house.

For the construction of more than one unit, it is necessary to obtain an additional release or multiple licenses from the publisher, architect or designer.

You may not copy or adapt home designs found in any plan book, on a CD-ROM or on the Internet.

Creating your own plan by copying even part of a home design is called creating a derivative work and is illegal without permission from the original designer.

Ignorance of the law is not a valid defense! To avoid legal complications and damages, it is critical that you be certain of the original plan source and refuse to be a party to any copying or borrowing of designs.

Delightful!

- A curved porch in the front and a garden sun room in the back make this home an all-seasons delight.
- Inside, the roomy kitchen is open to a five-sided, glassed-in dining room that overlooks the front porch.
- The living room features a fireplace nestled into a radiant glass wall that adjoins the bright garden room.
- Wrapped in windows, the garden room accesses the backyard as well as a storage area in the side-entry garage.
- Versatile future space above the kitchen and living room gives your family room to grow—add another bedroom or two, an office or a cool home theater.

Plan DD-1852	
Bedrooms: 3+	**Baths:** 2
Living Area:	
Main floor	1,680 sq. ft.
Garden room	240 sq. ft.
Total Living Area:	**1,920 sq. ft.**
Future area	316 sq. ft.
Attic	309 sq. ft.
Standard basement	1,680 sq. ft.
Garage and storage	570 sq. ft.
Exterior Wall Framing:	2x4
Foundation Options:	
Standard basement	
Crawlspace	
Slab	

(All plans can be built with your choice of foundation and framing. A generic conversion diagram is available. See order form.)

BLUEPRINT PRICE CODE: **B**

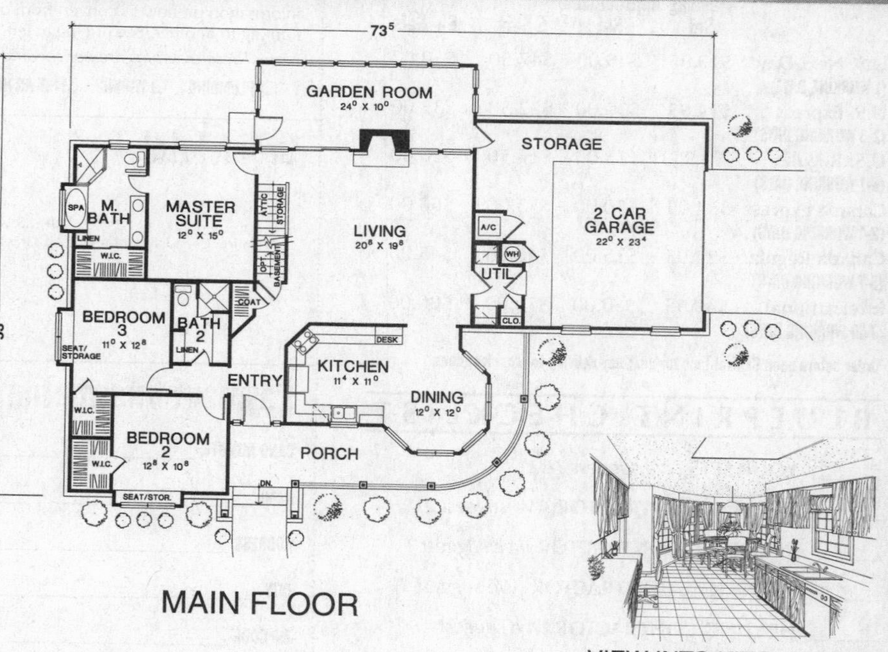

MAIN FLOOR

VIEW INTO KITCHEN AND DINING ROOM

Plan DD-1852

Plan copyright held by home designer/architect

Here and Now

- This country home's mammoth upper-floor future area can flex to meet your coming needs, but the main-floor amenities are fit to suit your lifestyle right here, right now.
- A cozy porch fronts the home, promising hours of relaxation.
- The bright Great Room boasts a media unit, a fireplace, a wet bar and French doors to a lovely screened porch.
- Guests in the formal dining room will enjoy looking out on the front yard through a wide bay window.
- The master bedroom features a bay window in the sleeping chamber, plus a long walk-in closet and a private bath with an oversized tub, a separate shower and a dual-sink vanity.
- Another bay window enhances one of the two secondary bedrooms.

Plan AX-00306

Bedrooms: 3+	**Baths:** 2
Living Area:	
Main floor	1,595 sq. ft.
Total Living Area:	**1,595 sq. ft.**
Future upper floor	813 sq. ft.
Screened porch	178 sq. ft.
Basement	1,595 sq. ft.
Garage	466 sq. ft.
Storage	24 sq. ft.
Utility room	22 sq. ft.
Exterior Wall Framing:	2x4
Foundation Options:	
Daylight basement	
Standard basement	
Crawlspace	
Slab	

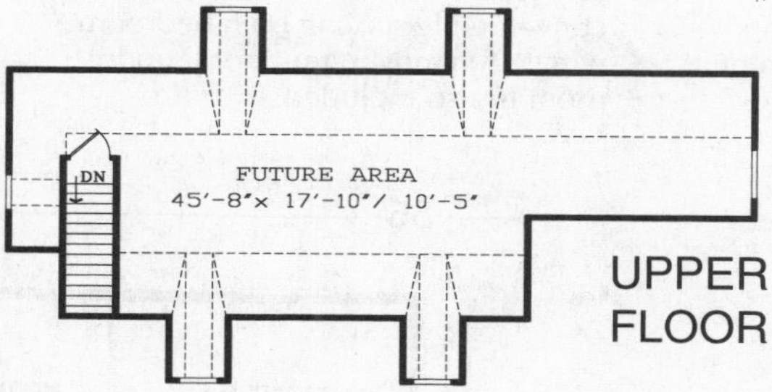

(All plans can be built with your choice of foundation and framing. A generic conversion diagram is available. See order form.)

BLUEPRINT PRICE CODE: B

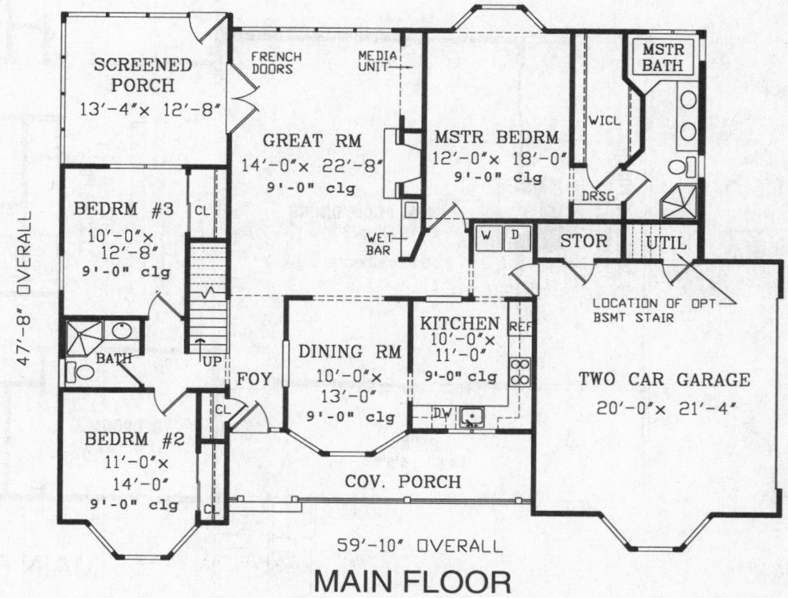

VIEW INTO GREAT ROOM

FUTURE AREA 45'-8"× 17'-10"/ 10'-5"

UPPER FLOOR

SCREENED PORCH 13'-4"× 12'-8"
GREAT RM 14'-0"× 22'-8" 9'-0" clg
MSTR BEDRM 12'-0"× 18'-0" 9'-0" clg
MSTR BATH
BEDRM #3 10'-0"× 12'-8" 9'-0" clg
DINING RM 10'-0"× 13'-0" 9'-0" clg
KITCHEN 10'-0"× 11'-0" 9'-0" clg
TWO CAR GARAGE 20'-0"× 21'-4"
BEDRM #2 11'-0"× 14'-0" 9'-0" clg
COV. PORCH
47'-8" OVERALL
59'-10" OVERALL

MAIN FLOOR

ORDER BLUEPRINTS ANYTIME! CALL TOLL-FREE 1-800-820-1296

Plan AX-00306

FOR MORE DETAILS, SEE PLAN AT familyhandyman.com/homeplans

Eight Is Just Enough

- Escape from the workaday world to this relaxing lakeside or ocean retreat.
- Four bedrooms border the exterior walls, affording a good deal of privacy while accommodating up to eight members of your family or good friends.
- A deck and a screened-in porch wrap the spectacular Great Room and dining area. You'll want to sit before the roaring fireplace and listen to the waves crashing on the shore.
- The large living space—and the rest of the home—is well endowed with glass so you can enjoy gorgeous views from all corners.
- Whenever there's a full house, the kitchen, featuring an oversized eating bar and work counter combination, will come in quite handy.
- Two full baths sit back-to-back, conveniently serving both bedroom wings. A handy main-floor laundry room is also included.

Plan PH-1600

Bedrooms: 4	**Baths:** 2
Living Area:	
Main floor	1,600 sq. ft.
Total Living Area:	**1,600 sq. ft.**
Screened porch	192 sq. ft.
Exterior Wall Framing:	2x6
Foundation Options:	
Crawlspace	
Pole	
Slab	

(All plans can be built with your choice of foundation and framing. A generic conversion diagram is available. See order form.)

BLUEPRINT PRICE CODE: **B**

56'

40'

BEDROOM 4
11'0" x 9'6"

MASTER BEDROOM
13'6" x 13'4"

BATH

WIC

KITCHEN
11'6" x 12'0"

BATH

LAUNDRY

SCREENED PORCH
8'0" x 24'0"
13'8" cathedral clg

GREAT ROOM/DINING
19'6" x 23'0"
13'8" cathedral clg

BEDROOM 3
11'0" x 9'6"

BEDROOM 2
11'0" x 9'6"

DECK
14'0" x 4'0"

MAIN FLOOR

Cool Contemporary

- Cool your heels in this impressive contemporary home. Its emphasis on windows, including a radiant sun room at the rear, creates a stunning visual effect and offers heating and cooling savings for the owners.
- The dramatic reception area introduces a breathtaking domed ceiling that tops the formal living and dining rooms. Skylights douse this space in sunshine, and three window walls offer a lovely view to the backyard. A central fireplace warms you when the sun sets.
- Casual living reigns in the open family room, dinette and kitchen, all of which share a vaulted ceiling. Another skylight tops the family room.
- Across the home, the master suite indulges you with a private terrace and a bath with dual sinks and a whirlpool tub. Your practical side will appreciate the abundance of closet space.
- Two ample secondary bedrooms share another full bath.

Plan K-812-S	
Bedrooms: 3	**Baths:** 2
Living Area:	
Main floor	1,690 sq. ft.
Sun room	109 sq. ft.
Total Living Area:	**1,799 sq. ft.**
Standard basement	1,714 sq. ft.
Garage	461 sq. ft.
Exterior Wall Framing:	2x4 or 2x6
Foundation Options:	
Standard basement	
Slab	

(All plans can be built with your choice of foundation and framing. A generic conversion diagram is available. See order form.)

BLUEPRINT PRICE CODE: B

VIEW INTO LIVING AND DINING ROOMS

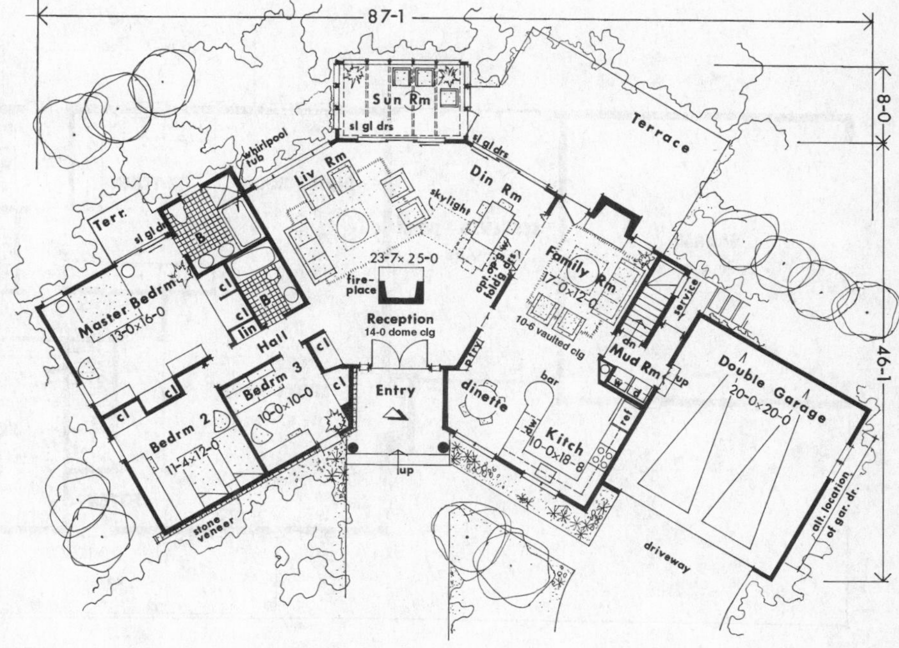

MAIN FLOOR

Shady Porches, Sunny Patio

- Designed with stylish country looks, this attractive one-story also has shady porches and a sunny patio for relaxed indoor/outdoor living.
- The inviting foyer flows into the spacious living room, which is warmed by a handsome fireplace.
- The adjoining dining room has a door to a screened-in porch, which opens to the backyard and serves as a breezeway to the nearby garage.
- The U-shaped kitchen has a pantry closet and plenty of counter space. Around the corner, a space-efficient laundry/utility room exits to a big backyard patio.
- The master bedroom is brightened by windows on two sides and includes a wardrobe closet. The compartmentalized master bath offers a separate dressing area and a walk-in closet.
- Another full bath serves two additional good-sized bedrooms.

Plan C-7557

Bedrooms: 3	**Baths:** 2
Living Area:	
Main floor	1,688 sq. ft.
Total Living Area:	**1,688 sq. ft.**
Screened porch	246 sq. ft.
Daylight basement	1,688 sq. ft.
Garage	400 sq. ft.
Exterior Wall Framing:	2x4
Foundation Options:	
Daylight basement	
Crawlspace	
Slab	

(All plans can be built with your choice of foundation and framing. A generic conversion diagram is available. See order form.)

BLUEPRINT PRICE CODE: B

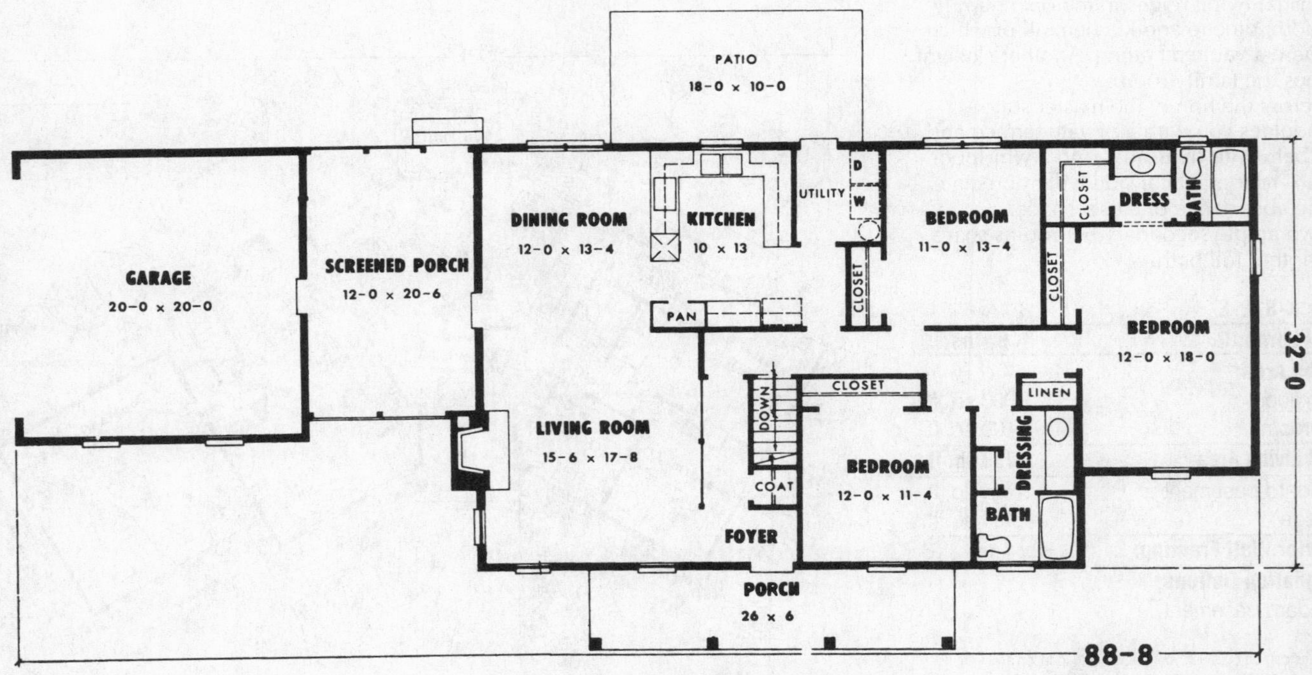

MAIN FLOOR

SEE ORDER INFO ON PAGES 12-15
familyhandyman.com/homeplans

REAR VIEW

Year-Round Comfort

FRONT VIEW

- Designed for the energy-conscious, this passive-solar home provides year-round comfort with much lower fuel costs.
- The open, airy interior is a delight. In the winter, sunshine penetrates deep into the living spaces. In the summer, wide overhangs shade the interior.
- The central living and dining rooms flow together, creating a bright, open space. Sliding glass doors open to a terrace and an enclosed sun spot.
- In the airy casual space, the kitchen has an eating bar and a sunny breakfast nook. The adjoining family room boasts a woodstove that warms the entire area.
- The master bedroom suite includes a private terrace, a personal bath and a walk-in closet. Two other bedrooms share another full bath.

Plan K-392-T

Bedrooms: 3	**Baths:** 2½
Living Area:	
Main floor	1,592 sq. ft.
Sun spot	125 sq. ft.
Total Living Area:	**1,717 sq. ft.**
Partial basement	634 sq. ft.
Garage	407 sq. ft.
Exterior Wall Framing:	2x4 or 2x6
Foundation Options:	
Partial basement	
Slab	

(All plans can be built with your choice of foundation and framing. A generic conversion diagram is available. See order form.)

BLUEPRINT PRICE CODE: **B**

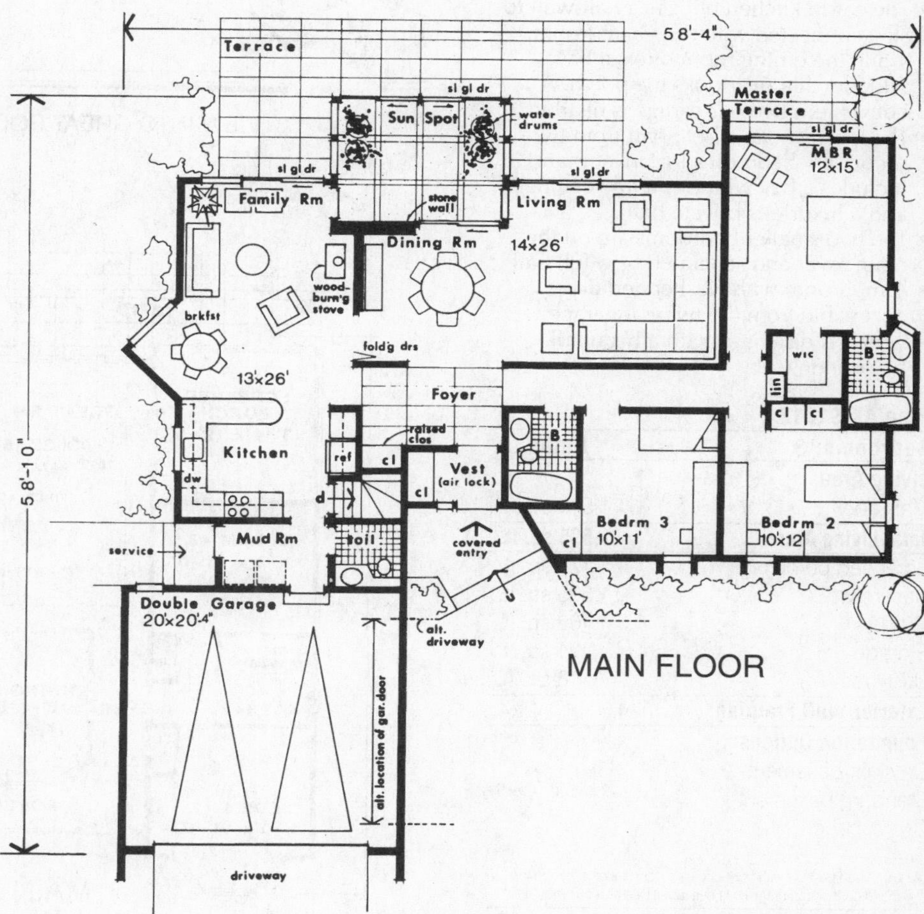

MAIN FLOOR

Anthony James Dugal

Single-Story with Sparkle

- A lovely facade with bay windows and dormers give this home extra sparkle.
- The Great Room anchors the floor plan, adjoining both the dining room and a screened porch. It also has a fireplace, a tray ceiling and a built-in wet bar.
- The eat-in kitchen utilizes a half-wall to stay connected with the Great Room, while the dining room offers a bay window that overlooks the porch. A convenient two-car garage is nearby.
- The master suite is set apart from two secondary bedrooms for privacy, and it includes a bay window, a tray ceiling, and a luxurious private bath.
- The two smaller bedrooms are off the main foyer and separated by a full bath.
- A mudroom with washer and dryer is accessible from the two-car garage, which is disguised with a beautiful bay window.

Plan AX-91312

Bedrooms: 3	**Baths:** 2
Living Area:	
Main floor	1,595 sq. ft.
Total Living Area:	**1,595 sq. ft.**
Screened porch	178 sq. ft.
Basement	1,595 sq. ft.
Garage	469 sq. ft.
Storage	21 sq. ft.
Utility room	18 sq. ft.
Exterior Wall Framing:	2x4

Foundation Options:
Daylight basement
Standard basement
Crawlspace
Slab
(All plans can be built with your choice of foundation and framing. A generic conversion diagram is available. See order form.)

BLUEPRINT PRICE CODE: **B**

NOTE:
The above photographed home may have been modified by the homeowner. Please refer to floor plan and/or drawn elevation shown for actual blueprint details.

VIEW INTO GREAT ROOM

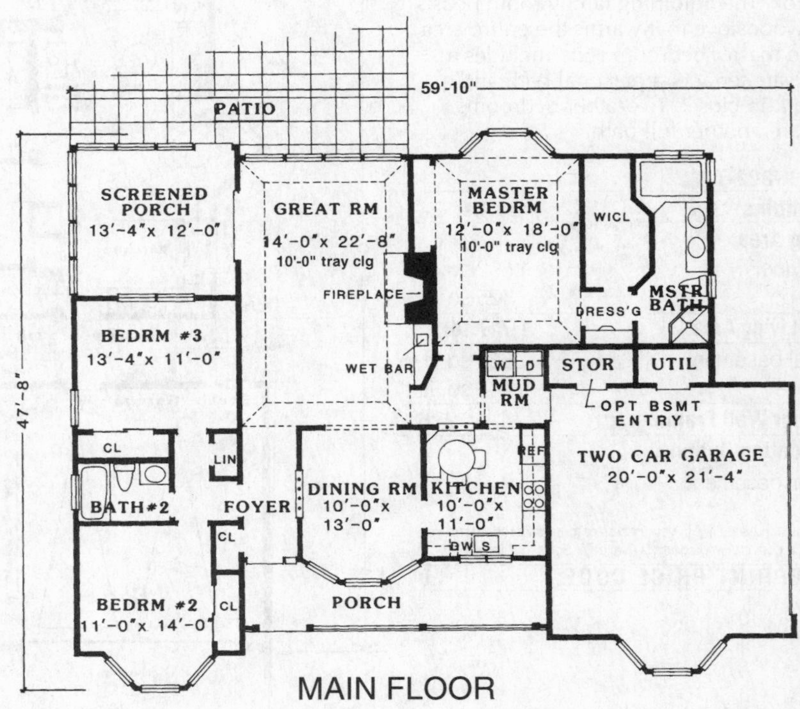

MAIN FLOOR

ORDER BLUEPRINTS ANYTIME!
CALL TOLL-FREE 1-800-820-1296

Plan AX-91312

Plan copyright held by home designer/architect

SEE ORDER INFO ON PAGES 12-15
familyhandyman.com/homeplans

Fresh Country Air

- A skylighted screen porch, a fun backyard deck and an abundance of windows infuse this country-style home with air and light.
- An inviting front porch ushers neighbors into the spacious family room, where a fireplace warms chilly nights. On sunny days, enjoy the screened-in back porch, or head out onto the rear deck.
- The roomy kitchen boasts a built-in desk, a closet pantry and serving bars overlooking both the breakfast nook and the family room.
- A tray ceiling, his-and-hers walk-in closets and a light-filled sitting area highlight the master bedroom. The private master bath flaunts a dual-sink vanity and a garden tub.
- A versatile future area above the garage offers expansion opportunities.

Plan APS-1717

Bedrooms: 3+	**Baths:** 2
Living Area:	
Main floor	1,787 sq. ft.
Total Living Area:	**1,787 sq. ft.**
Future area	263 sq. ft.
Screen porch	153 sq. ft.
Standard basement	1,787 sq. ft.
Garage	466 sq. ft.
Exterior Wall Framing:	2x4
Foundation Options:	
Standard basement	
Crawlspace	
Slab	

(All plans can be built with your choice of foundation and framing. A generic conversion diagram is available. See order form.)

BLUEPRINT PRICE CODE: B

REAR VIEW

VIEW INTO KITCHEN AND BREAKFAST NOOK

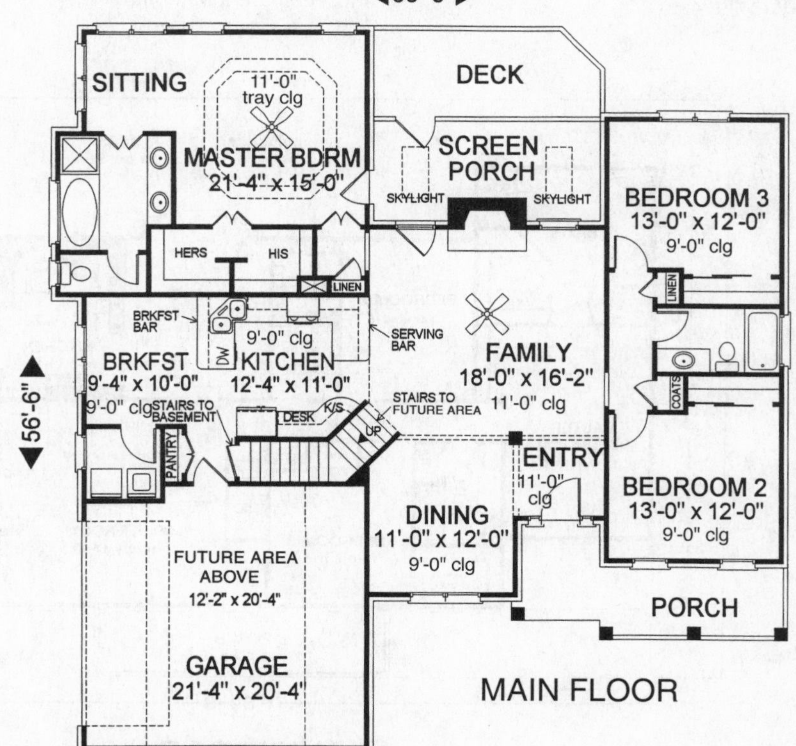

MAIN FLOOR

Breezy Beauty

- A nostalgic covered front porch, a backyard deck and a sprawling screened porch combine to make this beautiful one-story home a breezy delight.
- The front entry opens into the Great Room, which is crowned by a soaring cathedral ceiling. A handsome fireplace is flanked by built-in bookshelves and cabinets.
- The large, bayed dining room offers a tray ceiling and deck access through French doors.
- The adjoining kitchen boasts plenty of counter space and a handy recipe desk.
- From the kitchen, a side door leads to the screened porch. A wood floor and deck access highlight this cheery room.
- A quiet hall leads past a convenient utility room to the sleeping quarters.
- The secluded master bedroom is enhanced by a spacious walk-in closet. The private master bath includes a lovely garden tub, a separate shower, dual vanities, and a walk-in closet with room enough for every last shoe.
- Two more bedrooms with walk-in closets share a hall bath.

Plan C-8905

Bedrooms: 3	**Baths:** 2
Living Area:	
Main floor	1,811 sq. ft.
Total Living Area:	**1,811 sq. ft.**
Screened porch	240 sq. ft.
Daylight basement	1,811 sq. ft.
Garage	484 sq. ft.
Exterior Wall Framing:	2x4

Foundation Options:

Daylight basement
Crawlspace
Slab
(All plans can be built with your choice of foundation and framing. A generic conversion diagram is available. See order form.)

BLUEPRINT PRICE CODE: B

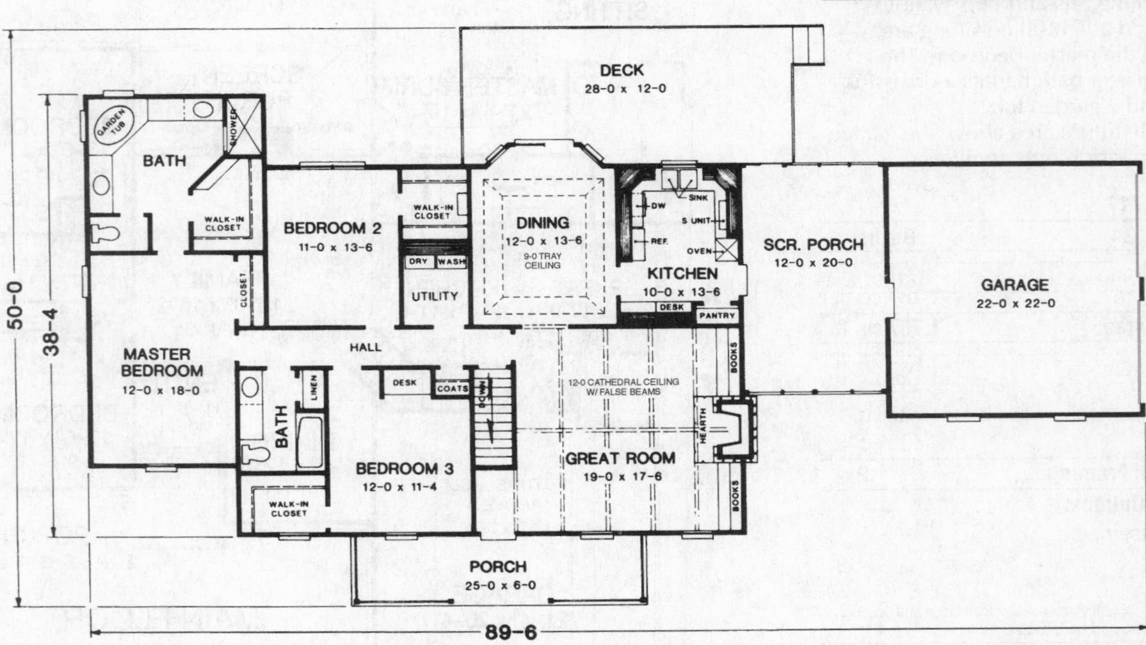

MAIN FLOOR

Plan C-8905

SEE ORDER INFO ON PAGES 12-15

Is This for You?

- Warning: This home plan is strictly reserved for fun-loving people who like to entertain friends and spend time outdoors. Sound like you? Read on.
- Not only a front porch—with room for a swing—but also a rear screened porch *and* a deck make up this design's impressive outdoor living spaces.
- A formal dining room, a breakfast room and a handy serving bar mean plenty of options for dining and entertaining.
- The cavernous family room hosts a cozy fireplace and access to the screened porch. A bay window graces the serene living room.
- The master bedroom adjoins a romantic sitting room and a fully loaded private bath with a large walk-in closet.
- Your houseguests will thank you for the thoughtful touch the other bedrooms offer—each has its own vanity, walk-in closet and access to the shared bath.
- A future area and a three-car garage give you plenty of room to expand.

Plan APS-1913

Bedrooms: 3+	**Baths:** 2½
Living Area:	
Main floor	1,982 sq. ft.
Total Living Area:	**1,982 sq. ft.**
Future area	386 sq. ft.
Screened porch	225 sq. ft.
Standard basement	1,982 sq. ft.
Three-car garage	681 sq. ft.
Exterior Wall Framing:	2x4
Foundation Options:	
Standard basement	
Crawlspace	

(All plans can be built with your choice of foundation and framing. A generic conversion diagram is available. See order form.)

BLUEPRINT PRICE CODE: **B**

REAR VIEW

SCREENED PORCH 16'-0" x 14'-3"
DECK 10'-11" x 8'-3"
MASTER SUITE 21'-4" x 14'-0" 12'-4" vltd clg
SITTING
BRKFST 11'-0" x 8'-4"
BEDROOM 3 13'-0" x 11'-0"
KITCHEN 13'-0" x 9'-4"
UP TO FUTURE AREA
FAMILY ROOM 16'-0" x 22'-0" 14'-4" vaulted clg
DINING 11'-0" x 13'-0" 10'-0" tray clg
BEDROOM 2 13'-0" x 11'-0"
LIVING 11'-0" x 13'-0" 14'-0" vltd clg
PORCH 15'-10" x 5'-0"
3 CAR GARAGE 21'-4" x 30'-9"
2 CAR GARAGE OPTION
63'-0"
58'-0"

MAIN FLOOR

Cozy One-Story

- This pleasing L-shaped design packs a lot of living space into its floor plan.
- The large family room at the center of the home extends to two outdoor living spaces: a screened porch and a big patio or deck. For colder days, the warm fireplace will come in handy.
- Formal occasions will be well received in the spacious living/dining room at the front of the home. Each area offers a nice view of the front porch.
- The airy kitchen includes a pantry, a windowed sink and lots of counter space. Attached is a cozy breakfast bay and, beyond that, a laundry room.
- Secluded to the rear of the sleeping wing, the master suite boasts a private symmetrical bath with a garden tub, a separate shower and his-and-hers vanities and walk-in closets.
- Two secondary bedrooms and another full bath complete the sleeping wing.

Plan C-8620

Bedrooms: 3	**Baths:** 2
Living Area:	
Main floor	1,955 sq. ft.
Total Living Area:	**1,955 sq. ft.**
Screened porch	120 sq. ft.
Daylight basement	1,822 sq. ft.
Garage	448 sq. ft.
Storage	45 sq. ft.
Exterior Wall Framing:	2x4
Foundation Options:	
Daylight basement	
Crawlspace	
Slab	

(All plans can be built with your choice of foundation and framing. A generic conversion diagram is available. See order form.)

BLUEPRINT PRICE CODE: **B**

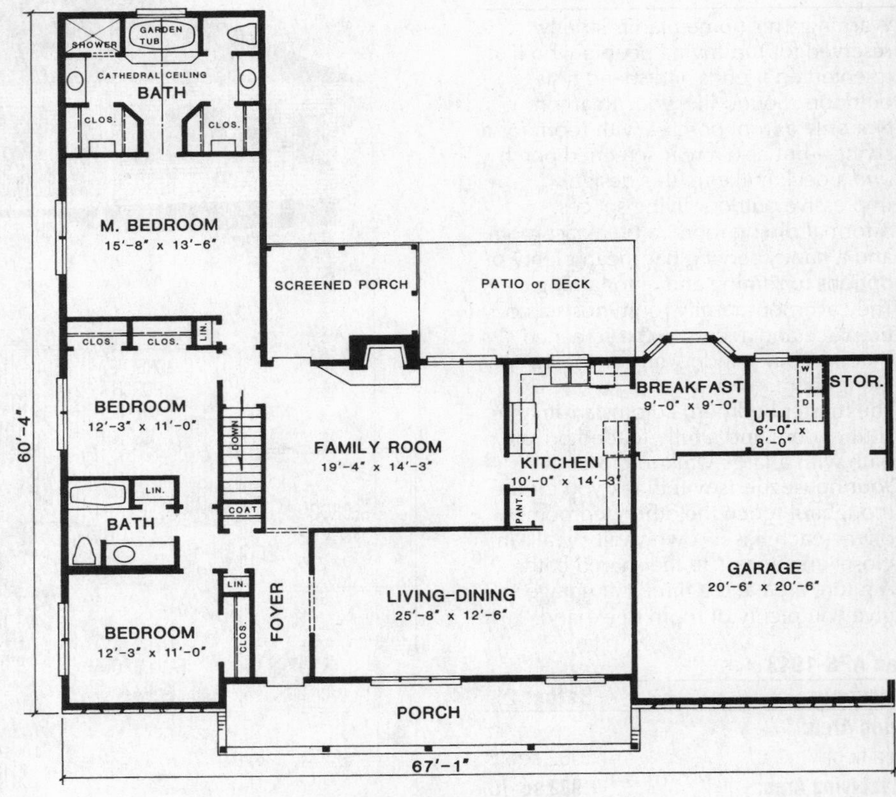

MAIN FLOOR

Plan C-8620

SEE ORDER INFO ON PAGES 12-15
familyhandyman.com/homeplans

You'll Love It!

- With its storybook-like exterior and delightful interior spaces, this plan will capture your heart.
- A partially enclosed foyer adjoins a handy powder room and continues straight past a coat closet into the central family room. Here, a fireplace and built-ins impart a warm ambience, while wide windows look out to a back patio and sun deck beyond.
- The formal dining room is open to the family room and convenient to the ultra-efficient island kitchen. If you prefer to keep the kitchen from your dinner guests' view, you'll appreciate the double swinging doors.
- Also adjacent to the family room, the nook offers more casual dining, plus direct access to the patio and a neat greenhouse.
- A bonus suite over the garage with an optional bath is a thoughtful feature.
- A luxurious, secluded master suite with all the trimmings, plus a secondary bedroom, comprise the home's sleeping quarters. A den at the front of the design provides built-ins appropriate to a study or home office.

Plan HDS-99-392	
Bedrooms: 2+	**Baths:** 2½–3½
Living Area:	
Main floor	1,997 sq. ft.
Bonus suite	310 sq. ft.
Total Living Area:	**2,307 sq. ft.**
Garage	502 sq. ft.
Exterior Wall Framing:	2x4
Foundation Options:	
Crawlspace	
(All plans can be built with your choice of foundation and framing. A generic conversion diagram is available. See order form.)	
BLUEPRINT PRICE CODE:	**C**

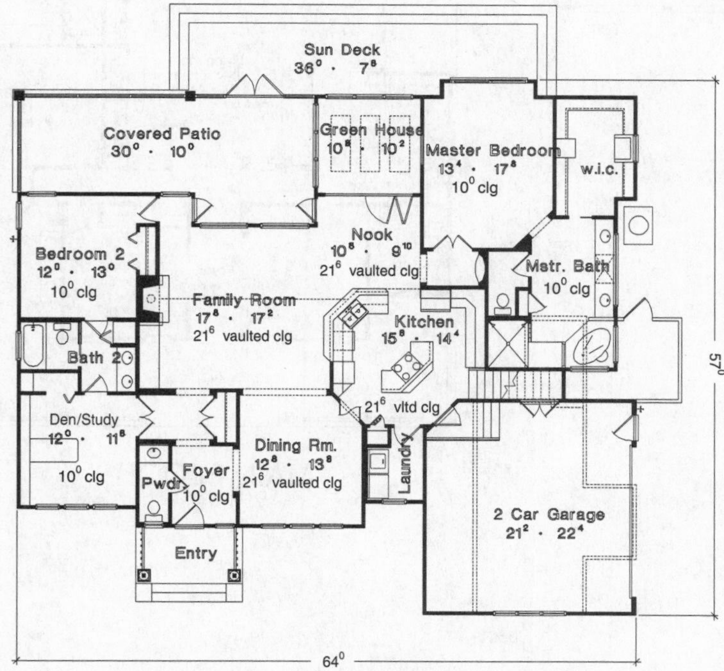

MAIN FLOOR

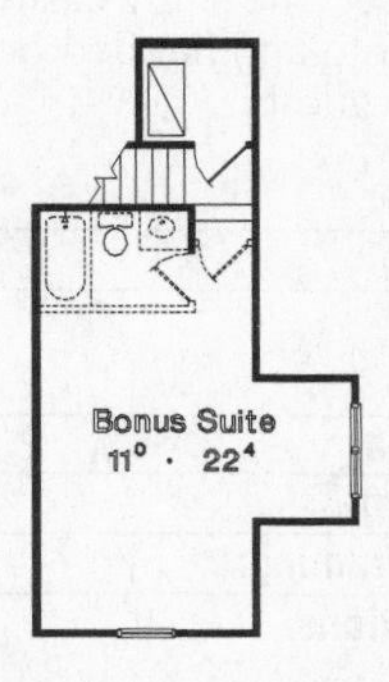

BONUS SUITE

Fabulous Farmhouse

- Tapered columns around the front porch and dormer windows set the tone for this sprawling country farmhouse.
- Inside, the foyer leads to the expansive central living room, which boasts a cozy fireplace, a built-in media center and bookshelves. Half-walls and columns set this space off from the other living areas.
- Perfectly placed between the formal dining room and the sunny breakfast area, the well-appointed kitchen features an island cooktop and a snack bar shared with the living room. A French door in the breakfast area accesses the rear porch.
- Set off from the living room by a solarium that doubles as a home office, the master bedroom offers a lavish private bath with his-and-hers walk-in closets, a garden tub and separate shower and a dual-sink vanity.
- The secondary bedroom sports a large walk-in closet. The study easily transforms into another bedroom for out-of-town guests.

Plan L-77-01B	
Bedrooms: 2+	**Baths:** 2
Living Area:	
Main floor	2,077 sq. ft.
Total Living Area:	**2,077 sq. ft.**
Detached garage	528 sq. ft.
Exterior Wall Framing:	2x4
Foundation Options:	
Slab (All plans can be built with your choice of foundation and framing. A generic conversion diagram is available. See order form.)	
BLUEPRINT PRICE CODE:	**C**

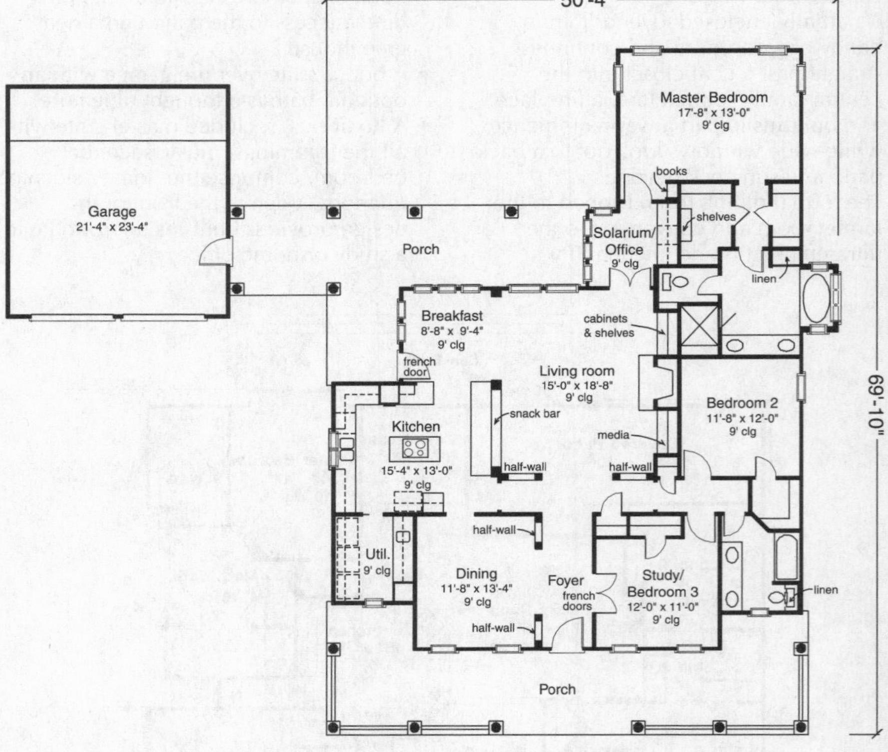

MAIN FLOOR

Plan L-77-01B

SEE ORDER INFO ON PAGES 12-15
familyhandyman.com/homeplans

Outdoor Odyssey

- Do you and your family members spend every available moment outside? If so, this remarkable home is for you.
- The wide front porch leads into the sidelighted entry, where double doors to the left enclose the peaceful living room. A single column marks the corner boundary of the formal dining room.
- The country kitchen includes an island cooktop and a large pantry, plus a casual eating area that's served by a wide snack counter.
- The snack counter also extends to the family room, which accesses a screened porch and a fun patio or deck beyond.
- Two bedrooms reside down a hallway off the family room. The master suite is sequestered on the opposite side of the home and features a luxurious private bath and access to the back patio for stargazing on a clear night.
- A future space above the three-car garage allows the home to expand as your family's needs do.

Plan APS-2020	
Bedrooms: 3+	**Baths:** 3
Living Area:	
Main floor	2,097 sq. ft.
Total Living Area:	**2,097 sq. ft.**
Future area	452 sq. ft.
Screened porch	155 sq. ft.
Garage	721 sq. ft.
Exterior Wall Framing:	2x4
Foundation Options:	
Crawlspace	
Slab	

(All plans can be built with your choice of foundation and framing. A generic conversion diagram is available. See order form.)

BLUEPRINT PRICE CODE: C

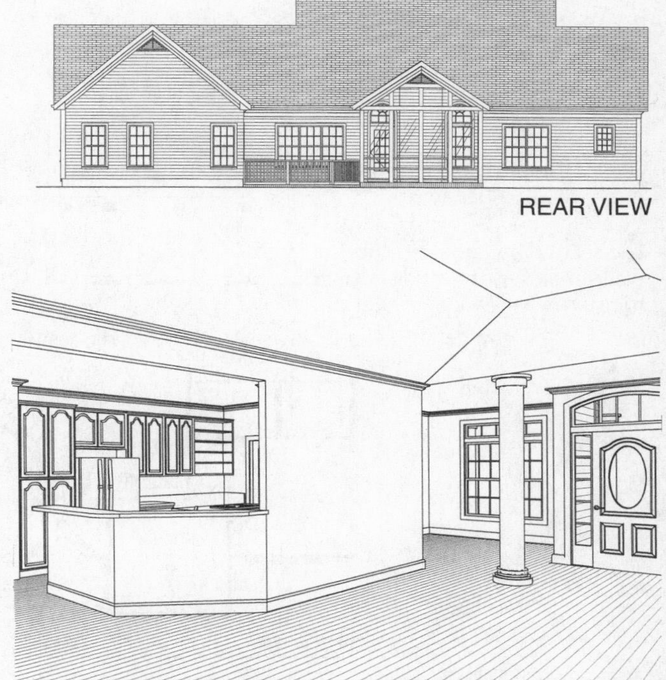

REAR VIEW

VIEW INTO KITCHEN, FAMILY ROOM AND FOYER

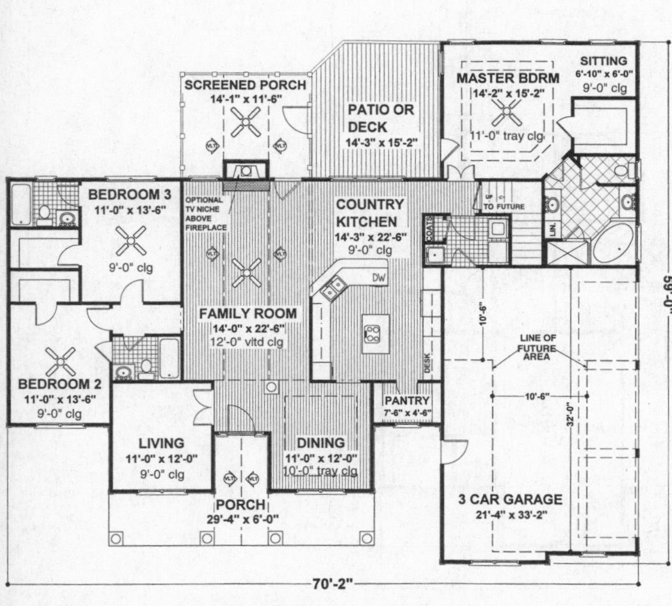

MAIN FLOOR

Subtle Surprises

- This three-bedroom design is packed with surprising touches, from the built-in entertainment center in the living room to the many walk-in closets and porches found throughout the home.
- The elegant exterior features half-round transom windows, quoins and sturdy brick. The garage is situated at the rear of the plan to highlight the classic symmetry of the French-inspired facade.
- Three covered porches—one in the front, one in back, and one off the study—allow for everything from summer barbecues with friends to quiet evening stargazing with loved ones.
- A kitchen bar overlooks the breakfast and living areas, so cooking doesn't get in the way of valuable family time.
- French doors lead into the sun room, which may serve as a transitional area to the backyard.
- The master suite boasts a private study that could be used as a home office. The luxurious bath includes a raised oval tub, a dual-sink vanity, a private toilet and his-and-hers walk-in closets.
- Two additional bedrooms share a full bath on the other side of the home.

Plan E-2009	
Bedrooms: 3	**Baths:** 2
Living Area:	
Main floor	2,000 sq. ft.
Sun room	160 sq. ft.
Total Living Area:	**2,160 sq. ft.**
Garage	499 sq. ft.
Storage	81 sq. ft.
Exterior Wall Framing:	2x4
Foundation Options:	
Crawlspace	
Slab	
(All plans can be built with your choice of foundation and framing. A generic conversion diagram is available. See order form.)	
BLUEPRINT PRICE CODE:	**C**

GARAGE 22'-0"x22'-0"
COVERED PORCH 20'-0"x8'-0"
BREAKFAST 11'-8"x13'-2" 9'-0" clg
UTIL
STOR 9'-0"x9'-0" 9'-0" clg
SUNROOM 16'-0"x10'-0" 9'-0" clg
LIVING ROOM 20'-0"x17'-0" 12'-0" clg
KITCHEN 13'-0"x11'-0" 9'-0" clg
DW
REF.
STUDY 11'-0"x9'-0" 9'-0" clg
PORCH
WIC
PANTRY
ENTERTAINMENT CENTER
BEDRM 3 12'-0"x12'-0" 9'-0" clg
FOYER 12'-0" clg
DINING ROOM 13'-0"x12'-0" 12'-0" clg
MASTER BEDRM 22'-0"x13'-0" 9'-0" clg
9'-0" clg
WIC
BEDRM 2 12'-0"x12'-0" 9'-0" clg
COVERED PORCH 20'-0"x6'-0"
68'-0"
64'-0"

MAIN FLOOR

ORDER BLUEPRINTS ANYTIME!
CALL TOLL-FREE 1-800-820-1296

Plan E-2009

SEE ORDER INFO ON PAGES 12-15
familyhandyman.com/homeplans

Elements of Elegance

- Elegant details adorn both the facade and the interior of this delightful home.
- A nostalgic covered porch introduces the sidelighted entry, which spills into the formal and informal gathering areas.
- To the left, the dramatic formal dining room is perfect for special meals.
- Double doors lead to a quiet study, warmed by its handsome fireplace and boxed-out window with curtains thrown open to the sun.
- Straight ahead, the ambience of the spacious family room is enhanced by a rustic corner fireplace and a stunning cathedral ceiling. French doors open to a comfortable screened porch, which accesses a deck only steps away.
- The island kitchen includes a long work island with a cooktop.
- A tray ceiling tops the master bedroom, which boasts private deck access. The master bath has a whirlpool garden tub separated from a shower by glass blocks.
- Two secondary bedrooms occupy the opposite side of the home.

Plan SDG-30616

Bedrooms: 3+	**Baths:** 2½
Living Area:	
Main floor	2,173 sq. ft.
Total Living Area:	**2,173 sq. ft.**
Screened porch	204 sq. ft.
Garage and storage	556 sq. ft.
Exterior Wall Framing:	2x4
Foundation Options:	
Slab	
(All plans can be built with your choice of foundation and framing. A generic conversion diagram is available. See order form.)	
BLUEPRINT PRICE CODE:	**C**

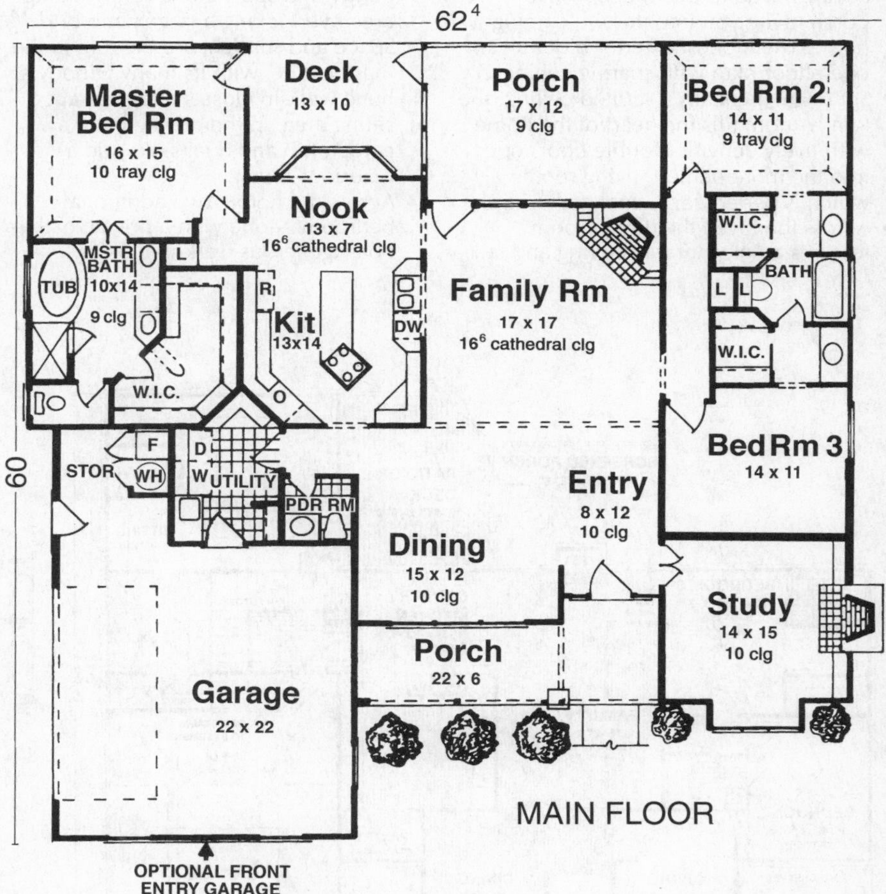

Inviting Design

- Lovely transoms and a deep, shady porch invite you into this welcoming home. The modest exterior hides a vast, open floor plan with soaring ceilings.
- Sprawling beneath a vaulted ceiling, the family room fills the heart of the home with lively activity. Double doors open into the more demure living room, which is perfect for formal gatherings.
- Across the foyer, the dining room features an elegant tray ceiling and tall windows. The grand country kitchen, only a step away, enjoys a huge walk-in pantry and spills into a sunny eating area overlooking a large patio or deck.
- Space and sunlight are the rule in the master suite, with its many windows, huge walk-in closets and pleasant sitting area. In the private bath, a garden tub and dual sinks add a luxurious touch.
- Across the home, two additional bedrooms—one with a private bath—boast generous walk-in closets.

Plan APS-2119

Bedrooms: 3+	**Baths:** 3
Living Area:	
Main floor	2,184 sq. ft.
Total Living Area:	**2,184 sq. ft.**
Future area	379 sq. ft.
Screened porch	166 sq. ft.
Daylight basement	2,184 sq. ft.
Garage	548 sq. ft.
Exterior Wall Framing:	2x4
Foundation Options:	
Daylight basement	
Crawlspace	
Slab	

(All plans can be built with your choice of foundation and framing. A generic conversion diagram is available. See order form.)

BLUEPRINT PRICE CODE: C

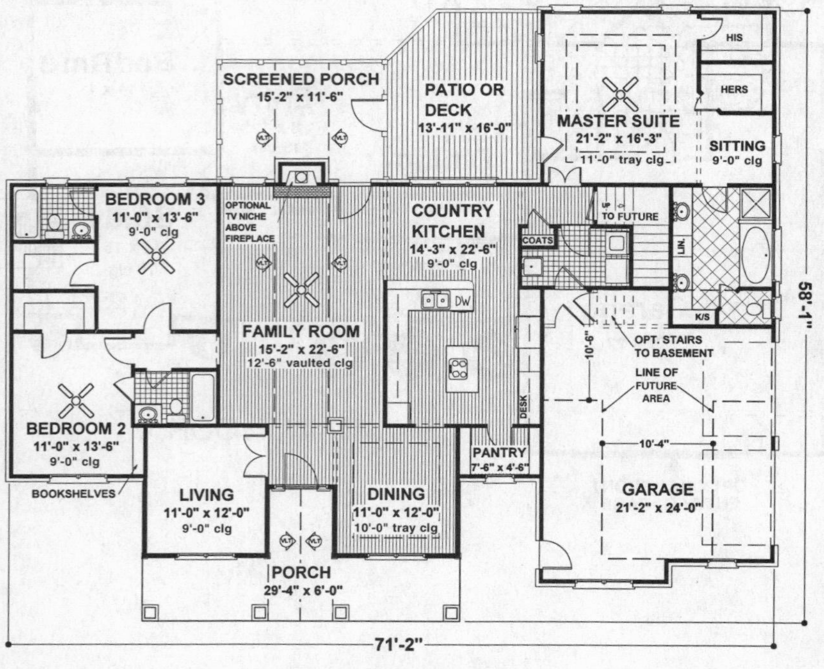

MAIN FLOOR

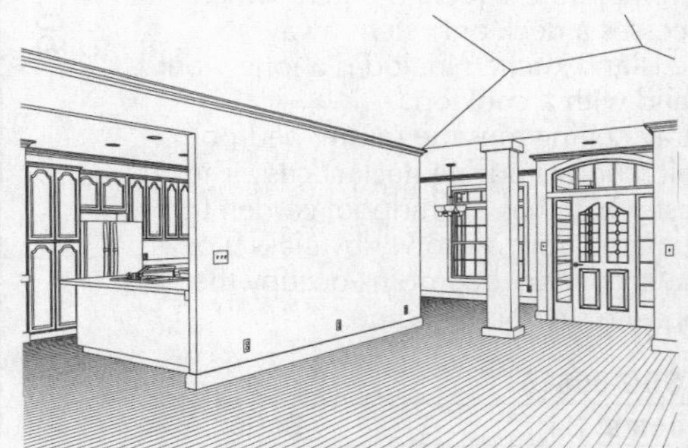

VIEW INTO KITCHEN, FAMILY ROOM AND FOYER

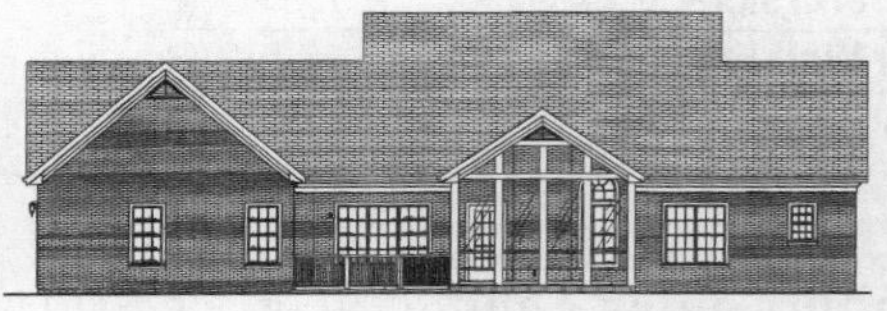

REAR VIEW

Plan APS-2119

SEE ORDER INFO ON PAGES 12-15

Rustic, Relaxed Living

- The screened porch of this rustic home offers a cool place to dine on warm summer days. The covered front porch provides an inviting welcome and a place for pure relaxation.
- With its warm fireplace, the home's spacious living room is ideal for unwinding. The living room unfolds to a dining area that overlooks a backyard patio and opens to the screened porch.
- The U-shaped kitchen is centrally located and features a nice windowed sink. A handy pantry and a laundry room adjoin to the right.
- Three large bedrooms make up the home's sleeping wing. The master bedroom boasts a roomy private bath with a step-up spa tub, a separate shower and two walk-in closets.
- The secondary bedrooms share a compartmentalized hall bath.

Plan C-8650

Bedrooms: 3	**Baths:** 2
Living Area:	
Main floor	1,773 sq. ft.
Total Living Area:	**1,773 sq. ft.**
Screened porch	246 sq. ft.
Daylight basement	1,773 sq. ft.
Garage	441 sq. ft.
Exterior Wall Framing:	2x4

Foundation Options:

Daylight basement
Crawlspace
Slab
(All plans can be built with your choice of foundation and framing. A generic conversion diagram is available. See order form.)

BLUEPRINT PRICE CODE: **B**

VIEW INTO LIVING ROOM

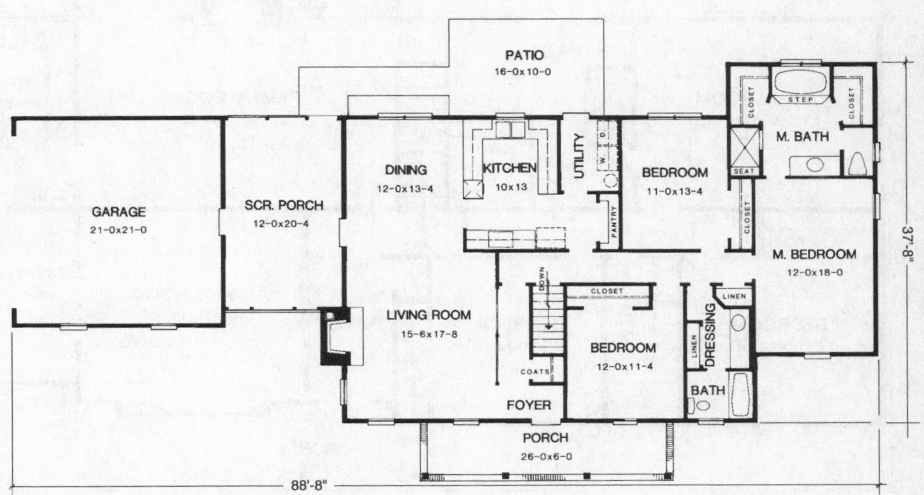

MAIN FLOOR

Endless Acreage

- Endless acreage will suit this expansive, wide home just fine; its outdoor living areas were made for enjoying grand landscapes—or at least pretending to.
- Columns frame the front porch, which leads to the sidelighted foyer. This area offers a clear view into the spacious living and dining rooms, each of which feature ample natural light.
- The nearby kitchen is roomy enough for lots of traffic, and easily serves the dining room and the adjoining breakfast nook. A sunny bay brightens this casual dining spot. A half-bath and a utility room are conveniently close at hand.
- A gorgeous fireplace anchors the family room, which will quickly become your favorite gathering spot. Doors lead to a screened porch out back—a delightful place to enjoy summer breezes and laughter with loved ones.
- Down the hall, the master suite boasts a large sleeping area with an equally impressive private bath. Amenities in this retreat include a dual-sink vanity and dressing area, a walk-in closet and a step-up tub. Two more bedrooms share a full hall bath.

Plan C-8625

Bedrooms: 3	**Baths:** 2½
Living Area:	
Main floor	2,306 sq. ft.
Total Living Area:	**2,306 sq. ft.**
Screened porch	276 sq. ft.
Daylight basement	2,306 sq. ft.
Garage and storage	583 sq. ft.
Exterior Wall Framing:	2x4
Foundation Options:	
Daylight basement	
Crawlspace	
Slab	

(All plans can be built with your choice of foundation and framing. A generic conversion diagram is available. See order form.)

BLUEPRINT PRICE CODE: C

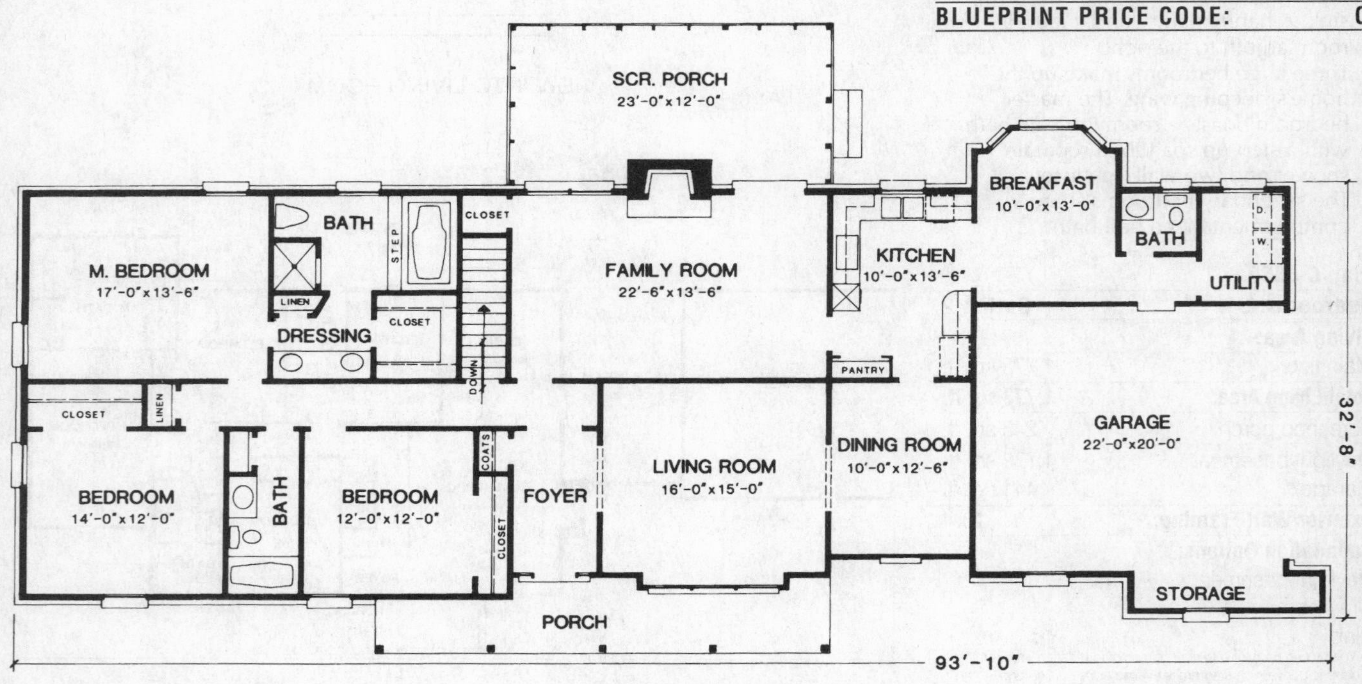

MAIN FLOOR

ORDER BLUEPRINTS ANYTIME!
CALL TOLL-FREE 1-800-820-1296

Plan C-8625

SEE ORDER INFO ON PAGES 12-15
familyhandyman.com/homeplans

Maximum Living Space

- Large rooms, high ceilings and a convenient traffic flow without hallways maximize the living space of this beautiful stucco home.
- At the heart of the floor plan, the kitchen, breakfast room and living room form an open activity area that combines work, dining and relaxation. Note the built-in entertainment center, the angled fireplace and the serving bar.
- Behind the fireplace, bold boxed columns separate the foyer from the formal dining room.
- French doors in the living room swing open to a soothing sun room, ideal for unwinding in inclement weather. Another French door offers entrance to a covered rear porch.
- The master and secondary bedrooms are distanced for privacy. With its own outdoor access, the study off the master suite also makes a great home office!

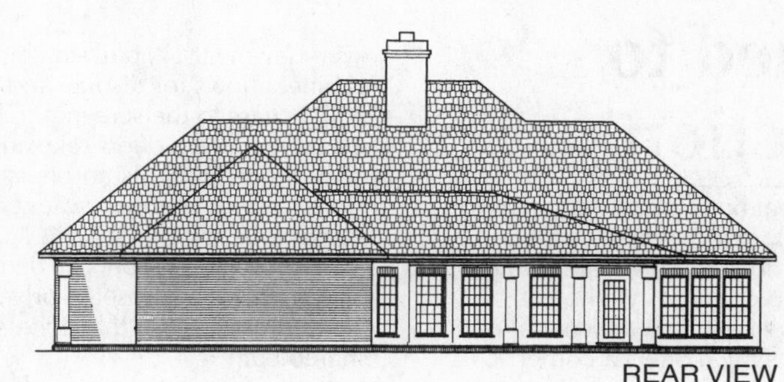

REAR VIEW

MAIN FLOOR

Plan E-2010	
Bedrooms: 3	**Baths:** 2
Living Area:	
Main floor	2,000 sq. ft.
Sun room	160 sq. ft.
Total Living Area:	**2,160 sq. ft.**
Garage	499 sq. ft.
Storage	81 sq. ft.
Exterior Wall Framing:	2x4
Foundation Options:	
Crawlspace	
Slab	
(All plans can be built with your choice of foundation and framing. A generic conversion diagram is available. See order form.)	
BLUEPRINT PRICE CODE:	**C**

Planned to Perfection

- From the great outdoor living spaces to the smart floor plan, you'll be hard-pressed to find a missing feature in this well-planned country-style home.
- A two-story ceiling tops the central living room, which offers a corner fireplace and a built-in media center.
- Two eating areas mean increased meal-service options. A pass-through between the well-appointed island kitchen and the casual eating area eases everyday meals. A built-in china cabinet allows for display and storage.
- With access to the screen porch, the master bedroom offers relaxation. A cozy sitting area, his-and-hers walk-in closets and a sizable private bath create a luxurious suite.
- Each of the two secondary bedrooms boasts a walk-in closet, a private vanity and a dressing area that accesses the shared bath.
- An upper-floor balcony overlooks the living room. Ample future space lets this home grow as your family's needs dictate: Add another bedroom, a home office or a music room.

Plan E-2310	
Bedrooms: 3+	**Baths:** 2½
Living Area:	
Upper floor	112 sq. ft.
Main floor	2,281 sq. ft.
Total Living Area:	**2,393 sq. ft.**
Screen porch	187 sq. ft.
Future space	912 sq. ft.
Garage	484 sq. ft.
Storage	86 sq. ft.
Exterior Wall Framing:	2x4
Foundation Options:	
Crawlspace	
Slab	

(All plans can be built with your choice of foundation and framing. A generic conversion diagram is available. See order form.)

BLUEPRINT PRICE CODE: **C**

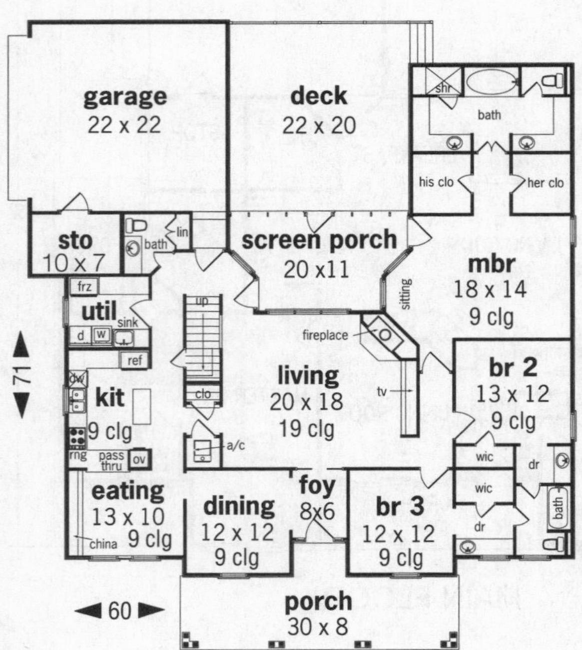

MAIN FLOOR

REAR VIEW

attic
future space
13 x 14
dn
open to lower level
hand railing
balcony 9 clg
future space
17 x 14
future space
30 x 12

UPPER FLOOR

Plan E-2310

SEE ORDER INFO ON PAGES 12-15

Wonderful Detailing

- The wonderfully detailed front porch, with its graceful arches, columns and railings, gives this home a character all its own. Dormer windows and arched transoms further accentuate the porch.
- The floor plan features a central living room with a high ceiling and a fireplace framed by French doors. These doors open to a covered porch or a sun room, and a sheltered deck beyond.
- Just off the living room, the island kitchen and breakfast area provide a spacious place for family or guests. The nearby formal dining room has arched transom windows.
- The unusual master suite includes a window alcove, access to the porch and a fantastic bath with a garden tub.
- A huge utility room, a storage area off the garage and a 1,000-sq.-ft. attic space are other bonuses of this design.

Plan J-90019	
Bedrooms: 3	**Baths:** 2½
Living Area:	
Main floor	2,410 sq. ft.
Total Living Area:	**2,410 sq. ft.**
Standard basement	2,410 sq. ft.
Garage	512 sq. ft.
Storage	86 sq. ft.
Exterior Wall Framing:	2x4
Foundation Options:	
Standard basement	
Crawlspace	
Slab	

(All plans can be built with your choice of foundation and framing. A generic conversion diagram is available. See order form.)

BLUEPRINT PRICE CODE: **C**

VIEW INTO LIVING ROOM

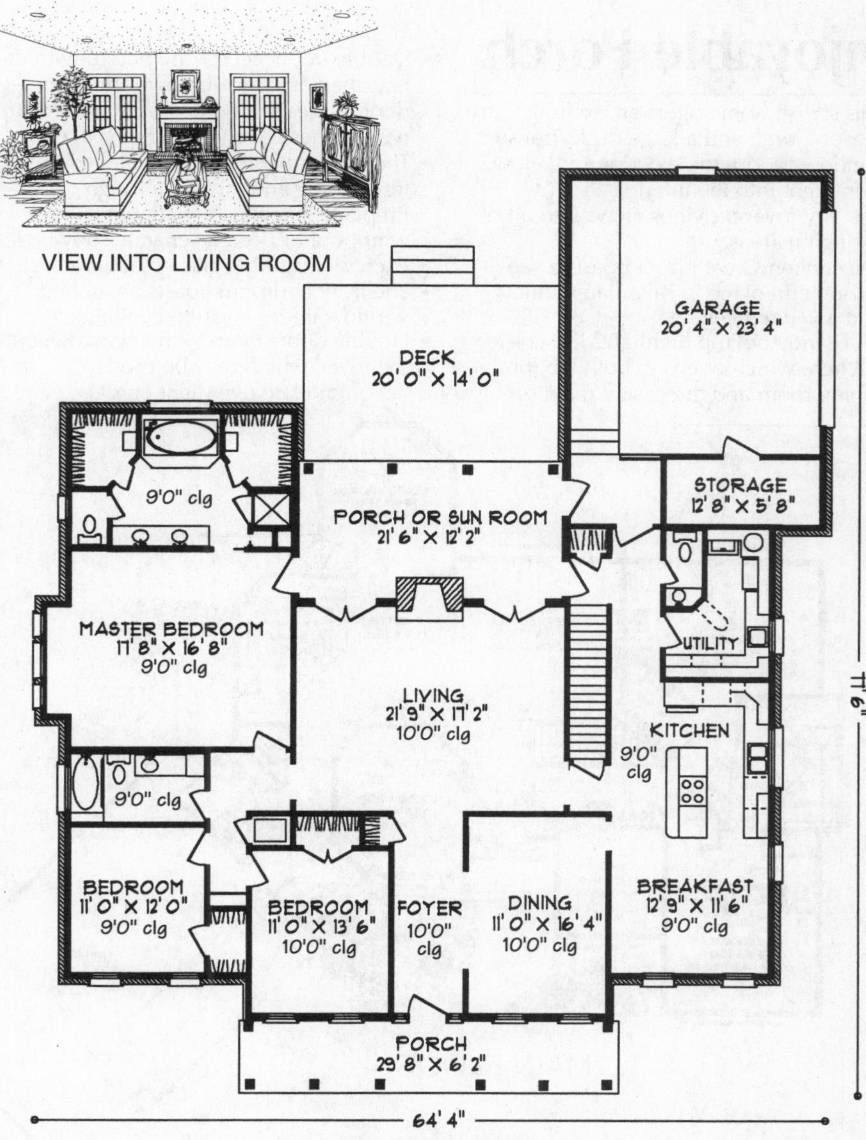

MAIN FLOOR

Plan J-90019

FOR MORE DETAILS, SEE PLAN AT
familyhandyman.com/homeplans

Enjoyable Porch

- This stylish home offers an exciting four-season porch and a large deck. Transom windows adorn the exterior and allow extra light into the interior.
- The airy foyer provides views into all of the living areas.
- The sunken Great Room boasts a see-through fireplace, a Palladian window and a vaulted ceiling.
- An island cooktop highlights the corner kitchen, which opens to both the formal dining room and the casual dinette.
- Double doors access the porch, with its bay, many sunny windows and French door to the inviting deck. Entertain with ease in these two wonderful spaces.
- The master bedroom is enhanced by a tray ceiling and the see-through fireplace. The master bath has a whirlpool tub and a separate shower, each with striking glass-block walls.
- The front bedroom boasts an arched window under a vaulted ceiling.
- Double doors open to the cozy den off the foyer, which may be used to accommodate overnight guests.

Plan PI-92-535

Bedrooms: 2+	**Baths:** 2½
Living Area:	
Main floor	2,302 sq. ft.
Four-season porch	208 sq. ft.
Total Living Area:	**2,510 sq. ft.**
Daylight basement	2,302 sq. ft.
Garage	912 sq. ft.
Exterior Wall Framing:	2x6
Foundation Options:	
Daylight basement	

(All plans can be built with your choice of foundation and framing. A generic conversion diagram is available. See order form.)

BLUEPRINT PRICE CODE: D

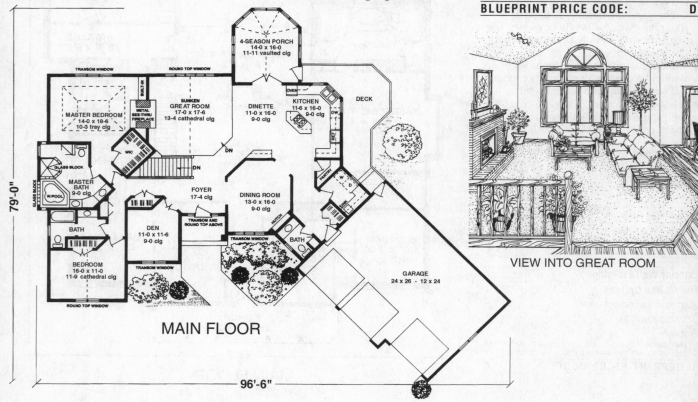

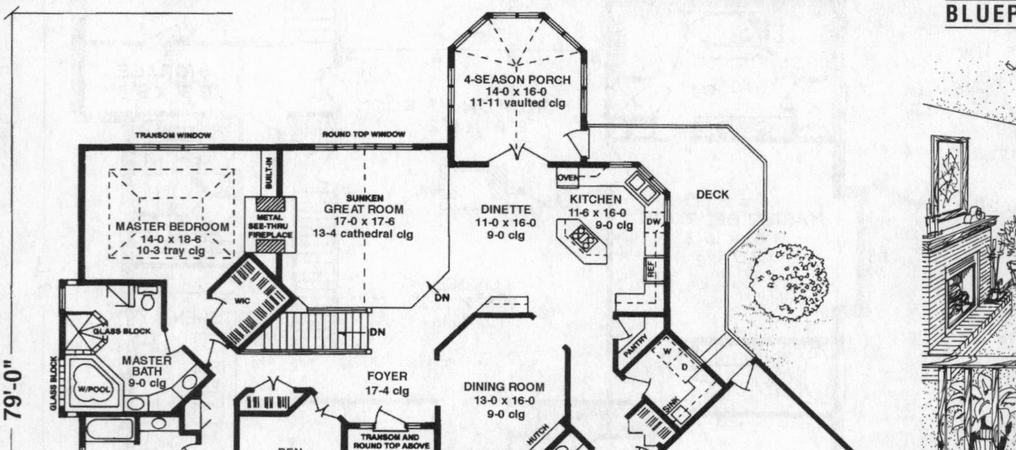

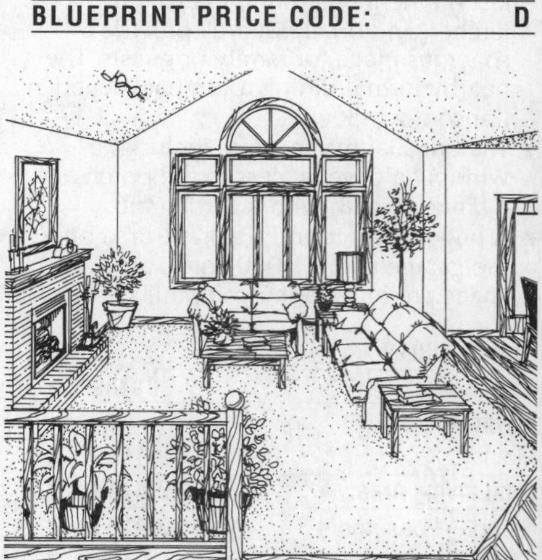

VIEW INTO GREAT ROOM

4-SEASON PORCH 14-0 x 16-0 11-11 vaulted clg
TRANSOM WINDOW
ROUND TOP WINDOW
BUILT-IN
DECK
MASTER BEDROOM 14-0 x 18-6 10-3 tray clg
METAL SEE-THRU FIREPLACE
SUNKEN GREAT ROOM 17-0 x 17-6 13-4 cathedral clg
DINETTE 11-0 x 16-0 9-0 clg
OVEN
KITCHEN 11-6 x 16-0 9-0 clg
DW
REF
WIC
DN
GLASS BLOCK
MASTER BATH 9-0 clg
W/POOL
FOYER 17-4 clg
DINING ROOM 13-0 x 16-0 9-0 clg
PANTRY
W D
SINK
HUTCH
BATH
DEN 11-0 x 11-6 9-0 clg
TRANSOM AND ROUND TOP ABOVE
TRANSOM WINDOW
BEDROOM 16-0 x 11-0 11-9 cathedral clg
TRANSOM WINDOW
ROUND TOP WINDOW
GARAGE 24 x 26 - 12 x 24
79'-0"
96'-6"

MAIN FLOOR

Plan PI-92-535

SEE ORDER INFO ON PAGES 12-15
familyhandyman.com/homeplans

Fresh Style

- Fashionably charming, this airy design produces fresh style. The lovely facade boasts intricate brickwork, attractive columns and tall, multipaned windows—a stunning combination.
- Entertaining is easy in this home, where formal rooms flank the foyer and an open family room provides recreational amenities. In the dining room, a clerestory dormer with a Palladian window brightens every dinner party.
- A TV niche and a handsome fireplace anchor the family room, while sliding glass doors lead out to a breezy screen porch and courtyard. A bayed eating nook flanks the family room, displaying a handy built-in china hutch.
- The kitchen is tucked away to conceal all your preparations, yet it is quite accessible to both eating areas. A smart utility room lies to one side, while a half-bath and the garage lie to the other.
- Secluded and peaceful, the master suite and the office comprise their own wing. A private entry makes the office ideal for receiving clients. Across the home, three more bedrooms share two baths.

Plan E-2611	
Bedrooms: 4+	**Baths:** 3½
Living Area:	
Main floor	2,682 sq. ft.
Total Living Area:	**2,682 sq. ft.**
Screen porch	211 sq. ft.
Garage	676 sq. ft.
Exterior Wall Framing:	2x4
Foundation Options:	
Crawlspace	
Slab	

(All plans can be built with your choice of foundation and framing. A generic conversion diagram is available. See order form.)

BLUEPRINT PRICE CODE: **D**

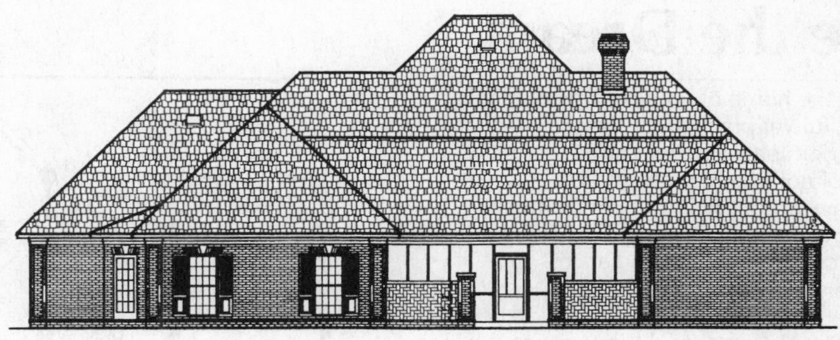

REAR VIEW

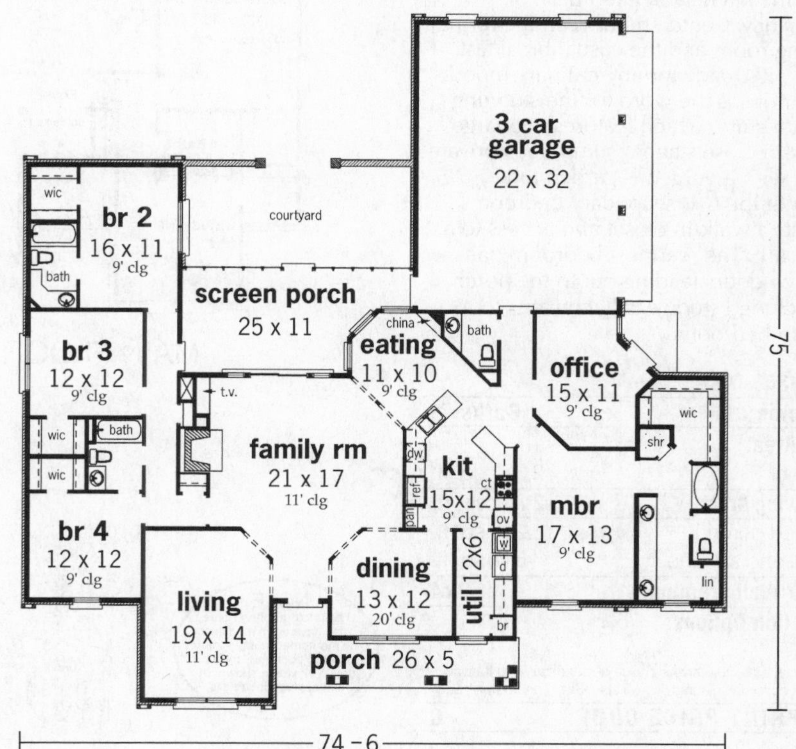

MAIN FLOOR

Live the Dream

- Enjoy the home of your dreams with this beautiful yet practical design.
- Brick dominates the exterior to give it a look of noble permanence.
- At the heart of the interior is the huge living room, which is highlighted by a cozy corner fireplace and access to a brilliant screened porch in back. A serving counter shared with the kitchen holds hors d'oeuvres during parties.
- A big corner pantry and a center island give the kitchen an extra dash of efficiency. Centered between the formal dining room and the casual breakfast nook, it's ready for any culinary mood.
- Luxurious is the word for the stunning master suite, which features two large walk-in closets and a sumptuous private bath with a gorgeous garden tub.
- Each of the two secondary bedrooms boasts a walk-in closet and access to a full bath. The rearmost bedroom has French doors leading out to the porch.
- A secluded study easily converts to a fourth bedroom.

Plan L-363-MSB

Bedrooms: 3+	**Baths:** 3
Living Area:	
Main floor	2,361 sq. ft.
Total Living Area:	**2,361 sq. ft.**
Screened porch	214 sq. ft.
Garage and storage	512 sq. ft.
Exterior Wall Framing:	2x4
Foundation Options:	
Slab	

(All plans can be built with your choice of foundation and framing. A generic conversion diagram is available. See order form.)

BLUEPRINT PRICE CODE: C

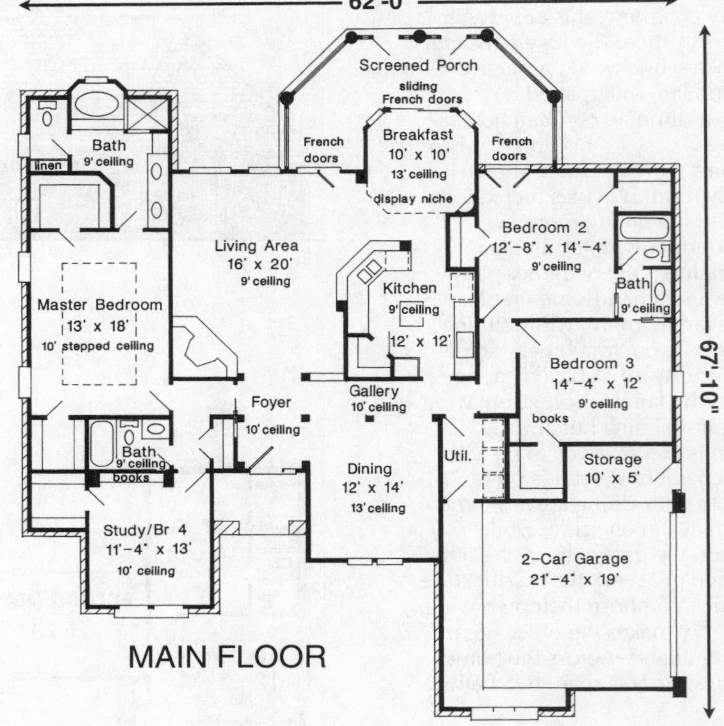

NOTE:
The photographed home may have been modified by the homeowner. Please refer to floor plan and/or drawn elevation shown for actual blueprint details.

REAR VIEW

ORDER BLUEPRINTS ANYTIME!
CALL TOLL-FREE 1-800-820-1296

Plan L-363-MSB

Plan copyright held by home designer/architect

SEE ORDER INFO ON PAGES 12-15
familyhandyman.com/homeplans

Fresh Air

- The most captivating feature of this home is its open atrium, which allows you a breath of fresh air from any part of the home whenever you desire.
- The master suite is just one of many areas that have direct access to the atrium. This sumptuous retreat includes a sitting room with a fireplace, a gorgeous bath with a spa tub that overlooks the atrium, and speedy access to both a study and an exercise room at opposite ends of the suite.
- When entertaining is on the agenda, this home fills the bill with its formal living and dining rooms, both in close proximity to the well-designed dual-island kitchen.
- Quiet time (or not) may be spent in the family room, which flows into a large game room that is the perfect size for an air hockey or ping pong table.
- During warm weather, small groups will enjoy relaxing on the screened porch.
- Two secondary bedrooms reside at the back of the home, just steps from the steam room and sauna. Coincidence? We think not!

Plan HDC-4228

Bedrooms: 3+	**Baths:** 3½
Living Area:	
Main floor	4,228 sq. ft.
Screened porch	247 sq. ft.
Total Living Area:	**4,228 sq. ft.**
Garage	932 sq. ft.
Exterior Wall Framing:	2x4
Foundation Options:	
Slab	

(All plans can be built with your choice of foundation and framing. A generic conversion diagram is available. See order form.)

BLUEPRINT PRICE CODE: G

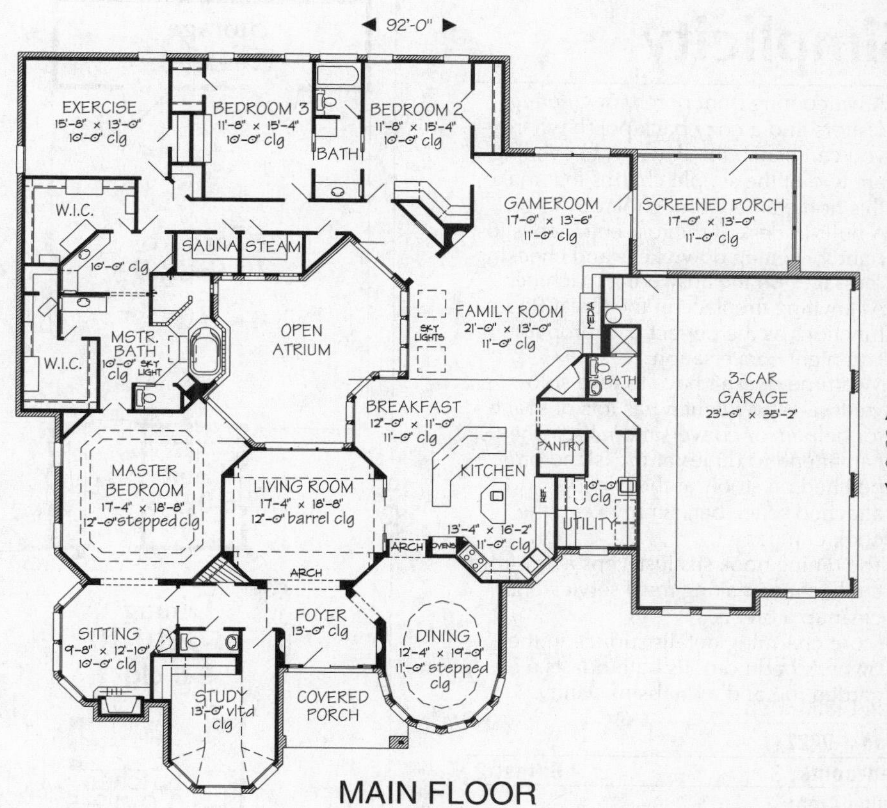

Plan HDC-4228

FOR MORE DETAILS, SEE PLAN AT familyhandyman.com/homeplans

Beautiful Simplicity

- A welcoming front porch for greeting visitors and a cozy back porch where you can watch the day turn to evening are two of the simple charms that make this home a beautiful choice.
- A built-in desk at the rear entrance is just right for setting down keys and checking messages on the answering machine.
- An inviting fireplace in the Great Room functions as the perfect backdrop for late-night conversation.
- Mealtime doesn't have to be a solo venture—this kitchen has lots of space for helpers or conversationalists. They can attend to duties at the island or, perched on stools at the island's attached snack bar, simply keep the cook company.
- The dining nook sits just steps away from the kitchen, making meal service and cleanup a breeze.
- More charming details surface in the owner's bedroom. Its bath boasts a garden tub and a dual-sink vanity.

Plan J-9722

Bedrooms: 3	**Baths:** 2
Living Area:	
Main floor	1,543 sq. ft.
Total Living Area:	**1,543 sq. ft.**
Carport	442 sq. ft.
Storage	120 sq. ft.
Exterior Wall Framing:	2x4
Foundation Options:	
Crawlspace	
Slab	

(All plans can be built with your choice of foundation and framing. A generic conversion diagram is available. See order form.)

BLUEPRINT PRICE CODE: **B**

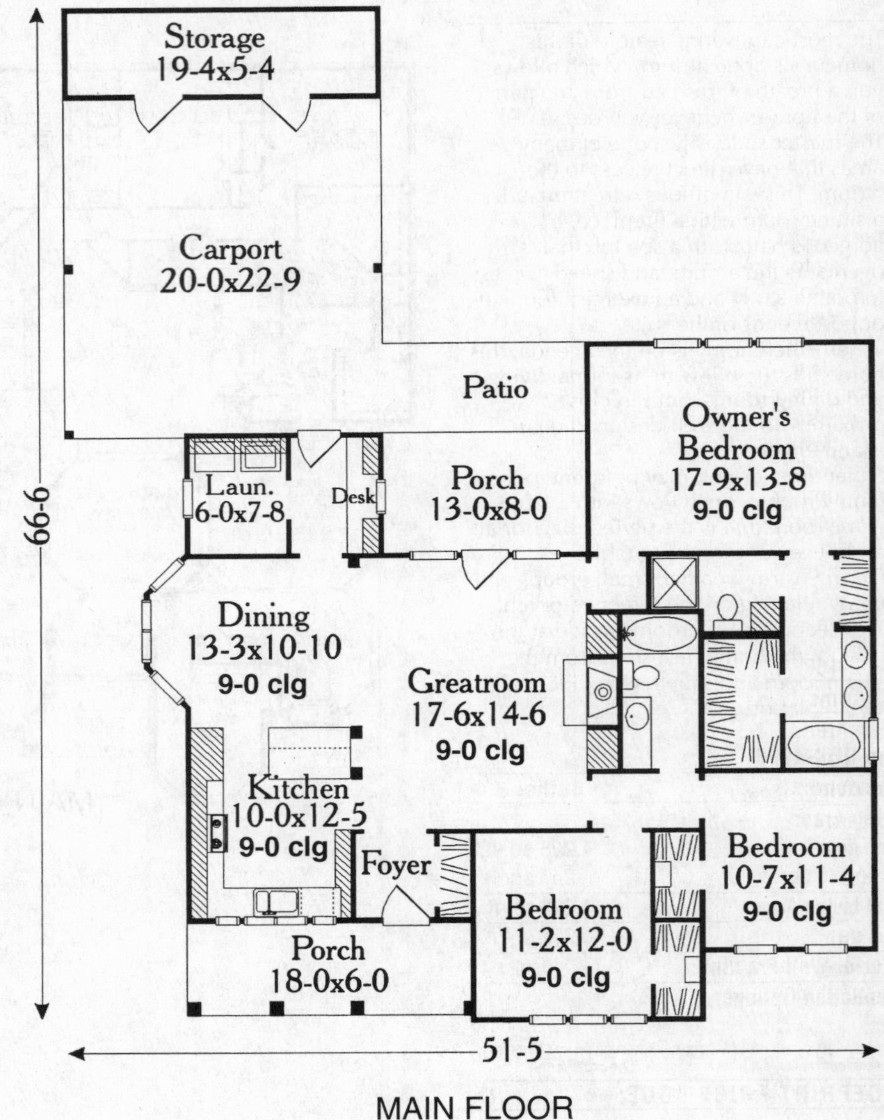

MAIN FLOOR

Plan J-9722

SEE ORDER INFO ON PAGES 12-15

Rustic Comfort

- Rustic charm highlights the exterior of this design, while the interior is filled with all the latest comforts.
- The front porch opens to the entry, where dividers with decorative railings offer views into the dining room.
- The sunken living room features a vaulted ceiling with exposed beams. The fireplace is fronted by fieldstone, adding to the rustic look. A rear door opens to a patio with luscious planters.
- The U-shaped kitchen features a china niche with glass shelves. Other bonuses include the adjacent sewing/hobby room, the oversized utility room and the garage's storage area and workbench.
- The master suite hosts a sunken sleeping area with built-in bookshelves. One step up is a sitting area that is defined by brick columns and a railed room divider. Double doors open to the bath, which offers a niche with glass shelves.
- Across the home, two more bedrooms share a second full bath.

Plan E-1607

Bedrooms: 3	**Baths:** 2
Living Area:	
Main floor	1,600 sq. ft.
Total Living Area:	**1,600 sq. ft.**
Standard basement	1,600 sq. ft.
Garage and workbench	484 sq. ft.
Storage	132 sq. ft.
Exterior Wall Framing:	2x6
Foundation Options:	
Standard basement	
Crawlspace	
Slab	

(All plans can be built with your choice of foundation and framing. A generic conversion diagram is available. See order form.)

BLUEPRINT PRICE CODE: **B**

VIEW INTO LIVING ROOM

REAR VIEW

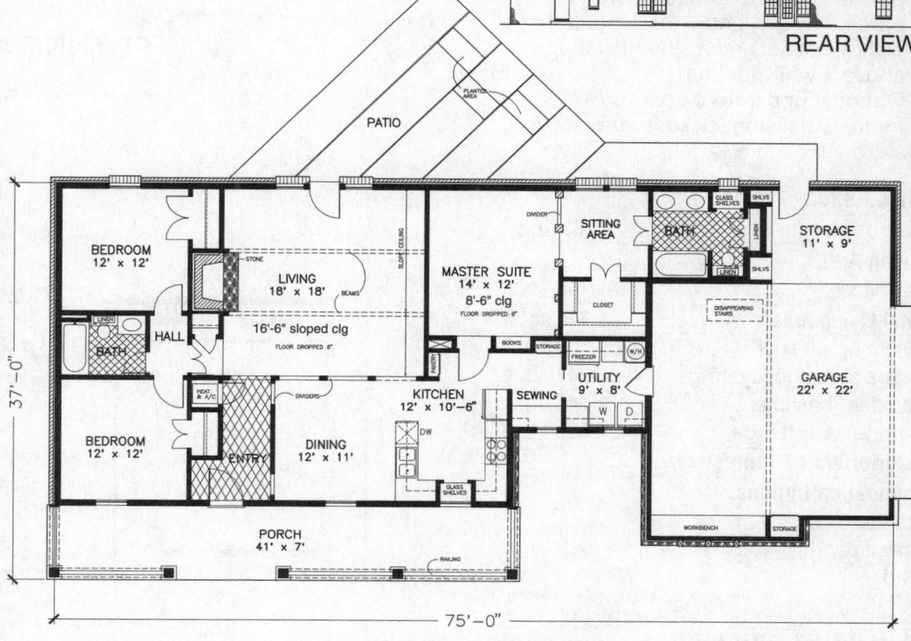

MAIN FLOOR

Breathtaking Open Space

- Soaring ceilings and an open floor plan add breathtaking volume to this charming country-style home.
- The inviting covered-porch entrance opens into the spacious living room, which boasts a spectacular cathedral ceiling. Two overhead dormers fill the area with natural light, while a fireplace adds warmth.
- Also under the cathedral ceiling, the kitchen and bayed breakfast room share an eating bar. Skylights brighten the convenient laundry room and the computer room, which provides access to a covered rear porch.
- The secluded master bedroom offers private access to another covered porch. The skylighted master bath has a walk-in closet and a sloped ceiling above a whirlpool tub.
- Optional upper-floor areas provide future expansion space for the needs of a growing family.

Plan J-9302	
Bedrooms: 3+	**Baths:** 2
Living Area:	
Main floor	1,745 sq. ft.
Total Living Area:	**1,745 sq. ft.**
Future upper floor	500 sq. ft.
Future area above garage	241 sq. ft.
Standard basement	1,745 sq. ft.
Garage and storage	559 sq. ft.
Exterior Wall Framing:	2x4
Foundation Options:	
Standard basement	
Crawlspace	
Slab	

(All plans can be built with your choice of foundation and framing. A generic conversion diagram is available. See order form.)

BLUEPRINT PRICE CODE: B

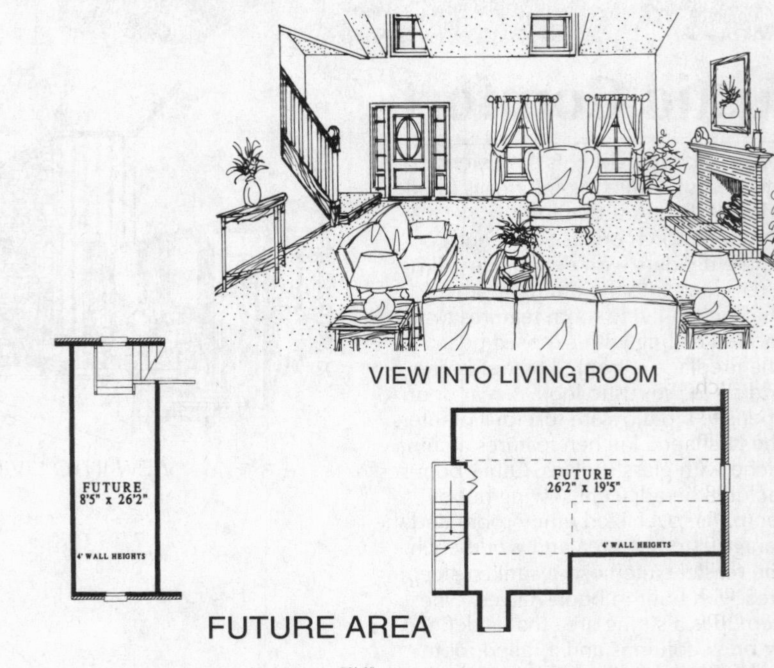

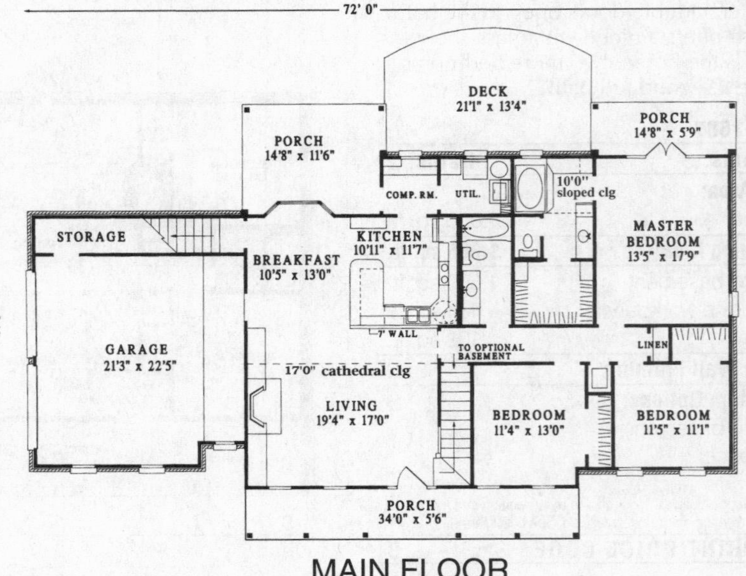

High Interest!

- Angles, high ceilings and an excellent use of space add interest and volume to the living areas of this efficient four-bedroom home.
- Beyond the beautiful stucco facade, the spacious central living room extends a warm welcome with its handsome fireplace; a French door whisks you outside to the covered back porch.
- The kitchen and breakfast room's unique designs ensure easy access and mobility for the family.
- A giant walk-in closet, a separate dressing room and an adjoining bath pamper you in the secluded master suite. The bath conveniently opens to the utility room, which houses the washer and dryer and an extra freezer.
- Three more bedrooms share another bath at the opposite end of the home.
- To the rear of the garage, a handy storage room and a built-in workbench help to organize your lawn and maintenance equipment.

Plan E-1828	
Bedrooms: 4	**Baths:** 2
Living Area:	
Main floor	1,828 sq. ft.
Total Living Area:	**1,828 sq. ft.**
Standard basement	1,828 sq. ft.
Garage and workbench	605 sq. ft.
Storage	120 sq. ft.
Exterior Wall Framing:	2x6
Foundation Options:	
Standard basement	
Crawlspace	
Slab	

(All plans can be built with your choice of foundation and framing. A generic conversion diagram is available. See order form.)

BLUEPRINT PRICE CODE: B

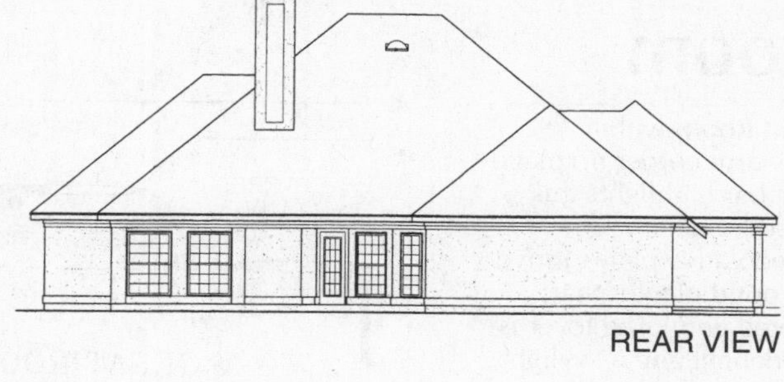

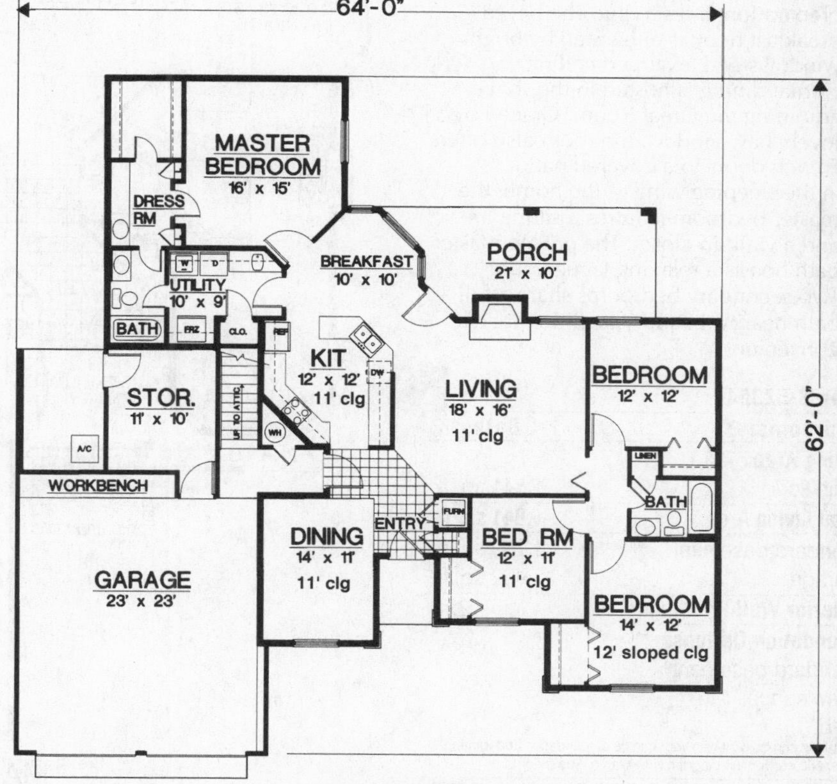

Plan E-1828

FOR MORE DETAILS, SEE PLAN AT familyhandyman.com/homeplans

Delightful Great Room

- An expansive Great Room with a vaulted ceiling, a warm corner fireplace and an angled wet bar highlights this tastefully appointed home.
- On the exterior, decorative plants thrive in the lush wraparound planter that leads to the sheltered entry. The foyer is brightened by a sidelight and a skylight.
- To the left, the kitchen offers an island cooktop with lots of room for food preparation and serving. The bayed breakfast nook is enhanced by bright windows and a vaulted ceiling.
- Formal dining is hosted in the space adjoining the Great Room. Graced by a lovely bay window, the room also offers French doors to a covered patio.
- In the sleeping wing of the home, the master bedroom features a sitting area and a walk-in closet. The private master bath boasts a relaxing Jacuzzi tub.
- Two secondary bedrooms share a full bath nearby. Laundry facilities are also convenient.

Plan S-52394

Bedrooms: 3 **Baths:** 2

Living Area:

Main floor	1,841 sq. ft.
Total Living Area:	**1,841 sq. ft.**
Standard basement	1,789 sq. ft.
Garage	432 sq. ft.
Exterior Wall Framing:	2x6

Foundation Options:

Standard basement
Crawlspace
Slab
(All plans can be built with your choice of foundation and framing. A generic conversion diagram is available. See order form.)

BLUEPRINT PRICE CODE: B

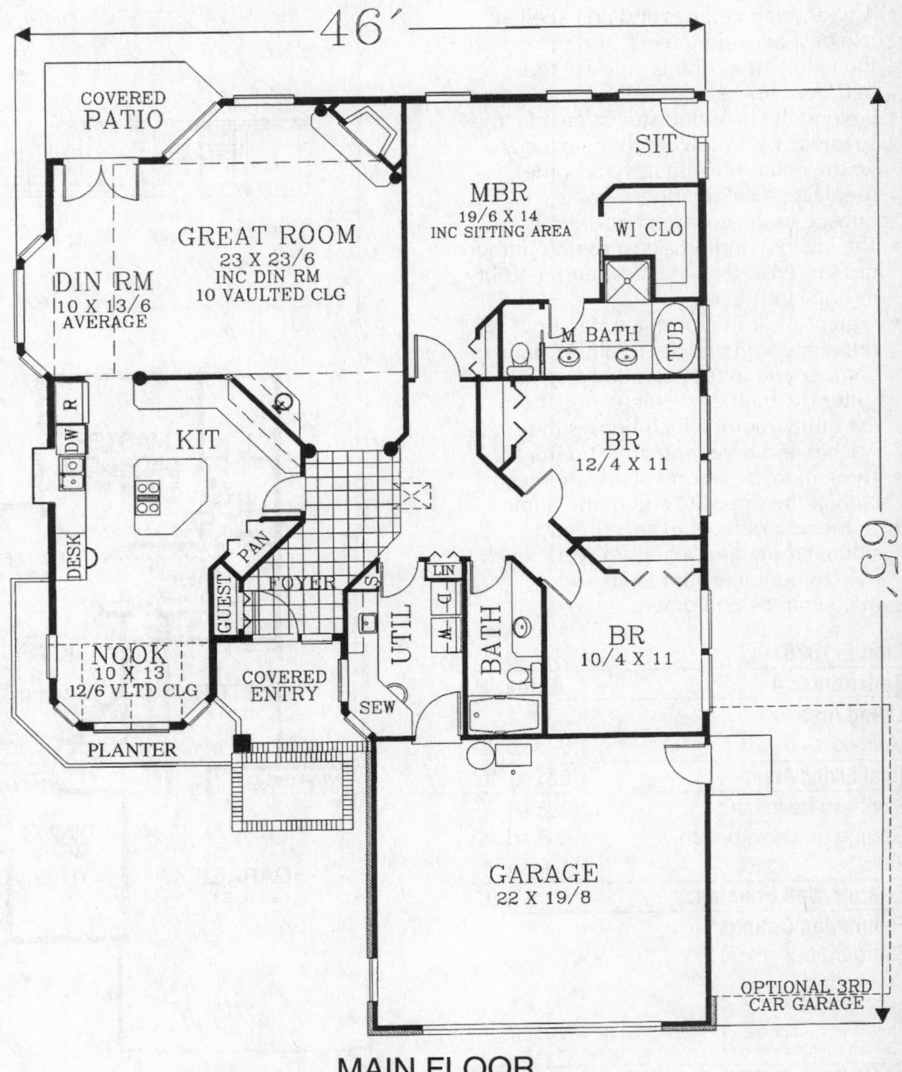

MAIN FLOOR

Plan S-52394

SEE ORDER INFO ON PAGES 12-15
familyhandyman.com/homeplans

Good Tidings

- The pretty exterior of this traditional home speaks wistfully of the calmer times of yesterday. Its up-to-date interior, however, promises comfortable living for years into the future.
- Inside, the columned dining room gives elegant meals a exquisite place of their own. Nearby access to the kitchen takes the labor out of even the most elaborate dinner parties.
- In the living room, also defined by columns, casual and formal times coexist easily. A warm fireplace provides a visual anchor to the room.
- The family cook will love the design of the kitchen, which opens to the living room and the breakfast nook, letting folks visit during meal preparation. When you're seated at the table in the bayed nook, Monday mornings will definitely seem brighter.
- For the resident do-it-yourselfer, the shop and extra storage space in the garage keep projects organized.
- Across the home, the master bedroom starts and ends each day in quiet seclusion. Private access to the porch lets you drink in a breath of fresh air, while the dual-sink vanity in the bath cuts down on traffic jams.

Plan J-9422

Bedrooms: 3	**Baths:** 2½
Living Area:	
Main floor	1,860 sq. ft.
Total Living Area:	**1,860 sq. ft.**
Standard basement	1,860 sq. ft.
Garage	610 sq. ft.
Shop/storage	130 sq.ft.
Storage	41 sq. ft.
Exterior Wall Framing:	2x4
Foundation Options:	
Standard basement	
Crawlspace	
Slab	

(All plans can be built with your choice of foundation and framing. A generic conversion diagram is available. See order form.)

BLUEPRINT PRICE CODE: B

HOBBY ROOMS & WORKSHOPS

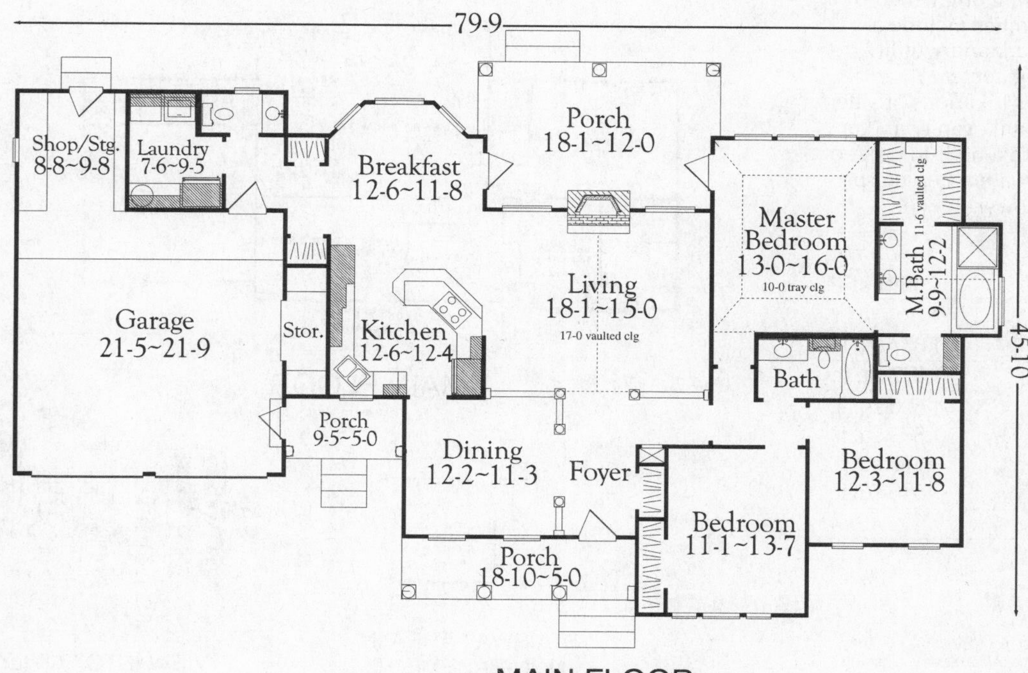

MAIN FLOOR

Upscale Charm

- Country charm and the very latest in conveniences mark this upscale home. For extra appeal, all of the living areas are on the main floor, while the upper floor hosts space for future expansion.
- Set off from the foyer, the dining room is embraced by elegant columns. Arched windows in the dining room and in the bedroom across the hall echo the front porch detailing. Straight ahead, a wall of French doors in the family room overlooks a back porch and a large deck.
- A curved island snack bar smoothly connects the gourmet kitchen to the sunny breakfast area, which features a dramatic vaulted ceiling brightened by skylights. Other amenities include a computer room and a laundry/utility room with a recycling center.
- The master bedroom's luxurious private bath includes a dual-sink vanity and a large storage unit with a built-in chest of drawers. Other extras are a step-up spa tub and a separate shower.

Plan J-92100	
Bedrooms: 3+	**Baths:** 2
Living Area:	
Main floor	1,877 sq. ft.
Total Living Area:	**1,877 sq. ft.**
Future upper floor	1,500 sq. ft.
Standard basement	1,877 sq. ft.
Garage	478 sq. ft.
Storage	46 sq. ft.
Exterior Wall Framing:	2x4
Foundation Options:	
Standard basement	
Crawlspace	
Slab	

(All plans can be built with your choice of foundation and framing. A generic conversion diagram is available. See order form.)

BLUEPRINT PRICE CODE: B

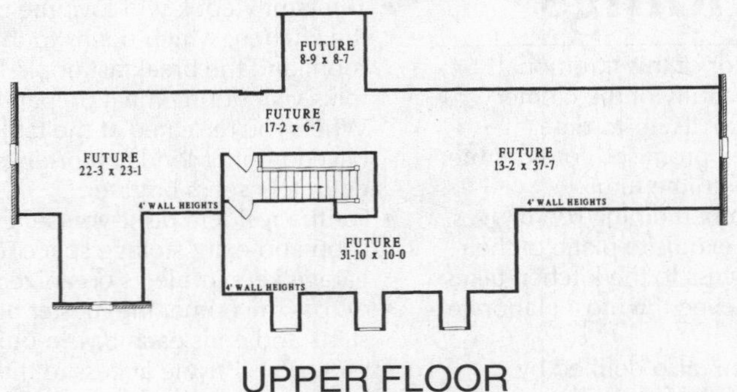

UPPER FLOOR

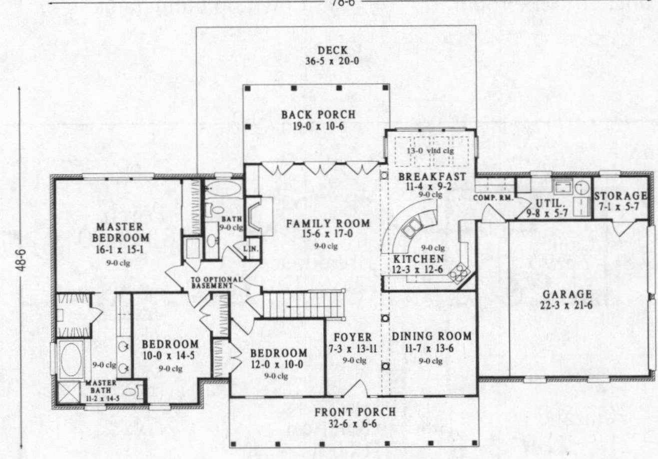

MAIN FLOOR

STAIRWAY AREA IN NON-BASEMENT VERSIONS

VIEW INTO FAMILY ROOM AND BREAKFAST NOOK

ORDER BLUEPRINTS ANYTIME! CALL TOLL-FREE 1-800-820-1296

Plan J-92100

SEE ORDER INFO ON PAGES 12-15

familyhandyman.com/homeplans

Graceful Windows

- Sunny windows, a prominent central dormer, a columned front porch, keystones and shutters give this home unparalleled grace.
- A sidelighted gallery introduces the Great Room. A volume ceiling, a fireplace and huge windows overlooking the rear patio make this room the natural center of activity.
- A serving bar connects the galley kitchen, handily located near the garage, with the other living areas. Meals may be served in the adjacent dining area, or on the patio during warm weather.
- Tucked away in a corner of the home for privacy, the master suite revels in luxury. A vaulted ceiling, a huge walk-in closet, a garden tub, a two-sink vanity and a private toilet provide total comfort.
- Two more bedrooms at the front of the home share a full bath.
- An extra room near the home's entry may serve as a formal dining room, a study, a den or a home office—the choice is yours!

Plan DD-1906-1

Bedrooms: 3+	**Baths:** 2
Living Area:	
Main floor	1,906 sq. ft.
Total Living Area:	**1,906 sq. ft.**
Standard basement	1,906 sq. ft.
Garage	630 sq. ft.
Exterior Wall Framing:	2x4
Foundation Options:	
Standard basement	
Crawlspace	
Slab	

(All plans can be built with your choice of foundation and framing. A generic conversion diagram is available. See order form.)

BLUEPRINT PRICE CODE: B

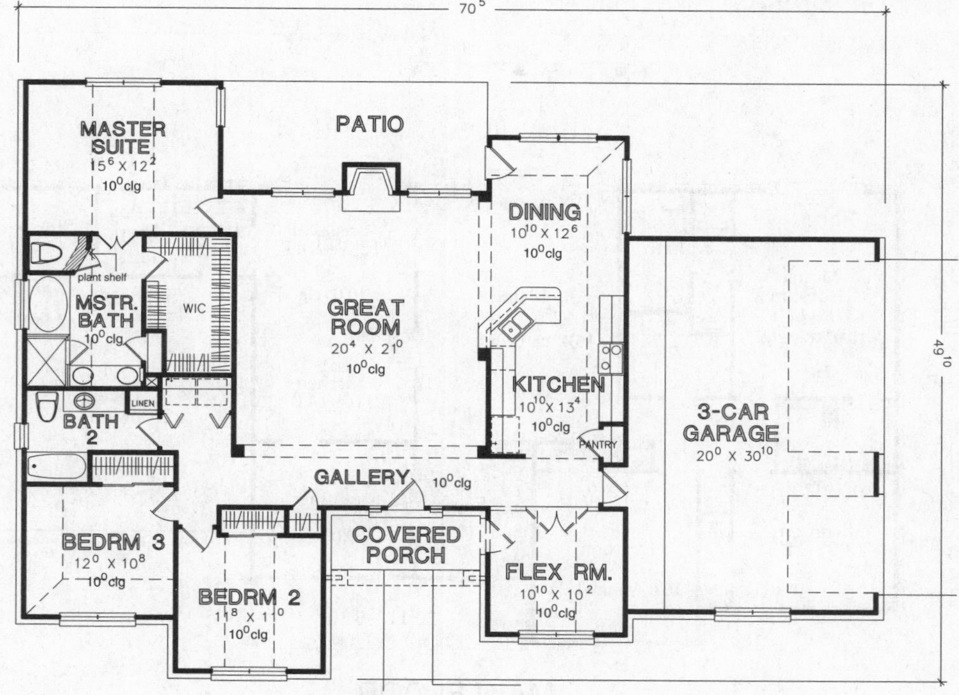

MAIN FLOOR

Plan DD-1906-1

FOR MORE DETAILS, SEE PLAN AT familyhandyman.com/homeplans

Memories in the Making

- You will enjoy years of memories in this peaceful country home.
- A tranquil covered porch opens into the foyer, where regal columns introduce the formal dining room. Raised ceilings enhance the foyer, dining room, kitchen and breakfast nook.
- Past two closets, a cathedral ceiling adds glamour to the living room. A grand fireplace flanked by French doors under beautiful quarter-round transoms will wow your guests! The French doors open to an inviting porch that is great for afternoon get-togethers.
- The sunny breakfast bay merges with the gourmet kitchen, which includes a large pantry and an island snack bar. Bi-fold doors above the sink create a handy pass-through to the living room.
- A neat computer room nearby allows the kids to do their homework under a parent's watchful eye.
- Across the home, a stylish tray ceiling crowns the master suite. The skylighted master bath features a refreshing whirlpool tub.
- A hall bath services two additional bedrooms. The larger bedroom is expanded by a vaulted ceiling.

Plan J-9294

Bedrooms: 3	**Baths:** 2
Living Area:	
Main floor	2,018 sq. ft.
Total Living Area:	**2,018 sq. ft.**
Standard basement	2,018 sq. ft.
Garage and storage	556 sq. ft.
Exterior Wall Framing:	2x4
Foundation Options:	
Standard basement	
Crawlspace	
Slab	

(All plans can be built with your choice of foundation and framing. A generic conversion diagram is available. See order form.)

BLUEPRINT PRICE CODE: C

74-11

49-2

Porch 17'10"~10'0"

Master Bedroom 13'0"~17'1" 10'0" tray clg

M.Bath

Bath

Living 21'0"~16'3" 15'4" cathedral clg

Breakfast 13'3"~8'11"

10'0" clg

Kitchen 13'0"~14'0"

Comp. Room

Laun.

Storage 8'1"~7'1"

Garage 20'11"~21'5"

Bedroom 13'0"~11'3"

Bedroom 13'1"~14'1" 10'0" vaulted clg

Foyer 10'0" clg

Dining 13'0"~10'11" 10'0" clg

Porch 22'11"~5'10"

MAIN FLOOR

Plan J-9294

SEE ORDER INFO ON PAGES 12-15

Handsome Facade

- This distinguished home's facade boasts a trio of dormers above a handsome front porch, complete with columns and room enough to enjoy a glass of lemonade with the neighbors.
- Inside, the entry leads to the versatile study and the expansive Great Room, which features a stunning corner fireplace and three large windows overlooking a large covered patio.
- The modern kitchen enjoys an island workstation and a walk-in pantry. These, along with a snack bar, help to serve the formal dining room, the Great Room and the sunny morning room.
- The exquisite master suite offers a pair of walk-in closets and a private bath with a garden spa tub, a separate shower and dual sinks.
- One of the secondary bedrooms features a full, private bath. The others share a full hall bath and each enjoys a built-in desk, making them perfect for the kids. A workshop off the garage is great for the family carpenter.

Plan DD-2096

Bedrooms: 4+	**Baths:** 3
Living Area:	
Main floor	2,088 sq. ft.
Total Living Area:	**2,088 sq. ft.**
Standard basement	2,088 sq. ft.
Garage and workshop	552 sq. ft.
Storage	64 sq. ft.
Exterior Wall Framing:	2x4

Foundation Options:
Standard basement
Crawlspace
Slab
(All plans can be built with your choice of foundation and framing. A generic conversion diagram is available. See order form.)

BLUEPRINT PRICE CODE: C

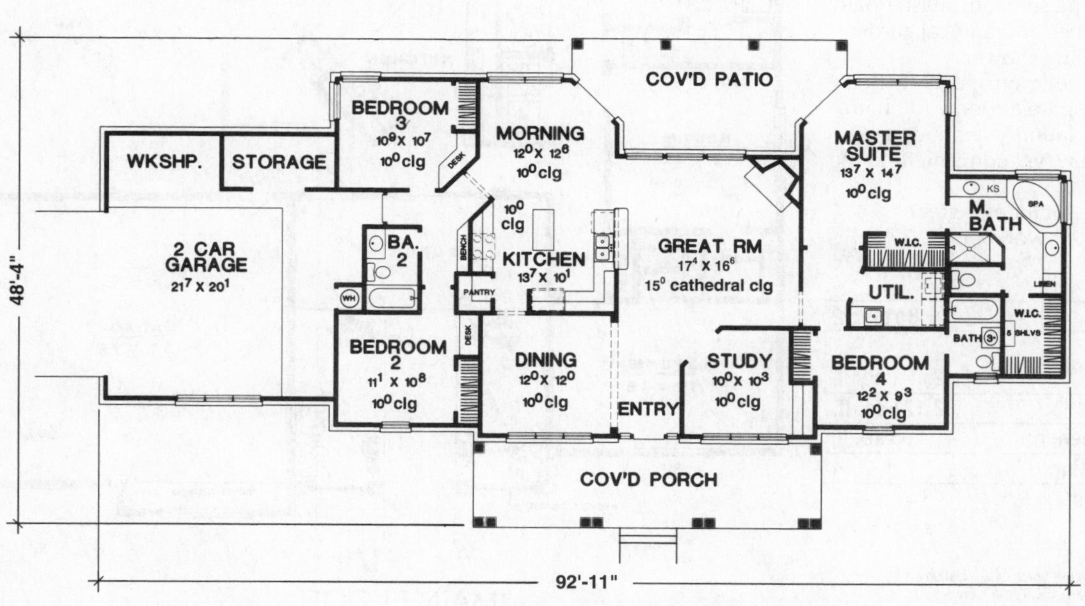

MAIN FLOOR

Attractive Angles

- Unique angles and open circulation define the interior of this traditional, Early American-style home. Its flowing family spaces accommodate the busiest schedules with flair.
- Centered around a stone fireplace, the Great Room and the dining room overlook a rear terrace. Easily serving this fine entertaining space, the central kitchen boasts a long eating bar for light appetizers or buffets—even snacks on the go!
- The angled master suite offers a huge walk-in closet, its own cozy fireplace, a panoramic rear view and private access to the terrace. The spacious master bath offers twin vanities and an oval garden tub with a separate shower.
- Two additional bedrooms, each with a walk-in closet, share a roomy full bath. Across the hall, laundry facilities are hidden from view, yet convenient to the sleeping quarters.
- Even the garage includes a great amenity: a well-lit workbench!

Plan VL-2121	
Bedrooms: 3	**Baths:** 2
Living Area:	
Main floor	2,121 sq. ft.
Total Living Area:	**2,121 sq. ft.**
Garage and workbench	483 sq. ft.
Exterior Wall Framing:	2x4
Foundation Options:	
Crawlspace	
Slab	
(All plans can be built with your choice of foundation and framing. A generic conversion diagram is available. See order form.)	
BLUEPRINT PRICE CODE:	**C**

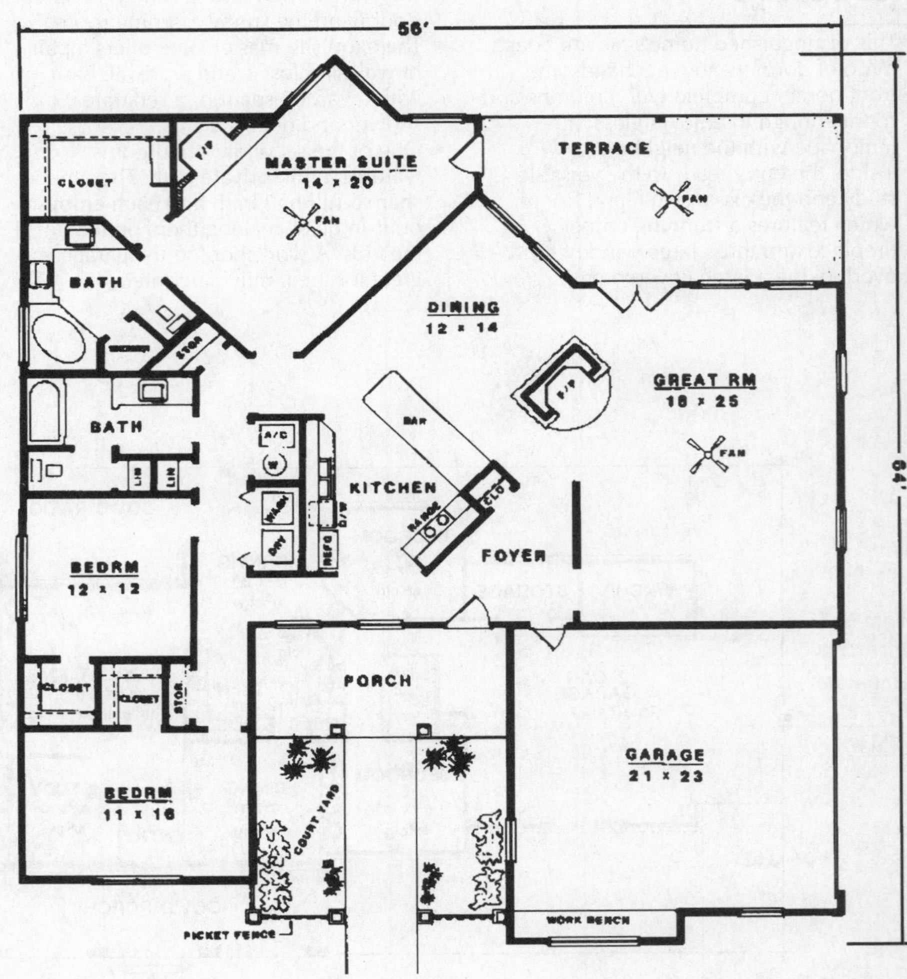

MAIN FLOOR

ORDER BLUEPRINTS ANYTIME!
CALL TOLL-FREE 1-800-820-1296

Plan VL-2121

SEE ORDER INFO ON PAGES 12-15
familyhandyman.com/homeplans

From the Past to Your Future

- With a trio of dormers up top and a classic porch out front, this stately traditional-style home steps straight from the past and into your future.
- Pass through the foyer into the living room, which features a tray ceiling and a window-flanked fireplace that warms not just that space, but the adjoining breakfast room, too.
- Mealtime is easy with a roomy kitchen offering lots of counter space, and with an angled counter serving both the living and breakfast rooms, you'll still be close by when guests come over.
- The owner's bedroom includes two walk-in closets and a private bath with a dual-sink vanity, while two secondary bedrooms share a full bath.
- Upstairs, future space abounds, with enough room for a wacky game room and even a home office.

Plan J-9513

Bedrooms: 3+	**Baths:** 2½
Living Area:	
Main floor	2,127 sq. ft.
Total Living Area:	**2,127 sq. ft.**
Future upper floor	1,095 sq. ft.
Standard basement	2,127 sq. ft.
Garage and storage	546 sq. ft.
Exterior Wall Framing:	2x4

Foundation Options:
Standard basement
Crawlspace
Slab
(All plans can be built with your choice of foundation and framing. A generic conversion diagram is available. See order form.)

BLUEPRINT PRICE CODE: **C**

UPPER FLOOR

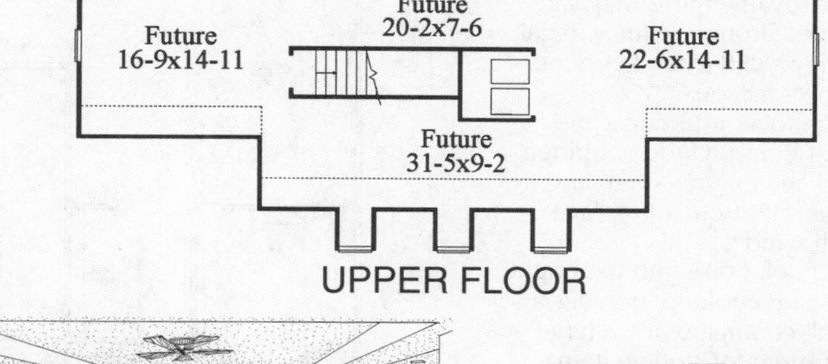
VIEW INTO LIVING ROOM

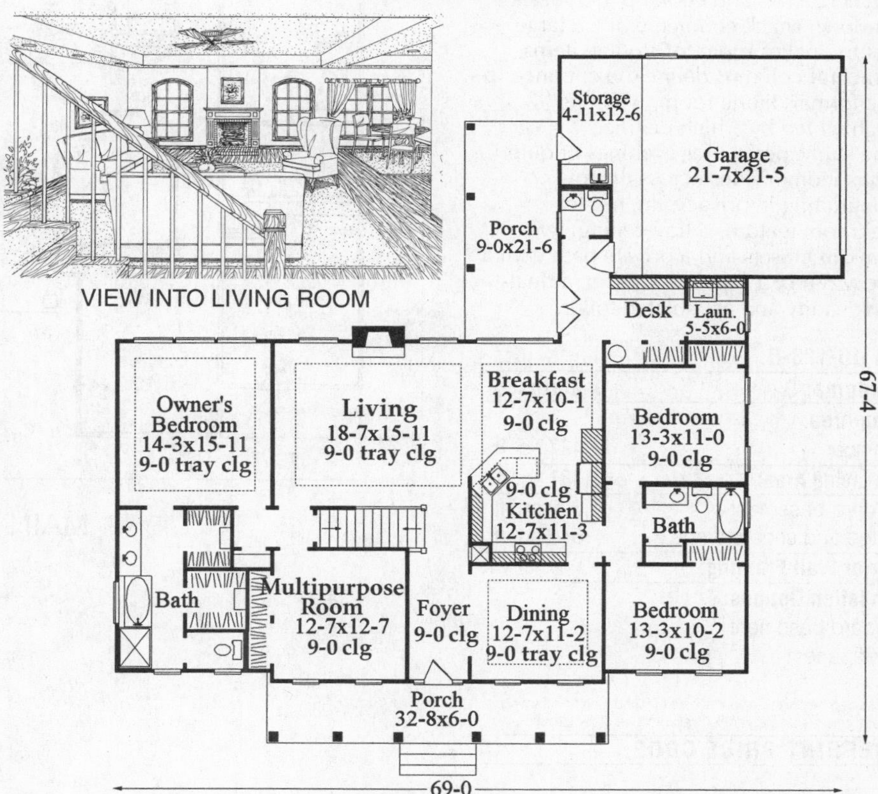

MAIN FLOOR

Plan J-9513

Royally Inspired

- You'll feel like royalty in this majestic one-story home. Strong rooflines, regal transom windows and smart keystone accents adorn its facade.
- Inside, the high foyer introduces the stunning Great Room. Under a unique barrel-vaulted ceiling, this sprawling area enjoys warmth from a fireplace flanked by tall windows.
- The breakfast nook flows into the bright kitchen. An island cooktop includes a sit-down snack counter, while a large pantry makes room for storage items.
- Graceful columns define the entrance to the formal dining room, which is highlighted by a high ceiling.
- The study, perfect for evenings of quiet relaxation, resides across the foyer.
- Luxuriating in privacy, the master bedroom features a tray ceiling, two walk-in closets and a private bath with a Jacuzzi tub, a separate shower, a dual-sink vanity and an isolated toilet.

Plan UD-123-D

Bedrooms: 3+	**Baths:** 2
Living Area:	
Main floor	2,437 sq. ft.
Total Living Area:	**2,437 sq. ft.**
Standard basement	2,649 sq. ft.
Garage and shop/storage	646 sq. ft.
Exterior Wall Framing:	2x4

Foundation Options:

Standard basement
Crawlspace
Slab
(All plans can be built with your choice of foundation and framing. A generic conversion diagram is available. See order form.)

BLUEPRINT PRICE CODE: C

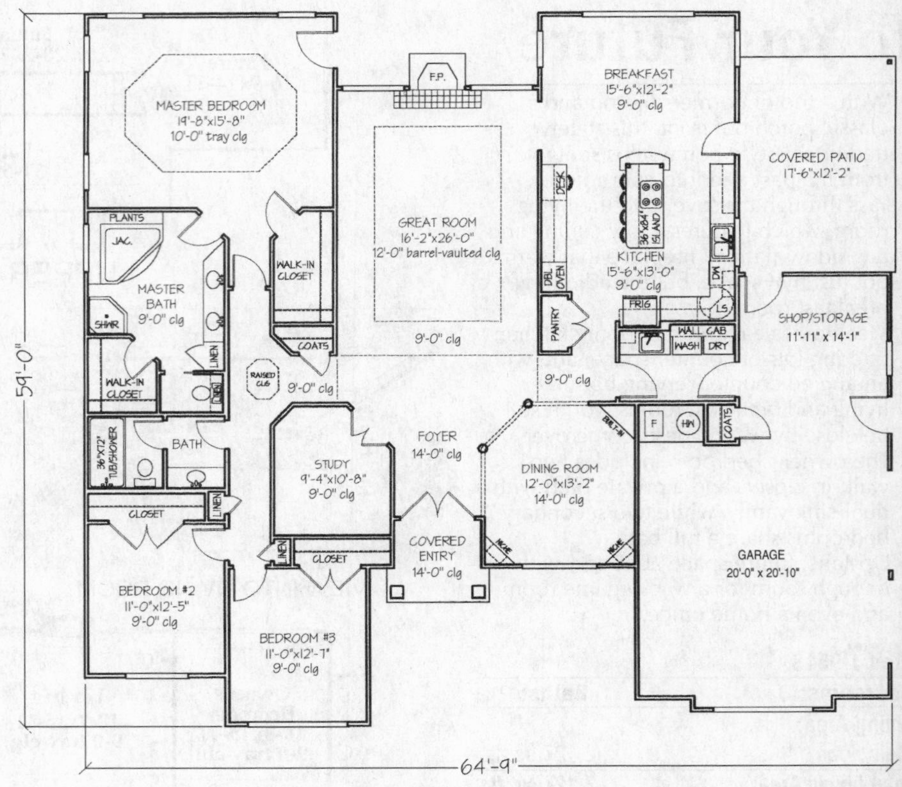

MAIN FLOOR

Plan UD-123-D

SEE ORDER INFO ON PAGES 12-15

Country Road

- The pretty countenance of this one-story home makes it look as if it was plucked straight from a winding country road. Whether rocking on the front porch, or reading a book by a sunny window, you will love the home's peaceful nature.
- An elegant gallery welcomes guests inside and leads through four handsome columns into the impressive living room. When you want to roll out the red carpet, this is the room.
- On the right, the breakfast nook and the kitchen merge together, creating an efficient space for casual meals. A neat serving counter between the two rooms holds dishes, platters and pitchers while serving dinner. In the kitchen, an island cooktop frees up counter space to chop vegetables for your stir-fry.
- The home's showstopper is the fantastic media room. Instead of driving to a crowded theater, settle into a comfortable easy chair for a night of entertainment in your own home.
- Across the home, the master bedroom boasts private access to a patio. As the day begins and ends, the amenity-packed bath offers luxurious treatment for the masters of the home. A large walk-in closet completes the suite.

Plan DD-2510

Bedrooms: 3+	**Baths:** 2
Living Area:	
Main floor	2,510 sq. ft.
Total Living Area:	**2,510 sq. ft.**
Standard basement	2,510 sq. ft.
Garage and workshop	508 sq. ft.
Exterior Wall Framing:	2x4
Foundation Options:	
Standard basement	
Crawlspace	
Slab	

(All plans can be built with your choice of foundation and framing. A generic conversion diagram is available. See order form.)

BLUEPRINT PRICE CODE: **D**

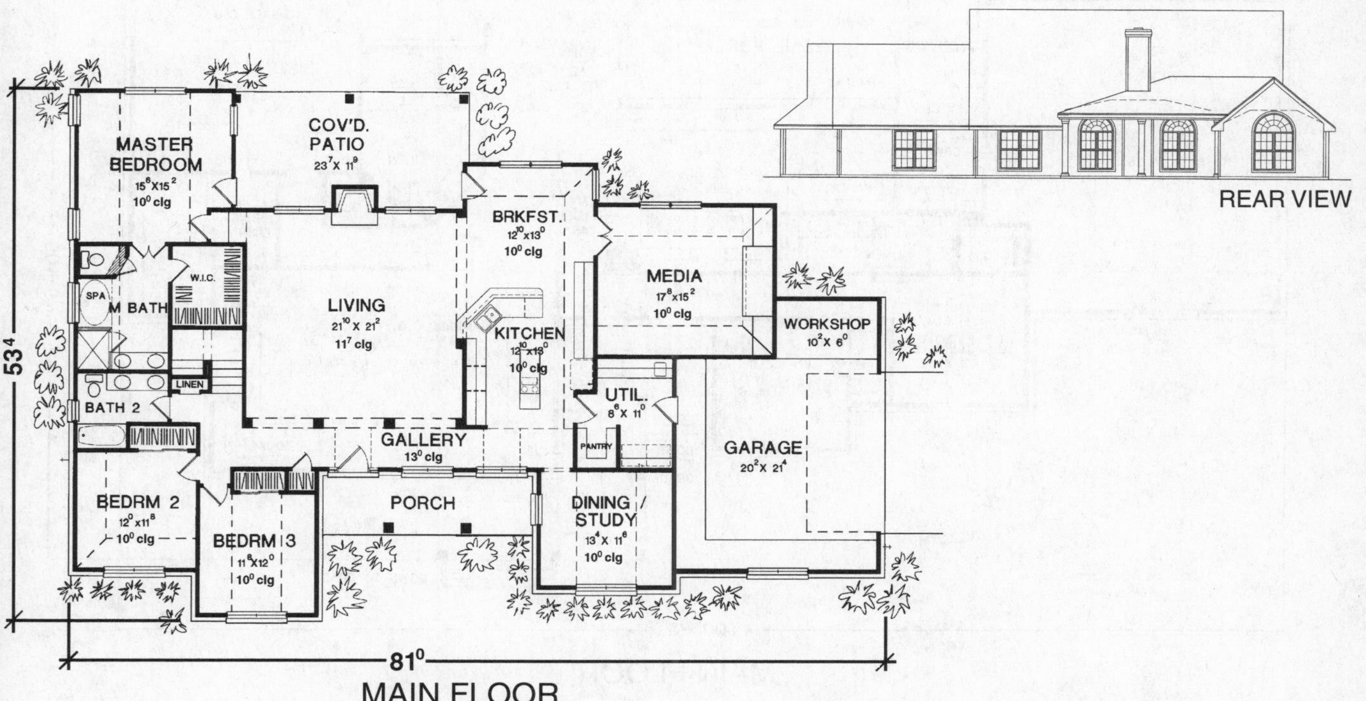

Exciting Ranch

- A wide wraparound porch and a brick exterior give this exciting ranch a rustic, yet sophisticated look.
- Past the porch, the entrance opens directly to the spacious Great Room, which boasts an elegant gambrel ceiling and a handsome brick fireplace centered between built-in bookshelves.
- To create a more open, airy feel, the Great Room flows into the kitchen and breakfast area.
- Complete with a large island cooktop, a handy snack bar, a walk-in pantry and a windowed sink, the kitchen is truly designed for the gourmet! The radiant breakfast bay expands to a covered backyard porch.
- A private porch and a relaxing spa bath reward the homeowners at the end of a long day! Convenient knee space is provided between the dual sinks.
- The two remaining bedrooms boast walk-in closets and share a second full bath. A service entrance is nearby.

Plan KLF-9303

Bedrooms: 3	**Baths:** 2
Living Area:	
Main floor	2,522 sq. ft.
Total Living Area:	**2,522 sq. ft.**
Garage and work area	738 sq. ft.
Exterior Wall Framing:	2x4
Foundation Options:	
Slab	

(All plans can be built with your choice of foundation and framing. A generic conversion diagram is available. See order form.)

BLUEPRINT PRICE CODE: D

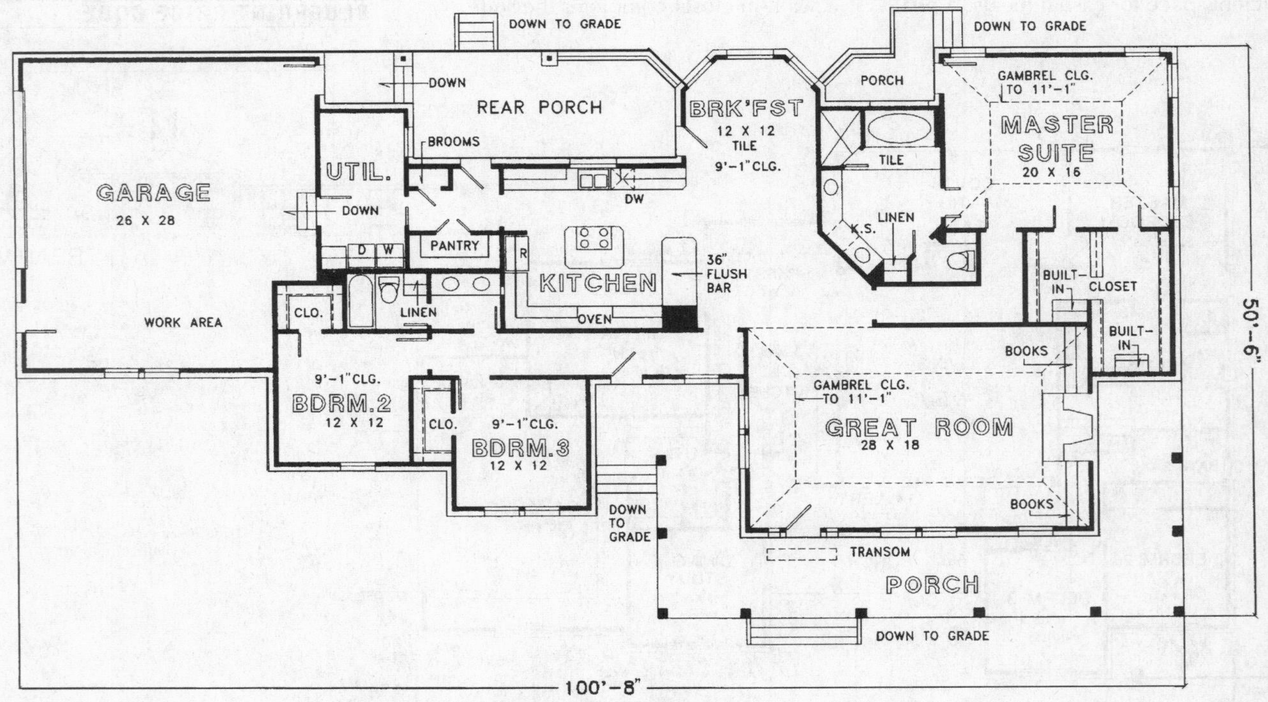

MAIN FLOOR

ORDER BLUEPRINTS ANYTIME! CALL TOLL-FREE 1-800-820-1296

Plan KLF-9303

SEE ORDER INFO ON PAGES 12-15

familyhandyman.com/homeplans

Grand Gallery

- Columns line the grand gallery that runs the length of this impressive, single-level home. The Great Room beyond is a flexible space, perfect for formal parties or family gatherings.
- Boasting exceptional counter space and a convenient island cooktop, the kitchen adjoins a bright breakfast room across a handy serving bar.
- A walk-in pantry boosts storage space in the utility area, which doubles as a mudroom. A generous-sized workshop is an added bonus in the garage.
- Imagine theater-quality entertainment in the vaulted media room. Its casual atmosphere makes it a great alternative for entertaining.
- Across the home, the master suite dominates the sleeping wing. Featuring plenty of windows and a vaulted ceiling, the suite also offers a walk-in closet and a fantastic bath with a garden tub and a separate shower.
- Vaulted ceilings crown the two secondary bedrooms, one of which enjoys a lovely, front-facing bay window. They share a full hall bath and two linen closets.

Plan DD-2545

Bedrooms: 3+	**Baths:** 2
Living Area:	
Main floor	2,543 sq. ft.
Total Living Area:	**2,543 sq. ft.**
Standard basement	2,543 sq. ft.
Garage and workshop	806 sq. ft.
Exterior Wall Framing:	2x4
Foundation Options:	
Standard basement	
Crawlspace	
Slab	

(All plans can be built with your choice of foundation and framing. A generic conversion diagram is available. See order form.)

BLUEPRINT PRICE CODE: D

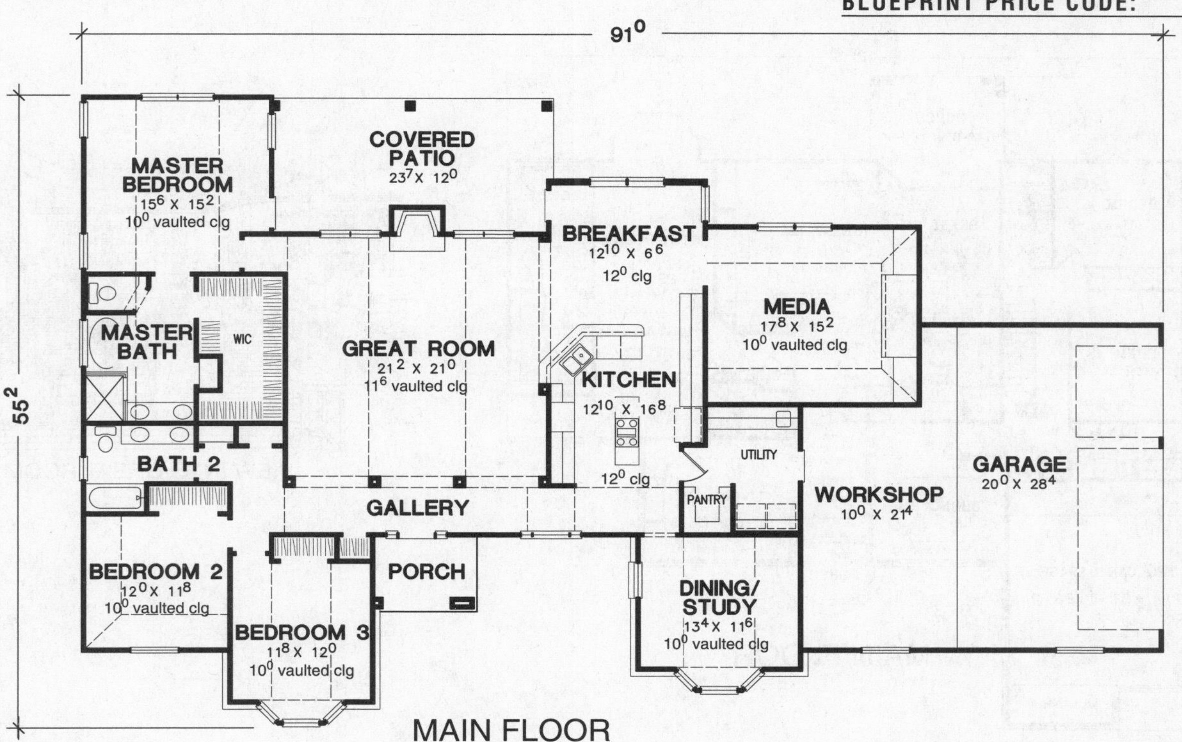

MAIN FLOOR

Luxurious and Sprawling

- This luxurious, sprawling brick home features elegantly zoned living spaces for everyone in your family.
- With its arched transom window, sidelights and a stepped ceiling, the entry makes a strong statement to arriving guests.
- Flanking the foyer, the formal living and dining rooms boast pillar-framed entrances and stepped ceilings. A fireplace warms the living room, while the dining room's proximity to the kitchen makes dinner parties easy.
- The island kitchen includes a walk-in pantry, plus an angled, combination snack and serving counter that extends to the Great Room and breakfast area.
- The dramatic Great Room contains a fireplace, access to the rear porch, and built-ins for a media center.
- The sensational master suite enjoys a bayed sitting area, a huge walk-in closet and a large private bath with two vanities and a windowed spa tub. An adjacent office accesses a side porch.
- Plans for an unfinished attic are included in the blueprints.

Plan AX-98364

Bedrooms: 3+	**Baths:** 3
Living Area:	
Main floor	2,585 sq. ft.
Total Living Area:	**2,585 sq. ft.**
Standard basement	2,585 sq. ft.
Garage and workshop	520 sq. ft.
Exterior Wall Framing:	2x4
Foundation Options:	
Standard basement	
Crawlspace	

(All plans can be built with your choice of foundation and framing. A generic conversion diagram is available. See order form.)

BLUEPRINT PRICE CODE: D

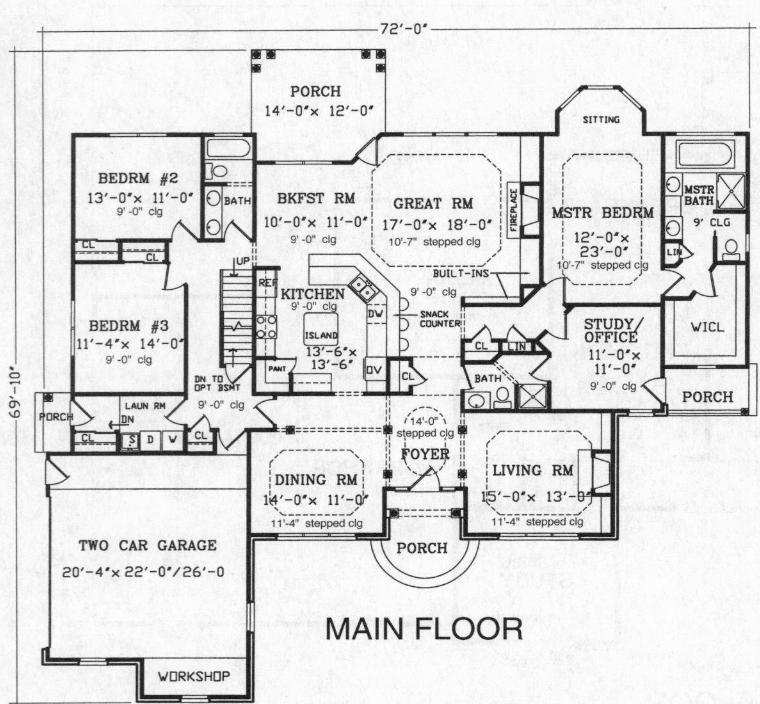

MAIN FLOOR

VIEW INTO GREAT ROOM

Plan AX-98364

SEE ORDER INFO ON PAGES 12-15
familyhandyman.com/homeplans

Room to Move

- Large rooms and high ceilings give this French-style home an expansive feel; ceiling fans lend atmosphere and grace to the main living spaces.
- Accessed from the soaring entry, the dining and living rooms also boast high ceilings. Lovely windows with arched transoms flood each room with natural light, while a fireplace and built-in bookshelves highlight the living room.
- Double doors from the dining room lead into the kitchen, which sports a large serving bar, a built-in desk and a central work island with cabinets. Two boxed-out windows above the sink let in the sun, while the breakfast nook basks in the light from a bay window.
- A stepped ceiling rises over the secluded master suite, which offers private access to the covered backyard porch. Behind double doors, the luxurious garden bath enjoys the bedroom's warm see-through fireplace.
- The secondary bedrooms have elevated ceilings and share a skylighted bath.
- The bonus room above the garage may be designed as an additional bedroom or a quiet office space.

Plan RD-2240

Bedrooms: 4+	**Baths:** 2½
Living Area:	
Main floor	2,240 sq. ft.
Bonus room	349 sq. ft.
Total Living Area:	**2,589 sq. ft.**
Garage and workbench	737 sq. ft.
Exterior Wall Framing:	2x4

Foundation Options:

Crawlspace

Slab

(All plans can be built with your choice of foundation and framing. A generic conversion diagram is available. See order form.)

BLUEPRINT PRICE CODE: D

VIEW INTO MASTER BATH

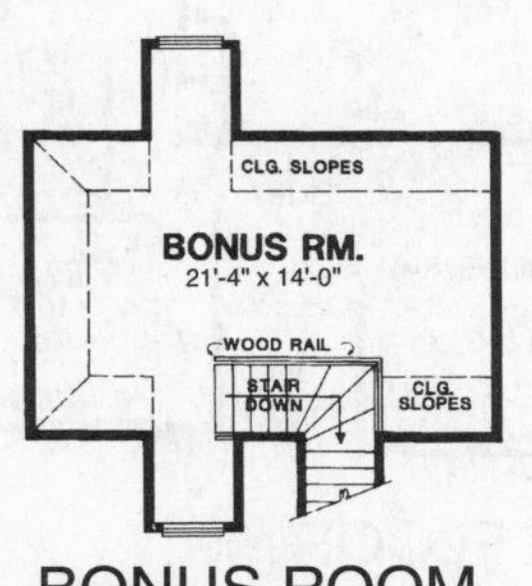

BONUS ROOM

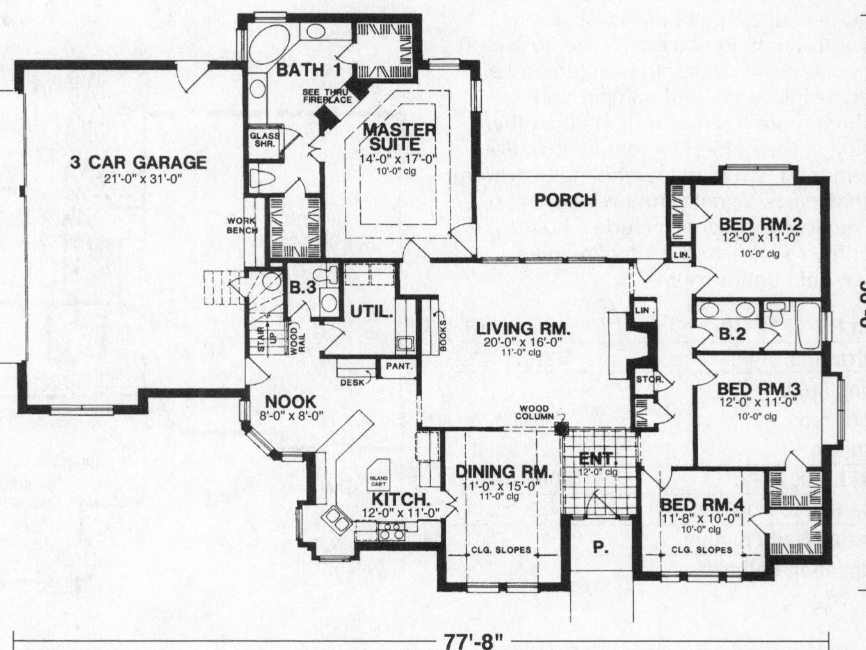

MAIN FLOOR

Graceful Lines

- Shining, arched windows and graceful rooflines enhance the distinctive facade of this one-story home.
- Inside, light from the entry floods the spacious living room, where three arched windows span the back wall. A handsome fireplace and a wet bar fulfill your entertaining needs.
- The well-appointed island kitchen sports boxed-out windows above the sink and adjoins a bayed nook. At the other end of the kitchen, double doors open into a formal dining room, which boasts one of the lovely front windows.
- Spend warm evenings on a back porch, which is accessible from the secluded master suite. The bedroom shares a see-through fireplace with the posh private bath, where an oval tub and a dual-sink vanity will pamper you.
- Three more bedrooms lie on the other side of the home. Two enjoy boxed-out windows, while the remaining bedroom showcases a grand front window.
- Practical highlights include a huge utility room near the kitchen and a versatile bonus room.

Plan RD-2316-7B	
Bedrooms: 4+	**Baths:** 2½
Living Area:	
Bonus room	349 sq. ft.
Main floor	2,320 sq. ft.
Total Living Area:	**2,669 sq. ft.**
Garage and workbench	735 sq. ft.
Exterior Wall Framing:	2x4
Foundation Options:	
Crawlspace	
Slab	

(All plans can be built with your choice of foundation and framing. A generic conversion diagram is available. See order form.)

BLUEPRINT PRICE CODE:	**D**

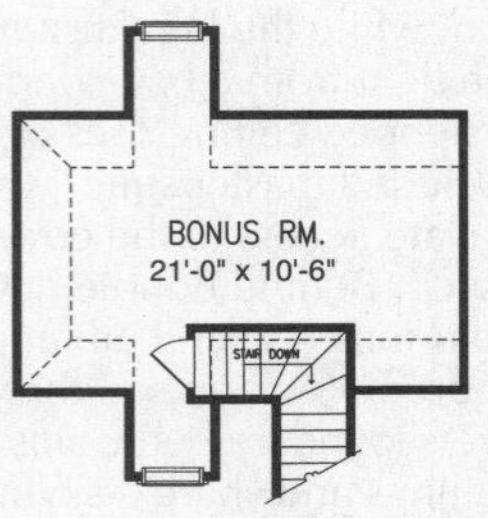

BONUS ROOM

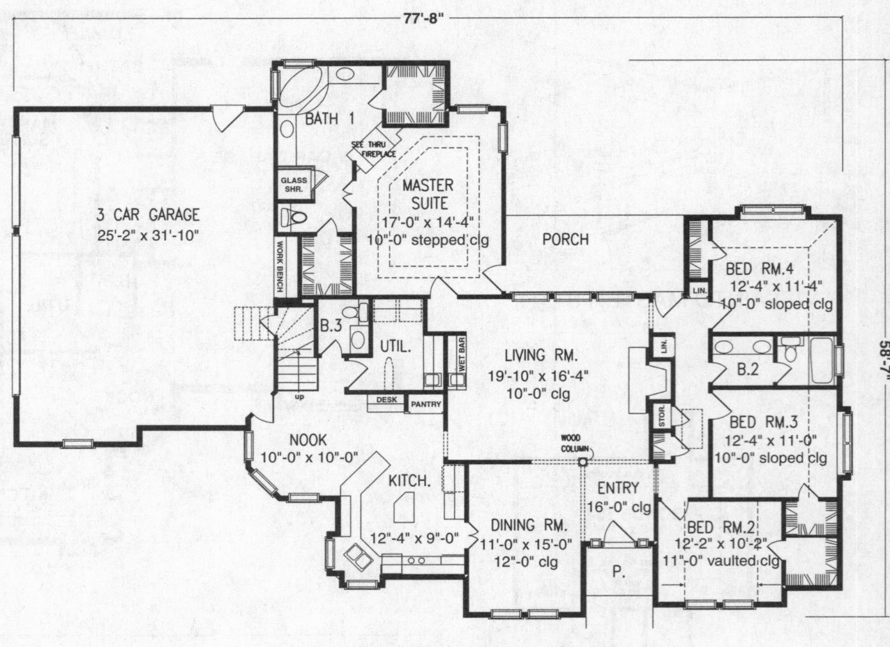

MAIN FLOOR

Plan RD-2316-7B

SEE ORDER INFO ON PAGES 12-15
familyhandyman.com/homeplans

Wonderful One-Story

- Countless up-to-date details make this one-story design a wonderful home.
- Beyond the arched entry, the foyer extends to the formal dining room, which is set off by regal columns.
- To the right, double doors introduce a computer room. With a walk-in closet and private access to a full bath, this space could also serve as a guest room.
- A stylish stepped ceiling tops the formal living room, which overlooks a large patio.
- In the home's casual living areas, a serving bar extends from the island kitchen into the breakfast nook and the family room. A fireplace and a wall of windows enhance the family room.
- Nearby, two good-sized secondary bedrooms share a hall bath.
- The secluded master suite features an elegant tray ceiling, a bayed sitting area and a private bath.

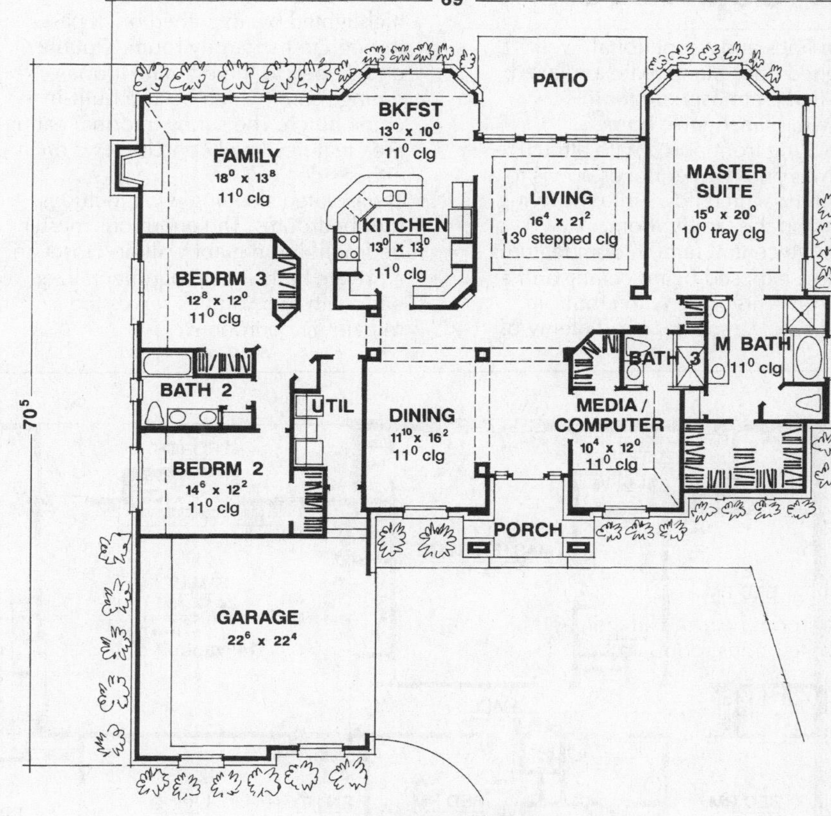

MAIN FLOOR

Plan DD-2710

Bedrooms: 3+	**Baths:** 3
Living Area:	
Main floor	2,710 sq. ft.
Total Living Area:	**2,710 sq. ft.**
Standard basement	2,710 sq. ft.
Garage	512 sq. ft.
Exterior Wall Framing:	2x4

Foundation Options:

Standard basement
Crawlspace
Slab
(All plans can be built with your choice of foundation and framing. A generic conversion diagram is available. See order form.)

BLUEPRINT PRICE CODE: **D**

Easy-Living Atmosphere

- Clean lines and a functional, well-designed floor plan create a relaxed, easy-living atmosphere for this sprawling ranch-style home.
- An inviting front porch with attractive columns and planter boxes opens to an airy entry, which flows into the living room and the family room.
- The huge central family room features a vaulted, exposed-beam ceiling and a handsome fireplace with a built-in wood box. A nice desk and plenty of bookshelves give the room a distinguished feel. A French door opens to a versatile covered rear porch.
- The large gourmet kitchen is highlighted by an arched brick pass-through to the family room. Double doors open to the intimate formal dining room, which hosts a built-in china hutch. The sunny informal eating area features lovely porch views on either side.
- The isolated sleeping wing includes four bedrooms. The enormous master bedroom has a giant walk-in closet and a private bath. A compartmentalized bath with two vanities serves the remaining bedrooms.

Plan E-2700

Bedrooms: 4	**Baths:** 2½
Living Area:	
Main floor	2,719 sq. ft.
Total Living Area:	**2,719 sq. ft.**
Garage	533 sq. ft.
Storage	50 sq. ft.
Exterior Wall Framing:	2x6
Foundation Options:	
Crawlspace	
Slab	

(All plans can be built with your choice of foundation and framing. A generic conversion diagram is available. See order form.)

BLUEPRINT PRICE CODE: D

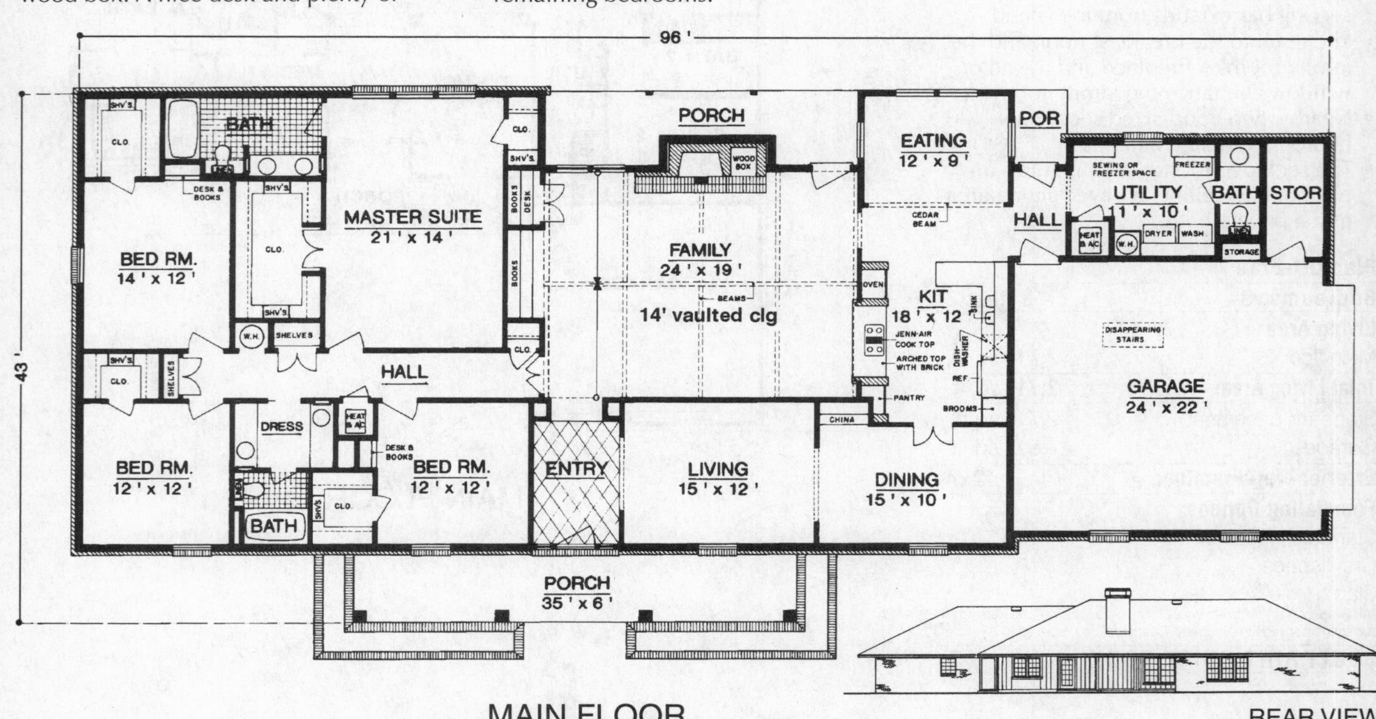

MAIN FLOOR

REAR VIEW

Plan E-2700

SEE ORDER INFO ON PAGES 12-15
familyhandyman.com/homeplans

Design Excellence

- This stunning one-story home features dramatic detailing and an exceptionally functional floor plan.
- The brick exterior and exciting window treatments beautifully hint at the spectacular interior design.
- High ceilings, a host of built-ins and angled window walls are just some of the highlights.
- The family room showcases a curved wall of windows and a three-way fireplace that can be enjoyed from the adjoining kitchen and breakfast room.
- The octagonal breakfast room offers access to a lovely porch and a handy half-bath. The large island kitchen boasts a snack bar and a unique butler's pantry that connects with the dining room. The sunken living room includes a second fireplace and a window wall.
- The master suite sports a coffered ceiling, a private sitting area and a luxurious bath with a gambrel ceiling.
- Each of the four possible bedrooms has private access to a bath.

Plan KLF-922

Bedrooms: 3+	**Baths:** 3½
Living Area:	
Main floor	3,450 sq. ft.
Total Living Area:	**3,450 sq. ft.**
Garage and workshop	904 sq. ft.
Exterior Wall Framing:	2x4

Foundation Options:

Slab

(All plans can be built with your choice of foundation and framing. A generic conversion diagram is available. See order form.)

BLUEPRINT PRICE CODE: E

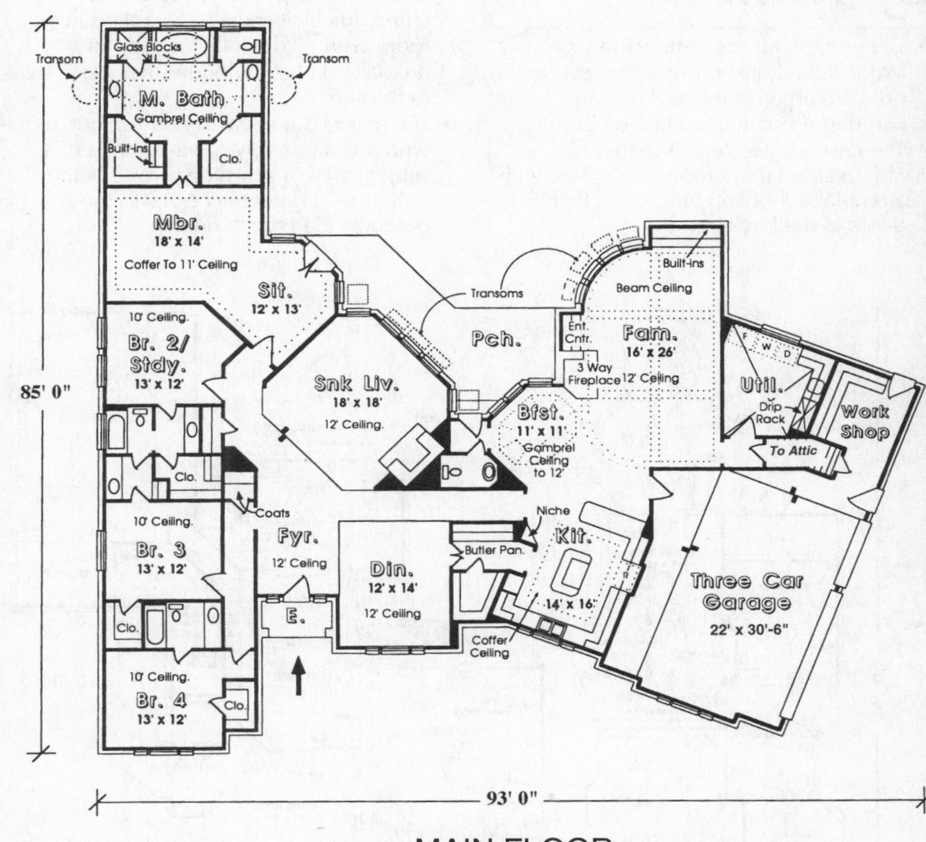

In a Class by Itself

- The endless number and variety of exquisite features ensures that every possible urge is met, and puts this wonderful home in a class by itself!
- The raised foyer steps into the remarkable family room, complete with a fireplace, book cabinets and French doors to the back porch.
- Interesting areas abound, including a media center designed to make movie nights as thrilling as the local multiplex.
- A raised dining room with its own china hutch sits next to a vaulted living room with a gorgeous focal-point fireplace. Lots of windows help to coax in the sun.
- The master suite leaves nothing out, with a wet bar, a two-way fireplace, a sitting room, a stunning private bath and three different accesses to the outdoors via French doors.

Plan L-062-EME	
Bedrooms: 4+	**Baths:** 3½
Living Area:	
Main floor	4,958 sq. ft.
Total Living Area:	**4,958 sq. ft.**
Optional loft	1,072 sq. ft.
Optional maid's quarters	608 sq. ft.
Garage and storage	866 sq. ft.
Exterior Wall Framing:	2x4
Foundation Options:	
Slab	
(All plans can be built with your choice of foundation and framing. A generic conversion diagram is available. See order form.)	
BLUEPRINT PRICE CODE:	**H**

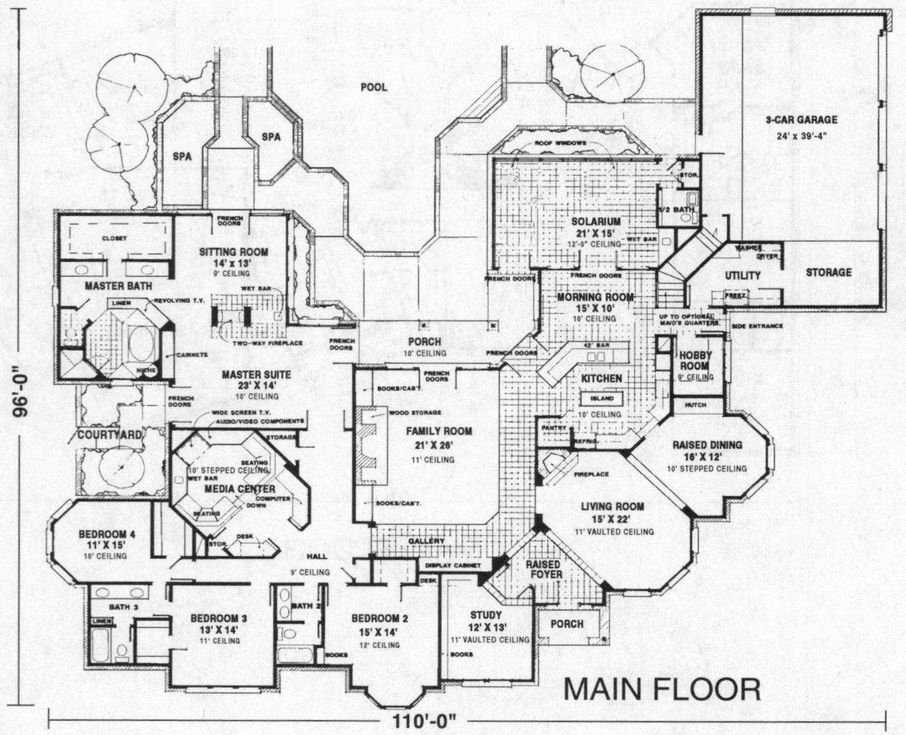

MAIN FLOOR

VIEW INTO MORNING ROOM AND KITCHEN

Superbly Done!

- A tile roof and extravagant glass are a just a prelude to the many amenities found in this superb home.
- The raised foyer offers a gorgeous view through French doors to a lanai and a potential pool area beyond.
- The grand living room has a curved wall of glass, plus a sloped ceiling with exposed rafters under a metal deck roof.
- Vaulted ceilings enhance both the nearby den and the sitting room in the posh master suite.
- The master suite offers a three-way fireplace and a raised exercise room with a private deck. A high ceiling tops the sleeping area and the bath, which boasts a whirlpool tub and a sit-down shower, each defined by a gorgeous glass-block wall.
- The formal dining room is enhanced by tall glass and a vaulted ceiling.
- High ceilings augment the bright morning room, the island kitchen and the family room, where a fireplace, a TV niche and deck access are featured.
- A nice ale bar has a pass-through for easy service to the pool area. A summer kitchen on the deck hosts barbecues.
- Three secondary bedrooms and two full baths complete this wing of the home.

Plan EOF-70

Bedrooms: 4+	**Baths:** 3½
Living Area:	
Main floor	5,013 sq. ft.
Total Living Area:	**5,013 sq. ft.**
Garage and shop	902 sq. ft.
Exterior Wall Framing:	8-in. concrete block
Foundation Options:	
Slab	

(All plans can be built with your choice of foundation and framing. A generic conversion diagram is available. See order form.)

BLUEPRINT PRICE CODE: I

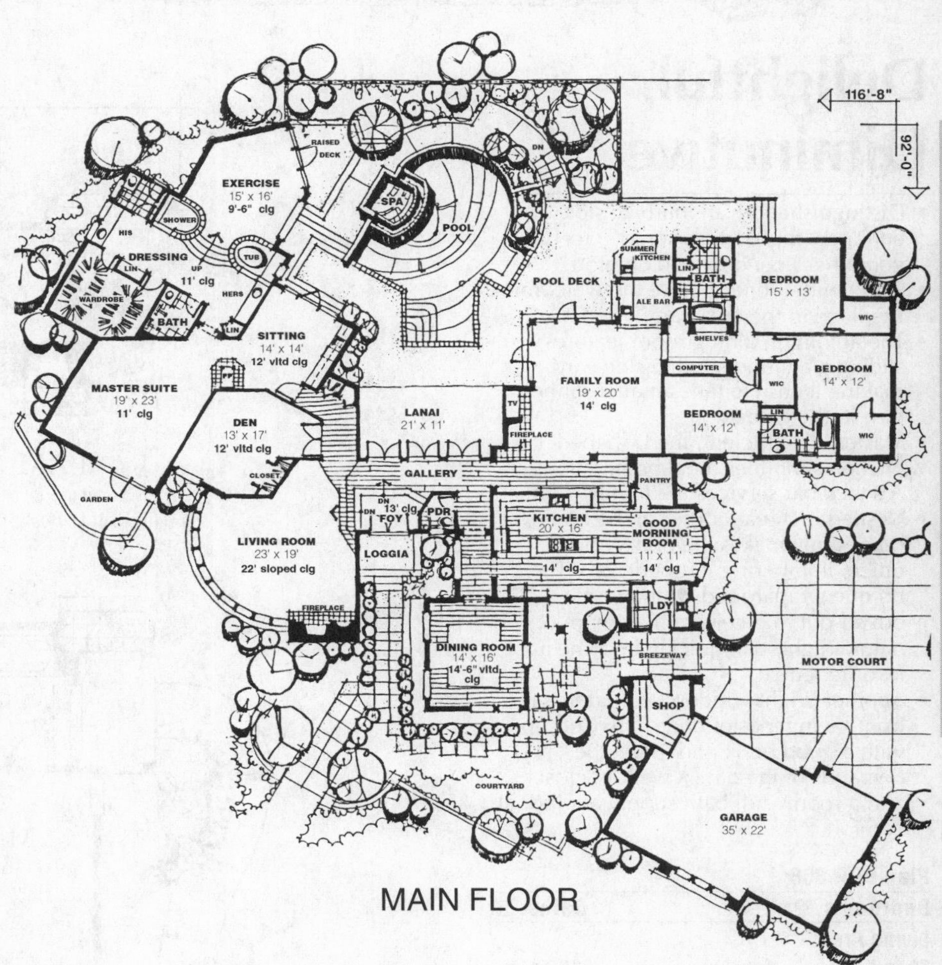

MAIN FLOOR

Delightful, Diminutive

- Distinguished by an intimate side entrance, this darling home gracefully combines economy and comfort.
- Relax with friends before the welcoming fireplace in the cozy family room.
- The adjoining dining room features sliding glass doors to the side yard, making it easy to take an after-dinner turn in the garden.
- Masterfully efficient, the L-shaped kitchen simplifies meal preparation. A snack bar services the family room.
- Nestled in a rear corner of the home, a quiet study makes the perfect home office, library or guest bedroom. The unique wraparound window seat, boxed-out to receive a maximum of natural light, will quickly become a favorite retreat.
- Another bright window seat adorns the front-facing master bedroom. Curl up with a good book and forget the demands of the day. A walk-in closet and a roomy full bath supply additional comfort.

Plan BRF-858	
Bedrooms: 2+	**Baths:** 2
Living Area:	
Main floor	858 sq. ft.
Total Living Area:	**858 sq. ft.**
Garage	237 sq. ft.
Exterior Wall Framing:	2x4
Foundation Options:	
Slab	
(All plans can be built with your choice of foundation and framing. A generic conversion diagram is available. See order form.)	
BLUEPRINT PRICE CODE:	**AA**

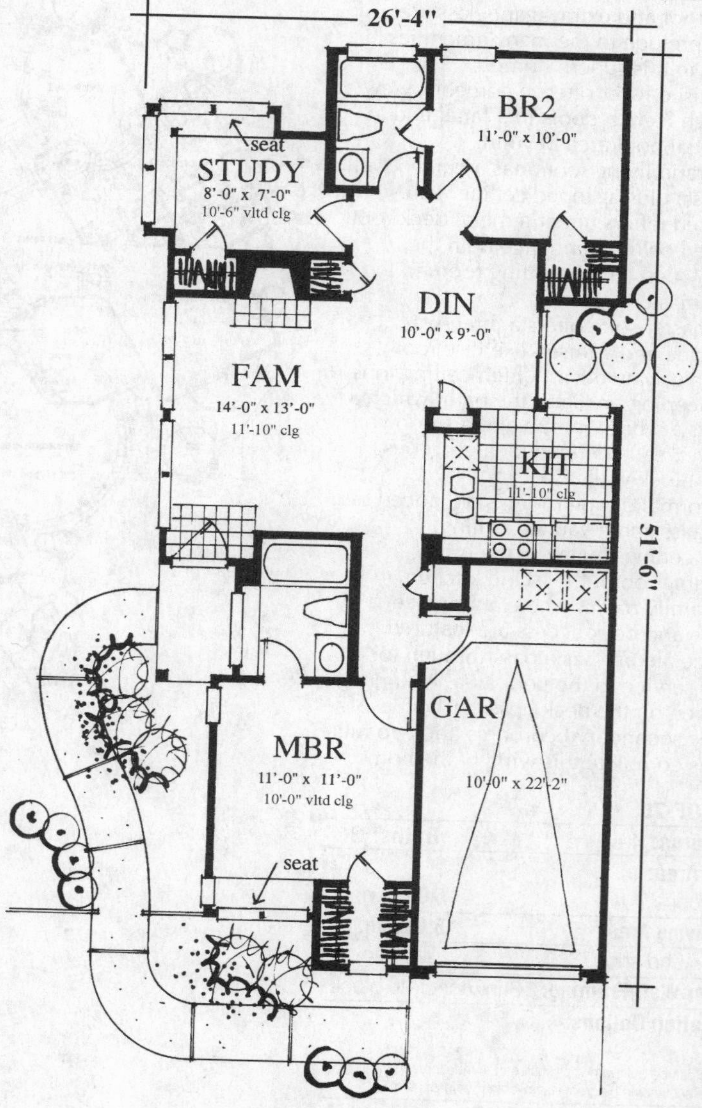

MAIN FLOOR

Plan BRF-858

SEE ORDER INFO ON PAGES 12-15
familyhandyman.com/homeplans

Welcoming Expanse

- Expanses of tall windows hint at the flowing spaces inside this welcoming home. With an astonishing number of amenities folded into its modest footprint, this design is sure to please.
- Past the covered entry, the foyer opens directly into the impressive Great Room, which includes built-ins for your entertainment center and a fireplace.
- An angled bar defines the nifty corner kitchen, where the counter space seems endless. Across the dining room, sliding glass doors invite meals on the patio.
- Tucked away in the rear corner of the home, the master bedroom offers a private patio as well as an impressive view. A large walk-in closet and a split bath round out the suite.
- Sunlight floods into the central hall through a unique skywell. The hall leads to a secondary bedroom, a full bath and a utility room.
- Completing the floor plan, the front-facing den enjoys a nice window arrangement and converts easily to an extra bedroom or guest room.

Plan S-62095

Bedrooms: 2+	**Baths:** 2
Living Area:	
Main floor	1,282 sq. ft.
Total Living Area:	**1,282 sq. ft.**
Garage	380 sq. ft.
Exterior Wall Framing:	2x6
Foundation Options:	
Crawlspace	
(All plans can be built with your choice of foundation and framing. A generic conversion diagram is available. See order form.)	
BLUEPRINT PRICE CODE:	**A**

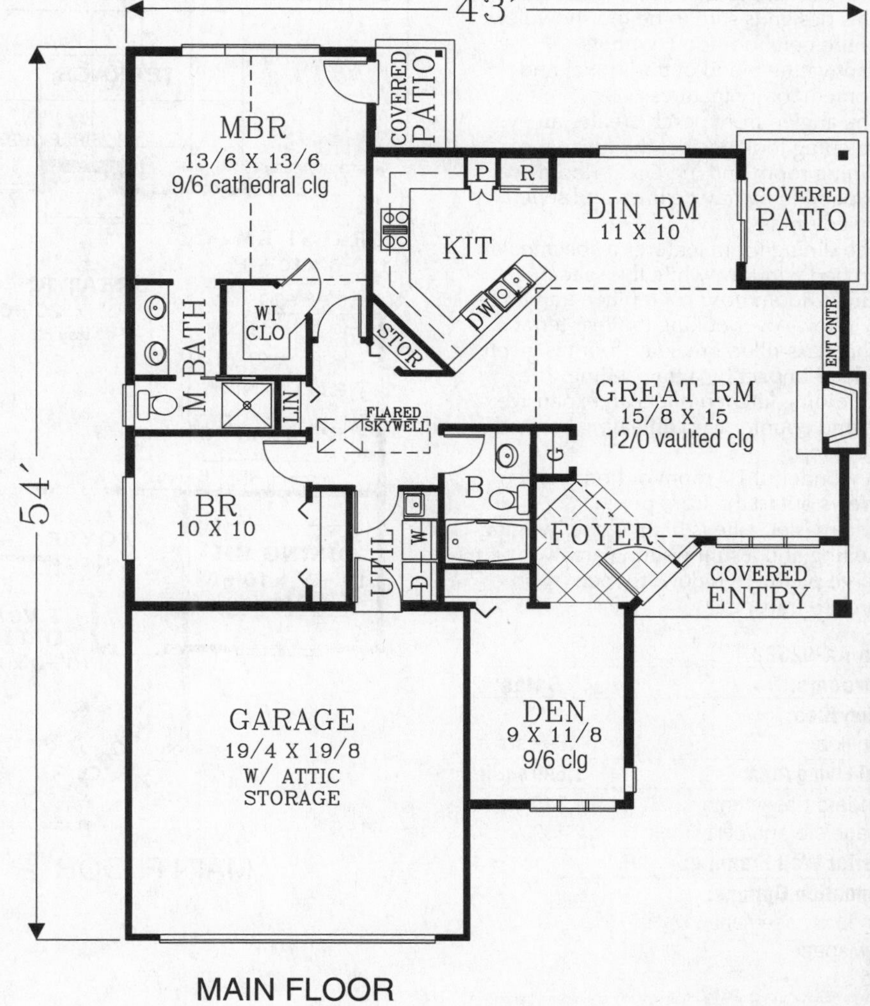

MAIN FLOOR

Plan S-62095

Captivating Showpiece

- This design is sure to be the showpiece of the neighborhood, with its captivating blend of traditional and contemporary features.
- The angled front porch creates an eye-catching look. Inside, the foyer, the dining room and the Great Room are expanded by tray ceilings and separated by columns.
- The dining room features a spectacular arched window, while the spacious Great Room hosts a fireplace framed by windows overlooking the rear terrace.
- The glass-filled breakfast room is given added impact by a tray ceiling. The adjoining kitchen offers an expansive island counter with an eating bar and a cooktop.
- A wonderful TV room or home office views out to the front porch.
- The master suite is highlighted by a tray ceiling and a sunny sitting area with a large picture window topped by an arched transom.

Plan AX-92322	
Bedrooms: 3+	**Baths:** 2
Living Area:	
Main floor	1,699 sq. ft.
Total Living Area:	**1,699 sq. ft.**
Standard basement	1,740 sq. ft.
Garage/storage/utility room	480 sq. ft.
Exterior Wall Framing:	2x4
Foundation Options:	
Standard basement	
Crawlspace	
Slab	
(All plans can be built with your choice of foundation and framing. A generic conversion diagram is available. See order form.)	
BLUEPRINT PRICE CODE:	**B**

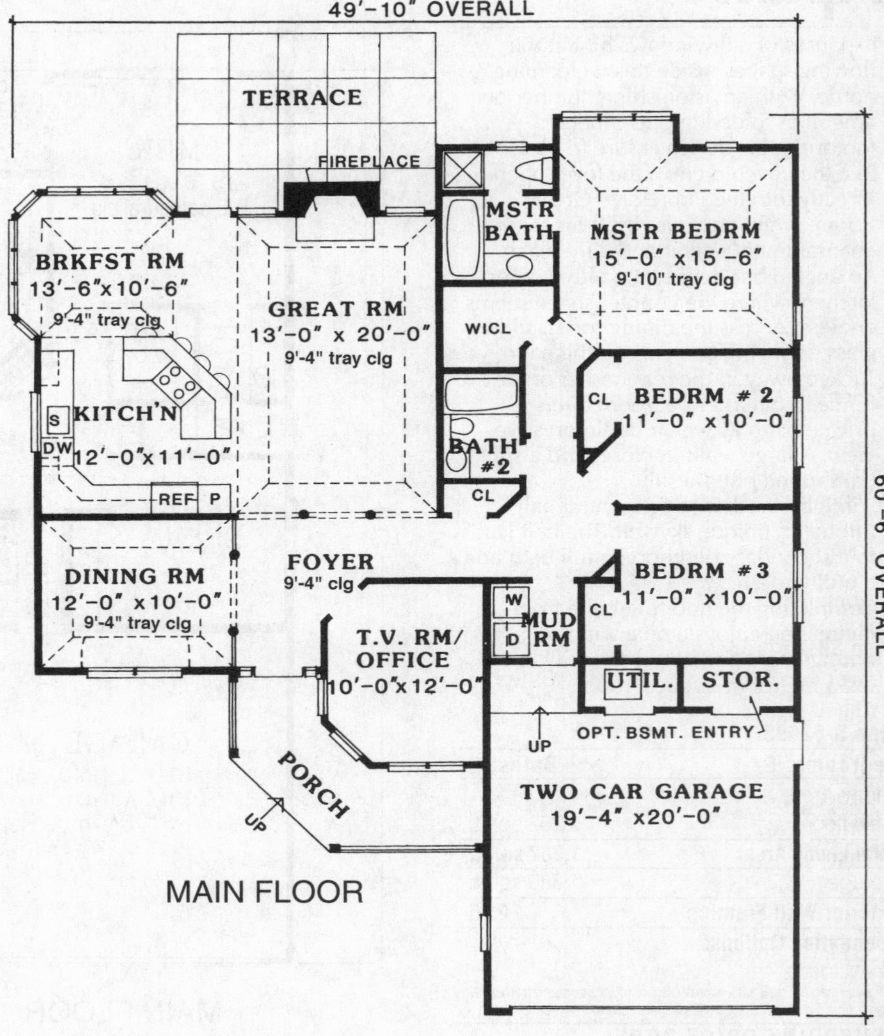

MAIN FLOOR

Plan AX-92322

SEE ORDER INFO ON PAGES 12-15

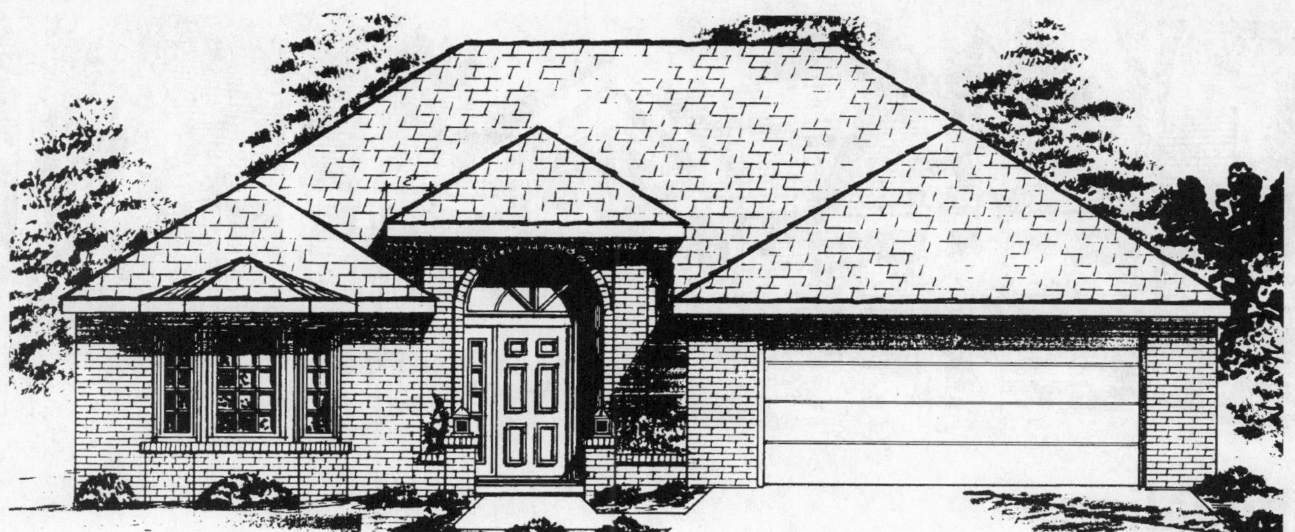

Large, Stylish Spaces

- This stylish brick home greets guests with a beautiful entry court that leads to the recessed front porch.
- Beyond the porch, the bright entry flows into the Great Room, which features a sloped ceiling. This airy space also offers a fireplace, a sunny dining area and sliding glass doors to a backyard patio.
- The kitchen has a walk-in pantry, an open serving counter above the sink and convenient access to the laundry facilities and the garage.
- Isolated from the secondary bedrooms, the master suite boasts a tray ceiling, an oversized walk-in closet and an exquisite bath with two distinct sink areas, a corner garden tub and a separate shower.
- The third bedroom, which features lovely double doors and a front-facing bay window, would also make a perfect home office.

Plan SDG-91188

Bedrooms: 2+	**Baths:** 2
Living Area:	
Main floor	1,704 sq. ft.
Total Living Area:	**1,704 sq. ft.**
Garage	484 sq. ft.
Exterior Wall Framing:	2x4
Foundation Options:	
Slab	

(All plans can be built with your choice of foundation and framing. A generic conversion diagram is available. See order form.)

BLUEPRINT PRICE CODE: B

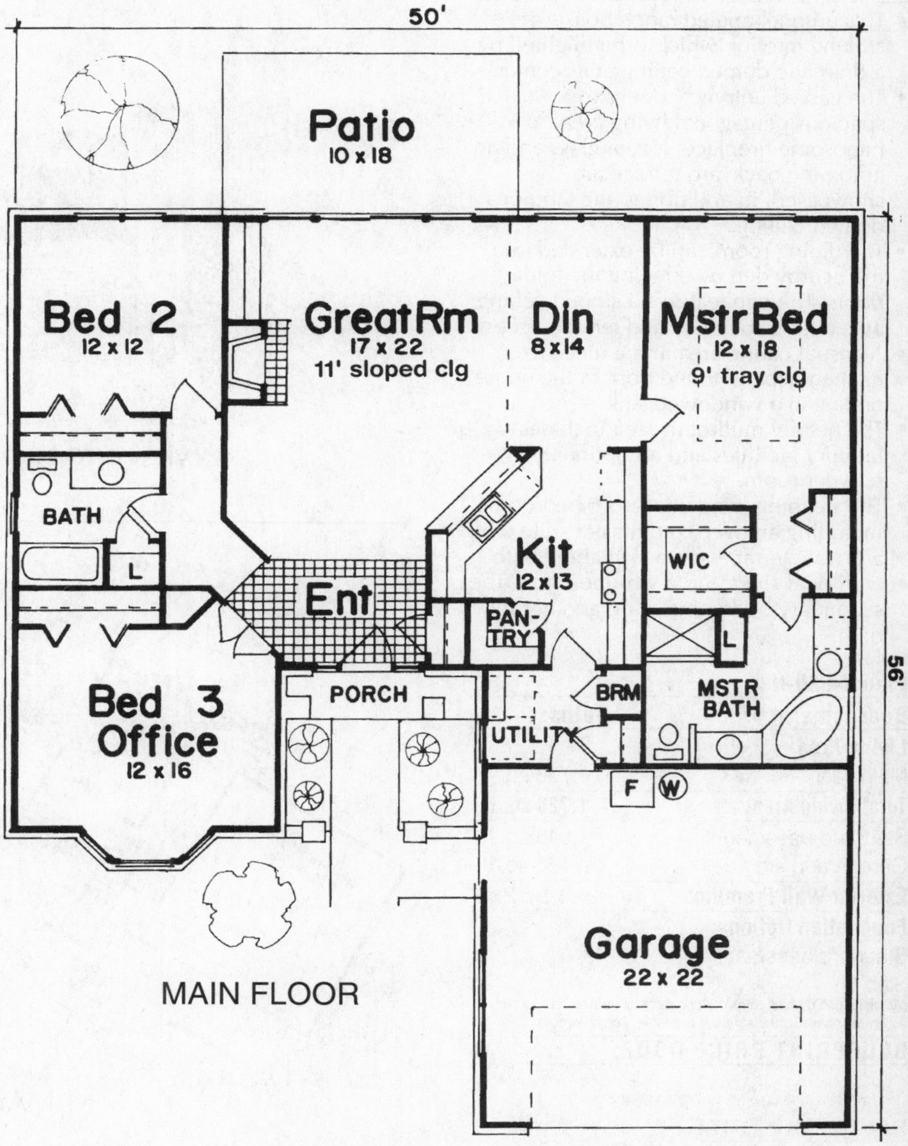

50'
56'
Patio
10 x 18
Bed 2
12 x 12
GreatRm
17 x 22
11' sloped clg
Din
8 x 14
MstrBed
12 x 18
9' tray clg
BATH
L
Kit
12 x 13
WIC
Ent
PAN-TRY
L
BRM
MSTR BATH
Bed 3 Office
12 x 16
PORCH
UTILITY
F
W
Garage
22 x 22

MAIN FLOOR

Plan SDG-91188

Appealing, Angled Ranch

- This unique, angled ranch boasts a striking interior, which is highlighted by a dramatic domed ceiling at its center.
- The gabled entryway opens to a spacious pentagonal living area. A handsome fireplace, lots of glass and an adjoining backyard terrace are showcased, in addition to the fabulous domed ceiling.
- The dining room can be extended into the nearby den by opening the folding doors. The den features a sloped ceiling, an exciting solar bay and terrace access.
- A casual eating area and a nice-sized kitchen expand to the front of the home, ending at a windowed sink.
- The nearby mudroom area includes laundry facilities and an optional powder room.
- The sleeping wing offers four bedrooms, including an oversized master suite with a private terrace and a skylighted bath with dual sinks and a whirlpool tub. The secondary bedrooms share another full bath.

Plan K-669-N

Bedrooms: 4	**Baths:** 2–2½
Living Area:	
Main floor	1,728 sq. ft.
Total Living Area:	**1,728 sq. ft.**
Standard basement	1,545 sq. ft.
Garage and storage	468 sq. ft.
Exterior Wall Framing:	2x4 or 2x6
Foundation Options:	
Standard basement	
Slab	

(All plans can be built with your choice of foundation and framing. A generic conversion diagram is available. See order form.)

BLUEPRINT PRICE CODE: B

VIEW INTO DINING AND LIVING ROOMS

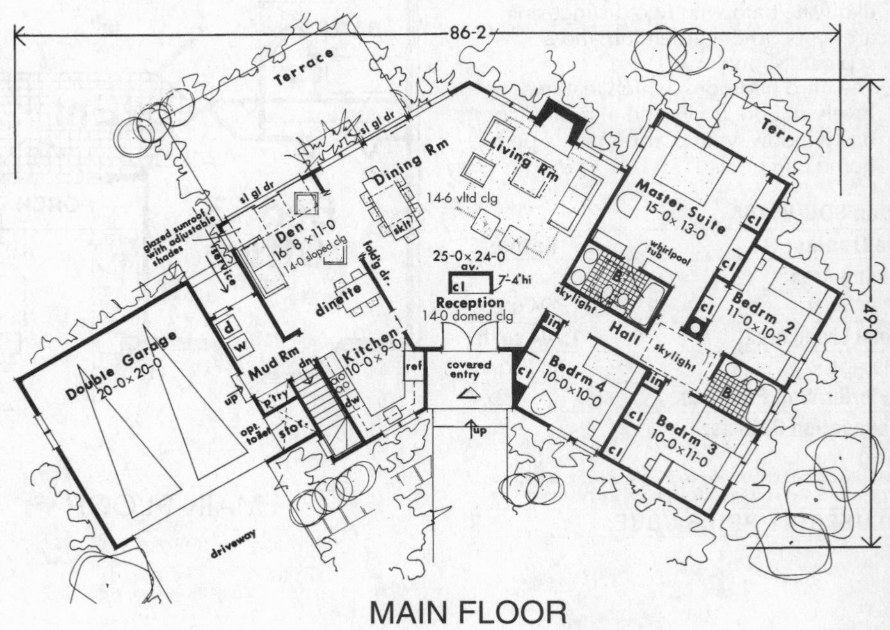

MAIN FLOOR

Plan K-669-N

SEE ORDER INFO ON PAGES 12-15

All-Around Pleaser

- With its charming front and large rear porches, this three-plus-bedroom home is an all-around pleaser.
- A welcoming foyer ushers visitors into the Great Room, where a handsome fireplace and a tray ceiling lend a dramatic touch to the home's central living area.
- The adjacent U-shaped kitchen with an angled snack bar leads into the formal dining room, partially framed by a column and a half-wall.
- To the left of the foyer, a study functions as a cozy home office. It also offers the possibility of an extra bedroom for surprise guests.
- Tucked behind the side-entry garage, the secluded master suite is crowned by a tray ceiling and graced by a private bath that features a garden tub, a separate seated shower, dual sinks and two enormous walk-in closets.
- At the opposite end of the home, an additional full bath serves two secondary bedrooms.

Plan VL-1771

Bedrooms: 3+	**Baths:** 2
Living Area:	
Main floor	1,771 sq. ft.
Total Living Area:	**1,771 sq. ft.**
Garage	480 sq. ft.
Exterior Wall Framing:	2x4
Foundation Options:	
Crawlspace	
Slab	
(All plans can be built with your choice of foundation and framing. A generic conversion diagram is available. See order form.)	
BLUEPRINT PRICE CODE:	**B**

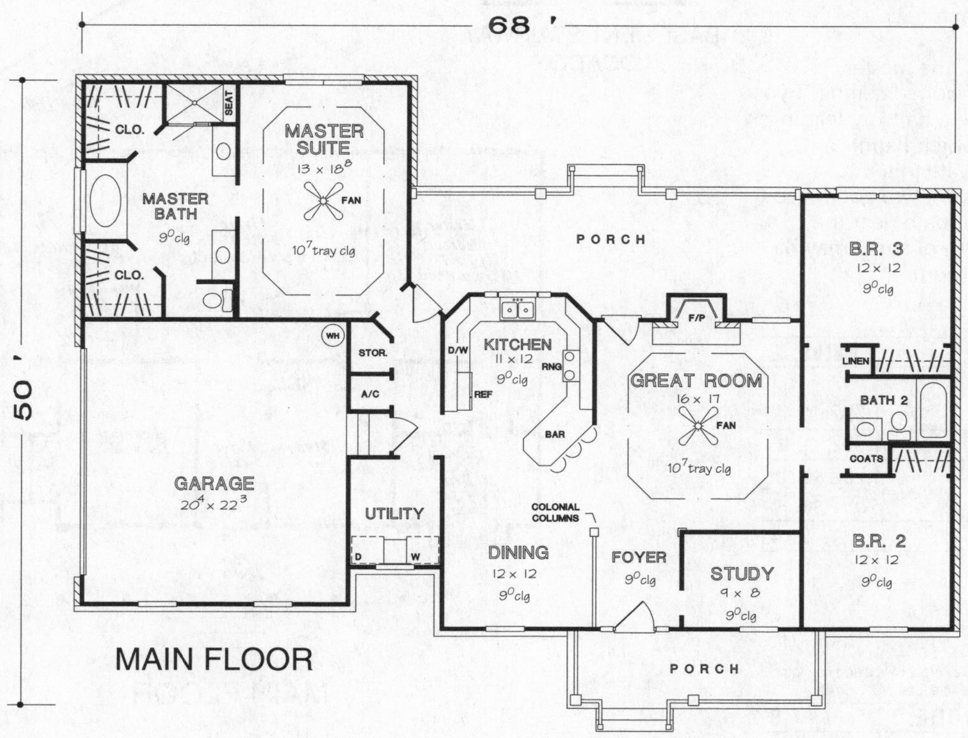

MAIN FLOOR

Plan VL-1771

Gracious Demeanor

- Elegant windows and a covered porch adorn the facade of this country-style home, giving it a gracious demeanor.
- Directly ahead of the ornate foyer, the skylighted living room boasts a cozy fireplace flanked by shelves and cabinets. An impressive vaulted ceiling rises overhead, while oversized windows provide great views of an expansive backyard patio.
- The adjoining dining room is topped by an elaborate vaulted ceiling and offers a door to a skylighted porch. The porch unfolds to the patio and accesses the sizable garage.
- Behind double doors, the master bedroom presents a vaulted ceiling. Two walk-in closets create a hallway leading to the master bath, which flaunts a garden tub and a private toilet.
- At the front of the home, two good-sized bedrooms share a full bath near the laundry room. The den or study may be used as an extra bedroom.

Plan J-9421	
Bedrooms: 3+	**Baths:** 2
Living Area:	
Main floor	1,792 sq. ft.
Total Living Area:	**1,792 sq. ft.**
Standard basement	1,792 sq. ft.
Garage and storage	597 sq. ft.
Exterior Wall Framing:	2x4
Foundation Options:	
Standard basement	
Crawlspace	
Slab	
(All plans can be built with your choice of foundation and framing. A generic conversion diagram is available. See order form.)	
BLUEPRINT PRICE CODE:	**B**

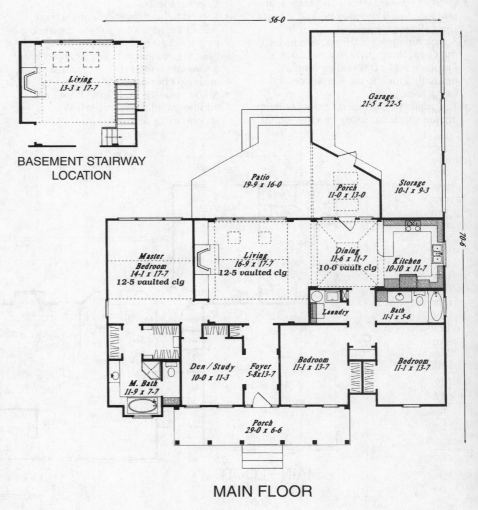

Living
13-3 x 17-7

BASEMENT STAIRWAY LOCATION

56-0
70-6
Garage
21-5 x 22-5
Patio
19-9 x 16-0
Porch
11-0 x 13-0
Storage
10-1 x 9-3
Master Bedroom
14-1 x 17-7
12-5 vaulted clg
Living
16-9 x 17-7
12-5 vaulted clg
Dining
11-6 x 11-7
10-0 vault clg
Kitchen
10-10 x 11-7
Laundry
Bath
11-1 x 5-6
M. Bath
11-9 x 7-7
Den / Study
10-0 x 11-3
Foyer
5-8x13-7
Bedroom
11-1 x 13-7
Bedroom
11-1 x 13-7
Porch
29-0 x 6-6

MAIN FLOOR

Plan J-9421

SEE ORDER INFO ON PAGES 12-15

Familiarity Breeds Content

- The familiar sight of this home's noble facade will bring ultimate contentment to you at the end of the day.
- From the foyer, double doors invite you into a quiet den or study. With its optional wet bar, this private space is a nice spot to unwind or surf the Internet before dinner.
- Presided over by a stunning fireplace, the huge central family room can host your larger gatherings. Sliding glass doors open to a covered patio that delivers a great view of the backyard. Why not line up some lawn chairs and cheer the participants of the family's croquet contest?
- A private entrance to the back patio enhances the master bedroom. Your morning will get off to the right start in the private bath, which boasts a large walk-in closet, a separate tub and shower, and a dual-sink vanity.
- When the kids stumble from their beds in the morning, they'll wake up quickly in the bright, bayed breakfast nook. The efficient layout of the kitchen lets you serve up their oatmeal in record time!

Plan HDS-99-287	
Bedrooms: 3+	**Baths:** 2
Living Area:	
Main floor	1,869 sq. ft.
Total Living Area:	**1,869 sq. ft.**
Garage	470 sq. ft.
Exterior Wall Framing:	2x4
Foundation Options:	
Slab	
(All plans can be built with your choice of foundation and framing. A generic conversion diagram is available. See order form.)	
BLUEPRINT PRICE CODE:	**B**

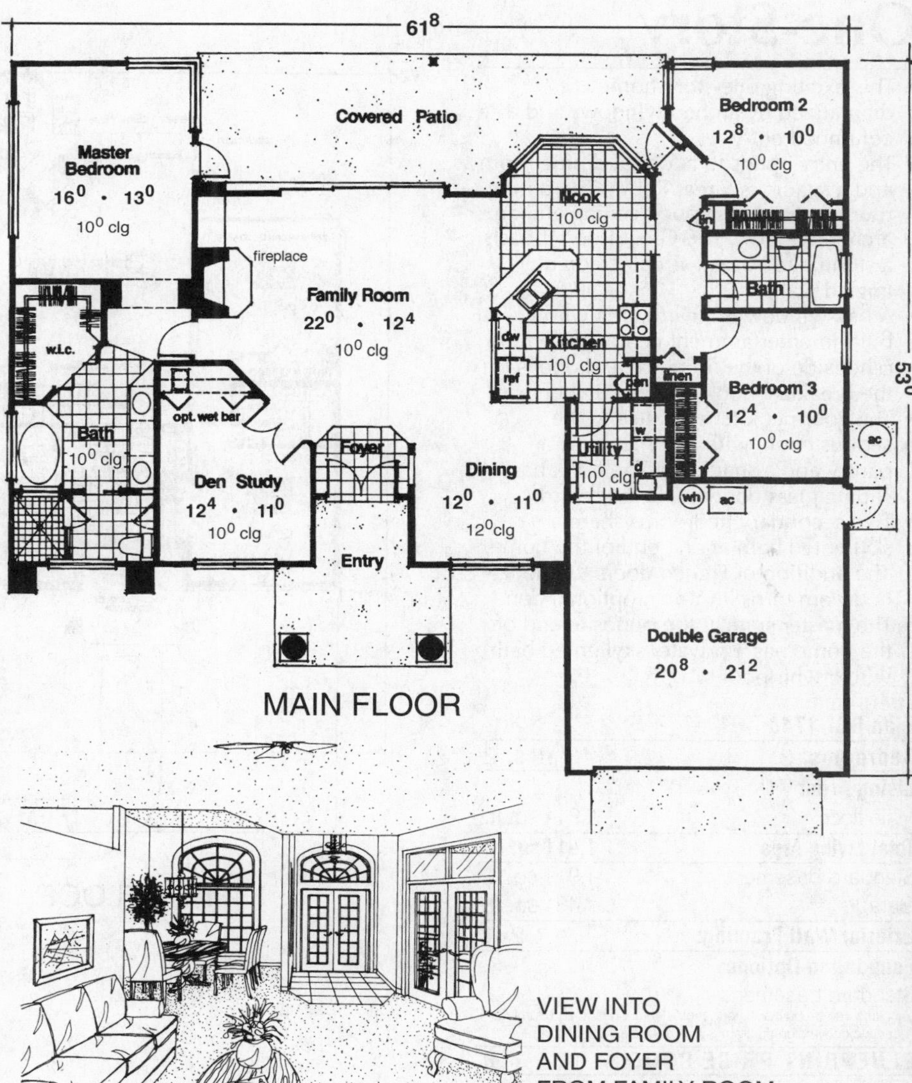

MAIN FLOOR

VIEW INTO DINING ROOM AND FOYER FROM FAMILY ROOM

Exciting One-Story

- This exciting one-story home is dramatized by arched windows and a columned entry.
- The entry opens to a formal dining room and a spacious Great Room. The dining room features a stepped ceiling and an arched window. The Great Room boasts a stunning two-way fireplace on an angled wall.
- A bay-windowed hearth area with a built-in entertainment center sits on the other side of the fireplace and opens to the breakfast nook and the kitchen.
- The gourmet kitchen caters to the serious cook, with a corner sink, a pantry and a snack bar. The nook has sliding glass doors to the backyard.
- Two secondary bedrooms share a skylighted bath at one end of the home. The addition of French doors to one bedroom turns it into an optional den.
- The master suite at the opposite end of the home has a private, skylighted bath with a whirlpool tub.

Plan DBI-1748	
Bedrooms: 3	**Baths:** 2
Living Area:	
Main floor	1,911 sq. ft.
Total Living Area:	**1,911 sq. ft.**
Standard basement	1,911 sq. ft.
Garage	481 sq. ft.
Exterior Wall Framing:	2x4
Foundation Options:	
Standard basement	
(All plans can be built with your choice of foundation and framing. A generic conversion diagram is available. See order form.)	
BLUEPRINT PRICE CODE:	**B**

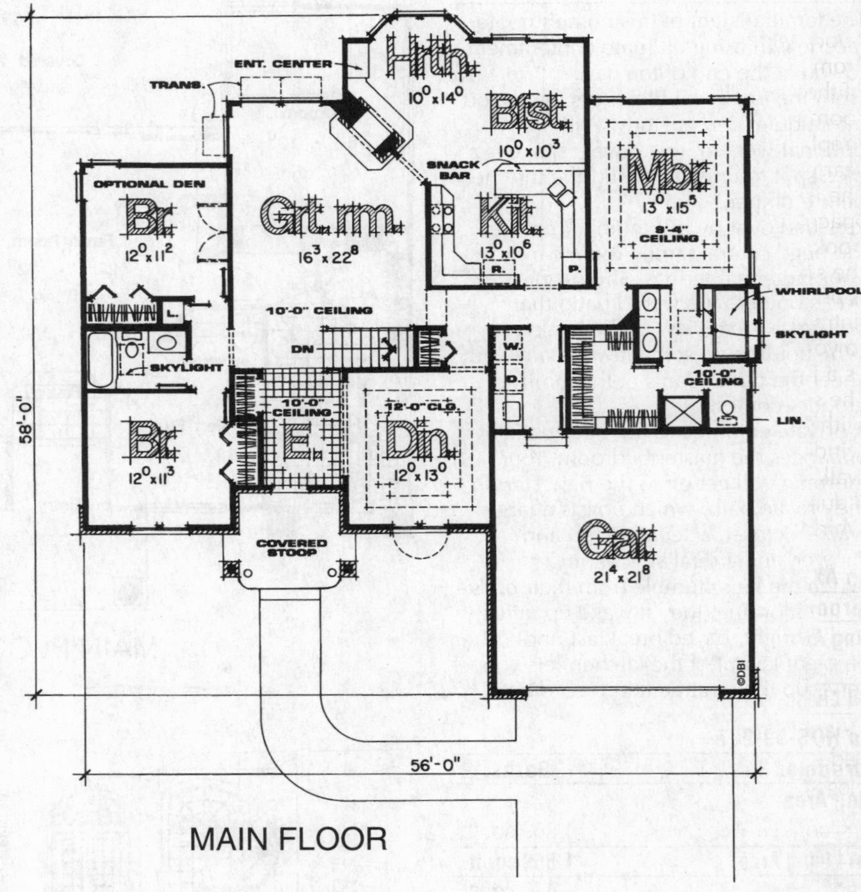

MAIN FLOOR

Plan DBI-1748

SEE ORDER INFO ON PAGES 12-15

Good Move!

- With its front porch, shutters and graceful dormers, this home exudes comfort and livability. When you invite them in for the first time, family and friends will congratulate you on your good move.
- From the foyer flows the open expanse of the Great Room and the dining room. The Great Room boasts a corner fireplace and sliding glass doors to the rear porch.
- The island kitchen offers ample work space and a lovely bayed breakfast nook; enjoy your morning coffee amid the sun's cheery rays!
- A private office with an outside entrance contributes privacy and quiet to your home business. It can also serve as a fourth bedroom.
- The secluded master suite charms you with a stepped ceiling and a bright bay window. Its amenities include two walk-in closets and a vaulted bath with a dual-sink vanity, a private toilet and a whirlpool tub.

Plan AX-5378	
Bedrooms: 3+	**Baths:** 2
Living Area:	
Main floor	1,914 sq. ft.
Total Living Area:	**1,914 sq. ft.**
Standard basement	1,925 sq. ft.
Garage and storage	482 sq. ft.
Enclosed storage	15 sq. ft.
Utility	18 sq. ft.
Exterior Wall Framing:	2x4
Foundation Options:	
Standard basement	
Crawlspace	
Slab	
(All plans can be built with your choice of foundation and framing. A generic conversion diagram is available. See order form.)	
BLUEPRINT PRICE CODE:	**B**

REAR VIEW

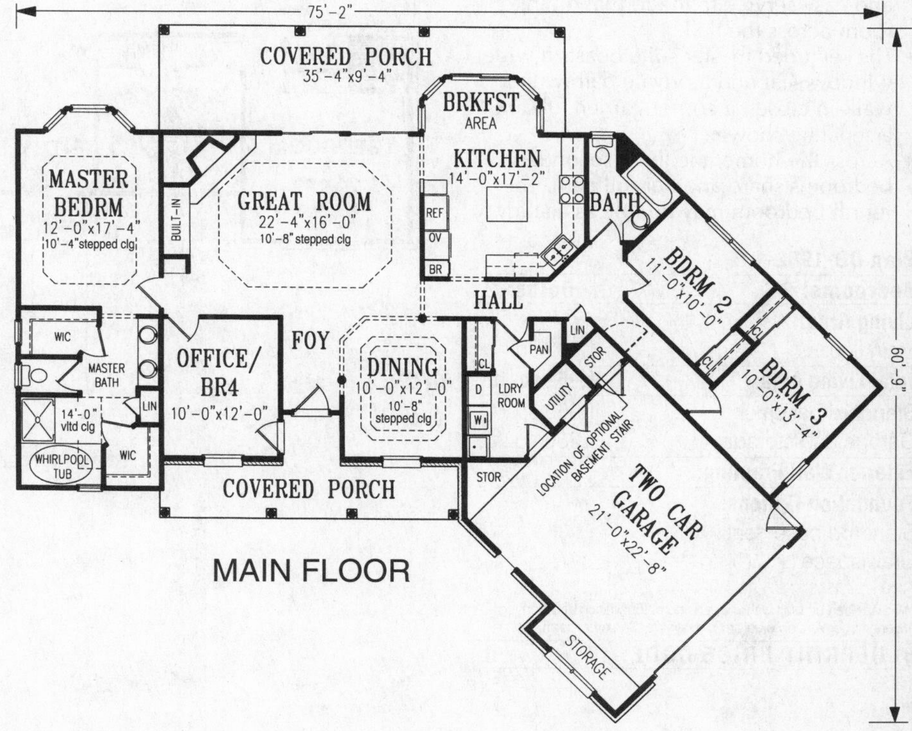

MAIN FLOOR

STUDIES, DENS & HOME OFFICES

Morning Room with a View

- This modern-looking ranch is stylishly decorated with a pair of arched-window dormers, handsome brick trim and a covered front porch.
- Inside, the dining room is set off by columns, as it merges with the entry.
- The main living areas are oriented to the rear, where a huge central family room offers a patio view and a fireplace that may also be enjoyed from the bayed morning room and adjoining kitchen.
- The walk-through kitchen features a pantry, a snack bar to the family room and easy service to the formal dining room across the hall.
- The secluded master suite boasts a wide window seat and a private bath with a walk-in closet, a corner garden tub and a separate shower.
- Across the home, the three secondary bedrooms share another full bath. The fourth bedroom may double as a study.

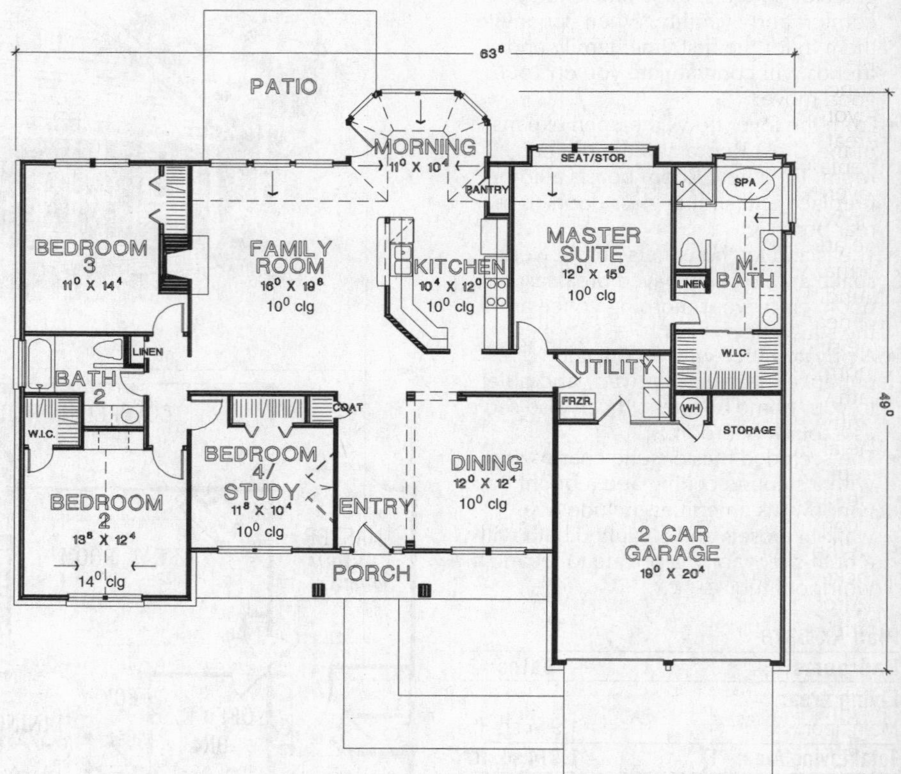

MAIN FLOOR

Plan DD-1962-1	
Bedrooms: 3+	**Baths:** 2
Living Area:	
Main floor	1,962 sq. ft.
Total Living Area:	**1,962 sq. ft.**
Standard basement	1,962 sq. ft.
Garage and storage	386 sq. ft.
Exterior Wall Framing:	2x4
Foundation Options:	
Standard basement	
Crawlspace	
Slab	
(All plans can be built with your choice of foundation and framing. A generic conversion diagram is available. See order form.)	
BLUEPRINT PRICE CODE:	**B**

Plan DD-1962-1

SEE ORDER INFO ON PAGES 12-15

Terrific Arched Transoms

- This terrific home greets guests with its wide arched transom windows and French doors that open to the foyer.
- Beyond the bright foyer, the expansive Great Room features a dynamic fireplace and sliding glass doors to a covered backyard patio.
- The walk-through kitchen easily services the adjoining breakfast area and the formal dining room. A pantry closet, laundry facilities and garage access are all nearby.
- The superb master bedroom boasts an enormous walk-in closet and an ideal bath with a step-up spa tub, a dual-sink vanity and a huge private shower.
- The alternate master bedroom offers a fireplace, a wet bar and a sitting room.
- The quiet den or study could be used to accommodate overnight guests.
- On the opposite end of the home, a pocket door introduces two secondary bedrooms, another full bath and private patio access.

Plan HDS-99-130

Bedrooms: 3+	**Baths:** 2
Living Area:	
Main floor	2,125 sq. ft.
Total Living Area:	**2,125 sq. ft.**
Garage	559 sq. ft.
Exterior Wall Framing:	2x4 or 8-in. concrete block
Foundation Options:	
Slab	

(All plans can be built with your choice of foundation and framing. A generic conversion diagram is available. See order form.)

BLUEPRINT PRICE CODE: C

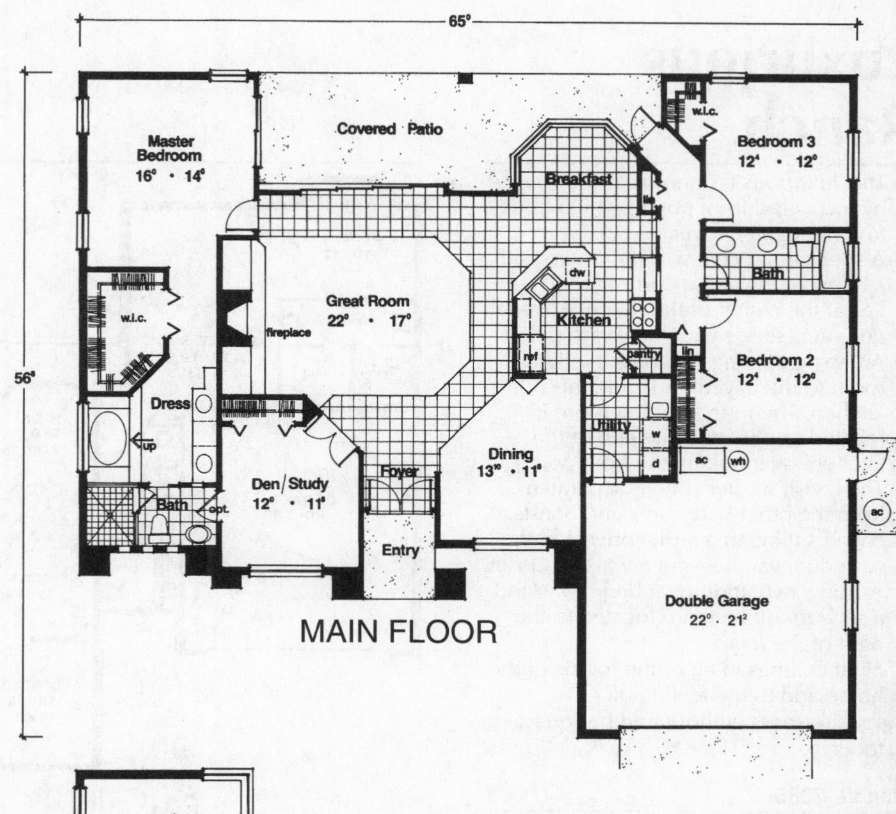

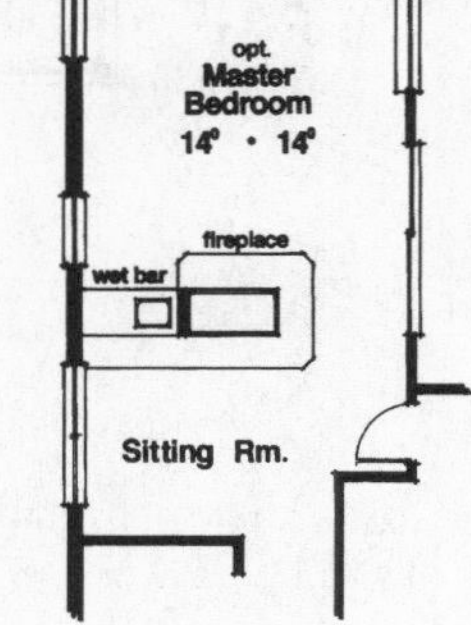

ALTERNATE MASTER BEDROOM

Luxurious Ranch

- This luxurious farmhouse is introduced by a covered front porch, which opens to a sidelighted foyer.
- A spectacular central living room with a high ceiling and a corner fireplace lies at the center of the home. A French door accesses a wide backyard porch.
- An angled eating bar joins the living room to the bayed nook and the kitchen. The formal dining room is located on the opposite end of the kitchen, overlooking the front porch.
- The lavish master suite is separated from the other bedrooms and boasts a bayed sitting area and a private bath with dual vanities and a walk-in closet.
- A study, two additional bedrooms and a second full bath are located to the right of the foyer.
- High ceilings in all of the rooms of the home add to the feeling of spaciousness without adding square footage.

Plan VL-2085	
Bedrooms: 3+	**Baths:** 2½
Living Area:	
Main floor	2,085 sq. ft.
Total Living Area:	**2,085 sq. ft.**
Garage	460 sq. ft.
Exterior Wall Framing:	2x4
Foundation Options:	
Crawlspace	
Slab	
(All plans can be built with your choice of foundation and framing. A generic conversion diagram is available. See order form.)	
BLUEPRINT PRICE CODE:	**C**

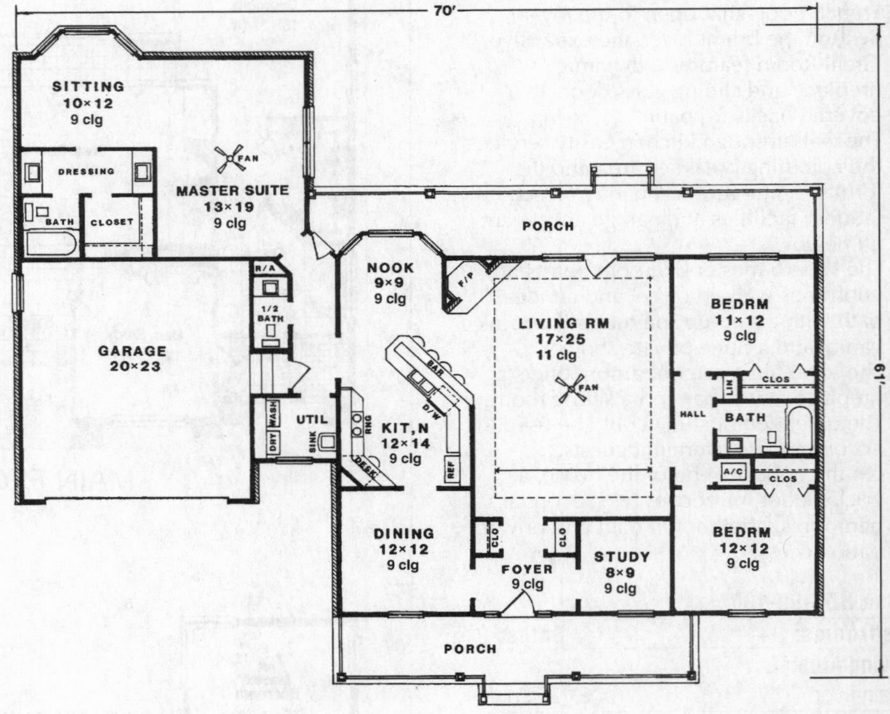

MAIN FLOOR

Plan VL-2085

SEE ORDER INFO ON PAGES 12-15

Modern Masterpiece

- This home's clean, modern lines, expansive windows and distinguished columns set the tone for the exciting floor plan found within.
- High ceilings and bright, open spaces are the hallmarks of the home. The impressive foyer, the dining room and the adjoining living room all have high ceilings. Elegant archways lead from the hall to the dining room and from the living room to the nook.
- The sunny nook and adjoining family room are filled with glass. The adjacent kitchen includes a generous snack counter and a high opening above the stove. The family room features a fireplace and built-in shelves.
- Double doors lead to the roomy den and the dynamite master suite, each with a high ceiling. The master suite features a superb bath with a spa tub and an oversized shower area.
- The cleverly designed hall bath serves guests from both indoors and out, while the two remaining bedrooms enjoy private access to another full bath.

Plan HDS-99-149

Bedrooms: 3+	**Baths:** 3
Living Area:	
Main floor	2,149 sq. ft.
Total Living Area:	**2,149 sq. ft.**
Garage	400 sq. ft.
Exterior Wall Framing:	2x4
Foundation Options:	
Slab	

(All plans can be built with your choice of foundation and framing. A generic conversion diagram is available. See order form.)

BLUEPRINT PRICE CODE: C

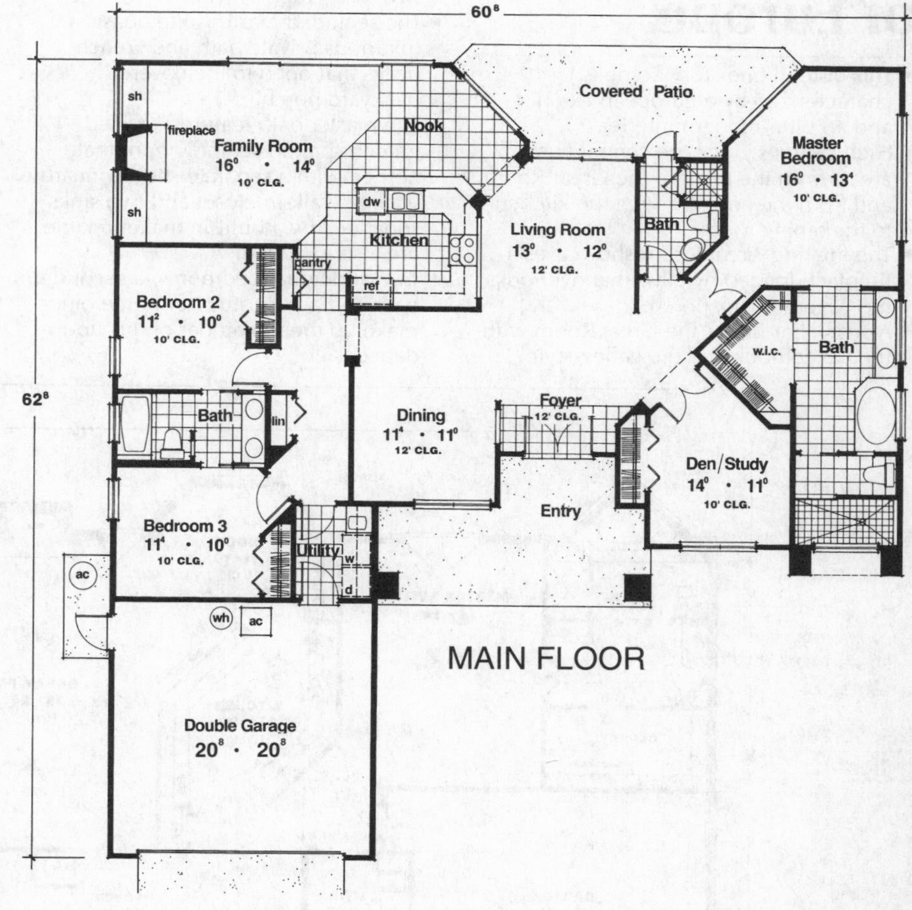

Plan HDS-99-149

Plan copyright held by home designer/architect

A Taste of Europe

- This tasteful one-story home is characterized by a European exterior and an ultra-modern interior.
- High ceilings grace the central living areas, from the foyer to the Great Room, and from the nook through the kitchen to the dining room.
- The inviting Great Room showcases a fireplace framed by glass that overlooks the covered back porch.
- A snack bar unites the Great Room with the bayed nook and the galley-style kitchen. A spacious utility room is just off the kitchen and accessible from the two-car garage as well.
- The secluded master suite boasts a luxurious private bath and French doors that open to the covered backyard porch.
- The master bath features a raised garden spa tub set into an intimate corner, with a separate shower nearby. A large walk-in closet and two sinks separated by a built-in makeup table are also included.
- Two additional bedrooms, a second full bath and a front study or home office make up the remainder of this up-to-date design.

Plan VL-2162

Bedrooms: 3+ **Baths:** 2

Living Area:

Main floor	2,162 sq. ft.
Total Living Area:	**2,162 sq. ft.**
Garage	498 sq. ft.
Exterior Wall Framing:	2x4

Foundation Options:

Crawlspace
Slab

(All plans can be built with your choice of foundation and framing. A generic conversion diagram is available. See order form.)

BLUEPRINT PRICE CODE: C

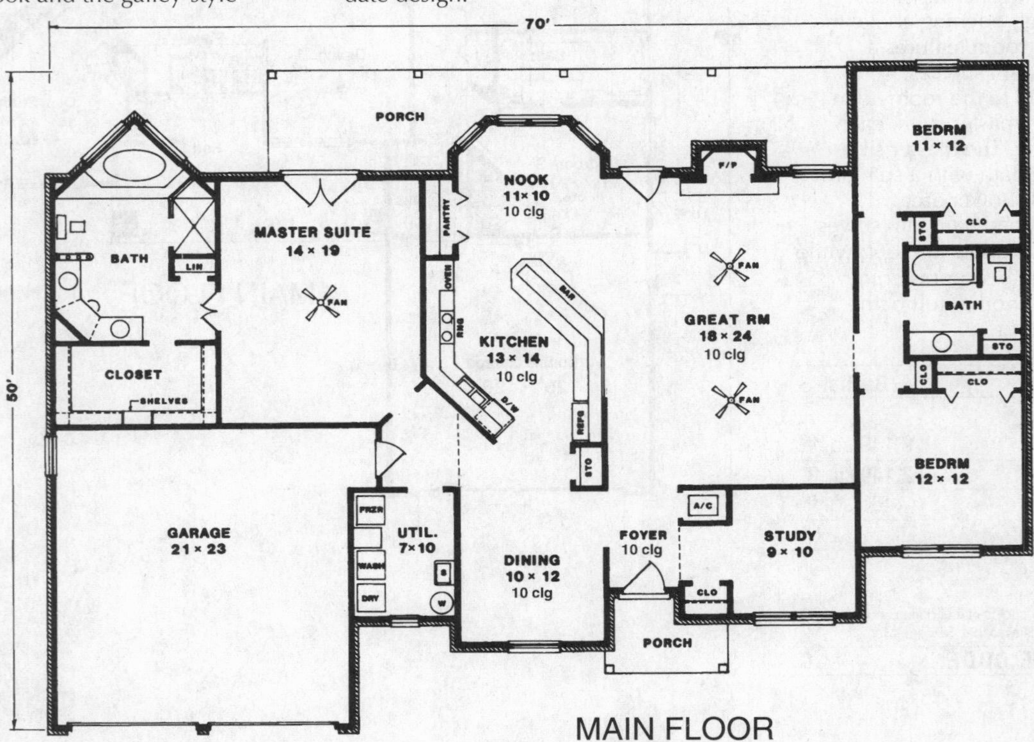

MAIN FLOOR

Plan VL-2162

SEE ORDER INFO ON PAGES 12-15

homeplans.com

One address. One stop.
One place to find and build your dream home.

Plan L-215-VSB

BIGGER SELECTION

If you like what you see in this magazine, but want more, visit us online at homeplans.com, where the biggest collection and best selection of home plans is at your fingertips. Our detailed search criteria include:

- **Square footage**
- **Number of bedrooms and baths**
- **Architectural style**
- **Number of floors**
- **Master suite location and features**
- **Special rooms**
- **Plus dozens more!**

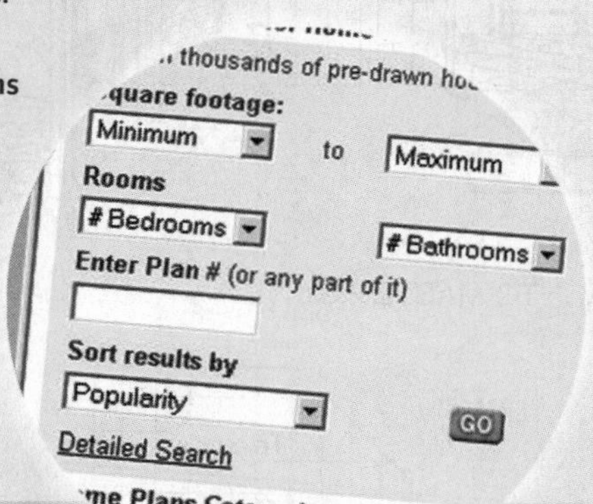

As specific as you want it to be.
To start your hunt, try a broad search on our home page or click "Detailed Search" to further narrow your selection.

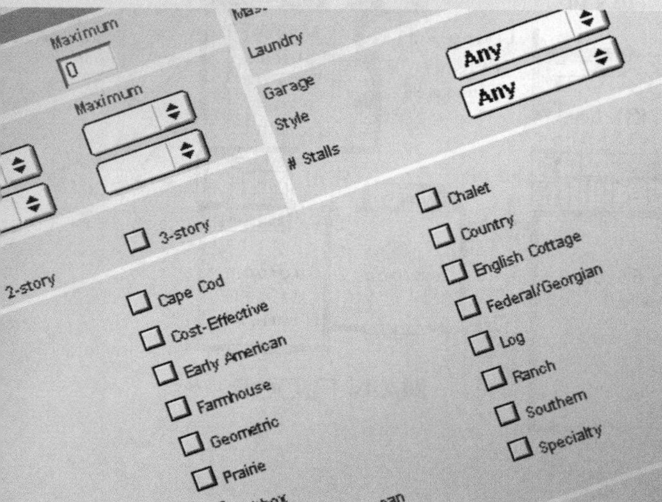

homestore™ plans and publications
213 E. 4th Street, Suite 400 • St. Paul, MN 55101

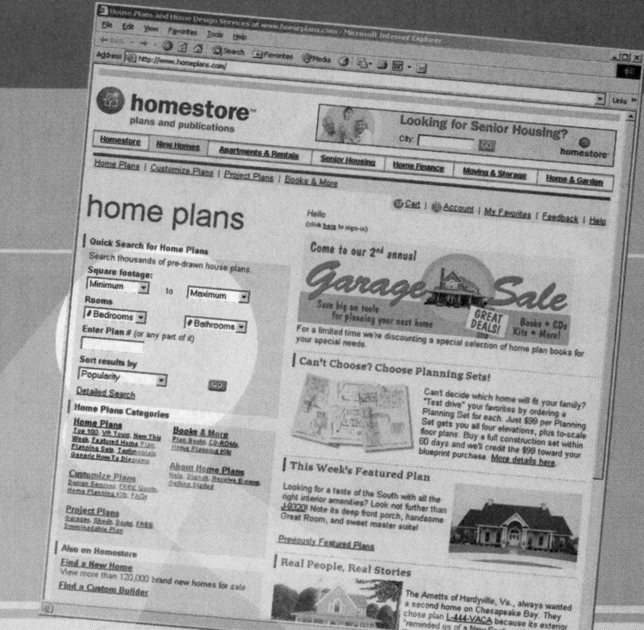

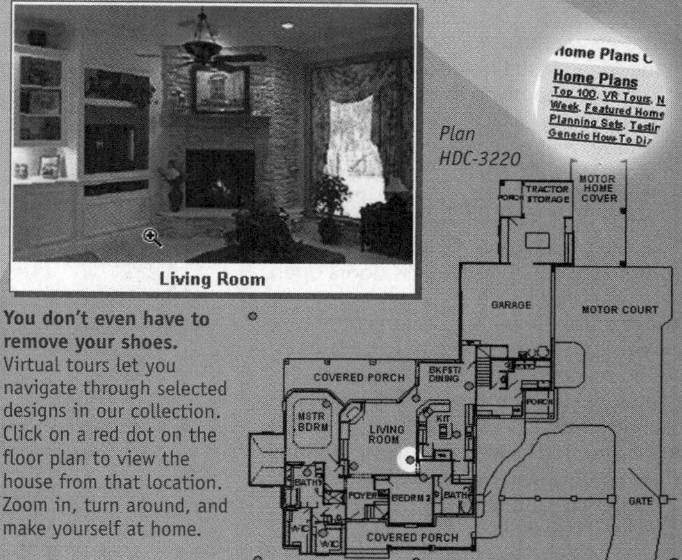

Living Room

Plan HDC-3220

You don't even have to remove your shoes. Virtual tours let you navigate through selected designs in our collection. Click on a red dot on the floor plan to view the house from that location. Zoom in, turn around, and make yourself at home.

SMART TOOLS

At homeplans.com you'll find a variety of helpful tools to guide you through the process of discovering your new home. It's like having a personal assistant at your beck and call!

- **Detailed plan specifications**
- **Printable plan summaries**
- **"Save your Favorites" tool—create a list of plans to review whenever you want**
- **Links to plans similar to the one you're viewing**
- **Rear views, virtual tours, color photos and artwork, and testimonials help you get to know a house before you make it your home**
- **Secure online ordering for your convenience and safety**

Finding your home plan is easy at homeplans.com

Luxury in a Small Package

- The elegant exterior of this design sets the tone for the luxurious spaces within.
- The foyer opens to the centrally located living room, which features a cathedral ceiling, a handsome fireplace and access to a lovely rear terrace.
- The unusual kitchen design includes an angled snack bar that lies between the bayed breakfast den and the formal dining room. Sliding glass doors open to another terrace.
- The master suite is a dream come true, with its romantic fireplace, built-in desk and tray ceiling. The private bath includes a whirlpool tub and a dual-sink vanity.
- Another full bath serves the remaining two bedrooms, one of which boasts a cathedral ceiling and a beautiful arched window.

VIEW INTO MASTER SUITE

Plan AHP-9300	
Bedrooms: 3	**Baths:** 2
Living Area:	
Main floor	1,513 sq. ft.
Total Living Area:	**1,513 sq. ft.**
Standard basement	1,360 sq. ft.
Garage	400 sq. ft.
Exterior Wall Framing:	2x4 or 2x6
Foundation Options:	
Standard basement	
Crawlspace	
Slab	
(All plans can be built with your choice of foundation and framing. A generic conversion diagram is available. See order form.)	
BLUEPRINT PRICE CODE:	**B**

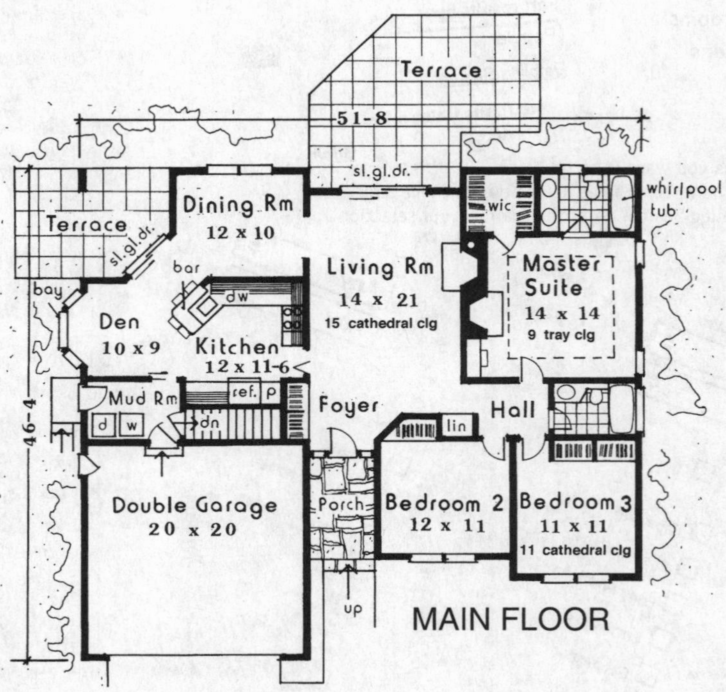

MAIN FLOOR

STUDIES, DENS & HOME OFFICES

ORDER BLUEPRINTS ANYTIME!
CALL TOLL-FREE 1-800-820-1296

Plan AHP-9300

Plan copyright held by home designer/architect

SEE ORDER INFO ON PAGES 12-15
familyhandyman.com/homeplans

Mark Englund/Homestore™ Plans and Publications

Spectacular One-Story!

- The angled, covered entry of this spectacular one-story home opens into its thoroughly up-to-date interior.
- Past the inviting foyer, the spacious dining area shares a soaring ceiling with the adjoining Great Room.
- Brightened by sliding glass doors to a covered backyard patio, the Great Room also includes an extensive built-in media center.
- The gourmet kitchen has a vaulted ceiling and serves a sunny bayed breakfast area over an angled counter. A convenient utility area with garage access is nearby.
- Enhanced by a lofty ceiling and windows on three sides, the master bedroom has an air of elegance. The lavish master bath boasts a spa tub, a separate shower, a dual-sink vanity and a roomy walk-in closet.
- Two additional bedrooms with high ceilings share a full bath.
- Featuring an enormous front window and a walk-in closet, the study would make a fantastic fourth bedroom.

Plan HDS-99-143	
Bedrooms: 3+	**Baths:** 2
Living Area:	
Main floor	1,865 sq. ft.
Total Living Area:	**1,865 sq. ft.**
Garage	377 sq. ft.
Exterior Wall Framing:	2x4
Foundation Options:	
Slab	
(All plans can be built with your choice of foundation and framing. A generic conversion diagram is available. See order form.)	
BLUEPRINT PRICE CODE:	**B**

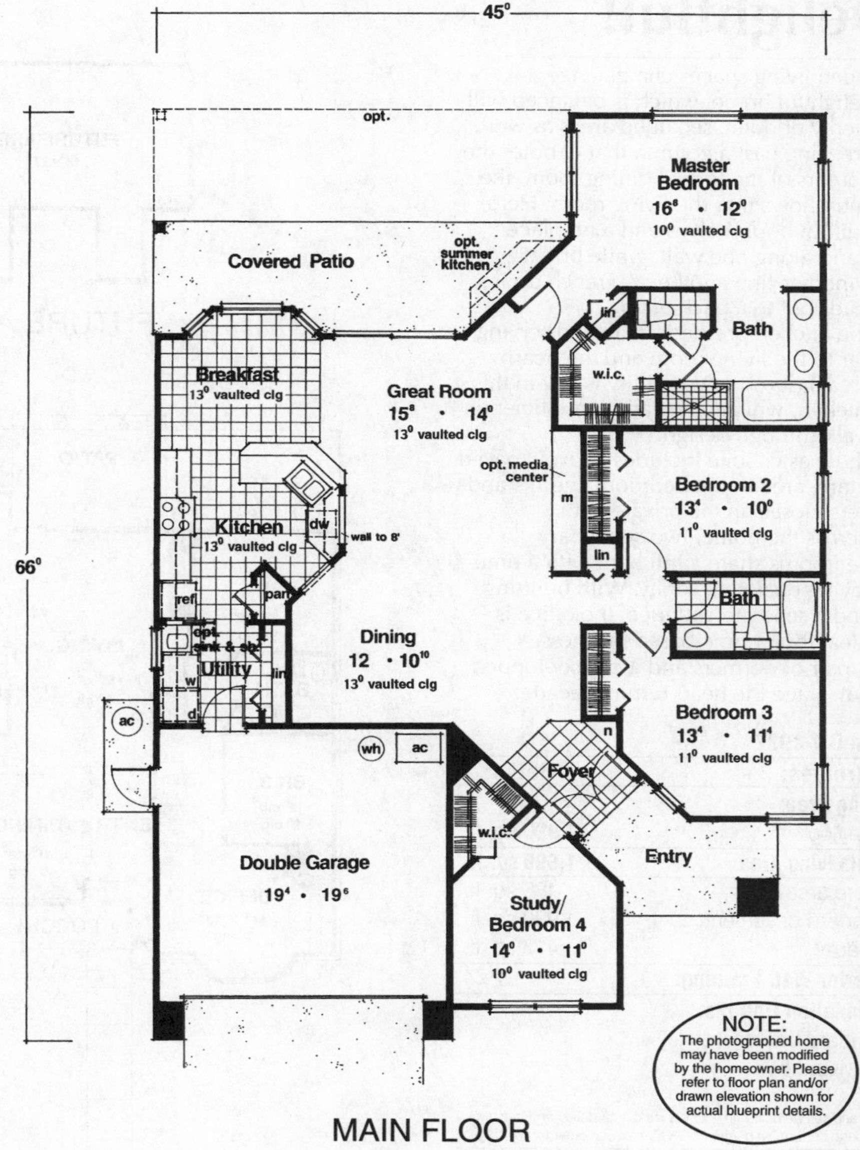

MAIN FLOOR

Plan HDS-99-143

Plan copyright held by home designer/architect

Delightful!

- Open living spaces characterize this delightful home, which is balanced with plenty of quiet, secluded areas as well.
- Breezing past a column that denotes the borders of the formal dining room, the entry flows into the living room. Here, built-in bookshelves and a fireplace stand along one wall, while bright windows line another. A French door leads out to a back patio.
- The kitchen presents an angled serving bar to the living room and the nearby breakfast room. Versatility is key in this kitchen, which offers an ultra-efficient walk-through design.
- The master suite includes a lovely bayed sitting area in the bedroom and his-and-hers closets in the private bath.
- Across the home, two secondary bedrooms share a full bath with a time-saving dual-sink vanity. With built-ins and a separate entrance, the office is ideal for a home-based business.
- A pair of dormers and a copper-topped bay grace the head-turning facade.

Plan DD-1992	
Bedrooms: 3+	**Baths:** 2
Living Area:	
Main floor	1,990 sq. ft.
Total Living Area:	**1,990 sq. ft.**
Future area	486 sq. ft.
Standard basement	1,990 sq. ft.
Garage	417 sq. ft.
Exterior Wall Framing:	2x4
Foundation Options:	
Standard basement	
Crawlspace	
Slab	
(All plans can be built with your choice of foundation and framing. A generic conversion diagram is available. See order form.)	
BLUEPRINT PRICE CODE:	**B**

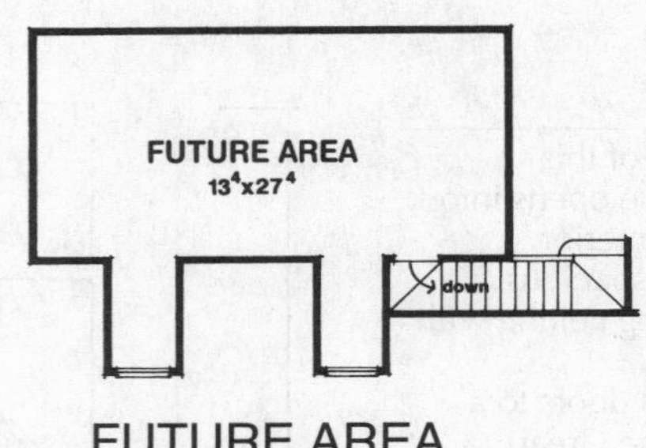

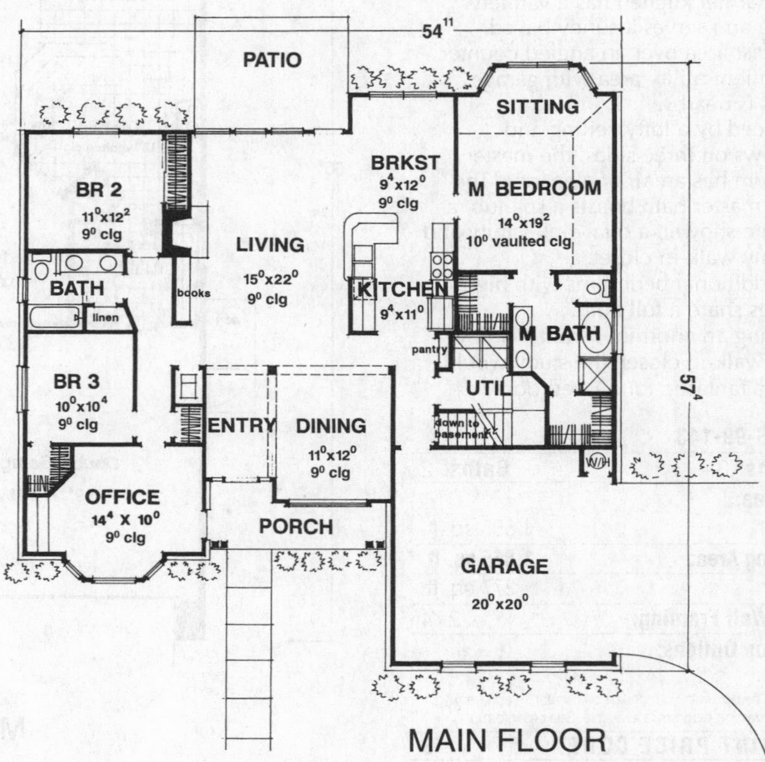

Plan DD-1992

SEE ORDER INFO ON PAGES 12-15

Modern Charmer

- This attractive plan combines country-style charm with a modern floor plan.
- The central foyer ushers guests past a study and on into the huge living room, which is highlighted by a tray ceiling, a corner fireplace and access to a big, covered backyard porch.
- An angled snack bar joins the living room to the bayed nook and the efficient kitchen. The formal dining room is easily reached from the kitchen and the foyer. A utility room and a half-bath are just off the garage entrance.
- The master suite, isolated for privacy, boasts a magnificent bath with a garden tub, a separate shower, double vanities and two walk-in closets.
- Two more bedrooms are located on the opposite side of the home and are separated by a hall bath.
- Ceilings in all rooms are raised for added spaciousness.

Plan VL-2069

Bedrooms: 3	**Baths:** 2½
Living Area:	
Main floor	2,069 sq. ft.
Total Living Area:	**2,069 sq. ft.**
Garage	460 sq. ft.
Exterior Wall Framing:	2x4
Foundation Options:	
Crawlspace	
Slab	

(All plans can be built with your choice of foundation and framing. A generic conversion diagram is available. See order form.)

BLUEPRINT PRICE CODE: C

REAR VIEW

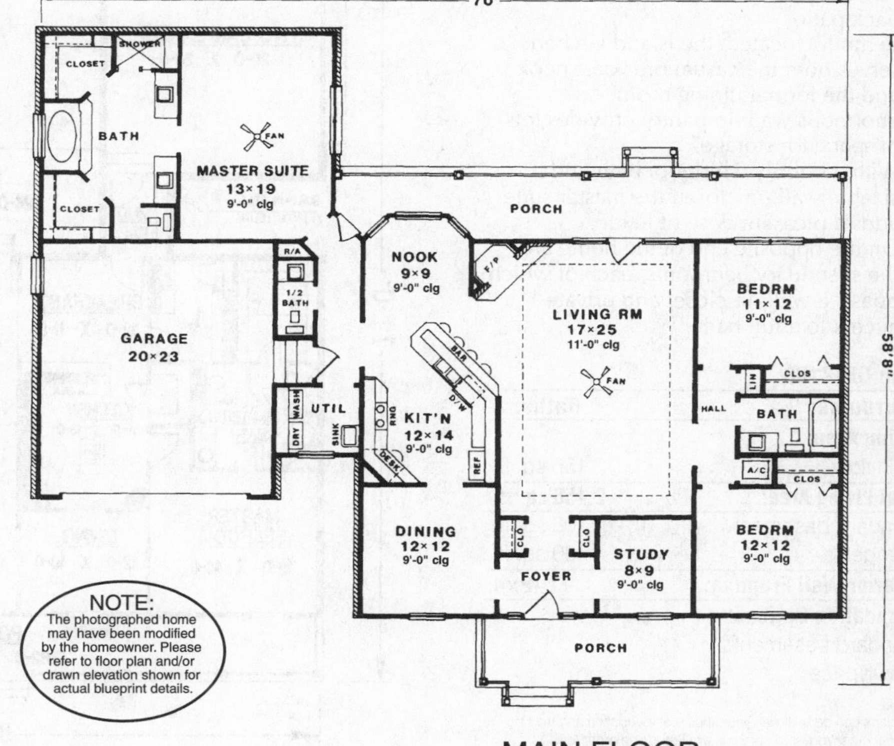

NOTE:
The photographed home may have been modified by the homeowner. Please refer to floor plan and/or drawn elevation shown for actual blueprint details.

MAIN FLOOR

Plan VL-2069

FOR MORE DETAILS, SEE PLAN AT familyhandyman.com/homeplans

DesignHouse Inc.

Porch Paradise

- You'll be tempted to spend all your time on the huge front porch of this perfect one-story home!
- Great for outdoor parties or relaxing on a rocking chair, the front porch has an endless variety of uses. The pretty railing makes a handy footrest.
- The interior offers room for casual and formal entertaining. The healthy-sized Great Room is the natural location for all your large gatherings. It features a tray ceiling and access to a spacious back patio.
- Centrally located, the island kitchen serves both the casual breakfast nook and the formal dining room. An enormous walk-in pantry provides lots of space for storage.
- With a bubbly whirlpool bath and a sizable walk-in closet, the master suite adds a pleasant dose of luxury.
- On the opposite end of the home are the secondary bedrooms, each of which boasts a walk-in closet and private access to a full bath.

Plan DP-2108	
Bedrooms: 3+	**Baths:** 3
Living Area:	
Main floor	2,156 sq. ft.
Total Living Area:	**2,156 sq. ft.**
Standard basement	2,108 sq. ft.
Garage	480 sq. ft.
Exterior Wall Framing:	2x4
Foundation Options:	
Standard basement	
Crawlspace	
Slab	
(All plans can be built with your choice of foundation and framing. A generic conversion diagram is available. See order form.)	
BLUEPRINT PRICE CODE:	**C**

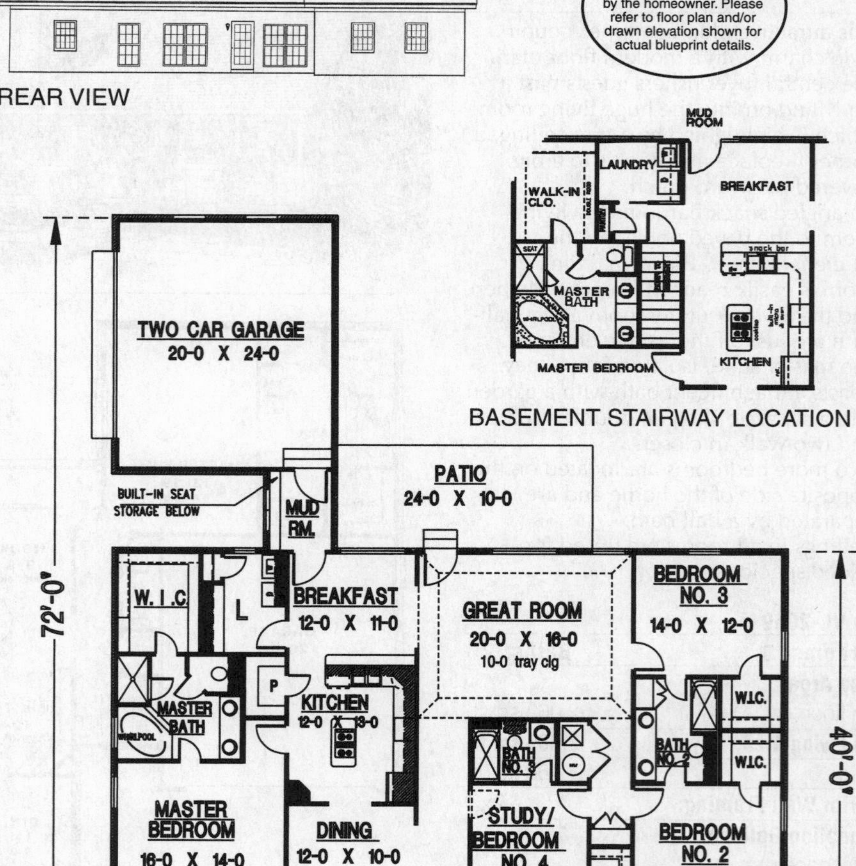

Plan DP-2108

SEE ORDER INFO ON PAGES 12-15

It's In the Details

- A wealth of interior details, including built-ins and decorative columns, proclaim this one-story design a winner.
- Keystones, quoins and wood shutters accent the home's rich stucco exterior.
- The centrally located living room includes a fireplace, built-in bookshelves, an entertainment center and access to a rear porch.
- Decorative columns and a tray ceiling define the elegant formal dining room.
- Everything is within reach of the family chef in the efficient kitchen. A snack bar serves the adjoining eating nook.
- Just off the foyer, built-in bookshelves flank one of two entries to a quiet den. The room also sports a built-in desk and a pair of closets, and could function as a study or as an additional bedroom.
- Secluded for privacy, the master suite boasts a well-appointed bath, a door to the nearby utility room and private access to the porch.

Plan E-2211	
Bedrooms: 3+	**Baths:** 3
Living Area:	
Main floor	2,200 sq. ft.
Total Living Area:	**2,200 sq. ft.**
Garage	502 sq. ft.
Storage	70 sq. ft.
Exterior Wall Framing:	2x4
Foundation Options:	
Crawlspace	
Slab	
(All plans can be built with your choice of foundation and framing. A generic conversion diagram is available. See order form.)	
BLUEPRINT PRICE CODE:	**C**

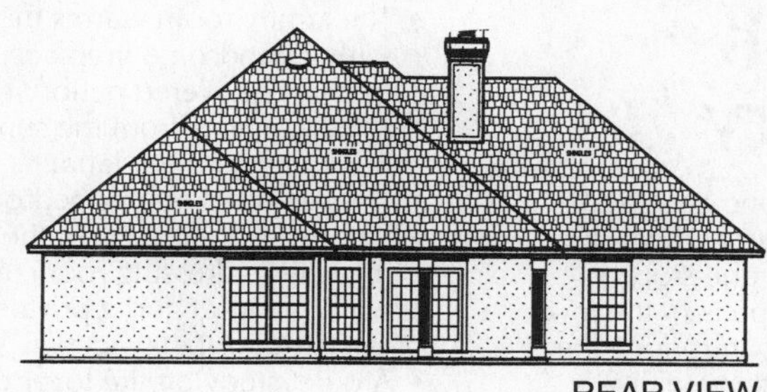

REAR VIEW

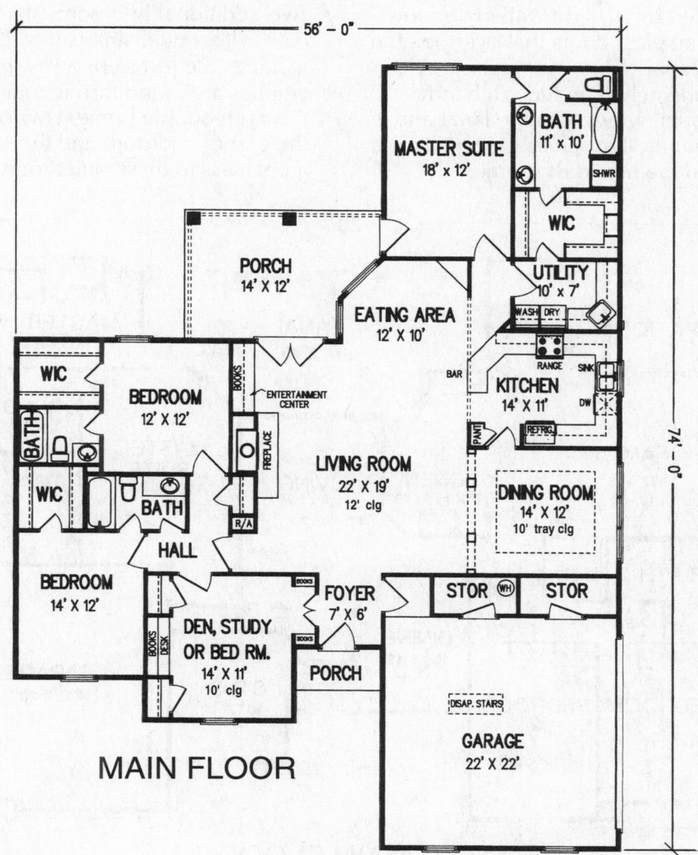

MAIN FLOOR

Plan E-2211

FOR MORE DETAILS, SEE PLAN AT
familyhandyman.com/homeplans

Mark Englund/Homestore™ Plans and Publications

Sprawling One-Story

- A high hip roof, a stone-accented facade and alluring arched windows adorn this sprawling one-story.
- The recessed entry opens to the foyer, where regal columns introduce the elegant formal dining room.
- The spacious living room ahead is highlighted by a bright wall of windows and sliding glass doors that overlook the covered lanai.
- The island kitchen includes a handy pass-through window to the lanai and a snack counter that serves the family room and the breakfast room.
- The family room warms the entire area with a handsome fireplace and opens to a cozy covered patio.
- A French door from the sunny breakfast nook accesses the lanai.
- The secluded master bedroom also features a great view of the lanai, and includes a dressing room, an enormous walk-in closet and a private bath with French-door lanai access.
- A quiet study off the foyer could also serve as a guest bedroom.
- Two additional bedrooms share a hall bath with a dual-sink vanity. Laundry facilities are just steps away. High ceilings are found throughout most of this comfortable home. Low ceilings in the corner bedroom and the study lend a coziness to these quiet rooms.

Plan DD-2241-1

Bedrooms: 3+	**Baths:** 2
Living Area:	
Main floor	2,256 sq. ft.
Total Living Area:	**2,256 sq. ft.**
Standard basement	2,256 sq. ft.
Garage	469 sq. ft.
Exterior Wall Framing:	2x4
Foundation Options:	
Standard basement	
Crawlspace	
Slab	

(All plans can be built with your choice of foundation and framing. A generic conversion diagram is available. See order form.)

BLUEPRINT PRICE CODE: C

NOTE: The photographed home may have been modified by the homeowner. Please refer to floor plan and/or drawn elevation shown for actual blueprint details.

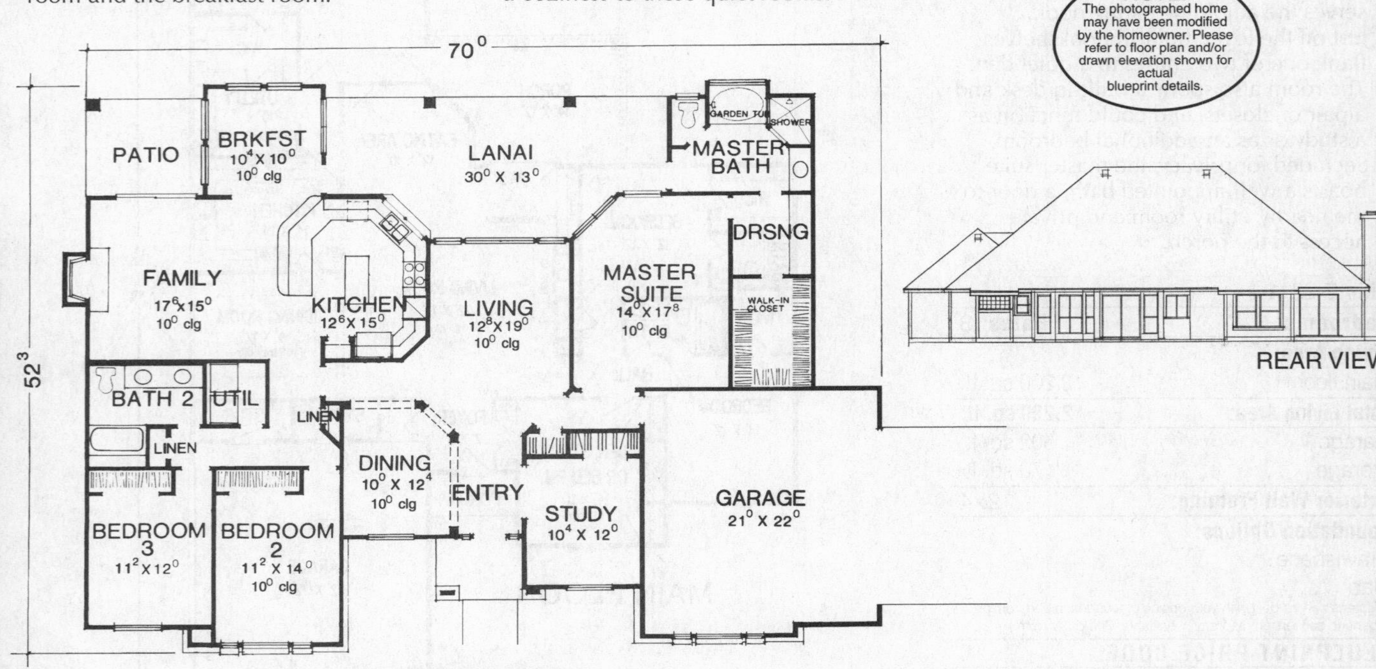

ORDER BLUEPRINTS ANYTIME!
CALL TOLL-FREE 1-800-820-1296

Plan DD-2241-1

SEE ORDER INFO ON PAGES 12-15
familyhandyman.com/homeplans

Sophisticated One-Story

- Beautiful windows accentuated by elegant keystones highlight the exterior of this sophisticated one-story design.
- An open floor plan is the hallmark of the interior. The foyer gives views of the study and the dining and living rooms.
- The spacious living room boasts a fireplace with built-in bookshelves and a rear window wall that stretches into the morning room.
- The sunny morning room has a snack bar to the kitchen. The island kitchen includes a walk-in pantry, a built-in desk and easy access to the utility room and the convenient half-bath.
- The master suite features private access to a nice covered patio, plus an enormous walk-in closet and a posh bath with a spa tub and glass-block shower.
- A hall bath serves the two secondary bedrooms, as well as the flexible study.

VIEW INTO LIVING ROOM

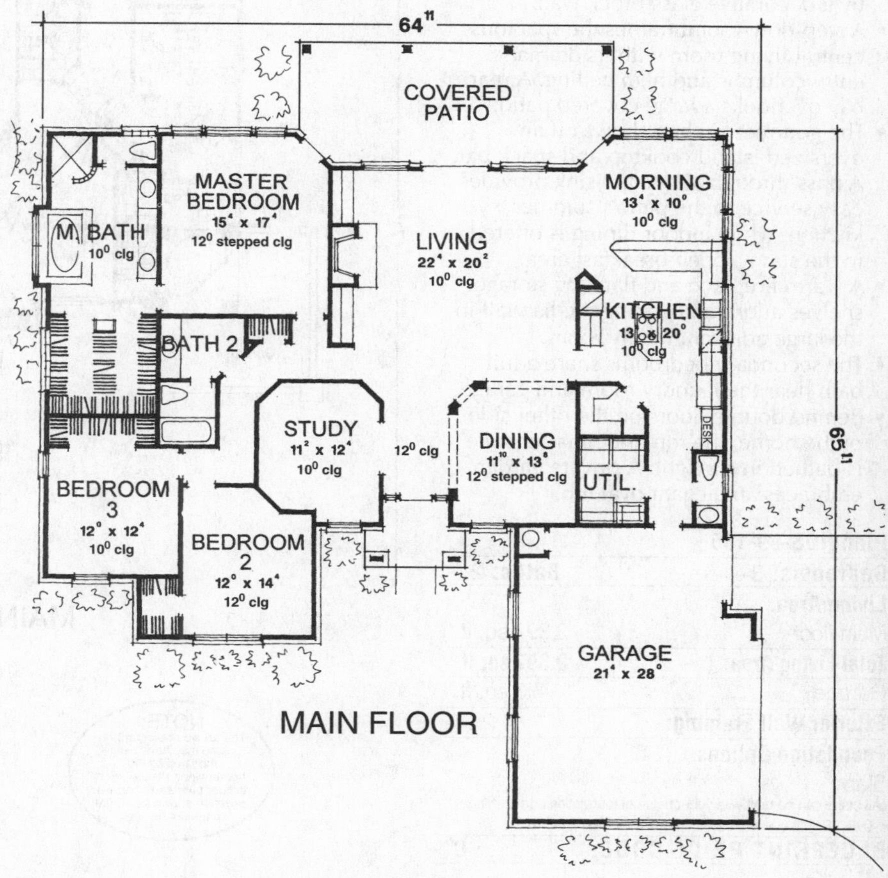

MAIN FLOOR

Plan DD-2455

Bedrooms: 3+	**Baths:** 2½
Living Area:	
Main floor	2,387 sq. ft.
Total Living Area:	**2,387 sq. ft.**
Standard basement	2,387 sq. ft.
Garage	585 sq. ft.
Exterior Wall Framing:	2x4
Foundation Options:	
Standard basement	
Crawlspace	
Slab	

(All plans can be built with your choice of foundation and framing. A generic conversion diagram is available. See order form.)

BLUEPRINT PRICE CODE: C

Plan DD-2455

FOR MORE DETAILS, SEE PLAN AT familyhandyman.com/homeplans

Mark Englund/Homestore™ Plans and Publications

Captivating Design

- This captivating and award-winning design is introduced by a unique entry landscape that includes striking columns, an exciting fountain courtyard and a private garden.
- The open interior commands attention with expansive glass and soaring ceilings throughout.
- The foyer's ceiling extends into the adjoining dining room, which is set off by a decorative glass-block wall.
- A step-down soffit frames the spacious central living room with its dramatic entry columns and high ceiling. A rear bay overlooks a large covered patio.
- The gourmet kitchen shows off an oversized island cooktop and snack bar. A pass-through above the sink provides easy service to the patio's summer kitchen, while indoor dining is offered in the sunny, open breakfast area.
- A warm fireplace and flanking storage shelves adorn an exciting media wall in the large adjacent family room.
- The secondary bedrooms share a full bath near the laundry room and garage.
- Behind double doors on the other side of the home, the romantic master suite is bathed in sunlight. A private garden embraces an elegant oval tub.

Plan HDS-99-185	
Bedrooms: 3+	**Baths:** 2½
Living Area:	
Main floor	2,397 sq. ft.
Total Living Area:	**2,397 sq. ft.**
Garage	473 sq. ft.
Exterior Wall Framing:	2x4
Foundation Options:	
Slab	
(All plans can be built with your choice of foundation and framing. A generic conversion diagram is available. See order form.)	
BLUEPRINT PRICE CODE:	**C**

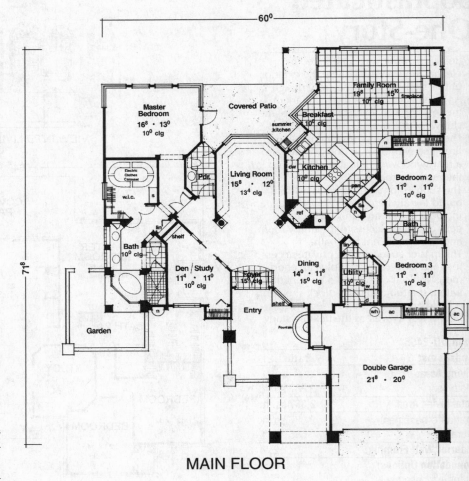

60^{0}

71^{8}

Master Bedroom $16^{8} \cdot 13^{0}$ 10^{0} clg

Covered Patio

Family Room $19^{8} \cdot 15^{10}$ 10^{0} clg

fireplace

Breakfast 10^{0} clg

summer kitchen

Electric Clothes Carousel

w.i.c.

Pdr.

Living Room $15^{8} \cdot 12^{0}$ 13^{4} clg

Kitchen 10^{0} clg

Bedroom 2 $11^{0} \cdot 11^{0}$ 10^{0} clg

Bath 10^{0} clg

Den / Study $11^{4} \cdot 11^{0}$ 10^{0} clg

Foyer 15^{0} clg

Dining $14^{0} \cdot 11^{8}$ 15^{0} clg

Utility 10^{0} clg

Bath

Bedroom 3 $11^{0} \cdot 11^{0}$ 10^{0} clg

Entry

Fountain

Garden

Double Garage $21^{8} \cdot 20^{0}$

MAIN FLOOR

NOTE:
The above photographed home may have been modified by the homeowner. Please refer to floor plan and/or drawn elevation shown for actual blueprint details.

Plan HDS-99-185

SEE ORDER INFO ON PAGES 12-15

Inviting Windows

- This comfortable home presents an impressive facade, with its large and inviting front window arrangement.
- A step down from the front entry, the Great Room boasts a sloped ceiling with a barrel-vaulted area that outlines the half-round front window. The striking angled fireplace can be enjoyed from the adjoining dining area.
- The galley-style kitchen hosts a half-round cutout above the sink and a breakfast area that accesses a backyard deck and patio. The kitchen, breakfast area and dining area also are enhanced by vaulted ceilings.
- The master bedroom features a boxed-out window, a walk-in closet and a dramatic sloped ceiling. The private bath includes a garden tub, a separate shower and a private toilet compartment.
- Another full bath serves the two remaining bedrooms, one of which has sliding glass doors to the deck and would make an ideal den.

VIEW INTO GREAT ROOM

REAR VIEW

Plan B-902	
Bedrooms: 2+	**Baths:** 2
Living Area:	
Main floor	1,368 sq. ft.
Total Living Area:	**1,368 sq. ft.**
Standard basement	1,368 sq. ft.
Garage	412 sq. ft.
Exterior Wall Framing:	2x4
Foundation Options:	
Standard basement	

All plans can be built with your choice of foundation and framing. A generic conversion diagram is available. See order form.)

BLUEPRINT PRICE CODE:	**A**

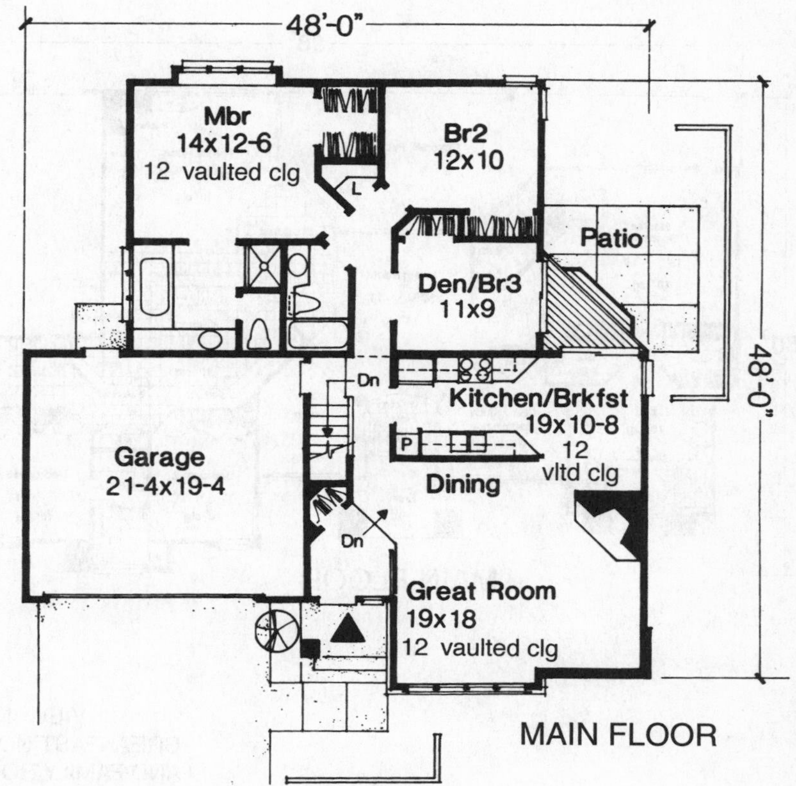

MAIN FLOOR

Plan B-902

FOR MORE DETAILS, SEE PLAN AT familyhandyman.com/homeplans

Mark Englund/Homestore™ Plans and Publications

Extraordinary Estate Living

- Extraordinary estate living is at its best in this palatial beauty.
- The double-doored entry opens to a large central living room that overlooks a covered patio with a vaulted ceiling. High ceilings are found in the living room, in the formal dining room and in the den or study, which may serve as a fourth bedroom.
- The gourmet chef will enjoy the spacious kitchen, which flaunts an island cooktop, a walk-in pantry and an island snack counter shared with the breakfast room and family room.
- This trio of informal living spaces also shares a panorama of glass and a corner fireplace centered between TV and media niches.
- Isolated at the opposite end of the home is the spacious master suite, which offers private patio access. Dual walk-in closets define the entrance to the adjoining master bath, complete with a garden Jacuzzi, a designer shower and separate dressing areas.
- The hall bath also opens to the outdoors for use as a pool bath.

Plan HDS-99-177

Bedrooms: 3+	**Baths:** 3
Living Area:	
Main floor	2,597 sq. ft.
Total Living Area:	**2,597 sq. ft.**
Garage	785 sq. ft.
Exterior Wall Framing:	2x4
Foundation Options:	
Slab	

(All plans can be built with your choice of foundation and framing. A generic conversion diagram is available. See order form.)

BLUEPRINT PRICE CODE: D

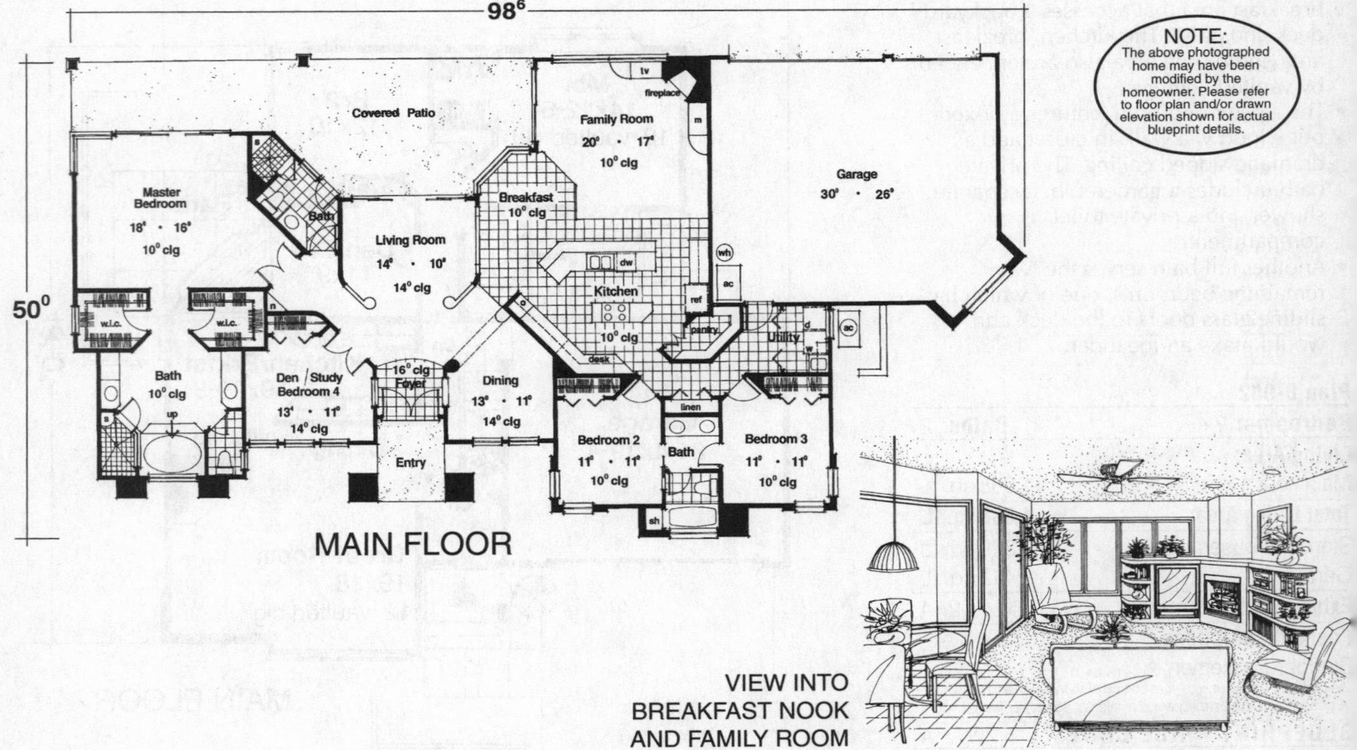

MAIN FLOOR

VIEW INTO BREAKFAST NOOK AND FAMILY ROOM

Plan HDS-99-177

SEE ORDER INFO ON PAGES 12-15
familyhandyman.com/homeplans

Double Take

- Family entertainment is a priority in one corner of this stunning home, where you'll find a joined family room and media room that will double your fun!
- For lively conversation, settle down in front of the family room's fireplace. When the evening calls for a movie, treat yourselves to a big-screen flick in the media room. Even your in-laws' home movies will look great!
- The nearby island kitchen lends itself easily to formal entertaining and daily chores. Note the big walk-in pantry and the wraparound serving bar.
- A morning room offers access to a partially covered backyard deck. Here you can barbecue, rain or shine; and there is plenty of room for a hot tub, if you like.
- Escape to the master suite for a little pampering. You can slip out to the deck on cool spring mornings or curl up with a crossword puzzle by the bay window. The master bath offers two walk-in closets and a dual-sink vanity.

Plan DD-2665

Bedrooms: 3+	**Baths:** 2½
Living Area:	
Main floor	2,666 sq. ft.
Total Living Area:	**2,666 sq. ft.**
Standard basement	2,666 sq. ft.
Garage	411 sq. ft.
Exterior Wall Framing:	2x4

Foundation Options:
Standard basement
Crawlspace
Slab
(All plans can be built with your choice of foundation and framing. A generic conversion diagram is available. See order form.)

BLUEPRINT PRICE CODE: D

REAR VIEW

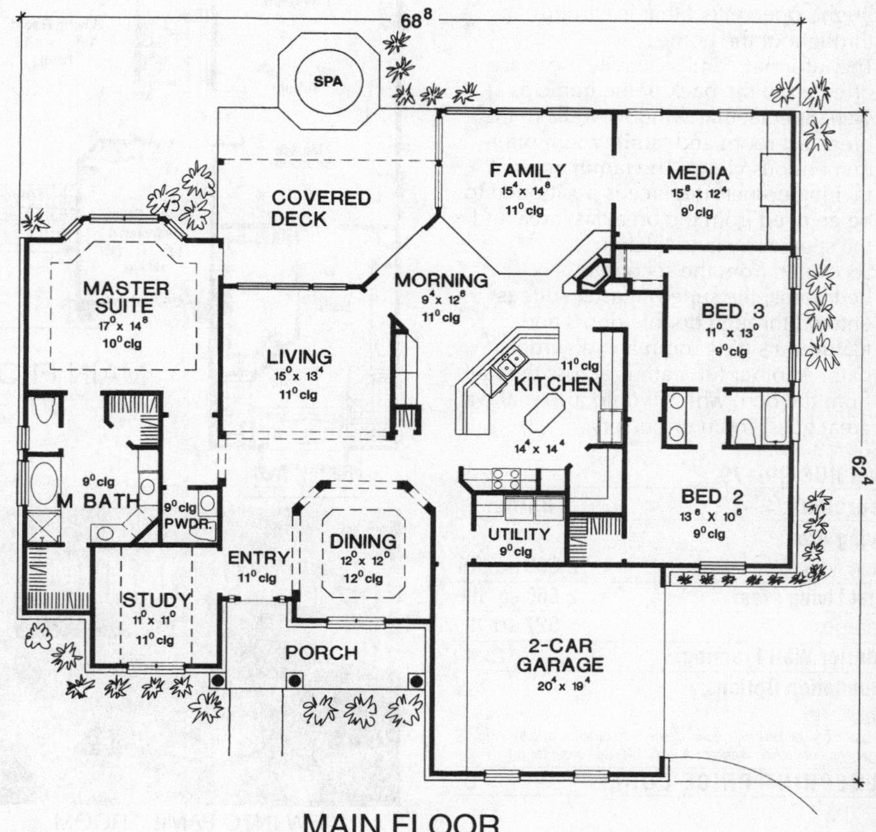

MAIN FLOOR

Builder: Williams Development
Photos by Mark Englund/Homestore™ Plans and Publications

Alluring Arches

- Massive columns, high, dramatic arches and expansive glass attract passersby to this alluring one-story home.
- Inside, coffered ceilings are found in the foyer, dining room and living room. A bank of windows in the living room provides a sweeping view of the covered backyard patio, creating a bright, open effect that is carried throughout the home.
- The informal, family activity areas are oriented to the back of the home as well. Spectacular window walls in the breakfast room and family room offer tremendous views. The family room's inviting corner fireplace is positioned to be enjoyed from the breakfast area and the spacious island kitchen.
- Separated from the secondary bedrooms, the superb master suite is entered through double doors and features a sitting room and a garden bath. Another full bath is across the hall from the den, which would also make a great guest room or nursery.

Plan HDS-99-179	
Bedrooms: 3+	**Baths:** 3
Living Area:	
Main floor	2,660 sq. ft.
Total Living Area:	**2,660 sq. ft.**
Garage	527 sq. ft.
Exterior Wall Framing:	2x4
Foundation Options:	
Slab	
(All plans can be built with your choice of foundation and framing. A generic conversion diagram is available. See order form.)	
BLUEPRINT PRICE CODE:	**D**

VIEW INTO FAMILY ROOM

NOTE:
The above photographed home may have been modified by the homeowner. Please refer to floor plan and/or drawn elevation shown for actual blueprint details.

Plan HDS-99-179

SEE ORDER INFO ON PAGES 12-15

Innovative Use of Space

- Strategic angles, built-in shelving and multi-access rooms exemplify the innovative use of space in this exciting stucco and stone home.
- Elaborate ceilings and windows further enhance the volume of the living areas.
- Adjacent to the airy foyer, the living room's built-in cabinets, shelves and plant niches add function to its beautiful fireplace wall.
- More shelves display your personal library in the double-doored study.
- Wraparound counter space frames the octagonal kitchen, which can be accessed from the foyer and formal dining room, as well as from the casual spaces on the other side.
- A luxurious garden bath and a winding walk-in closet adjoin the spacious master bedroom; a compartmentalized bath serves the secondary bedrooms.
- The unfinished bonus room upstairs is available for future use as an extra bedroom, game room or hobby area.

Plan KLF-9710

Bedrooms: 3+	**Baths:** 2½
Living Area:	
Main floor	2,747 sq. ft.
Total Living Area:	**2,747 sq. ft.**
Future area	391 sq. ft.
Garage and storage	504 sq. ft.
Exterior Wall Framing:	2x4
Foundation Options:	
Slab	

(All plans can be built with your choice of foundation and framing. A generic conversion diagram is available. See order form.)

BLUEPRINT PRICE CODE: D

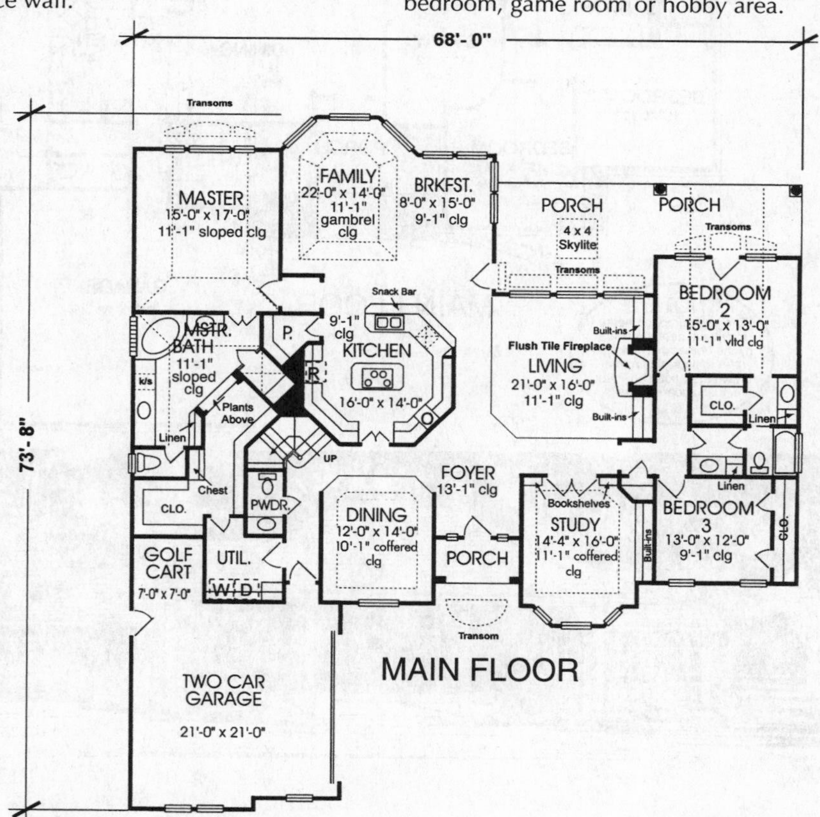

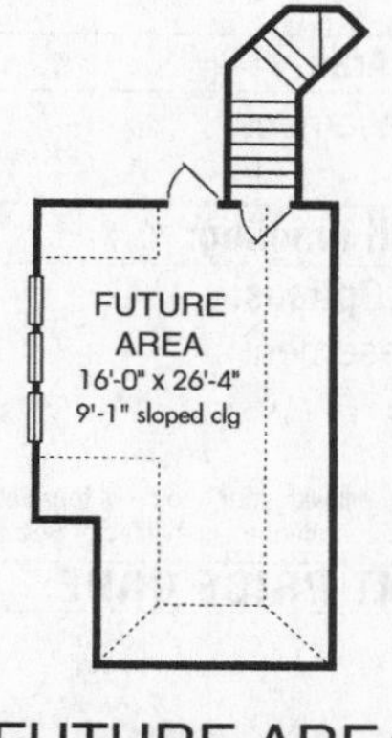

ORDER BLUEPRINTS ANYTIME!
CALL TOLL-FREE 1-800-820-1296

Plan KLF-9710

FOR MORE DETAILS, SEE PLAN AT familyhandyman.com/homeplans

Angled Interior

- This plan gives new dimension to one-story living. The exterior has graceful arched windows and a sweeping roofline. The interior is marked by unusual angles and stately columns.
- The living areas are clustered around a large lanai, or covered porch. French doors provide lanai access from the family room, the living room and the master bedroom.
- The central living room also offers arched windows and shares a two-sided fireplace with the family room.
- The island kitchen and the bayed morning room are open to the family room, which features a wet bar next to the striking fireplace.
- The master bedroom features an irresistible bath with a spa tub, a separate shower, dual vanities and two walk-in closets. Two more good-sized bedrooms share another full bath.
- A cathedral ceiling enhances the third bedroom. Most other rooms boast terrific high ceilings as well.

Plan DD-2802	
Bedrooms: 3+	**Baths:** 2½
Living Area:	
Main floor	2,899 sq. ft.
Total Living Area:	**2,899 sq. ft.**
Standard basement	2,899 sq. ft.
Garage	568 sq. ft.
Exterior Wall Framing:	2x4
Foundation Options:	
Standard basement	
Crawlspace	
Slab	
(All plans can be built with your choice of foundation and framing. A generic conversion diagram is available. See order form.)	
BLUEPRINT PRICE CODE:	**D**

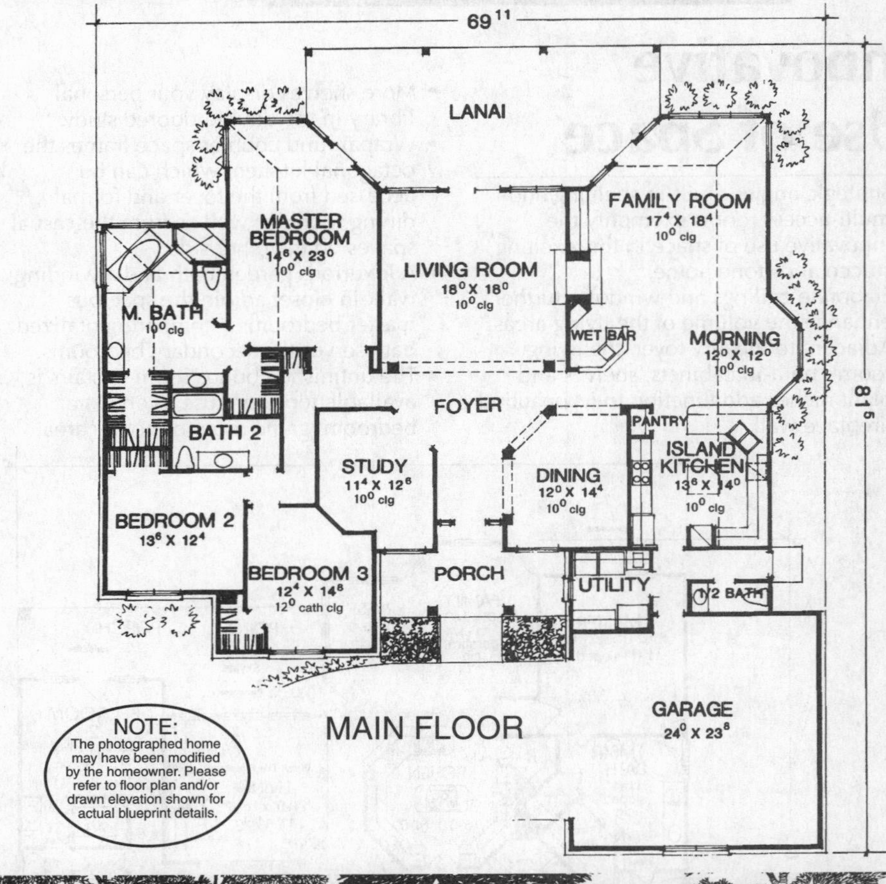

REAR VIEW

Plan DD-2802

Plan copyright held by home designer/architect

SEE ORDER INFO ON PAGES 12-15

Walk Right In

- A walk-in closet in every bedroom is one of the thoughtful touches you'll find in this home, which displays a gracious, Southern-style facade.
- The home is anchored by a central Great Room big enough for entertaining on a grand scale.
- The smartly designed kitchen extends a handy snack bar to the bright breakfast area. An island cooktop frees up coveted counter space. A gourmet walk-in pantry gives you all the storage space you've ever dreamed of, and a built-in desk helps you get organized. French doors access the dining room.
- The generous laundry room boasts lots of cabinet and closet space, plus a built-in, fold-down ironing board.
- The secluded master suite becomes the owners' retreat. A dressing area with a dual-sink vanity opens to a big walk-in closet and a private bath with a whirlpool tub and a separate shower.
- Across the home, two bedrooms have private access to a shared full bath.
- A quiet study doubles as a guest room.
- The blueprints for this design include plans for a detached, two-car garage.

Plan DP-2189

Bedrooms: 3+	**Baths:** 2½
Living Area:	
Main floor	2,189 sq. ft.
Total Living Area:	**2,189 sq. ft.**
Detached garage	480 sq. ft.
Exterior Wall Framing:	2x4
Foundation Options:	
Slab	

(All plans can be built with your choice of foundation and framing. A generic conversion diagram is available. See order form.)

BLUEPRINT PRICE CODE: C

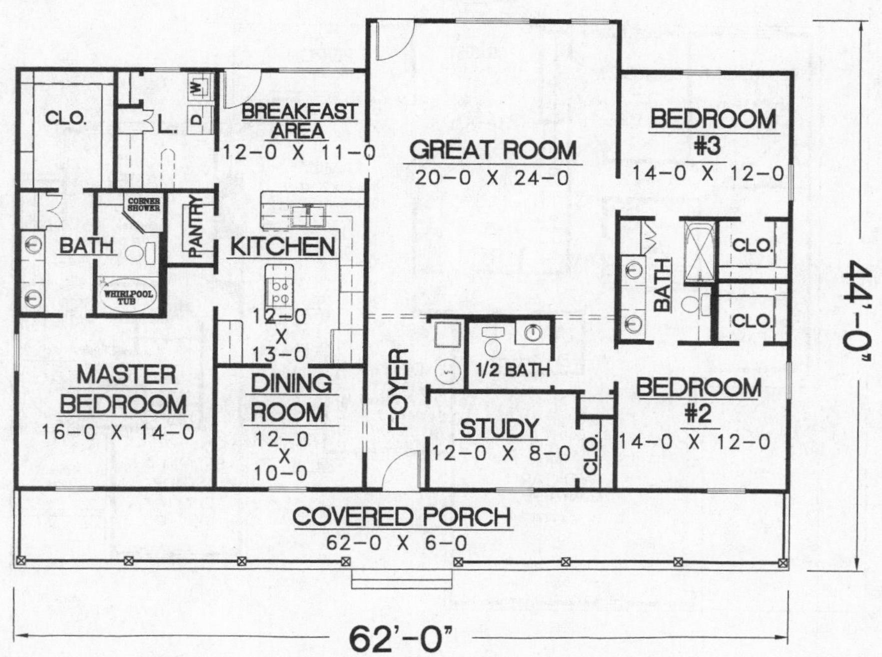

MAIN FLOOR

Plan DP-2189

FOR MORE DETAILS, SEE PLAN AT familyhandyman.com/homeplans

Incredible Brick Beauty

- This incredible one-story brick home offers you a beautiful way to live.
- A bold arched window and a stylish, oval window help to create a sparkling front facade.
- At the center of the home is the family room, which is large enough to handle big events. Its coffered ceiling and cozy fireplace are perfect for intimate evenings as well.
- The spacious island kitchen boasts a handy corner pantry and a convenient eating bar. A bay-windowed breakfast nook makes a sunny spot for a quick morning bagel; if the weather's irresistible, step out to the back porch and soak it up!
- A great example of grand living is the master bedroom. Two huge walk-in closets flank the secluded bath, where you can enjoy a private bath in the corner garden tub.
- Two additional bedrooms and a study that easily converts to a fourth bedroom complete the design.

Plan KLF-973	
Bedrooms: 3+	**Baths:** 2
Living Area:	
Main floor	2,244 sq. ft.
Total Living Area:	**2,244 sq. ft.**
Garage	791 sq. ft.
Exterior Wall Framing:	2x4
Foundation Options:	
Slab	
(All plans can be built with your choice of foundation and framing. A generic conversion diagram is available. See order form.)	
BLUEPRINT PRICE CODE:	**C**

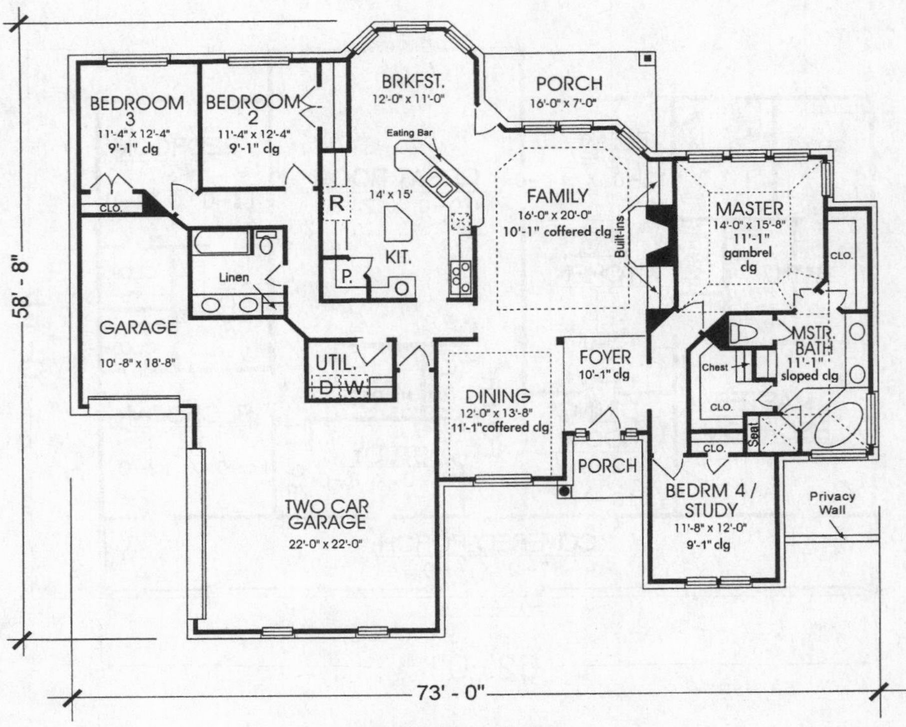

MAIN FLOOR

Plan KLF-973

SEE ORDER INFO ON PAGES 12-15

First Glimpse of Elegance

- The eye-catching dining room—with its tray ceiling and built-in china cabinet—presents a first glimpse of the elegance this home's interior has to offer.
- Across the foyer, a study is just the spot for a secluded home office, a quiet library or even a guest bedroom.
- At the heart of it all, the Great Room enjoys a fireplace and a built-in TV shelf. To one side, a window wall lets in plenty of sunlight, while to another side, the kitchen's angled snack bar promises an open, casual atmosphere.
- Servicing the Great Room and the bayed morning room, the kitchen includes a large walk-in pantry, lots of counter space and a center island workstation.
- The master bedroom enjoys a door to the patio, great views of the backyard and a private bath with two walk-in closets and a whirlpool tub.
- In addition to a sizable closet in each secondary bedroom, the two rooms also boast private access to a nice compartmentalized bath with a handy dual-sink vanity.

Plan DD-2291

Bedrooms: 3+	**Baths:** 2½
Living Area:	
Main floor	2,296 sq. ft.
Total Living Area:	**2,296 sq. ft.**
Standard basement	2,296 sq. ft.
Garage	487 sq. ft.
Exterior Wall Framing:	2x4
Foundation Options:	
Standard basement	
Crawlspace	
Slab	

(All plans can be built with your choice of foundation and framing. A generic conversion diagram is available. See order form.)

BLUEPRINT PRICE CODE: C

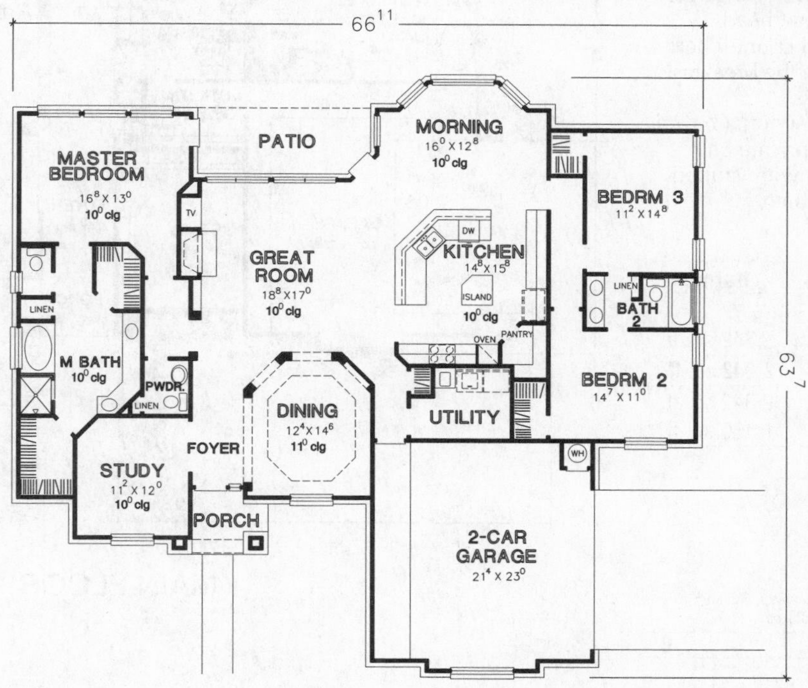

MAIN FLOOR

Plan DD-2291

Impressive Columns

- Impressive columns and striking stucco give this home a distinguished look.
- Inside, a high ceiling extends above the foyer, the formal living and dining rooms and the inviting family room.
- The stunning raised dining room is set off by decorative wood columns that support a wraparound overhead plant shelf. A two-way fireplace is shared with the family room, which also features built-in shelves and arched windows that overlook a large deck.
- The study includes built-in bookshelves and a ceiling that vaults overhead.
- The kitchen has an angled counter bar and a corner pantry while the breakfast nook provides deck access.
- The large master suite shows off a bayed sitting area and a roomy, private bath.
- Two secondary bedrooms with vaulted ceilings share a nice hall bath.

Plan DW-2342

Bedrooms: 3+	**Baths:** 2
Living Area:	
Main floor	2,342 sq. ft.
Total Living Area:	**2,342 sq. ft.**
Standard basement	2,342 sq. ft.
Garage	460 sq. ft.
Exterior Wall Framing:	2x4
Foundation Options:	
Standard basement	
Crawlspace	
Slab	

(All plans can be built with your choice of foundation and framing. A generic conversion diagram is available. See order form.)

BLUEPRINT PRICE CODE: C

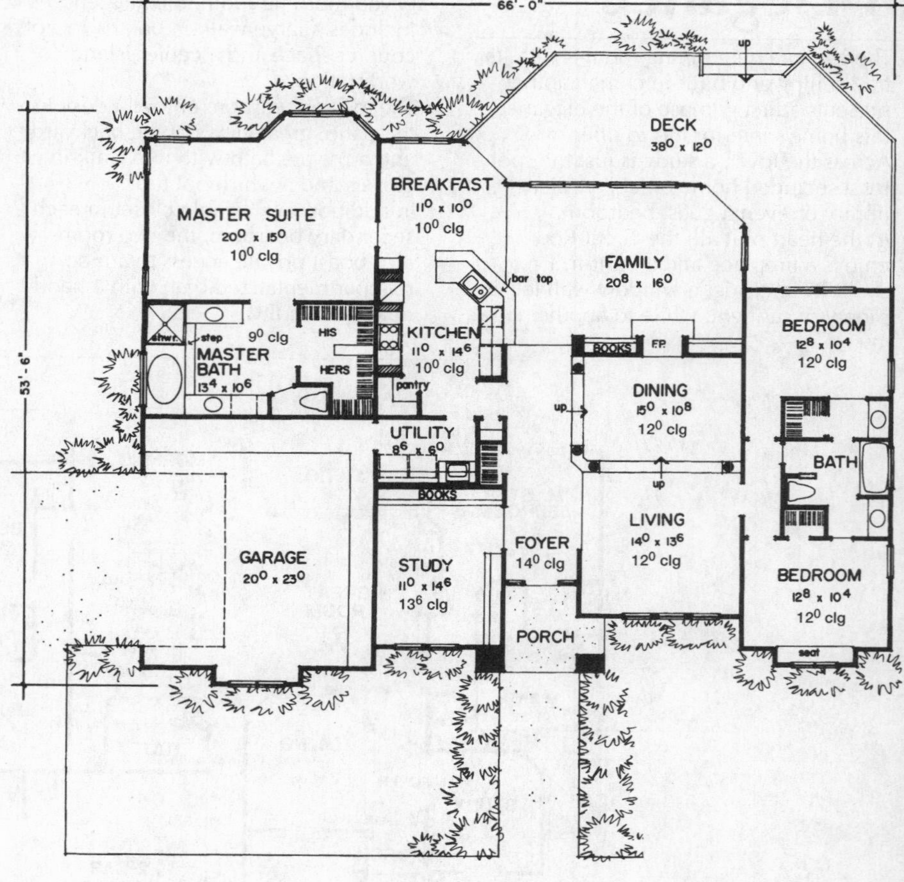

MAIN FLOOR

Plan DW-2342

SEE ORDER INFO ON PAGES 12-15

Distinguished Facade

- A distinguished facade featuring arches, columns and brick creates this home's traditional look. Inside, this theme continues with an arched foyer flanked by a study and the formal dining room.
- Past a large butler's pantry, the kitchen offers an island workstation and shares a wide snack bar with the living room.
- The sunny breakfast nook features access to a backyard patio, while the central living room offers plenty of space and a prominent corner fireplace.
- One wing of the home hosts the master bedroom, which boasts a large window overlooking the front yard and a private bath with a walk-in closet, a dual-sink vanity and a garden tub. Another wing provides two more bedrooms—each with a walk-in closet—and a full bath.
- The blueprints include plans for a detached two-car garage.

Plan DD-2374	
Bedrooms: 3+	**Baths:** 2½
Living Area:	
Main floor	2,373 sq. ft.
Total Living Area:	**2,373 sq. ft.**
Future area	818 sq. ft.
Standard basement	2,373 sq. ft.
Detached garage	480 sq. ft.
Porte cochere	355 sq. ft.
Exterior Wall Framing:	2x4
Foundation Options:	
Standard basement	
Crawlspace	
Slab	

(All plans can be built with your choice of foundation and framing. A generic conversion diagram is available. See order form.)

BLUEPRINT PRICE CODE: C

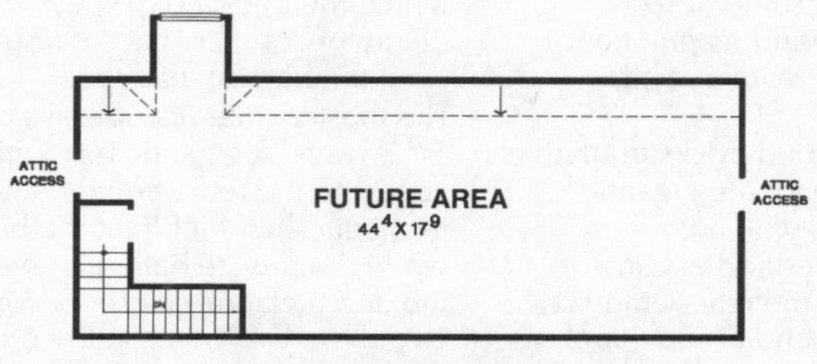

FUTURE AREA

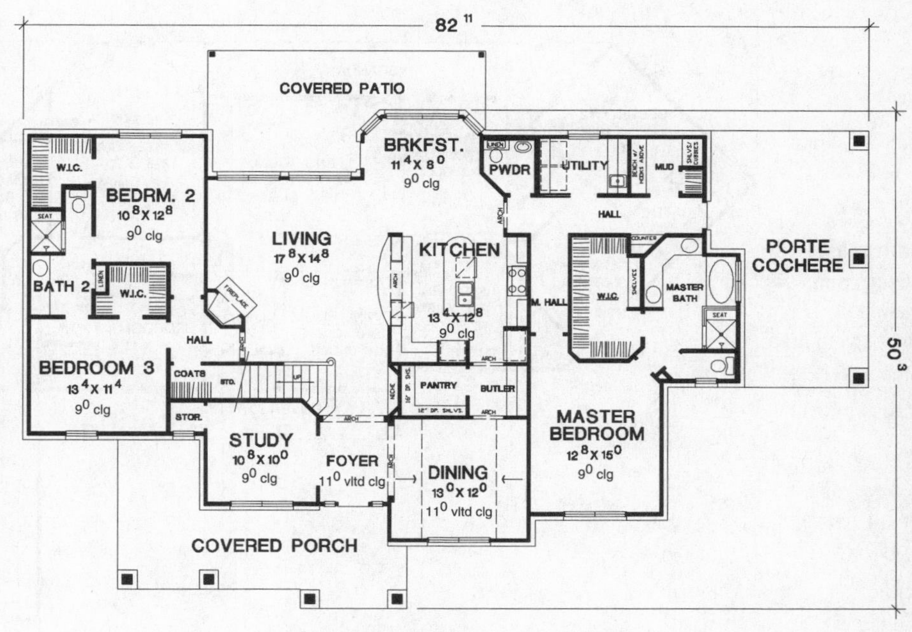

MAIN FLOOR

Plan DD-2374

FOR MORE DETAILS, SEE PLAN AT familyhandyman.com/homeplans

Villa Royale

- An opulent floor plan, sumptuous Mediterranean styling and magnificent windows throughout create a royal-caliber villa.
- Inside, the entry is framed by decorative columns. Directly ahead, the gigantic living room welcomes with a corner fireplace, media shelves and expansive windows overlooking the rear veranda.
- A formal dining room and a study flank the entryway. The study can also serve as a fourth bedroom.
- The kitchen extends a snack bar to the living room and the breakfast nook, which includes a bayed window seat. Plenty of counter space can handle even the biggest feasts.
- The master suite occupies its own wing for privacy. A gigantic bay window, access to the rear veranda, and a built-in media shelf highlight the bedroom, while the private bath features a garden tub and a walk-in closet beyond.
- Two more bedrooms at the other end of the home enjoy walk-in closets and a shared bath.

Plan DD-2403

Bedrooms: 3+	**Baths:** 2½
Living Area:	
Main floor	2,388 sq. ft.
Total Living Area:	**2,388 sq. ft.**
Garage	490 sq. ft.
Exterior Wall Framing:	2x4
Foundation Options:	
Crawlspace	
Slab	

(All plans can be built with your choice of foundation and framing. A generic conversion diagram is available. See order form.)

BLUEPRINT PRICE CODE: C

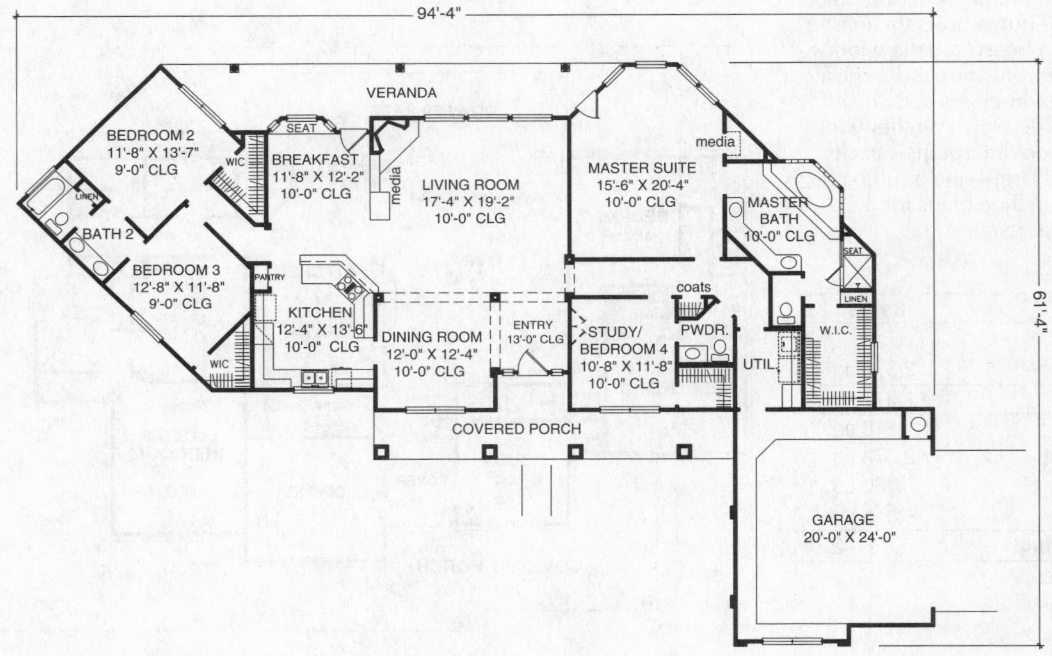

MAIN FLOOR

Plan DD-2403

SEE ORDER INFO ON PAGES 12-15

A Splashy Introduction

- This home's entry makes a statement before visitors even step through the front door. An exterior fountain provides a splashy introduction, arches accentuate the handsome facade and a built-in plant shelf is sure to bring out the green thumb in anyone.
- Once inside, guests will admire the tiled foyer, which opens into the home's formal spaces. Ahead, a stepped ceiling and a big bay window adorn the living room, while to the right, a high ceiling distinguishes the open dining room.
- On the left of the home, a secluded den or study lies behind sliding doors. With built-in bookshelves and a handy closet, this room also makes for an excellent guest bedroom.
- To the back of the home, the family room features a lovely fireplace and smoothly merges with the breakfast nook and the well-appointed kitchen.
- Offering extravagance at every turn, the master suite enjoys a private bath and a walk-in closet so luxurious that it has its own electric clothes carousel.

Plan HDS-99-204

Bedrooms: 3+	**Baths:** 2½
Living Area:	
Main floor	2,397 sq. ft.
Total Living Area:	**2,397 sq. ft.**
Garage	772 sq. ft.
Exterior Wall Framing:	2x4
Foundation Options:	
Slab	
(All plans can be built with your choice of foundation and framing. A generic conversion diagram is available. See order form.)	
BLUEPRINT PRICE CODE:	**C**

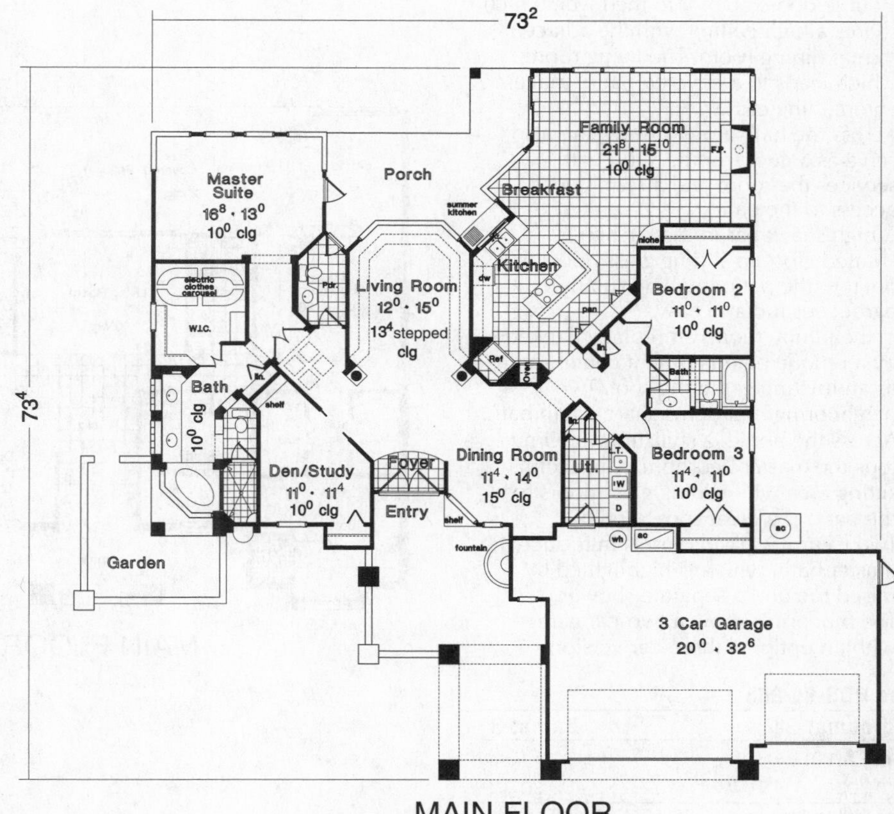

MAIN FLOOR

Regal Entry

- An entry accented by regal columns and a beautiful arched window arrangement introduces this Mediterranean home.
- Double doors open into the foyer, which shares a high ceiling with the adjacent formal dining room. The living room, which leads to a covered patio, makes entertaining easy.
- Across the hall, a quiet study can also serve as a guest room. A full bath services the room and also includes access to the patio.
- A high snack bar in the kitchen is located close to sliding glass doors that open to the patio, making summer barbecues fun and easy.
- In the family room, a fireplace flanked by a unique entertainment center serves as an inviting gathering spot. Two neighboring bedrooms share a hall bath.
- Across the home, a stylish tray ceiling tops the master bedroom. A peaceful sitting area with sliding glass doors to the patio is a great spot to relax.
- Two roomy walk-in closets introduce the master bath, which is highlighted by a raised tub and a separate shower.
- The blueprints show a two-car garage with an optional three-car version.

Plan HDS-99-205

Bedrooms: 3+	**Baths:** 3
Living Area:	
Main floor	2,409 sq. ft.
Total Living Area:	**2,409 sq. ft.**
Two-car garage	495 sq. ft.
Three-car garage	759 sq. ft.
Exterior Wall Framing:	8-in. concrete block
Foundation Options:	
Slab	
(All plans can be built with your choice of foundation and framing. A generic conversion diagram is available. See order form.)	
BLUEPRINT PRICE CODE:	**C**

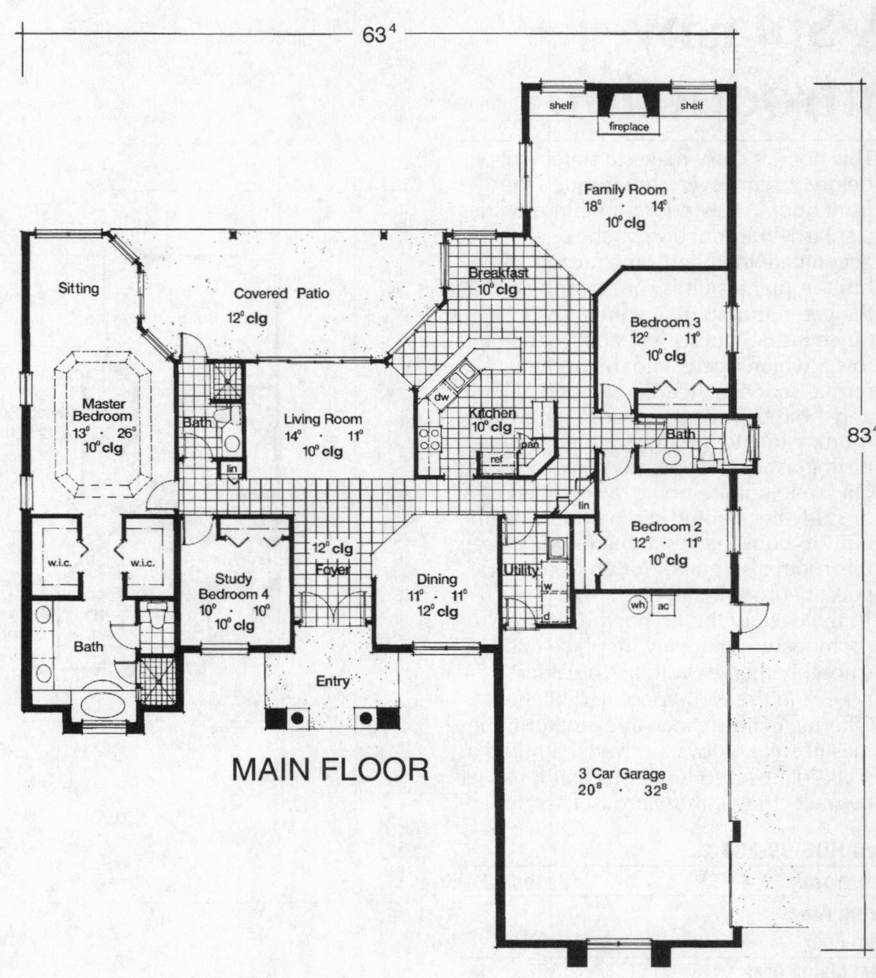

MAIN FLOOR

Plan HDS-99-205

SEE ORDER INFO ON PAGES 12-15
familyhandyman.com/homeplans

The Look of Yesteryear

- A wraparound porch, quaint dormers and nostalgic window treatments give this home the look of yesteryear. Inside, you'll find a thoroughly modern floor plan that caters to today's families.
- The central living room enjoys a large hearth area and a door that leads to a covered backyard patio.
- Smells of delicious home-cooked meals will drift from the well-stocked kitchen into the sunny breakfast nook. The nook overlooks the patio and features a convenient serving bar.
- All bedrooms are located on the opposite side of the home, creating an effective separation between sleeping and living quarters.
- The master suite boasts a tray ceiling, a walk-in closet and a private bath with a tub that offers a lovely garden view.
- Two additional bedrooms with sloped ceilings and large closets share a hall bath with a dual-sink vanity.
- The fourth bedroom may be converted to a study or a home office. Double doors can be added so that the room is accessible from the foyer.

Plan DD-2495

Bedrooms: 3+	**Baths:** 2½
Living Area:	
Main floor	2,420 sq. ft.
Total Living Area:	**2,420 sq. ft.**
Standard basement	2,420 sq. ft.
Exterior Wall Framing:	2x4

Foundation Options:
Standard basement
Crawlspace
Slab
(All plans can be built with your choice of foundation and framing. A generic conversion diagram is available. See order form.)

BLUEPRINT PRICE CODE: C

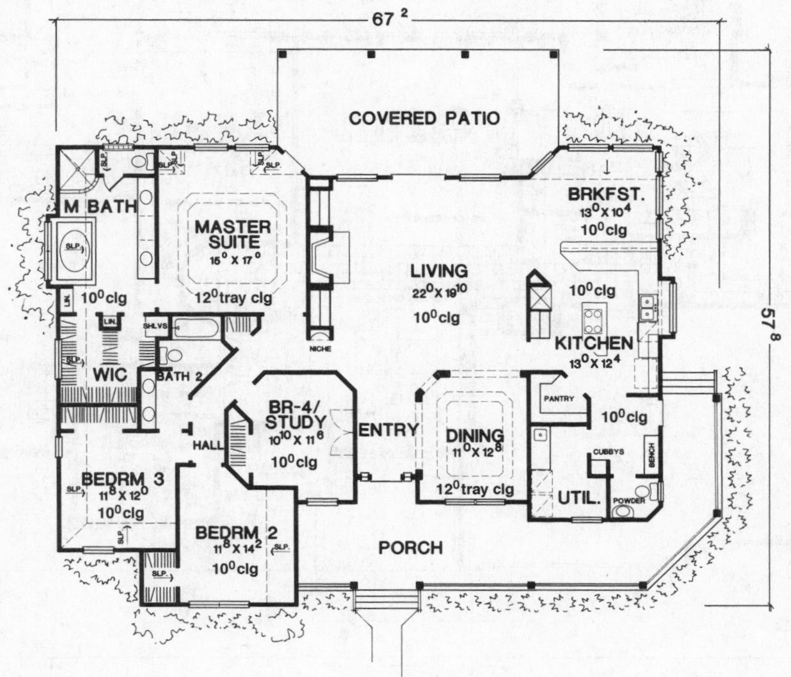

MAIN FLOOR

Plan DD-2495

Excitingly Different

- This unusual design is filled with spaces that are far from boring. The entry opens to a semi-circular stairway with a spectacular vaulted, domed ceiling.
- Domed ceilings are repeated in the breakfast nook and the master bath. The nook faces a unique hearth room and the island kitchen, which includes a snack bar, a built-in desk and a convenient wet bar.
- The Great Room is nothing short of extraordinary, with its see-through fireplace, volume ceiling and stunning arched windows. Across the hall, the dining room is defined by columns and an elegant tray ceiling.
- The succulent master suite has a volume ceiling and high transom windows. The bath is showcased by the domed tub area, his-and-hers sinks, a shower framed by a glass-block wall and a roomy walk-in closet.
- The second bedroom and the den or optional third bedroom have direct access to a bath.

Plan DBI-1232

Bedrooms: 2+	**Baths:** 2½
Living Area:	
Main floor	2,422 sq. ft.
Total Living Area:	**2,422 sq. ft.**
Standard basement	2,422 sq. ft.
Garage	642 sq. ft.
Exterior Wall Framing:	2x4

Foundation Options:

Standard basement

(All plans can be built with your choice of foundation and framing. A generic conversion diagram is available. See order form.)

BLUEPRINT PRICE CODE: C

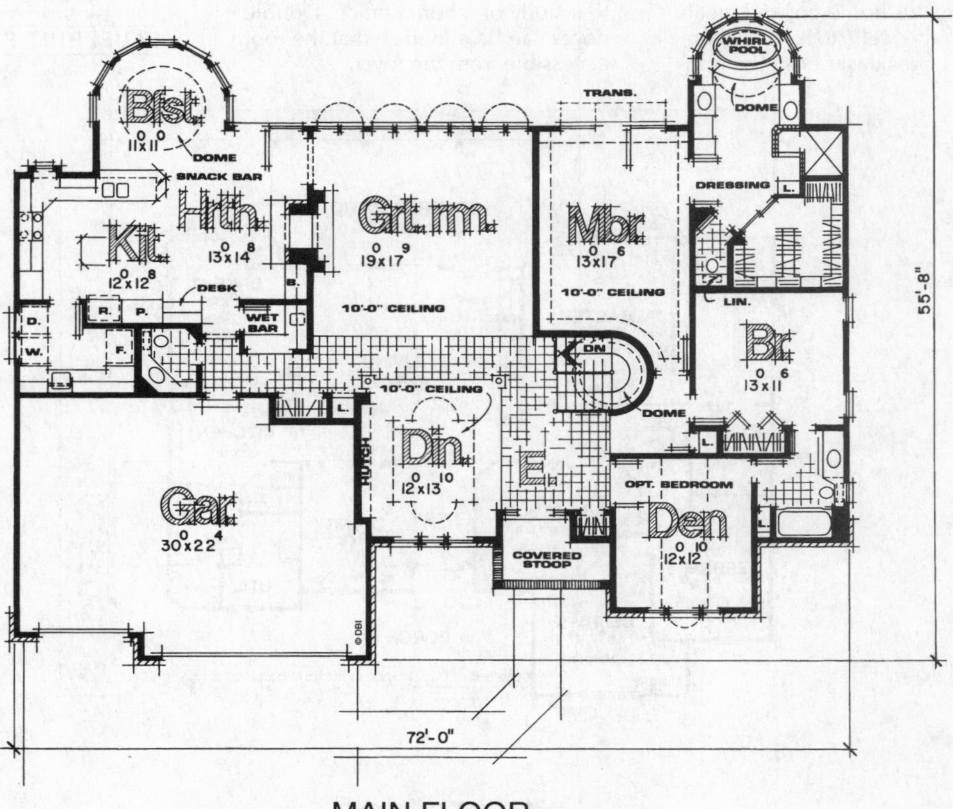

MAIN FLOOR

Plan DBI-1232

Pretty and Promising

- This one-story home promises all the luxury and convenience any family could want. Entering through a door flanked by sidelights, you'll find a quiet study to the left and the formal dining room to the right.
- Walk into the living room to be awed by a handsome fireplace with snazzy built-in bookshelves. Off the living room you'll find the breakfast nook—a perfect spot to enjoy a cup of coffee.
- The spacious kitchen boasts an island cooktop and plenty of counter space. A nearby utility room lies opposite a convenient half-bath.
- The master bedroom enjoys private access to a covered patio. The master bath includes a large walk-in closet, a lovely spa tub and a dual-sink vanity.
- Two additional bedrooms, both with generous closets, share a full bath.

Plan DD-2455-B

Bedrooms: 3+	**Baths:** 2½
Living Area:	
Main floor	2,424 sq. ft.
Total Living Area:	**2,424 sq. ft.**
Standard basement	2,424 sq. ft.
Garage	605 sq. ft.
Exterior Wall Framing:	2x4

Foundation Options:

Standard basement

Crawlspace

Slab

(All plans can be built with your choice of foundation and framing. A generic conversion diagram is available. See order form.)

BLUEPRINT PRICE CODE: C

MAIN FLOOR

Perfect—Inside and Out

- Charming as can be on the outside, it's the thoughtful interior of this country-style gem that sets it apart from the rest.
- Distinguished by handsome columns, the Great Room truly is the heart of the design. A corner fireplace casts a cozy glow on winter nights. A matching set of French doors leads out to a covered patio for warm-weather fun.
- The kitchen is fronted by a long serving bar for ease in entertaining, and it boasts a walk-in pantry as well. The nearby bayed breakfast nook provides a sunny spot for casual meals.
- A mudroom is handily located near the utility room. An adjacent powder room may serve as a pool bath.
- The formal dining room just off the foyer may be converted into a home office, a bedroom or a hobby room.
- At day's end, relax in the quiet master suite. Two walk-in closets flank the hall to the private bath, which has a garden tub, a separate shower and a dual-sink vanity. French doors open to the patio.
- Two more bedrooms share a split bath featuring a dual-sink vanity.

Plan DD-2436	
Bedrooms: 3+	**Baths:** 2½
Living Area:	
Main floor	2,436 sq. ft.
Total Living Area:	**2,436 sq. ft.**
Standard basement	2,436 sq. ft.
Garage	478 sq. ft.
Exterior Wall Framing:	2x4
Foundation Options:	
Standard basement	
Crawlspace	
Slab	
(All plans can be built with your choice of foundation and framing. A generic conversion diagram is available. See order form.)	
BLUEPRINT PRICE CODE:	**C**

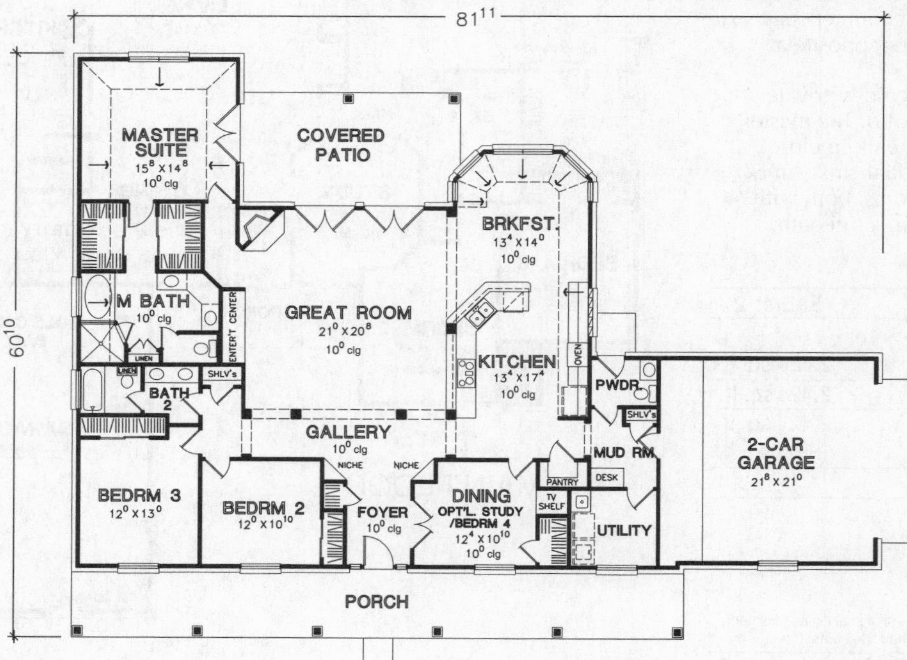

MAIN FLOOR

ORDER BLUEPRINTS ANYTIME! CALL TOLL-FREE 1-800-820-1296

Plan DD-2436

SEE ORDER INFO ON PAGES 12-15

familyhandyman.com/homeplans

Regal Poise

- With its stately brick facade, gorgeous half-round transoms and striking gables, this regal home will grace the most upscale neighborhood.
- A warmly appointed family room anchors the home, boasting a prominent fireplace flanked by built-in cabinets. French doors lead to a rear porch. Transom windows add dazzle.
- The exciting wraparound kitchen boasts an angled bar and stacked ovens with cookie sheet storage above. The adjoining bayed breakfast nook nestles between two porches.
- Shielded from kitchen noise by double doors, the formal dining room provides an intimate space for special meals.
- Natural light floods the master suite through a brilliant bayed window arrangement. In the master bath, a lush plant shelf overlooks a whirlpool tub and a neat split vanity with knee space.
- In the opposite wing of the home, two good-sized secondary bedrooms share a compartmentalized bath, allowing the kids an extra measure of privacy.
- To the right of the sidelighted foyer, French doors introduce a peaceful study that may also be used as a bedroom.

Plan KLF-941

Bedrooms: 3+	**Baths:** 2½
Living Area:	
Main floor	2,437 sq. ft.
Total Living Area:	**2,437 sq. ft.**
Garage and storage	589 sq. ft.
Exterior Wall Framing:	2x4
Foundation Options:	
Slab	
(All plans can be built with your choice of foundation and framing. A generic conversion diagram is available. See order form.)	
BLUEPRINT PRICE CODE:	**C**

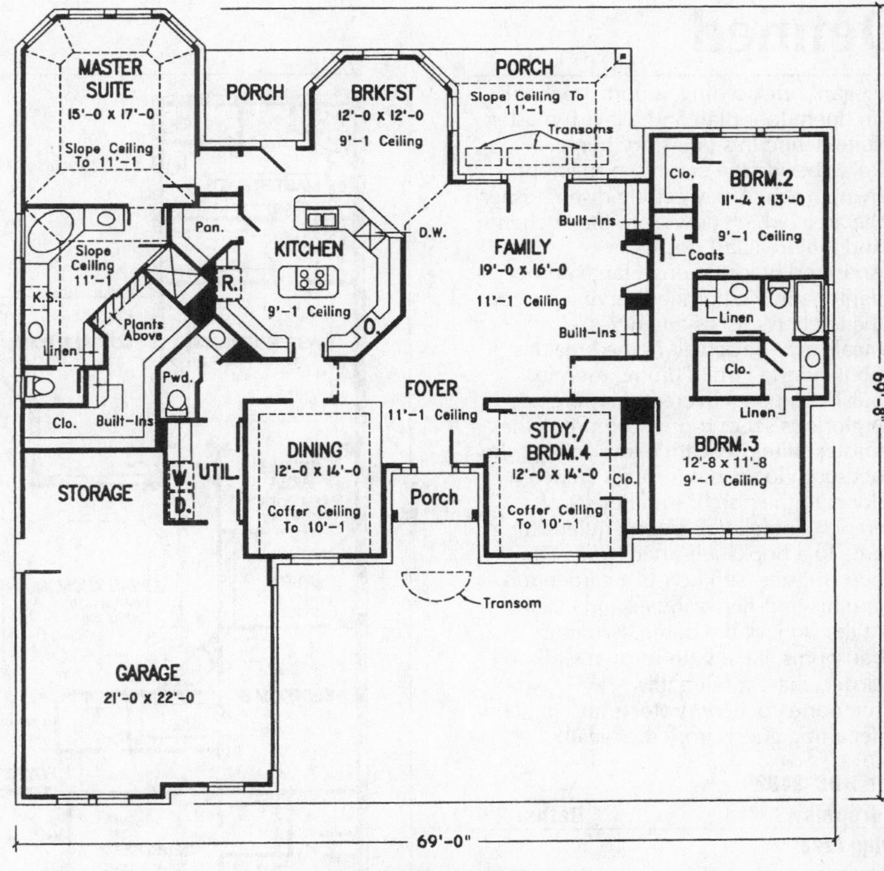

MAIN FLOOR

Elegance Defined

- Elegant brick styling, a porte cochere, an open floor plan and a lavish master suite define this one-story home.
- Relax beside the fire in the spacious living room. A tray ceiling distinguishes the area, which flows into the kitchen and the breakfast nook.
- An island workstation, a large corner pantry and a columned serving bar top the kitchen's list of amenities.
- Meals may be served in the breakfast nook, in the formal dining room or outside on the covered rear porch.
- A glorious set of rooms comprises the master suite. Beneath a tray ceiling, the bedroom looks out through French doors to the porch. Another set of French doors leads from a quiet sitting area to a bookshelf-lined study. The posh master bath boasts a garden tub and his-and-hers vanities and closets.
- At the front of the home, two more bedrooms, each with its own walk-in closet, share a full bath.
- The porte cochere protects arriving and departing guests from the weather.

Plan HDC-2482

Bedrooms: 3	**Baths:** 2½
Living Area:	
Main floor	2,482 sq. ft.
Total Living Area:	**2,482 sq. ft.**
Garage	663 sq. ft.
Exterior Wall Framing:	2x4

Foundation Options:

Slab

(All plans can be built with your choice of foundation and framing. A generic conversion diagram is available. See order form.)

BLUEPRINT PRICE CODE: **C**

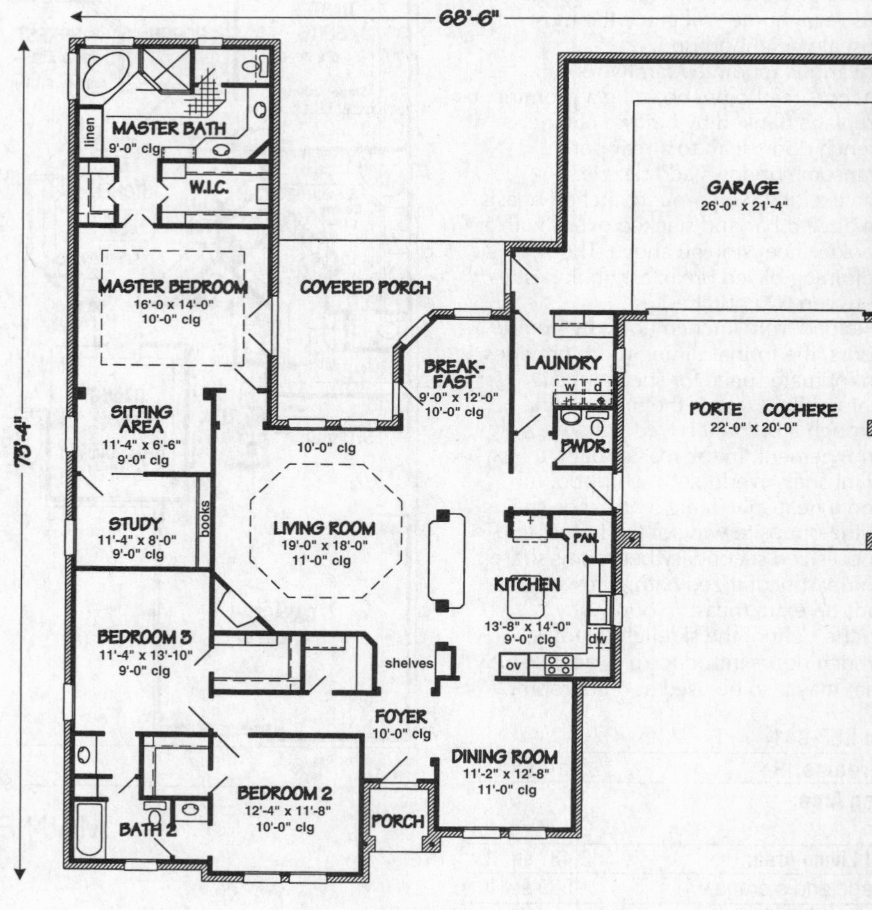

MAIN FLOOR

SEE ORDER INFO ON PAGES 12-15
familyhandyman.com/homeplans

Nostalgic Facade

- This lovely home is characterized by a nostalgic facade that disguises a uniquely modern floor plan.
- The covered front porch leads guests to the bright, sidelighted foyer. The foyer is flanked by the formal dining room and a quiet study as it flows to the sumptuous living room.
- The spacious living room boasts a stepped ceiling and a handsome corner fireplace. French doors open to a covered back porch.
- The walk-through kitchen features a sunny bayed breakfast nook, a nifty work desk and an angled sink and snack counter.
- A half-bath, a laundry room and access to the two-car garage are all close by.
- The isolated master suite boasts two walk-in closets and a lavish private bath with a bayed garden tub, a separate shower and a dual-sink vanity.
- At the opposite end of the home, three additional bedrooms are serviced by two full baths.

Plan VL-2483

Bedrooms: 4	**Baths:** 3½
Living Area:	
Main floor	2,483 sq. ft.
Total Living Area:	**2,483 sq. ft.**
Garage	504 sq. ft.
Exterior Wall Framing:	2x4
Foundation Options:	
Crawlspace	
Slab	

(All plans can be built with your choice of foundation and framing. A generic conversion diagram is available. See order form.)

BLUEPRINT PRICE CODE: C

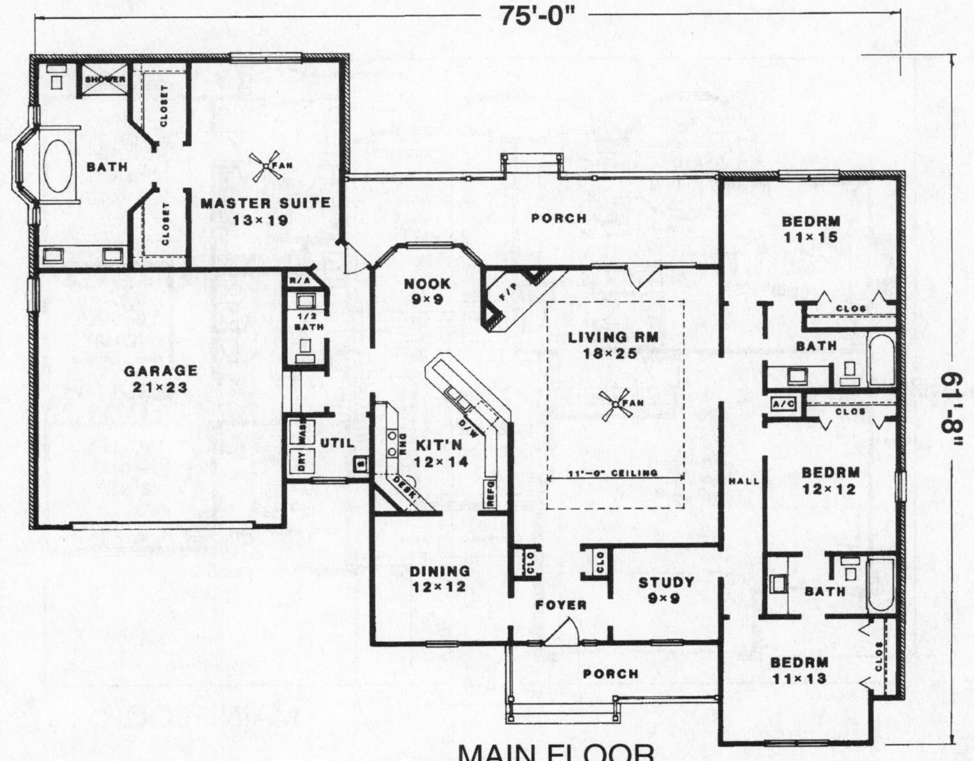

MAIN FLOOR

Elegant Effects

- Repeating arches accent the covered entry of this elegant one-story home.
- The volume entry opens to the formal spaces. The dining room features a high ceiling and a built-in hutch. The living room shows off a dramatic boxed window topped with high glass.
- The gourmet kitchen unfolds to a gazebo dinette and a spacious family room with a fireplace and flanking bookshelves. A handy snack bar is incorporated into the kitchen's central island cooktop.
- A nice-sized laundry room sits near the entrance to the garage and offers room for an extra freezer.
- The sleeping wing consists of three bedrooms, two baths and a versatile den that could serve as a fourth bedroom. With the addition of double doors, one bedroom easily converts to a sitting area for the master suite.
- The luxurious master bath offers a huge walk-in closet and his-and-hers vanities. An exciting oval whirlpool tub is set into a bay window.
- A full basement offers expansion possibilities when the time arrives.

Plan DBI-2206

Bedrooms: 2+	**Baths:** 2½
Living Area:	
Main floor	2,498 sq. ft.
Total Living Area:	**2,498 sq. ft.**
Standard basement	2,498 sq. ft.
Garage	710 sq. ft.
Exterior Wall Framing:	2x4
Foundation Options:	
Standard basement	
(All plans can be built with your choice of foundation and framing. A generic conversion diagram is available. See order form.)	
BLUEPRINT PRICE CODE:	**C**

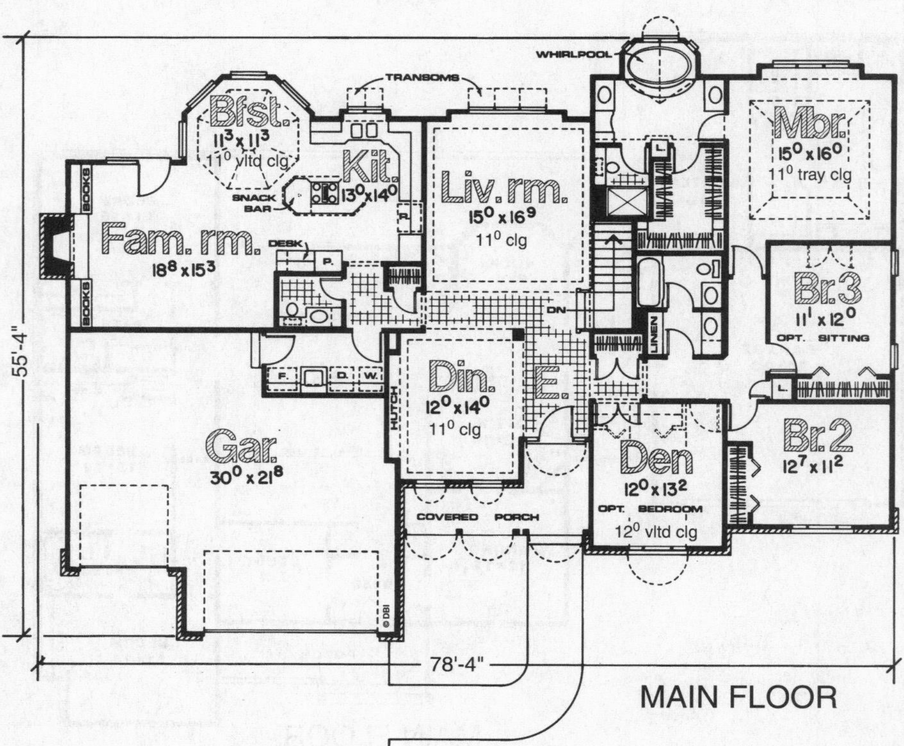

MAIN FLOOR

Sunny Entry

- A dramatic columned entry highlighted by a sunny window arrangement greets visitors to this glorious home.
- Double doors open to the tiled foyer, which shares a high ceiling with the formal living and dining rooms. A tray ceiling tops the dining room, and sliding glass doors in the living room open to a tranquil covered patio.
- The secluded family room boasts a fireplace flanked by bookshelves, plus sliding glass doors to the backyard.
- An island serving bar links the family room to the kitchen and the breakfast nook. A desk and a walk-in pantry are some of the kitchen's features. A wall of windows bathes the nook in sunlight.
- Two bedrooms nearby include private access to a separated bath.
- Across the home, beautiful French doors open to the master suite, which flaunts patio access and two walk-in closets. The master bath boasts a garden tub and two vanities.
- A quiet study off the foyer could accommodate overnight guests. A hall bath nearby features patio access.
- All rooms are enhanced by 10-ft. ceilings, unless otherwise noted.

Plan HDS-99-207

Bedrooms: 3+	**Baths:** 3
Living Area:	
Main floor	2,593 sq. ft.
Total Living Area:	**2,593 sq. ft.**
Garage	508 sq. ft.
Exterior Wall Framing:	2x4 or 8-in. concrete block
Foundation Options:	
Slab	

(All plans can be built with your choice of foundation and framing. A generic conversion diagram is available. See order form.)

BLUEPRINT PRICE CODE: D

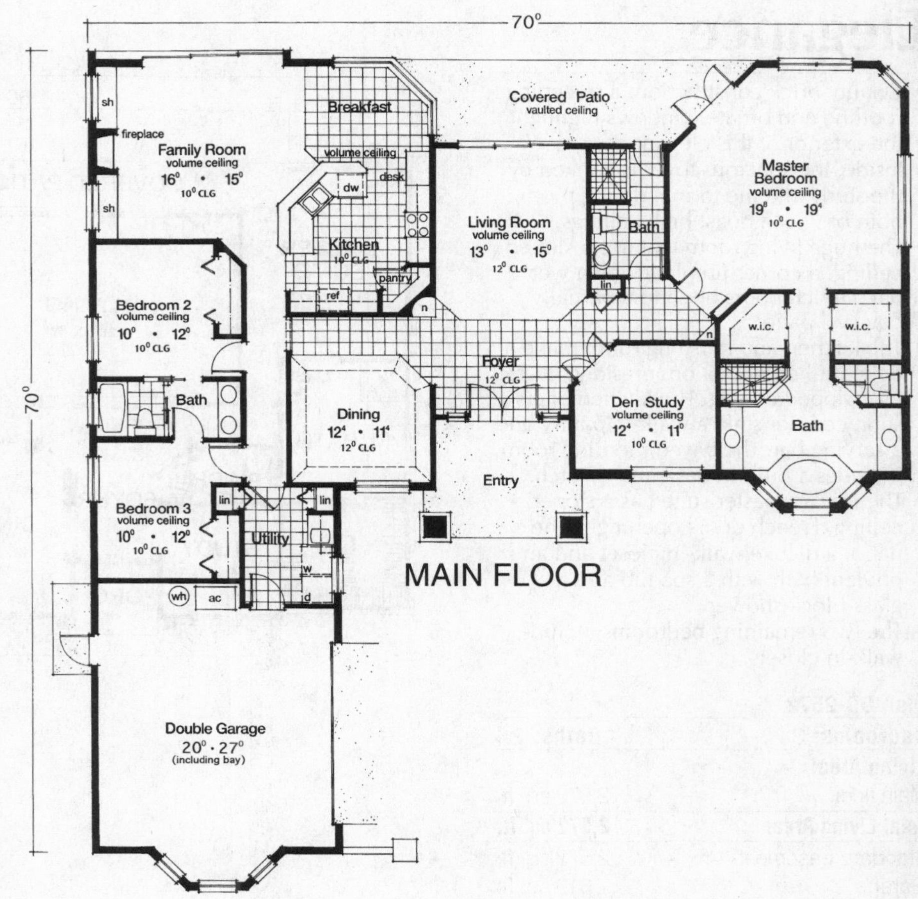

Plan HDS-99-207

Quality and Elegance

- Quality brick construction, a sweeping roofline and ornate windows highlight the exterior of this elegant design.
- Inside, the spacious foyer is flanked by the study and the formal dining room, both of which boast high ceilings.
- The huge living room features a sloped ceiling, a corner fireplace and a wet bar. French doors open to a partially covered patio.
- The kitchen and morning room make a delightful combination, presided over by a sloped ceiling. The kitchen offers a sunny corner sink, a walk-in pantry and a serving bar. The bayed morning room includes a built-in desk and a hutch.
- The private master suite has a sloped ceiling, French doors opening to the patio, a deluxe walk-in closet and an opulent bath with a spa tub and a glass-block shower.
- The two remaining bedrooms include walk-in closets.

Plan DD-2572	
Bedrooms: 3+	**Baths:** 2½
Living Area:	
Main floor	2,572 sq. ft.
Total Living Area:	**2,572 sq. ft.**
Standard basement	2,572 sq. ft.
Garage	619 sq. ft.
Exterior Wall Framing:	2x4
Foundation Options:	
Standard basement	
Crawlspace	
Slab	
(All plans can be built with your choice of foundation and framing. A generic conversion diagram is available. See order form.)	
BLUEPRINT PRICE CODE:	D

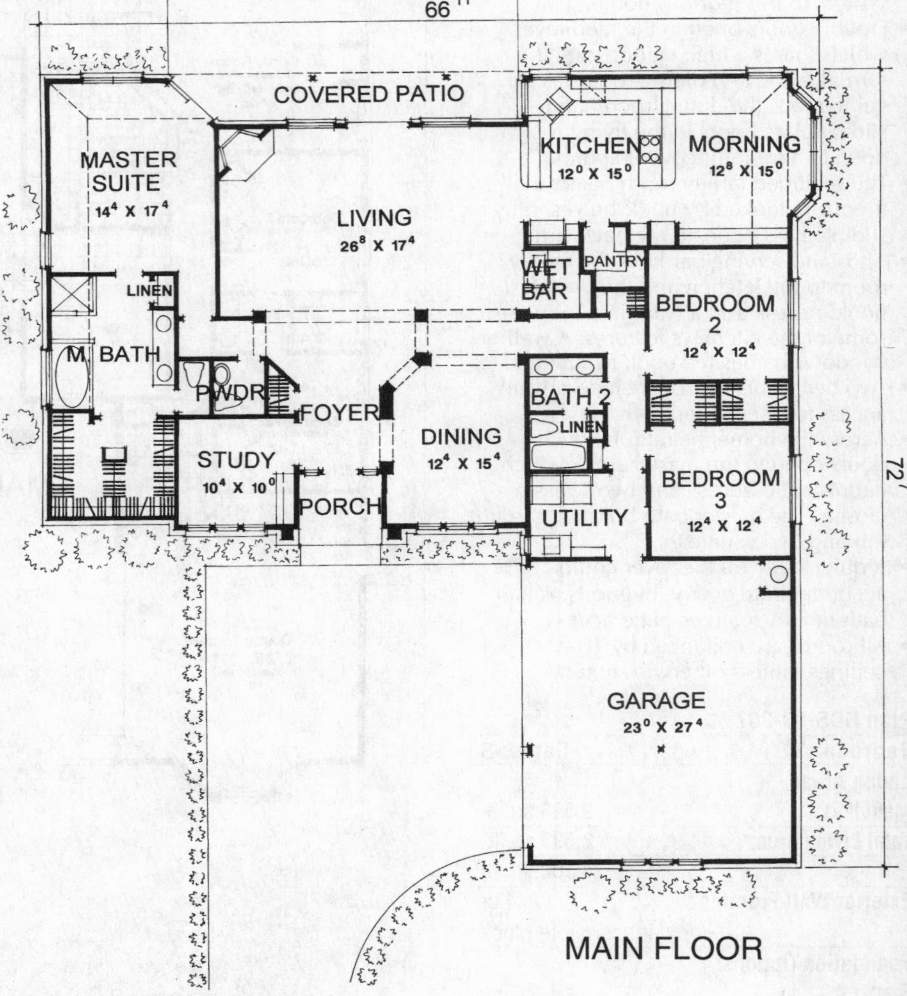

MAIN FLOOR

Plan DD-2572

SEE ORDER INFO ON PAGES 12-15

Creative Luxury

- A stunning facade and a creative floor plan combine to produce a truly luxurious home.
- The high foyer is flanked by a den with a nearby full bath, and the sunken formal dining room.
- Straight ahead, the sunken living room is topped by a high ceiling and offers access to a covered patio through sliding glass doors. A summer kitchen services the patio on warm evenings.
- Patio access through sliding glass doors enhances the master bedroom.
- Twin walk-in closets with plant shelves above line the path to the sunken master bath. Here, amenities include a raised tub and a glass-block shower.
- Connected to the living room by a wet bar, the open kitchen is bordered by a quaint breakfast nook. From the nook, French and sliding doors open to the summer kitchen and patio.
- A beautiful fireplace warms the family room, while window-lined walls let in cheery sunlight.
- Two large secondary bedrooms flaunt exotic plant shelves and private access to a split bath.

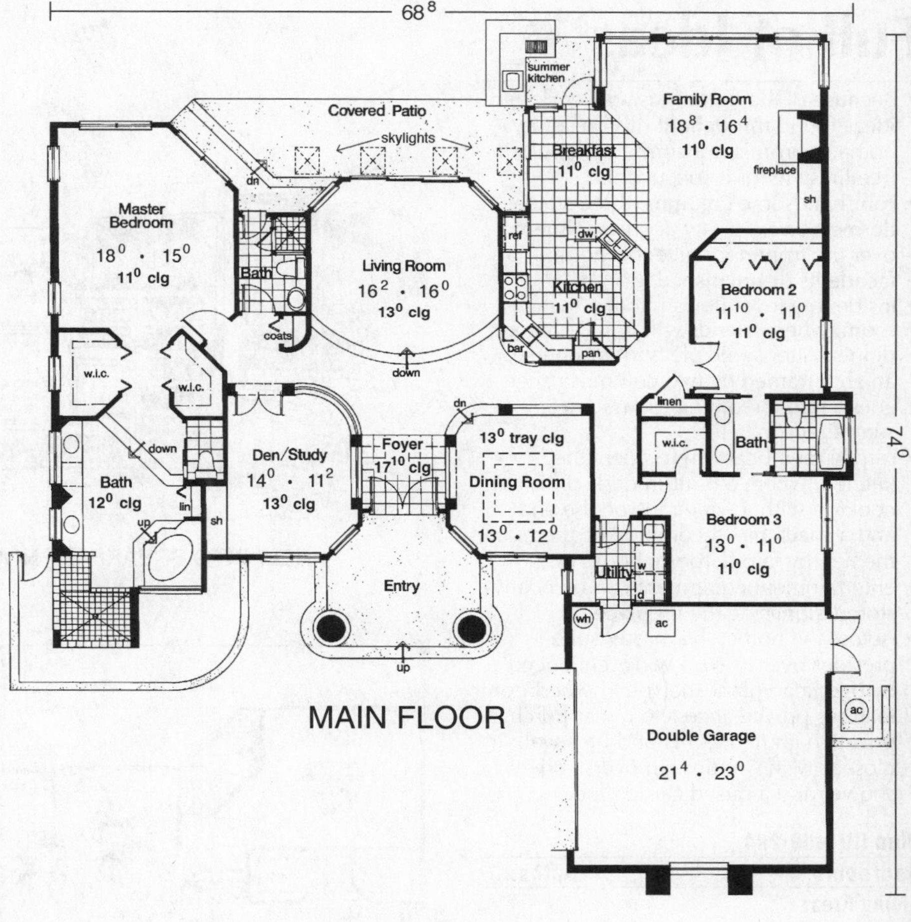

Plan HDS-99-237

Bedrooms: 3+	**Baths:** 3
Living Area:	
Main floor	2,636 sq. ft.
Total Living Area:	**2,636 sq. ft.**
Garage	536 sq. ft.
Exterior Wall Framing:	8-in. concrete block
Foundation Options:	
Slab	

(All plans can be built with your choice of foundation and framing. A generic conversion diagram is available. See order form.)

BLUEPRINT PRICE CODE: D

Plan HDS-99-237

FOR MORE DETAILS, SEE PLAN AT
familyhandyman.com/homeplans

Full of Ideas

- Because of the numerous, clever design ideas found throughout this one-story home, it promises a comfortable, worry-free lifestyle for its occupants.
- Four handsome columns, three stately dormers and a pretty acorn pediment over the front door give this home's facade its distinguished air.
- Inside, the foyer flows into the living room, where friends will mingle before dinner. After some pleasant discourse, an arch framed by two columns ushers guests into the dining room for a sumptuous meal.
- Family members will frequent the kitchen, where a built-in desk, an island cooktop with a wine rack on the end and a snack bar accommodate them. In the nearby family room, books and entertainment equipment can be neatly stored alongside the fireplace.
- Across the home, the master suite presides over its own wing, enhanced by overhead plant shelves. The bedroom features private access to a rear porch. A private bath flaunts his-and-hers walk-in closets, twin vanities, an oversized shower and a raised garden tub.

Plan HDS-99-294

Bedrooms: 3+	**Baths:** 3
Living Area:	
Main floor	2,636 sq. ft.
Total Living Area:	**2,636 sq. ft.**
Garage	789 sq. ft.
Exterior Wall Framing:	2x4
Foundation Options:	
Slab	

(All plans can be built with your choice of foundation and framing. A generic conversion diagram is available. See order form.)

BLUEPRINT PRICE CODE: D

VIEW INTO BREAKFAST NOOK, FAMILY ROOM AND KITCHEN

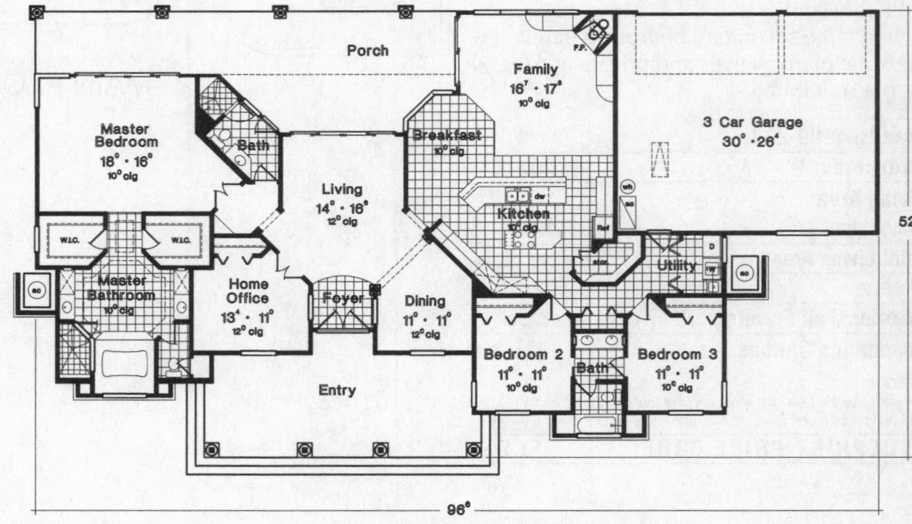

MAIN FLOOR

Plan HDS-99-294

SEE ORDER INFO ON PAGES 12-15

Elegant Arches

- Elegant arched windows and decorative dormers grace this home's entry.
- A cozy study with a sloped ceiling lies just to the left of the entry, while columns set off the formal dining room on the right.
- Straight ahead, the spacious Great Room, the kitchen and the breakfast nook all flow into each other. An angled snack bar serves both the Great Room and the breakfast nook, while the island in the center of the kitchen facilitates easy meal preparation.
- Secluded in its own wing, the comforting master bedroom features a bayed sitting area, a tray ceiling and a private bath with two walk-in closets, dual sinks, a spa tub and a separate shower. Ahh, the pleasures of home.
- On the other side of the home, three secondary bedrooms share two full baths. One of these baths has outdoor access—just another excuse to put in a pool out back!

Plan DD-2579	
Bedrooms: 4+	**Baths:** 3½
Living Area:	
Main floor	2,587 sq. ft.
Total Living Area:	**2,587 sq. ft.**
Standard basement	2,587 sq. ft.
Garage	411 sq. ft.
Exterior Wall Framing:	2x4
Foundation Options:	
Standard basement	
Crawlspace	
Slab	
(All plans can be built with your choice of foundation and framing. A generic conversion diagram is available. See order form.)	
BLUEPRINT PRICE CODE:	**D**

REAR VIEW

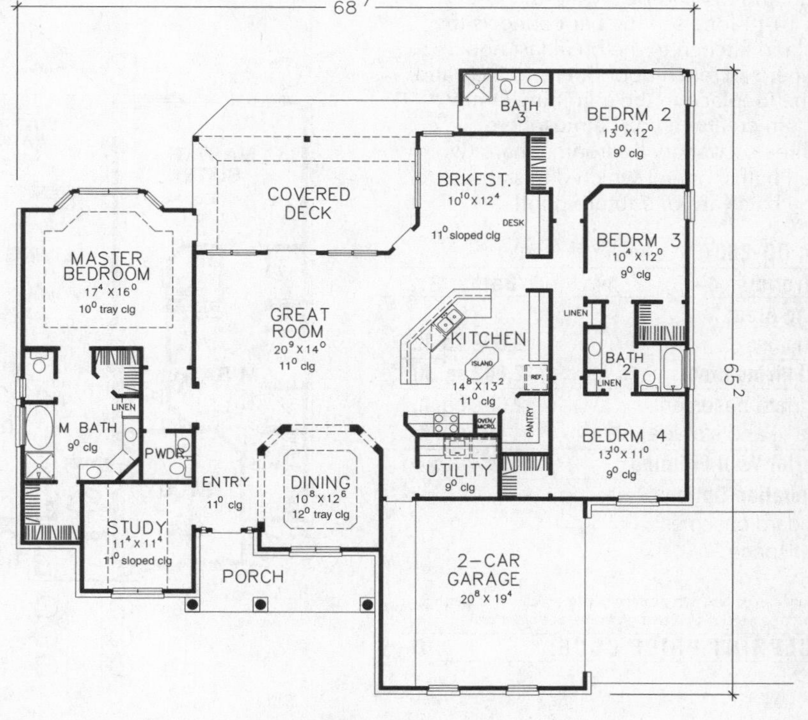

MAIN FLOOR

Splendid Glass

- Splendid half-round-topped windows add a taste of high class to the facade of this inviting European-style home.
- Adjacent to the sidelighted foyer, double doors introduce a study that can also be used to sleep overnight guests.
- A tray ceiling crowns the bright, formal dining room.
- The living room's windows offer great views of a covered patio and the backyard beyond.
- Private patio access enhances the posh master suite. The master bath is entered through double doors, and hosts a spa tub and his-and-hers walk-in closets.
- A 14-ft.-long serving bar connects the island kitchen to the breakfast nook, where a French door opens to the patio. The fireplace in the adjoining family room creates a cozy atmosphere.
- Three secondary bedrooms share two full baths, one of which offers access to the backyard or a future pool!

Plan DD-2607

Bedrooms: 4+	**Baths:** 3½
Living Area:	
Main floor	2,602 sq. ft.
Total Living Area:	**2,602 sq. ft.**
Standard basement	2,602 sq. ft.
Garage and storage	487 sq. ft.
Exterior Wall Framing:	2x4

Foundation Options:
Standard basement
Crawlspace
Slab
(All plans can be built with your choice of foundation and framing. A generic conversion diagram is available. See order form.)

BLUEPRINT PRICE CODE: D

REAR VIEW

67^0

70^0

BEDRM 2 14^0 x 12^0

FAMILY 16^0 x 11^8 10^0 clg

W.I.C.

W.I.C.

COVERED PATIO 16^5 x 8^4

MASTER SUITE 16^4 x 12^8 10^0 clg

BEDRM 4 10^6 x 12^{10}

BRKFST 11^0 x 9^0 10^0 clg

LIVING 12^{10} x 14^8 10^0 clg

KITCHEN 14^0 x 14^4 10^0 clg

LINEN

W.I.C.

LINEN

SPA

PANTRY

M BATH

PWDR.

LINEN

DINING 11^6 x 13^4 11^0 tray clg

BEDRM 3 14^0 x 10^8

UTIL.

W.I.C.

W.I.C.

FOYER

STORAGE

STUDY 10^{10} x 11^8 10^0 clg

PORCH

GARAGE 21^0 x 22^8

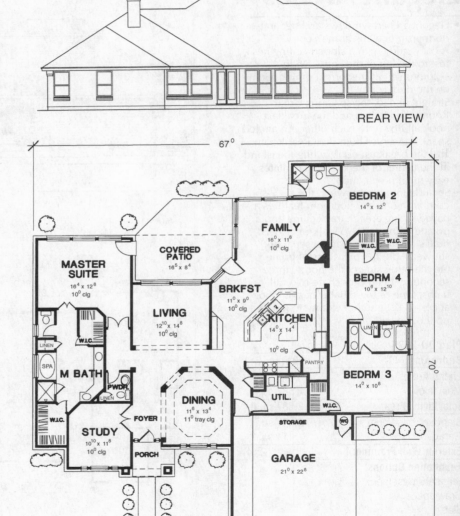

MAIN FLOOR

ORDER BLUEPRINTS ANYTIME!
CALL TOLL-FREE 1-800-820-1296

Plan DD-2607

SEE ORDER INFO ON PAGES 12-15
familyhandyman.com/homeplans

Patio Living

- A well-executed floor plan sets this impeccable design apart from the ordinary. Rooms of various shapes are arranged to maintain openness and to take advantage of a wonderful patio.
- The granite-paved foyer is open to the large living room, which provides a terrific view of the covered patio.
- The octagonal dining room and den or study flank the foyer and also face the living room.
- The uniquely shaped family room, with a fireplace centered between built-in shelves, gives a dynamic view of the outdoors and is open to the kitchen.
- The spacious kitchen includes an island range, a wide serving counter and an octagonal breakfast nook.
- Two secondary bedrooms enjoy plenty of privacy in their hidden wing of the home. They share a full bath, which is also accessible from the patio.
- The master suite constitutes a wing in itself. The bedroom boasts a fireplace, walls of glass and a high ceiling. The luxurious bath includes a whirlpool tub, a separate shower and twin dressing areas.

Plan HDS-99-137	
Bedrooms: 3+	**Baths:** 2½
Living Area:	
Main floor	2,656 sq. ft.
Total Living Area:	**2,656 sq. ft.**
Garage	503 sq. ft.
Exterior Wall Framing:	2x4 and 8-in. concrete block
Foundation Options:	
Slab	
(All plans can be built with your choice of foundation and framing. A generic conversion diagram is available. See order form.)	
BLUEPRINT PRICE CODE:	**D**

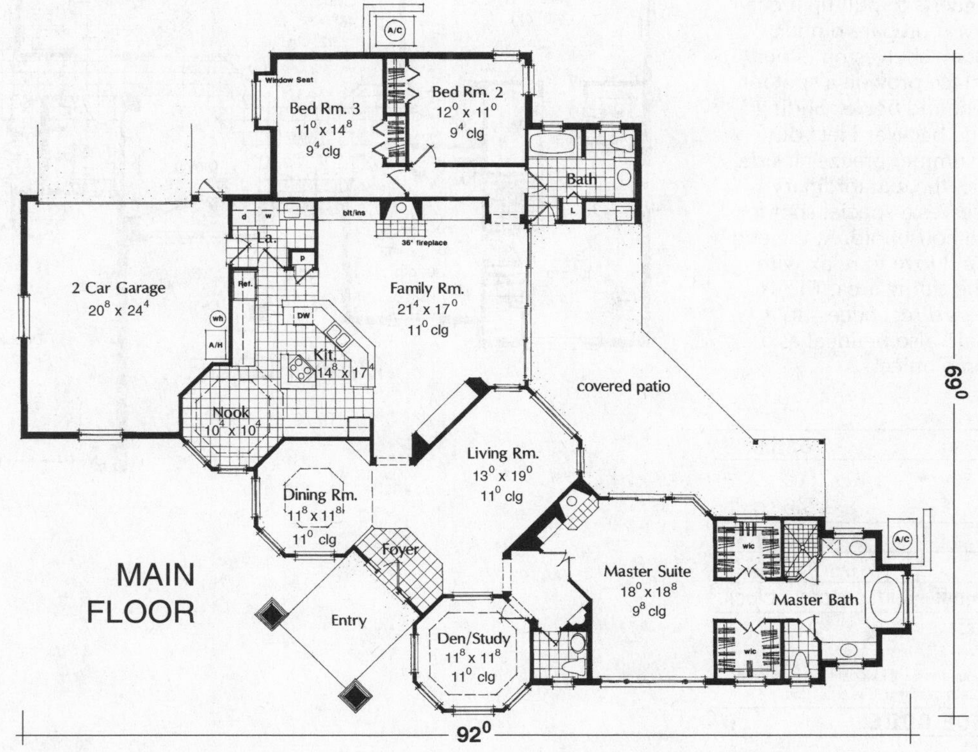

Fresh Look!

- Unique angles and bright mitred-glass walls give this home a fresh look.
- Grand double doors open into the stunning tiled foyer. Straight ahead, a dazzling mitred-glass wall in the living room overlooks a backyard porch.
- On the right, the formal dining room sets an elegant tone when you entertain. A decorative plant shelf crowns an inset where you can display fine collectibles.
- A lovely arch leads into the nearby kitchen, where a walk-in pantry includes room for all your favorite delectables. A serving counter between the kitchen and the breakfast nook is a great place for guests to pull up a chair and visit while you prepare dinner.
- In the family room, shelves on either side of the fireplace provide a spot for stereo equipment and books. Sliding glass doors to the backyard let you enjoy pleasant summer breezes inside.
- Across the home, the extraordinary master suite reserves a special spot for the adults of the household. At the end of each day, you'll love to relax with a good book in the sitting area. The master bath offers direct access to a den, which would also be ideal as a nursery or a home office.

Plan HDS-99-247

Bedrooms: 4+	**Baths:** 3
Living Area:	
Main floor	2,746 sq. ft.
Total Living Area:	**2,746 sq. ft.**
Garage	459 sq. ft.
Exterior Wall Framing:	8-in. concrete block
Foundation Options:	
Slab	

(All plans can be built with your choice of foundation and framing. A generic conversion diagram is available. See order form.)

BLUEPRINT PRICE CODE: **D**

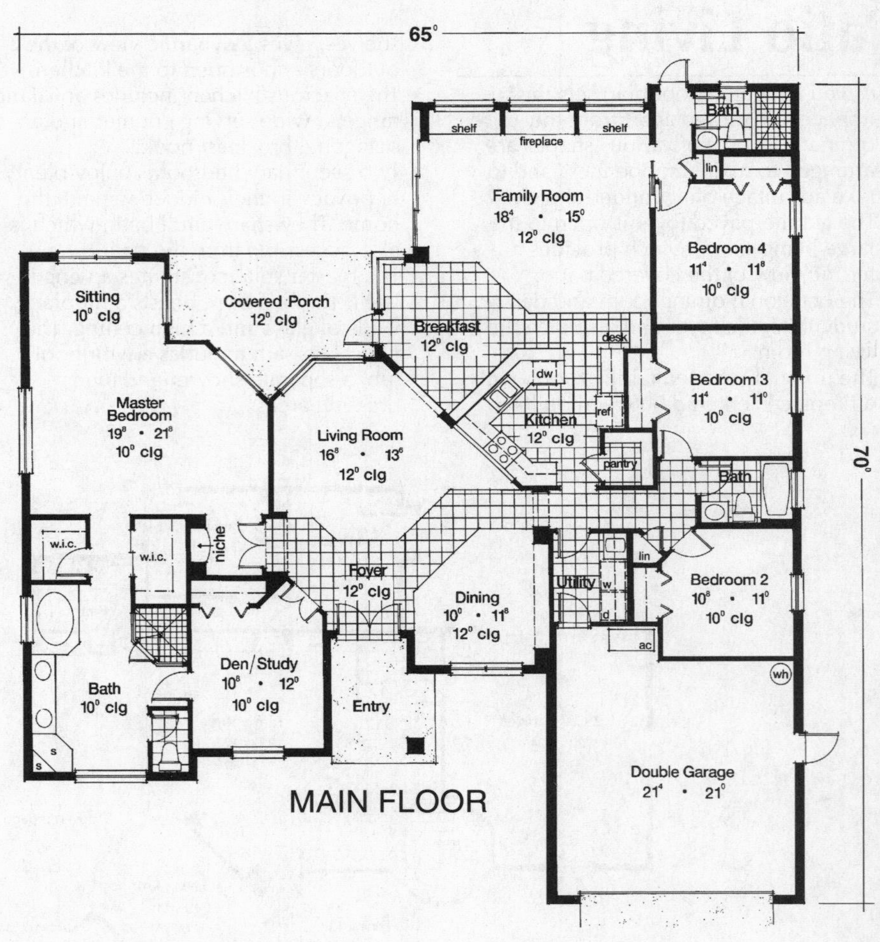

MAIN FLOOR

ORDER BLUEPRINTS ANYTIME!
CALL TOLL-FREE 1-800-820-1296

Plan HDS-99-247

SEE ORDER INFO ON PAGES 12-15
familyhandyman.com/homeplans

Magnetic Personality

- Dramatic rooflines, durable stucco and keystone-topped windows will draw you irresistibly to this classy one-story.
- Marvelous entertainment options abound inside, where a demure dining room defined by a column awaits the culinary delights of the kitchen.
- A central skylight and a dazzling sun room flood the kitchen with natural light. Dramatic window walls offer panoramic views of the backyard. Breakfast will taste better on the skylighted porch via a French door.
- After-dinner conversation will warm your heart, as will the family room's majestic fireplace flanked by shelves.
- In the master suite, peace is assured by the soothing bath, which includes a lush plant shelf and a whirlpool tub under a glass-block wall. A handy passage connects the walk-in closet to the laundry room.
- If your family outgrows the secondary bedrooms, a large future area above the garage may be finished.

Plan KLF-951	
Bedrooms: 3+	**Baths:** 2½
Living Area:	
Main floor	2,750 sq. ft.
Total Living Area:	**2,750 sq. ft.**
Future area	391 sq. ft.
Garage and storage	504 sq. ft.
Exterior Wall Framing:	2x4
Foundation Options:	
Slab	
(All plans can be built with your choice of foundation and framing. A generic conversion diagram is available. See order form.)	
BLUEPRINT PRICE CODE:	**D**

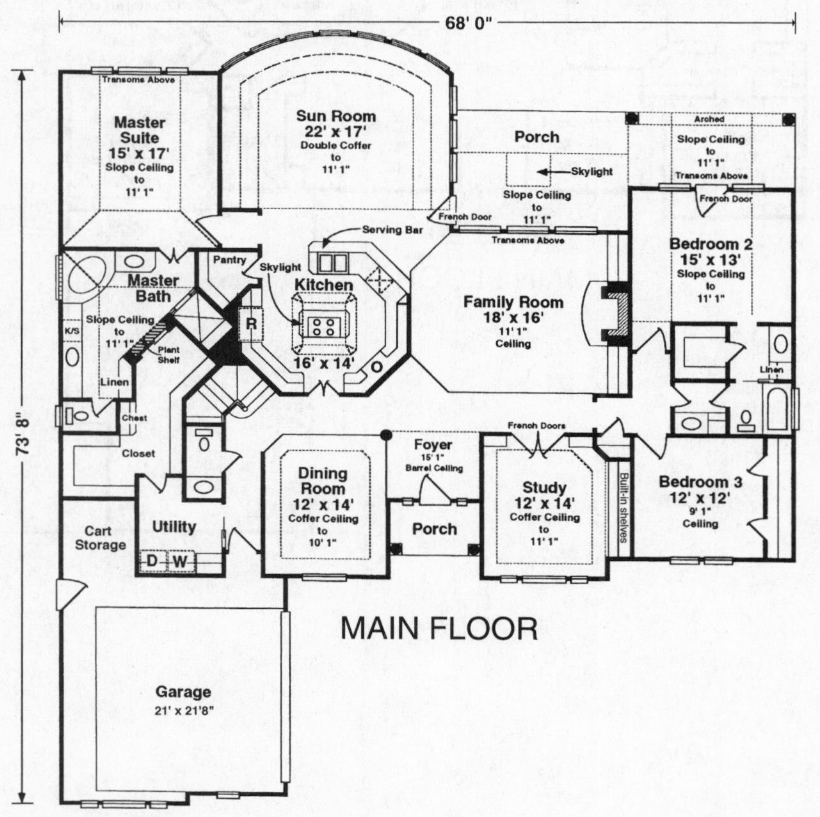

MAIN FLOOR

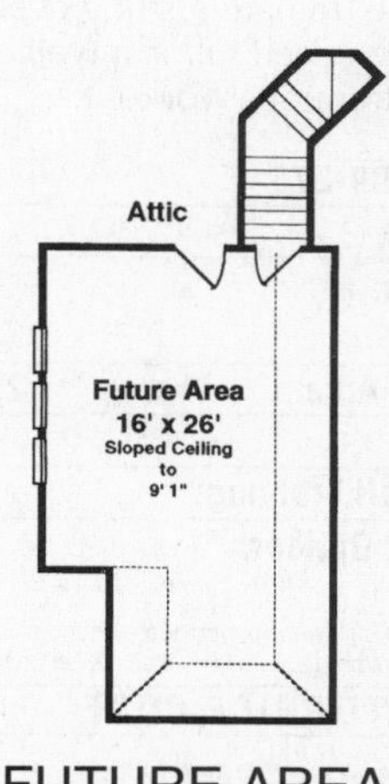

FUTURE AREA

Ray of Sunshine

- This gorgeous home features numerous dazzling windows and glass walls that bring cheery sunshine to both your home and your family.
- A bright stucco exterior with decorative keystones, arched windows and a dramatic entry between two regal columns brings a touch of Spanish-style flair to the neighborhood.
- Inside, the living and dining rooms await the formal dinners and Sunday brunches that you'll cherish preparing. Open the French doors to the patio and enjoy the gentle days of spring.
- When family members return home, they will congregate in the family room to do homework or read the paper.
- The open design of the kitchen allows the family chef to visit with family members working on other business. An island worktop with a vegetable sink makes meal preparation fun.
- Across the home, double doors introduce the gorgeous master suite. In the bath, his-and-hers closets and vanities eliminate jostling over space, while the raised tub is a welcome sight after a strenuous workout.

Plan HDS-99-276

Bedrooms: 3+	**Baths:** 3
Living Area:	
Main floor	2,766 sq. ft.
Total Living Area:	**2,766 sq. ft.**
Garage	887 sq. ft.
Exterior Wall Framing:	2x4
Foundation Options:	
Slab	
(All plans can be built with your choice of foundation and framing. A generic conversion diagram is available. See order form.)	
BLUEPRINT PRICE CODE:	**D**

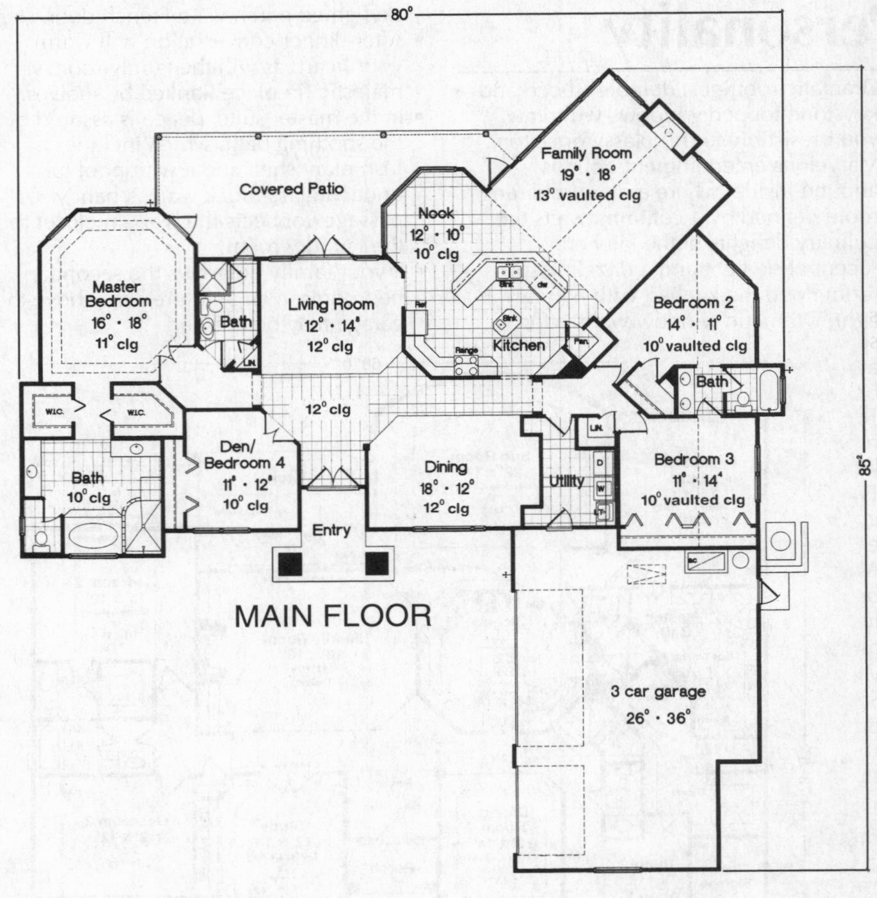

Plan HDS-99-276

SEE ORDER INFO ON PAGES 12-15

All You Need

- This home has everything you need and more, including three bedrooms and three baths. For proof that one level is enough, look no further.
- The formal dining room on the left and the living room straight ahead make a lasting impression on guests entering through the front door. Columns add to the elegant effect.
- Down the hall and to the right, the sprawling, comfortable family room is sure to be the hub of the home. It shares a see-through fireplace, flanked by bookshelves, with the living room.
- The sunny nook opens to the family room and lies adjacent to the spacious kitchen.
- Two secondary bedrooms, which are connected by a shared split bath, each enjoy a walk-in closet.
- Across the home, spend time just before bed in the cozy sitting area of your luxurious master bedroom. Built-in mirrors and dual walk-in closets line the walkway to the private bath.
- Set the study up as a home office or fun project room.

Plan RD-2854

Bedrooms: 3+	**Baths:** 3
Living Area:	
Main floor	2,854 sq. ft.
Total Living Area:	**2,854 sq. ft.**
Garage and storage	522 sq. ft.
Exterior Wall Framing:	2x4
Foundation Options:	
Crawlspace	
Slab	

(All plans can be built with your choice of foundation and framing. A generic conversion diagram is available. See order form.)

BLUEPRINT PRICE CODE: D

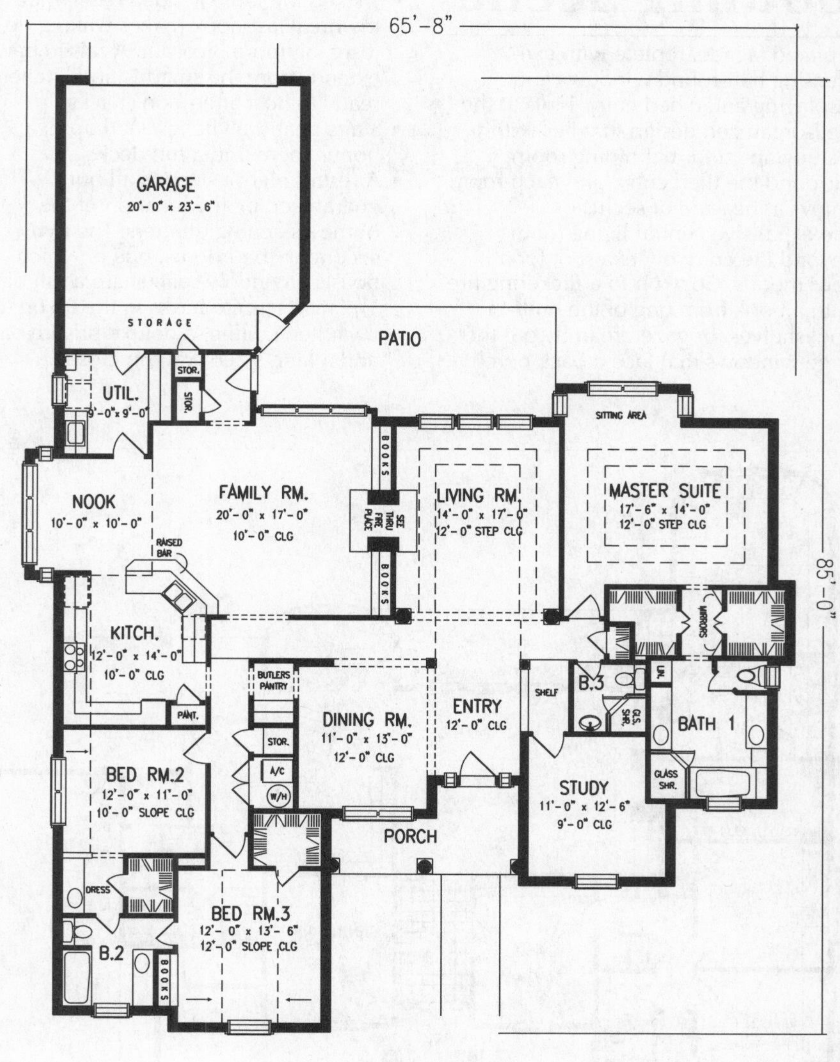

MAIN FLOOR

Plan RD-2854

FOR MORE DETAILS, SEE PLAN AT familyhandyman.com/homeplans

Soothing Scene

- A placid facade, replete with eye-pleasing half-round windows and displaying an arched entry, hints at the well-organized design that lies within.
- A study and a formal dining room surround the tiled entry, and each room enjoys a measure of seclusion.
- The expansive central living room beyond the entry offers a spot for all your moods. Cozy up to a flickering fire with a book from one of the built-in bookshelves, or gaze dreamily out the large windows that face a back porch.
- Tucked into an extended bay window, the breakfast nook makes waking up just a bit more pleasant. A raised bar extends from the smart island kitchen, ready to host afternoon snacks.
- Stairs near the kitchen lead up to a bonus room and a fun deck.
- A restful night's sleep is all but guaranteed by the location of the home's sleeping quarters. The two secondary bedrooms, one of which boasts a window seat, share a full bath. The master suite basks in the luxury of a vaulted ceiling, a deluxe private bath and a king-sized walk-in closet.

Plan RD-2585

Bedrooms: 3+	**Baths:** 2½
Living Area:	
Main floor	2,585 sq. ft.
Bonus room	316 sq. ft.
Total Living Area:	**2,901 sq. ft.**
Standard basement	2,585 sq. ft.
Garage and storage	783 sq. ft.
Exterior Wall Framing:	2x4
Foundation Options:	
Standard basement	
Crawlspace	
Slab	

(All plans can be built with your choice of foundation and framing. A generic conversion diagram is available. See order form.)

BLUEPRINT PRICE CODE: D

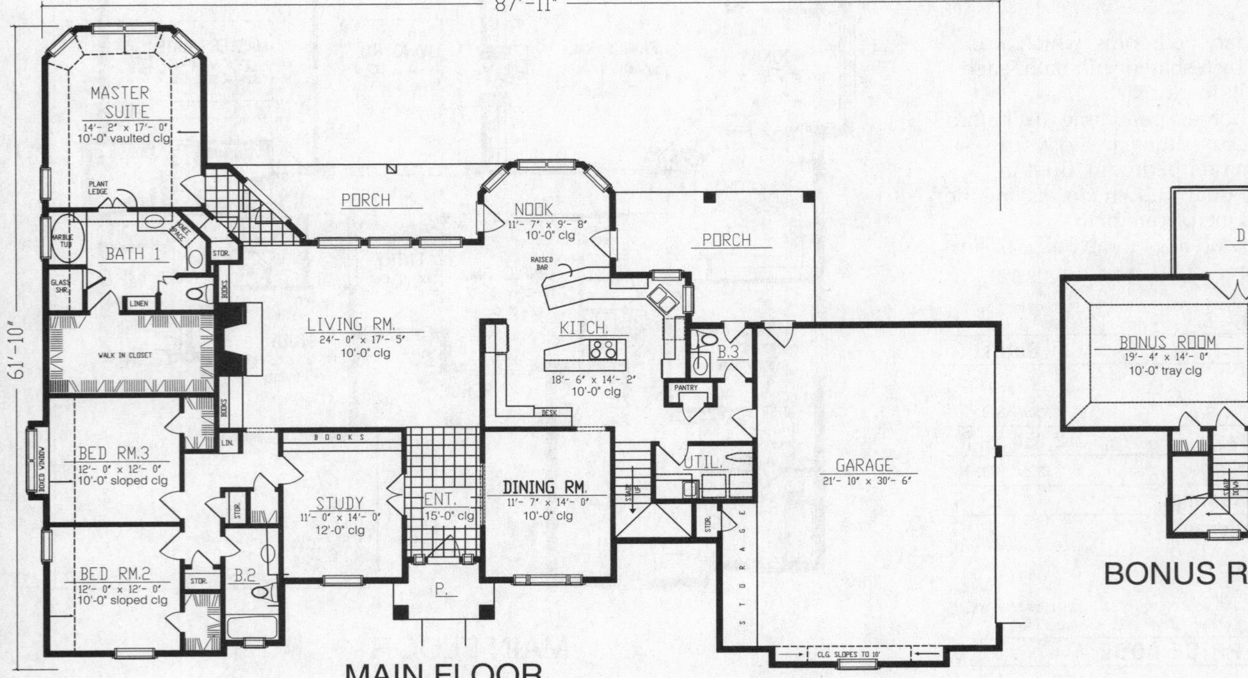

Plan RD-2585

SEE ORDER INFO ON PAGES 12-15
familyhandyman.com/homeplans

Designed with You in Mind

- This elegant stucco home was designed with the master of the house in mind.
- Over 600 sq. ft. has been reserved for the astounding master suite. An angled sitting area accesses a rear patio, while dual walk-in closets frame the elegant double-doored entry of the private bath. Front and center is a large Jacuzzi, joined by a private toilet, a separate shower and time-saving twin vanities.
- The formal living areas extend from the foyer. The central living room features a vaulted ceiling and a spectacular window wall overlooking the adjoining covered patio with a summer kitchen.
- The large gourmet kitchen merges with a breakfast area and a spacious family room. The breakfast area boasts a fascinating curved glass wall and opens to the patio. A handy snack bar serves refreshments to guests in the family room, which features a warm fireplace flanked by bookshelves.
- Two secondary bedrooms, a den or guest room, and a hall or pool bath complete this stunning floor plan.

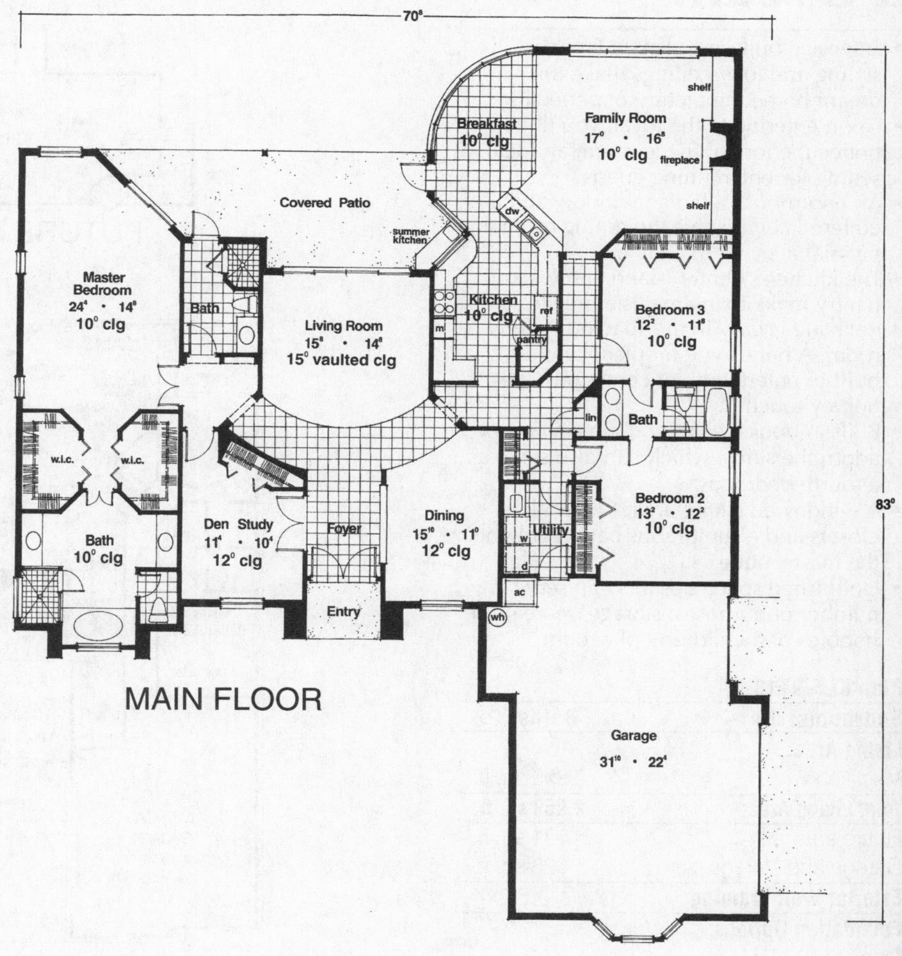

MAIN FLOOR

Plan HDS-99-178	
Bedrooms: 3+	**Baths:** 3
Living Area:	
Main floor	2,931 sq. ft.
Total Living Area:	**2,931 sq. ft.**
Garage	703 sq. ft.
Exterior Wall Framing:	8-in. concrete block
Foundation Options:	
Slab	
(All plans can be built with your choice of foundation and framing. A generic conversion diagram is available. See order form.)	
BLUEPRINT PRICE CODE:	**D**

Plan HDS-99-178

FOR MORE DETAILS, SEE PLAN AT familyhandyman.com/homeplans

Step into a Dream

- Extensive built-ins, elegant French styling and lofty ceilings make this dream home the picture of perfection.
- Upon entering to the foyer, you'll first notice the formal living room, an ideal setting for entertaining guests.
- An enormous Palladian window and a coffered ceiling give the dining room a palatial air.
- The kitchen's center island and walk-in pantry make fixing meals a breeze.
- Relaxing is easy in the spacious family room. A handsome fireplace and a built-in entertainment center provide homey touches.
- Built-in bookshelves and a bay window adorn the study, which can also serve as a fourth bedroom.
- A windowed sitting area, two walk-in closets and a sumptuous bath highlight the master suite.
- Unfinished space upstairs can serve any number of purposes: storage, recreation, hobbies or a children's playroom.

Plan KLF-9713	
Bedrooms: 3+	**Baths:** 2½
Living Area:	
Main floor	2,959 sq. ft.
Total Living Area:	**2,959 sq. ft.**
Future area	531 sq. ft.
Garage and storage	628 sq. ft.
Exterior Wall Framing:	2x4
Foundation Options:	
Slab	
(All plans can be built with your choice of foundation and framing. A generic conversion diagram is available. See order form.)	
BLUEPRINT PRICE CODE:	D

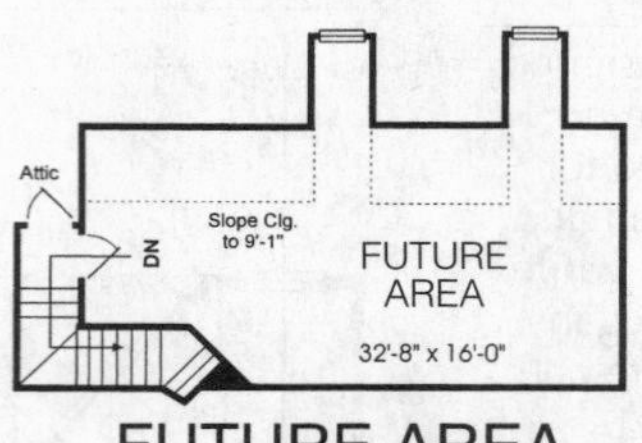

FUTURE AREA

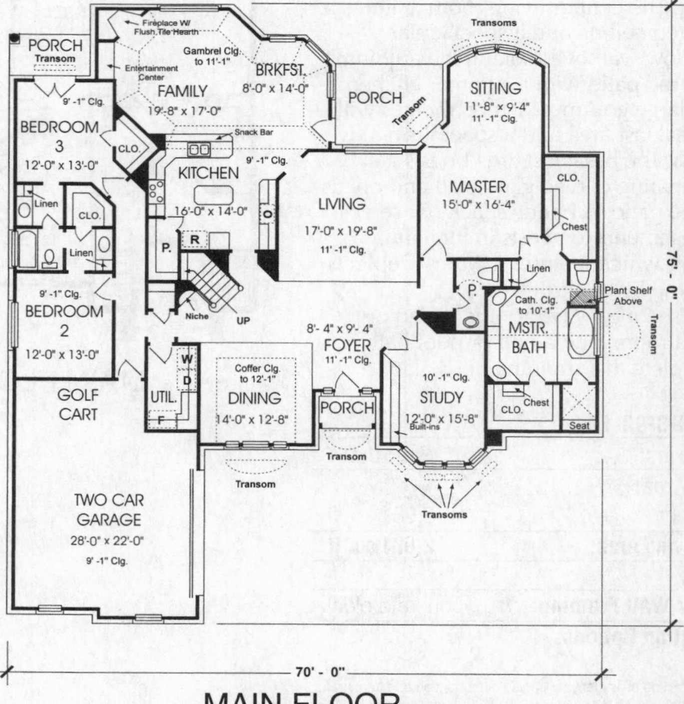

MAIN FLOOR

Plan KLF-9713

SEE ORDER INFO ON PAGES 12-15

Pump Up the Volume

- With high ceilings in nearly every room, this beautiful home's focal point is the voluminous living room, which boasts a cozy fireplace, built-in bookshelves and a view out over a back porch.
- The master suite includes expansive dimensions and a big bay of windows. Its private bath offers a dual-sink vanity, a marble tub and a roomy walk-in closet.
- Two secondary bedrooms show off more exciting amenities. One features a cute boxed-out window; both share a full bath and each enjoys a walk-in closet.
- Adjacent to the entry, a private study with built-in bookshelves can be used as a home office or a media room.
- Off the living room, the expansive kitchen satisfies all your cooking needs. With an island cooktop, ample counter space and a raised serving bar, this kitchen guarantees convenience.
- Upstairs, a bonus room promises opportunity for expansion and offers access to a large deck.

Plan RD-2654

Bedrooms: 3+	**Baths:** 2½
Living Area:	
Main floor	2,654 sq. ft.
Bonus room	311 sq. ft.
Total Living Area:	**2,965 sq. ft.**
Garage and storage	807 sq. ft.
Exterior Wall Framing:	2x4
Foundation Options:	
Crawlspace	
Slab	

(All plans can be built with your choice of foundation and framing. A generic conversion diagram is available. See order form.)

BLUEPRINT PRICE CODE: D

WOOD RAIL

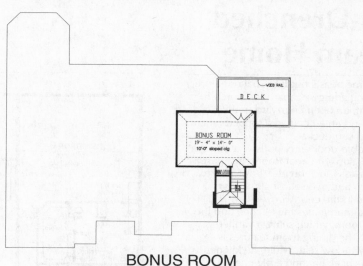

DECK

BONUS ROOM
19'- 4" x 14'- 0"
10'-0" sloped clg

BONUS ROOM

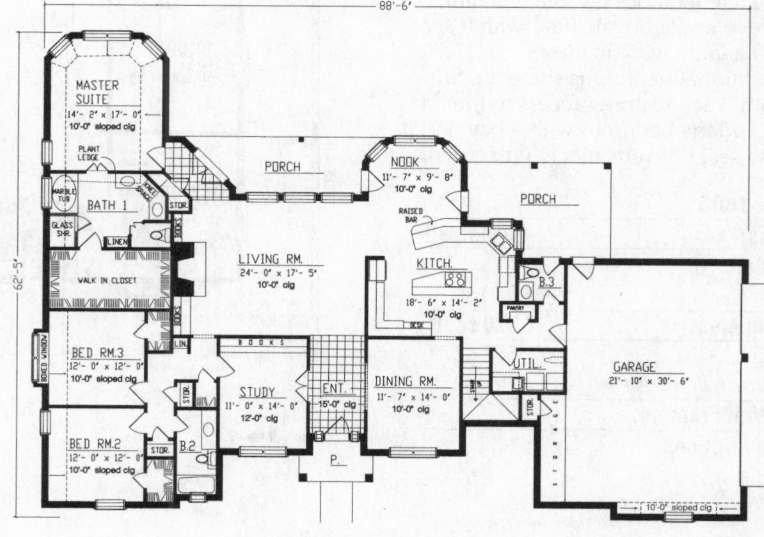

MAIN FLOOR

Sun-Drenched Dream Home

- This home boasts outdoor spaces galore, including a huge wraparound porch in the front, an open courtyard in the center and an arched area topped by an optional sun deck.
- The double-door entry pulls you into the vaulted, sunken Great Room, just past a clever glass block divider. Beyond are a fireplace and two sets of glass doors opening to the courtyard.
- Sunlight illuminates the kitchen and the dining room, which share a vaulted ceiling. The dining room features a bayed window seat, while the kitchen offers a snack bar and a big pantry.
- Across the courtyard, a sizable den/bedroom that may become a master suite includes a vaulted ceiling, a fireplace and a private bath with a spa tub and a large walk-in closet.
- Two additional bedrooms share the full hall bath. Each features access to the porch, and the bedroom with a bay window seat converts nicely into a den.

Plan SUN-1805	
Bedrooms: 1+	**Baths:** 2½
Living Area:	
Main floor	2,970 sq. ft.
Total Living Area:	**2,970 sq. ft.**
Garage	887 sq. ft.
Utility	14 sq. ft.
Exterior Wall Framing:	2x6
Foundation Options:	
Crawlspace	
Slab	

(All plans can be built with your choice of foundation and framing. A generic conversion diagram is available. See order form.)

BLUEPRINT PRICE CODE: D

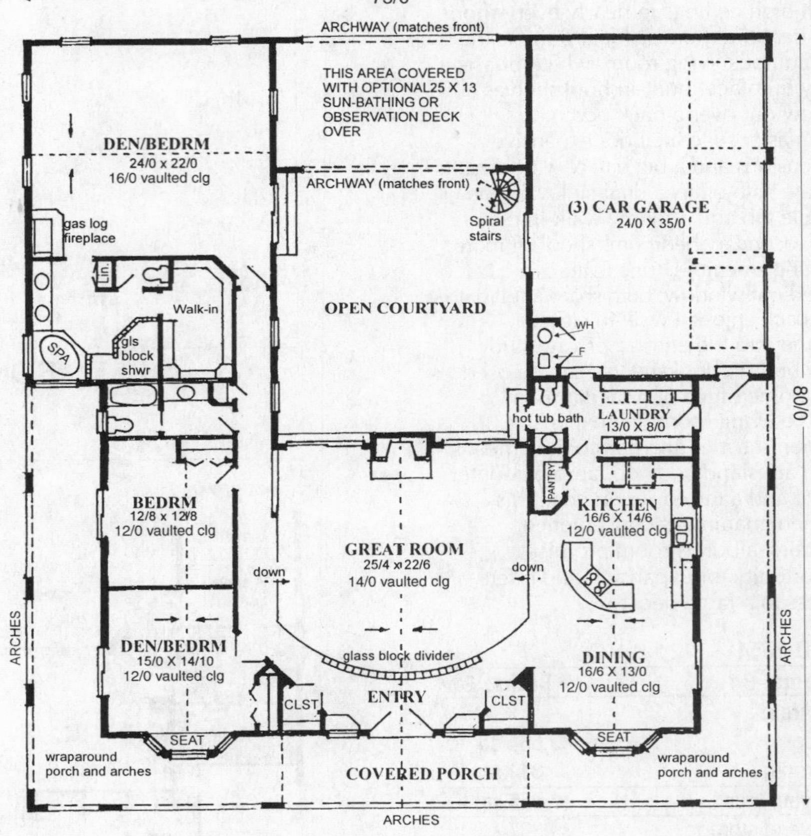

MAIN FLOOR

SEE ORDER INFO ON PAGES 12-15

Manor Defined

- This grand manor is defined from the outset, with stylish gables, artistic masonry and tall, arched windows.
- Inside the home, raised ceilings add to the elegance throughout. At the front, a grand entry flows between a study and the formal dining room.
- A wall of windows in the tray-ceilinged living room brightens any occasion.
- Around the corner, the gourmet kitchen offers plenty of space for meal planning and preparation. Not without style though, the kitchen's breakfast area shares a see-through fireplace with the family room.
- A corner window in the family room directs the focus out of doors, where an inviting patio offers a built-in spa tub.
- The master bedroom has its own door to the covered portion of the back patio. The master bath boasts twin walk-in closets, a dual-sink vanity and a marble tub with a neighboring shower.
- Across the home, three more bedrooms each deliver private access to one of two additional baths. The rear bath also serves the outdoor spa area.

Plan DD-3029	
Bedrooms: 4+	**Baths:** 3½
Living Area:	
Main floor	3,029 sq. ft.
Total Living Area:	**3,029 sq. ft.**
Standard basement	3,029 sq. ft.
Garage and storage	484 sq. ft.
Exterior Wall Framing:	2x4
Foundation Options:	
Standard basement	
Crawlspace	
Slab	

(All plans can be built with your choice of foundation and framing. A generic conversion diagram is available. See order form.)

BLUEPRINT PRICE CODE: E

REAR VIEW

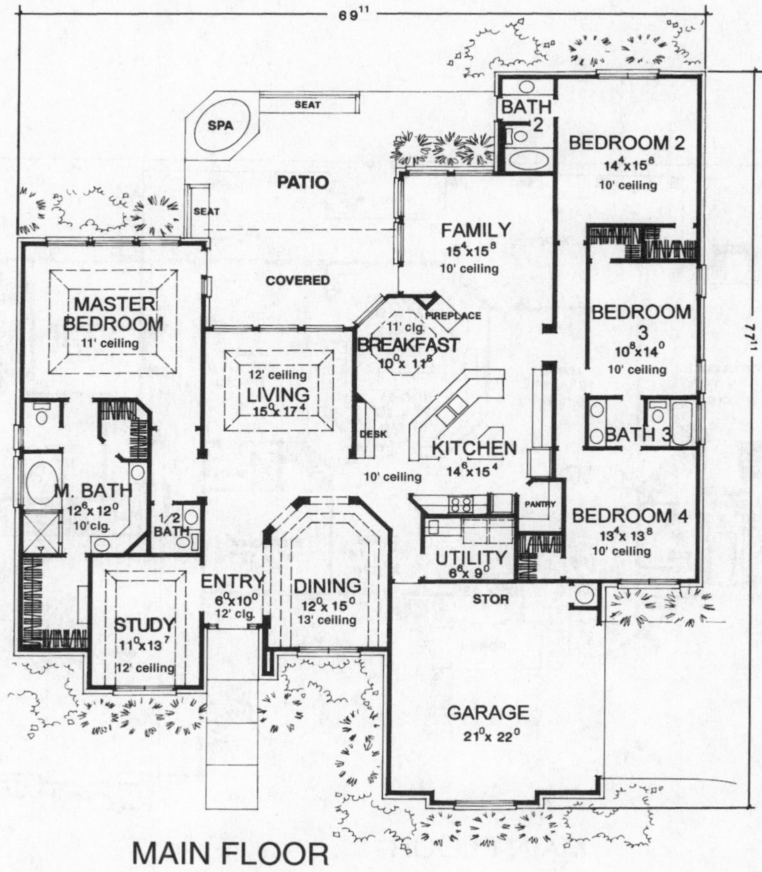

MAIN FLOOR

Plan DD-3029

FOR MORE DETAILS, SEE PLAN AT familyhandyman.com/homeplans

One-Floor Gracious Living

- An impressive roofscape, stately brick with soldier coursing and an impressive columned entry grace the exterior of this exciting single-story home.
- The entry opens to the the free-flowing interior, where the formal areas merge near the den, or guest room.
- The living room offers a window wall to a wide backyard deck, and the dining room is convenient to the kitchen.
- The octagonal island kitchen area offers a sunny breakfast nook with a large corner pantry.
- The spacious family room adjoins the kitchen and features a handsome fireplace flanked by built-in bookshelves, and deck access. Laundry facilities and garage access are nearby.
- The lavish master suite has a fireplace and a state-of-the-art bath, and is privately situated in the left wing.
- Three secondary bedrooms with abundant closet space share two baths on the right side of the home. Two of the bedrooms have window seats.

Plan DD-3076

Bedrooms: 4+	**Baths:** 3
Living Area:	
Main floor	3,132 sq. ft.
Total Living Area:	**3,132 sq. ft.**
Standard basement	3,132 sq. ft.
Garage	648 sq. ft.
Exterior Wall Framing:	2x4

Foundation Options:

Standard basement
Crawlspace
Slab

(All plans can be built with your choice of foundation and framing. A generic conversion diagram is available. See order form.)

BLUEPRINT PRICE CODE: E

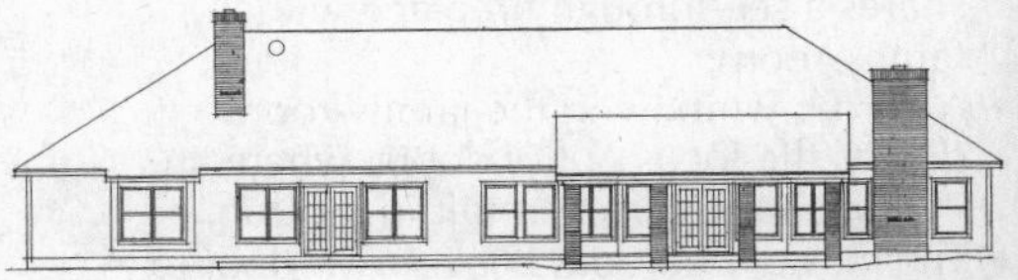

REAR VIEW

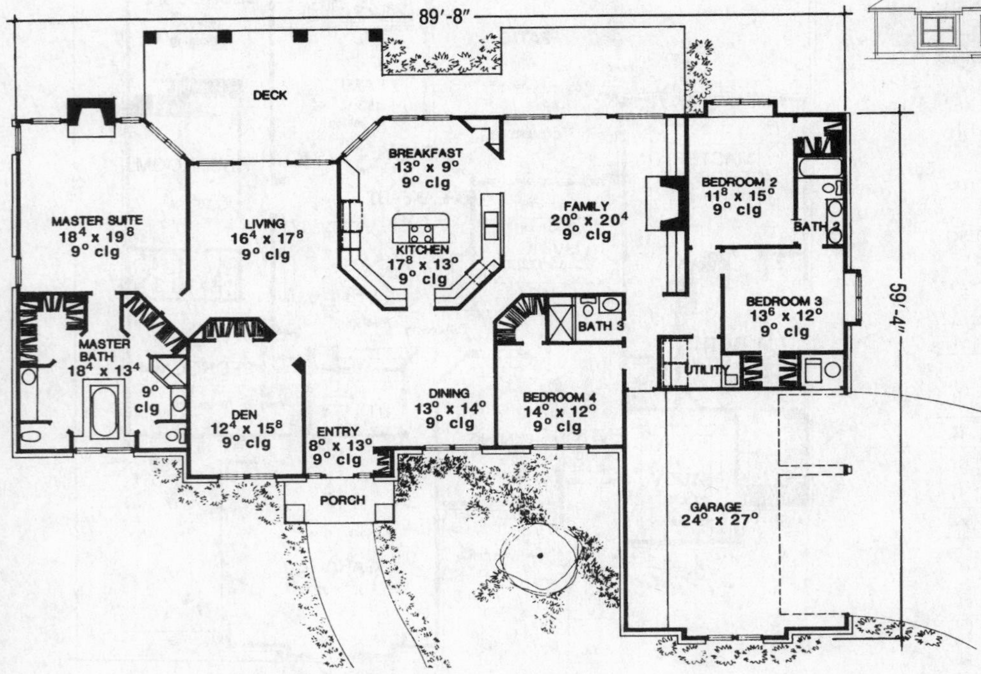

89'-8"
59'-4"
DECK
BREAKFAST $13^{0} \times 9^{0}$ 9^{0} clg
MASTER SUITE $18^{4} \times 19^{8}$ 9^{0} clg
LIVING $16^{4} \times 17^{8}$ 9^{0} clg
FAMILY $20^{0} \times 20^{4}$ 9^{0} clg
KITCHEN $17^{8} \times 13^{0}$ 9^{0} clg
BEDROOM 2 $11^{8} \times 15^{0}$ 9^{0} clg
BATH
BEDROOM 3 $13^{6} \times 12^{0}$ 9^{0} clg
BATH 3
UTILITY
MASTER BATH $18^{4} \times 13^{4}$
9^{0} clg
DEN $12^{4} \times 15^{8}$ 9^{0} clg
ENTRY $8^{0} \times 13^{0}$ 9^{0} clg
DINING $13^{0} \times 14^{0}$ 9^{0} clg
BEDROOM 4 $14^{0} \times 12^{0}$ 9^{0} clg
PORCH
GARAGE $24^{0} \times 27^{0}$

MAIN FLOOR

Plan DD-3076

SEE ORDER INFO ON PAGES 12-15
familyhandyman.com/homeplans

Graceful Estate

- Bright, beautiful windows, distinctive brickwork and a stylish floor plan give this graceful home an elegant feel.
- Beyond the impressive arched entry, the inviting foyer is highlighted by a fantail transom window.
- Off the foyer, the living and dining rooms boast stunning window walls.
- The gourmet island kitchen includes a corner pantry, a built-in planning desk, an angled bar and a lazy Susan. The adjoining breakfast room offers access to a covered back porch.
- The spacious family room showcases a handsome marble-hearthed fireplace flanked by stunning windows.
- The luxurious master suite features a bayed sitting area. The private master bath offers a garden tub, a separate shower and a dual-sink vanity with knee space.
- Easily convertible to an in-law or guest suite, the good-sized study has private bathroom access.
- Two additional bedrooms occupy the opposite side of the home and offer private access to a shared bath. A laundry/utility room is close by.

Plan KLF-9305

Bedrooms: 4	**Baths:** 3
Living Area:	
Main floor	3,100 sq. ft.
Total Living Area:	**3,100 sq. ft.**
Garage	760 sq. ft.
Exterior Wall Framing:	2x4
Foundation Options:	
Slab	

(All plans can be built with your choice of foundation and framing. A generic conversion diagram is available. See order form.)

BLUEPRINT PRICE CODE: **E**

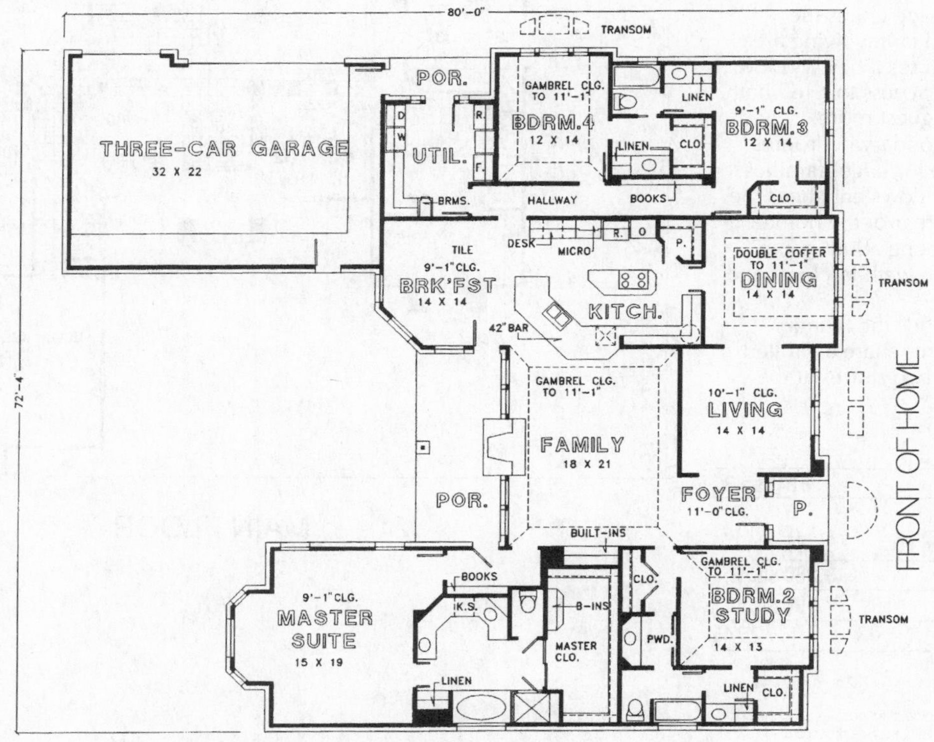

MAIN FLOOR

Plan KLF-9305

Master-Suite Marvel

- This home's master suite has every lavish amenity you could dream of. Rejuvenate in the atrium spa, enjoy the walk-in closet's clothes carousel, or lounge in the vaulted sitting room, which opens to a rear lanai.
- Architectural columns define the striking octagonal dining room, which adjoins the island kitchen and the sunny breakfast nook.
- A see-through fireplace unites the spacious formal and family living areas.
- The den, which features a bay window, a roomy closet and access to a full bath, easily doubles as a guest room.
- Generous-sized secondary bedrooms make life enjoyable for larger families. A bayed wall of windows enhances the suite nestled at the rear of the home. The front-facing "young adult" room benefits from a large walk-in closet and a built-in desk.
- A high ceiling expands the laundry room. All other rooms share a vaulted ceiling that rises to two stories at the center of the home.

Plan HDS-99-279

Bedrooms: 3+	**Baths:** 3
Living Area:	
Main floor	3,280 sq. ft.
Total Living Area:	**3,280 sq. ft.**
Garage	596 sq. ft.
Exterior Wall Framing:	2x4
Foundation Options:	
Slab	
(All plans can be built with your choice of foundation and framing. A generic conversion diagram is available. See order form.)	
BLUEPRINT PRICE CODE:	**E**

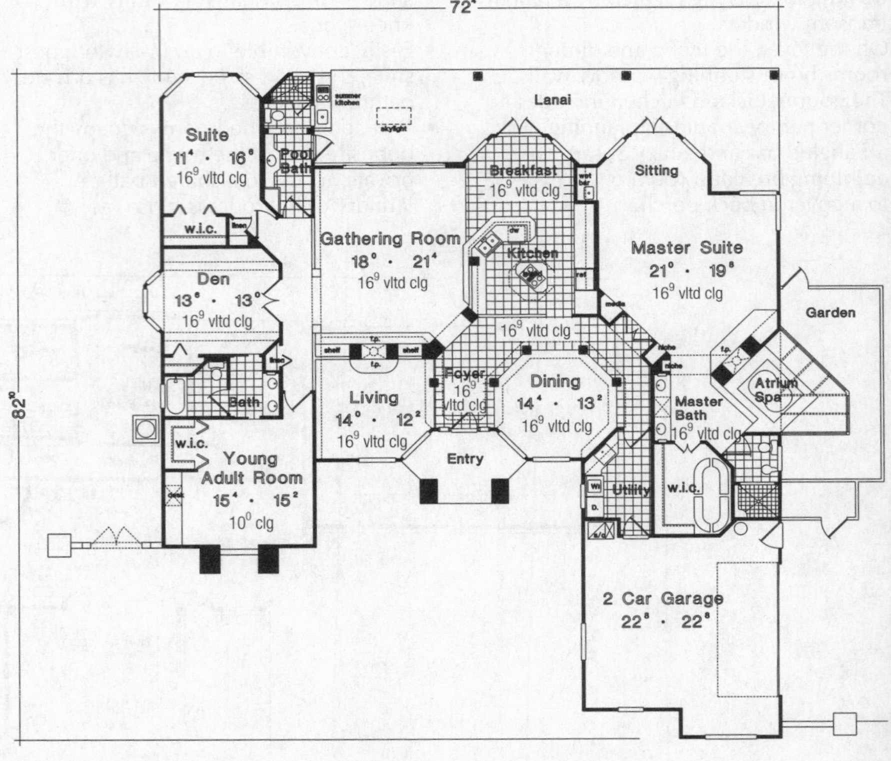

MAIN FLOOR

Plan HDS-99-279

SEE ORDER INFO ON PAGES 12-15
familyhandyman.com/homeplans

Exquisitely Expansive

- "Exquisite!" is what you'll exclaim as you explore this memorable home's expansive and artfully detailed interior.
- Enter the raised foyer and choose whether to step down to the columned gallery, the living room or the dining room. The gallery provides passage through double doors to the cozy study—where you'll be able to work by fireside—and the neighboring library, with its built-in bookshelves.
- The living room is a grand space that centers on the fireplace, which is nicely framed by built-ins, and French doors to the back porch.
- At the heart of the home is the island kitchen, accented by the adjoining bayed breakfast room for casual dining.
- The magnificent master retreat enjoys a bayed sitting area, an enormous walk-in closet and a deluxe bath that luxuriates in abundant storage space, a dual-sink vanity, and a raised spa tub where you'll soak for hours.
- Three secondary bedrooms enjoy private access to adjacent baths.

Plan L-3538-FC	
Bedrooms: 4+	**Baths:** 3½
Living Area:	
Main floor	3,538 sq. ft.
Total Living Area:	**3,538 sq. ft.**
Garage	773 sq. ft.
Exterior Wall Framing:	2x6
Foundation Options:	
Slab	

All plans can be built with your choice of foundation and framing. A generic conversion diagram is available. See order form.)

BLUEPRINT PRICE CODE: **F**

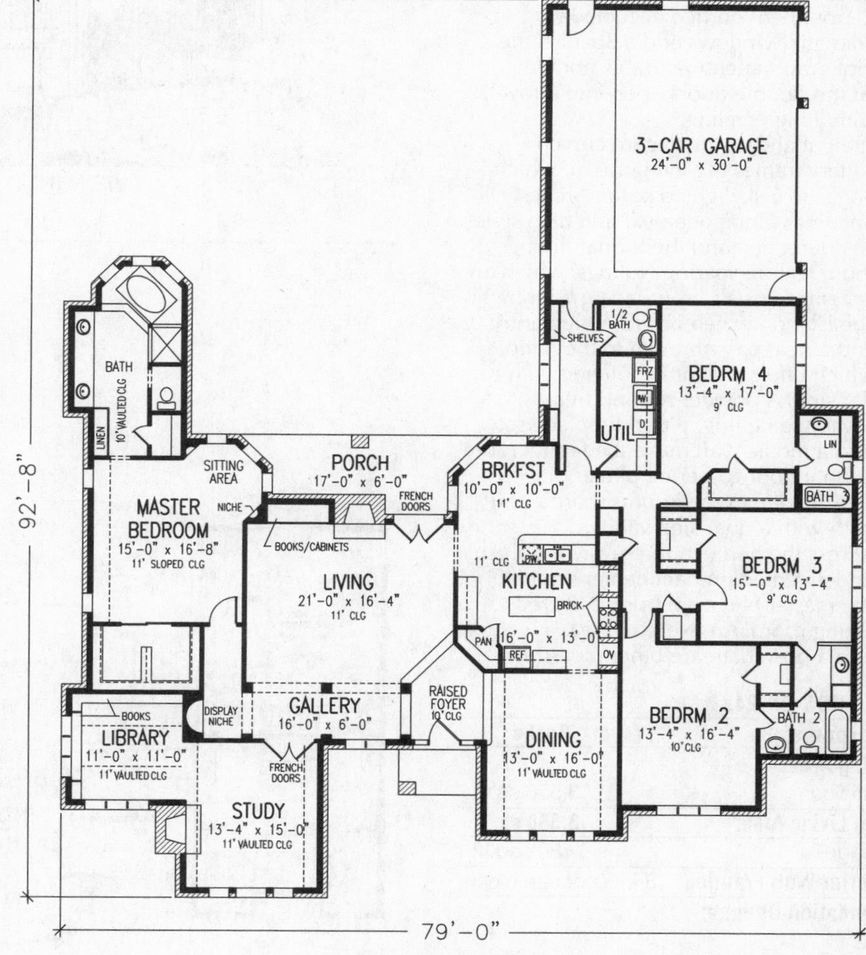

MAIN FLOOR

Prominent Portico

- A prominent portico accented by dramatic windows and a Spanish tile roof draws attention to this home. Grand double doors open into a foyer with a high ceiling.
- Straight ahead, an elegant curved gallery frames the living room, which opens to a skylighted patio. Arched openings along one wall add high style.
- The quiet den and the formal dining room feature soaring ceilings, which are accented by tall, front-facing windows.
- The island kitchen boasts a big pantry and a neat pass-through to the patio, which offers a summer kitchen with a bar sink. A powder room is nearby.
- A vaulted ceiling, plus a fireplace set into a media wall make the family room a fun indoor gathering place.
- Two secondary bedrooms share a split bath with a dual-sink vanity.
- Across the home, a three-way fireplace and an entertainment center separate the master bedroom from its bayed sitting room. An exercise area, a wet bar and a posh bath are other pleasures!

Plan HDS-99-242	
Bedrooms: 3+	**Baths:** 3½
Living Area:	
Main floor	3,556 sq. ft.
Total Living Area:	**3,556 sq. ft.**
Garage	809 sq. ft.
Exterior Wall Framing:	8-in. concrete block
Foundation Options:	
Slab	
(All plans can be built with your choice of foundation and framing. A generic conversion diagram is available. See order form.)	
BLUEPRINT PRICE CODE:	**F**

VIEW INTO MASTER SUITE

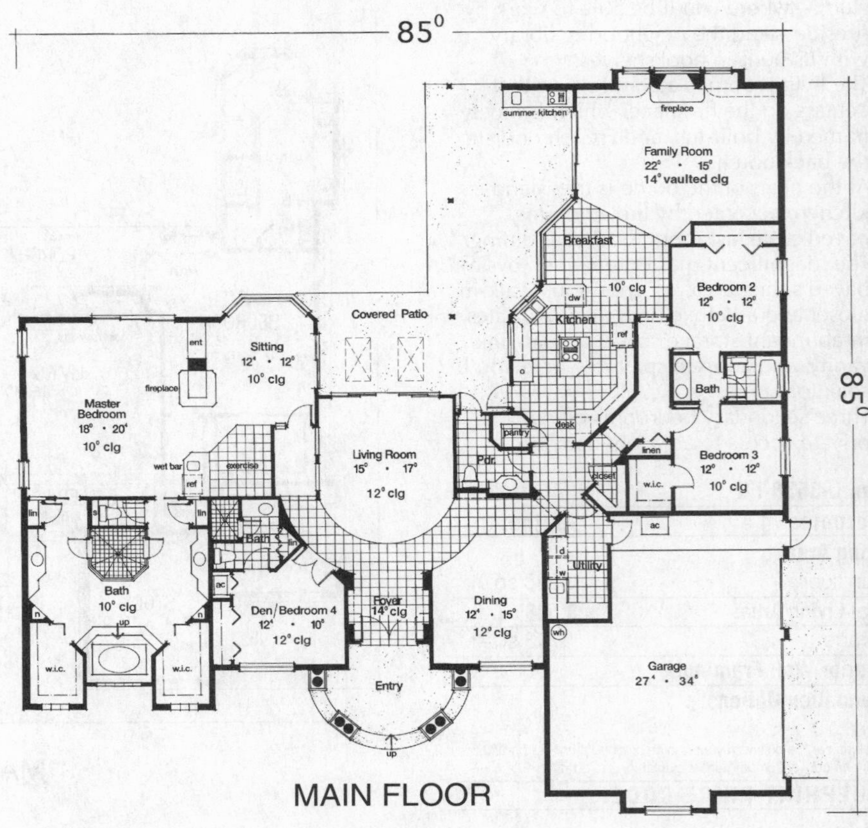

MAIN FLOOR

Plan HDS-99-242

SEE ORDER INFO ON PAGES 12-15
familyhandyman.com/homeplans

Mediterranean Allure

- This home's half-round transoms, exciting arches, stucco exterior and clay tile roof exude Mediterranean allure.
- An octagonal tray ceiling tops the elegant raised dining room, setting it apart from the surrounding rooms. The nearby skylighted breakfast nook peers out to the back deck, while the roomy kitchen boasts a large pantry, an angled counter and a snack bar.
- The living room features a high ceiling and a handsome corner fireplace, while through a barrel-vaulted passageway, the spacious family room offers a built-in bookcase.
- Full of classic details, the master suite boasts a volume ceiling, a washer and dryer, and a barrel arch leading to a huge walk-in closet. The private bath shows off a refreshing spa tub, a dual-sink vanity and a sizable glassed-in shower.
- Three additional bedrooms on the other wing share two full hall baths.

Plan SUN-1295

Bedrooms: 4+	**Baths:** 3½
Living Area:	
Main floor	3,600 sq. ft.
Total Living Area:	**3,600 sq. ft.**
Garage	744 sq. ft.
Exterior Wall Framing:	2x6
Foundation Options:	
Crawlspace	
Slab	

(All plans can be built with your choice of foundation and framing. A generic conversion diagram is available. See order form.)

BLUEPRINT PRICE CODE: F

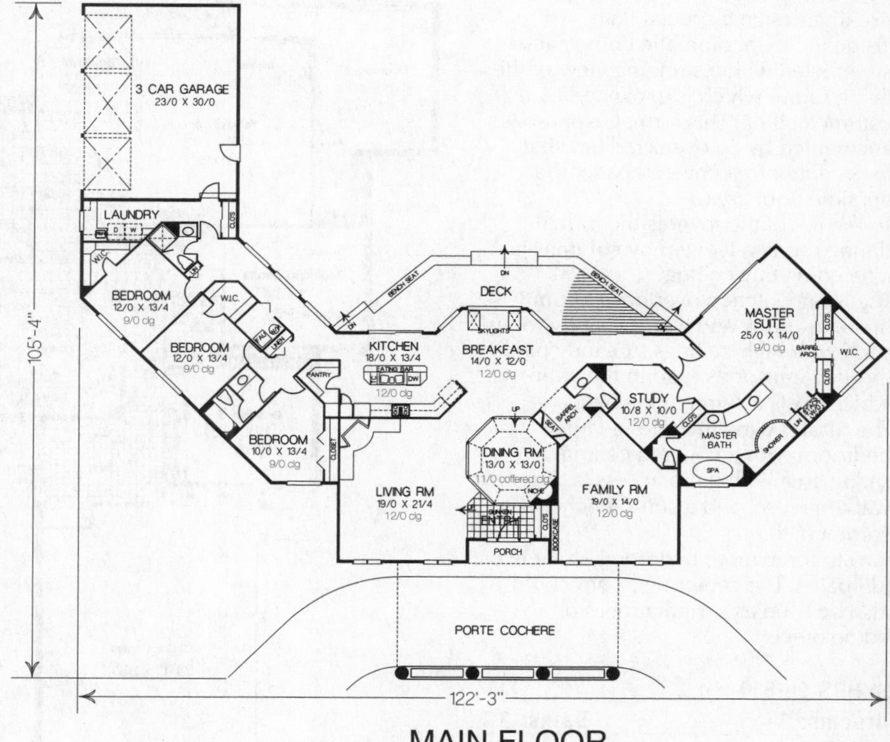

MAIN FLOOR

Bright Design

- Sweeping rooflines, arched transom windows and a stucco exterior give this exciting design a special flair.
- Inside the high, dramatic entry, guests are greeted with a stunning view of the living room, which is expanded by a volume ceiling. This formal expanse is augmented by an oversized bay that looks out onto a covered patio and possible pool area.
- To the left of the foyer is the formal dining room, accented by columns and a receding tray ceiling.
- The island kitchen overlooks a sunny breakfast nook and a large family room, each with high ceilings. A handy pass-through transports food to the patio, which hosts a summer kitchen.
- The master wing includes a large bedroom with a coffered ceiling, a sitting area with patio access, a massive walk-in closet and a sun-drenched garden bath.
- Two to three more bedrooms share two full baths. The center bedroom could also be used as a media room or a home office.

Plan HDS-90-814	
Bedrooms: 3+	**Baths:** 3½
Living Area:	
Main floor	3,743 sq. ft.
Total Living Area:	**3,743 sq. ft.**
Garage	725 sq. ft.
Exterior Wall Framing:	2x4 or 8-in. concrete block
Foundation Options:	
Slab	
(All plans can be built with your choice of foundation and framing. A generic conversion diagram is available. See order form.)	
BLUEPRINT PRICE CODE:	**F**

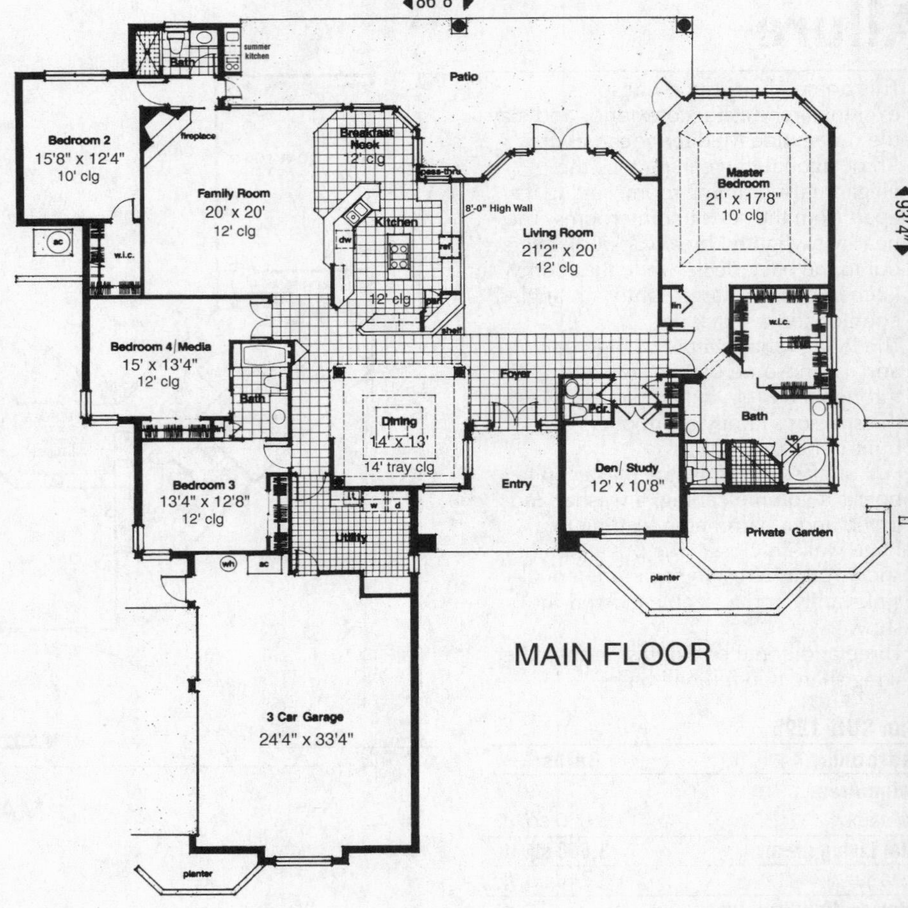

MAIN FLOOR

Plan HDS-90-814

SEE ORDER INFO ON PAGES 12-15
familyhandyman.com/homeplans

Sensational Southern-Style

- This stately home is reminiscent of the Old South, but features an interior filled with modern luxuries.
- From the front porch, visitors enter the high-ceilinged foyer. Ahead, the light-filled family room offers a dramatic corner fireplace and outdoor views.
- Elegant double doors open to the formal living spaces on either side of the foyer.
- The large gourmet kitchen boasts a handy island counter, a walk-in pantry, a snack bar and a bright eating area with an exciting wet bar!
- The luxurious master suite flaunts a romantic sitting area with a corner fireplace and porch access, a big walk-in closet and a private bath with an angled whirlpool tub.
- Three more bedrooms with private bath access are located on the opposite end of the home. An exciting sun room adjoins the bedrooms and opens to the back porch.

Plan E-4001	
Bedrooms: 3+	**Baths:** 4½
Living Area:	
Main floor	4,083 sq. ft.
Total Living Area:	**4,083 sq. ft.**
Standard basement	4,083 sq. ft.
Garage	816 sq. ft.
Storage	242 sq. ft.
Exterior Wall Framing:	2x6
Foundation Options:	
Standard basement	
Crawlspace	
Slab	

(All plans can be built with your choice of foundation and framing. A generic conversion diagram is available. See order form.)

BLUEPRINT PRICE CODE: G

REAR VIEW

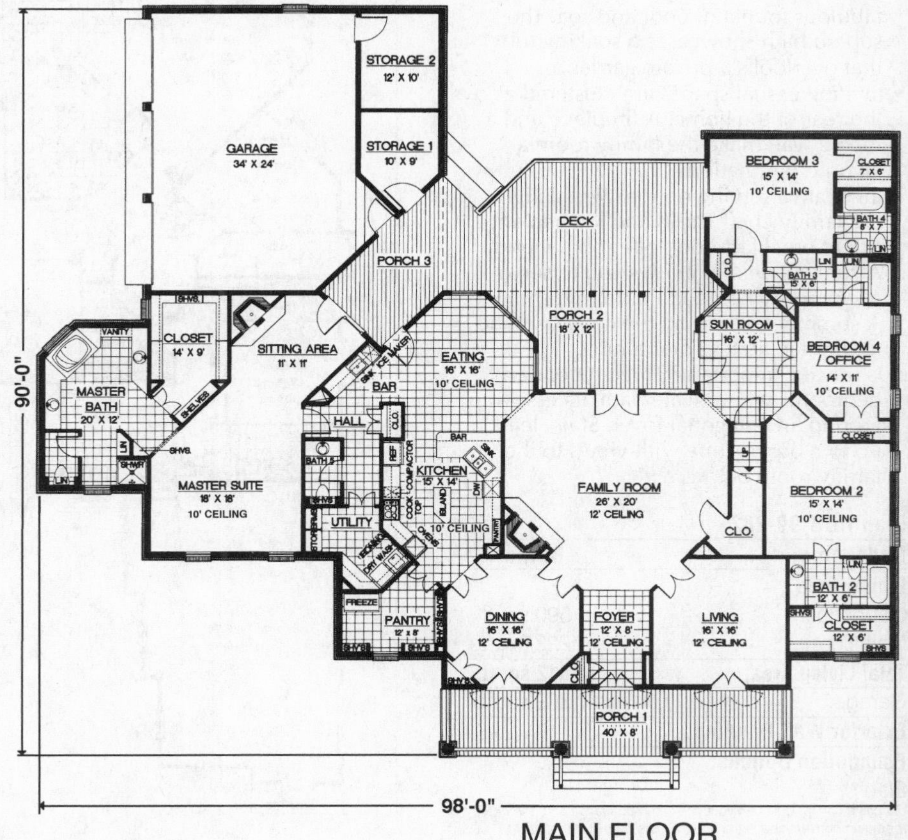

MAIN FLOOR

It's All Here!

- It's hard to think of a missing feature in this grand Mediterranean design!
- Inside the columned entry, ten more columns define the living and dining rooms and the welcoming foyer.
- Imagine a relaxing afternoon devouring a novel in the quiet den or office.
- Isolated to the right, the posh master bedroom's French doors give way to a fabulous fountain, pool and spa. The superb bath showcases a soaking tub that overlooks a private garden.
- Inviting casual spaces are clustered at the rear of the home. A fireplace and a media wall make the family room a favorite destination.
- Innovative serving options will delight the family chef! The island kitchen and bright breakfast nook offer pool views. A sunken wet bar allows you to serve swimmers who need liquid refreshment. A summer kitchen on the covered patio further facilitates entertaining.
- Is privacy important? Three secondary bedrooms with private bath access wrap around an octagonal foyer. Stairs lead up to a bonus suite with views to the family room below.

Plan HDS-99-282	
Bedrooms: 4+	**Baths:** 6
Living Area:	
Upper floor	590 sq. ft.
Main floor	4,222 sq. ft.
Total Living Area:	**4,812 sq. ft.**
Garage	869 sq. ft.
Exterior Wall Framing:	2x6
Foundation Options:	
Slab (All plans can be built with your choice of foundation and framing. A generic conversion diagram is available. See order form.)	

BLUEPRINT PRICE CODE: **H**

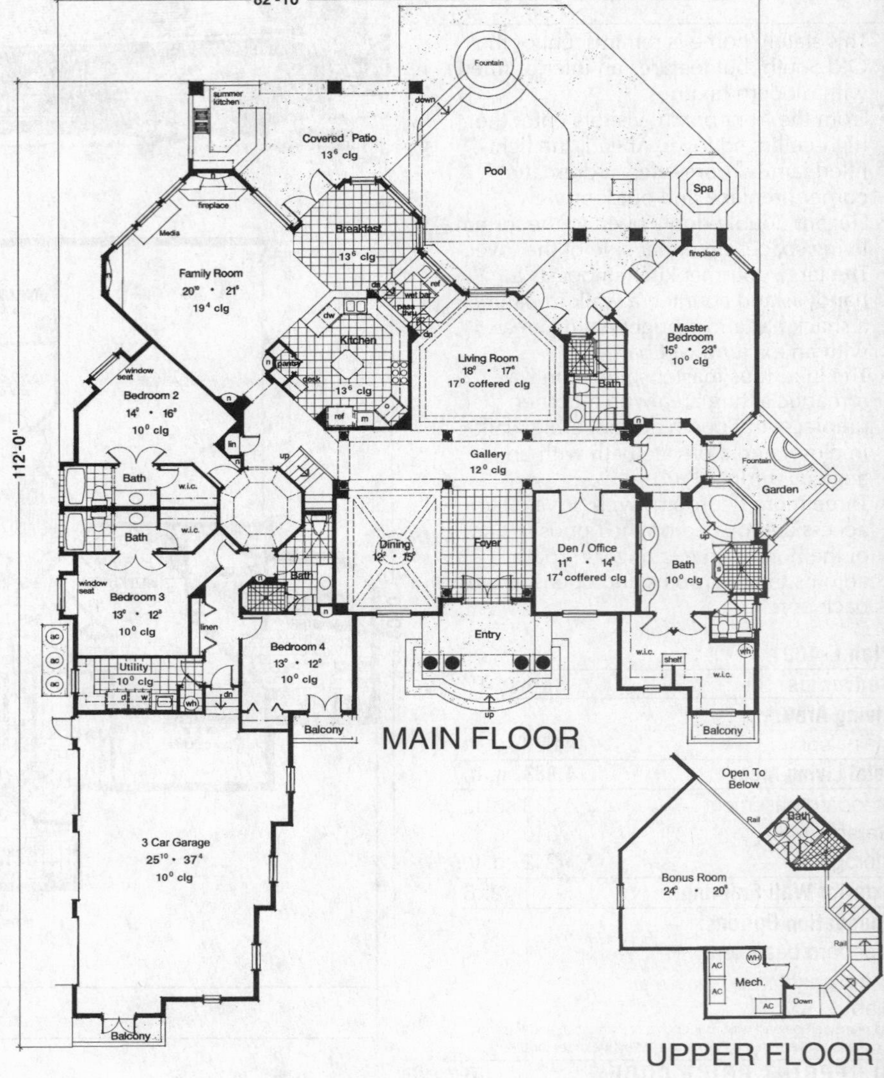

ORDER BLUEPRINTS ANYTIME!
CALL TOLL-FREE 1-800-820-1296

Plan HDS-99-282

SEE ORDER INFO ON PAGES 12-15
familyhandyman.com/homeplans

Outdoor Surprises!

- A private entry courtyard topped by an intricate trellis draws attention to this beautiful brick home.
- The drama continues inside, where you'll find high ceilings, sprawling openness and breathtaking views of the many outdoor living spaces.
- The central hearth room is a great spot to welcome your guests and keep them entertained with its dazzling fireplace.
- Appetizers and refreshments can be served at the long snack bar extending from the triangular kitchen.
- Plenty of space for formal mingling is offered in the spacious living and dining room expanse beyond. The screened porch, adjoining patio and panoramic views will inspire hours of conversation.
- Ideal for the empty nester, this home includes two private bedroom suites. The master suite boasts his-and-hers closets, vanities and toilets.
- The studio at the front of the home could also serve as an extra bedroom.

Plan EOF-86-B

Bedrooms: 2+	**Baths:** 2½
Living Area:	
Main floor	1,830 sq. ft.
Total Living Area:	**1,830 sq. ft.**
Screened porch	134 sq. ft.
Garage	433 sq. ft.
Storage	12 sq. ft.
Exterior Wall Framing:	2x4
Foundation Options:	
Slab	
(All plans can be built with your choice of foundation and framing. A generic conversion diagram is available. See order form.)	
BLUEPRINT PRICE CODE:	**B**

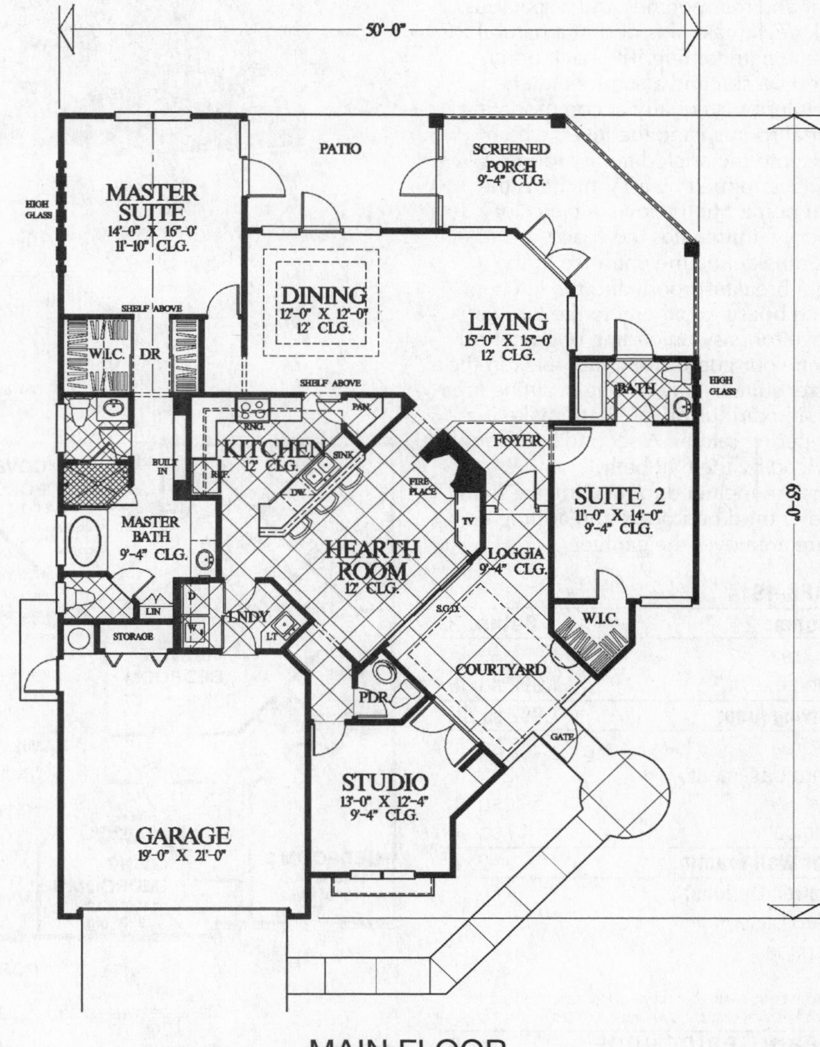

MAIN FLOOR

Outdoor Fête

- Who doesn't love an outdoor party? Front and rear porches and a spacious back deck make this design a natural for outside entertaining. The back porch features a spa and a summer kitchen.
- The interior is equally accommodating. Formal rooms flank the foyer, which leads into the angled family room. A fireplace topped by a TV niche is the focal point. High above, a clerestory window illuminates the space.
- Columns define the entrance to the bright breakfast room and the kitchen, which boasts proximity to the two-car garage for easy unloading of groceries.
- When your guests are gone, relax in the master suite. A tray ceiling, a sitting area and a luxurious private bath make it a pampering retreat. A second bedroom is serviced by the hall bath.
- Plans are included for making the living room a third bedroom, and adding a future area over the garage.

Plan APS-1914	
Bedrooms: 2+	**Baths:** 3
Living Area:	
Main floor	1,992 sq. ft.
Total Living Area:	**1,992 sq. ft.**
Future area	247 sq. ft.
Standard basement	1,992 sq.ft.
Garage	590 sq. ft.
Mechanical	19 sq. ft.
Exterior Wall Framing:	2x4
Foundation Options:	
Standard basement	
Crawlspace	
Slab	

(All plans can be built with your choice of foundation and framing. A generic conversion diagram is available. See order form.)

BLUEPRINT PRICE CODE:	**B**

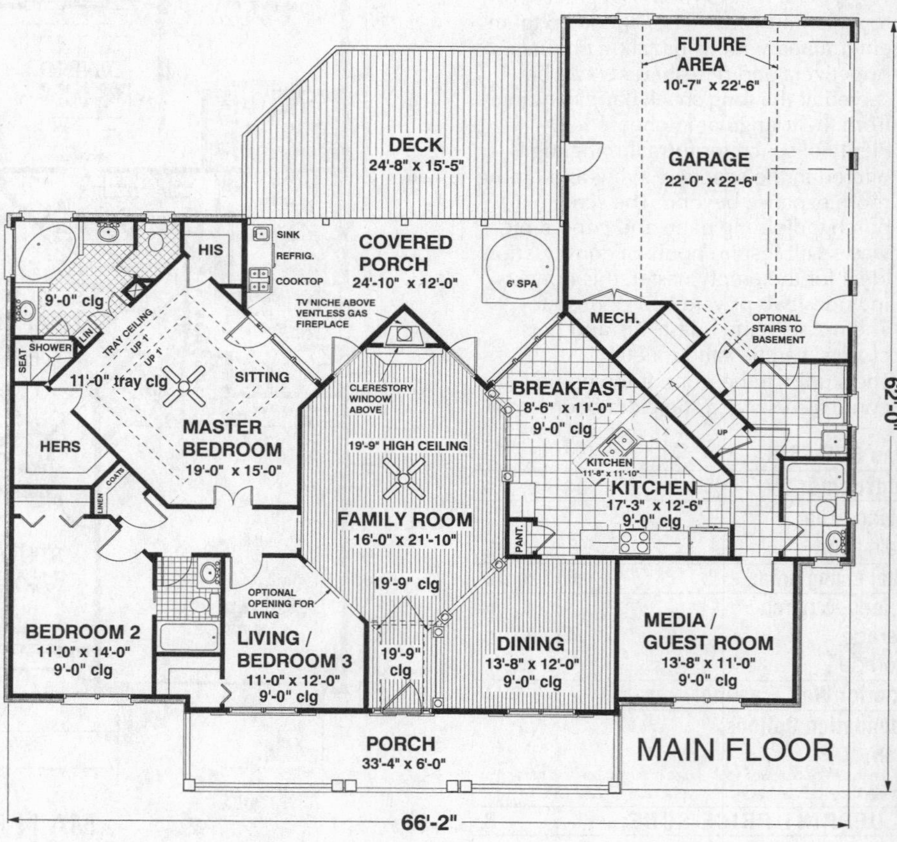

Plan APS-1914

SEE ORDER INFO ON PAGES 12-15

Versatile Spaces

- This home is jam-packed with versatile spaces. Up front, an office offers private access to the front porch. In back, a secluded guest bedroom is ideal for older children or visiting in-laws.
- Perfect for rowdy Super Bowl parties or quiet evenings, the central Great Room features a toasty fireplace flanked by windows overlooking a covered patio.
- The open kitchen's handy pantry, ample counter space and convenient serving bar provide plenty of room for gourmet pursuits. Take your brunch in the adjoining breakfast nook or step out onto the cozy covered patio.
- The master bedroom's high ceiling and big windows usher in light. The private master bath is the ideal spot to beautify yourself. Bathe in the splashy garden tub, primp and preen at the dual-sink vanity, then grab your finest duds from the big walk-in closet.
- Nearby, two additional bedrooms boast high ceilings and closet space aplenty.
- Loaded with storage nooks, the attached two-car garage opens to the laundry room. At the back of the home, the mudroom leads to a full bath.

Plan DD-2260-A	
Bedrooms: 4+	**Baths:** 3
Living Area:	
Main floor	2,321 sq. ft.
Total Living Area:	**2,321 sq. ft.**
Standard basement	2,321 sq. ft.
Garage	427 sq. ft.
Exterior Wall Framing:	2x4
Foundation Options:	
Standard basement	
Crawlspace	
Slab	
(All plans can be built with your choice of foundation and framing. A generic conversion diagram is available. See order form.)	
BLUEPRINT PRICE CODE:	**C**

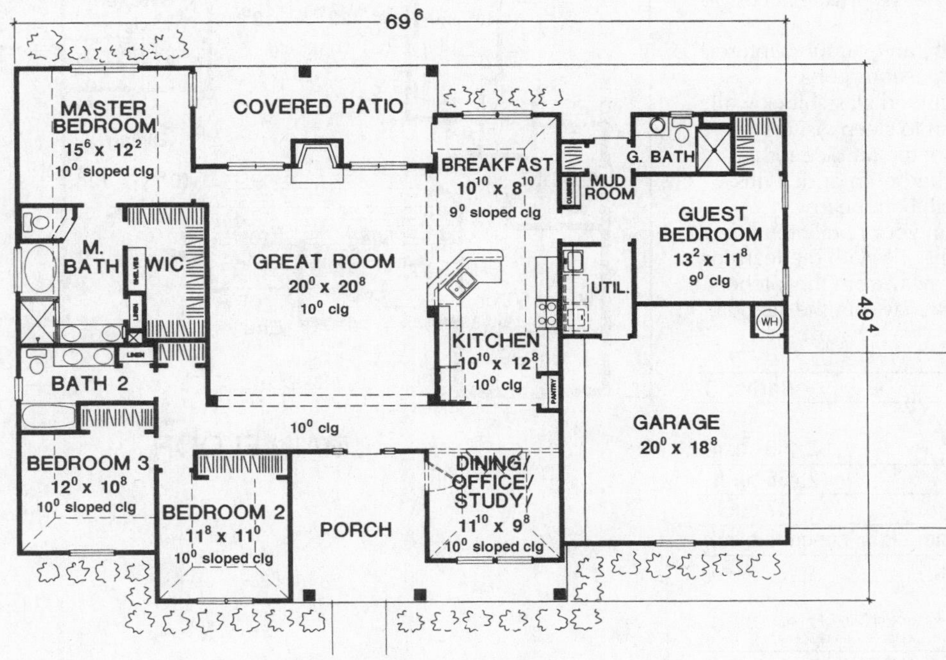

MAIN FLOOR

Conclusive Evidence

- The verdict is in on this spicy Mediterranean home: magnificent!
- From the moment you step down into the huge family room and view its stunning fireplace flanked by media nooks, you begin to understand the excitement that this house generates.
- Beyond the family room, a covered patio beckons from behind sliding glass doors. There's room enough here to entertain your family and the in-laws!
- Seclusion reigns in the master suite, which is a study of good design. A plant shelf overlooks the entry to the sleeping chamber, which boasts private access to the back patio.
- In the master bath, an oval tub captures the eye with its sensuous curves spooned into a curved glass-block wall.
- Whether you plan to sleep visitors or just get away from the rat race for a while, the guest bedroom or den fills the bill, with a full bath nearby.
- Do the students in your family tend to burn the midnight oil? With the learning center just steps away from the kitchen, a late-night snack may join the agenda!

Plan HDS-99-266

Bedrooms: 3+	**Baths:** 3
Living Area:	
Main floor	2,456 sq. ft.
Total Living Area:	**2,456 sq. ft.**
Garage	447 sq. ft.
Exterior Wall Framing:	8-in. concrete block
Foundation Options:	
Slab	

(All plans can be built with your choice of foundation and framing. A generic conversion diagram is available. See order form.)

BLUEPRINT PRICE CODE: C

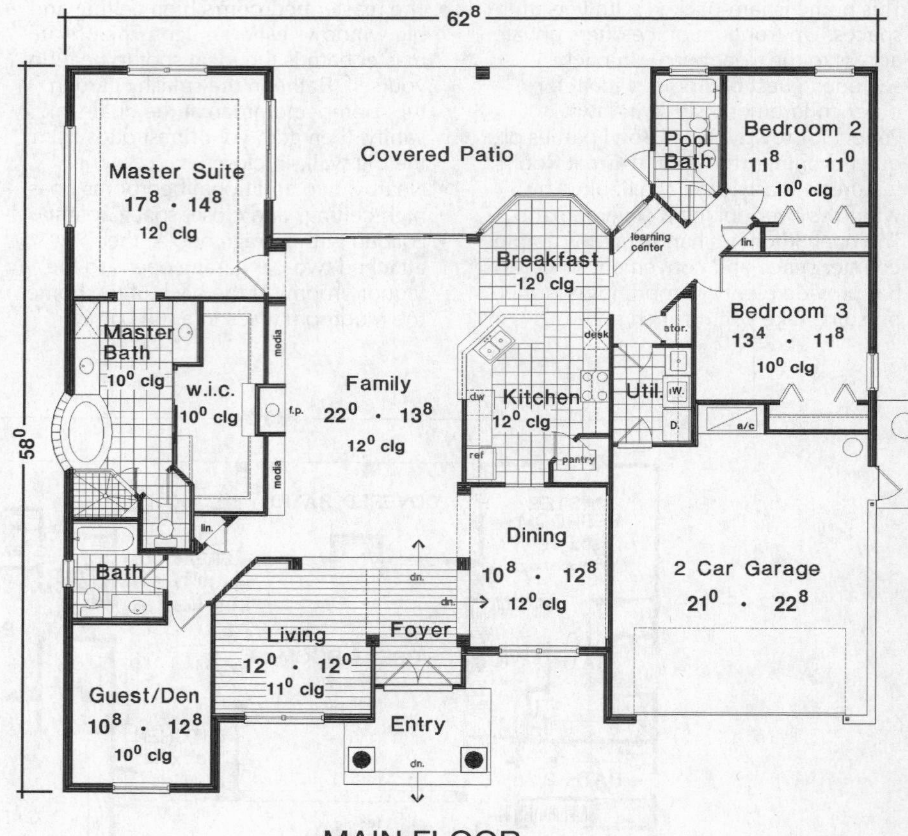

MAIN FLOOR

Enlightened Simplicity

- This stunning home draws its restful, nostalgic quality and elegant styling from its Craftsman heritage. But the comforts and amenities found inside reveal that the style is only a point of departure. You'll find luxuries you've only dreamed of!
- The front door opens into a gallery, perfect for displaying your artwork, textiles or pottery.
- Columns announce the Great Room beyond. A cheery fireplace anchors this expansive communal living space.
- The spacious island kitchen, served by a walk-in pantry and an angled counter bar, adjoins both the breakfast room and the formal dining room.
- An enormous walk-in closet, a garden tub, a separate shower and a dual-sink vanity update the master suite, which enjoys a sloped ceiling.
- The lavish guest quarters (the perfect in-law suite or media room) are nestled in a corner of the home for privacy.

Plan DD-2541-1B

Bedrooms: 4	**Baths:** 3
Living Area:	
Main floor	2,541 sq. ft.
Total Living Area:	**2,541 sq. ft.**
Standard basement	2,541 sq. ft.
Garage and workshop	498 sq. ft.
Exterior Wall Framing:	2x4

Foundation Options:
Standard basement
Crawlspace
Slab
(All plans can be built with your choice of foundation and framing. A generic conversion diagram is available. See order form.)

BLUEPRINT PRICE CODE: D

VIEW INTO GREAT ROOM, NOOK AND KITCHEN

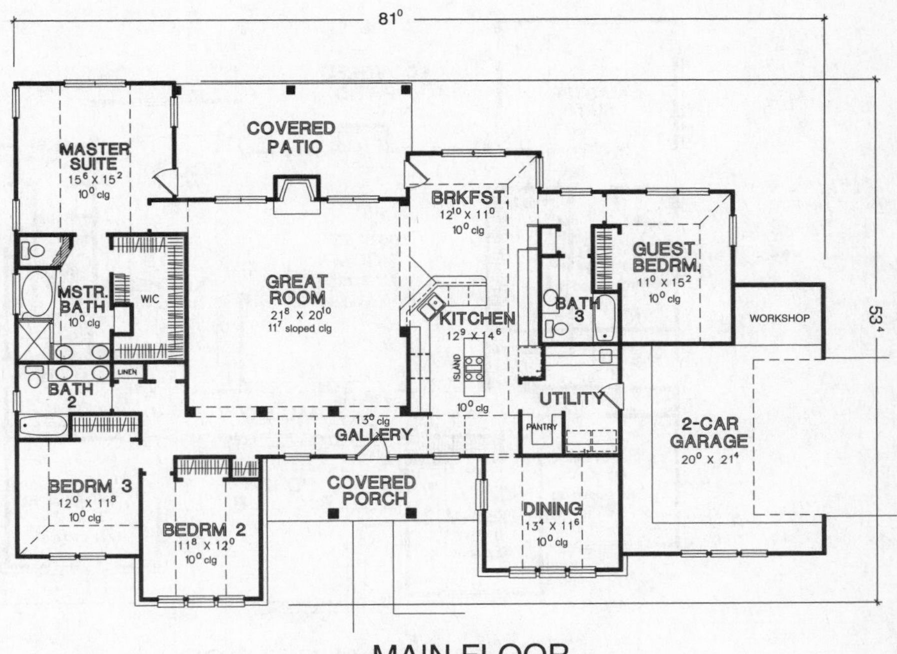

MAIN FLOOR

Sun-Drenched

- Revel in the sun-drenched interior of this sprawling, single-level home. Traditional touches, such as shuttered windows, cool columns and endearing dormers, invite you inside.
- Warmed by an impressive fireplace, the Great Room hosts rowdy family gatherings and elegant parties with equal ease. Easy access to the kitchen's snack bar accommodates hungry guests.
- Inside the kitchen, a wide island cooktop joins ample counter space and a walk-in pantry in creating a chef's paradise. The dining room across the gallery enjoys a sloped ceiling and plenty of sunlight.
- Visitors lack nothing in the posh guest bedroom, with its large windows and convenient access to a full bath. On the other side of the home, two additional bedrooms offer high ceilings and share another hall bath.
- Kick back and enjoy the sunlight in the great master suite, which includes private patio access. The private bath boasts a luxurious garden tub with a separate shower, not to mention a cavernous walk-in closet.

Plan DD-2541-1

Bedrooms: 4	**Baths:** 3
Living Area:	
Main floor	2,542 sq. ft.
Total Living Area:	**2,542 sq. ft.**
Standard basement	2,542 sq. ft.
Garage and storage	498 sq. ft.
Exterior Wall Framing:	2x4
Foundation Options:	
Standard basement	
Crawlspace	
Slab	

(All plans can be built with your choice of foundation and framing. A generic conversion diagram is available. See order form.)

BLUEPRINT PRICE CODE: D

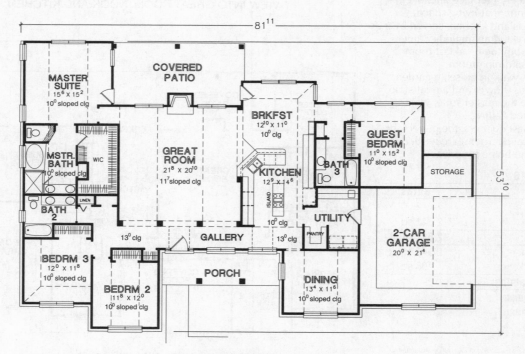

81^{11}
COVERED PATIO
MASTER SUITE 15^6 x 15^2 10^0 sloped clg
MSTR. BATH 10^0 sloped clg
WIC
LINEN
BATH 2
GREAT ROOM 21^8 x 20^{10} 11^7 sloped clg
BRKFST 12^{10} x 11^0 10^0 clg
KITCHEN 12^9 x 14^6
ISLAND
10^0 clg
GUEST BEDRM 11^0 x 15^2 10^0 sloped clg
BATH 3
STORAGE
53^{10}
UTILITY
PANTRY
2-CAR GARAGE 20^0 x 21^4
13^0 clg
GALLERY
13^0 clg
BEDRM 3 12^0 x 11^8 10^0 sloped clg
BEDRM 2 11^8 x 12^0 10^0 sloped clg
PORCH
DINING 13^4 x 11^6 10^0 sloped clg

MAIN FLOOR

Plan DD-2541-1

SEE ORDER INFO ON PAGES 12-15

Twice as Nice

- Graced with two deluxe master suites, this beautiful Mediterranean-style home is comfortable and elegant.
- The impressive columned entrance opens into the bright and airy foyer, which is highlighted by an arched transom window. The adjacent formal dining salon features a coffered ceiling and a stunning window wall.
- The gourmet kitchen includes a pantry, a snack counter and a morning room with a bay window, which offers access to a covered back porch.
- Warmed by a fireplace, the spacious central parlour boasts a high ceiling and French doors to the porch.
- The first master suite features a sitting area nestled into a bay window, plus his-and-hers walk-in closets and private porch access. The second suite offers a roomy walk-in closet and access to a private backyard patio. Both master baths include corner garden tubs, dual vanities and sit-down makeup counters.
- The library/guest room, with convenient private bath access, would make a great third bedroom.

Plan EOF-68	
Bedrooms: 2+	**Baths:** 3
Living Area:	
Main floor	2,690 sq. ft.
Total Living Area:	**2,690 sq. ft.**
Garage	732 sq. ft.
Exterior Wall Framing:	2x6
Foundation Options:	
Slab (All plans can be built with your choice of foundation and framing. A generic conversion diagram is available. See order form.)	
BLUEPRINT PRICE CODE:	**D**

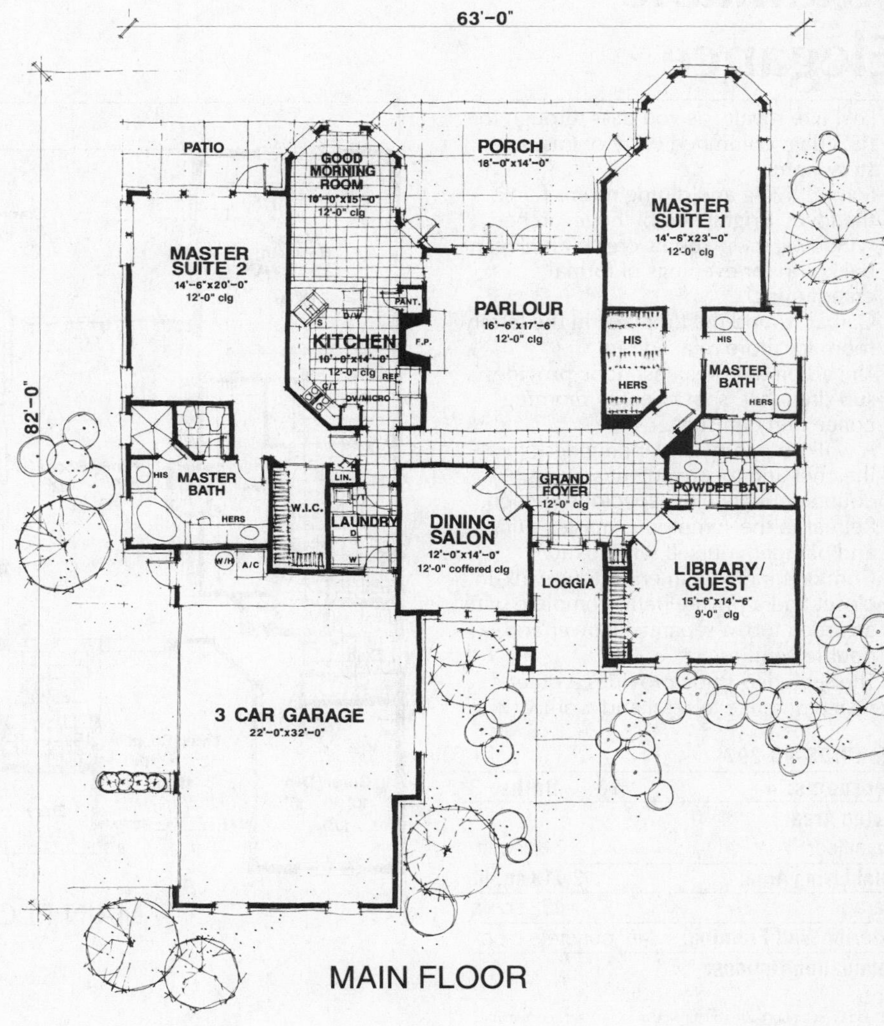

MAIN FLOOR

Attainable Elegance

- Feel like royalty as you pass through the dazzling, columned entry of this one-story home.
- Formal living and dining rooms flank the foyer. Brightened by huge, arched windows, these rooms create an elegant backdrop for evenings of formal entertaining.
- Gather 'round the fireplace in the family room for more relaxed fun.
- The adjoining breakfast nook provides a sun-drenched spot to enjoy morning coffee and danishes.
- A walk-in pantry, a planning desk for the chef and a convenient serving counter enhance the spacious kitchen.
- Retreat to the sumptuous master suite and pamper yourself with luxury. Comforts include an enormous walk-in closet and a private bath, complete with a garden tub, a separate shower and double vanities.
- The secluded study provides a quiet, peaceful place to read and work.

Plan HDS-99-297

Bedrooms: 4+	**Baths:** 3
Living Area:	
Main floor	2,718 sq. ft.
Total Living Area:	**2,718 sq. ft.**
Garage	452 sq. ft.
Exterior Wall Framing:	8-in. concrete block
Foundation Options:	
Slab	

(All plans can be built with your choice of foundation and framing. A generic conversion diagram is available. See order form.)

BLUEPRINT PRICE CODE: D

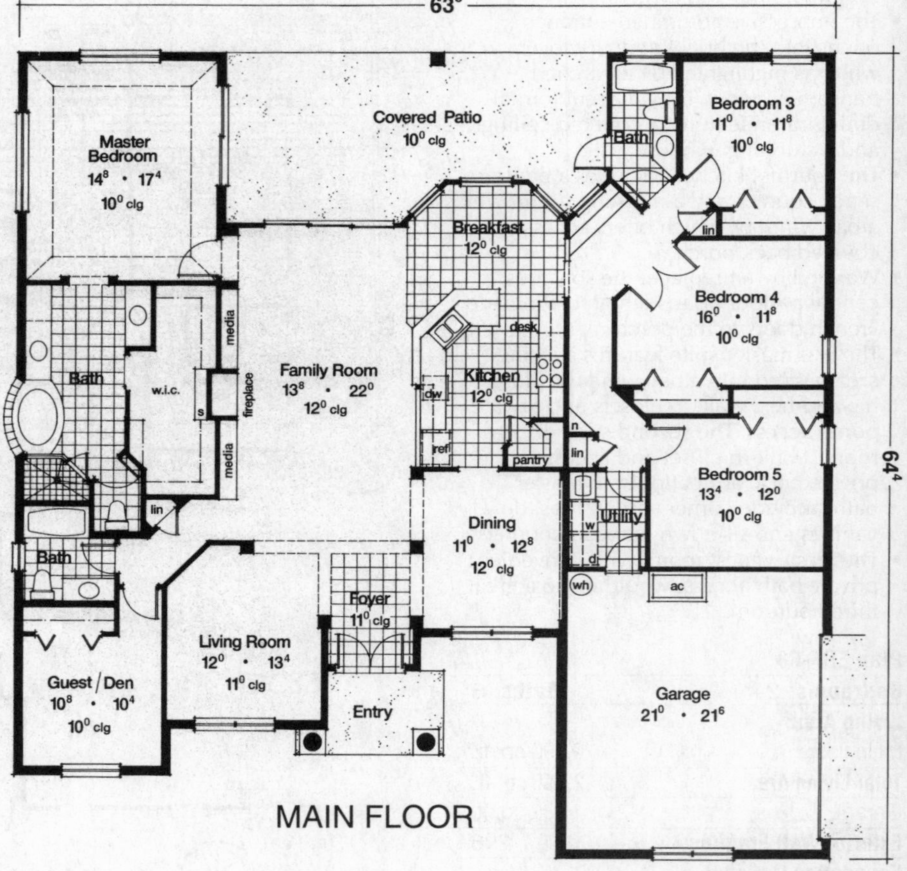

MAIN FLOOR

Plan HDS-99-297

Open Spaces

- The open design of this home includes front and rear porches that contribute to its indoor/outdoor feel. You'll appreciate the extra space for relaxing.
- Through the foyer lies the central Great Room, which boasts a handsome fireplace, built-in shelves and sidelighted French doors that open onto the rear porch.
- Cook up a gourmet meal in the modern kitchen, then serve it in the dignified dining room. Casual meals may be served at the handy snack bar or in the spacious breakfast nook, which is illuminated by an adjoining sun room.
- The master suite's private bath flaunts a large tub and two sinks, while the bedroom enjoys a wall of windows looking out to the backyard, and his-and-hers walk-in closets.
- A guest bedroom overlooking the front porch offers a private bath.
- Two secondary bedrooms share a private, compartmentalized bath that features a dual-sink vanity.
- This wing also features a walk-in pantry, a computer room and a large laundry room with plenty of space for your washer, dryer and freezer.

Plan DP-2726	
Bedrooms: 4	**Baths:** 3½
Living Area:	
Main floor	2,726 sq. ft.
Total Living Area:	**2,726 sq. ft.**
Garage and storage	598 sq. ft.
Exterior Wall Framing:	2x4
Foundation Options:	
Slab	

(All plans can be built with your choice of foundation and framing. A generic conversion diagram is available. See order form.)

BLUEPRINT PRICE CODE: **D**

REAR VIEW

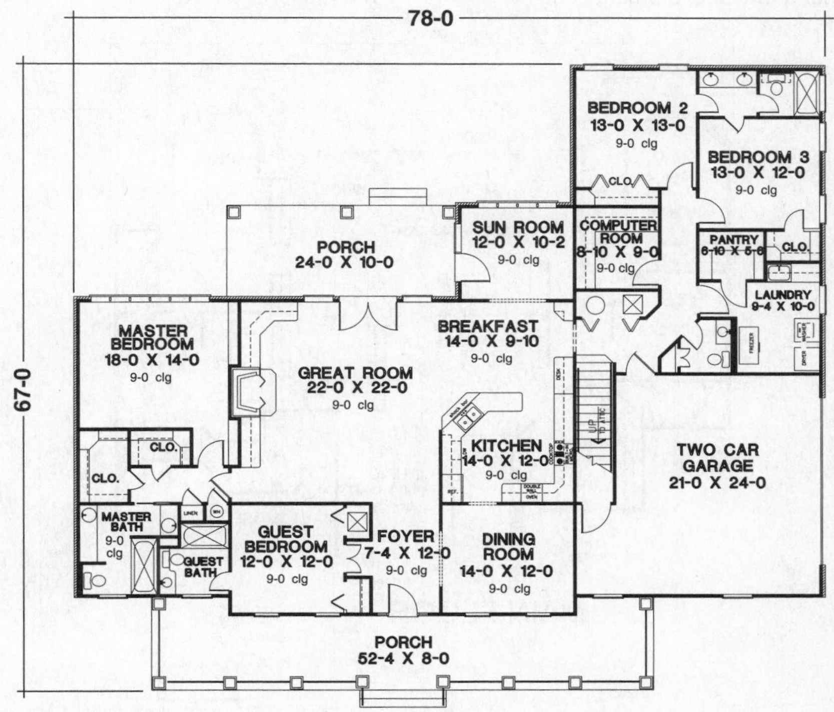

MAIN FLOOR

Your Hard Work Pays Off!

- A smile will come to your face as you realize that all the years you've worked and saved have paid off handsomely with a great life in this luxurious home!
- Quoins, keystones and exquisite window treatments highlight a stylish stucco and brick exterior that treats visitors to a strong first impression.
- Inside, the enormous family room is the center of attention. Guests can gather around the entertainment center or soak up the cool evening air while sipping drinks and sampling hors d'oeuvres out on a huge back porch.
- Incredibly appointed, the fantastic master suite offers its occupants a pair of walk-in closets, a dreamy private bath and a beautiful bayed sitting area.
- On the opposite side of the home is a guest bedroom with its own access to a full bath. Another bedroom and a cozy study, which easily converts to a fourth bedroom, are also found here.
- An unfinished bonus room above the garage can be utilized as a home office, a hobby room or an extra bedroom when the need arises.

Plan KLF-9712

Bedrooms: 3+ **Baths:** 3

Living Area:

Main floor	2,958 sq. ft.
Total Living Area:	**3,213 sq. ft.**
Bonus room	255 sq. ft.
Garage/golf cart storage	672 sq. ft.
Exterior Wall Framing:	2x4

Foundation Options:

Slab

(All plans can be built with your choice of foundation and framing. A generic conversion diagram is available. See order form.)

BLUEPRINT PRICE CODE: E

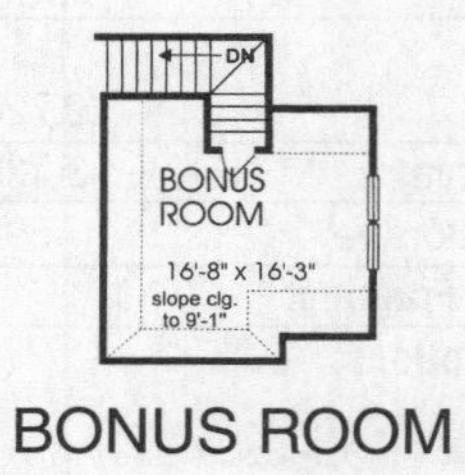

BONUS ROOM

ORDER BLUEPRINTS ANYTIME!
CALL TOLL-FREE 1-800-820-1296

Plan KLF-9712

Plan copyright held by home designer/architect

SEE ORDER INFO ON PAGES 12-15
familyhandyman.com/homeplans

Master Suite Fit for a King

- This sprawling one-story features an extraordinary master suite that stretches from the front of the home to the back.
- Eye-catching windows and columns introduce the foyer, which flows back to the Grand Room. French doors open to the covered veranda, which offers a fabulous summer kitchen.
- The kitchen and bayed morning room are nestled between the Grand Room and a warm Gathering Room. A striking fireplace, an entertainment center and an ale bar are found here.
- The isolated master suite features a stunning two-sided fireplace and an octagonal lounge area with veranda access. His-and-hers closets, separate dressing areas and a garden tub are other amenities. Across the home, three additional bedroom suites have private access to one of two more full baths.
- The private dining room at the front of the home has a coffered ceiling and a niche for a china cabinet.
- An oversized laundry room is located across from the kitchen and near the entrance to the three-car garage.

Plan EOF-60	
Bedrooms: 4	**Baths:** 3
Living Area:	
Main floor	3,002 sq. ft.
Total Living Area:	**3,002 sq. ft.**
Garage	660 sq. ft.
Exterior Wall Framing:	2x6
Foundation Options:	
Slab	
(All plans can be built with your choice of foundation and framing. A generic conversion diagram is available. See order form.)	
BLUEPRINT PRICE CODE:	**E**

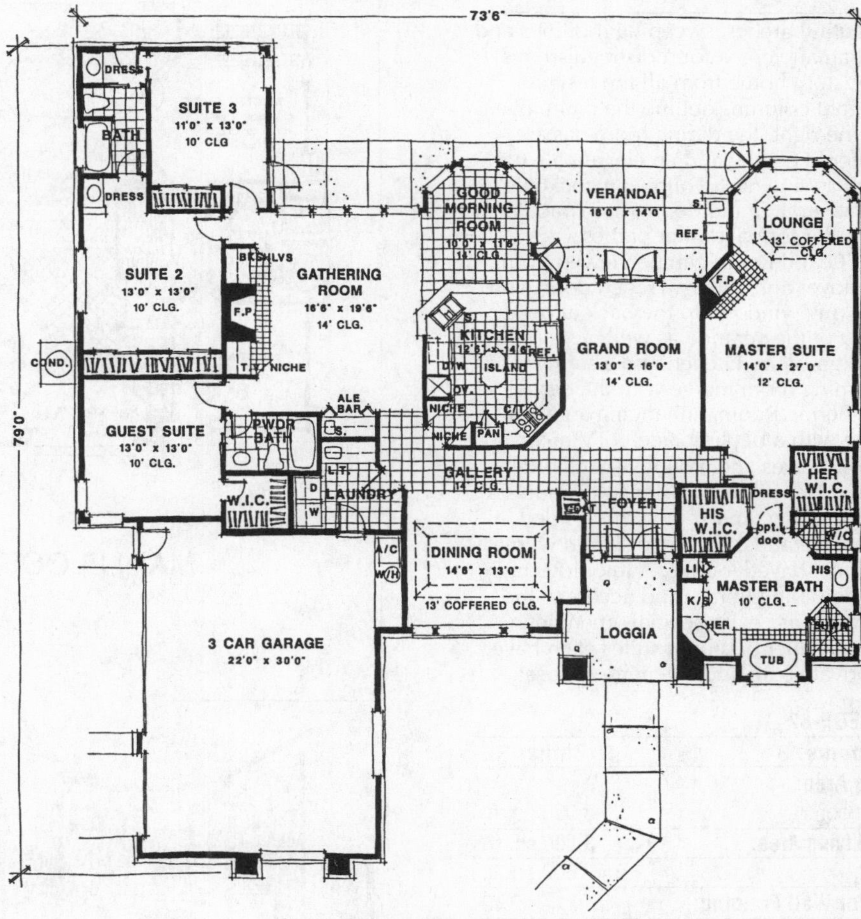

MAIN FLOOR

Distinguished Living

- Beautiful arches, sweeping rooflines and a dramatic entry court distinguish this one-story home from all the rest.
- Elegant columns outline the main foyer. To the right, the dining room has a coffered ceiling and an elegant ale bar with a wine rack. Following cocktails in the central Grand Room, this space is ideal for formal dinner parties.
- The Grand Room can be viewed from the foyer and gallery. French doors and flanking windows to the back allow a view of the veranda as well.
- A large island kitchen and a sunny morning room merge with the casual Gathering Room, enhancing together time with a big fireplace, a TV niche, bookshelves and a handy snack bar.
- The extraordinary master suite flaunts a high ceiling, an exciting three-sided fireplace and a TV niche shared with a private, bayed lounge. A luxurious bath, an adjoining library and access to the veranda are extra-special amenities.
- Two smaller bedroom suites each have a private bath and a generous closet.

Plan EOF-62	
Bedrooms: 3+	**Baths:** 3½
Living Area:	
Main floor	3,090 sq. ft.
Total Living Area:	**3,090 sq. ft.**
Garage	660 sq. ft.
Exterior Wall Framing:	2x6
Foundation Options:	
Slab	

(All plans can be built with your choice of foundation and framing. A generic conversion diagram is available. See order form.)

BLUEPRINT PRICE CODE: E

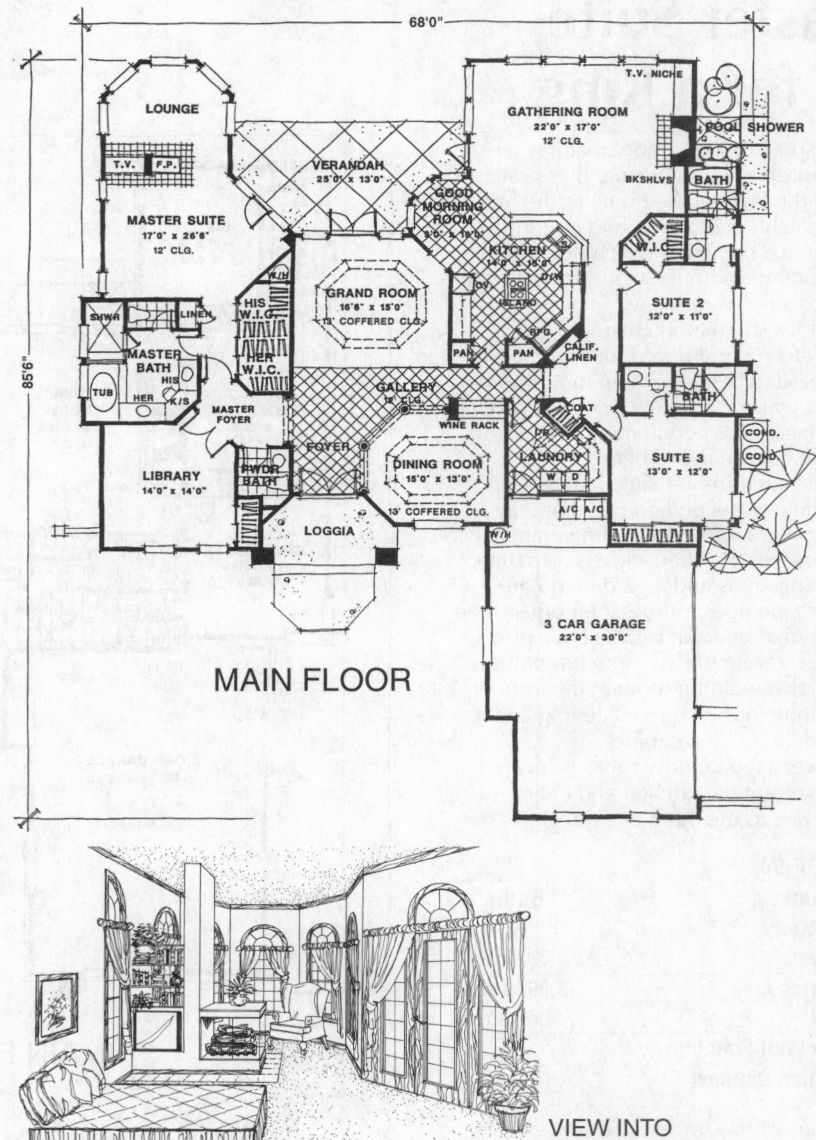

VIEW INTO MASTER SUITE

All Good Things

- This stone-sturdy home pleases the eye with a rustic, country facade and a multitude of interior luxuries.
- Designed with your loved ones in mind, the family room, island kitchen and bayed breakfast nook flow into each other for a feeling of togetherness. From the nook, a huge backyard deck is quickly accessible.
- For formal gatherings, the living and dining rooms serve effortlessly. The living room hosts a cozy fireplace, and columns distinguish the dining room.
- The master suite epitomizes comfort, with its private deck and adjoining office space. Opulence is apparent in the master bath, which features a spa tub, a separate shower, a dual-sink vanity and two walk-in closets.
- Two additional bedrooms share a full hall bath. The foremost bedroom boasts a cheery bay window, and could serve as a comfortable study.
- A stunning guest suite delivers a private deck and a kitchen area. With its full bath, it's the perfect spot for long-term guests or relatives who are enjoying their golden years.

Plan DD-3152

Bedrooms: 3+	**Baths:** 3½
Living Area:	
Main floor	3,164 sq. ft.
Total Living Area:	**3,164 sq. ft.**
Standard basement	3,164 sq. ft.
Garage and storage	736 sq. ft.
Exterior Wall Framing:	2x4
Foundation Options:	
Standard basement	
Crawlspace	
Slab	

(All plans can be built with your choice of foundation and framing. A generic conversion diagram is available. See order form.)

BLUEPRINT PRICE CODE: E

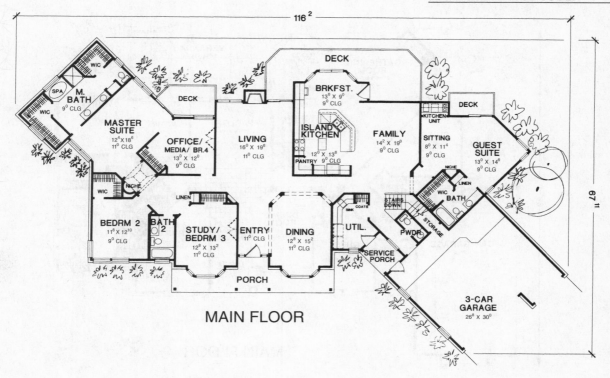

116²
67¹¹
DECK
BRKFST. 13⁶ X 9⁰ 9⁰ CLG
DECK
SPA
M. BATH 9⁰ CLG
WIC
WIC
MASTER SUITE 12⁴ X 18⁶ 11⁰ CLG
OFFICE/ MEDIA/ BR.4 13⁰ X 12⁰ 9⁰ CLG
LIVING 16⁰ X 19⁶ 11⁰ CLG
ISLAND KITCHEN 12⁰ X 13⁶ 9⁰ CLG
PANTRY
FAMILY 14² X 19⁰ 9⁰ CLG
KITCHEN UNIT
DECK
SITTING 8⁰ X 11⁴ 9⁰ CLG
GUEST SUITE 13⁰ X 14⁶ 9⁰ CLG
NICHE
WIC
NICHE
LINEN
WIC
BATH
LINEN
STAIRS DOWN
SINK
COATS
BEDRM 2 11⁶ X 12¹⁰ 9⁰ CLG
BATH 2
STUDY/ BEDRM 3 12⁸ X 13² 11⁰ CLG
ENTRY 11⁰ CLG
DINING 12⁸ X 15² 11⁰ CLG
UTIL.
PWDR.
STORAGE
SERVICE PORCH
PORCH
3-CAR GARAGE 26⁸ X 30⁰

MAIN FLOOR

Lap of Luxury

- Entering this stunning, feature-filled one-story estate means entering a world of luxury and comfort.
- The open foyer is brightened by an arched transom window. Introduced by an archway, the adjacent formal dining room features a unique ale bar.
- The bright and airy parlor offers French doors to a covered backyard veranda. An outside stairway accesses the partial daylight basement.
- The island kitchen includes a menu desk, a pantry and a panoramic morning room.
- A handsome fireplace with a built-in wood box and a media center enhance the inviting Gathering Room.
- Double doors lead into the master suite, which features built-in bookshelves and cabinets. A sitting room provides private outdoor access. The master bath showcases a corner garden tub, a separate shower, dual vanities and roomy his-and-hers walk-in closets.
- A second bedroom, a guest suite, and a library or fourth bedroom complete the home's innovative floor plan.
- High ceilings add spaciousness to the main living areas, the bedrooms, the library and all three baths.

Plan EOF-63

Bedrooms: 3+	**Baths:** 3
Living Area:	
Main floor	3,316 sq. ft.
Total Living Area:	**3,316 sq. ft.**
Partial daylight basement	550 sq. ft.
Garage	496 sq. ft.
Exterior Wall Framing:	2x6
Foundation Options:	
Partial daylight basement	

(All plans can be built with your choice of foundation and framing. A generic conversion diagram is available. See order form.)

BLUEPRINT PRICE CODE: E

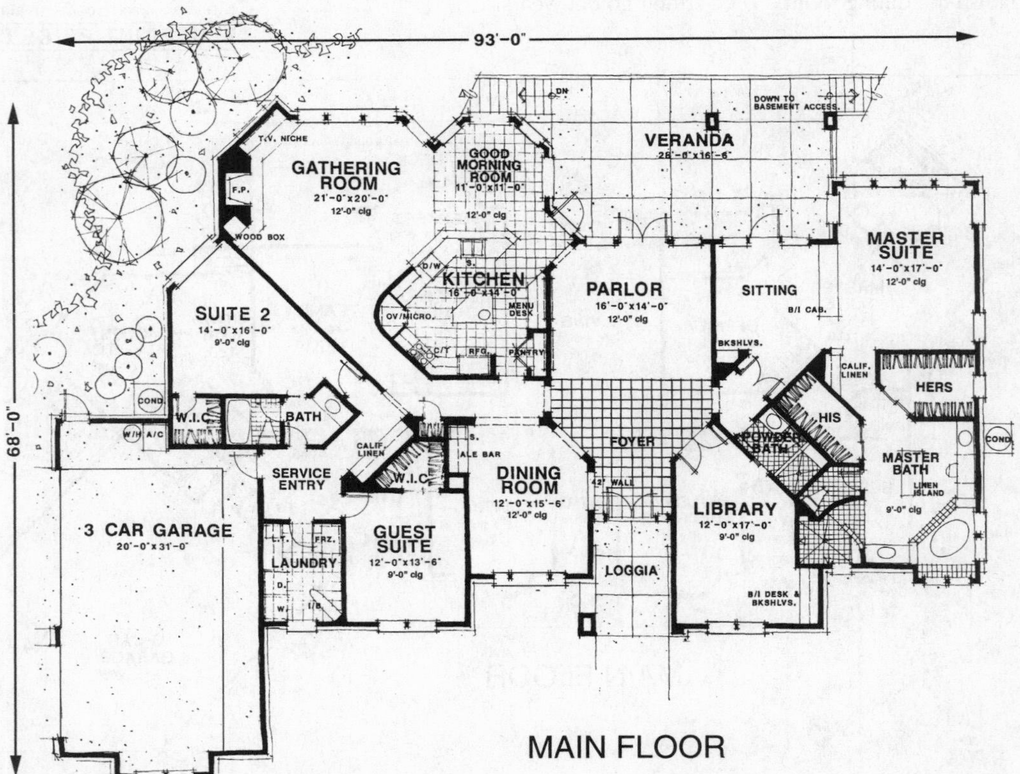

MAIN FLOOR

Plan EOF-63

SEE ORDER INFO ON PAGES 12-15

Beautiful Blend

- This home features an eclectic blend of amenities, beginning with a shady wraparound front porch, and ending with a soothing courtyard that is dominated by a pool, a spa, planters and access from all areas of the home.
- Inside, the foyer is flanked by the formal dining room and a columned music room. A gathering room straight ahead has a vaulted ceiling and three sets of French doors leading to the courtyard.
- The island kitchen features easy access to a nearby office and laundry room, plus an eating nook, a wet bar and a pass-through to a fireside library.
- The relaxing library is lined with built-in bookshelves and warmed by a fireplace. Nearby, a guest suite features a walk-in closet and a private bath.
- Just past the exciting home theater, the master bedroom boasts a large walk-in closet, three sets of French doors opening to the courtyard, and a private bath with an oversized shower, a corner garden tub and a dual-sink vanity.
- Two more bedrooms share a full hall bath, which also serves the pool area.

Plan HDS-99-325

Bedrooms: 4+	**Baths:** 3½
Living Area:	
Main floor	3,386 sq. ft.
Total Living Area:	**3,386 sq. ft.**
Future area	444 sq. ft.
Garage	765 sq. ft.
Exterior Wall Framing:	2x4
Foundation Options:	
Slab	

(All plans can be built with your choice of foundation and framing. A generic conversion diagram is available. See order form.)

BLUEPRINT PRICE CODE: E

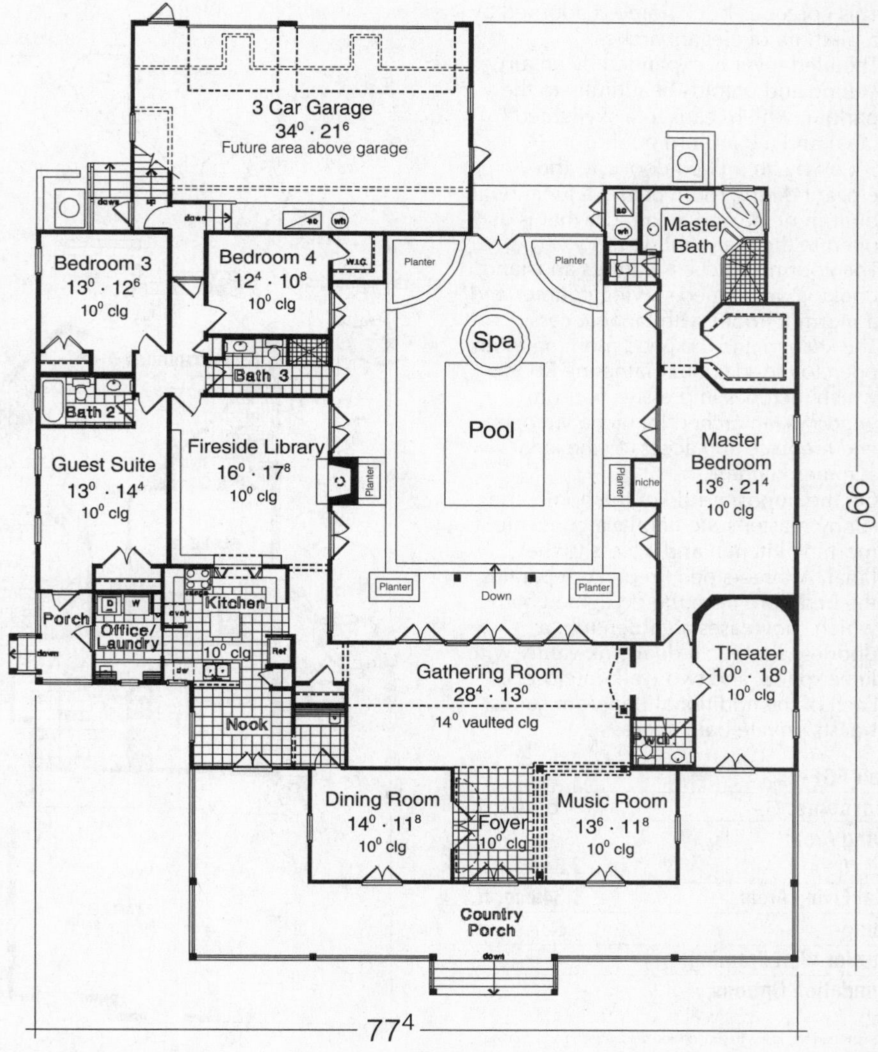

MAIN FLOOR

Elegant Arches

- This gorgeous brick home is adorned by a plethora of elegant arches.
- The tiled foyer is expanded by an airy ceiling and unfolds beautifully to the parlour, which leads to a skylighted lanai and a backyard pool.
- Set off by an arched doorway, the elegant dining room boasts a functional built-in niche and an ale bar that is open to the main hallway.
- The gourmet kitchen features an island cooktop, an angled serving counter and a morning room with lanai access.
- The kitchen and the good morning room open to the spacious Gathering Room, which includes impressive transom windows, an arched TV niche, an open-end fireplace and access to the lanai's summer kitchen.
- On the opposite side of the home, the sunny master suite flaunts a convenient morning kitchen and access to the lanai. A three-sided fireplace separates the bedroom from the skylighted bath, which showcases a garden tub, a doorless shower, a dual-sink vanity with knee space, and two walk-in closets.
- Each of the additional bedroom suites boasts private bath access.

Plan EOF-74

Bedrooms: 3+	**Baths:** 4
Living Area:	
Main floor	3,349 sq. ft.
Total Living Area:	**3,349 sq. ft.**
Garage	527 sq. ft.
Exterior Wall Framing:	2x6
Foundation Options:	
Slab	

(All plans can be built with your choice of foundation and framing. A generic conversion diagram is available. See order form.)

BLUEPRINT PRICE CODE: E

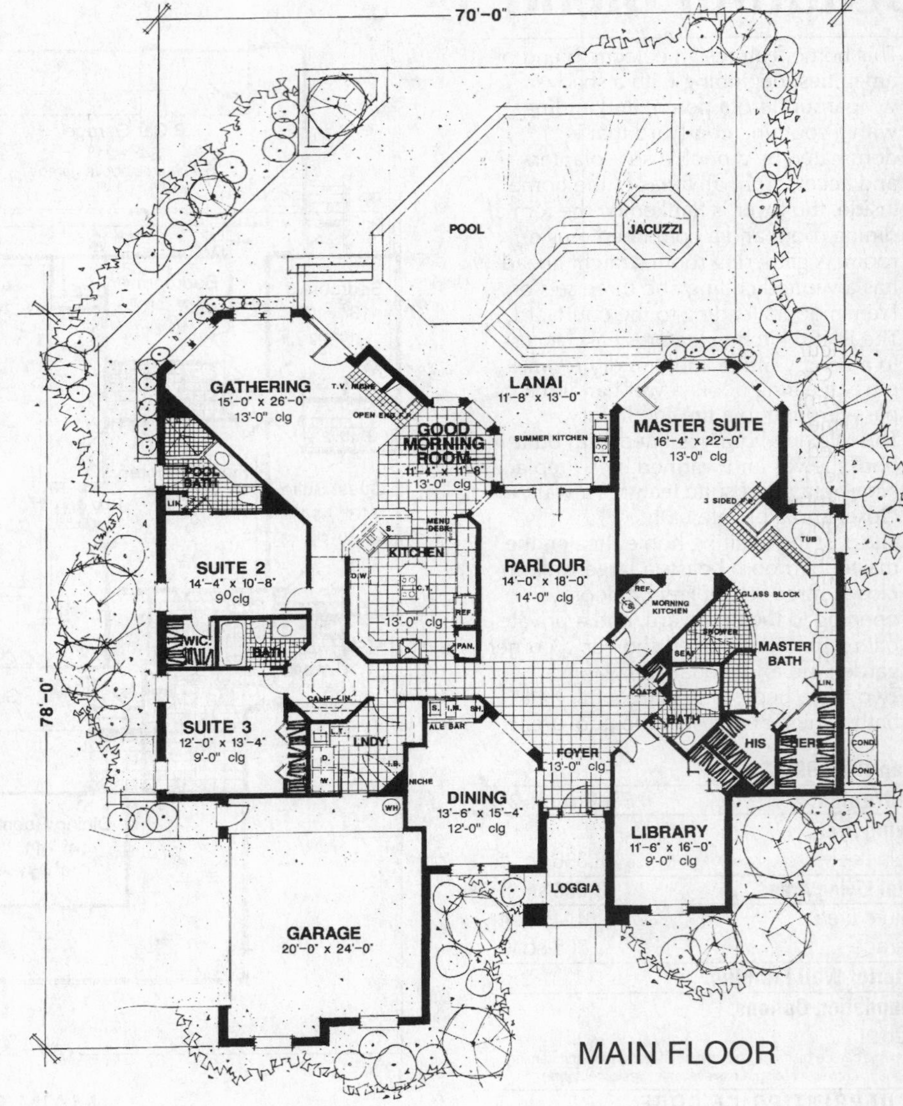

MAIN FLOOR

Opulence Rules

- Opulence is the rule in this spectacular home. Volume ceilings and striking columns create an atmosphere of grandeur, while the modern design ensures livability.
- Welcome guests in the foyer, which offers views to the home's formal areas.
- Tapered columns lead to either the sunken living room, flooded with light from a spectacular arched window, or the elegant dining room, where French doors open to the starry night.
- Spectacular columns frame the fireplace in the Great Room. Built-in shelves hold everything from family photos to media equipment. Sliding glass doors access a screened patio that sports a sizzling summer kitchen.
- A columned serving bar wraps around the island kitchen between the dining room and the sunny breakfast nook.
- Bold angles, volume ceilings and a circular glass-block shower distinguish the master suite. The whirlpool tub basks in light from two large windows, and French doors lead from the bayed bedroom onto the screened patio.

Plan HDS-99-217

Bedrooms: 5	**Baths:** 4
Living Area:	
Main floor	3,448 sq. ft.
Total Living Area:	**3,448 sq. ft.**
Screened patio	680 sq. ft.
Garage	782 sq. ft.

Exterior Wall Framing:
2x4 and 8-in. concrete block

Foundation Options:
Slab
(All plans can be built with your choice of foundation and framing. A generic conversion diagram is available. See order form.)

BLUEPRINT PRICE CODE: E

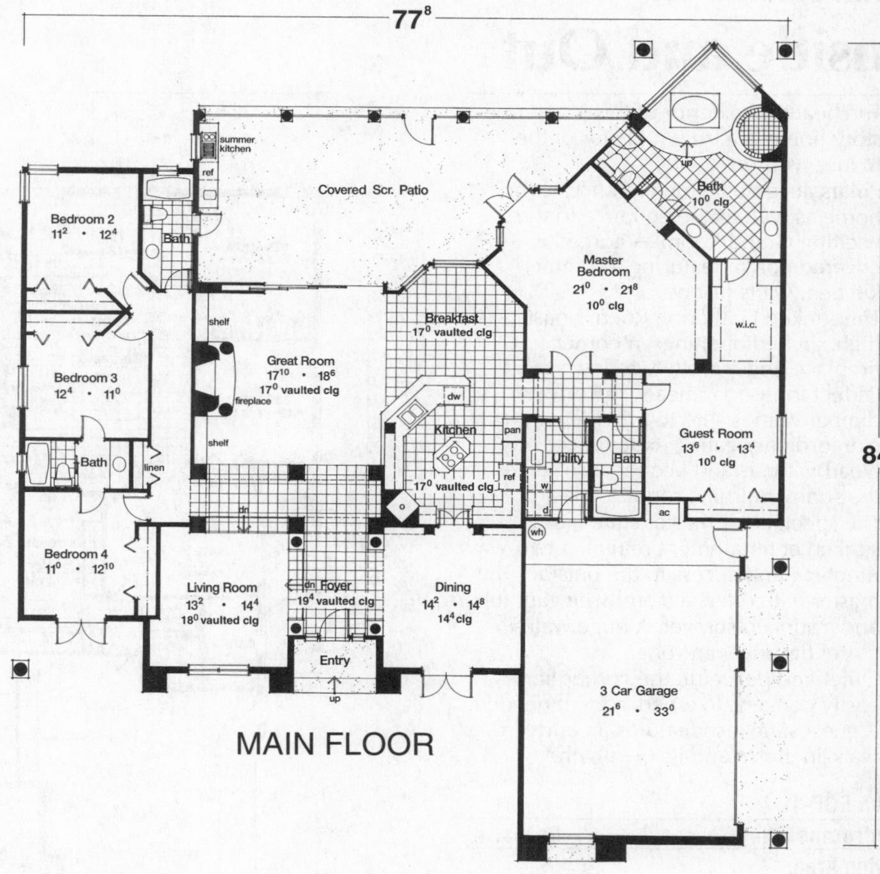

MAIN FLOOR

Luxurious Inside and Out

- The beautiful exterior of this grand one-story home is a true indicator of the luxury within.
- Pillars accentuate the entrance of the home as well as the entrance to the exciting Grand Room. A gorgeous covered porch, featuring a summer kitchen, waits just beyond.
- The sunken Gathering Room boasts high, arched openings, a corner fireplace and a pretty window seat.
- Perfect for formal meals, the private dining room is sure to provide an extraordinary eating experience. Nearby, the island kitchen also serves the sunny morning room.
- The spectacular master suite has a sunken entertainment retreat, a two-way fireplace and access to the outside. The master bath offers a sinfully elegant tub and a sunken shower. A huge walk-in closet fits any wardrobe.
- Quiet and peaceful, the corner library easily converts to a bedroom, if needed.
- A guest suite also features a courtyard, a walk-in closet and its own bath.

Plan EOF-1

Bedrooms: 4+	**Baths:** 4
Living Area:	
Main floor	3,903 sq. ft.
Total Living Area:	**3,903 sq. ft.**
Garage	748 sq. ft.
Exterior Wall Framing:	2x4
Foundation Options:	
Slab	

(All plans can be built with your choice of foundation and framing. A generic conversion diagram is available. See order form.)

BLUEPRINT PRICE CODE: F

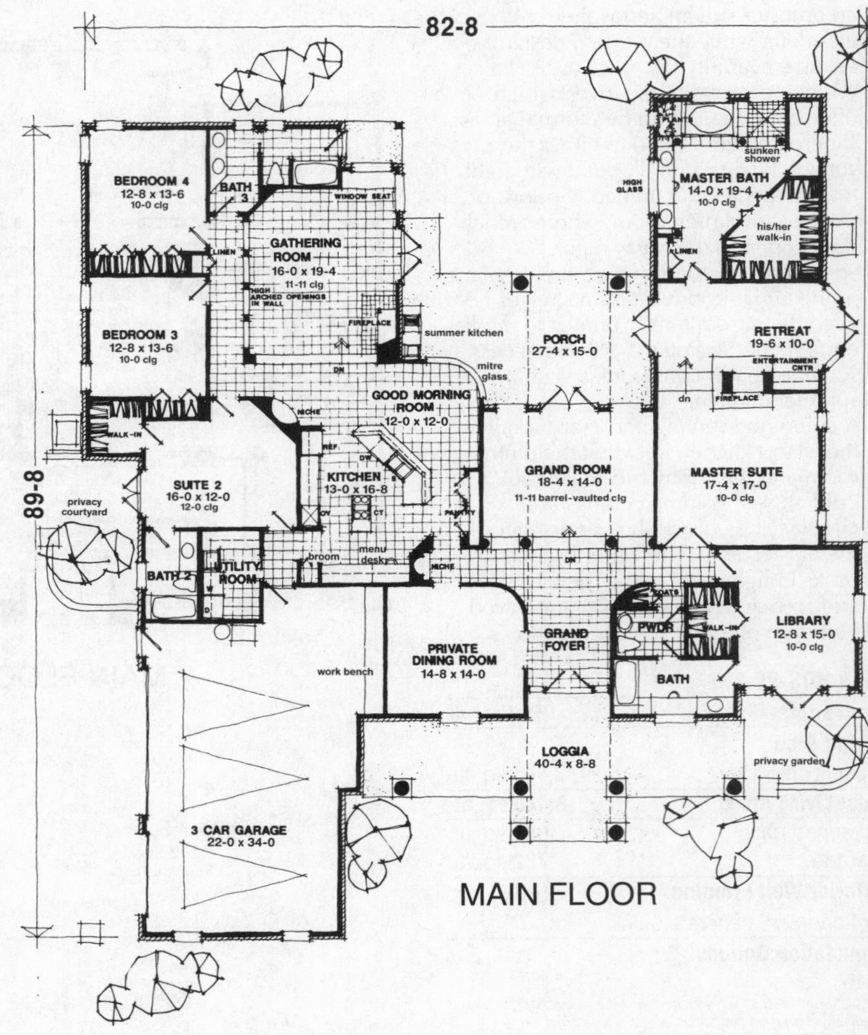

Grand Hall

- Imagine welcoming guests in the grand entry hall of this fantastic home. Guide them into the formal living room, with its intriguing window arrangements, and then into the formal dining room for a gourmet feast.
- Prepare that feast in the roomy, central kitchen, which boasts every amenity from a walk-in pantry to an eating bar. The adjacent vaulted nook is perfect for casual meals.
- Step down into the sun-brightened family room, which is warmed by a handsome fireplace. Help yourself to a drink from the wet bar and step out onto the huge rear deck and patio.
- Luxury reigns in the fabulous master suite. Step in from a private patio and settle into the sitting area, which shares a three-sided fireplace with a raised whirlpool tub; the open bath beyond includes a huge walk-in closet.
- Twin sets of French doors open from either end into the angled den. The option room beyond the large laundry room includes a full bath and private access to the patio, making it ideal as a guest suite.

Plan P-7740-4A	
Bedrooms: 2+	**Baths:** 3½
Living Area:	
Main floor	3,653 sq. ft.
Option room	271 sq. ft.
Total Living Area:	**3,924 sq. ft.**
Garage A	535 sq. ft.
Garage B	351 sq. ft.
Patio storage	30 sq. ft.
Exterior Wall Framing:	2x6
Foundation Options:	
Crawlspace	

(All plans can be built with your choice of foundation and framing. A generic conversion diagram is available. See order form.)

BLUEPRINT PRICE CODE: F

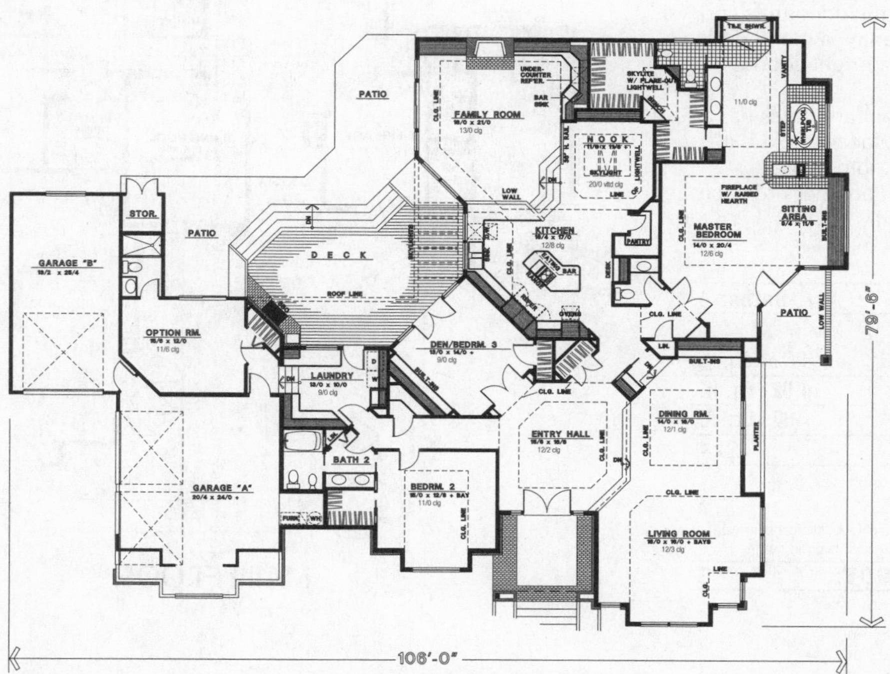

MAIN FLOOR

Tall and Proud

- This stately home's proud exterior gives way to a luxurious and impressive interior.
- The step-down parlour is the home's centerpiece, and boasts a high ceiling and a full-wall fireplace and entertainment center.
- The master suite features a step-down sitting room and a corner fireplace. The opulent master bath has a linen island, a morning kitchen and a bidet.
- The library offers private access to the main hall bath.
- Graceful arches and a high, coffered ceiling adorn the formal dining room.
- The spacious kitchen includes an island cooktop, a walk-in pantry, a menu desk, a vegetable sink and a bright good morning room.
- Each of the three secondary suites has a large closet and direct access to a bath.
- The huge Gathering Room boasts wraparound glass and another fireplace and entertainment wall.

Plan EOF-58

Bedrooms: 4+ **Baths:** 4

Living Area:

Main floor 4,021 sq. ft.

Total Living Area: 4,021 sq. ft.

Garage 879 sq. ft.

Exterior Wall Framing: 2x4

Foundation Options:

Slab

(All plans can be built with your choice of foundation and framing. A generic conversion diagram is available. See order form.)

BLUEPRINT PRICE CODE: G

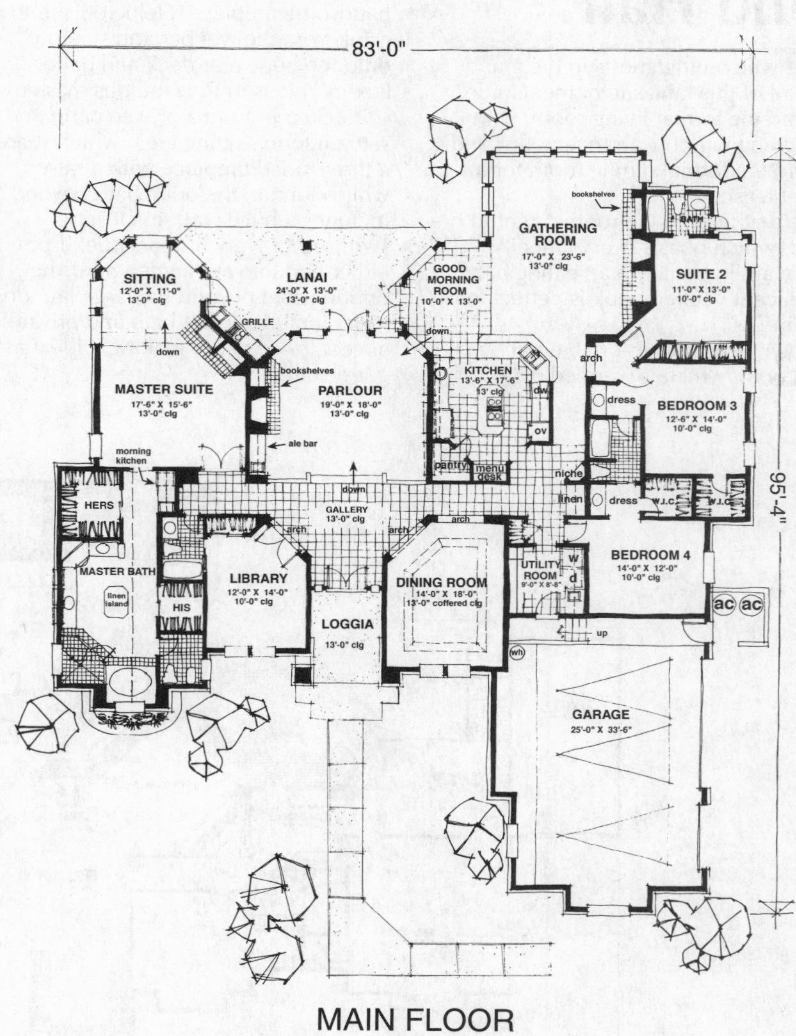

MAIN FLOOR

Plan EOF-58

SEE ORDER INFO ON PAGES 12-15

Sprawl Appeal

- This sprawling one-story offers plenty of room for relaxation and recreation.
- Striking columns and a stepped ceiling set off the formal dining room, which shows off a handsome arched hutch. Weary travelers may stay the night in the neighboring guest bedroom.
- A coffered ceiling adorns the huge sunken living room. Above the central fireplace is a gorgeous mantel; alongside are beautiful glass and wood cabinets, and adjustable shelves. French doors give way to a covered deck.
- Serenity reigns in the secluded master bedroom, which is crowned by a stepped ceiling and furnished with French doors that open to the backyard. The adjoining office space may double as a restful sitting room.
- The master bath promises ultimate comfort, with a fabulous tub under a glass-block wall, plus a separate shower and a dual-sink vanity. Two walk-in closets and a private toilet round out the amenities.
- French doors open to the deck from both the bright family room and the adjoining morning room. A long snack bar unites the morning room with the kitchen, which has an island cooktop.
- Near the library is a cluster of four spacious bedrooms that share two full baths. Built-in desks and shelves grace all four bedrooms.

Plan DD-4286

Bedrooms: 6+	**Baths:** 4
Living Area:	
Main floor	4,666 sq. ft.
Total Living Area:	**4,666 sq. ft.**
Standard basement	4,666 sq. ft.
Garage	925 sq. ft.
Exterior Wall Framing:	2x4
Foundation Options:	
Standard basement	
Crawlspace	
Slab	

(All plans can be built with your choice of foundation and framing. A generic conversion diagram is available. See order form.)

BLUEPRINT PRICE CODE: H

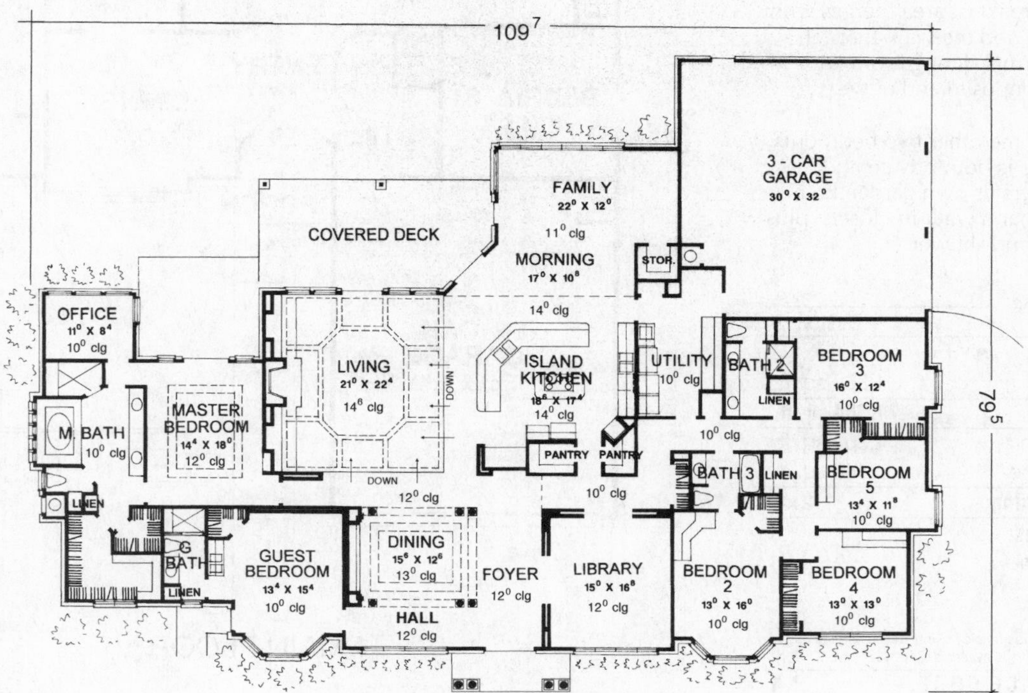

MAIN FLOOR

Compact Home Big on Style

- While compact in size, this stylish one-story presents an open, flowing floor plan with little wasted space.
- Staggered rooflines, elaborate brick accents and beautiful arched windows smarten the exterior.
- The interior offers a large central living room with a high ceiling and a warming fireplace flanked by sparkling windows. A comfortable back patio is the perfect spot to relax on a warm spring day.
- The spacious breakfast area merges with the living room and the walk-through kitchen. The formal dining room is located at the opposite end of the kitchen.
- Separated from the other two bedrooms, the master suite is both private and spacious. It offers its own garden bath with twin sinks and walk-in closets, plus a separate tub and shower.

Plan DD-1296	
Bedrooms: 3	**Baths:** 2
Living Area:	
Main floor	1,364 sq. ft.
Total Living Area:	**1,364 sq. ft.**
Standard basement	1,364 sq. ft.
Garage and storage	443 sq. ft.
Exterior Wall Framing:	2x4
Foundation Options:	
Standard basement	
Crawlspace	
Slab	

(All plans can be built with your choice of foundation and framing. A generic conversion diagram is available. See order form.)

BLUEPRINT PRICE CODE: A

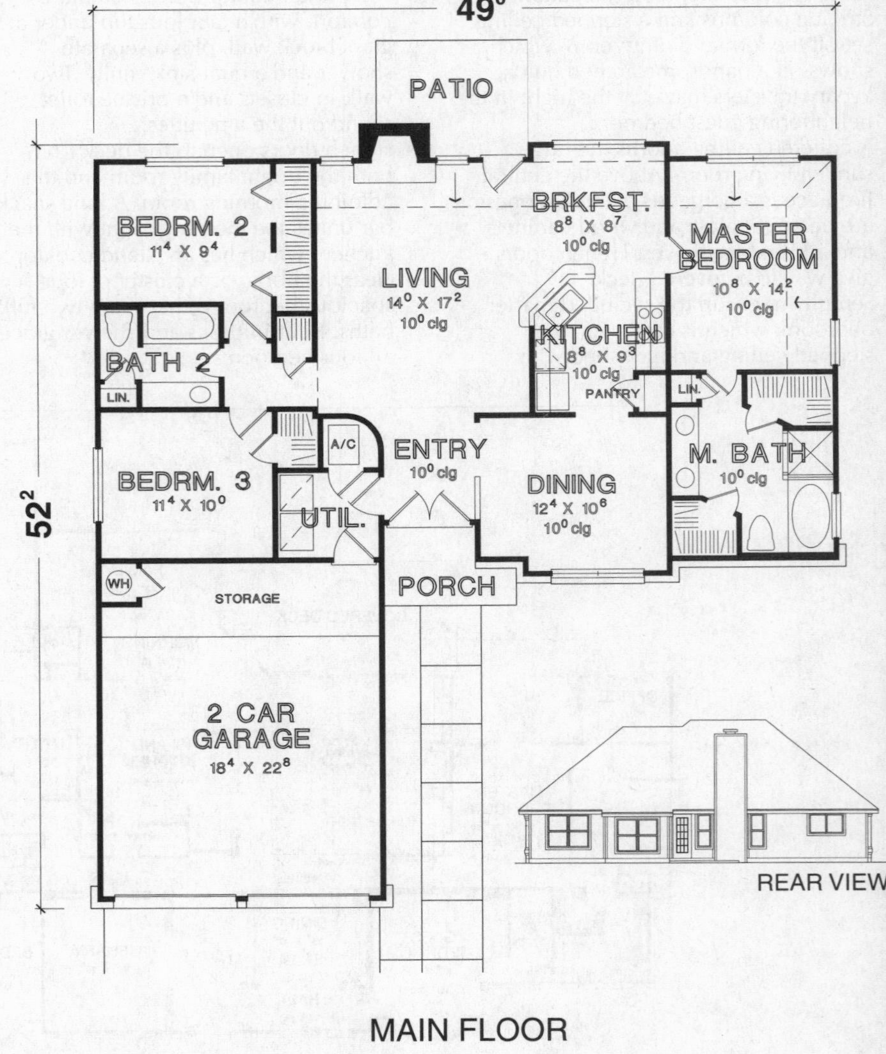

Plan DD-1296

SEE ORDER INFO ON PAGES 12-15
familyhandyman.com/homeplans

Victorian Form

- This beautiful home flaunts true-to-form Victorian styling in a modest one-story.
- A delightful, covered front porch and a stunning, sidelighted entry give way to the welcoming foyer.
- The foyer flows into the Great Room, which is warmed by a corner fireplace and topped by a stepped ceiling.
- Sliding French doors open to the backyard from both the Great Room and the adjoining formal dining room.
- On the other side of the open kitchen, a turreted breakfast room overlooks the front porch with cheery windows under an incredible high ceiling!
- The restful master suite is graced by a charming window seat and crowned by a stepped ceiling. A dressing area leads to the master bath, which offers a separate tub and shower.
- To the right of the foyer, two more bedrooms share a hall bath. One bedroom features an impressive vaulted ceiling.

VIEW INTO BREAKFAST ROOM

Plan AX-94319	
Bedrooms: 3	**Baths:** 2
Living Area:	
Main floor	1,466 sq. ft.
Total Living Area:	**1,466 sq. ft.**
Standard basement	1,498 sq. ft.
Garage, storage and utility	483 sq. ft.
Exterior Wall Framing:	2x4
Foundation Options:	
Standard basement	
Crawlspace	
Slab	

(All plans can be built with your choice of foundation and framing. A generic conversion diagram is available. See order form.)

BLUEPRINT PRICE CODE: **A**

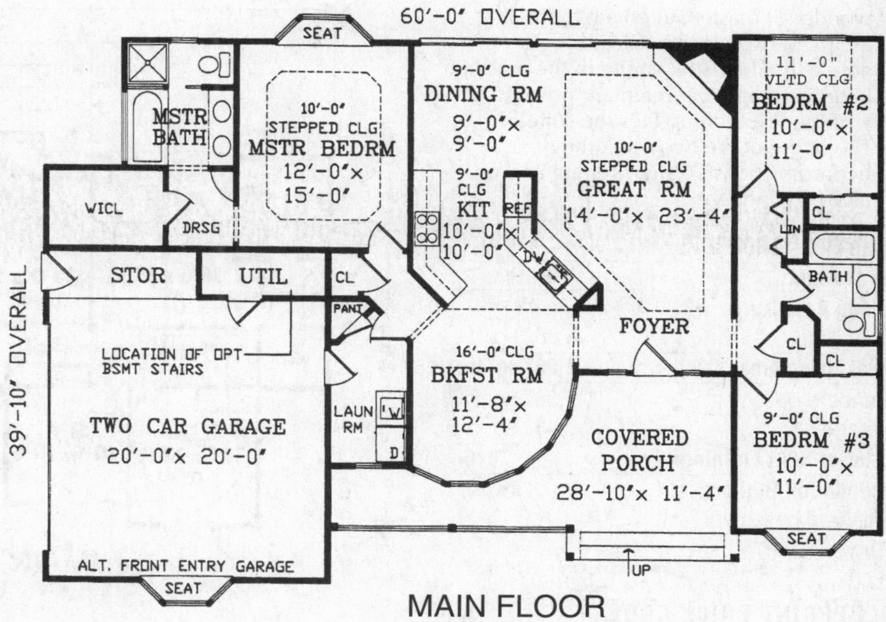

MAIN FLOOR

All in One!

- This plan puts today's most luxurious home-design features into one attractive, economical package.
- The covered front porch and the gabled roofline, accented by an arched window and a round louver vent, give the exterior a homey yet stylish appeal.
- Just inside the front door, the raised ceiling offers an impressive greeting. The living room is flooded with light through a central skylight and a pair of French doors that frame the fireplace.
- The living room flows into the nice-sized dining room, also with a raised ceiling. The adjoining kitchen offers a handy laundry closet, lots of counter space and a sunny dinette that opens to an expansive backyard terrace.
- The bedroom wing includes a wonderful master suite with a dressing area and two closets. Glass blocks above the dual-sink vanity in the master bath let in light yet maintain privacy. A whirlpool tub completes the suite.
- The larger of the two remaining bedrooms boasts a high ceiling and an arched window.

Plan HFL-1680-FL	
Bedrooms: 3	**Baths:** 2
Living Area:	
Main floor	1,367 sq. ft.
Total Living Area:	**1,367 sq. ft.**
Standard basement	1,367 sq. ft.
Garage	431 sq. ft.
Exterior Wall Framing:	2x6
Foundation Options:	
Standard basement	
Slab	

(All plans can be built with your choice of foundation and framing. A generic conversion diagram is available. See order form.)

BLUEPRINT PRICE CODE: A

VIEW INTO LIVING ROOM

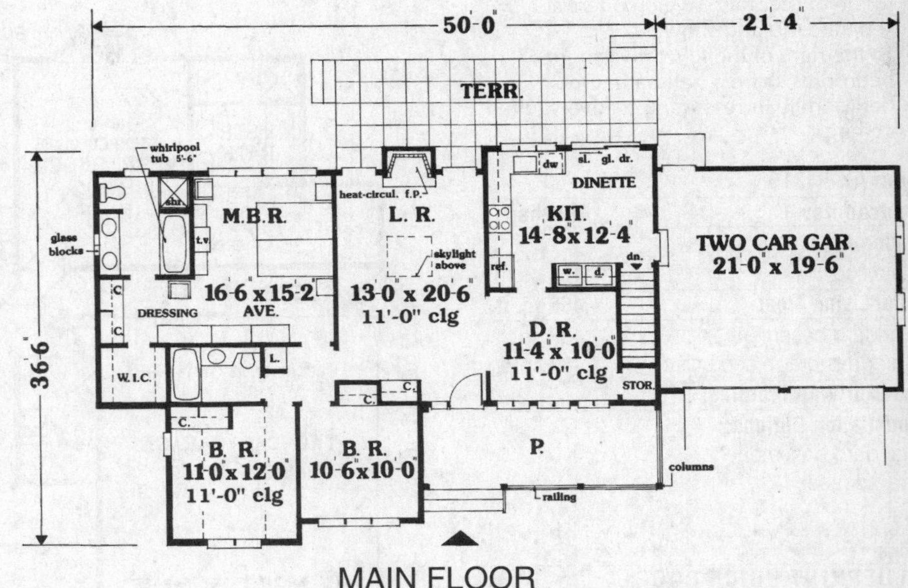

MAIN FLOOR

Plan HFL-1680-FL

SEE ORDER INFO ON PAGES 12-15
familyhandyman.com/homeplans

Ceilings to Notice

- Distinctive windows and lofty ceilings abound throughout this home, providing stylish spaciousness.
- An open arrangement allows easy communication in the home's common areas. The dining room is designed for formal use, yet remains exposed to the Great Room, allowing you to incorporate it into your day-to-day activities if you choose.
- A snack bar between the kitchen and the Great Room is perfect for serving evening TV snacks, while the bayed breakfast room is just right for a leisurely weekend brunch.
- The master suite offers a large walk-in closet and a luxurious private bath.
- Across the hall from the master suite, two bedrooms—both with dramatic vaulted ceilings—share a full bath. One bedroom is adorned with an arched, transom-topped window, while the other enjoys a bayed window seat.

Plan AX-1301

Bedrooms: 3	**Baths:** 2
Living Area:	
Main floor	1,489 sq. ft.
Total Living Area:	**1,489 sq. ft.**
Standard basement	1,489 sq. ft.
Garage	432 sq. ft.
Exterior Wall Framing:	2x6
Foundation Options:	
Standard basement	
Crawlspace	
Slab	

(All plans can be built with your choice of foundation and framing. A generic conversion diagram is available. See order form.)

BLUEPRINT PRICE CODE: A

VIEW INTO GREAT ROOM, KITCHEN AND BREAKFAST ROOM

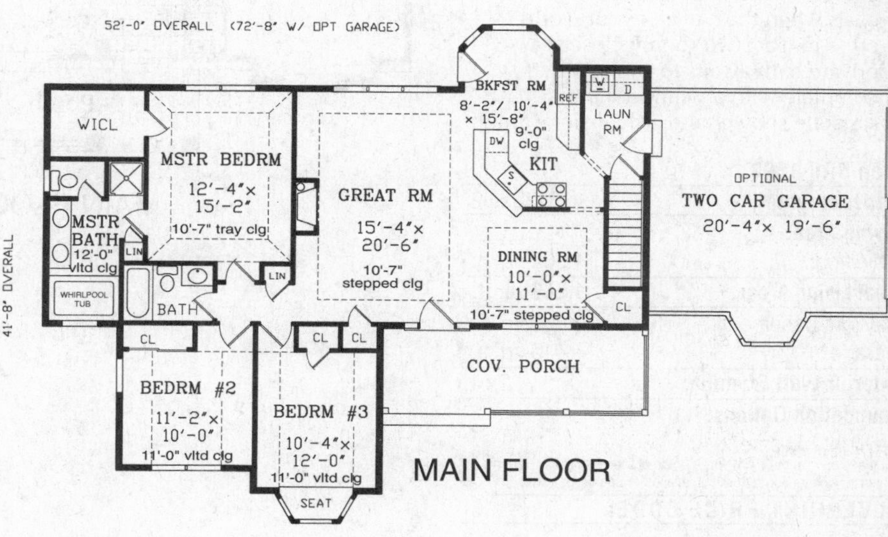

MAIN FLOOR

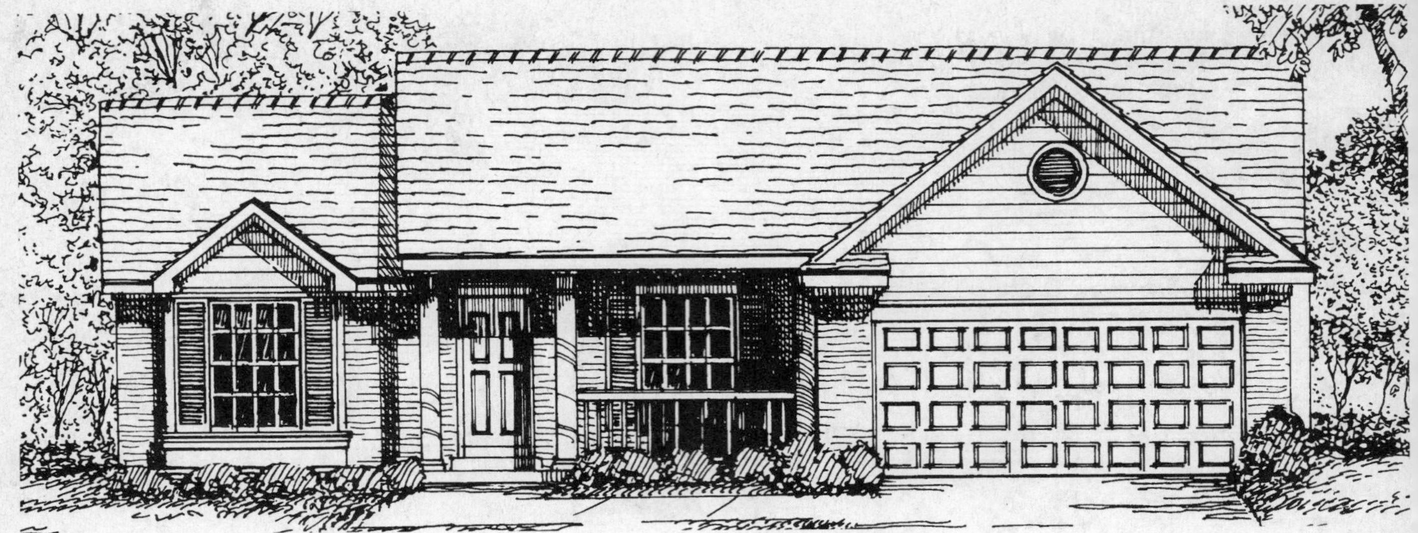

Wish You Were Here?

- This home's inviting front porch and welcoming interior is enough to make anyone wish for the sweet life within.
- With an air of mystery, the foyer allows guests a glimpse of the elegant dining room over a half-wall to the right.
- Ahead, the open living room leaves no room for guessing; its prominent fireplace practically begs you to pull up a chair and relax in the warmth.
- A serving bar brings a casual tone to your gatherings, and joins the living room to the kitchen. Here, you'll find vast counter space and an adjoining breakfast nook that should slow you down on those busy weekday mornings!
- Corner windows spruce up the master bedroom, which provides a pleasant oasis when the cares of your world press in. Past two roomy closets, a private bath awaits to spoil you, complete with a whirlpool tub, a separate shower and a dual-sink vanity.

Plan BRF-1502

Bedrooms: 3	**Baths:** 2
Living Area:	
Main floor	1,502 sq. ft.
Total Living Area:	**1,502 sq. ft.**
Daylight basement	1,502 sq. ft.
Garage	413 sq. ft.
Exterior Wall Framing:	2x4
Foundation Options:	
Daylight basement	
(All plans can be built with your choice of foundation and framing. A generic conversion diagram is available. See order form.)	
BLUEPRINT PRICE CODE:	**B**

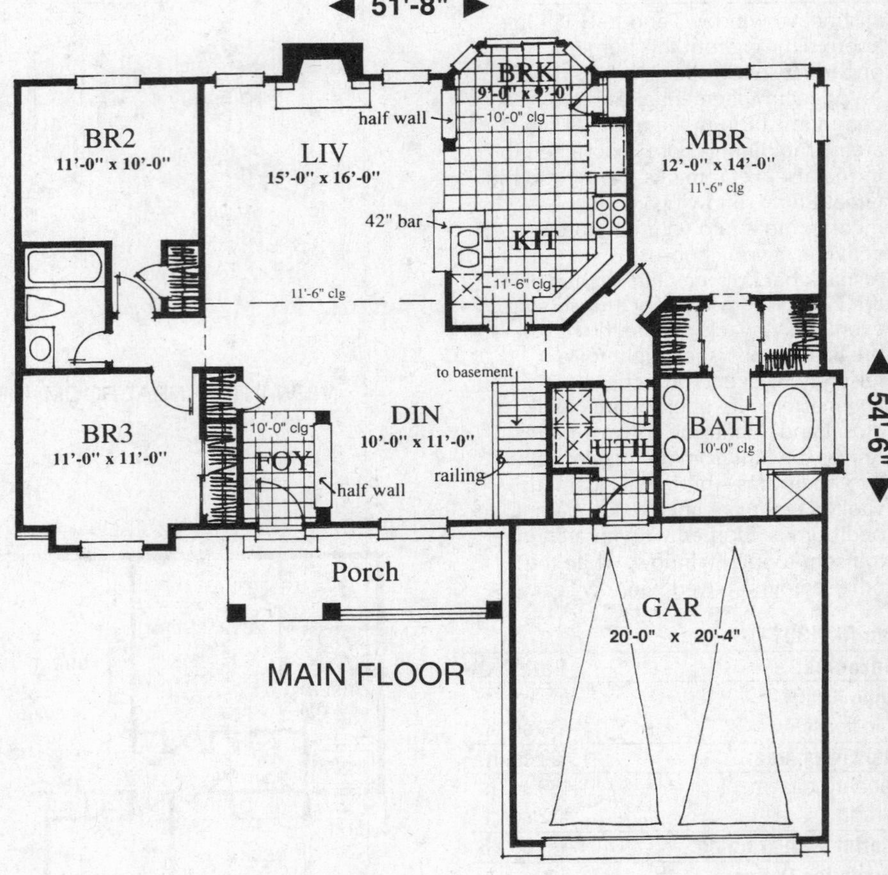

Mediterranean Mystique

- This home's keystone-enhanced stucco exterior and sweeping roofline give it a Mediterranean mystique.
- A double-door entry leads to the foyer, which is open to the formal living and dining areas. A vaulted ceiling crowns this space.
- Adjacent to the formal area, the family room offers plenty of room for relaxed gatherings. Another vaulted ceiling soars overhead.
- The open kitchen features a service counter and a high ceiling that is shared with the breakfast nook. An optional bay window and a high plant shelf enhance the nook.
- In the sleeping wing of the home, the master bedroom promises a calm retreat with its walk-in closet and lavish vaulted ceiling. The master bath flaunts a garden tub and a separate shower.
- Two secondary bedrooms off the formal areas share a full bath. All three bedrooms are dressed up with high plant shelves.

Plan HDS-99-222

Bedrooms: 3	**Baths:** 2
Living Area:	
Main floor	1,565 sq. ft.
Total Living Area:	**1,565 sq. ft.**
Garage	397 sq. ft.
Exterior Wall Framing:	2x4 or 8-in. concrete block

Foundation Options:

Slab

(All plans can be built with your choice of foundation and framing. A generic conversion diagram is available. See order form.)

BLUEPRINT PRICE CODE: B

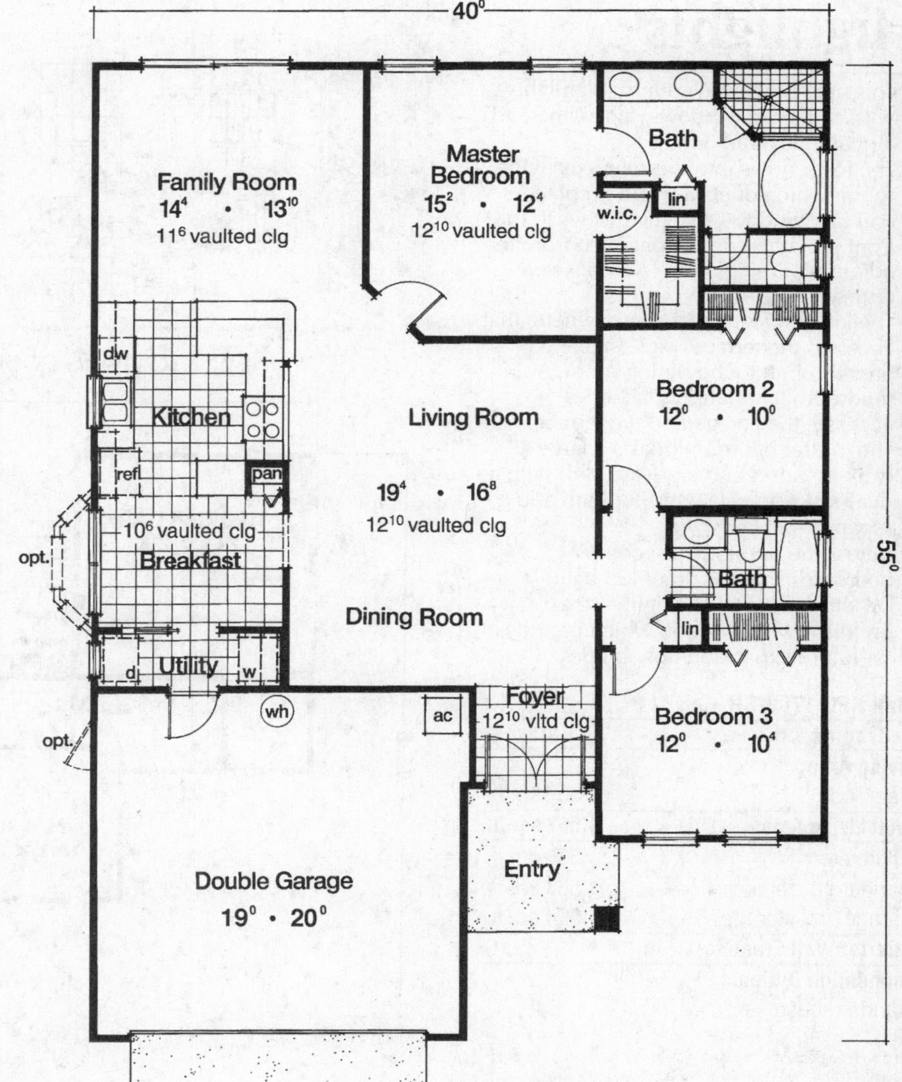

MAIN FLOOR

Country Highlights

- This nice home has country highlights, with shuttered windows, lap siding and a quaint covered porch.
- The foyer flows into the spacious living room, which offers a warm fireplace and tall windows that give views to the front porch. French doors open from the adjoining dining room to a backyard terrace.
- The kitchen features a sunny dinette that accesses the terrace, plus an angled pass-through to the dining room. A nifty mudroom with laundry facilities accesses the garage and the terrace.
- The master bedroom boasts a large walk-in closet and a private bath with a dual-sink vanity, a whirlpool tub and a separate shower.
- Across the home, two secondary bedrooms share another full bath.
- Dormered windows brighten the unfinished upper floor, which provides for future expansion possibilities.

Plan HFL-1700-SR	
Bedrooms: 3+	**Baths:** 2
Living Area:	
Main floor	1,567 sq. ft.
Total Living Area:	**1,567 sq. ft.**
Future area	338 sq. ft.
Standard basement	1,567 sq. ft.
Garage and storage	504 sq. ft.
Exterior Wall Framing:	2x6
Foundation Options:	
Standard basement	
Slab	

(All plans can be built with your choice of foundation and framing. A generic conversion diagram is available. See order form.)

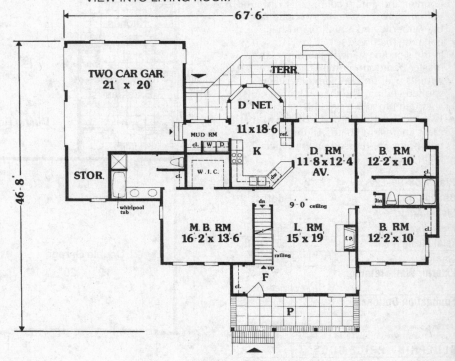

BLUEPRINT PRICE CODE: B

VIEW INTO LIVING ROOM

67'-6"
46'-8"
TWO CAR GAR.
21' x 20'
STOR.
TERR.
D' NET.
11 x 18'-6"
MUD RM
cl.
W
D
ref.
K
W.I.C.
dw
D. RM
11'-8"x 12'-4"
AV.
B. RM
12'-2"x 10'
cl.
lin
whirlpool tub
dn
9'-0" ceiling
M. B. RM
16'-2"x 13'-6"
L. RM
15' x 19'
f.p.
B. RM
12'-2"x 10'
cl.
railing
up
F
cl.
P

MAIN FLOOR

Plan HFL-1700-SR

SEE ORDER INFO ON PAGES 12-15

Elegance with Economy

- This handsome design offers the rich look of brick and an open floor plan with multipurpose living areas that cut down on wasted space.
- A sidelighted entry opens to the central Great Room. A cathedral ceiling and windows on either side of an inviting fireplace add volume to this family activity area.
- Between the adjoining breakfast room and the formal dining room is a see-through wet bar. The breakfast room also features a bay window with sliding glass doors to the backyard, a built-in work desk, a pantry and a snack bar.
- The fully equipped kitchen has a lovely window box above the sink and easy access to both eating areas.
- The sleeping wing's master bedroom has a private bath with a plant shelf, a skylighted dressing area, a whirlpool tub and a large walk-in closet. Two secondary bedrooms share a convenient hall bath.

Plan DBI-1767

Bedrooms: 3	**Baths:** 2
Living Area:	
Main floor	1,604 sq. ft.
Total Living Area:	**1,604 sq. ft.**
Standard basement	1,604 sq. ft.
Garage	466 sq. ft.
Exterior Wall Framing:	2x4
Foundation Options:	
Standard basement	
(All plans can be built with your choice of foundation and framing. A generic conversion diagram is available. See order form.)	
BLUEPRINT PRICE CODE:	**B**

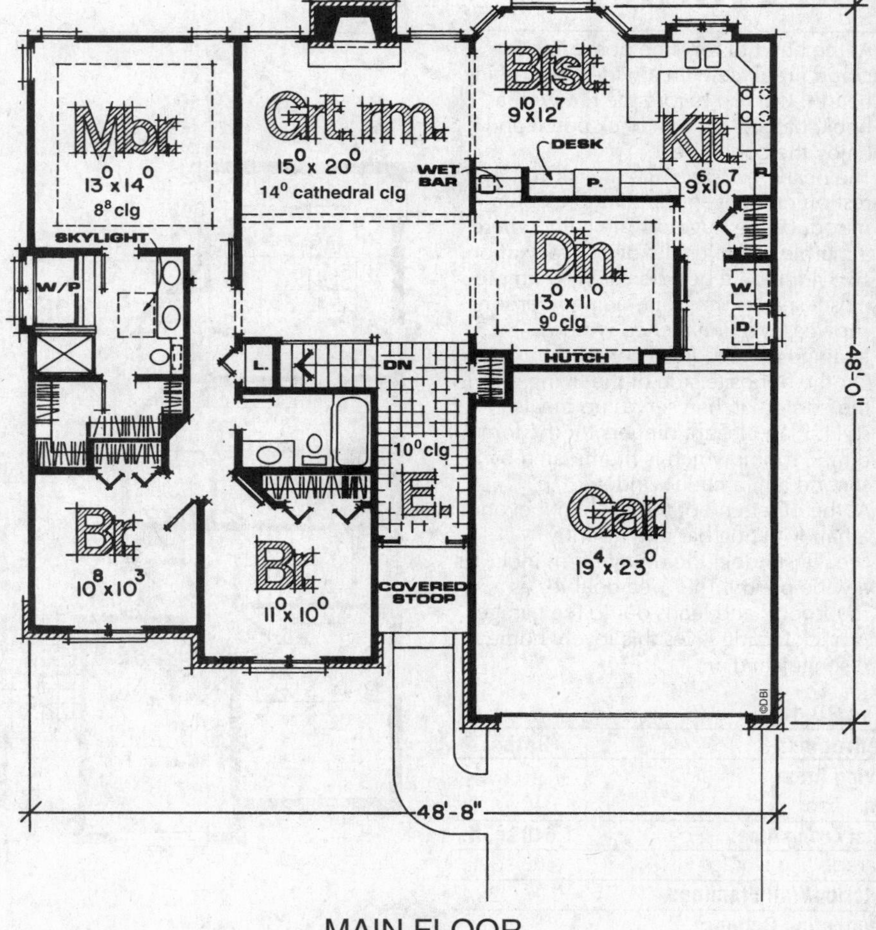

MAIN FLOOR

Hearth and Home

- At the heart of this fine home lies a grand fireplace with a wide, welcoming hearth. Curl up before the fire with a book, or step out to a back porch and enjoy the cool breeze.
- The nearby master suite invites you to rest on quiet evenings. Double doors introduce the huge private bath, where a marble tub offers luxurious relaxation.
- Two additional bedrooms enjoy ample closet space. The front-facing bedroom showcases a fine arched window—imagine officing from here!
- On the opposite side of the living room, the corner kitchen serves up meals in style. Plan elegant dinners for the formal dining room, which is illuminated by a second tall, arched window.
- At the other end of the kitchen, beyond a handy eating bar and a sunny breakfast nook, the utility room includes a wide pantry. This area doubles as a mudroom, and leads out to the garage.
- A brick facade gives this lovely home a distinguished air.

Plan RD-1640

Bedrooms: 3 **Baths:** 2

Living Area:

Main floor	1,640 sq. ft.
Total Living Area:	**1,640 sq. ft.**
Garage and storage	468 sq. ft.
Exterior Wall Framing:	2x4

Foundation Options:

Crawlspace

Slab

(All plans can be built with your choice of foundation and framing. A generic conversion diagram is available. See order form.)

BLUEPRINT PRICE CODE: B

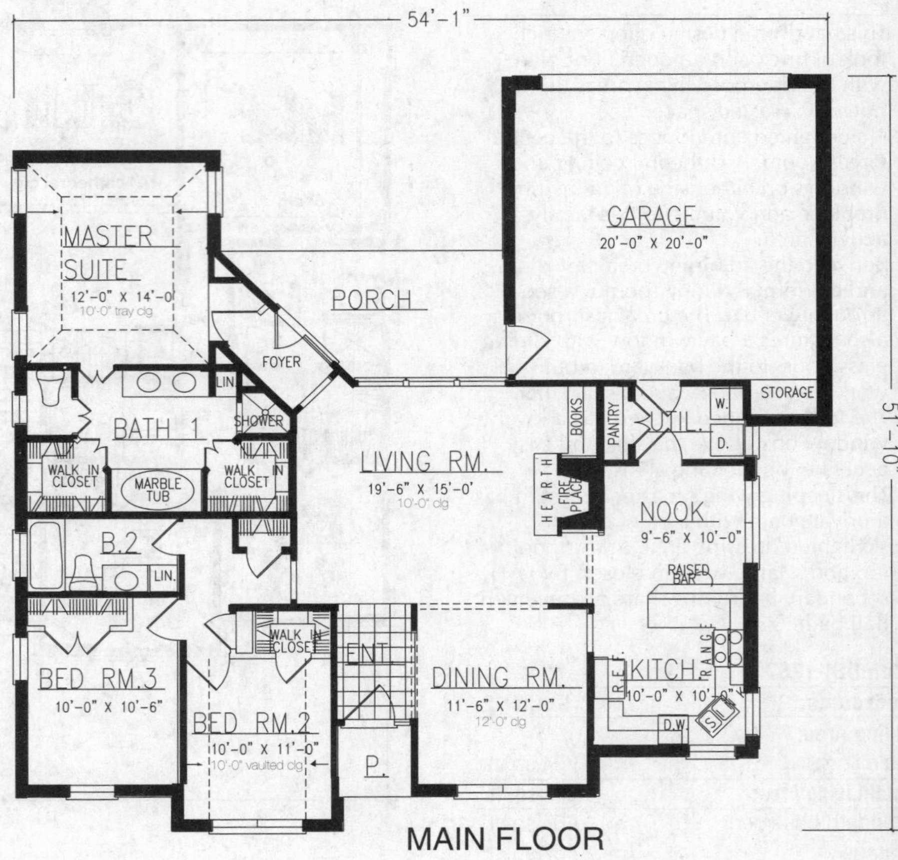

MAIN FLOOR

All-Inclusive

- The stylish facade of this one-story home welcomes all, with its assortment of windows and columned front porch.
- Inside, another column graces the entry, which flows into the dining room on the left and straight ahead to the central living room.
- The crossroads of the home are in the living room, where a window wall expands the area to a backyard deck. The soothing fireplace may be enjoyed throughout the living spaces.
- The kitchen offers an L-shaped serving counter to both the living room and the sunny breakfast bay.
- Secluded behind the kitchen, the master bedroom has a nice sitting bay and an elaborate private bath. Found here are a dual-sink vanity, a dual walk-in closet, a garden bath and a separate shower.
- Across the home, two good-sized secondary bedrooms each have private access to a roomy full bath.

Plan DD-1596

Bedrooms: 3	**Baths:** 2
Living Area:	
Main floor	1,680 sq. ft.
Total Living Area:	**1,680 sq. ft.**
Standard basement	1,680 sq. ft.
Garage	413 sq. ft.
Exterior Wall Framing:	2x4
Foundation Options:	
Standard basement	
Crawlspace	
Slab	

(All plans can be built with your choice of foundation and framing. A generic conversion diagram is available. See order form.)

BLUEPRINT PRICE CODE: B

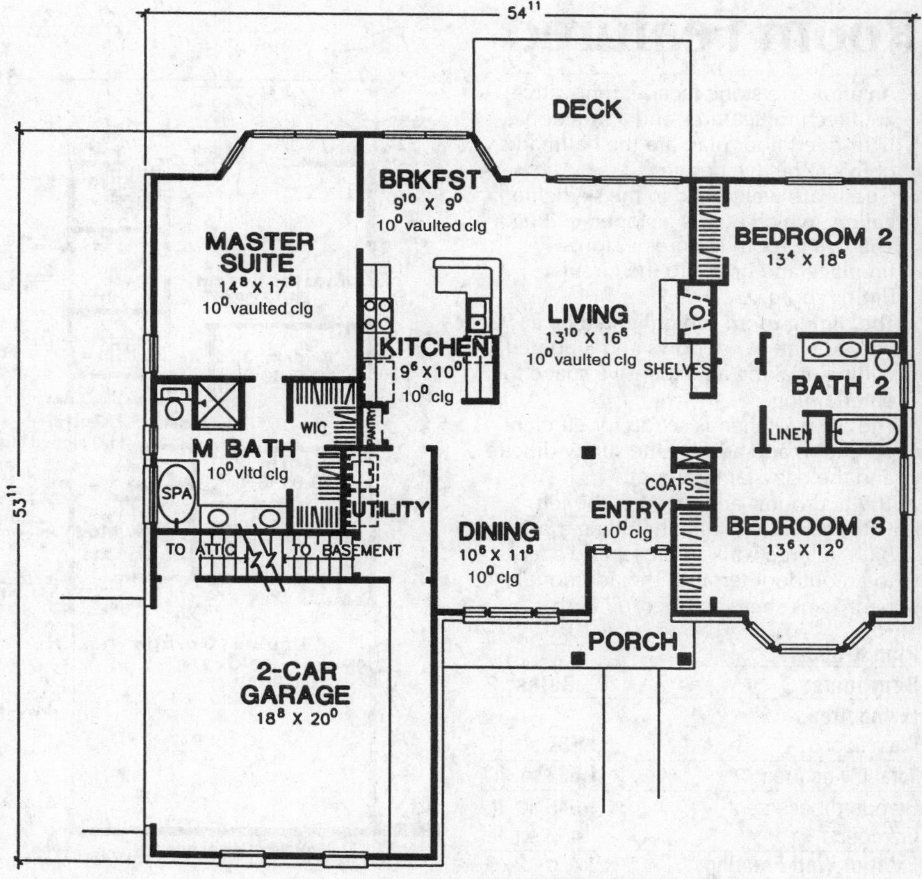

MAIN FLOOR

Circular Dining Room Featured

- An attractive stone facade, innovative architectural features and a functional, light-filled floor plan are the hallmarks of this attractive design.
- Guests are welcomed in the skylighted gallery, which boasts a sloped ceiling. The living room features a stone fireplace and opens to the circular dining room.
- The dining room is highlighted by a curved wall of windows and a domed ceiling, making an expansive space for entertaining.
- The open kitchen is set up for efficient operation and adjoins the sunny dinette and the cozy family room.
- The bedrooms are zoned to the left, with the master suite including a private bath, a large walk-in closet and access to an outdoor terrace. The additional bedrooms share another full bath.

Plan K-663-N	
Bedrooms: 3	**Baths:** 2
Living Area:	
Main floor	1,682 sq. ft.
Total Living Area:	**1,682 sq. ft.**
Standard basement	1,645 sq. ft.
Garage	453 sq. ft.
Exterior Wall Framing:	2x4 or 2x6
Foundation Options:	
Standard basement	
Slab	

(All plans can be built with your choice of foundation and framing. A generic conversion diagram is available. See order form.)

BLUEPRINT PRICE CODE: B

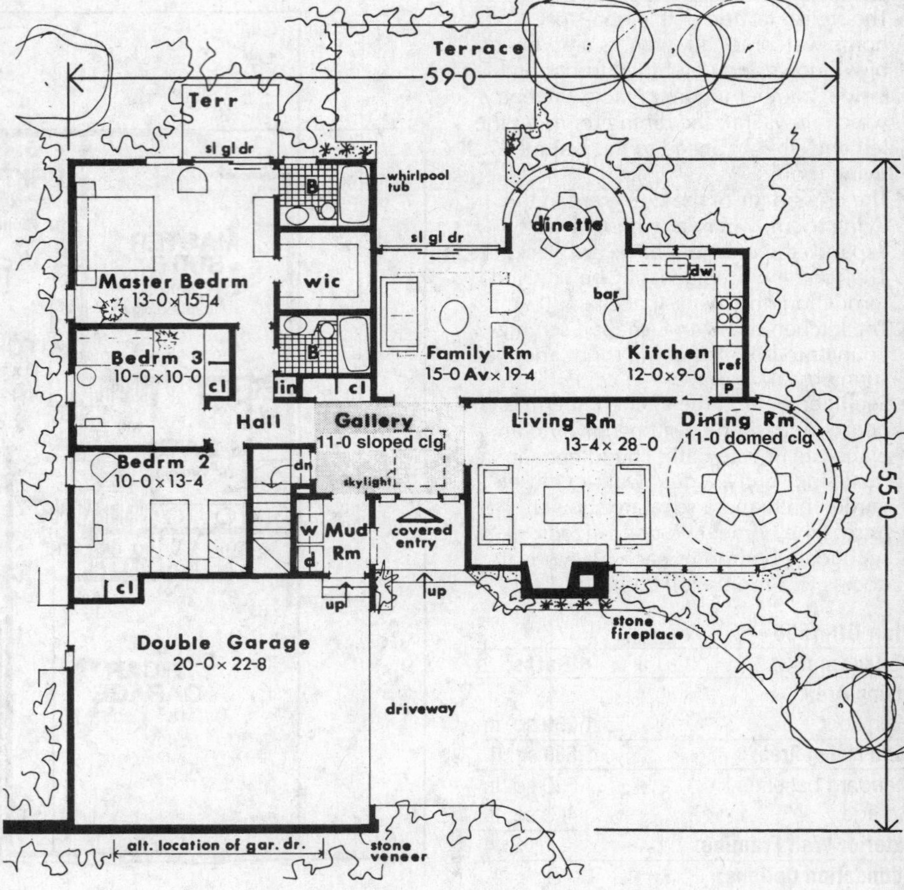

MAIN FLOOR

ORDER BLUEPRINTS ANYTIME!
CALL TOLL-FREE 1-800-820-1296

Plan K-663-N

SEE ORDER INFO ON PAGES 12-15
familyhandyman.com/homeplans

French Charm

- The charming exterior of this French home exhibits an ornate assortment of keystones, quoins and arches.
- Inside the home, a high plant ledge adorns the tiled entry, which boasts a dramatic ceiling.
- To the left, the elegant formal dining room extends to the living room, which boasts a warm fireplace, neat built-in bookshelves and functional cabinets to store CDs or family photos. A striking ceiling soars above both rooms.
- A convenient serving bar links the gourmet kitchen to the sunny bayed breakfast nook. The adjacent utility room includes a handy pantry closet.
- Across the home, a rear foyer offers entrance to a covered porch and to the luxurious master suite. The master suite features a sloped ceiling, a window seat and a lush garden bath highlighted by a marble tub!
- A hall bath serves the two secondary bedrooms, one of which has a sloped ceiling, a walk-in closet and a useful built-in desk.

Plan RD-1714

Bedrooms: 3	**Baths:** 2
Living Area:	
Main floor	1,714 sq. ft.
Total Living Area:	**1,714 sq. ft.**
Garage and storage	470 sq. ft.
Exterior Wall Framing:	2x4

Foundation Options:
Crawlspace
Slab
(All plans can be built with your choice of foundation and framing. A generic conversion diagram is available. See order form.)

BLUEPRINT PRICE CODE: B

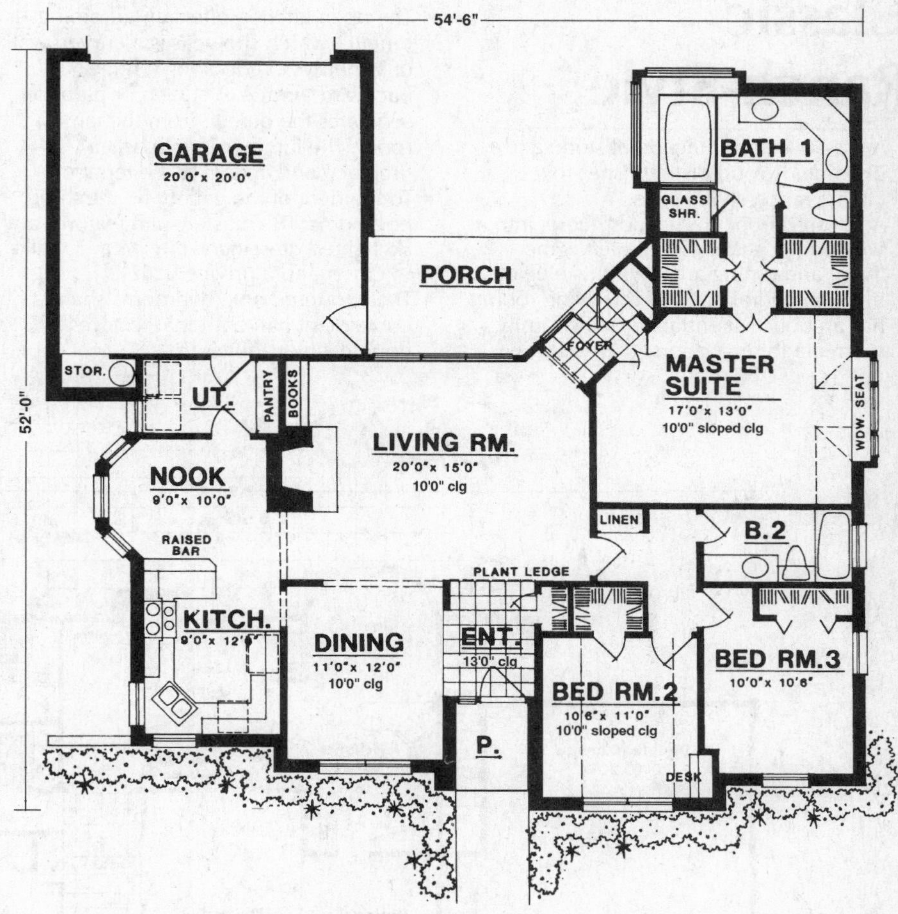

MAIN FLOOR

Plan RD-1714

FOR MORE DETAILS, SEE PLAN AT
familyhandyman.com/homeplans

Classic Ranch-Style

- A classic exterior facade of stone and unpainted wood distinguishes this classic ranch-style home.
- A covered front entry leads guests into a welcoming gallery. At the left is the living and dining area, with its elegant, high, cathedral ceiling. The living room has an optional entrance to the family room via folding doors.
- The open kitchen offers an adjoining dinette, which showcases a curved wall of windows overlooking a huge backyard terrace. A screen or partition separates the dinette from the family room. The family room boasts a fireplace and access to the terrace.
- To the right of the gallery lie the three bedrooms. The master suite features a skylighted dressing/vanity area, a walk-in closet and a private bath.
- The two remaining bedrooms share a convenient hall bath that features a double-sink vanity.

Plan K-162-J	
Bedrooms: 3	**Baths:** 2
Living Area:	
Main floor	1,721 sq. ft.
Total Living Area:	**1,721 sq. ft.**
Standard basement	1,672 sq. ft.
Garage and storage	496 sq. ft.
Exterior Wall Framing:	2x4 or 2x6
Foundation Options:	
Standard basement	
Slab	

(All plans can be built with your choice of foundation and framing. A generic conversion diagram is available. See order form.)

BLUEPRINT PRICE CODE: B

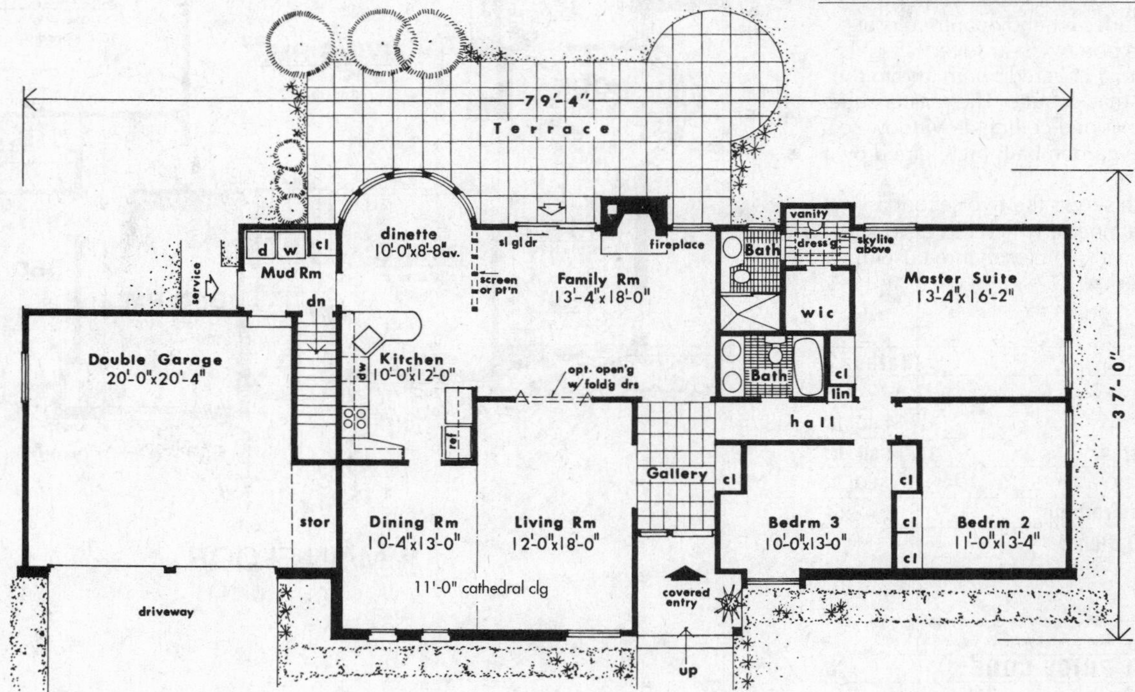

MAIN FLOOR

Plan K-162-J

SEE ORDER INFO ON PAGES 12-15

Skylighted Country Kitchen

- This country ranch-style home combines rustic wood posts and shutters with stylish curved glass.
- The foyer unfolds to the flowing formal areas. The living room and the dining room each offer a stepped ceiling and a view of one of the two porches.
- The skylighted country kitchen shares the family room's warm fireplace. The kitchen's central island cooktop and snack bar make serving a breeze!
- In addition to the fireplace, the family room also boasts gliding French doors to the adjacent porch.
- The bedroom wing houses three bedrooms and two full baths. The skylighted master bath flaunts a whirlpool tub and a dual-sink vanity.
- Each of the secondary bedrooms has a high ceiling area above its lovely arched window.

Plan AX-92321

Bedrooms: 3	**Baths:** 2
Living Area:	
Main floor	1,735 sq. ft.
Total Living Area:	**1,735 sq. ft.**
Standard basement	1,735 sq. ft.
Garage	449 sq. ft.
Storage	28 sq. ft.
Utility	28 sq. ft.
Exterior Wall Framing:	2x4

Foundation Options:
Standard basement
Crawlspace
Slab
(All plans can be built with your choice of foundation and framing. A generic conversion diagram is available. See order form.)

BLUEPRINT PRICE CODE: **B**

REAR VIEW

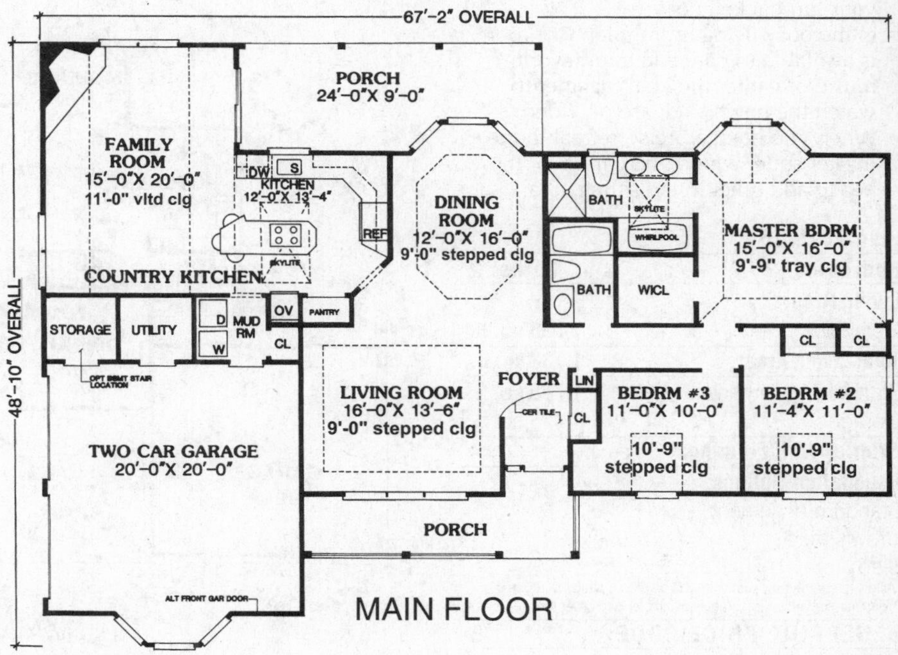

MAIN FLOOR

Plan AX-92321

This Is It!

- This comfortable design is just the plan you're looking for. The affordable design includes all the features—both inside and out—today's family needs.
- The first days of spring will feel even better when you settle into a rocker on the porch and watch the kids play a game of Kick the Can in the front yard.
- Inside, the dining room awaits formal dinners. Built-in china cabinets replace the stairway to the basement in the crawlspace and slab versions.
- In the kitchen, a snack bar is the perfect place to feed the kids a snack. The sunshine that pours into the morning room will rouse the spirits of even the sleepiest family member.
- Friends and family will show up at your home to celebrate the Fourth of July on your fun-packed deck.
- In the busy living room, plenty of room is available to dance to your favorite music or gather the clan together to watch the newest release on video.
- When you need a break, retreat to the master suite, where you can savor the peace and quiet in the sitting area.

Plan DD-1716

Bedrooms: 3 **Baths:** 2

Living Area:

Main floor	1,738 sq. ft.
Total Living Area:	**1,738 sq. ft.**
Standard basement	1,738 sq. ft.
Garage	425 sq. ft.
Exterior Wall Framing:	2x4

Foundation Options:

Standard basement
Crawlspace
Slab

(All plans can be built with your choice of foundation and framing. A generic conversion diagram is available. See order form.)

BLUEPRINT PRICE CODE: B

REAR VIEW

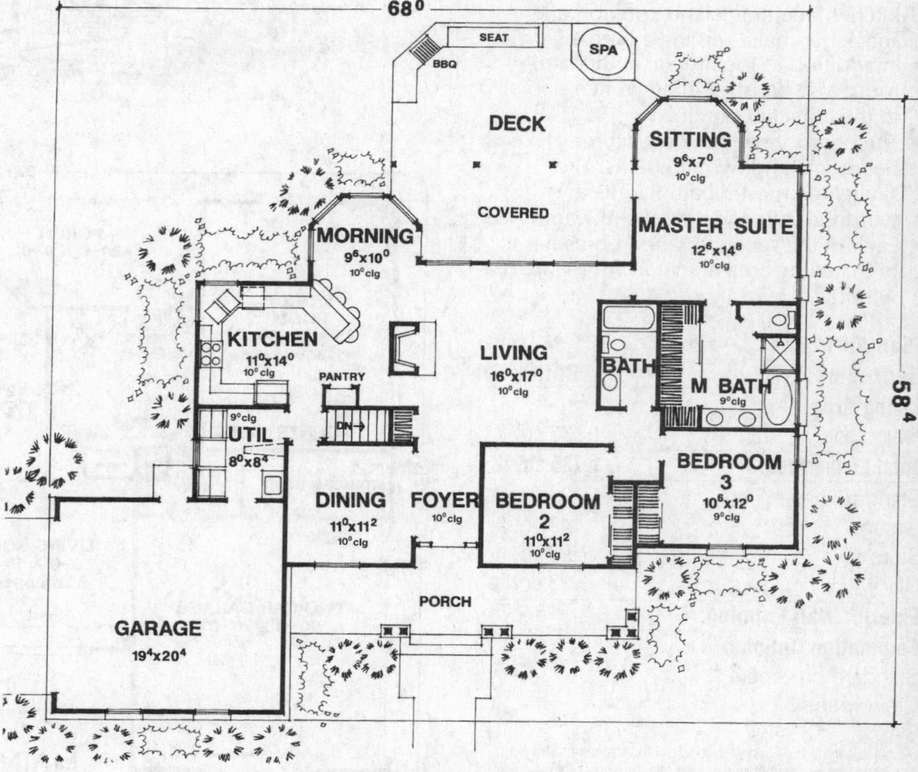

MAIN FLOOR

Plan DD-1716

SEE ORDER INFO ON PAGES 12-15
familyhandyman.com/homeplans

Updated Creole

- This Louisiana-style raised cottage features a tin roof, shuttered windows and three pairs of French doors, all of which add to the comfort and nostalgic appeal of this Creole classic.
- The French doors enter from the cool and relaxing front porch to the formal living areas and a front bedroom.
- The central living room merges with the dining room and the kichen's eating area. Two sets of French doors access a rear porch.
- The efficient kitchen offers a raised ceiling, an angled snack bar and a bayed nook with a sloped ceiling.
- A secluded master suite showcases a private bath, fit for the most demanding tastes. Across the home, the secondary bedrooms include abundant closet space and share a full bath.
- This full-featured, energy-efficient design also includes a large utility room and extra storage space in the garage.

Plan E-1823	
Bedrooms: 3	**Baths:** 2
Living Area:	
Main floor	1,800 sq. ft.
Total Living Area:	**1,800 sq. ft.**
Garage and storage	574 sq. ft.
Enclosed storage	60 sq. ft.
Exterior Wall Framing:	2x6

Foundation Options:

Crawlspace

Slab

(All plans can be built with your choice of foundation and framing. A generic conversion diagram is available. See order form.)

BLUEPRINT PRICE CODE: **B**

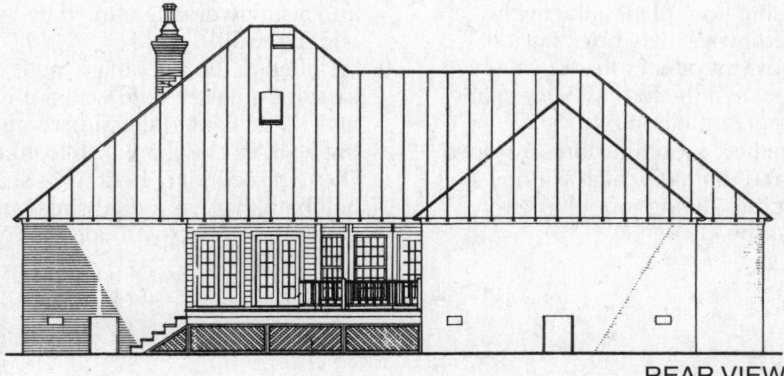

REAR VIEW

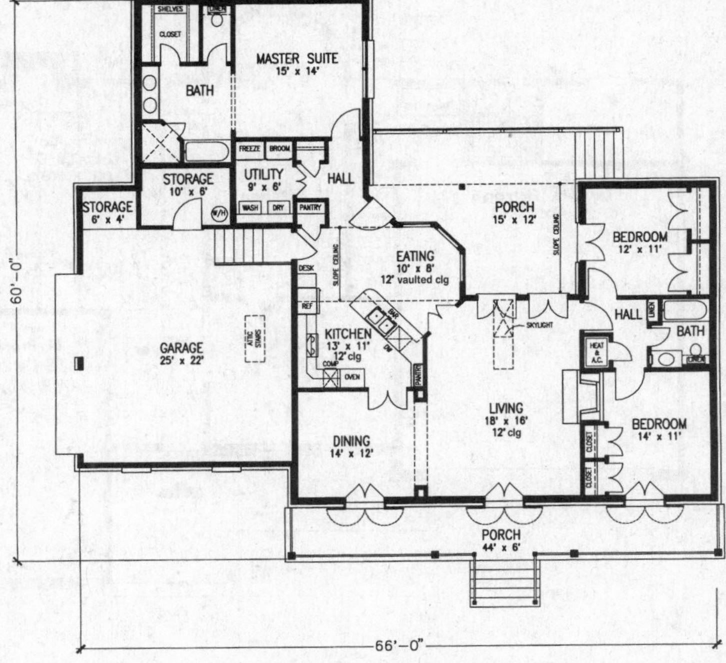

MAIN FLOOR

Outstanding One-Story

- This sharp one-story home has an outstanding floor plan, attractively enhanced by a stately brick facade.
- A vestibule introduces the foyer, which flows between the formal living spaces at the front of the home.
- The large living room features a sloped ceiling and dramatic, high windows. The spacious dining room has easy access to the kitchen.
- The expansive family room is the center of the home, with a beamed cathedral ceiling, a slate-hearth fireplace and sliding glass doors to a backyard terrace.
- The adjoining kitchen offers a snack bar and a sunny dinette framed by a curved window wall.
- Included in the sleeping wing is a luxurious master suite with a private bath. A skylighted dressing room and a big walk-in closet are also featured.
- The two secondary bedrooms share a hall bath that has a dual-sink vanity. A half-bath is near the mud/laundry room.

Plan K-278-M	
Bedrooms: 3	**Baths:** 2½
Living Area:	
Main floor	1,803 sq. ft.
Total Living Area:	**1,803 sq. ft.**
Standard basement	1,778 sq. ft.
Garage	493 sq. ft.
Storage	58 sq. ft.
Exterior Wall Framing:	2x4 or 2x6
Foundation Options:	
Standard basement	
Slab	

(All plans can be built with your choice of foundation and framing. A generic conversion diagram is available. See order form.)

BLUEPRINT PRICE CODE: B

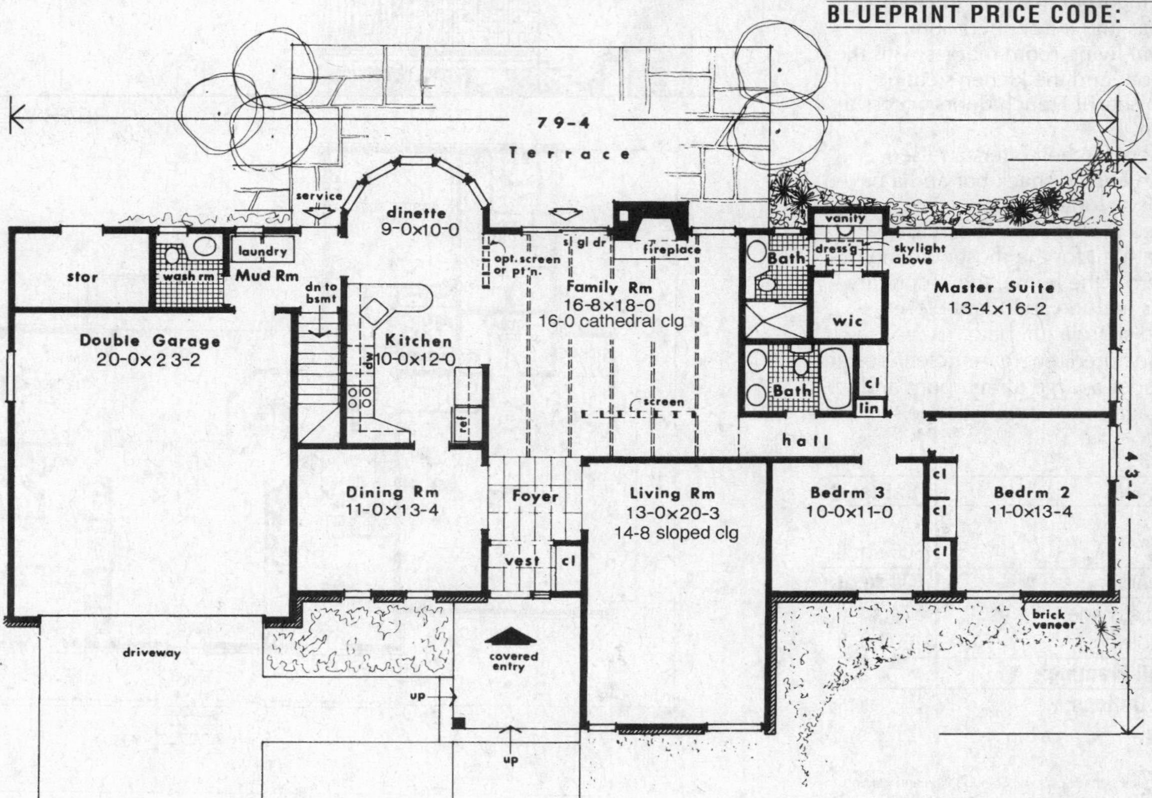

MAIN FLOOR

Plan K-278-M

SEE ORDER INFO ON PAGES 12-15

Country Charm, Cottage Look

- An interesting combination of stone and stucco gives a charming cottage look to this attractive country home.
- Off the inviting sidelighted entry, the formal dining room is defined by striking columns.
- The dining room expands into the living room, which boasts a fireplace and built-in shelves. A French door provides access to a cute backyard patio.
- The galley-style kitchen unfolds to a sunny morning room.
- All of the living areas are expanded by high ceilings.
- The master bedroom features a nice bayed sitting area. The luxurious master bath boasts an exciting garden tub and a glass-block shower, as well as a big walk-in closet and a dressing area with two sinks.
- Across the home, two additional bedrooms with walk-in closets and private dressing areas share a tidy compartmentalized bath.

Plan DD-1790

Bedrooms: 3	**Baths:** 2½
Living Area:	
Main floor	1,812 sq. ft.
Total Living Area:	**1,812 sq. ft.**
Standard basement	1,812 sq. ft.
Garage	438 sq. ft.
Exterior Wall Framing:	2x4
Foundation Options:	
Standard basement	
Crawlspace	
Slab	

(All plans can be built with your choice of foundation and framing. A generic conversion diagram is available. See order form.)

BLUEPRINT PRICE CODE: B

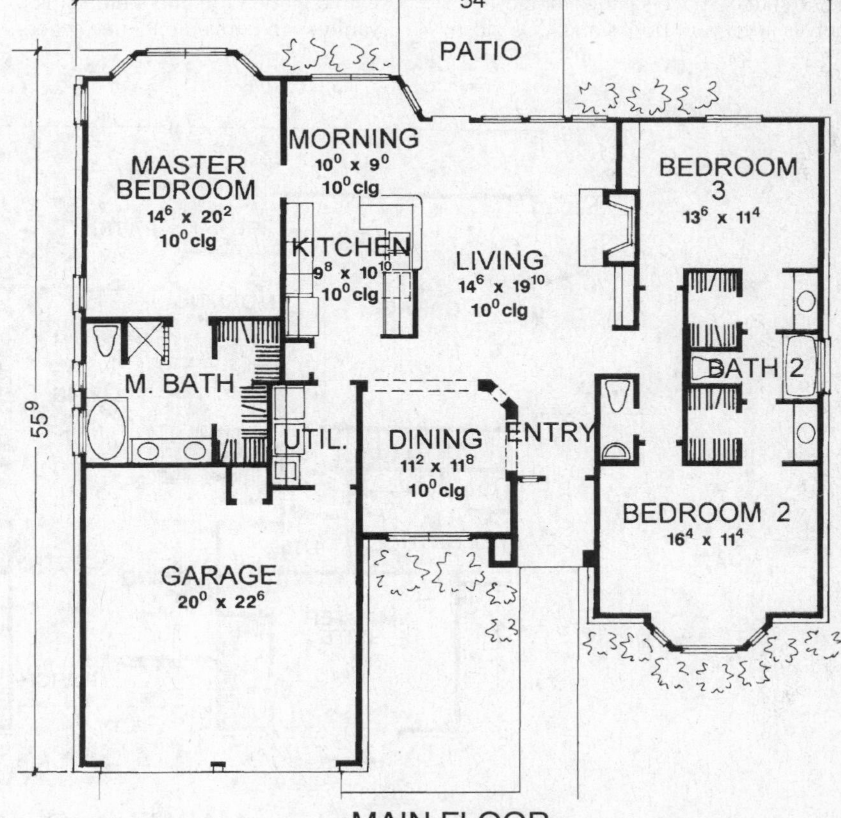

MAIN FLOOR

Plan DD-1790

FOR MORE DETAILS, SEE PLAN AT
familyhandyman.com/homeplans

Spatially Smart!

- Handsome columns and stylish metal-roofed bays adorn this good-looking brick home.
- High ceilings and carefree, open living spaces spatially enhance the interior and make the most of the economical square footage.
- A dressy fluted column sets off the entry and allows a dramatic view of the living room and the backyard patio. Next to the fireplace, space-saving storage shelves keep your books and CDs close at hand. A French door swings open to the patio.
- Half-round windows fashionably brighten the dining room–designed for your most formal occasions.
- A pantry and breakfast bar accessorize the airy kitchen, which overlooks a delightful morning room.
- The big-sized master bedroom, like the living areas, is augmented by a high ceiling.
- The private master bath is furnished with a garden tub and a dual-sink vanity with convenient knee space.

Plan DD-1796

Bedrooms: 4	**Baths:** 2
Living Area:	
Main floor	1,827 sq. ft.
Total Living Area:	**1,827 sq. ft.**
Standard basement	1,827 sq. ft.
Garage and storage	472 sq. ft.
Exterior Wall Framing:	2x4

Foundation Options:

Standard basement
Crawlspace
Slab
(All plans can be built with your choice of foundation and framing. A generic conversion diagram is available. See order form.)

BLUEPRINT PRICE CODE: B

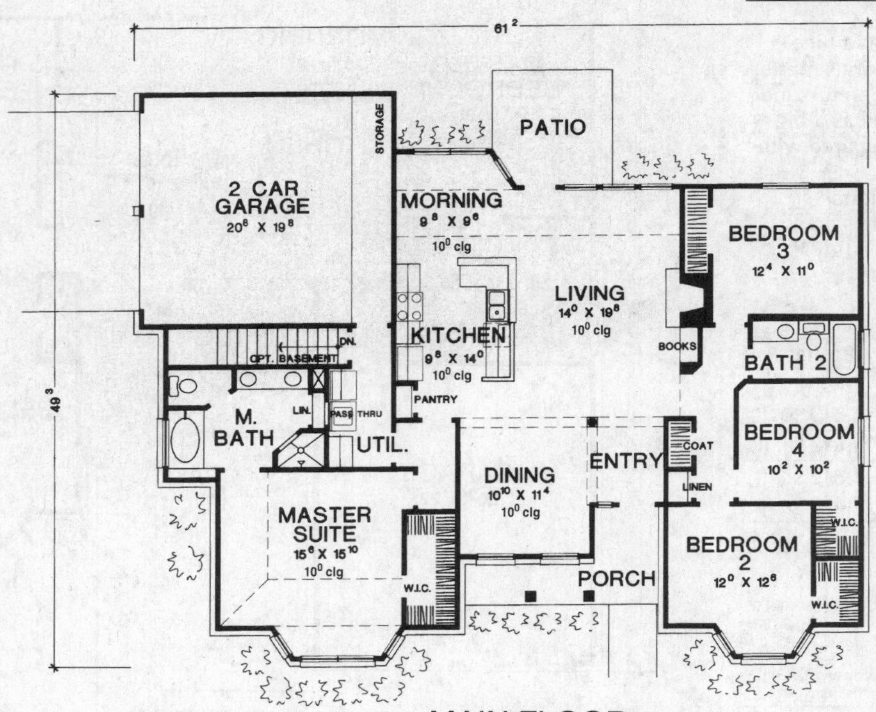

MAIN FLOOR

ORDER BLUEPRINTS ANYTIME!
CALL TOLL-FREE 1-800-820-1296

Plan DD-1796

SEE ORDER INFO ON PAGES 12-15
familyhandyman.com/homeplans

Healthy Appetite

- There's plenty of opportunity for fun and food in this home, which boasts a big backyard porch that's tailor-made for your active lifestyle!
- From the sheltered front entry, the foyer forks to introduce the living areas. To the left, a dramatic glass-block wall nicely defines the formal dining room.
- The centerpiece of the home is the angled family room, where a prominent fireplace promises countless evenings of warmth and togetherness. Banks of windows deliver great views to the porch and beyond.
- If you like to greet nature face-to-face each morning, you'll love the master bedroom's private porch access. The master bath is equally well appointed, and includes a garden tub, a corner shower and a sink for each of you.
- Hectic meals are a thing of the past in the wide-open kitchen. Here, an island cooktop and lots of counter space work to your advantage. A cute nook with a corner window seat has porch access.

Plan DW-1830	
Bedrooms: 3	**Baths:** 2
Living Area:	
Main floor	1,830 sq. ft.
Total Living Area:	**1,830 sq. ft.**
Standard basement	1,830 sq. ft.
Garage	490 sq. ft.
Exterior Wall Framing:	2x4
Foundation Options:	
Standard basement	
Crawlspace	
Slab	
(All plans can be built with your choice of foundation and framing. A generic conversion diagram is available. See order form.)	
BLUEPRINT PRICE CODE:	**B**

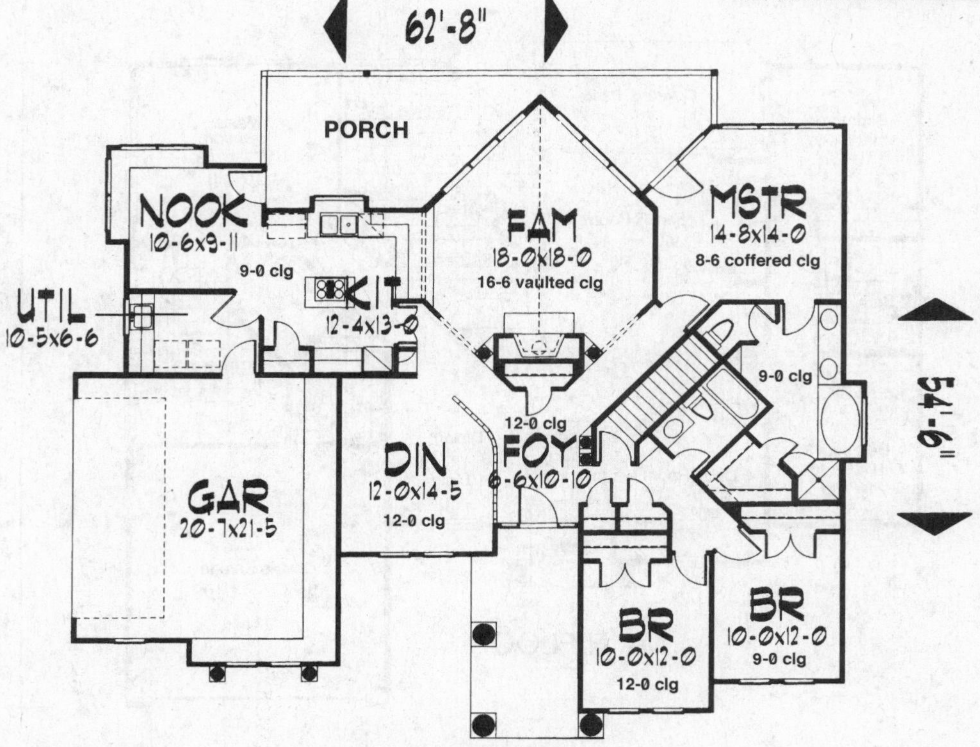

MAIN FLOOR

Sunny Delight

- The unmistakable Mediterranean flavor of this one-story home evokes pleasing, restful images of easygoing days. Inside, high ceilings and the minimal use of hallways and walls foster the home's cool, open feel.
- On either side of the foyer, the living room and the dining room each reserve a quiet, elegant space for special events. Built-in niches offer a great way to display artwork and photos.
- Casual affairs have a place of their own in the family room. Here, built-in shelving flanks the fireplace, providing ideal spots for media equipment.
- The walls that set off the kitchen stop two feet below the ceiling, creating great shelves to display greenery.
- Adjacent to the kitchen, sunny sliding glass doors in the breakfast nook let you enjoy morning coffee inside or out.
- As an extra bonus, the master suite also includes pretty sliding glass doors that open to the backyard.

Plan HDS-99-286

Bedrooms: 3	**Baths:** 2
Living Area:	
Main floor	1,833 sq. ft.
Total Living Area:	**1,833 sq. ft.**
Garage	392 sq. ft.
Exterior Wall Framing:	2x4
Foundation Options:	
Slab	

(All plans can be built with your choice of foundation and framing. A generic conversion diagram is available. See order form.)

BLUEPRINT PRICE CODE: B

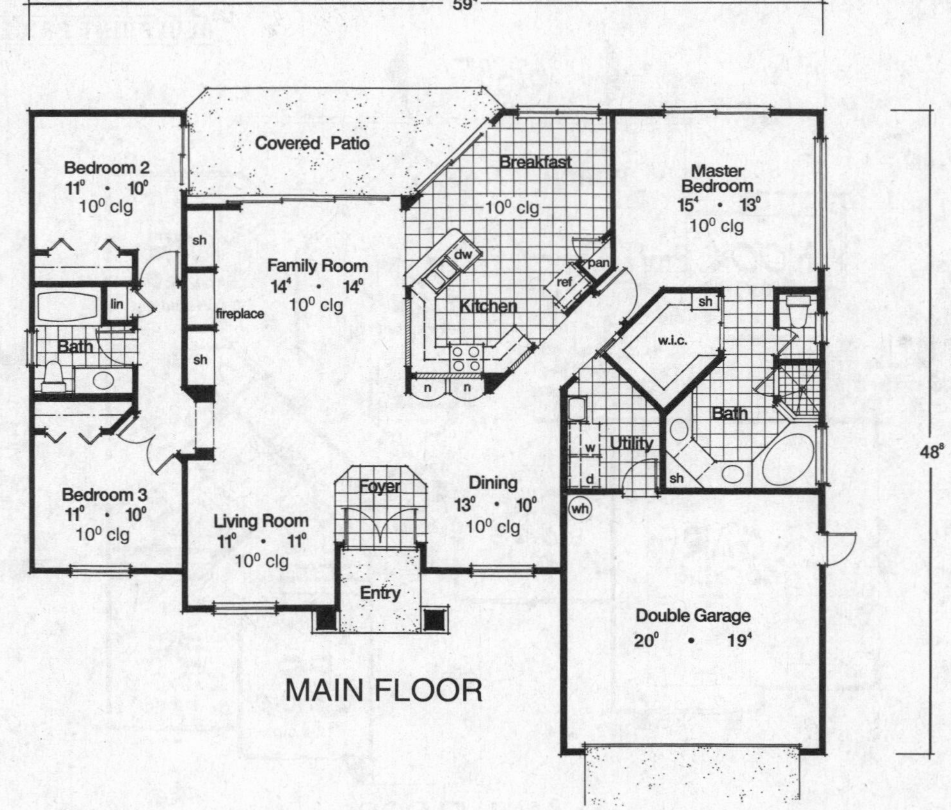

MAIN FLOOR

Plan HDS-99-286

SEE ORDER INFO ON PAGES 12-15

Elegance End to End

- Elegance roams end to end in this sprawling one-story brick home.
- Beneath a beautiful half-round window, the dramatic entry's high ceiling amplifies the volume throughout the rest of the floor plan.
- A breathtaking expanse of glass sheds light on the spacious central living room, anxiously awaiting your next family function.
- The formal dining room commands attention with an exquisite Palladian window showpiece.
- When casual meals suit your schedule, relax in the lovely bayed breakfast nook. Or step up for a snack at the kitchen's raised bar.
- An angled hall reaches the secluded master suite, which caters to both its occupants with a wraparound dual-sink vanity, a separate tub and shower, plus a pair of walk-in closets.
- The home's two baths nicely isolate the master bedroom from the secondary bedrooms. The foremost bedroom boasts a desk and a walk-in closet.

Plan RD-1841

Bedrooms: 3	**Baths:** 2
Living Area:	
Main floor	1,841 sq. ft.
Total Living Area:	**1,841 sq. ft.**
Garage	534 sq. ft.
Exterior Wall Framing:	2x4
Foundation Options:	
Crawlspace	
Slab	

(All plans can be built with your choice of foundation and framing. A generic conversion diagram is available. See order form.)

BLUEPRINT PRICE CODE: B

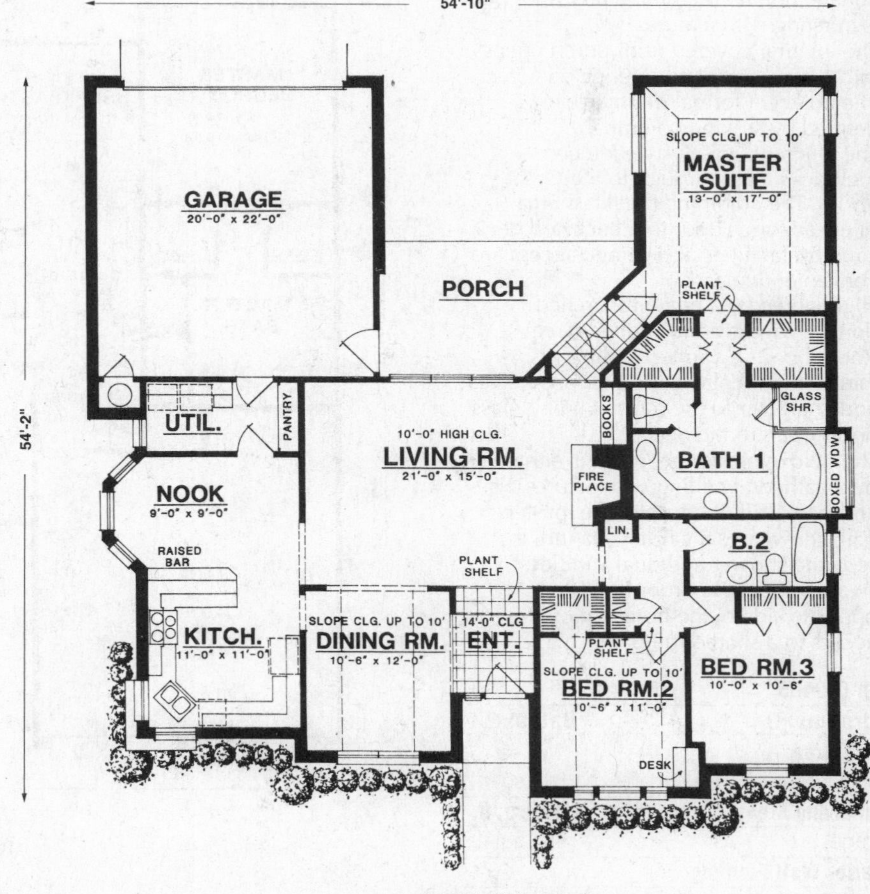

MAIN FLOOR

Lovely Cottage

- Past its quaint exterior, this lovely cottage home's bright and airy floor plan is bursting with features.
- The inviting covered front porch opens into a high-ceilinged sidelighted foyer. The adjacent formal dining room is defined by striking columns.
- The efficient, galley-style kitchen includes a pass-through to the Great Room. The adjoining breakfast area offers a French door to a backyard deck. Laundry facilities and garage access are conveniently nearby.
- Highlighted by a beautiful arched dormer window, the vaulted Great Room boasts a vaulted ceiling. A handsome fireplace and built-in shelves add character to the room. Sliding glass doors open to the deck.
- The deluxe master bedroom is enhanced by a cathedral ceiling and features his-and-hers walk-in closets. The master bath showcases a garden spa tub, a separate shower and dual vanities.
- Two additional bedrooms on the opposite side of the home enjoy private access to a shared full bath.

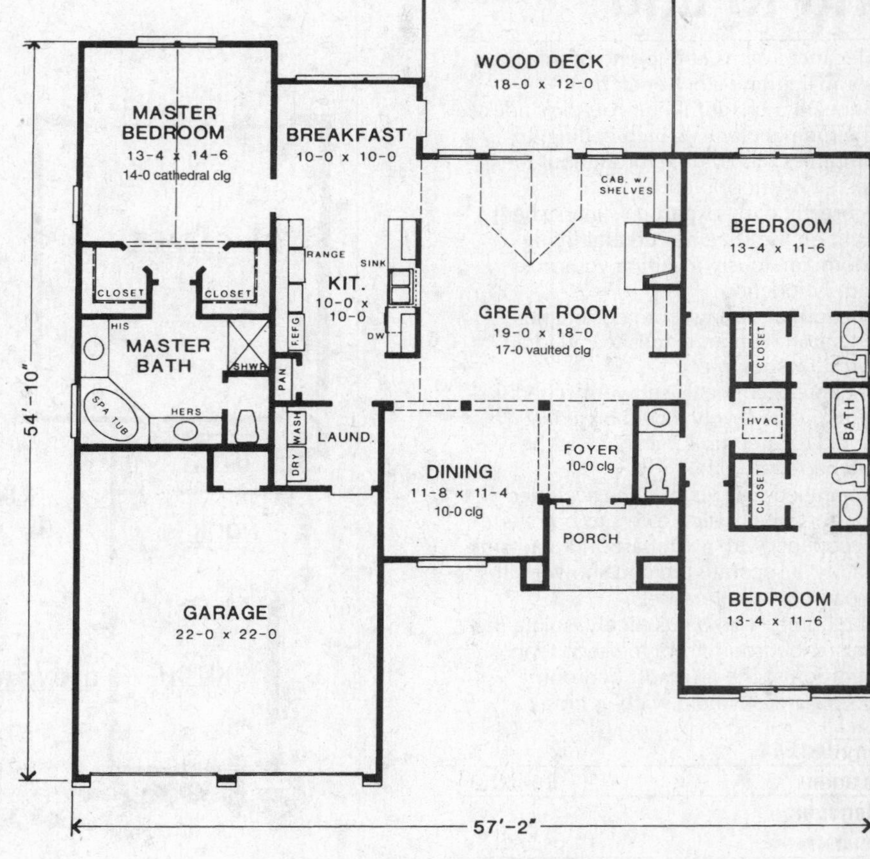

MAIN FLOOR

Plan C-9405

Bedrooms: 3	**Baths:** 2½
Living Area:	
Main floor	1,845 sq. ft.
Total Living Area:	**1,845 sq. ft.**
Garage	484 sq. ft.
Exterior Wall Framing:	2x4
Foundation Options:	
Crawlspace	
Slab	

(All plans can be built with your choice of foundation and framing. A generic conversion diagram is available. See order form.)

BLUEPRINT PRICE CODE: B

Plan C-9405

SEE ORDER INFO ON PAGES 12-15

Attainable Luxury

- This traditional ranch home offers a large, central living room with a raised ceiling, a corner fireplace and an adjoining patio.
- The U-shaped kitchen easily services both the formal dining room and the bayed eating area.
- The luxurious master suite features a large bath with separate vanities and dressing areas.
- Two secondary bedrooms share a second full bath.
- A covered carport boasts a decorative brick wall and attic space above. Two additional storage areas provide plenty of room for gardening supplies and sports equipment.

Plan E-1812

Bedrooms: 3	**Baths:** 2
Living Area:	
Main floor	1,860 sq. ft.
Total Living Area:	**1,860 sq. ft.**
Carport	484 sq. ft.
Storage	132 sq. ft.
Exterior Wall Framing:	2x6
Foundation Options:	
Crawlspace	
Slab	

(All plans can be built with your choice of foundation and framing. A generic conversion diagram is available. See order form.)

BLUEPRINT PRICE CODE: B

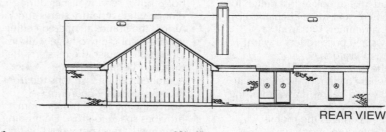

REAR VIEW

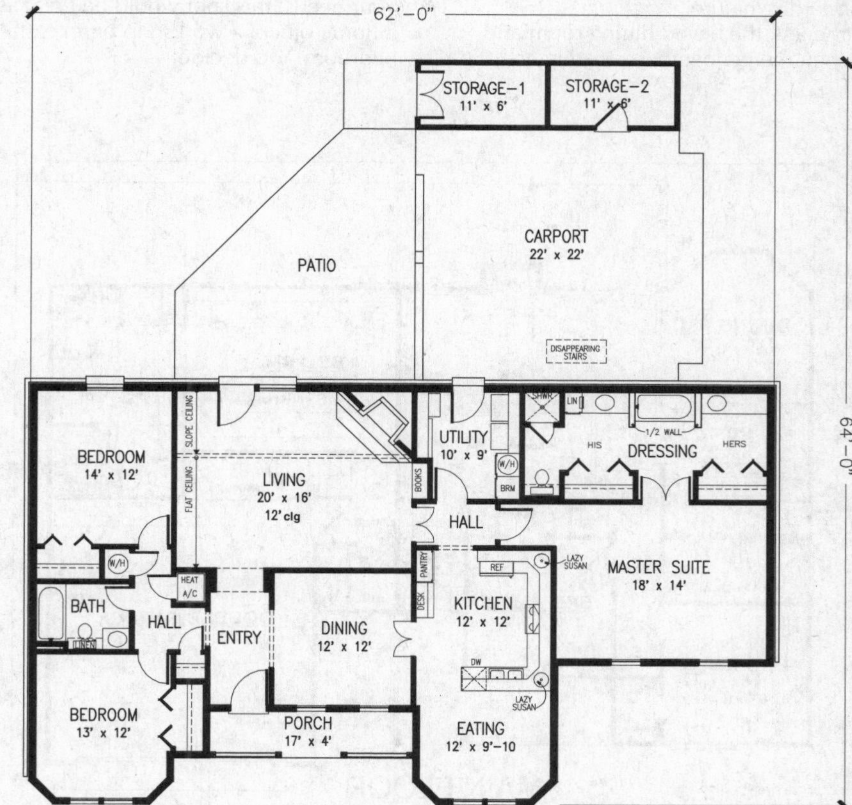

MAIN FLOOR

Take a Look!

- Once you take a look at this delightful home, you're sure to be enchanted by its many amenities. Out front, a perfectly sized porch offers a warm welcome to visitors.
- Inside, the entry leads back to the Great Room, where a cathedral ceiling with exposed wood beams draws admiring glances from guests. The handsome fireplace maximizes the room's comforting nature.
- To the left, the bayed dining room and kitchen merge together, creating an efficient space for family meals. A breakfast bar between the two rooms holds bulky serving dishes during dinner, while a pantry stores sundries.
- Across the home, a coffered ceiling, a private bath and two huge walk-in closets distinguish the master suite from the other bedrooms.
- A vaulted ceiling also tops the front-facing secondary bedroom.
- Above the garage, a bonus room provides space to grow. Depending on your needs, this spot would be great as a home office, a workshop or an extra bedroom. You decide!

Plan KD-1577

Bedrooms: 3+	**Baths:** 2
Living Area:	
Main floor	1,577 sq. ft.
Bonus room	274 sq. ft.
Total Living Area:	**1,851 sq. ft.**
Garage	438 sq. ft.
Exterior Wall Framing:	2x4
Foundation Options:	
Crawlspace	
Slab	

(All plans can be built with your choice of foundation and framing. A generic conversion diagram is available. See order form.)

BLUEPRINT PRICE CODE: B

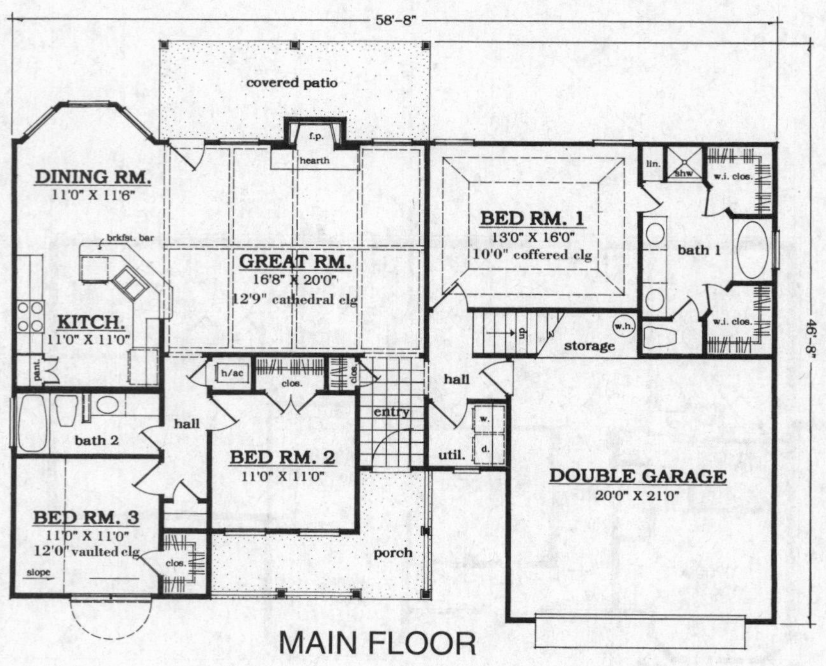

MAIN FLOOR

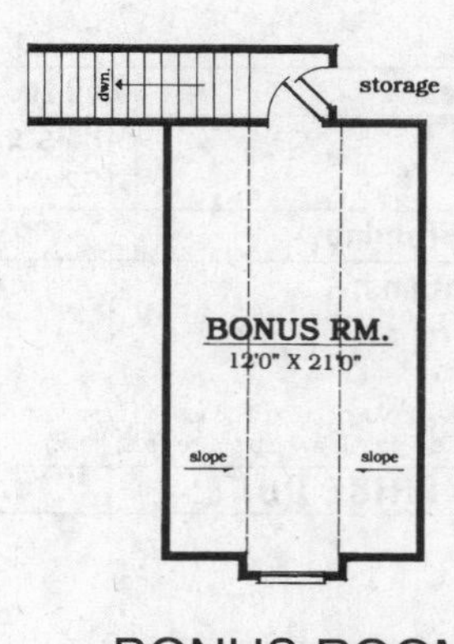

BONUS ROOM

Plan KD-1577

SEE ORDER INFO ON PAGES 12-15
familyhandyman.com/homeplans

Impressive Master Suite

- This attractive one-story home features an impressive master suite. Located apart from the secondary bedrooms, it hosts a lavish private bath with a spa tub, a separate shower and his-and-hers dressing areas. Plenty of closet space rounds out the suite's many amenities.
- A lovely front porch opens to the entry, which flows into a formal dining room, the sizable living room and the secondary bedroom wing.
- The living room boasts a large corner fireplace, a sloped ceiling and access to a huge back patio.
- Double doors separate the dining room from the U-shaped kitchen, which adjoins a comfortable, casual eating area. A built-in desk and a handy pantry closet, plus access to the nearby utility room and carport, give the kitchen's layout extra points.
- The carport keeps vehicles out of sight at the back of the home. Ample storage holds yard tools and other outdoor equipment.

Plan E-1818	
Bedrooms: 3	**Baths:** 2
Living Area:	
Main floor	1,868 sq. ft.
Total Living Area:	**1,868 sq. ft.**
Carport	484 sq. ft.
Storage	132 sq. ft.
Exterior Wall Framing:	2x6
Foundation Options:	
Crawlspace	
Slab	
(All plans can be built with your choice of foundation and framing. A generic conversion diagram is available. See order form.)	
BLUEPRINT PRICE CODE:	**B**

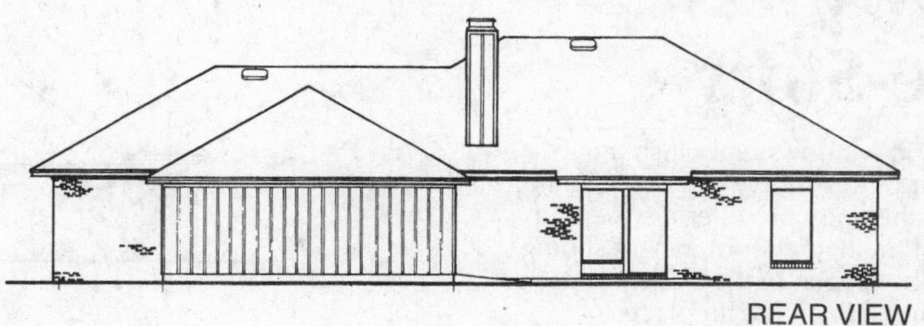
REAR VIEW

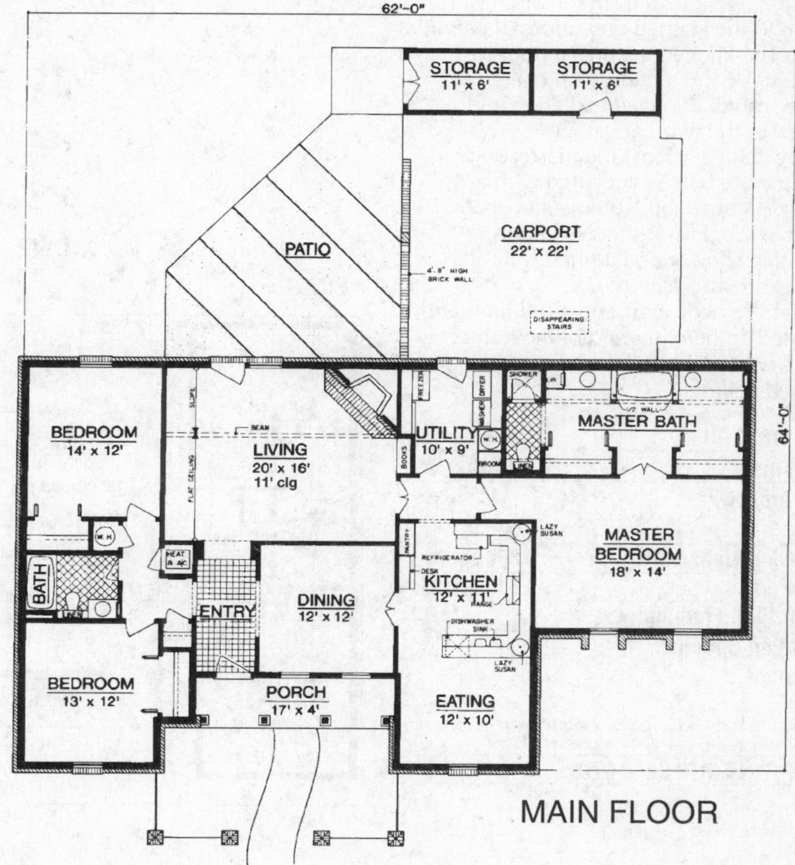

MAIN FLOOR

Plan E-1818

FOR MORE DETAILS, SEE PLAN AT familyhandyman.com/homeplans

Showy One-Story

- Dramatic windows embellish the exterior of this showy one-story home.
- Inside, the entry provides a sweeping view of the living room, where sliding glass doors open to the backyard patio and flank a dramatic fireplace.
- Skylights accent the living room's sloped ceiling, while arched openings define the formal dining room.
- Double doors lead from the dining room to the kitchen and informal eating area. The kitchen features a built-in work desk and a pantry. An oversized utility room adjoins the kitchen and accesses the two-car garage.
- A tray ceiling adorns the master suite. The private bath is accented with a skylight above the fabulous fan-shaped marble tub. His-and-hers vanities, a separate shower and a huge walk-in closet are also featured.
- Two more bedrooms and a full bath are located at the other end of the home.
- The front-facing bedroom boasts a sloped ceiling.

Plan E-1830	
Bedrooms: 3	**Baths:** 2
Living Area:	
Main floor	1,868 sq. ft.
Total Living Area:	**1,868 sq. ft.**
Garage and storage	616 sq. ft.
Exterior Wall Framing:	2x6
Foundation Options:	
Crawlspace	
Slab	

(All plans can be built with your choice of foundation and framing. A generic conversion diagram is available. See order form.)

BLUEPRINT PRICE CODE: B

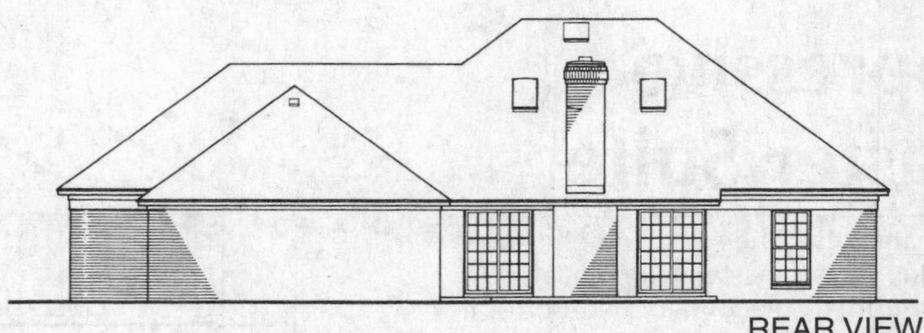

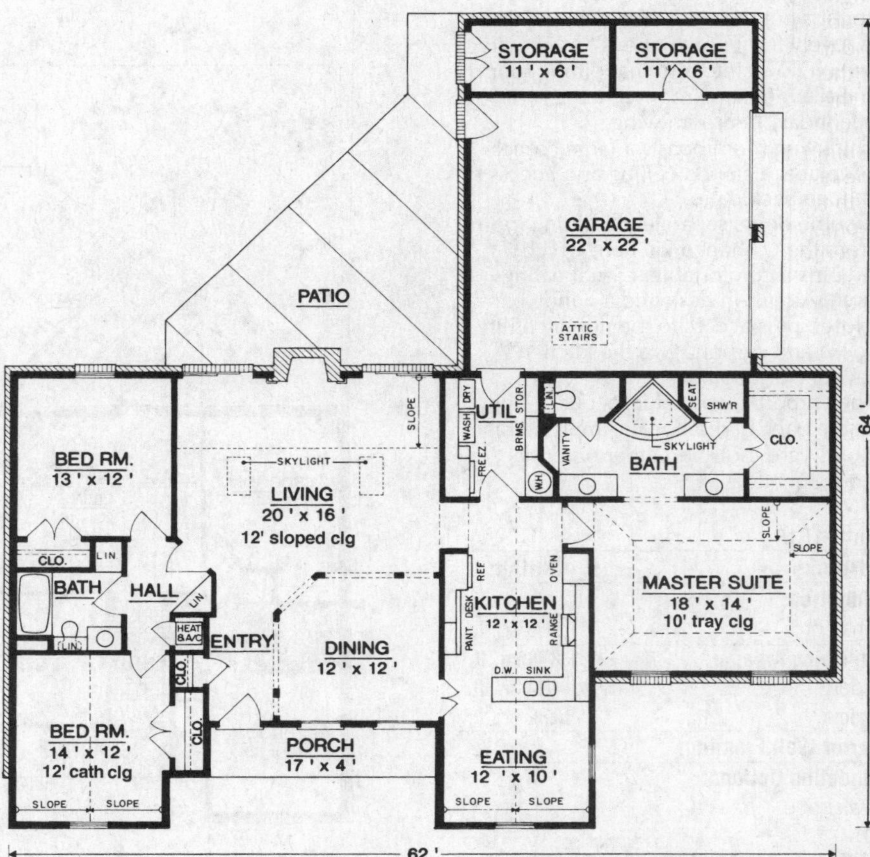

MAIN FLOOR

Plan E-1830

Distinguished Durability

- Sturdy tapered columns with brick pedestals give this unique home a feeling of durability and security.
- Off the foyer, the spacious living room is brightened by the incoming light of the double dormers above. The high ceiling and the glass-framed fireplace add further ambience. An atrium door opens to the wraparound porch.
- Decorative wood columns and a high ceiling enhance the dining room.
- The neat kitchen shares serving counters with the breakfast nook and the living room, for easy service to both locations. A central cooktop island and a built-in desk are other conveniences.
- The main bath has twin sinks and is easily accessible from the secondary bedrooms and the living areas.
- An oval garden tub, an isolated toilet and dual sinks are featured in the master bath. The master suite also boasts a cathedral ceiling, a huge walk-in closet and a private porch.

Plan DW-1883

Bedrooms: 3	**Baths:** 2
Living Area:	
Main floor	1,883 sq. ft.
Total Living Area:	**1,883 sq. ft.**
Standard basement	1,883 sq. ft.
Exterior Wall Framing:	2x4

Foundation Options:
Standard basement
Crawlspace
Slab
(All plans can be built with your choice of foundation and framing. A generic conversion diagram is available. See order form.)

BLUEPRINT PRICE CODE: **B**

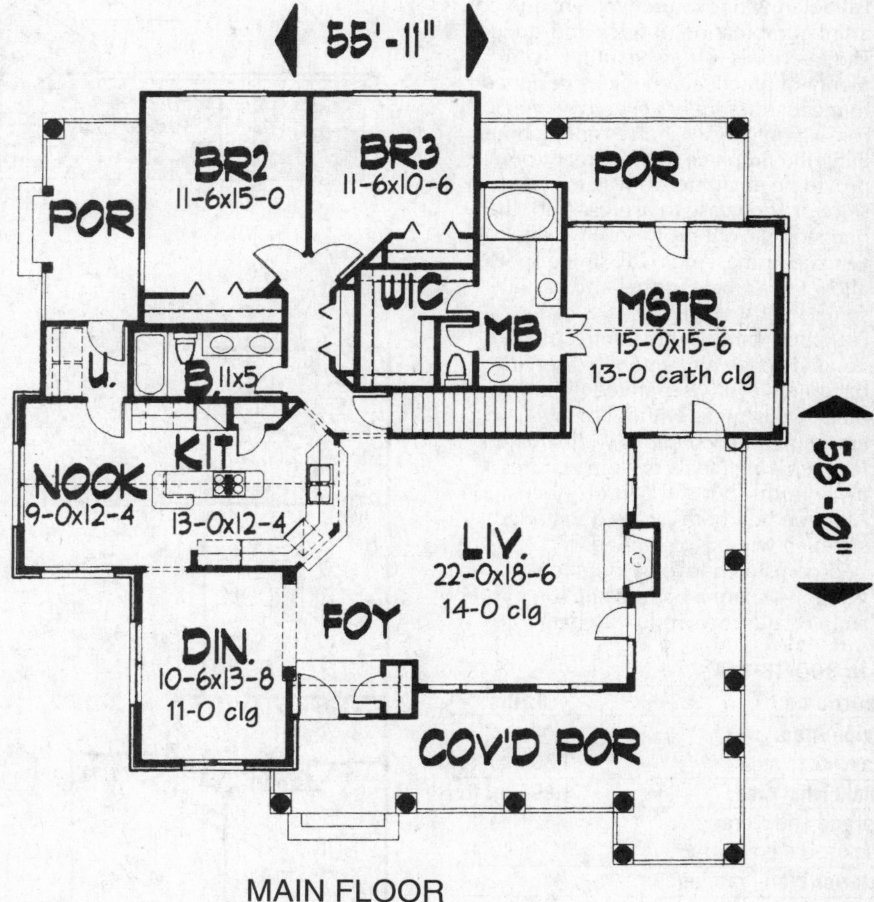

MAIN FLOOR

FOR MORE DETAILS, SEE PLAN AT familyhandyman.com/homeplans

Practical Grace

- Graceful, stylish features adorn this home's facade, such as tall shutters, a Palladian window arrangement and an artful combination of brick and stucco.
- The interior is just as beautiful, with plenty of practical amenities designed to meet your family's everyday needs.
- For example, bookshelves and cabinets flank the fireplace in the Great Room, providing an attractive way for you to store or showcase treasures. Also, the one-story layout promises livability for years to come. And dual dining spots allow you to host formal and casual soirees with equal ease.
- Equipped with a large pantry, plentiful counter space and an angled serving bar, and cleverly separated from the other living areas without being confining, the kitchen is well-situated for preparing meals or doing chores away from—but still part of—the action.
- All three bedrooms share a secluded sleeping wing. Two secondary bedrooms with lovely front-facing windows share a bath, while the master suite hoards its own luxury bath.

Plan BOD-18-11A

Bedrooms: 3	**Baths:** 2
Living Area:	
Main floor	1,890 sq. ft.
Total Living Area:	**1,890 sq. ft.**
Garage and storage	521 sq. ft.
Enclosed storage	44 sq. ft.
Exterior Wall Framing:	2x4
Foundation Options:	
Crawlspace	
Slab	

(All plans can be built with your choice of foundation and framing. A generic conversion diagram is available. See order form.)

BLUEPRINT PRICE CODE: B

REAR VIEW

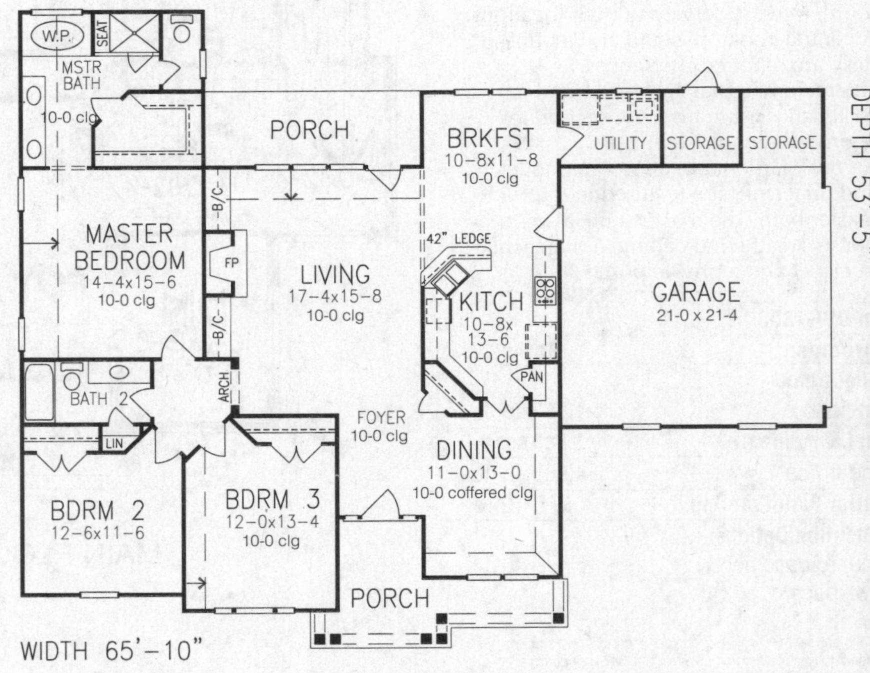

MAIN FLOOR

Plan BOD-18-11A

SEE ORDER INFO ON PAGES 12-15

A Peek at Country

- Three charming dormers peek out from this fantastic country home. The large front porch below provides plenty of room for outdoor family activities.
- Beyond the entry lies the cavernous Great Room, which includes a handsome fireplace, a curved serving bar looking into the kitchen, and access to the backyard patio through French doors.
- The airy country kitchen boasts a large central island, lots of counter space and a sizable pantry with built-in shelves. The kitchen serves a sun-drenched breakfast nook with a built-in window seat; the formal dining room is also within easy reach.
- Luxury is king in the master bedroom, which features a bayed sitting area, a walk-in closet and private access to the backyard patio. The master bath boasts another walk-in closet and a garden tub.
- Two secondary bedrooms share a full hall bath.

Plan DD-1890

Bedrooms: 3	**Baths:** 2½
Living Area:	
Main floor	1,890 sq. ft.
Total Living Area:	**1,890 sq. ft.**
Standard basement	1,890 sq. ft.
Garage and storage	455 sq. ft.
Exterior Wall Framing:	2x4

Foundation Options:

Standard basement
Crawlspace
Slab
(All plans can be built with your choice of foundation and framing. A generic conversion diagram is available. See order form.)

BLUEPRINT PRICE CODE: B

BREAKFAST NOOKS & MORNING ROOMS

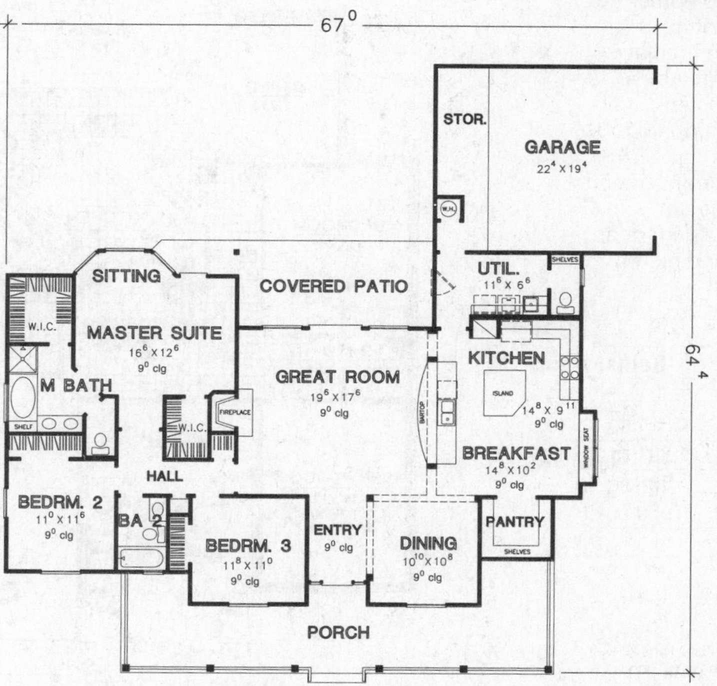

MAIN FLOOR

Garden Home with a View

- This clever design proves that privacy doesn't have to be compromised even in high-density urban neighborhoods. From within, views are oriented to a beautiful, lush entry courtyard and a covered rear porch.
- The exterior appearance is sheltered, but warm and welcoming.
- The innovative interior design centers on a unique kitchen, which directs traffic away from the working areas while still serving the entire home.
- The sunken family room features a vaulted ceiling and a warm fireplace.
- The master suite is highlighted by a sumptuous master bath with an oversized shower and a whirlpool tub, plus a large walk-in closet.
- The formal living room is designed and placed in such a way that it can become a third bedroom, a den, or an office or study room, depending on family needs and lifestyles.

Plan E-1824	
Bedrooms: 2+	**Baths:** 2
Living Area:	
Main floor	1,891 sq. ft.
Total Living Area:	**1,891 sq. ft.**
Garage	506 sq. ft.
Storage	60 sq. ft.
Exterior Wall Framing:	2x4
Foundation Options:	
Crawlspace	
Slab	

(All plans can be built with your choice of foundation and framing. A generic conversion diagram is available. See order form.)

BLUEPRINT PRICE CODE: B

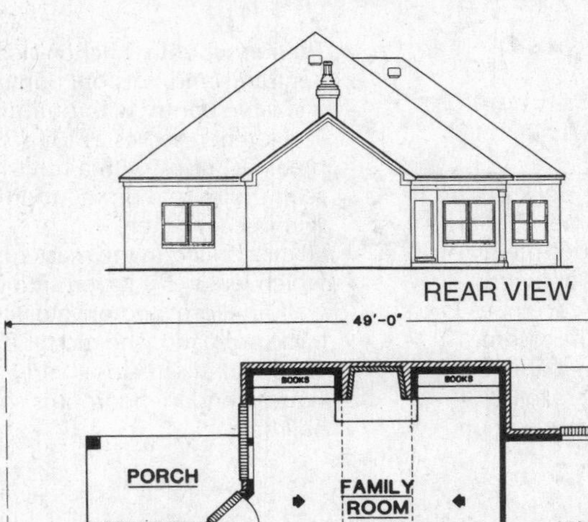
REAR VIEW

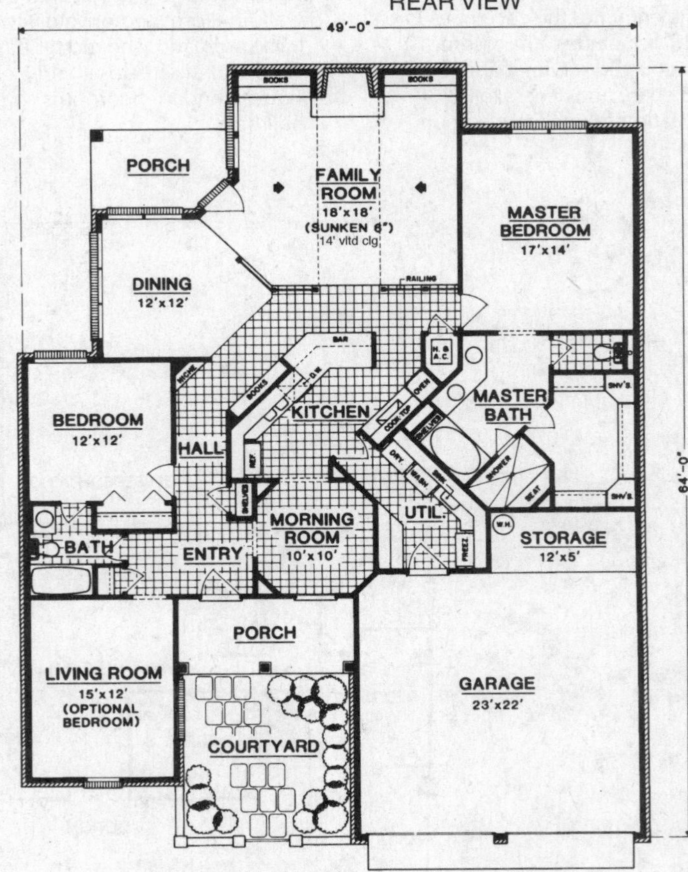

MAIN FLOOR

Sweet Home

- The sweet facade of this charming home looks as if it were plucked straight out of a European hamlet. The stone exterior, decorated dormers and cute porch combine to present a charming invitation to guests.
- Inside, the floor plan takes advantage of the compact square footage. A tiled foyer leads into a unique curved gallery that wraps around the central Great Room. On the left, a half-wall allows a view into the dining room.
- A wall of windows adds brightness and cheer to the Great Room, where a shuttered pass-through to the kitchen lets the chef visit with guests. French doors open to a railed deck that is the perfect site for drinks with friends.
- Between the kitchen and the breakfast nook, a serving counter provides a spot to set snacks. The kitchen's island cooktop makes meal preparation easier.
- The Great Room, the breakfast nook and the kitchen boast high ceilings.
- The master suite's sunny bay serves as a cozy sitting area to retreat to each day.

Plan DW-1892

Bedrooms: 3	**Baths:** 2
Living Area:	
Main floor	1,892 sq. ft.
Total Living Area:	**1,892 sq. ft.**
Standard basement	1,892 sq. ft.
Exterior Wall Framing:	2x4
Foundation Options:	
Standard basement	
Crawlspace	
Slab	

(All plans can be built with your choice of foundation and framing. A generic conversion diagram is available. See order form.)

BLUEPRINT PRICE CODE: B

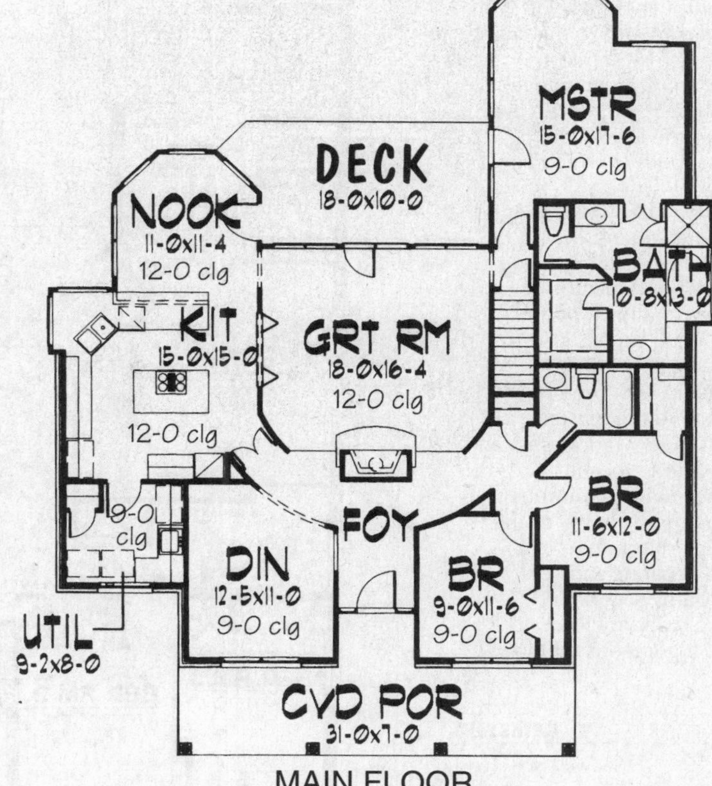

MAIN FLOOR

Ultimate French Comfort

- Delightful interior touches coupled with a striking French facade make this home the ultimate in one-story comfort.
- In the sidelighted entry, an attractive overhead plant ledge captures the eye.
- The entry opens to the formal dining and living rooms—both of which boast high ceilings.
- In the living room, a handy wet bar and a media center flank a handsome fireplace. Large windows frame wide backyard views. Around the corner, French doors open to a back porch.
- Adjacent to the dining room, the kitchen offers a speedy serving bar. A bayed nook lights up with morning sun.
- Double doors open to the master bedroom, with its cute window seat and TV shelf. A high ceiling tops it off.
- Two walk-in closets with glamorous mirror doors flank the walkway to the master bath, which offers an exotic garden tub and a separate shower.
- One of the two roomy secondary bedrooms offers a walk-in closet, a built-in desk and a gorgeous window.

Plan RD-1895	
Bedrooms: 3	**Baths:** 2
Living Area:	
Main floor	1,895 sq. ft.
Total Living Area:	**1,895 sq. ft.**
Garage and storage	485 sq. ft.
Exterior Wall Framing:	2x4
Foundation Options:	
Crawlspace	
Slab	
(All plans can be built with your choice of foundation and framing. A generic conversion diagram is available. See order form.)	
BLUEPRINT PRICE CODE:	**B**

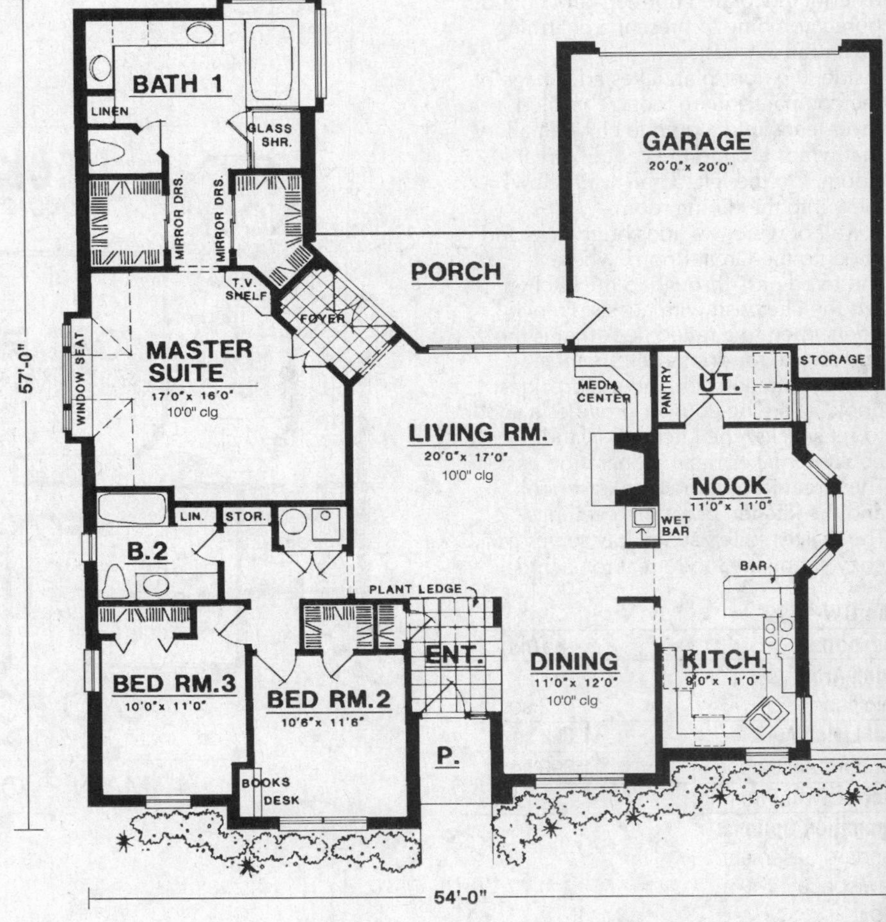

MAIN FLOOR

Plan RD-1895

SEE ORDER INFO ON PAGES 12-15

While Away an Afternoon

- The pretty porch that fronts this home provides plenty of room for whiling away an afternoon. Try a porch swing on one end and a cluster of comfortable wicker furniture on the other.
- Inside, columns introduce the living room and the dining room, on either side of the foyer. A tray ceiling lends elegance to the living room.
- At the rear of the home, the Great Room, the breakfast nook and the kitchen flow into one another, creating an easygoing, casual spot for family fun. In the Great Room, a neat media wall holds the TV, the DVD player and the stereo. An angled fireplace adds a bit of rustic charm to the setting.
- Tucked away for privacy, the master bedroom provides a pleasant retreat. A stepped ceiling crowns the room, while a bay window serves as a sitting area.

Plan AX-5374

Bedrooms: 3	**Baths:** 2
Living Area:	
Main floor	1,902 sq. ft.
Total Living Area:	**1,902 sq. ft.**
Standard basement	1,925 sq. ft.
Garage and storage	534 sq. ft.
Utility room	18 sq. ft.
Exterior Wall Framing:	2x4

Foundation Options:

Standard basement
Crawlspace
Slab
(All plans can be built with your choice of foundation and framing. A generic conversion diagram is available. See order form.)

BLUEPRINT PRICE CODE: **B**

VIEW INTO GREAT ROOM

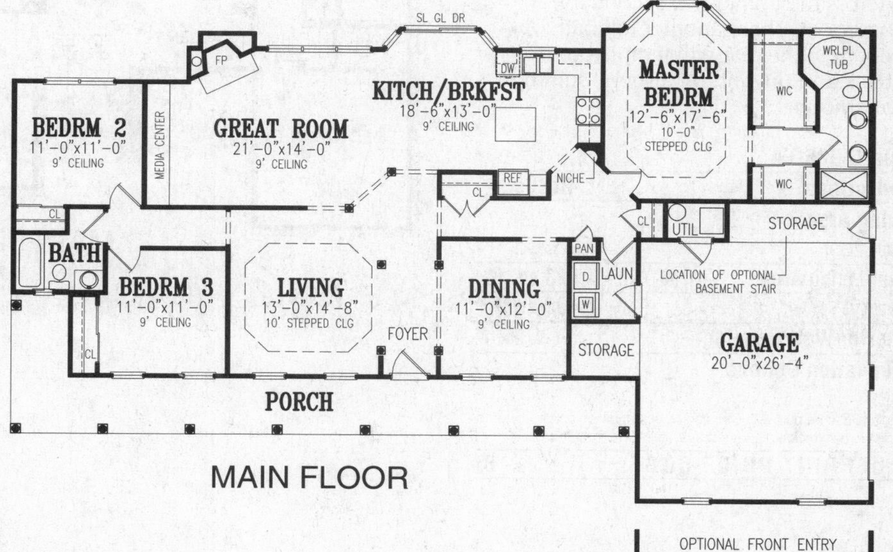

MAIN FLOOR

Plan AX-5374

Fond of French?

- Old country elegance and comfort are yours with this beautiful French traditional home.
- Central to all activities in the home, the large living room boasts the warmth of a fireplace and is complemented by built-in bookshelves.
- The convenient galley kitchen features a handy snack bar shared with the living room, and a breakfast nook for casual meals. A formal dining room lies between the kitchen and the foyer.
- "Luxurious" best describes the master suite, with an art niche to display your favorite sculpture, and a lavish bath that boasts dual sinks and a Jacuzzi tub. A roomy walk-in closet and built-in shelves are welcome additions, providing plenty of space for clothing and storage.
- Across the home, two secondary bedrooms share another full bath. A porch in the rear will tempt you to sit back and unwind on a sunny summer afternoon.

Plan L-925-FA	
Bedrooms: 3	**Baths:** 2
Living Area:	
Main floor	1,923 sq. ft.
Total Living Area:	**1,923 sq. ft.**
Garage	490 sq. ft.
Exterior Wall Framing:	2x4
Foundation Options:	
Slab	
(All plans can be built with your choice of foundation and framing. A generic conversion diagram is available. See order form.)	
BLUEPRINT PRICE CODE:	**B**

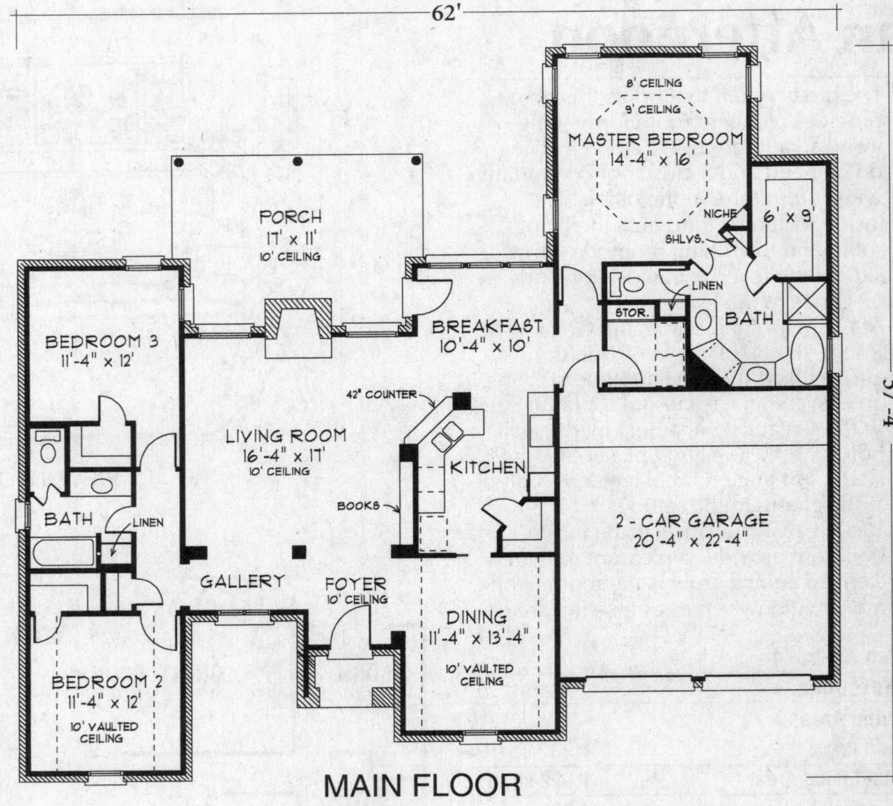

MAIN FLOOR

Plan L-925-FA

SEE ORDER INFO ON PAGES 12-15

Tasteful Charm

- Columned covered porches lend warmth and charm to the front and rear of this tasteful traditional home.
- Sidelight and transom glass brightens the entry foyer, which shares a high ceiling with the elegant dining room.
- The dining room provides a quiet spot for formal meals, while a Palladian window arrangement adds light and flair.
- The spacious living room offers a warming fireplace and an adjacent TV cabinet. The dramatic ceiling vaults to an exciting height. French doors give way to the skylighted rear porch, which is finished with lovely brick pavers. Two brick steps descend to an adjoining patio, which is also beautifully paved with brick.
- The gourmet kitchen offers a built-in oven/microwave cabinet, a separate cooktop and an island snack bar with a sink. Its high ceiling extends into the sunny breakfast nook.
- The oversized laundry room includes a handy half-bath, a wall-to-wall storage cabinet, a hanging rod, a large sink and nearby porch access.
- The secluded master bedroom boasts a vaulted ceiling and a large walk-in closet. In the private master bath, a glass-block divider separates the whirlpool tub from the shower stall.

Plan J-9414

Bedrooms: 3	**Baths:** 2½
Living Area:	
Main floor	1,974 sq. ft.
Total Living Area:	**1,974 sq. ft.**
Standard basement	1,974 sq. ft.
Garage and storage	518 sq. ft.
Exterior Wall Framing:	2x4
Foundation Options:	
Standard basement	
Crawlspace	
Slab	

(All plans can be built with your choice of foundation and framing. A generic conversion diagram is available. See order form.)

BLUEPRINT PRICE CODE: B

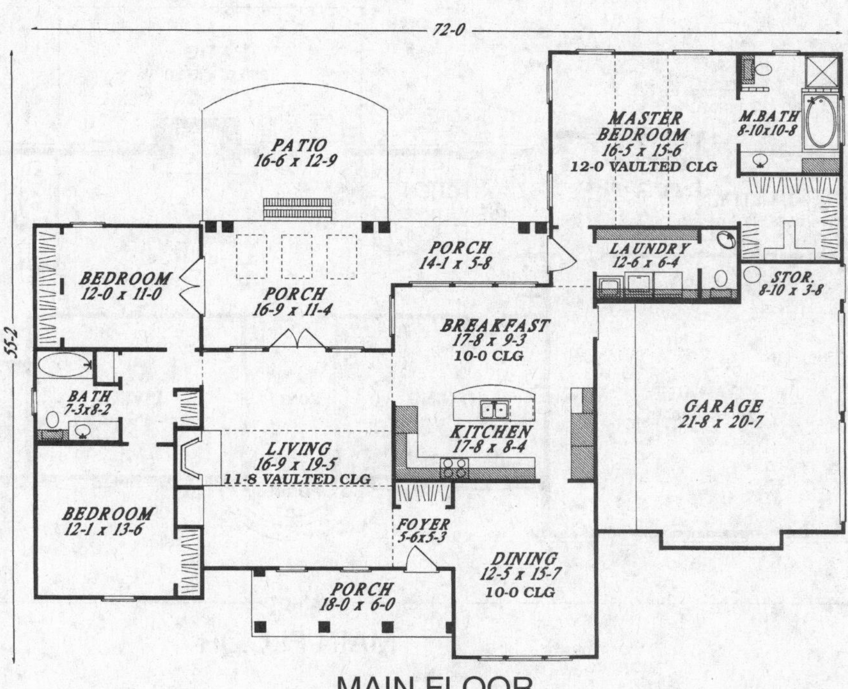

BASEMENT STAIRWAY LOCATION

MAIN FLOOR

Plan J-9414

FOR MORE DETAILS, SEE PLAN AT familyhandyman.com/homeplans

Family Home, Formal Accents

- Captivating roof angles and European detailing highlight the exterior of this graceful home.
- The generous foyer is flanked by the spacious living and dining rooms, both with tall, ornate windows.
- Beyond the foyer lies an expansive family room, highlighted by a dramatic fireplace and sliding glass doors that open to a sunny patio.
- The kitchen makes use of an L-shaped counter and a central island to maximaze efficiency. The adjacent breakfast room offers casual dining. A nearby utility room features a washer and dryer and a door to the backyard.
- The large master suite boasts two closets and a private bath with a dual-sink vanity and a step-up tub.
- Across the hall, two additional bedrooms share a second full bath.

Plan C-8103

Bedrooms: 3	**Baths:** 2
Living Area:	
Main floor	1,940 sq. ft.
Total Living Area:	**1,940 sq. ft.**
Daylight basement	1,870 sq. ft.
Garage	400 sq. ft.
Exterior Wall Framing:	2x4
Foundation Options:	
Daylight basement	
Crawlspace	
Slab	

(All plans can be built with your choice of foundation and framing. A generic conversion diagram is available. See order form.)

BLUEPRINT PRICE CODE: B

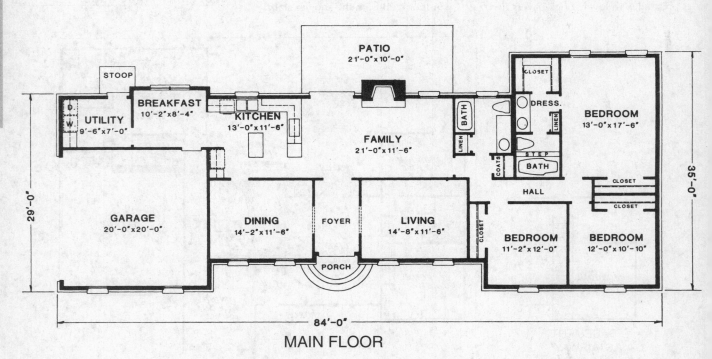

PATIO
21'-0"x10'-0"
STOOP
BREAKFAST
10'-2"x8'-4"
UTILITY
9'-6"x7'-0"
D.
W.
KITCHEN
13'-0"x11'-6"
FAMILY
21'-0"x11'-6"
BATH
LINEN
CLOSET
DRESS.
LINEN
STEP
BATH
COATS
BEDROOM
13'-0"x17'-6"
HALL
CLOSET
CLOSET
GARAGE
20'-0"x20'-0"
DINING
14'-2"x11'-6"
FOYER
LIVING
14'-8"x11'-6"
CLOSET
BEDROOM
11'-2"x12'-0"
BEDROOM
12'-0"x10'-10"
PORCH
29'-0"
35'-0"
84'-0"

MAIN FLOOR

ORDER BLUEPRINTS ANYTIME!
CALL TOLL-FREE 1-800-820-1296

Plan C-8103

SEE ORDER INFO ON PAGES 12-15
familyhandyman.com/homeplans

Quite a Cottage

- This cottage's inviting wraparound veranda is topped by an eye-catching metal roof that will draw admiring gazes from neighbors out for a stroll.
- Inside, the raised foyer ushers guests into your home in style. Straight ahead, built-in bookshelves line one wall in the living room. A pass-through to the wet bar in the kitchen saves trips back and forth when entertaining.
- The family chef will love the gourmet kitchen, where an island cooktop frees counter space for other projects. For morning coffee and casual meals, the breakfast nook sets a cheery, relaxed tone. When appearances count, move out to the formal dining room.
- Across the home, the master suite serves as an oasis of peace and quiet. First thing in the morning, step out to the veranda to watch the rising sun soak up the mist. When you want a little extra special treatment, sink into the oversized garden tub for a long bath.
- The foremost bedroom boasts a large walk-in closet and built-in bookshelves.
- The blueprints for this home include plans for a detached two-car garage.

Plan L-893-VSA

Bedrooms: 3	**Baths:** 2
Living Area:	
Main floor	1,891 sq. ft.
Total Living Area:	**1,891 sq. ft.**
Detached garage	576 sq. ft.
Exterior Wall Framing:	2x4

Foundation Options:

Slab

(All plans can be built with your choice of foundation and framing. A generic conversion diagram is available. See order form.)

BLUEPRINT PRICE CODE: **B**

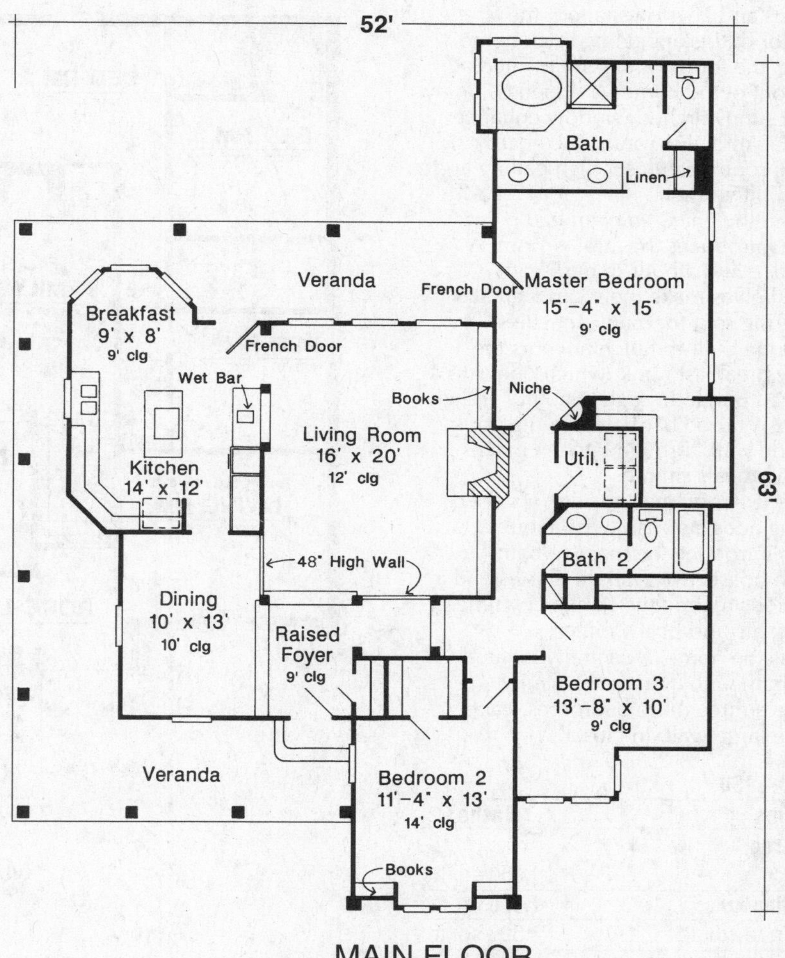

MAIN FLOOR

Appealing Brick

- Quoins and keystones adorn the exterior of this appealing brick home.
- Inside, the formal areas are located at the front of the home. A sloped ceiling and a sunny arched window enhance the elegant living room. The nearby dining room features a high ceiling and a decorative shelf.
- Beyond the entry, an overhead plant ledge introduces the family room. A fireplace and a built-in desk with bookshelves make the room a great gathering spot for many activities.
- A unique built-in hutch anchors the sunny breakfast nook, which opens to a covered porch through beautiful French doors. A raised bar between the nook and the walk-through kitchen makes serving meals simple.
- In the secluded master suite, a sloped ceiling adds a stylish twist. Double doors introduce the massive bath, which boasts two walk-in closets and a luxurious marble tub flanked by time-saving his-and-hers vanities.
- Across the home, a centrally located split bath with a dual-sink vanity services three more bedrooms, each with a large walk-in closet.

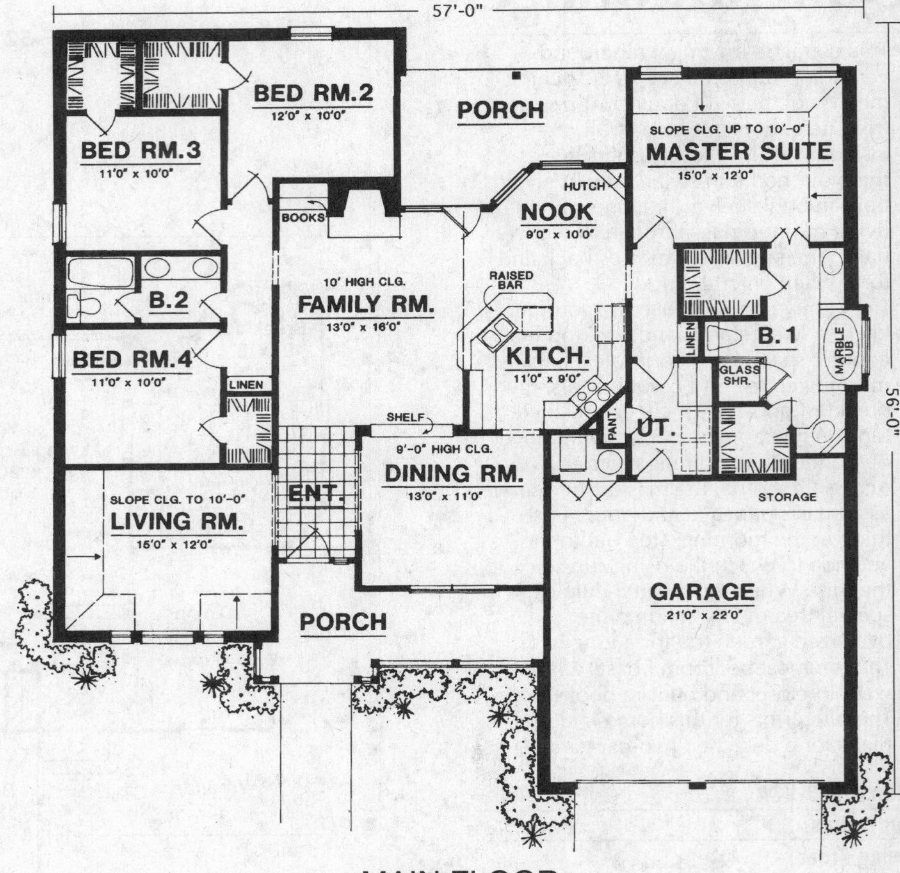

MAIN FLOOR

Plan RD-1950	
Bedrooms: 4	**Baths:** 2
Living Area:	
Main floor	1,950 sq. ft.
Total Living Area:	**1,950 sq. ft.**
Garage and storage	523 sq. ft.
Exterior Wall Framing:	2x4
Foundation Options:	
Crawlspace	
Slab	
(All plans can be built with your choice of foundation and framing. A generic conversion diagram is available. See order form.)	
BLUEPRINT PRICE CODE:	**B**

Plan RD-1950

SEE ORDER INFO ON PAGES 12-15
familyhandyman.com/homeplans

Southern Comfort

- This sprawling three-bedroom design exemplifies the comfort and charm of Southern-style architecture.
- The columned front porch beckons you to relax on a Sunday afternoon.
- Inside, the formal dining room opens to the left of the foyer, which leads to the home's focal point—the large living room. Complete with a built-in entertainment center, a cozy fireplace and a snack bar, this space will attract plenty of attention. Windows flanking the fireplace overlook the rear porch.
- Among the kitchen's many amenities are an island cooktop, a pantry closet and an adjoining breakfast area. The breakfast area accesses the rear porch through a French door.
- Secluded from the other bedrooms for privacy, the master suite is highlighted by two walk-in closets, a garden tub, a separate shower and a dual-sink vanity. The suite also enjoys private access to the rear porch.
- Across the home, two secondary bedrooms, one with a walk-in closet, share another full bath.

Plan L-1990-02A	
Bedrooms: 3	**Baths:** 2½
Living Area:	
Main floor	1,990 sq. ft.
Total Living Area:	**1,990 sq. ft.**
Garage	522 sq. ft.
Exterior Wall Framing:	2x4
Foundation Options:	
Slab	
(All plans can be built with your choice of foundation and framing. A generic conversion diagram is available. See order form.)	
BLUEPRINT PRICE CODE:	**B**

83'-6"
62'-10"
MASTER BEDROOM 13'-4" x 18' 9' CEILING
W.I.C
LINEN
9' CEILING
CAB'TS
MASTER-BATH 10'-8" x 13'
W.I.C
LINEN
BATH
36" HIGH COUNTER
2 - CAR GARAGE 21'-4" x 21'-4"
PORCH
FRENCH DOOR
PORCH
FRENCH DOOR
BREAKFAST AREA 10' x 9'-4" 9' CEILING
KITCHEN 13'-8" x 12'-8"
9' CEILING
PANTRY
42" COUNTER
WIDE SCREEN T.V.
CABINETS
CABINETS
LIVING ROOM 16'-4" x 18' 10' CEILING
BEDROOM 3 11'-8" x 11' 9' CEILING
LINEN
BATH 2
UTILITY 7'-8" x 8'-8" 9' CEILING
DINING 11'-4" x 13' 9' CEILING
FOYER 9' CEILING
BEDROOM 2 11'-4" x 13' 9' CEILING
SHELVES
PORCH

MAIN FLOOR

Traditional Curb Appeal

- With an expansive front porch topped by a charming trio of dormers, this traditional country-style home offers the curb appeal you seek.
- Accessing both the formal dining room and a bayed morning room, the kitchen boasts a work island and an attractive, bow-shaped counter serving the living room. The mudroom and laundry facilities are just around the corner.
- Step through the spacious living room's French doors to the deck area. An optional barbecue and an outdoor spa make entertaining a breeze.
- The master suite enjoys a bayed sitting area, deck access, two walk-in closets and a private bath with separate vanities and a garden tub.
- Two more bedrooms share a full hall bath. Future space upstairs can be used as you desire.

Plan DD-1984	
Bedrooms: 3+	**Baths:** 3
Living Area:	
Main floor	1,994 sq. ft.
Total Living Area:	**1,994 sq. ft.**
Future upper floor	1,316 sq. ft.
Standard basement	1,994 sq. ft.
Garage and storage	466 sq. ft.
Exterior Wall Framing:	2x4
Foundation Options:	
Standard basement	
Crawlspace	
Slab	

(All plans can be built with your choice of foundation and framing. A generic conversion diagram is available. See order form.)

BLUEPRINT PRICE CODE: **B**

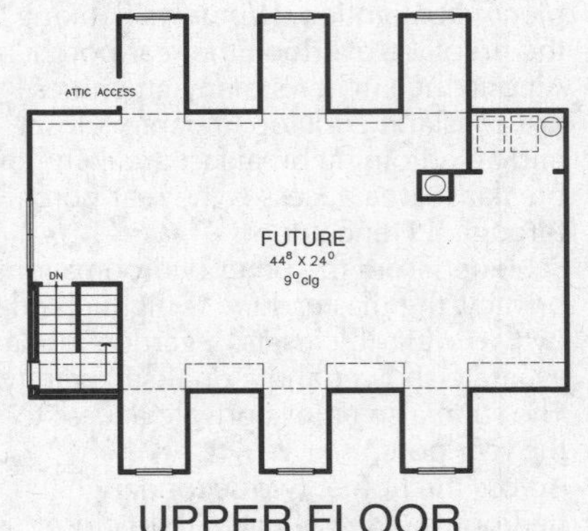

UPPER FLOOR

VIEW INTO LIVING ROOM

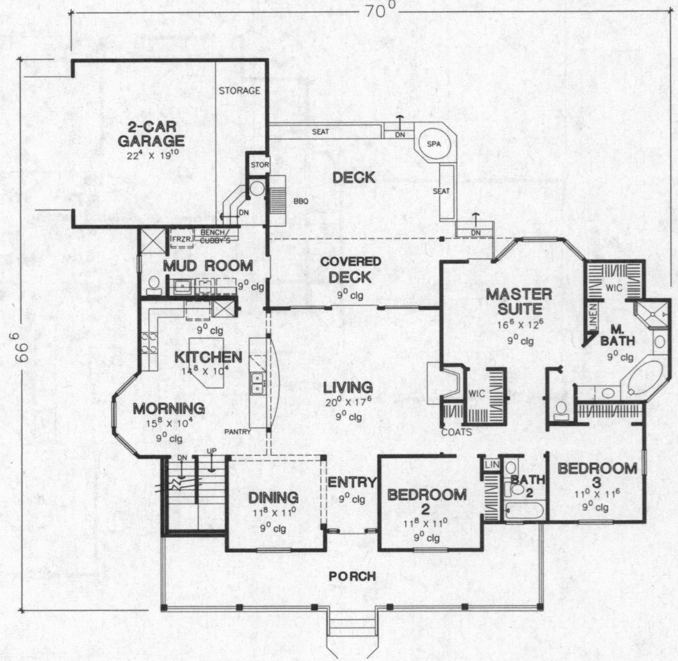

MAIN FLOOR

ORDER BLUEPRINTS ANYTIME!
CALL TOLL-FREE 1-800-820-1296

Plan DD-1984

SEE ORDER INFO ON PAGES 12-15
familyhandyman.com/homeplans

Interior Angles Add Excitement

- Interior angles add a touch of excitement to this one-story home.
- A pleasantly charming exterior combines wood and stone to give the plan a solid, comfortable look for any neighborhood.
- Formal living and dining rooms flank the entry, which leads into the large family room, featuring a fireplace, a vaulted ceiling and built-in bookshelves. A covered porch and a sunny patio are just steps away.
- The adjoining eating area with a built-in china cabinet angles off the roomy kitchen. Note the pantry and the convenient utility room.
- The master bedroom suite is both spacious and private, and includes a dressing room, a large walk-in closet and a secluded bath.
- The three secondary bedrooms are also zoned for privacy, and share a compartmentalized bath.

Plan E-1904

Bedrooms: 4	**Baths:** 2½
Living Area:	
Main floor	1,997 sq. ft.
Total Living Area:	**1,997 sq. ft.**
Garage	484 sq. ft.
Storage	104 sq. ft.
Exterior Wall Framing:	2x4
Foundation Options:	
Crawlspace	
Slab	

(All plans can be built with your choice of foundation and framing. A generic conversion diagram is available. See order form.)

BLUEPRINT PRICE CODE: B

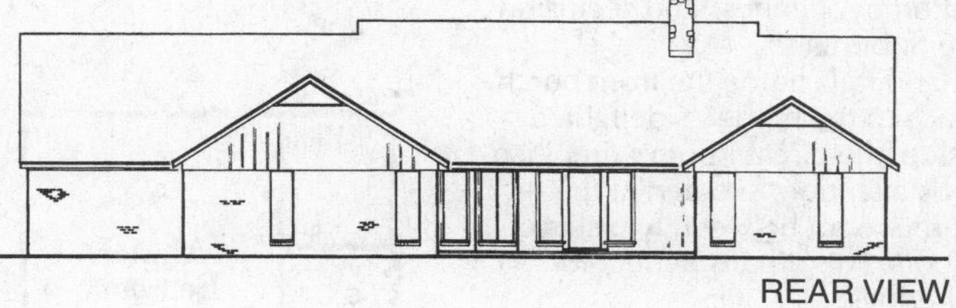
REAR VIEW

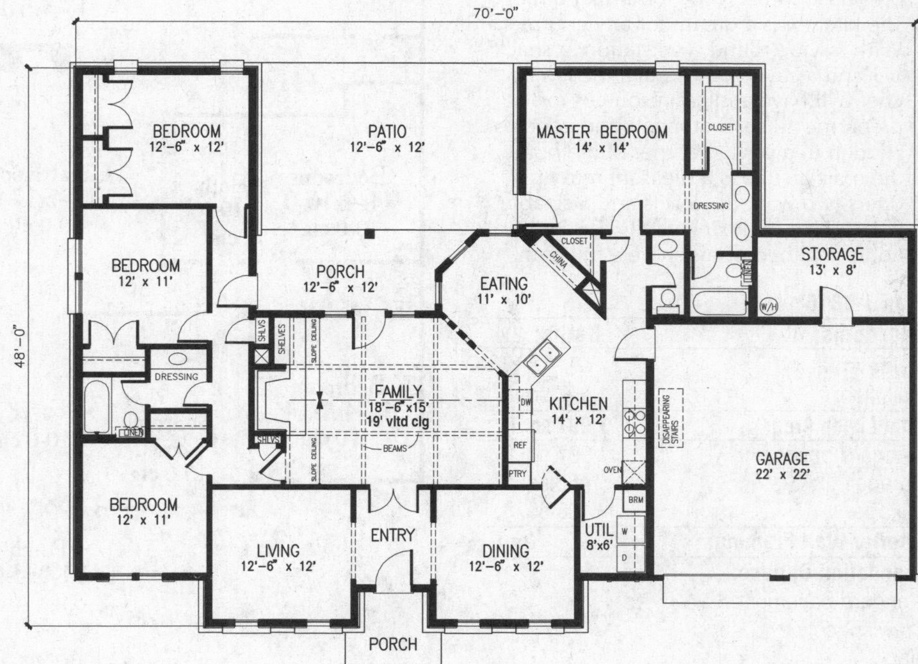

MAIN FLOOR

Clever Balance

- Beauty and balance are the hallmarks of this home's exterior, while a clever combination of openness and seclusion marks the floor plan.
- Columns and rails frame the front porch, which leads to the home's sidelighted entry. Inside, the Great Room's fireplace commands attention, situated at the center of the room between two sets of French doors. This area is perfect for large gatherings.
- The spacious dining room is equally accommodating for guests, while the breakfast nook is nice for casual dining.
- The kitchen is a dream for any gourmet. With a wide island workstation, a snack bar and a cavernous pantry, the family chef will have endless resources for preparing all sorts of meals and goodies.
- Hidden in a private corner of the home, the master suite is a pleasant retreat. It offers two walk-in closets and a sizable bath with a dual-sink vanity. Three additional bedrooms share a full bath.

Plan J-9816

Bedrooms: 4	**Baths:** 2½
Living Area:	
Main floor	1,997 sq. ft.
Total Living Area:	**1,997 sq. ft.**
Standard basement	1,997 sq. ft.
Garage	465 sq. ft.
Storage	105 sq. ft.
Exterior Wall Framing:	2x4

Foundation Options:

Standard basement
Crawlspace
Slab
(All plans can be built with your choice of foundation and framing. A generic conversion diagram is available. See order form.)

BLUEPRINT PRICE CODE: B

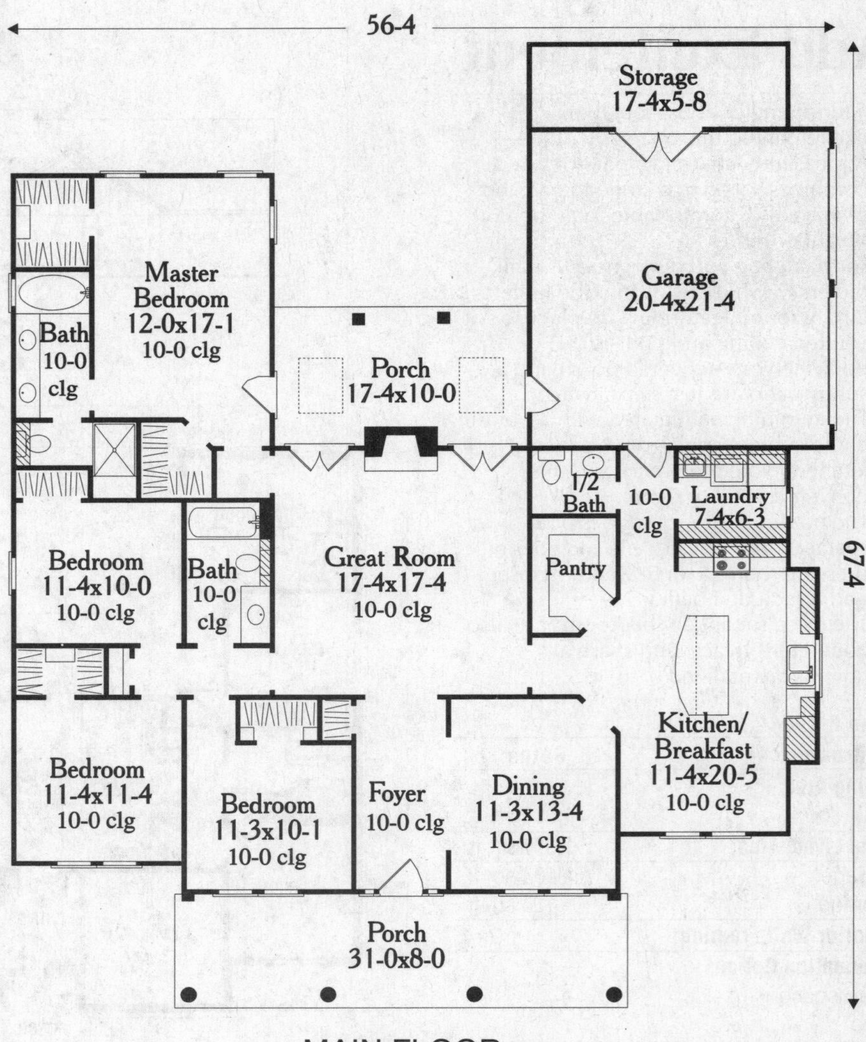

MAIN FLOOR

Plan J-9816

SEE ORDER INFO ON PAGES 12-15
familyhandyman.com/homeplans

Handsome Porch

- This home's handsome porch wraps around a lovely sidelighted entry and a bayed breakfast nook—so comfortable, you'll hardly want to go inside!
- When you finally step through the front door, however, you'll be glad you did. The entry spills gracefully into the Great Room, which boasts an ideal central location and three transom-topped windows overlooking a back patio.
- The well-planned kitchen features an island workstation and an angled snack bar, which serves the Great Room and the bayed formal dining room.
- The peaceful master suite offers the relaxation you crave at the end of a long day. Pamper yourself in the private bath's oval garden tub or oversized shower, then rest beneath the sleeping room's vaulted ceiling.
- At the front of the home, two additional bedrooms share a full hall bath.
- Plans for a detached, two-car garage are included with the blueprints.

Plan DD-1970	
Bedrooms: 3	**Baths:** 2
Living Area:	
Main floor	2,001 sq. ft.
Total Living Area:	**2,001 sq. ft.**
Standard basement	2,001 sq. ft.
Detached garage	440 sq. ft.
Exterior Wall Framing:	2x4
Foundation Options:	
Standard basement	
Crawlspace	
Slab	

(All plans can be built with your choice of foundation and framing. A generic conversion diagram is available. See order form.)

BLUEPRINT PRICE CODE: C

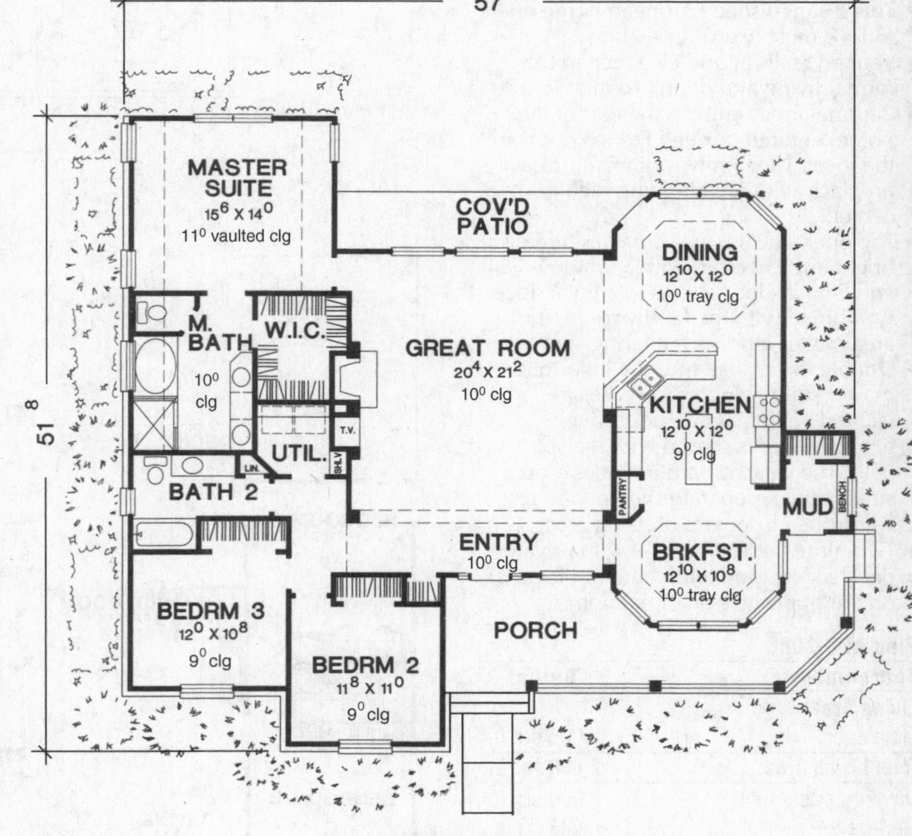

MAIN FLOOR

Plan DD-1970

FOR MORE DETAILS, SEE PLAN AT familyhandyman.com/homeplans

European Charm

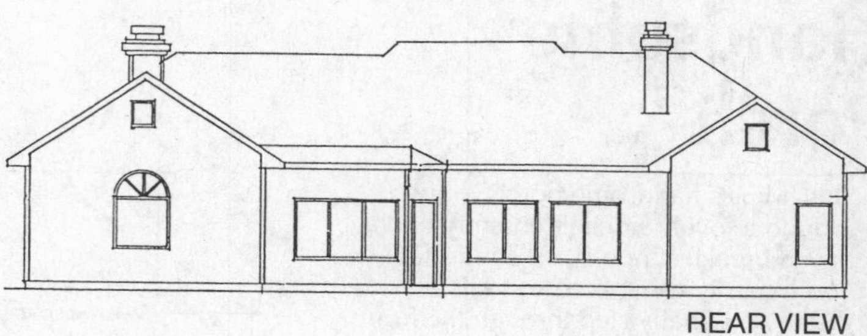

- This distinguished European home offers today's most luxurious features.
- Vaulted ceilings add elegance to the formal living and dining rooms.
- Informal areas enliven the rear of the home, entered through French doors in the foyer. The family room features a fireplace with an adjoining media center.
- The open kitchen and breakfast area is bright and cheerful, with a window wall and French-door access to a back deck. Combined with the family room, this area makes a prime gathering spot.
- Double doors lead into the luxurious master suite, which showcases a vaulted ceiling and a see-through fireplace that is shared with the spa bath. The splashy bath includes a dual-sink vanity, a separate shower and a wardrobe closet and dressing area.
- Two more bedrooms, one with private deck access, and a full bath are located on the opposite side of the home.

Plan APS-2006

Bedrooms: 3	**Baths:** 2
Living Area:	
Main floor	2,006 sq. ft.
Total Living Area:	**2,006 sq. ft.**
Daylight basement	2,006 sq. ft.
Garage	448 sq. ft.
Exterior Wall Framing:	2x4
Foundation Options:	
Daylight basement	
Crawlspace	
Slab	

(All plans can be built with your choice of foundation and framing. A generic conversion diagram is available. See order form.)

BLUEPRINT PRICE CODE: C

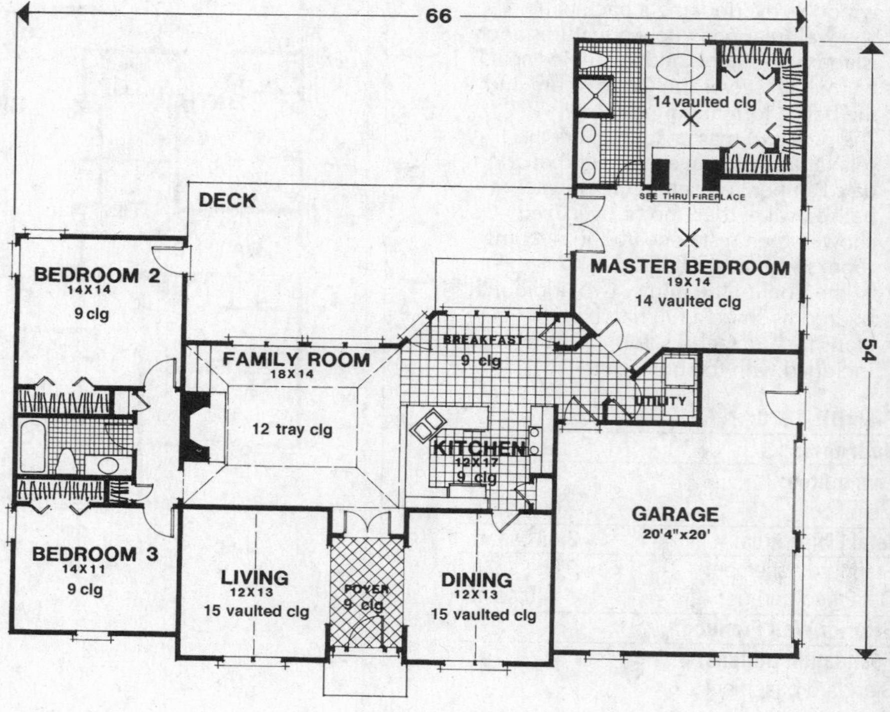

MAIN FLOOR

Plan APS-2006

SEE ORDER INFO ON PAGES 12-15
familyhandyman.com/homeplans

Magnificent Mediterranean

- High windows and noble arches highlight the magnificent facade of this comfortable Mediterranean home.
- Past dramatic entry columns, double doors introduce the high foyer. The adjoining formal living and dining rooms also have high ceilings.
- The open family room boasts a media wall and a central fireplace. Sliding glass doors open to a great covered patio in the backyard.
- A serving bar connects the family room to the kitchen, which adjoins a bright breakfast nook. The nook's vaulted ceiling rises over the kitchen as well.
- Isolated from household bustle, the master bedroom flaunts a private bath and its own access to the backyard. The bath sports a garden tub, a separate shower and a private toilet.
- On the opposite side of the home, a convenient hall bath services three secondary bedrooms with overhead plant shelves. The rear bedroom offers patio access.

Plan HDS-99-231	
Bedrooms: 4	**Baths:** 2
Living Area:	
Main floor	2,010 sq. ft.
Total Living Area:	**2,010 sq. ft.**
Garage	416 sq. ft.
Exterior Wall Framing:	2x4
Foundation Options:	
Slab (All plans can be built with your choice of foundation and framing. A generic conversion diagram is available. See order form.)	
BLUEPRINT PRICE CODE:	**C**

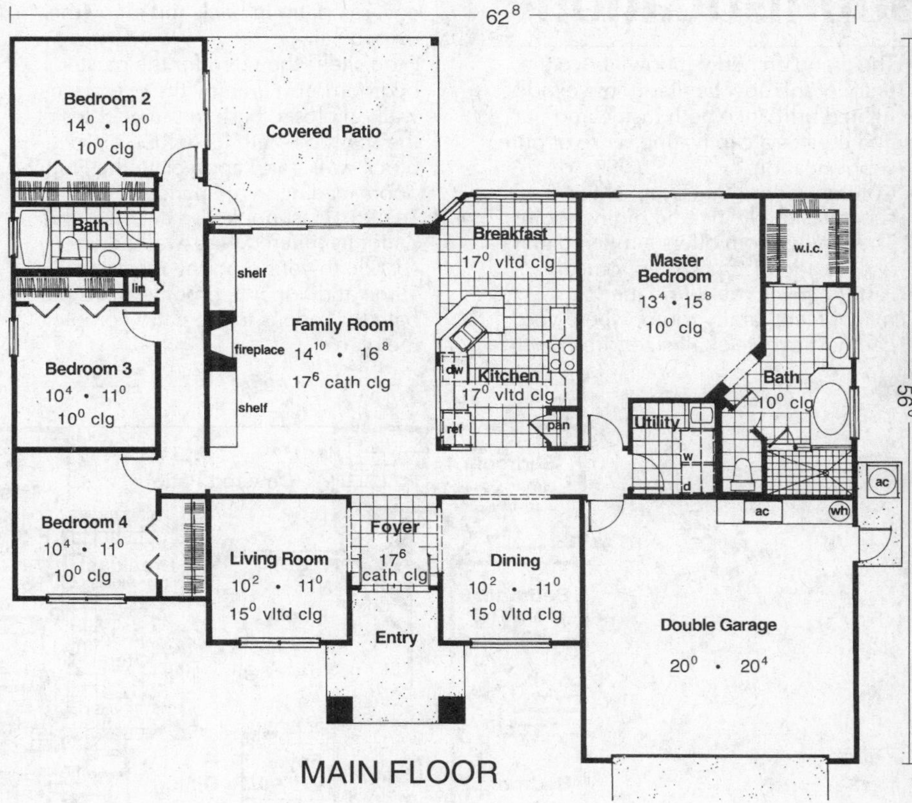

MAIN FLOOR

ORDER BLUEPRINTS ANYTIME!
CALL TOLL-FREE 1-800-820-1296

Plan HDS-99-231

FOR MORE DETAILS, SEE PLAN AT
familyhandyman.com/homeplans

Pure Sophistication

- The grand arched window above the entry of this spectacular home exudes lighted brilliance both inside and out, and creates a captivating sense of pure sophistication.
- Columns adorn the foyer, which separates the living and dining rooms. The dining room offers a mitered glass wall to add pizzazz to your meal.
- Past the foyer you'll find the magnificent family room, where you can host events of all sizes, from boisterous birthday bashes to intimate evenings by the cozy fireplace. If the night is warm and starry, escape to the covered patio in back and enjoy the evening air.
- Exquisite is the word for the master bedroom. You'll enjoy the oversized walk-in closet, bask in the bubbles of the spa tub—with its unique glass-block wall—and appreciate the French doors leading to the patio.
- The breakfast nook also accesses the patio. Its mitered glass wall adds sparkle to your morning meal.
- Three additional bedrooms and a full bath that opens to the patio complete the plan.

Plan HDS-99-255

Bedrooms: 4	**Baths:** 2
Living Area:	
Main floor	2,060 sq. ft.
Total Living Area:	**2,060 sq. ft.**
Garage	478 sq. ft.
Exterior Wall Framing:	2x4
Foundation Options:	
Slab	

(All plans can be built with your choice of foundation and framing. A generic conversion diagram is available. See order form.)

BLUEPRINT PRICE CODE: C

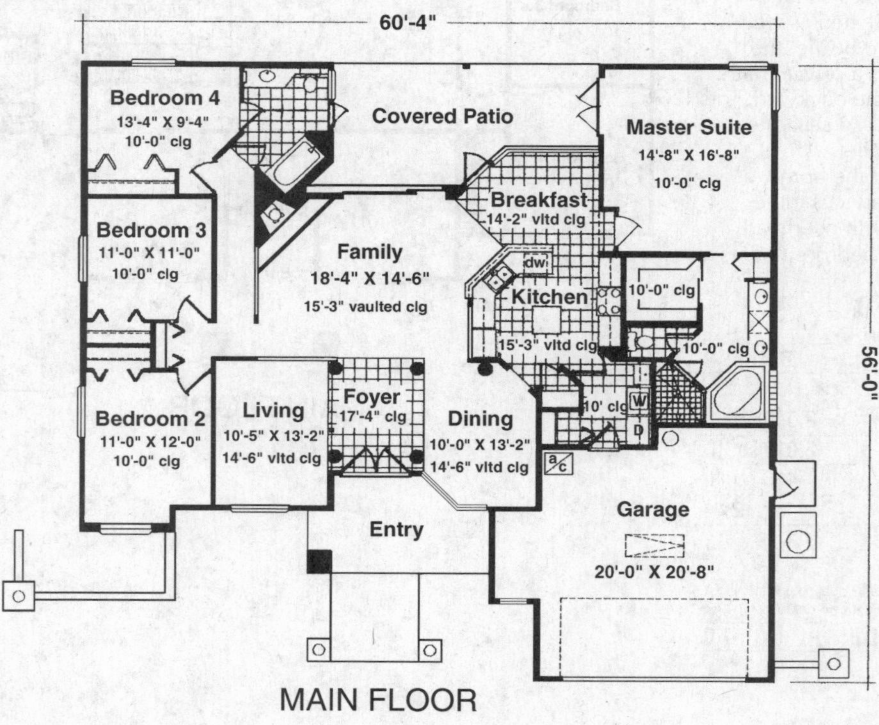

MAIN FLOOR

Plan HDS-99-255

SEE ORDER INFO ON PAGES 12-15
familyhandyman.com/homeplans

Mark Englund/Homestore™ Plans and Publications

French Garden Design

- A creative, angular design gives this traditional French garden home an exciting, open and airy floor plan.
- Guests enter through a covered, columned porch that opens into the large, angled living and dining rooms.
- High ceilings highlight the living and dining area, which also features corner windows, a wet bar, a cozy fireplace and access to a huge backyard porch.
- The angled walk-through kitchen, also with a high ceiling, offers plenty of work space and an adjoining informal eating nook that faces a delightful private courtyard. The nearby utility area has extra freezer space, a walk-in pantry and garage access.
- The home's bedrooms are housed in two separate wings. One wing boasts a luxurious master suite, which features a large walk-in closet, an angled tub and a separate shower.
- Two large bedrooms in the other wing share a hall bath. Each bedroom has a walk-in closet.

Plan E-2004	
Bedrooms: 3	**Baths:** 2
Living Area:	
Main floor	2,023 sq. ft.
Total Living Area:	**2,023 sq. ft.**
Garage	484 sq. ft.
Storage	87 sq. ft.
Exterior Wall Framing:	2x6
Foundation Options:	
Crawlspace	
Slab	

(All plans can be built with your choice of foundation and framing. A generic conversion diagram is available. See order form.)

BLUEPRINT PRICE CODE: C

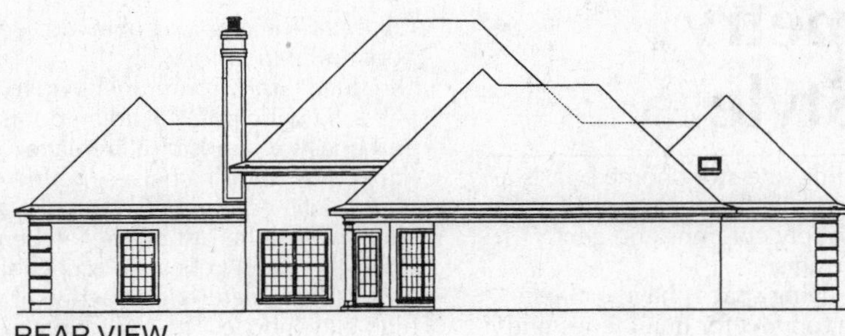

REAR VIEW

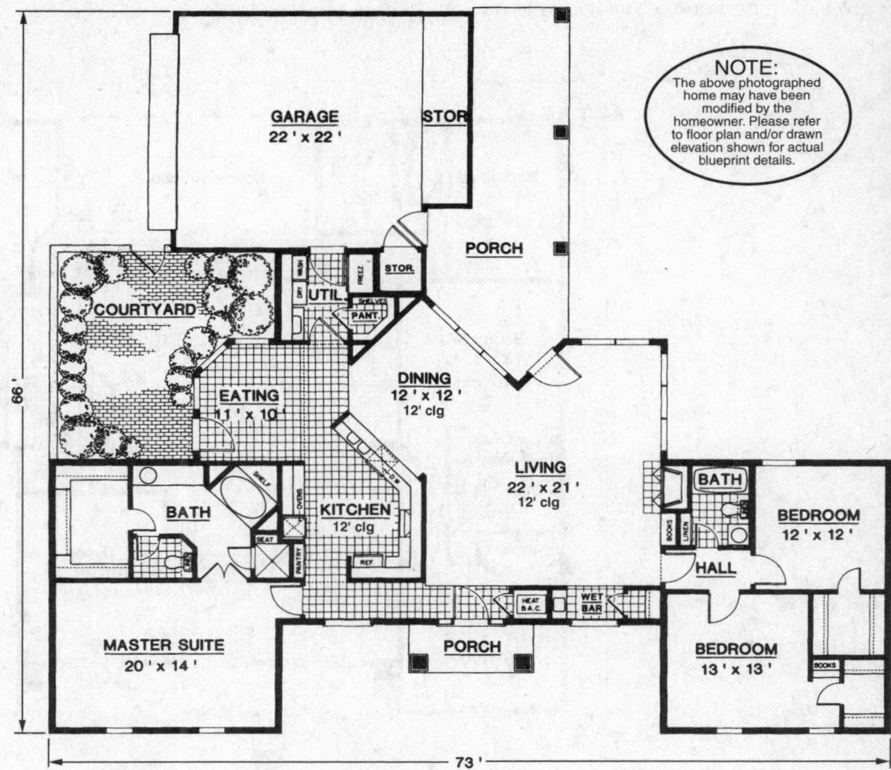

NOTE: The above photographed home may have been modified by the homeowner. Please refer to floor plan and/or drawn elevation shown for actual blueprint details.

MAIN FLOOR

BREAKFAST NOOKS & MORNING ROOMS

Plan E-2004

FOR MORE DETAILS, SEE PLAN AT familyhandyman.com/homeplans

Symmetry and Style

- This appealing one-story home boasts a striking facade with symmetrical rooflines, stately columns and gently curved transoms.
- The formal living spaces have a classic split design, perfect for quiet times and conversation.
- The unique layout of the bedroom wing gives each bedroom easy access to a full bath. The rear bedroom also enjoys pool and patio proximity.
- The huge family room opens up to the patio via wide pocket sliding doors, and boasts a handsome fireplace flanked by built-in shelves, perfect for your media equipment.
- The master suite just off the kitchen and nook is private, yet easily accessible. One unique feature is its bed wall with high glass above. The master bath offers a huge walk-in closet, a relaxing corner tub, a step-down shower, dual sinks and a private toilet.

Plan HDS-99-147	
Bedrooms: 4	**Baths:** 3
Living Area:	
Main floor	2,089 sq. ft.
Total Living Area:	**2,089 sq. ft.**
Garage	415 sq. ft.
Exterior Wall Framing:	2x4
Foundation Options:	
Slab	
(All plans can be built with your choice of foundation and framing. A generic conversion diagram is available. See order form.)	
BLUEPRINT PRICE CODE:	**C**

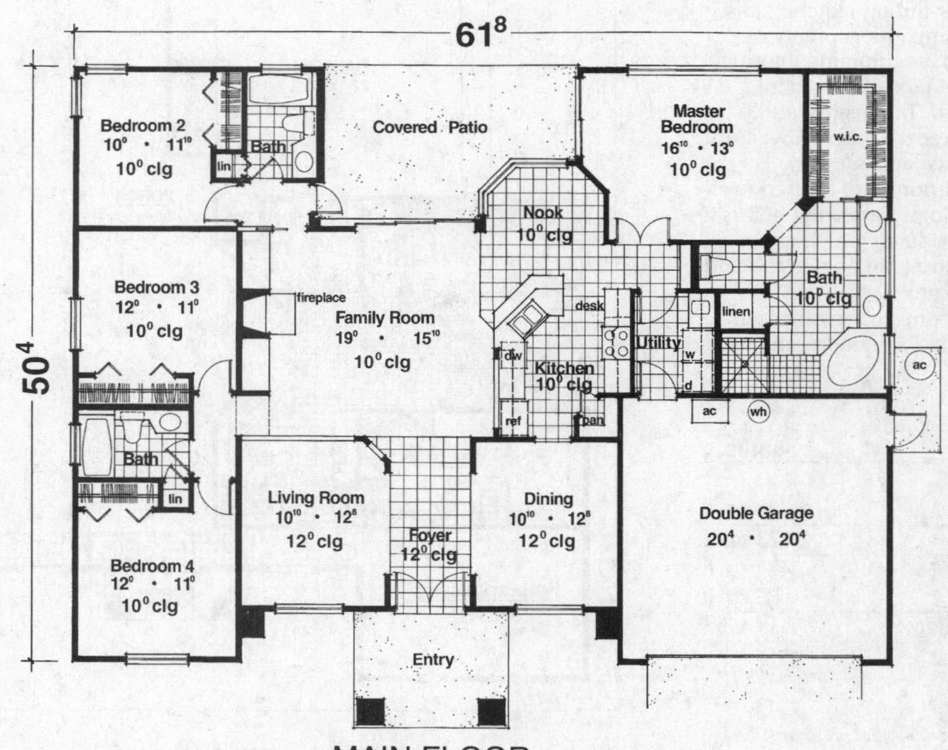

MAIN FLOOR

Plan HDS-99-147

SEE ORDER INFO ON PAGES 12-15

Picture Perfect!

- With graceful arches, columns and railings, this home's wonderful front porch makes it the picture of country charm. Decorative chimneys, shutters and dormers complete the portrait.
- Illuminated by sidelights and a fantail transom, the foyer enjoys a dramatic view of the living room and the back porch. Extra-high ceilings adorn the living room, the foyer and the adjoining dining room and bedroom.
- French doors nicely frame the living room's grand fireplace while they offer access to the skylighted porch.
- The L-shaped kitchen has a big island cooktop and a sunny breakfast nook.
- A Palladian window arrangement brightens the sitting alcove in the master suite, which also has its own entrance to the porch. The fantastic garden bath includes dual walk-in closets and a handy double-sink vanity.
- Future expansion space is available on the upper floor.

Plan J-9401

Bedrooms: 3+	**Baths:** 2½
Living Area:	
Main floor	2,089 sq. ft.
Total Living Area:	**2,089 sq. ft.**
Future upper floor	878 sq. ft.
Standard basement	2,089 sq. ft.
Garage	492 sq. ft.
Storage	38 sq. ft.
Exterior Wall Framing:	2x4

Foundation Options:

Standard basement
Crawlspace
Slab

(All plans can be built with your choice of foundation and framing. A generic conversion diagram is available. See order form.)

BLUEPRINT PRICE CODE: C

VIEW INTO KITCHEN AND BREAKFAST NOOK

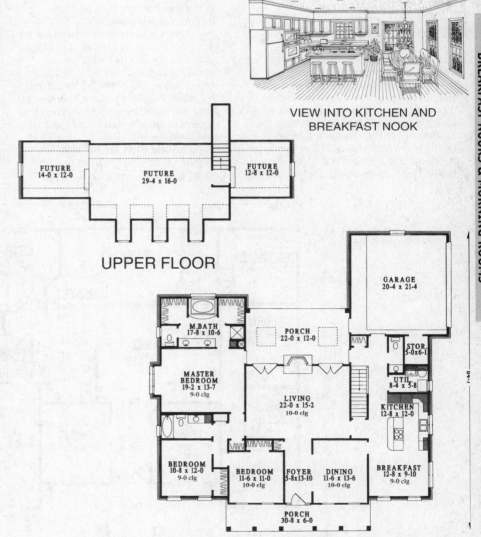

FUTURE 14-0 x 12-0
FUTURE 29-4 x 16-0
FUTURE 12-8 x 12-0

UPPER FLOOR

GARAGE 20-4 x 21-4
M.BATH 17-8 x 10-6
PORCH 22-0 x 12-0
STOR. 5-0x6-1
MASTER BEDROOM 19-2 x 13-7 9-0 clg
UTIL. 8-4 x 5-8
LIVING 22-0 x 15-2 10-0 clg
KITCHEN 12-8 x 12-0
BEDROOM 10-8 x 12-0 9-0 clg
BEDROOM 11-6 x 11-0 10-0 clg
FOYER 5-8x13-10
DINING 11-6 x 13-6 10-0 clg
BREAKFAST 12-8 x 9-10 9-0 clg
PORCH 30-8 x 6-0
63-10

MAIN FLOOR

Plan J-9401

Splendor in the Sun

- Oversized arched windows flood the interior of this Mediterranean-style home with plenty of splendid sunlight.
- The airy foyer opens directly into the formal living and dining rooms, each of which is crowned by a high ceiling.
- At the heart of the design, the large family room includes a wall of windows overlooking a covered patio. A fireplace flanked by built-in media shelves warms chilly evenings. Set out popcorn and other munchies on the snack bar fronting the adjoining kitchen.
- The kitchen also features a large pantry, plus easy access to the sunny breakfast nook and the dining room.
- Set off for absolute privacy, the master suite offers views of the backyard and the patio. The posh private bath boasts a big walk-in closet, plant shelves, twin vanities, a splashy garden tub and an oversized shower.
- Blueprints for this plan include chimney details in the front perspective drawing.

Plan HDS-99-302

Bedrooms: 4	**Baths:** 3
Living Area:	
Main floor	2,089 sq. ft.
Total Living Area:	**2,089 sq. ft.**
Garage	415 sq. ft.
Exterior Wall Framing:	2x4
Foundation Options:	
Slab	

(All plans can be built with your choice of foundation and framing. A generic conversion diagram is available. See order form.)

BLUEPRINT PRICE CODE: C

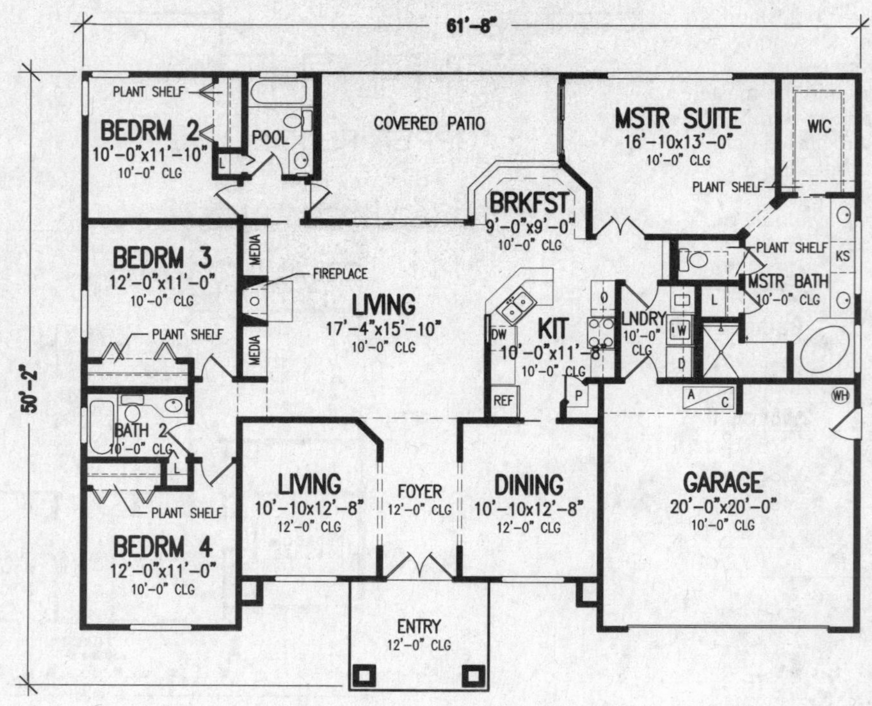

MAIN FLOOR

Plan HDS-99-302

SEE ORDER INFO ON PAGES 12-15
familyhandyman.com/homeplans

Stunning Porch

- This home's stunning wraparound porch and covered rear patio provide fantastic spaces for outdoor entertaining.
- Through the entry, the living room boasts a cathedral ceiling, a built-in entertainment center, a handsome fireplace and access to the covered patio at the back of the design.
- The gourmet kitchen's angled snack bar serves the bayed morning room. A nearby desk is the perfect spot for the kids to surf the Internet under a parent's watchful eye. The formal dining room gives your family a place to share special holiday meals together.
- The opulent master bedroom boasts a cathedral ceiling and a private bath, which features a dual-sink vanity, two walk-in closets, a garden tub and an oversized shower.
- Two additional bedrooms are blessed with generous closet space. The bedrooms share a full hall bath that includes its own dual-sink vanity—a must-have amenity for a busy family.

Plan DD-2117	
Bedrooms: 3	**Baths:** 2½
Living Area:	
Main floor	2,104 sq. ft.
Total Living Area:	**2,104 sq. ft.**
Standard basement	2,112 sq. ft.
Garage	544 sq. ft.
Exterior Wall Framing:	2x4
Foundation Options:	
Standard basement	
Crawlspace	
Slab	

(All plans can be built with your choice of foundation and framing. A generic conversion diagram is available. See order form.)

BLUEPRINT PRICE CODE: C

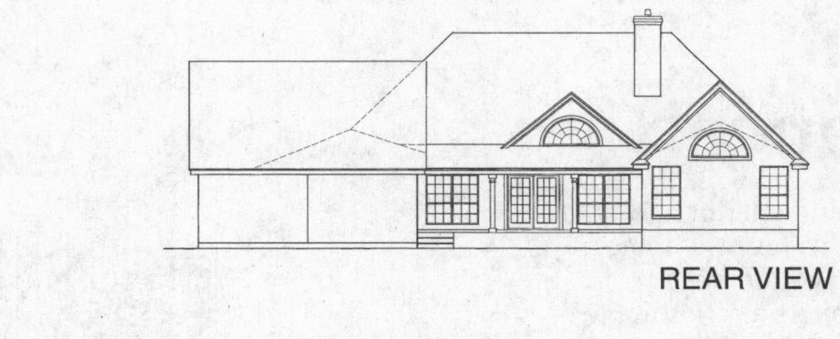

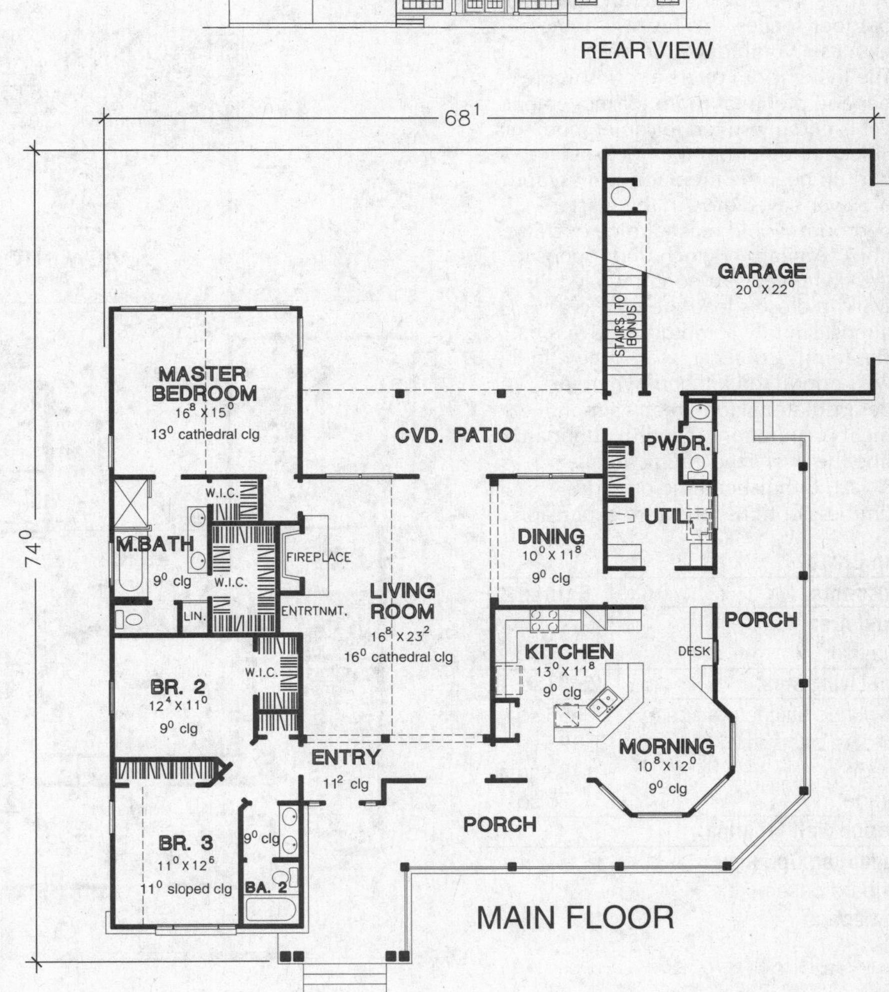

Plan DD-2117

Plan copyright held by home designer/architect

FOR MORE DETAILS, SEE PLAN AT familyhandyman.com/homeplans

Youthful Exuberance!

- With its free-flowing interior and breezy outdoor spaces, this historic home exudes a youthful exuberance.
- The living room offers a refreshing wet bar and plenty of room for movement, yet is equally suited for quiet moments. Select a book from the bookshelves, curl up near the fireplace and escape!
- A clever bayed area in the master bedroom would make a nice exercise nook. A nearby French door opens to the skylighted sun porch, while twin walk-in closets lead the way to an almost sinfully sumptuous private bath.
- The family cook can work magic in the well-appointed kitchen, where a peninsula cooktop greatly simplifies meal preparation. Plentiful cupboards line the oversized eating area.
- A vast, unfinished attic provides limitless options for future expansion.

Plan E-2107	
Bedrooms: 3+	**Baths:** 2½
Living Area:	
Main floor	2,123 sq. ft.
Total Living Area:	**2,123 sq. ft.**
Unfinished attic/future space	556 sq. ft.
Standard basement	2,123 sq. ft.
Garage	483 sq. ft.
Storage	76 sq. ft.
Exterior Wall Framing:	2x6
Foundation Options:	
Standard basement	
Crawlspace	
Slab	

(All plans can be built with your choice of foundation and framing. A generic conversion diagram is available. See order form.)

BLUEPRINT PRICE CODE: C

VIEW INTO LIVING ROOM

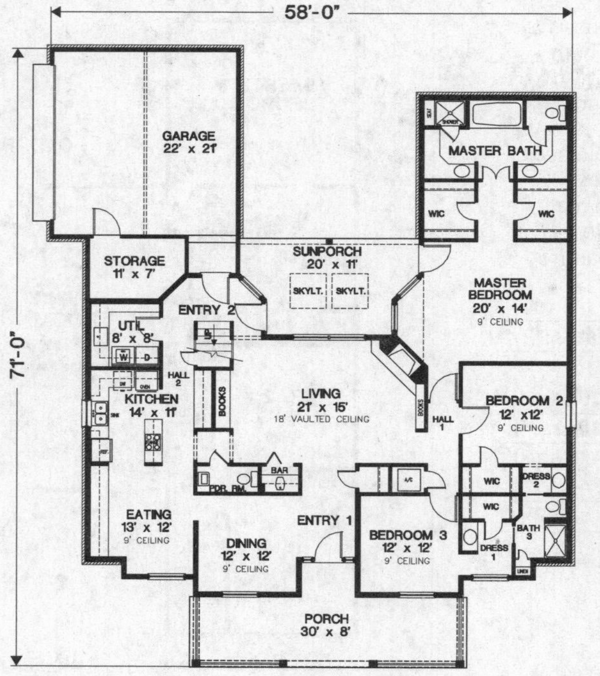

MAIN FLOOR

REAR VIEW

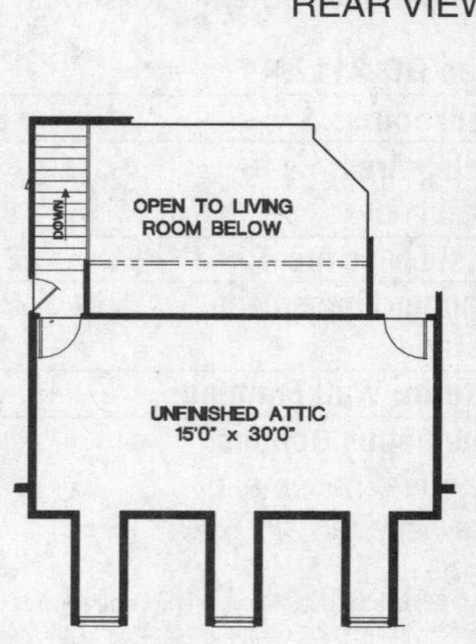

UPPER FLOOR

ORDER BLUEPRINTS ANYTIME!
CALL TOLL-FREE 1-800-820-1296

Plan E-2107

SEE ORDER INFO ON PAGES 12-15
familyhandyman.com/homeplans

You Found It!

- You've always wanted a home with a wraparound porch—nothing pretentious or fancy, just a place to enjoy grand vistas or feel the breeze in the shade. Your one stipulation: It's got to be big. I mean HUGE. Guess what? You found it.
- Imagine the countless hours you'll spend on your porch, chatting, napping, reading, writing, daydreaming, eating, then back to napping, reading, et cetera. When it's time to move inside, however, you won't be disappointed: Airy, wide-open spaces await you.
- The living areas flow easily into one another, guaranteeing quality time as a family no matter where you choose to sit. Bay windows expand your space in both the living room and breakfast nook, while a single wall in the kitchen—complete with a handy pass-through—conceals dirty dishes.
- In the sleeping wing, peace and privacy reign supreme. Two bedrooms with sizable closets share a full bath, while the master suite—large and sunny—enjoys a private bath.
- Other amenities include pantry shelves, laundry facilities and a huge garage.

Plan SUN-1730

Bedrooms: 3	**Baths:** 2
Living Area:	
Main floor	2,134 sq. ft.
Total Living Area:	**2,134 sq. ft.**
Daylight basement	1,375 sq. ft.
Garage	700 sq. ft.
Exterior Wall Framing:	2x6
Foundation Options:	
Daylight basement	
Slab	

(All plans can be built with your choice of foundation and framing. A generic conversion diagram is available. See order form.)

BLUEPRINT PRICE CODE: C

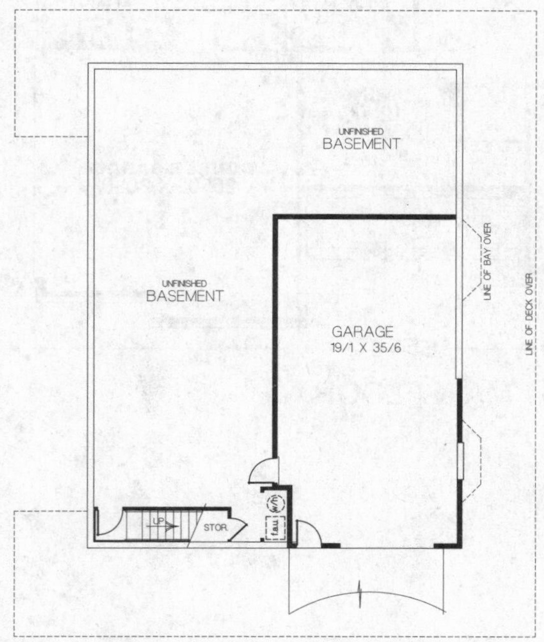

DAYLIGHT BASEMENT

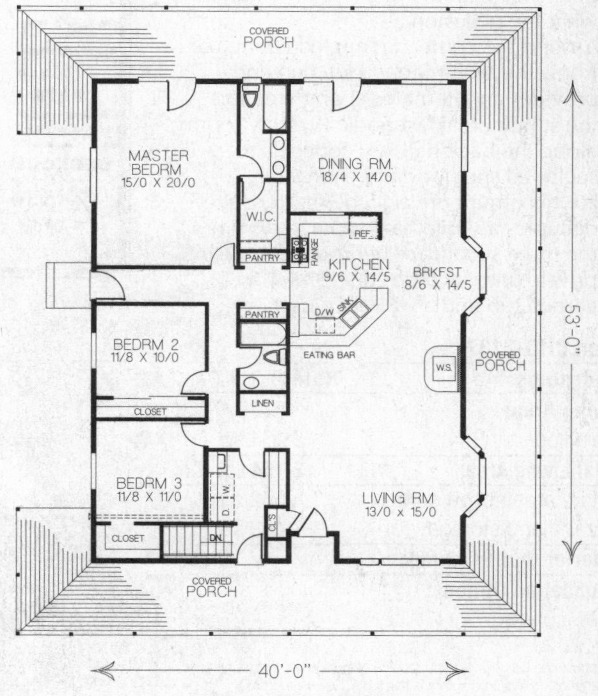

MAIN FLOOR

You're the One

- Want a beautiful family home that will serve your needs for years to come? Look no further—you've found the one!
- A stately exterior marked by corner quoins and alluring arches gives this design true curb appeal. The one-story layout allows you to plan ahead for accessibility needs, while a future area over the garage provides versatile living space for a growing family.
- A graceful column separates the foyer from the dining room and the Great Room, which features a central fireplace and built-in bookshelves. These areas offer the flexibility you need no matter what the occasion.
- Around the corner, an angled eating bar fronts the well-planned kitchen and provides an alternate serving area for the sunny breakfast nook. A utility room along the back hallway conceals a secluded spot for daily chores.
- For maximum privacy, the master suite occupies a wing that's separated from the three secondary bedrooms. Its lush private bath includes dual sinks, a garden tub and a walk-in closet.

Plan CHD-2137

Bedrooms: 4+	**Baths:** 2½–3½
Living Area:	
Main floor	2,154 sq. ft.
Total Living Area:	**2,154 sq. ft.**
Future area above garage	572 sq. ft.
Garage and storage	469 sq. ft.
Exterior Wall Framing:	2x4

Foundation Options:

Crawlspace

Slab

(All plans can be built with your choice of foundation and framing. A generic conversion diagram is available. See order form.)

BLUEPRINT PRICE CODE: C

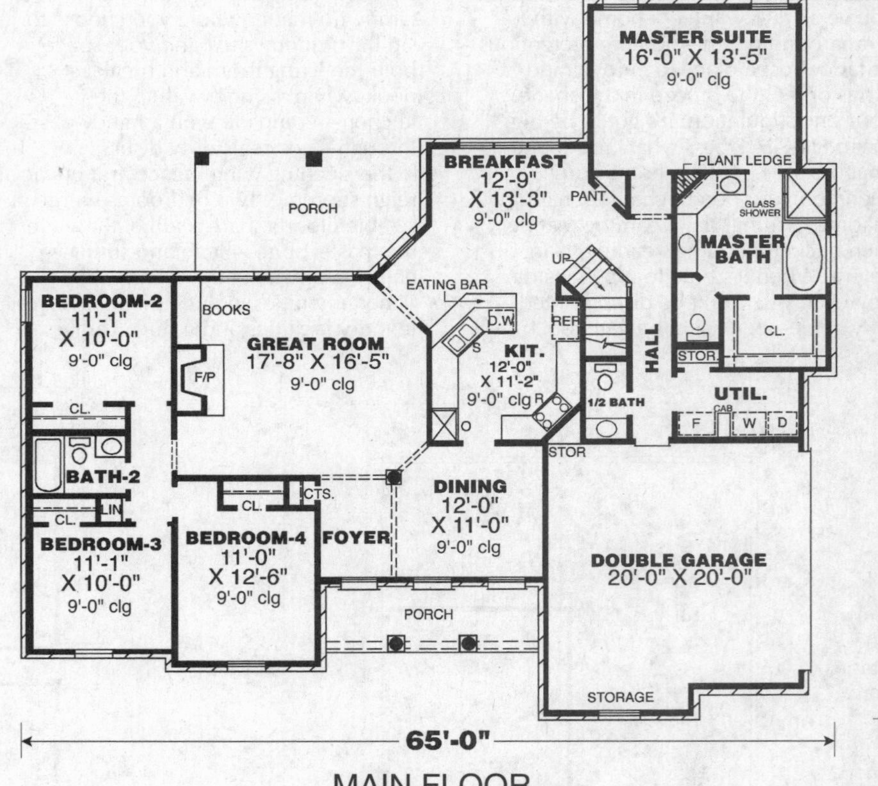

MAIN FLOOR

Plan CHD-2137

SEE ORDER INFO ON PAGES 12-15

Picture-Perfect Porches

- Come home to traditional country living, where picture-perfect front and rear porches let you stretch out and relax at day's end.
- The fantastic Great Room, with a tray ceiling, a warm fireplace and access to the rear porch, could easily become your family's favorite room.
- Savor a casual meal in the sunny breakfast room or, if the weather is nice, enjoy it out on the rear porch. The cook in the family will appreciate the adjoining kitchen with its island cooktop, walk-in pantry and oversized snack bar.
- The secluded master suite spans the depth of the home. Steal a moment for yourself and relax in the soothing whirlpool tub. A huge walk-in closet, a dual-sink vanity and a private toilet round out the bath.
- Two secondary bedrooms boast walk-in closets and share a full hall bath. A third secondary bedroom offers a large standard closet and private access to the hall bath.

Plan DP-2172

Bedrooms: 4	**Baths:** 2
Living Area:	
Main floor	2,172 sq. ft.
Total Living Area:	**2,172 sq. ft.**
Detached garage	480 sq. ft.
Exterior Wall Framing:	2x4

Foundation Options:

Crawlspace

Slab

(All plans can be built with your choice of foundation and framing. A generic conversion diagram is available. See order form.)

BLUEPRINT PRICE CODE: C

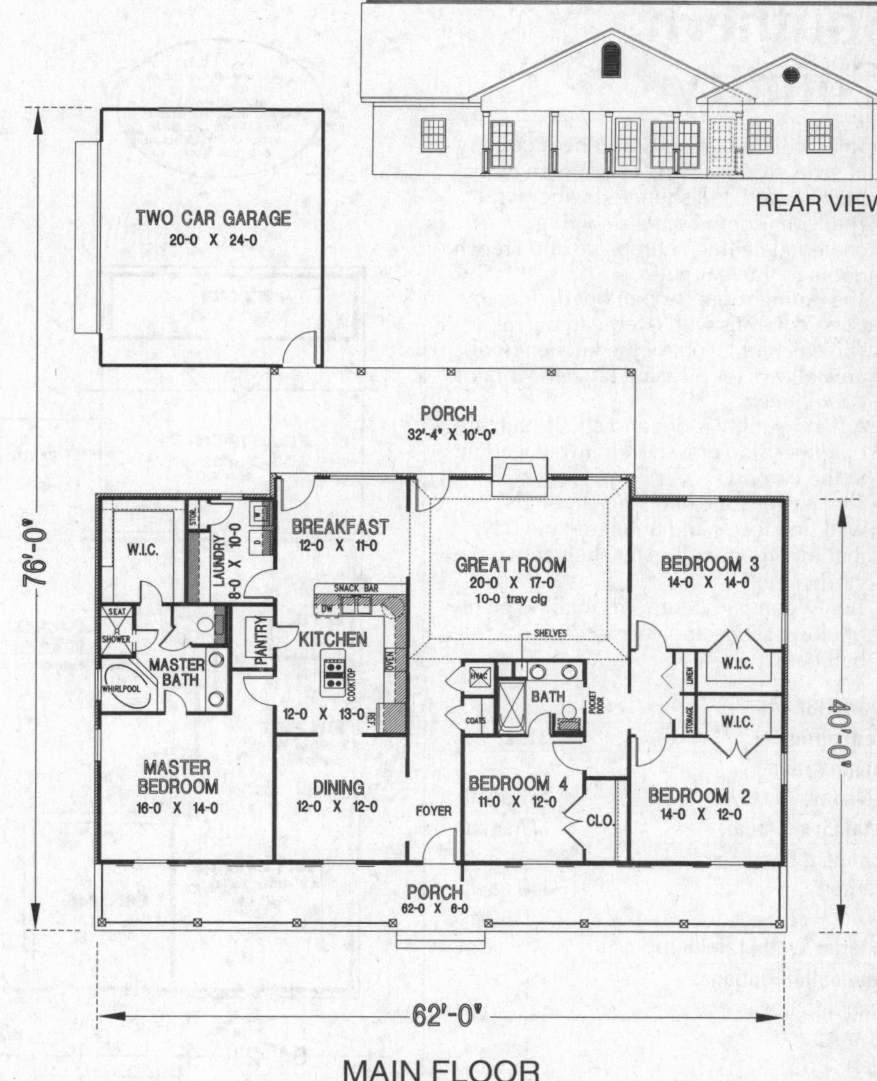

MAIN FLOOR

Southern Country

- This home is distinctly Southern country in style, from its wide front porch to its multi-paned and shuttered windows.
- The living room boasts a soaring cathedral ceiling, a fireplace and French doors to the rear patio.
- The dining room is open but defined by three columns with overhead beams.
- The efficient layout of the kitchen/nook area allows for pleasant kitchen working conditions.
- A handy utility room and a half-bath are on either side of a short hallway leading to the carport.
- The master suite offers his-and-hers walk-in closets and an incredible bath that incorporates a plant shelf above the garden tub.
- Two secondary bedrooms include plenty of closet space and easy access to a full hall bath.

Plan J-86140	
Bedrooms: 3	**Baths:** 2½
Living Area:	
Main floor	2,177 sq. ft.
Total Living Area:	**2,177 sq. ft.**
Standard basement	2,177 sq. ft.
Carport	440 sq. ft.
Storage	120 sq. ft.
Exterior Wall Framing:	2x4
Foundation Options:	
Standard basement	
Crawlspace	
Slab	

(All plans can be built with your choice of foundation and framing. A generic conversion diagram is available. See order form.)

BLUEPRINT PRICE CODE: C

NOTE: The above photographed home may have been modified by the homeowner. Please refer to floor plan and/or drawn elevation shown for actual blueprint details.

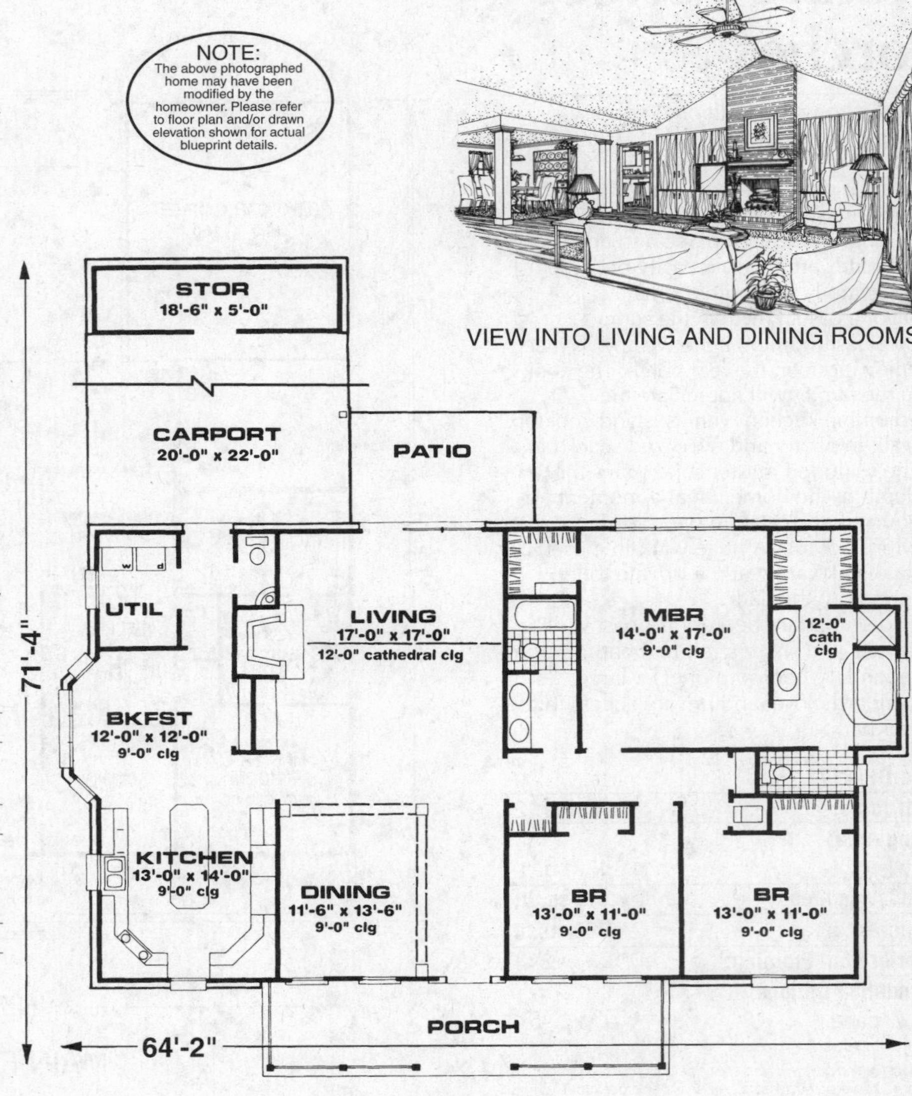

VIEW INTO LIVING AND DINING ROOMS

MAIN FLOOR

Plan J-86140

SEE ORDER INFO ON PAGES 12-15

Gorgeous Glass

- Two glorious half-round window arrangements give this one-story home a stunning countenance.
- Inside, a dramatic see-through fireplace lends a comforting air to both the living room and the family room, which is further accented by a bay window, a stepped ceiling and access to an intimate rear porch.
- The raised serving bar between the breakfast nook and the kitchen makes a fun spot to grab a quick afternoon snack. The dining room adjoins the kitchen as well, allowing for easy food service during formal affairs.
- A handy utility room off the kitchen provides space for a freezer.
- A sloped ceiling in the bedroom and a perfectly planned bath highlight the opulent master suite. Enjoy the luxurious garden tub, the separate shower, the dual sinks and the two walk-in closets.
- The large, two-stall garage includes storage space for tools, golf clubs or sports equipment.

Plan RD-2195

Bedrooms: 4	**Baths:** 2
Living Area:	
Main floor	2,195 sq. ft.
Total Living Area:	**2,195 sq. ft.**
Garage and storage	505 sq. ft.
Enclosed utility	14 sq. ft.
Exterior Wall Framing:	2x4
Foundation Options:	
Crawlspace	
Slab	

(All plans can be built with your choice of foundation and framing. A generic conversion diagram is available. See order form.)

BLUEPRINT PRICE CODE: C

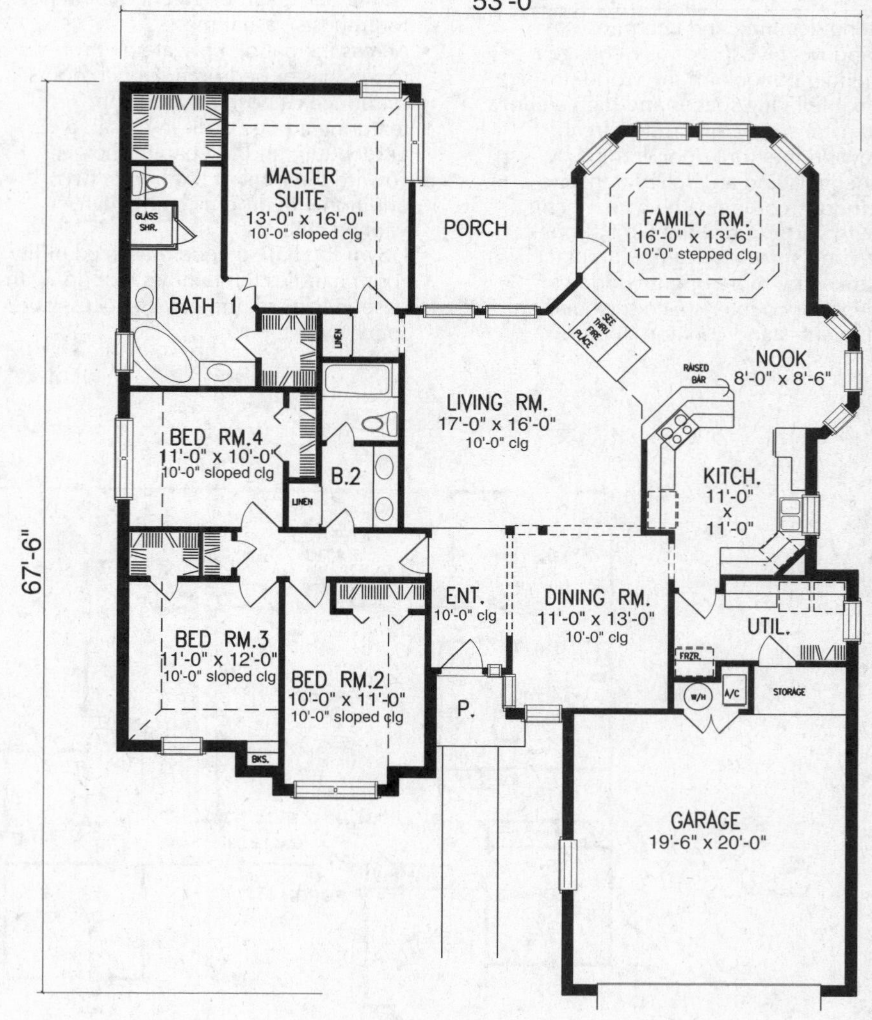

MAIN FLOOR

Family Cottage

- Stone detailing and charming bay windows give this family cottage a friendly outlook on the world. Inside, flexible living spaces and high ceilings create a sunny, spacious retreat.
- Beyond the front door, framed by sidelights and an arched transom window, columns line a connecting gallery. The sprawling Great Room beyond showcases a fine fireplace flanked by more bright windows.
- Plenty of counter space surround an efficient island cooktop in the well-appointed kitchen. Just across the eating bar, a sun-brightened breakfast room hosts casual meals.
- Across the patio, a private door opens to the master bedroom. French doors introduce its posh private bath, featuring a huge walk-in closet, a garden tub, and a separate shower.
- Toward the front of the home, two additional bedrooms enjoy high, vaulted ceilings.
- Down the hall, a generous-sized utility room handles the family's laundry with ease. Backyard and garage access add to its convenience.

Plan DD-2228-B

Bedrooms: 3	**Baths:** 2
Living Area:	
Main floor	2,228 sq. ft.
Total Living Area:	**2,228 sq. ft.**
Standard basement	2,228 sq. ft.
Garage	431 sq. ft.
Exterior Wall Framing:	2x4
Foundation Options:	
Standard basement	
Crawlspace	
Slab	

(All plans can be built with your choice of foundation and framing. A generic conversion diagram is available. See order form.)

BLUEPRINT PRICE CODE: C

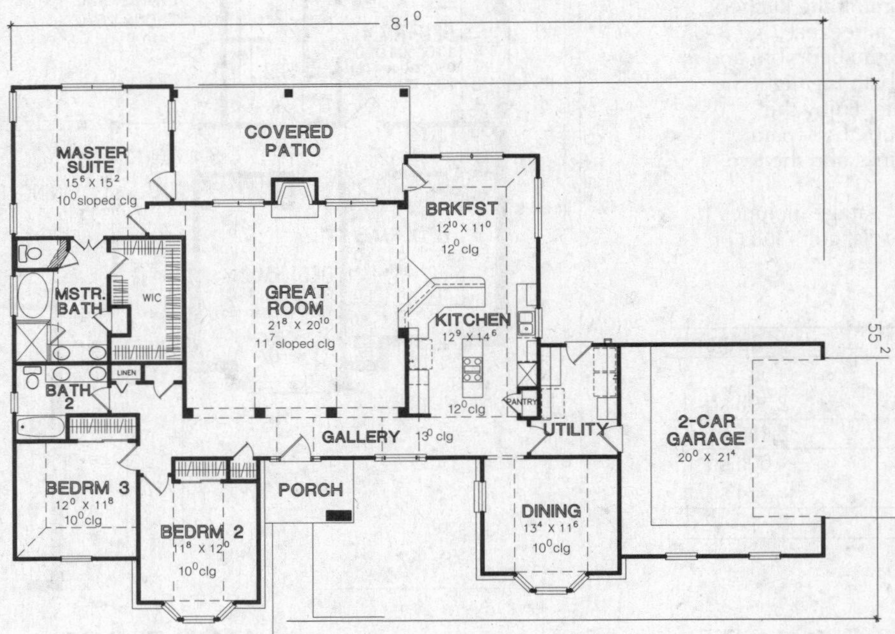

MAIN FLOOR

Mark Englund/Homestore™ Plans and Publications

Luxurious Living on One Level

- The elegant exterior of this spacious one-story presents a classic air of quality and distinction.
- Three French doors brighten the inviting entry, which flows into the roomy living room. Boasting a high ceiling, the living room enjoys a fireplace with a wide hearth and adjoining built-in bookshelves. A wall of glass, including a French door, provides views of the sheltered backyard porch.
- A stylish angled counter joins the open kitchen to the sunny bay-windowed eating nook.
- Secluded for privacy, the master suite features a nice dressing area, a large walk-in closet and private backyard access. A convenient laundry/utility room is adjacent to the master bath.
- At the opposite end of the home, double doors lead to three more bedrooms, a compartmentalized bath and lots of closet space.

Plan E-2208

Bedrooms: 4	**Baths:** 2
Living Area:	
Main floor	2,252 sq. ft.
Total Living Area:	**2,252 sq. ft.**
Standard basement	2,252 sq. ft.
Garage	528 sq. ft.
Storage	64 sq. ft.
Exterior Wall Framing:	2x6
Foundation Options:	
Standard basement	
Crawlspace	
Slab	

(All plans can be built with your choice of foundation and framing. A generic conversion diagram is available. See order form.)

BLUEPRINT PRICE CODE: C

NOTE: The above photographed home may have been modified by the homeowner. Please refer to floor plan and/or drawn elevation shown for actual blueprint details.

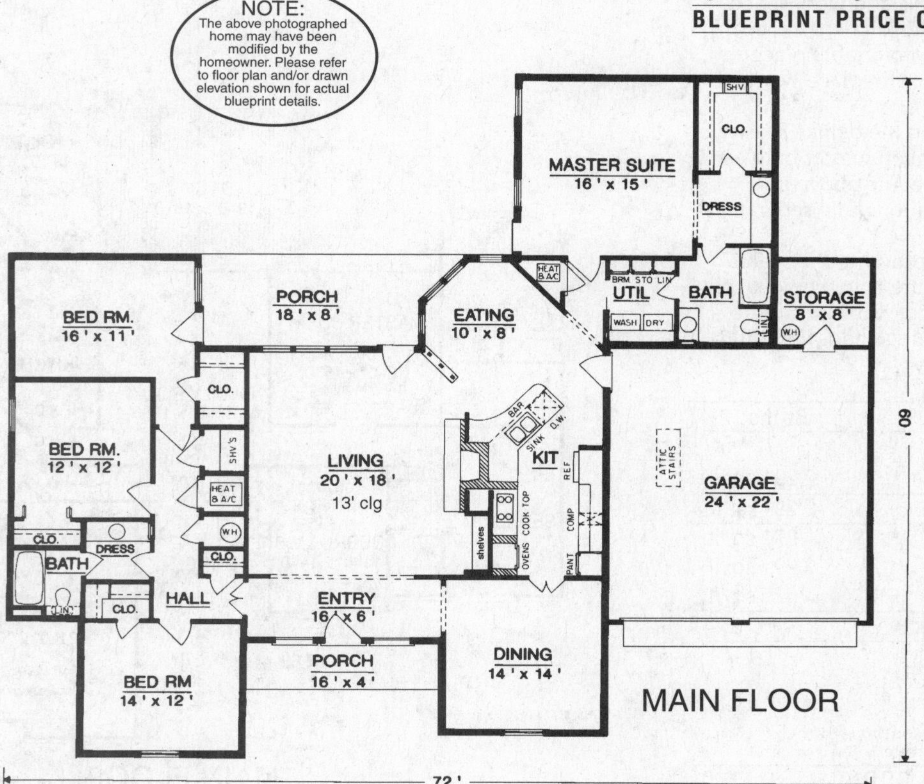

Sunny and Spacious

- Ceilings soar throughout this sunny and spacious family home. Add to this a unique, angled floor plan, and you'll have the home of your dreams.
- Light pours into a stunning bayed dining room through a wall of windows that looks out to the backyard. Between the dining room and the cavernous family room, the central kitchen hosts two eating bars and an island work space.
- Spilling out from the kitchen, the hearth room provides a comfortable place to relax. A cozy corner fireplace warms the room.
- Bask in more sun in the deluxe master suite, where the bayed master bath flaunts a vaulted ceiling above twin vanities, a garden tub, and a separate, oversized shower.
- Two additional bedrooms, one with a vaulted ceiling, share a convenient split bath with a dual-sink vanity. A future room above the garage adds versatility.

Plan APS-2220	
Bedrooms: 3+	**Baths:** 2½
Living Area:	
Main floor	2,291 sq. ft.
Total Living Area:	**2,291 sq. ft.**
Future room	271 sq. ft.
Daylight basement	2,291 sq. ft.
Garage	525 sq. ft.
Exterior Wall Framing:	2x4
Foundation Options:	
Daylight basement	
Crawlspace	

(All plans can be built with your choice of foundation and framing. A generic conversion diagram is available. See order form.)

BLUEPRINT PRICE CODE: C

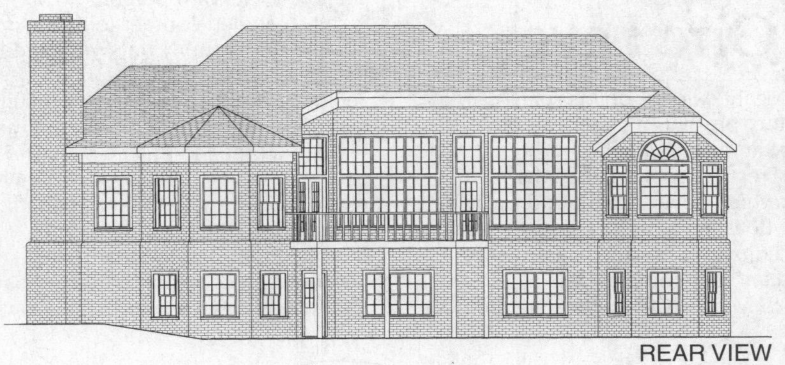

REAR VIEW

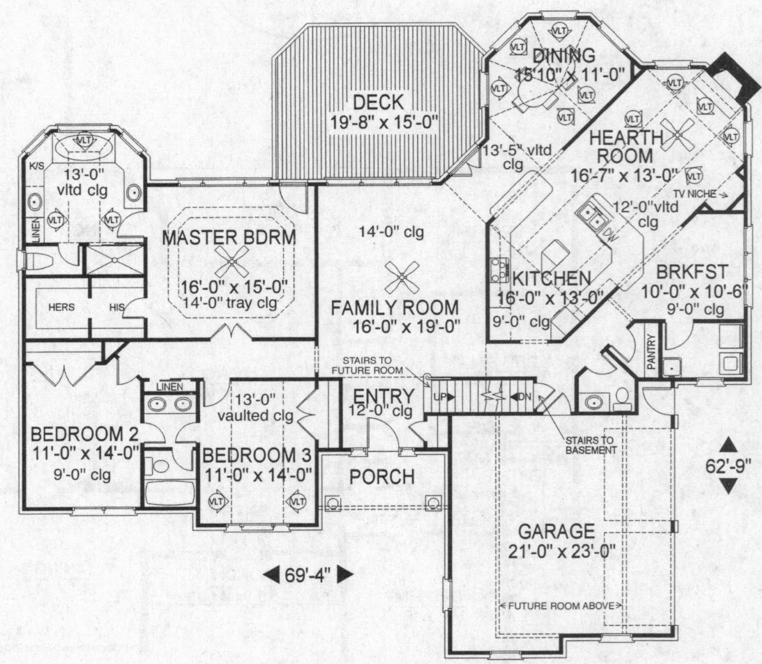

MAIN FLOOR

Ultra-Modern Mediterranean

- Soaring ceilings, a luxurious master suite and a clean stucco exterior with stylish arched windows give this nouveau-Mediterranean home its unique appeal.
- The magnificent living room and the elegant dining room combine to form one large, open area. The dining room has a tall, arched window and a coffered ceiling. The living room boasts a convenient wet bar and sliding glass doors to the covered patio.
- The informal family room is warmed by a fireplace and shares a soaring ceiling with the sunny breakfast area and the large, modern kitchen.
- The kitchen easily accesses the family room and the formal dining room, and features an eating bar and a big pantry.
- The luxurious master suite offers patio access and is enhanced by an elegant tray ceiling and his-and-hers walk-in closets. The huge master bath features a dual-sink vanity, a large tiled shower and a whirlpool tub.

Plan HDS-99-158

Bedrooms: 4	**Baths:** 3
Living Area:	
Main floor	2,352 sq. ft.
Total Living Area:	**2,352 sq. ft.**
Garage	440 sq. ft.
Exterior Wall Framing:	2x4 and 8-in. concrete block
Foundation Options:	
Slab	

(All plans can be built with your choice of foundation and framing. A generic conversion diagram is available. See order form.)

BLUEPRINT PRICE CODE: **C**

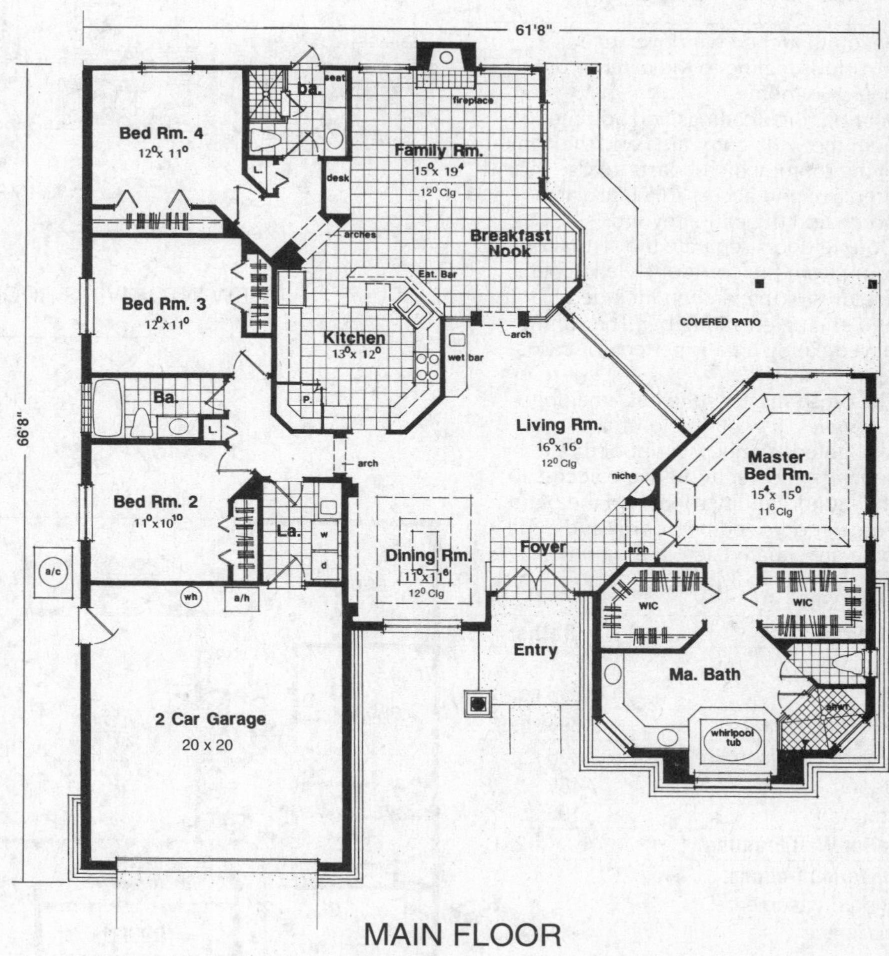

MAIN FLOOR

High Luxury in One Story

VIEW INTO LIVING ROOM

- Beautiful arched windows lend a luxurious feeling to the exterior of this one-story home.
- Soaring, high ceilings add volume to both the wide entry area and the central living room, which boasts a large fireplace and access to a backyard porch and the patio beyond.
- Double doors separate the formal dining room from the corridor-style kitchen. Features of the kitchen include a pantry and an angled eating bar. The sunny, bayed eating area is perfect for casual family meals.
- The plush master suite has amazing amenities: a walk-in closet, a skylighted, angled whirlpool tub, a separate shower and private access to the laundry/utility room and the patio.
- Three good-sized bedrooms and a full bath are situated across the home.

Plan E-2302

Bedrooms: 4	**Baths:** 2
Living Area:	
Main floor	2,396 sq. ft.
Total Living Area:	**2,396 sq. ft.**
Standard basement	2,396 sq. ft.
Garage	484 sq. ft.
Storage	103 sq. ft.
Exterior Wall Framing:	2x6

Foundation Options:

Standard basement
Crawlspace
Slab
(All plans can be built with your choice of foundation and framing. A generic conversion diagram is available. See order form.)

BLUEPRINT PRICE CODE: **C**

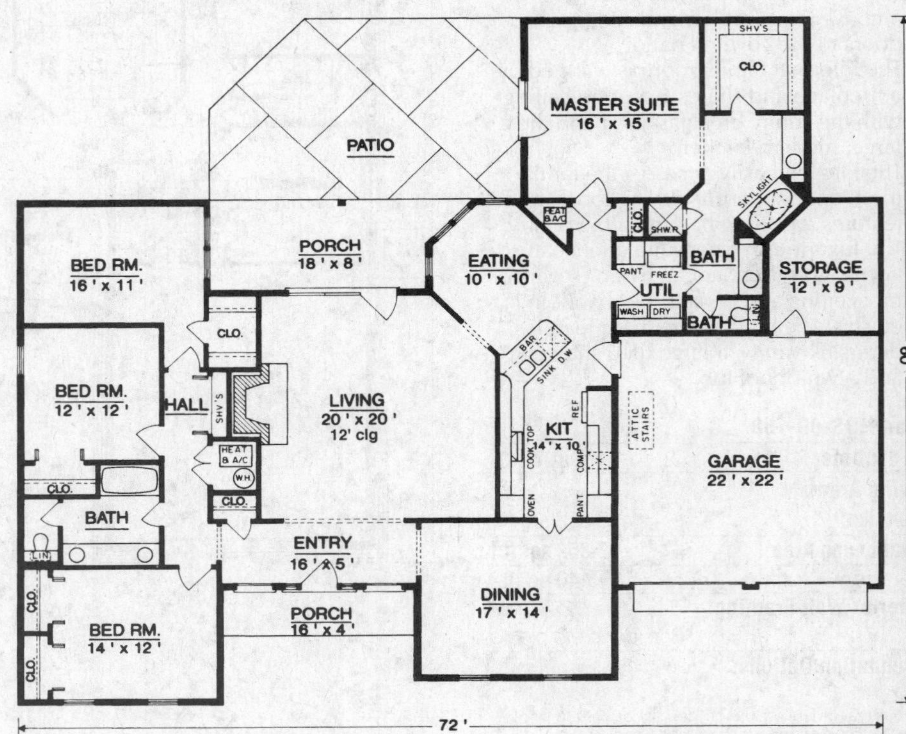

MAIN FLOOR

ORDER BLUEPRINTS ANYTIME!
CALL TOLL-FREE 1-800-820-1296

Plan E-2302

SEE ORDER INFO ON PAGES 12-15
familyhandyman.com/homeplans

High Drama

- Enormous arched windows, decorative corner quoins and a high, sweeping roofline give this dazzling brick home its dramatic appeal.
- The formal living spaces flank the foyer, each with a vaulted ceiling and attractive windows. The living room also boasts a handsome fireplace.
- The U-shaped kitchen easily serves the dining room and the sunny breakfast nook, which offers French doors to a large backyard lanai.
- Two more sets of French doors brighten the family room, which is further expanded by a sloped ceiling. A unique fireplace with a built-in log bin is adjacent to a handy set of shelves.
- Secluded in its own wing, the luxurious master bedroom has private access to the lanai. The master bath showcases a spa tub, a separate shower, a dual-sink vanity with knee space and his-and-hers walk-in closets.
- Three additional bedrooms occupy a second sleeping wing and share a convenient hallway bath.

Plan DW-2403

Bedrooms: 4	**Baths:** 2½
Living Area:	
Main floor	2,403 sq. ft.
Total Living Area:	**2,403 sq. ft.**
Standard basement	2,403 sq. ft.
Garage	380 sq. ft.
Exterior Wall Framing:	2x4
Foundation Options:	
Standard basement	
Crawlspace	
Slab	

(All plans can be built with your choice of foundation and framing. A generic conversion diagram is available. See order form.)

BLUEPRINT PRICE CODE: C

70'- 11"

47'- 5"

LANAI $27^{0} \times 10^{0}$

MASTER BEDROOM $15^{0} \times 19^{4}$ 11^{0} tray clg

BEDROOM 4 $10^{0} \times 9^{6}$ 9^{0} clg

BATH

BEDROOM 3 $10^{0} \times 10^{8}$ 9^{0} clg

slp clg

BREAKFAST $12^{0} \times 10^{0}$ 10^{0} clg

HALL

FAMILY $16^{6} \times 17^{6}$ 10^{0} clg

UTILITY

BEDROOM 2 $11^{0} \times 10^{0}$ 9^{0} clg

HERS

KITCHEN $14^{0} \times 10^{6}$ 10^{0} clg

M. BATH 10^{0} clg

PWDR

GARAGE $20^{4} \times 18^{8}$

HIS

LIVING $15^{0} \times 15^{0}$ 13^{0} cathedral clg

FOYER $10^{6} \times 8^{6}$ 10^{0} clg

DINING $12^{0} \times 15^{0}$ 13^{0} cathedral clg

PORCH

MAIN FLOOR

Breath of Life

- Lush plant shelves and panoramic windows breathe life into this refreshing one-story home.
- As guests step through the double doors, the dramatic living room unfolds ahead. Tasteful niches enhance the receiving hall. A striking column introduces the formal dining room.
- When the weather allows, escort visitors through the living room's sliding glass doors to the back porch. There's plenty of room for crowds, and the little ones can pursue their brands of fun in safety.
- On those calm nights when a little bonding is on the agenda, the family room quietly comes through, with its warm fireplace and media shelves.
- Offer the kids a bedtime snack in the island kitchen. The two baths near their bedrooms let them brush their teeth with less hassle.
- Catch the late news and then retire to the master suite, where sliding glass doors to the back porch let you stargaze privately with a nightcap.
- The master bath is the stuff of fantasy, with twin walk-in closets and a soothing tub tucked into a bayed window. The separate shower will help to recharge your batteries on weekday mornings.

Plan HDS-99-245

Bedrooms: 4	**Baths:** 3
Living Area:	
Main floor	2,431 sq. ft.
Total Living Area:	**2,431 sq. ft.**
Garage	465 sq. ft.
Exterior Wall Framing:	8-in. concrete block
Foundation Options:	
Slab	

(All plans can be built with your choice of foundation and framing. A generic conversion diagram is available. See order form.)

BLUEPRINT PRICE CODE: C

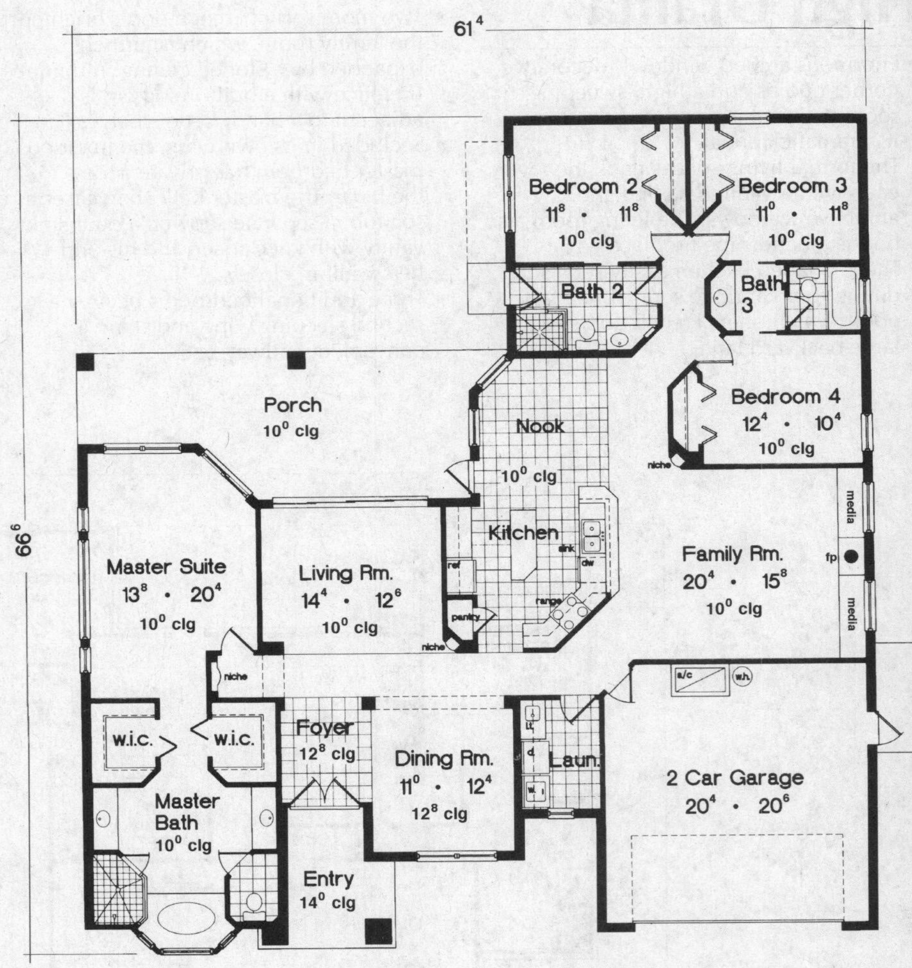

MAIN FLOOR

Plan HDS-99-245

SEE ORDER INFO ON PAGES 12-15

Imagination Run Wild

- This home features a multi-purpose room that awaits your creative touch. The space could become a media room, a library, a home office—simply let your imagination run wild!
- An exceptional living room anchors the home. Defined by elegant columns, this open area offers a wet bar, a fireplace and a bright wall of windows that overlooks a rear porch.
- The adjoining formal dining room looks out on a front courtyard, enclosed by an attractive privacy wall.
- The spacious island kitchen makes it a breeze to whip up culinary delights. The nearby breakfast nook provides a cozy spot for casual meals.
- Secluded for optimum privacy, the master suite includes an intimate sitting area and a walk-in closet. A corner spa tub, a separate shower and a dual-sink vanity adorn the master bath.

Plan HOM-2401

Bedrooms: 3+	**Baths:** 3
Living Area:	
Main floor	2,442 sq. ft.
Total Living Area:	**2,442 sq. ft.**
Standard basement	2,442 sq. ft.
Garage and storage	558 sq. ft.
Exterior Wall Framing:	2x6

Foundation Options:

Standard basement
Crawlspace
Slab
(All plans can be built with your choice of foundation and framing. A generic conversion diagram is available. See order form.)

BLUEPRINT PRICE CODE: C

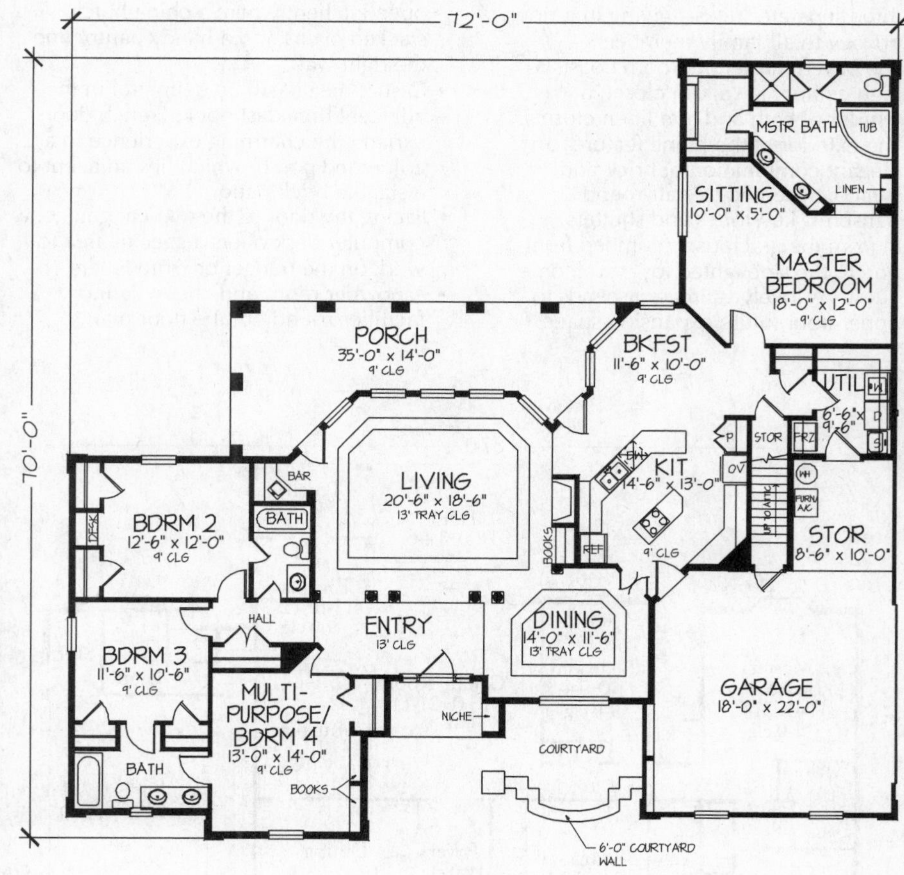

MAIN FLOOR

Suite Trio

- This gorgeous home's symmetrical facade conceals a sleeping wing with three separate suites—giving luxurious privacy to all family members!
- The bayed master bedroom boasts a high ceiling, a walk-in closet, a whirlpool bath and two linen closets.
- The exterior of the home features an elegant combination of brick and stucco, accented by half-round transoms, keystones and shutters.
- In from the gracious, columned front porch, the sidelighted foyer welcomes guests. A lovely staircase ascends to upper-floor future expansion space.
- The bright and spacious Great Room is warmed by a fireplace, making it a great spot for entertaining or relaxing.
- A curved serving bar highlights the open kitchen, where a china hutch, stacked ovens and a handy pantry line the right wall.
- Casual meals will be delightful in the adjacent breakfast nook; French doors expand the charming experience to a columned porch, which lies adjacent to a sizable brick patio.
- Facing the door to the two-car garage, a computer desk offers a special area to work on the budget or write letters.
- A powder room and cheery laundry facilities round out the floor plan.

Plan J-9307

Bedrooms: 3+	**Baths:** 3½
Living Area:	
Main floor	2,497 sq. ft.
Total Living Area:	**2,497 sq. ft.**
Future area	966 sq. ft.
Standard basement	2,497 sq. ft.
Garage and storage	587 sq. ft.
Exterior Wall Framing:	2x4

Foundation Options:

Standard basement
Crawlspace
Slab

(All plans can be built with your choice of foundation and framing. A generic conversion diagram is available. See order form.)

BLUEPRINT PRICE CODE: **C**

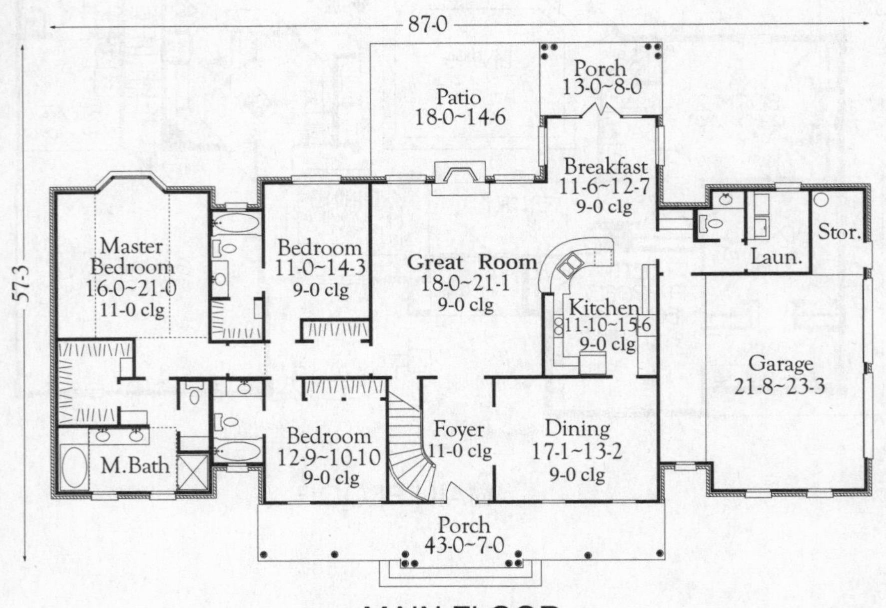

MAIN FLOOR

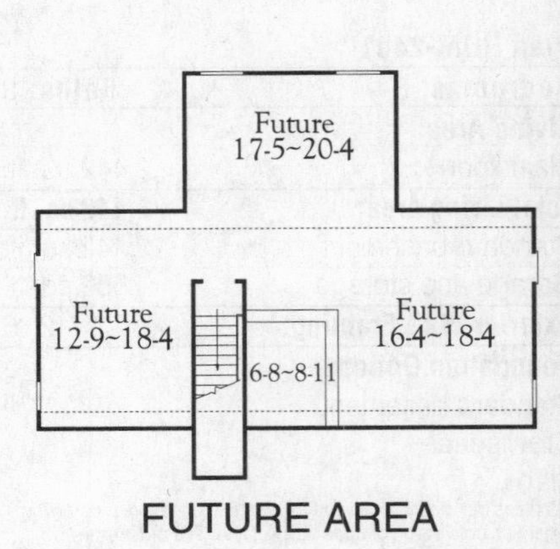

FUTURE AREA

Plan J-9307

SEE ORDER INFO ON PAGES 12-15

Sun-Splashed Retreat

- Lots of windows fill this beautiful Mediterranean-style home with light, while a free-flowing floor plan makes entertaining easy. At the end of the day, retreat to the spacious master suite.
- At the elegant entry, pass under stately columns and through French doors into the Great Room, which boasts a majestic window wall and built-in shelves flanking the fireplace.
- The island kitchen hosts a handy walk-in pantry and an angled serving bar accessible from both the bayed breakfast nook and the Great Room. Sliding glass doors lead out to a breezy covered patio.
- The patio may also be accessed from the master suite's bayed sitting area. The master bath features a dual-sink vanity, one of two walk-in closets and a garden tub set in a bowed, glass-block window.
- Each secondary bedroom boasts a nearby bath and a walk-in closet.
- The two-car garage has a golf cart bay.

Plan HDS-99-359

Bedrooms: 3	**Baths:** 3
Living Area:	
Main floor	2,503 sq. ft.
Total Living Area:	**2,503 sq. ft.**
Garage	716 sq. ft.
Exterior Wall Framing:	8-in. concrete block
Foundation Options:	
Slab	

(All plans can be built with your choice of foundation and framing. A generic conversion diagram is available. See order form.)

BLUEPRINT PRICE CODE: D

VIEW INTO GREAT ROOM AND DINING ROOM

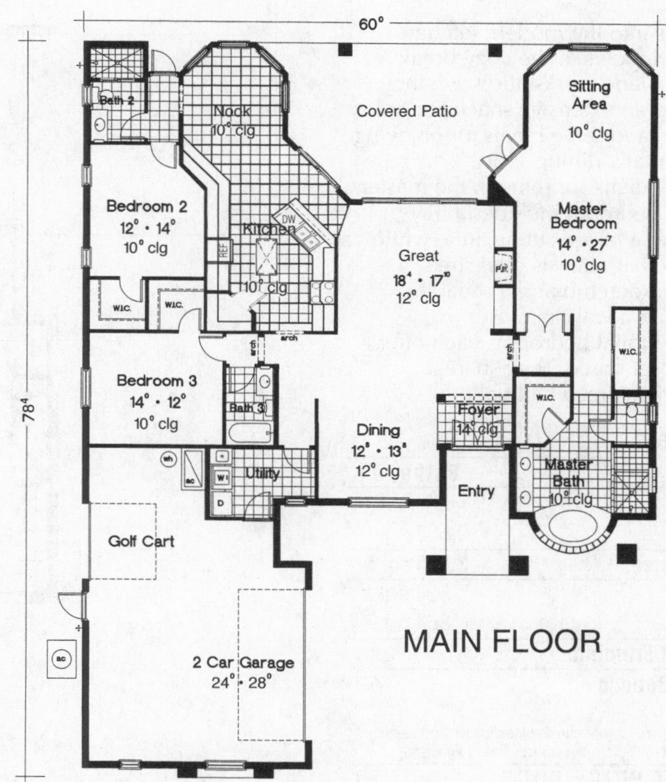

MAIN FLOOR

Captivating Accents

- Captivating accents grace the facade of this exquisite home, which offers elegant arched windows and a recessed entry with sidelights and a transom.
- The foyer leads past handy display niches to the central living room, which provides a handsome tray ceiling and a view of a back porch through a wall of windows.
- Light spills into the modern kitchen through windows in the cozy breakfast nook. An island workstation, a handy pantry and an extensive snack bar help you create and serve meals for enjoying in one of many dining spots.
- Opulence reigns supreme in the master suite. The bedroom includes a tray ceiling and a bayed sitting area, while the private bath boasts dual sinks, a relaxing garden tub and a separate shower, and a walk-in closet.
- Three additional bedrooms each offer ample closet space. They share a compartmentalized hall bath.

Plan HDC-2553

Bedrooms: 4	**Baths:** 2½
Living Area:	
Main floor	2,553 sq. ft.
Total Living Area:	**2,553 sq. ft.**
Garage	524 sq. ft.
Porte cochere	364 sq. ft.
Exterior Wall Framing:	2x4
Foundation Options:	
Slab	

(All plans can be built with your choice of foundation and framing. A generic conversion diagram is available. See order form.)

BLUEPRINT PRICE CODE: D

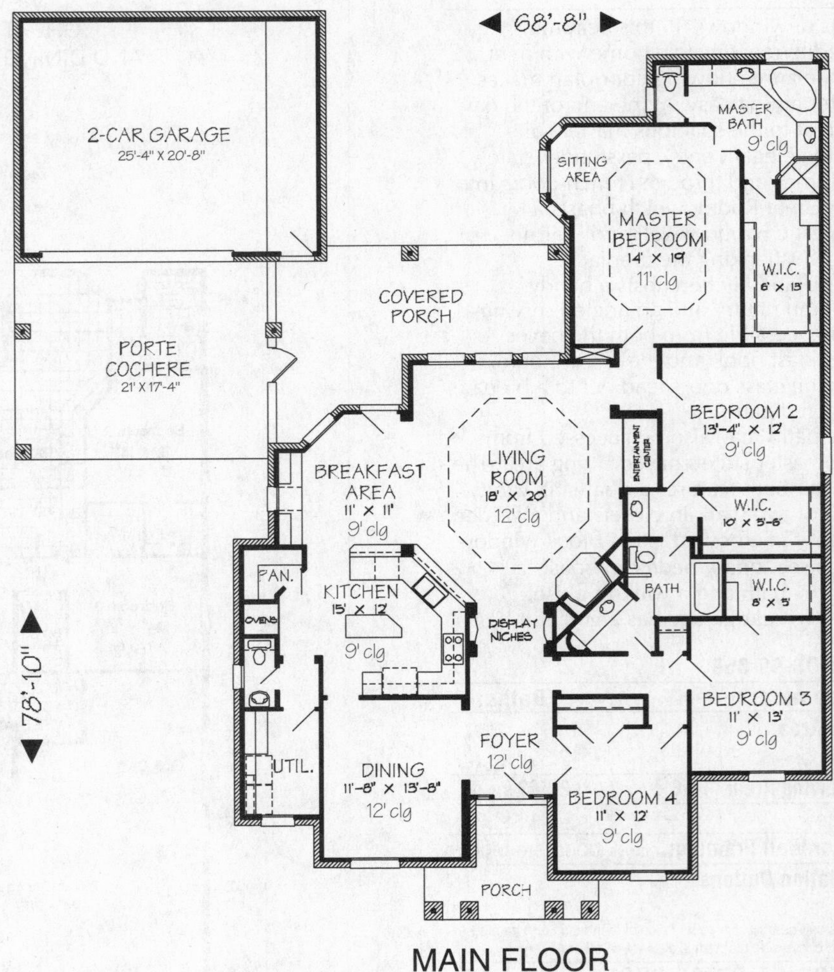

MAIN FLOOR

Plan HDC-2553

SEE ORDER INFO ON PAGES 12-15

Stately Brick Facade

- This home's stately brick facade showcases a columned entry crowned by an elegant pediment.
- At the center of the home, the Great Room features built-in bookshelves and a fireplace flanked by stunning French doors leading to a skylighted back porch.
- The spacious kitchen's snack bar serves the airy breakfast nook and the formal dining room.
- The best part of your day may be when you retire to the luxurious master suite, which features a windowed sitting area and flaunts private access to the back porch. The master bath boasts two tremendous walk-in closets, a relaxing spa tub and a separate shower.
- All three secondary bedrooms enjoy roomy walk-in closets and share a full bath that includes a dual-sink vanity.

Plan J-9823

Bedrooms: 4 **Baths:** 2½

Living Area:

Main floor	2,585 sq. ft.
Total Living Area:	**2,585 sq. ft.**
Standard basement	2,585 sq. ft.
Garage	581 sq. ft.
Storage	276 sq. ft.
Exterior Wall Framing:	2x4

Foundation Options:

Standard basement
Crawlspace
Slab
(All plans can be built with your choice of foundation and framing. A generic conversion diagram is available. See order form.)

BLUEPRINT PRICE CODE: D

VIEW INTO GREAT ROOM

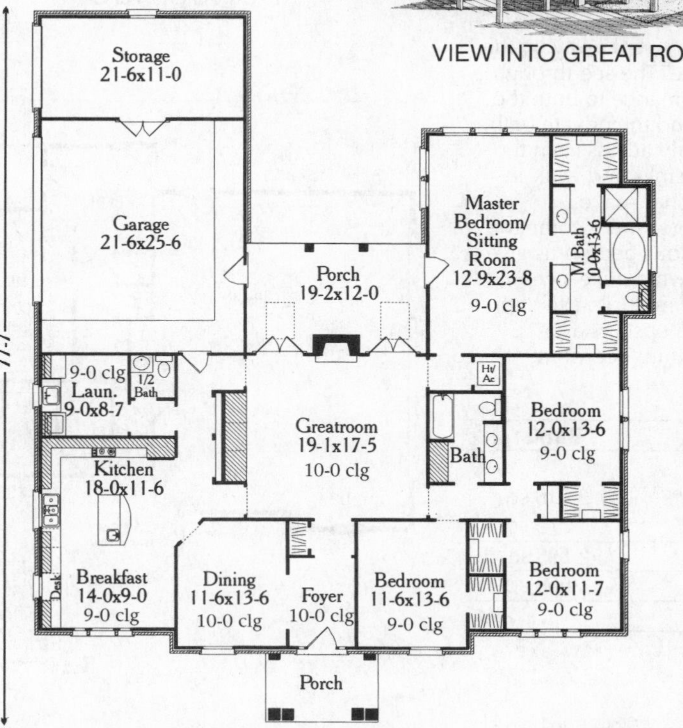

MAIN FLOOR

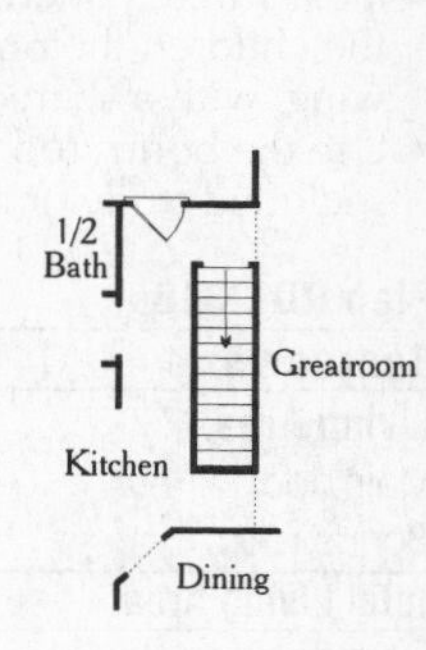

BASEMENT STAIRWAY LOCATION

Plan J-9823

FOR MORE DETAILS, SEE PLAN AT familyhandyman.com/homeplans

Personal Palace

- This elegant home makes you feel like royalty, without the formality. It's both comfortable and stylish—a perfect combination!
- Position your "throne" in front of the living room fireplace and put up your feet. Restless? Step out to the back porch and enjoy the night air.
- Make meals fit for a king or queen in the welcoming kitchen. The adjoining breakfast nook features a bay window that sheds light on early morning conversations.
- Allow yourself to be swept away by the majestic master suite. The see-through fireplace delivers romance to both the sleeping chamber and the private bath. The spa tub is directly across from the fireplace, and dual sinks and walk-in closets ensure personal space.
- Lower the drawbridge—here come the kids! Three tremendous bedrooms give the children their own deluxe sleeping wing, with a shared multiple-use bath.
- Use the bonus room upstairs as a secluded study or a fifth bedroom.

Plan RD-2316	
Bedrooms: 4+	**Baths:** 2½
Living Area:	
Main floor	2,316 sq. ft.
Bonus room	379 sq. ft.
Total Living Area:	**2,695 sq. ft.**
Garage	869 sq. ft.
Exterior Wall Framing:	2x4
Foundation Options:	
Crawlspace	
Slab	

(All plans can be built with your choice of foundation and framing. A generic conversion diagram is available. See order form.)

BLUEPRINT PRICE CODE: **D**

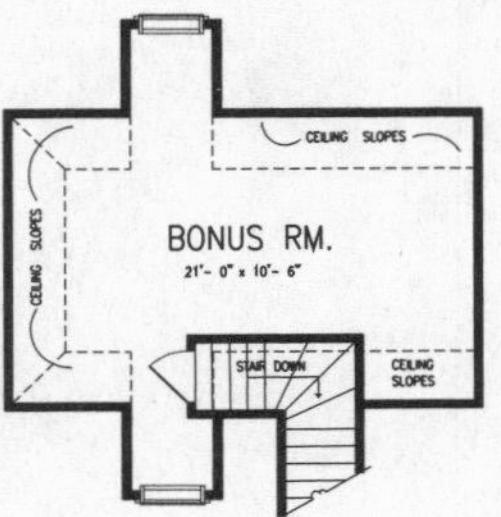

BONUS ROOM

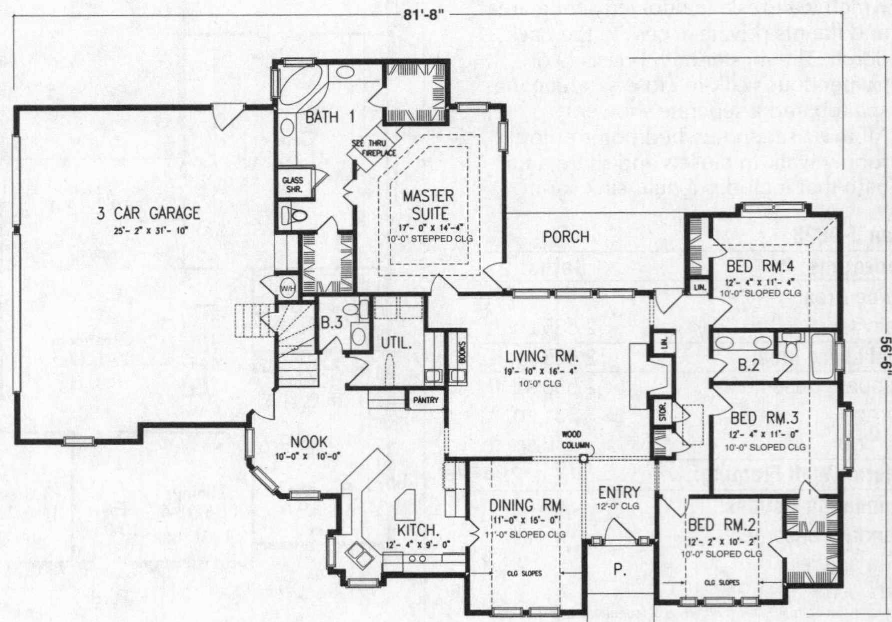

MAIN FLOOR

ORDER BLUEPRINTS ANYTIME!
CALL TOLL-FREE 1-800-820-1296

Plan RD-2316

SEE ORDER INFO ON PAGES 12-15
familyhandyman.com/homeplans

Classic Arches

- A stucco facade and exterior arches lend a classic flavor to this elegant home.
- The coffered foyer is entered through double doors and flanked by the formal areas. Flooded by sunlight from clerestory windows, this area is expanded by a high ceiling.
- The focal point of the home is the open family room, which showcases a handsome fireplace surrounded by built-ins and offers access to the back patio through sliding glass doors.
- The adjacent kitchen provides an island work area, a planning desk and a peninsular bar that serves the family room and the bayed breakfast nook. These three areas share a high ceiling.
- Secluded in the corner of the home is the spectacular master suite, highlighted by a three-way fireplace and a wet bar that separates the bedroom and the sitting area. The luxurious bath includes a garden tub, a separate shower and a dual-sink vanity with knee space.
- Three additional bedrooms and two full baths complete this exciting design.
- Unless otherwise specified, all rooms have high ceilings.

Plan HDS-99-189

Bedrooms: 4	**Baths:** 3
Living Area:	
Main floor	2,726 sq. ft.
Total Living Area:	**2,726 sq. ft.**
Garage	506 sq. ft.
Exterior Wall Framing:	2x4
Foundation Options:	
Slab	

(All plans can be built with your choice of foundation and framing. A generic conversion diagram is available. See order form.)

BLUEPRINT PRICE CODE:	**D**

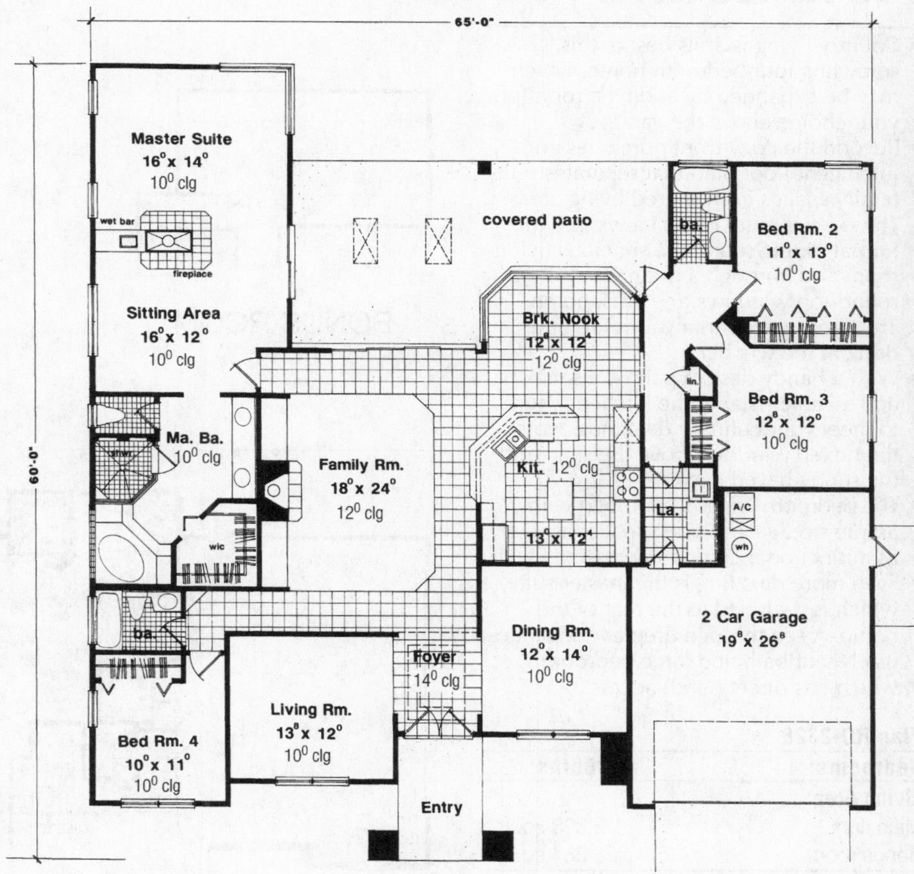

MAIN FLOOR

New Country

- Country living is at its best in this sprawling four-bedroom home, which may be expanded by adding a room of your choice above the garage.
- Beyond the cozy front porch lies an intelligent floor plan that separates quiet family spaces from shared living areas.
- The home's entry offers views into the formal dining room, the spacious living room and, through a dramatic wall of round-top windows, the back porch. Treat your guests to a warm fire or a drink at the wet bar.
- With a handy desk, a pantry, a snack bar and a center island, the kitchen is sure to meet your culinary demands. Note the boxed window above the sink, and the sunny bayed nook.
- The bedroom wing is equipped with ample storage and linen space, as well as a functional compartmentalized bath.
- Even more dazzling is the master suite, which is secluded to the rear of the home. A see-through fireplace separates its elegant bath and large bedroom, which has direct porch access.

Plan RD-2328	
Bedrooms: 4+	**Baths:** 2½
Living Area:	
Main floor	2,328 sq. ft.
Bonus room	384 sq. ft.
Total Living Area:	**2,712 sq. ft.**
Garage and workbench	874 sq. ft.
Exterior Wall Framing:	2x4
Foundation Options:	
Crawlspace	
Slab	

(All plans can be built with your choice of foundation and framing. A generic conversion diagram is available. See order form.)

BLUEPRINT PRICE CODE: **D**

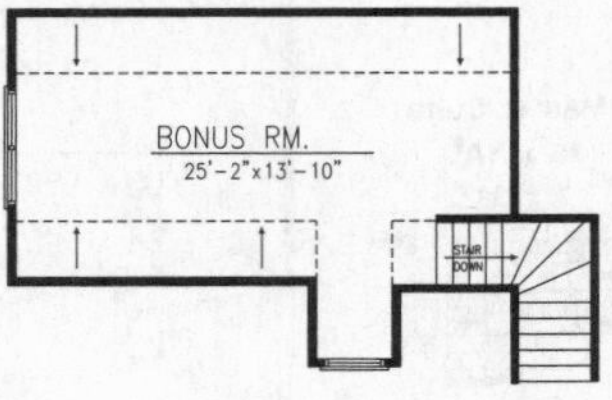

BONUS ROOM

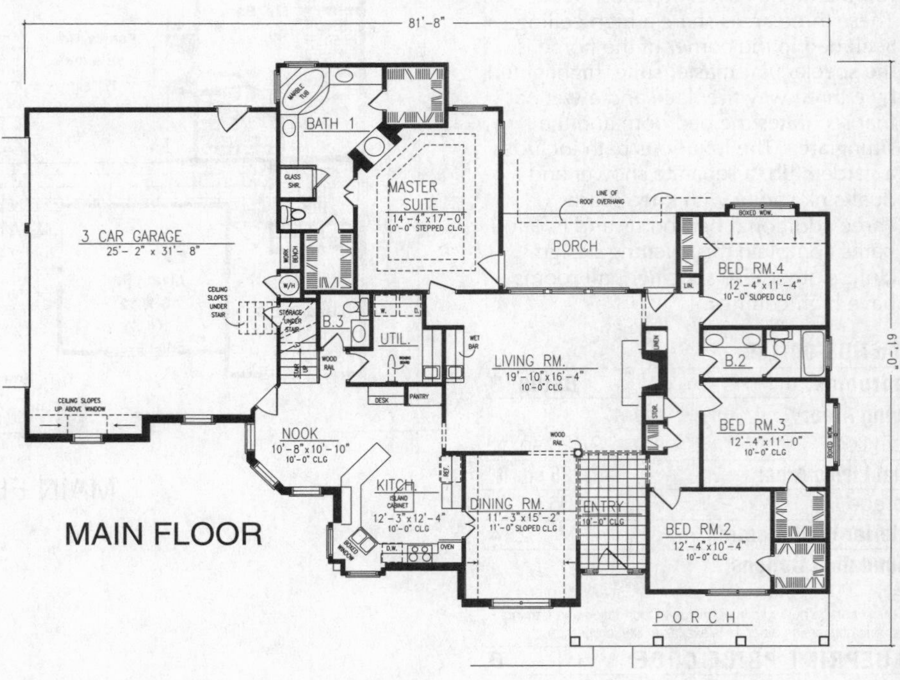

MAIN FLOOR

ORDER BLUEPRINTS ANYTIME!
CALL TOLL-FREE 1-800-820-1296

Plan RD-2328

SEE ORDER INFO ON PAGES 12-15
familyhandyman.com/homeplans

Magical Multi-Level

- An attractive stucco exterior imbues this multi-level home with magical charm.
- Dramatic double doors open into the foyer and Great Room, which share a vaulted ceiling. A guest closet resides beneath a decorative plant shelf. A romantic two-way fireplace adds an intimate glow to the Great Room and the adjacent formal dining room.
- A neat pass-through between the dining room and the kitchen eases the strain of formal meals. A handy island with a cooktop and a snack bar for four serves as the focal point of the kitchen. The family cook will love the unique vegetable sink near the pass-through.
- A half-level up, an open library with a built-in desk and shelving allows young children to work on homework while parents visit in the Great Room nearby.
- In the master suite, a quiet sitting area with a wet bar makes the room an inviting adult retreat. A private deck is a great place to enjoy a nightcap.
- In the daylight basement, a good-sized family room that is open to the breakfast nook above is a great informal area for both boisterous get-togethers and quiet moments with loved ones.

Plan S-61394

Bedrooms: 4	**Baths:** 3
Living Area:	
Main floor	2,213 sq. ft.
Partial daylight basement	680 sq. ft.
Total Living Area:	**2,893 sq. ft.**
Garage	390 sq. ft.
Exterior Wall Framing:	2x6
Foundation Options:	
Partial daylight basement	

(All plans can be built with your choice of foundation and framing. A generic conversion diagram is available. See order form.)

BLUEPRINT PRICE CODE: D

DAYLIGHT BASEMENT

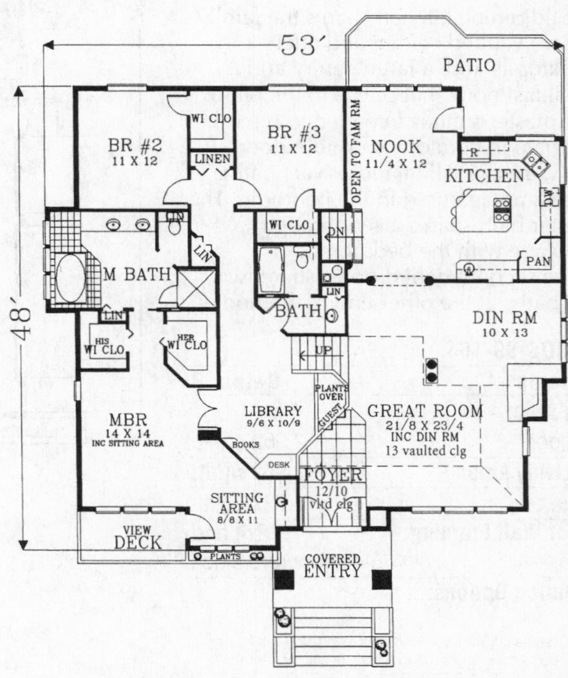

MAIN FLOOR

Super Features!

- Super indoor/outdoor living features are the main ingredients of this sprawling one-story home.
- Beyond the columned entry, the foyer features a high ceiling and is brightened by a fantail transom. The dining room and the living room enjoy ceilings that vault over arched transoms.
- The vaulted family room sits at the center of the floor plan and extends to the outdoor living spaces. A handsome fireplace flanked by built-in shelves adds excitement.
- The adjoining kitchen shares the family room's vaulted ceiling and offers a cooktop island, a large pantry and a breakfast nook that opens to the patio.
- The master suite is intended to offer the ultimate in comfort. A double-door entry, a tray ceiling and private patio access are featured in the bedroom. The master bath shares a see-through fireplace with the bedroom.
- Three secondary bedrooms share two full baths at the other end of the home.

Plan HDS-99-164	
Bedrooms: 4	**Baths:** 3
Living Area:	
Main floor	2,962 sq. ft.
Total Living Area:	**2,962 sq. ft.**
Garage	737 sq. ft.
Exterior Wall Framing:	2x4 and 8-in. concrete block
Foundation Options:	
Slab	

(All plans can be built with your choice of foundation and framing. A generic conversion diagram is available. See order form.)

BLUEPRINT PRICE CODE: D

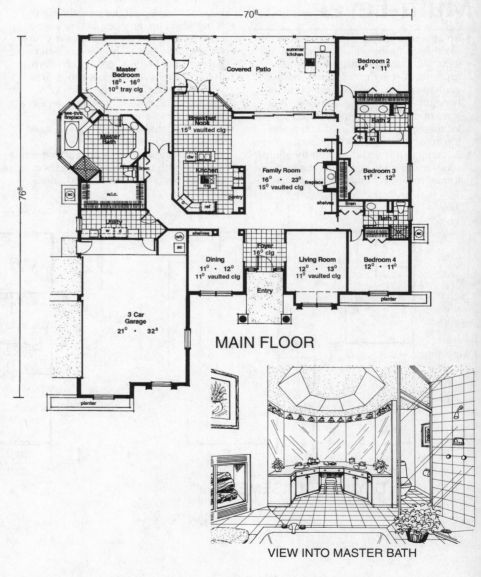

MAIN FLOOR

VIEW INTO MASTER BATH

ORDER BLUEPRINTS ANYTIME! CALL TOLL-FREE 1-800-820-1296

Plan HDS-99-164

SEE ORDER INFO ON PAGES 12-15

familyhandyman.com/homeplans

Hidden Courtyard

- This traditional home has generous living spaces both inside and out.
- Columns define the doorways of the dining and living rooms, which face each other across the entry hall.
- The U-shaped kitchen shares an eating bar with the spacious Keeping Room. A built-in pantry and a china hutch flank the door to the formal dining room.
- The back porch looks out over a secluded courtyard, shielded on three sides by the house and on the fourth by an attractive brick privacy wall.
- The master suite features a large bedroom with a corner fireplace. The skylighted master bath boasts a whirlpool tub, a separate shower, a private toilet and a giant walk-in closet.
- A huge area upstairs allows for future expansion.

Plan VL-3084

Bedrooms: 4+	**Baths:** 3½
Living Area:	
Main floor	3,084 sq. ft.
Total Living Area:	**3,084 sq. ft.**
Future area	868 sq. ft.
Garage	570 sq. ft.
Storage	102 sq. ft.
Exterior Wall Framing:	2x6
Foundation Options:	
Crawlspace	
Slab	

(All plans can be built with your choice of foundation and framing. A generic conversion diagram is available. See order form.)

BLUEPRINT PRICE CODE: E

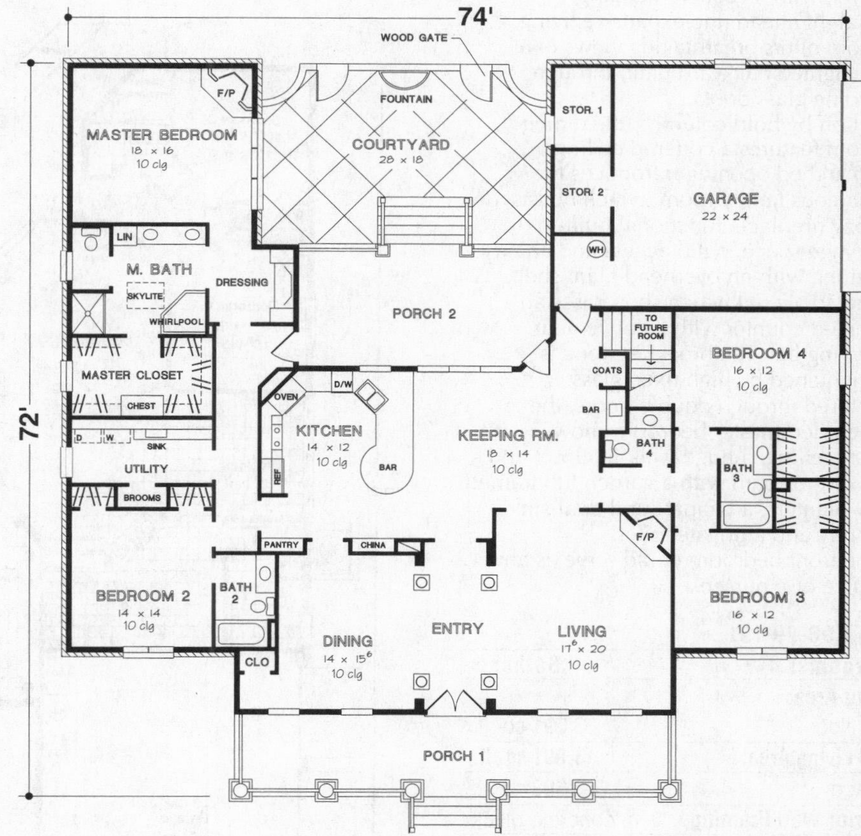

MAIN FLOOR

Soaring Ceilings

- This irresistible home is adorned with soaring ceilings in every room.
- Decorative planters flank the columned entry, where double doors open to the foyer, with its coffered ceiling.
- Straight ahead, the expansive living room offers breathtaking views of a skylighted backyard patio through sliding glass doors.
- Set off by bold columns, the dining room features a coffered ceiling.
- An arched opening introduces the spacious family room, which boasts a cozy fireplace, functional built-in storage space, patio access and an airy ceiling with an overhead plant shelf.
- The adjacent kitchen showcases an angled counter with a convenient serving bar. The breakfast nook is brightened by high fixed glass.
- Entered through double doors, the secluded master bedroom showcases a tray ceiling, a huge walk-in closet and a luxurious bath with a garden tub framed by planters, a wraparound dual-sink vanity and a private toilet.
- The front bedroom could serve as an office or a nursery.

Plan HDS-99-191

Bedrooms: 4	**Baths:** 3
Living Area:	
Main floor	3,091 sq. ft.
Total Living Area:	**3,091 sq. ft.**
Garage	698 sq. ft.
Exterior Wall Framing:	8-in. concrete block
Foundation Options:	
Slab	

(All plans can be built with your choice of foundation and framing. A generic conversion diagram is available. See order form.)

BLUEPRINT PRICE CODE: **E**

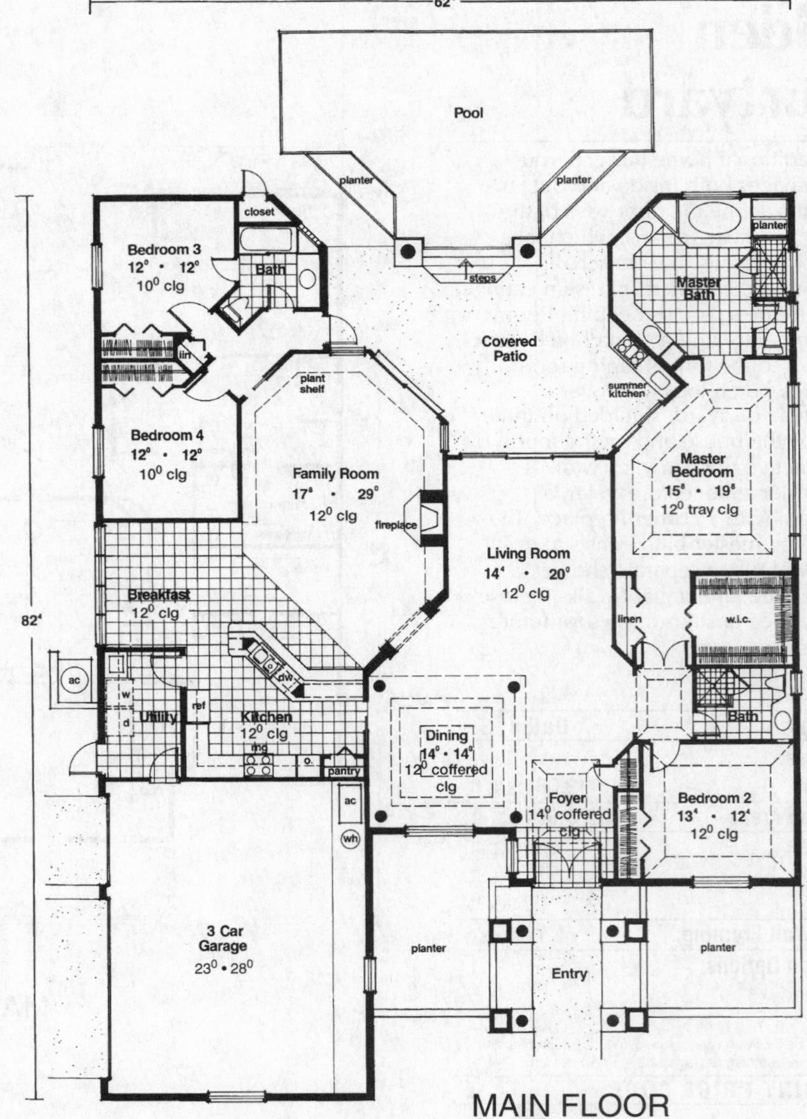

MAIN FLOOR

Plan HDS-99-191

SEE ORDER INFO ON PAGES 12-15

Intriguing Combination

- This intriguing home is finished with a combination of wood siding and brick, giving it a warm, rustic look.
- Geared for formal entertaining as well as family living, the home offers distinct activity zones. A built-in china hutch and a fireplace add style and function to the formal spaces at the front of the home. Both the living and dining rooms are set off by decorative columns.
- The large-scale family room features a high ceiling, a fireplace and a built-in entertainment center. The skylighted sun room and the breakfast area include sloped ceilings and French doors opening to the patio.
- The master suite has a high vaulted ceiling, private access to the patio and its own fireplace. The adjoining bath offers abundant storage space and a garden tub with glass-block walls.

Plan E-3102

Bedrooms: 4	**Baths:** 3
Living Area:	
Main floor	3,158 sq. ft.
Total Living Area:	**3,158 sq. ft.**
Standard basement	3,158 sq. ft.
Garage	559 sq. ft.
Storage	64 sq. ft.
Exterior Wall Framing:	2x6

Foundation Options:
Standard basement
Crawlspace
Slab
(All plans can be built with your choice of foundation and framing. A generic conversion diagram is available. See order form.)

BLUEPRINT PRICE CODE: E

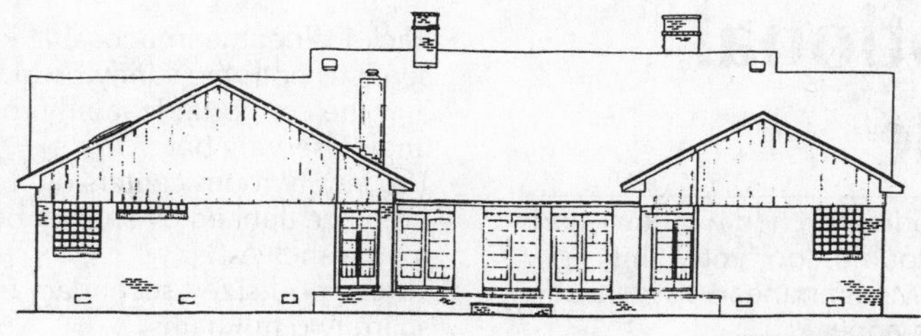

REAR VIEW

PATIO
BEDROOM 20'x13' 9' clg
MASTER SUITE 20'x16' 14' vaulted clg
MASTER BATH
BATH
DRESS
BEDROOM 16'x11' 9' clg
SUNROOM 15'x8' 9' clg
BREAKFAST 15'x8' 9' clg
HALL
UTIL
STORAGE 8'x8'
KITCHEN 19'x10' 13' clg
FAMILY 20'x20' 13' clg
GARAGE 24'x22'
BEDROOM 16'x13' 9' clg
ENTRY
DINING 14'-6"x13' 9' clg
LIVING 18'x14' 9' clg
PORCH 24'x6'
72'-0"
70'-0"

MAIN FLOOR

Exceptional Facade

- Featuring glorious arched windows and a dramatic double-door entry, this exceptional Mediterranean-style facade radiates curb appeal.
- Inside, the airy foyer connects the formal dining room and the octagonal living room. Lovely French doors lead onto an expansive rear porch that boasts a well-placed summer kitchen.
- Back inside, the impeccable kitchen services both the sunny breakfast area and the comfortable family room via an angled serving bar.
- The family room centers on a cheery fireplace flanked by snappy built-in media shelves.
- Three good-sized secondary bedrooms share two full baths.
- On the other side of the home, the sensational master suite is stocked with every amenity, including two walk-in closets, a sparkling garden tub and a separate shower.

Plan HDS-99-298

Bedrooms: 5+	**Baths:** 4
Living Area:	
Main floor	3,424 sq. ft.
Bonus room	507 sq. ft.
Total Living Area:	**3,931 sq. ft.**
Garage	814 sq. ft.
Exterior Wall Framing:	8-in. concrete block

Foundation Options:

Slab

(All plans can be built with your choice of foundation and framing. A generic conversion diagram is available. See order form.)

BLUEPRINT PRICE CODE: F

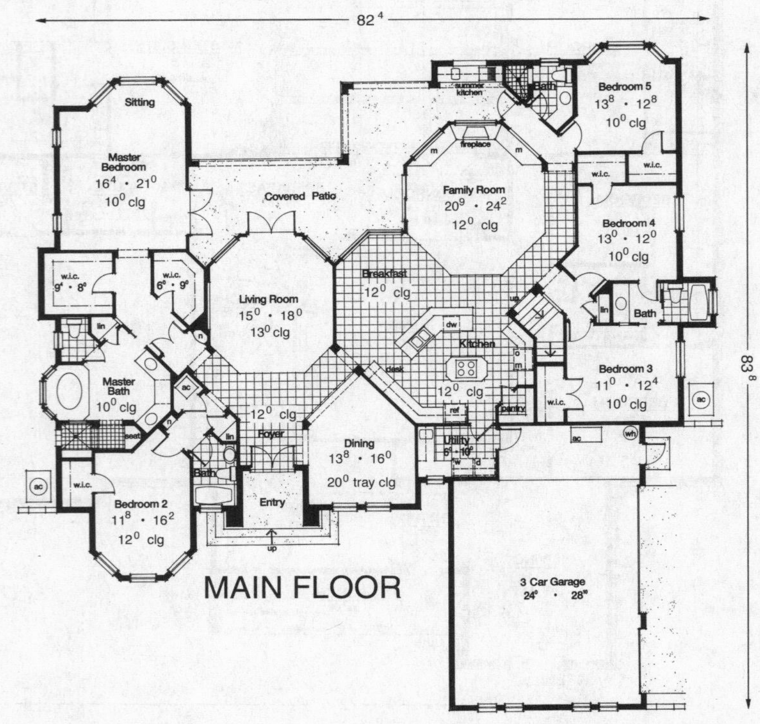

MAIN FLOOR

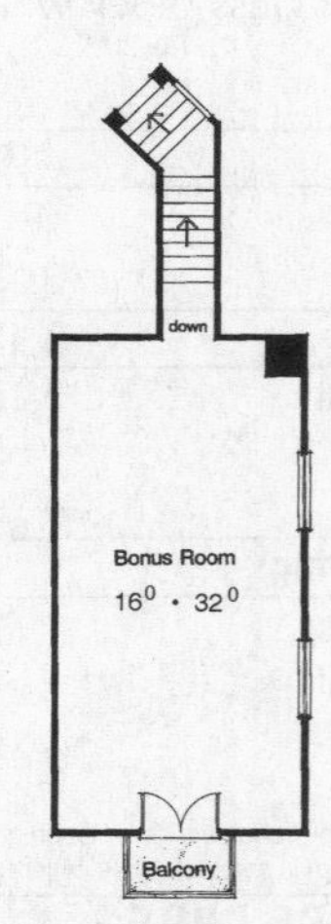

BONUS ROOM

Luxuries Galore

- Ideally suited for a scenic site, this deluxe walk-out design offers panoramic views of the outdoors and a long list of luxuries.
- Warm brick accents highlight the exterior, where a covered porch leads to a large entry. Straight ahead, the sunken living room and the spacious family room feature window walls overlooking a huge covered deck.
- The strategically placed woodstove warms the family room as well as the adjoining kitchen and nook. The island kitchen boasts deck access, a large walk-in pantry, a glass-filled nook and a top-notch laundry room.
- The nearby dining room features a charming window seat.
- The master bedroom features private deck access, a roomy walk-in closet and a superb bath that offers a bayed step-up spa tub, a separate shower and a built-in desk or makeup table.
- Another bedroom and an innovative hall bath complete the main floor.
- Downstairs, you'll find two more bedrooms, a large bath, two storage areas and a recreation room with a woodstove and a full-service wet bar. The storage areas are not included in the basement square footage.

Plan NW-744

Bedrooms: 4	**Baths:** 3½
Living Area:	
Main floor	2,539 sq. ft.
Daylight basement	1,461 sq. ft.
Total Living Area:	**4,000 sq. ft.**
Garage	904 sq. ft.
Large storage room	718 sq. ft.
Small storage room	230 sq. ft.
Exterior Wall Framing:	2x6

Foundation Options:

Daylight basement

(All plans can be built with your choice of foundation and framing. A generic conversion diagram is available. See order form.)

BLUEPRINT PRICE CODE: G

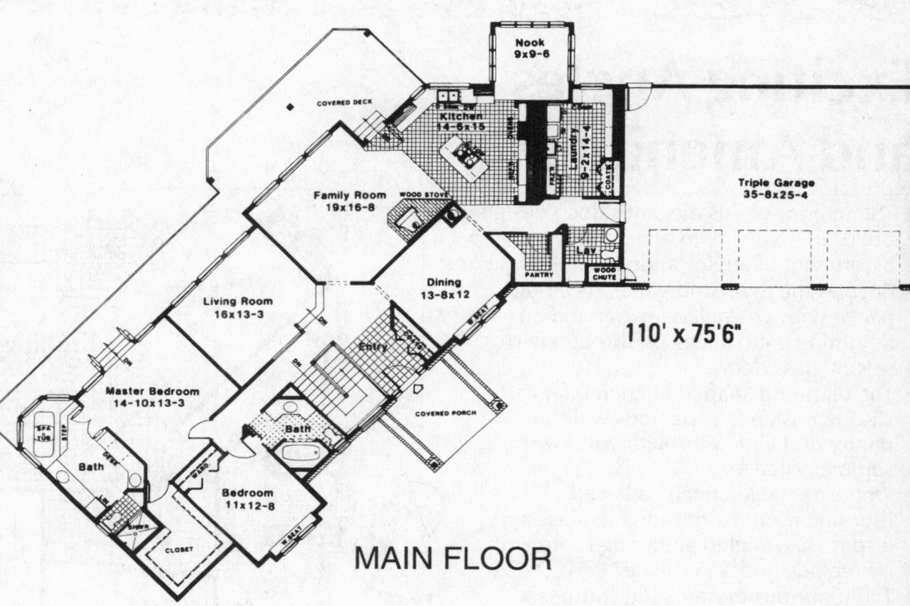

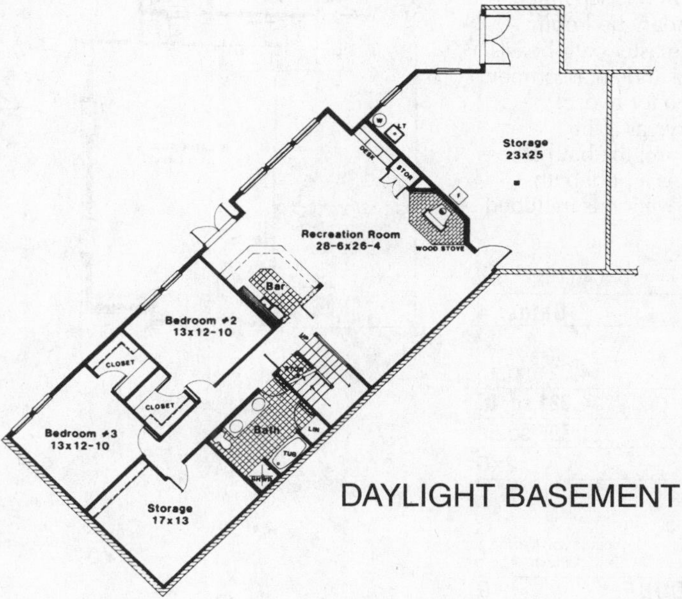

Exciting Angles and Amenities

- The interior of this elegant stucco design oozes in luxury, with an exciting assortment of angles and glass.
- Beyond the foyer and gallery is a huge parlor with an angled ale bar and an adjoining patio accessed through two sets of glass doors.
- The diamond-shaped kitchen offers a sit-down island, a spacious walk-in pantry and a pass-through window to a summer kitchen.
- Opposite the kitchen is a bayed morning room surrounded in glass and a spacious, angled gathering room with a fireplace and a TV niche.
- The luxurious master suite features a glassed lounge area and a spectacular two-sided fireplace, and is separated from the three secondary bedroom suites. The stunning master bath boasts a central linen island and an assortment of amenities designed for two.
- The library could serve as a fifth bedroom or guest room; the bath across the hall could serve as a pool bath.
- An alternate brick elevation is included in the blueprints.

Plan EOF-59

Bedrooms: 4+	**Baths:** 4
Living Area:	
Main floor	4,021 sq. ft.
Total Living Area:	**4,021 sq. ft.**
Garage	737 sq. ft.
Exterior Wall Framing:	2x6
Foundation Options:	
Slab	

(All plans can be built with your choice of foundation and framing. A generic conversion diagram is available. See order form.)

BLUEPRINT PRICE CODE: **G**

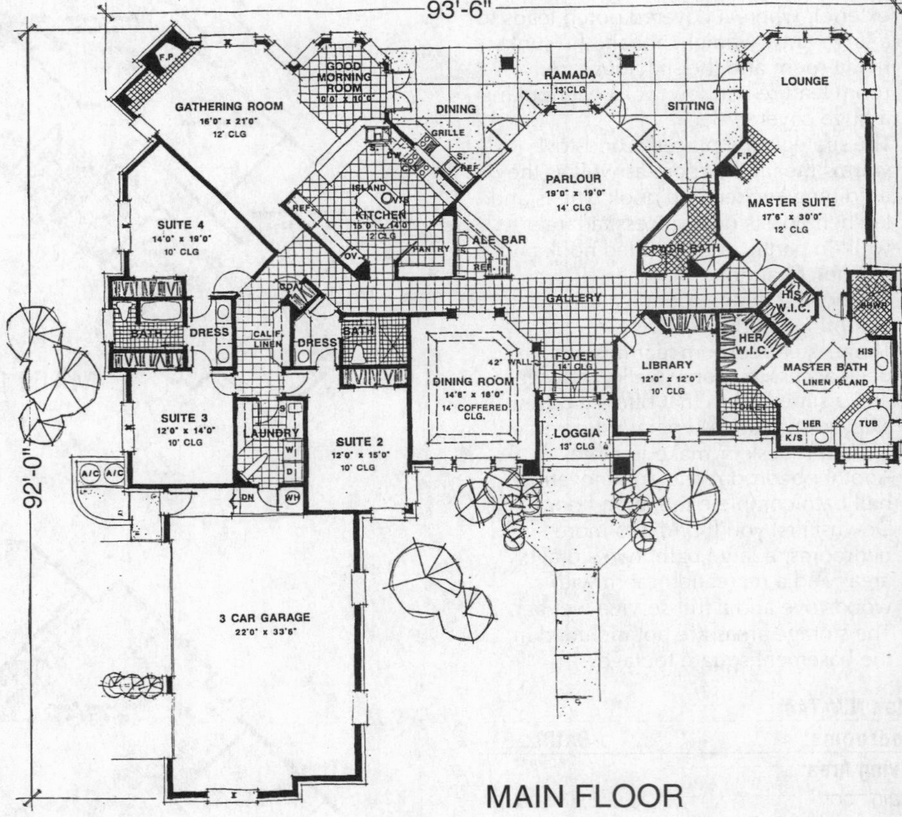

MAIN FLOOR

ORDER BLUEPRINTS ANYTIME!
CALL TOLL-FREE 1-800-820-1296

Plan EOF-59

SEE ORDER INFO ON PAGES 12-15
familyhandyman.com/homeplans

Elegant Touch

- A stunning exterior of brick, siding and copper flashing adds an elegant touch to this feature-filled one-story home.
- The recessed, sidelighted entry opens directly into the bright and airy family room, which boasts a high ceiling and a striking window-flanked fireplace.
- The adjacent formal dining room features a tray ceiling and includes a French door to a backyard patio.
- Designed with the gourmet in mind, the kitchen offers a pantry, an angled eating bar and a sunny breakfast area. A French door accesses a rear porch.
- Enhanced by a cathedral ceiling and decorative plant shelves, the master suite unfolds to a sitting area and a roomy walk-in closet. The vaulted master bath showcases a garden tub, a separate shower and a functional dual-sink vanity with knee space.
- On the opposite side of the home, two more bedrooms share another full bath.
- A laundry room is conveniently located between the entry and the garage.

Plan APS-1516	
Bedrooms: 3	**Baths:** 2
Living Area:	
Main floor	1,593 sq. ft.
Total Living Area:	**1,593 sq. ft.**
Standard basement	1,593 sq. ft.
Garage and storage/mechanical	482 sq. ft.
Exterior Wall Framing:	2x4
Foundation Options:	
Standard basement	
Crawlspace	
Slab	
(All plans can be built with your choice of foundation and framing. A generic conversion diagram is available. See order form.)	
BLUEPRINT PRICE CODE:	**B**

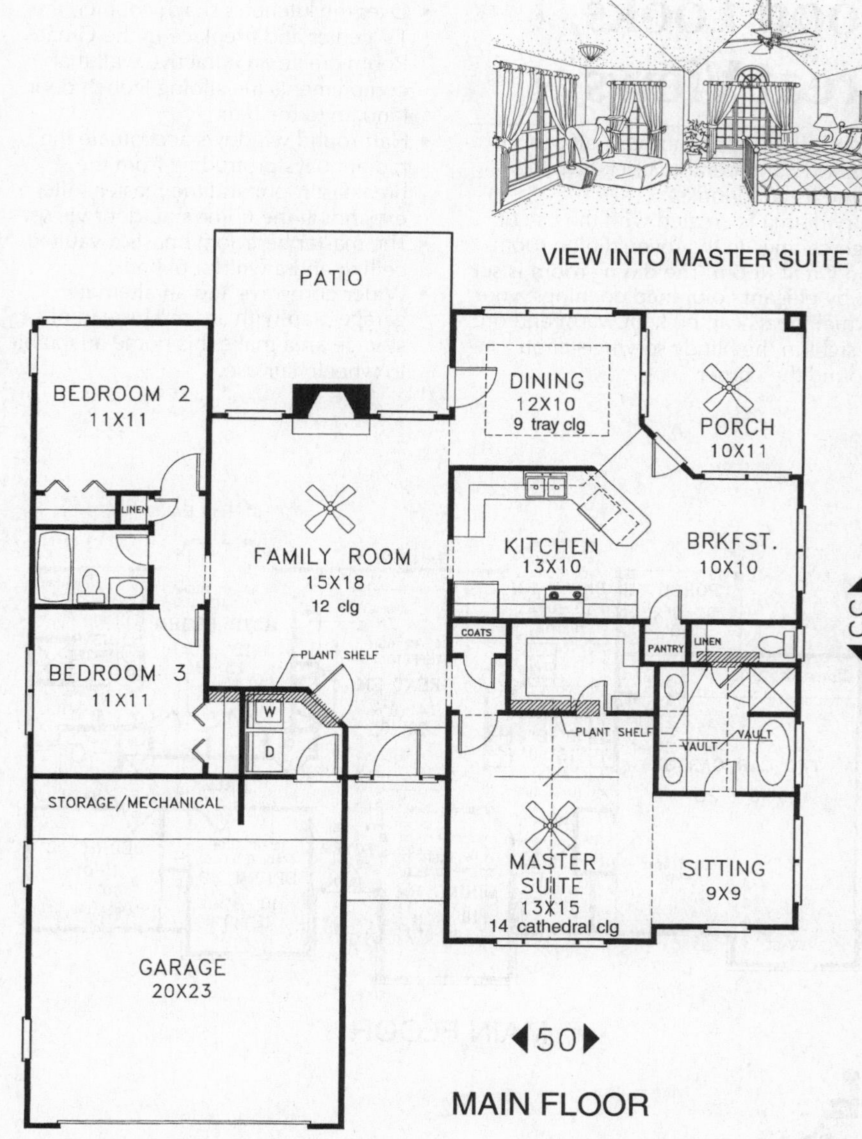

MAIN FLOOR

Good Looks, Great Views

- Wood shutters, glamorous half-round windows and durable brick give this home its good looks.
- Entry drama is created with the use of high ceilings in the foyer, dining room and Great Room. The dining room is set off by elegant columned openings; your formal meals can be kept warm and out of sight in the handy serving station around the corner.
- Over the kitchen's snack counter, the TV center and fireplace in the Great Room create an attractive wall that complements the sliding French door tandem to the rear.
- Half-round windows accentuate the radiant bays protruding from the breakfast room and the master suite, expanding the home's outdoor views.
- The master bedroom boasts a vaulted ceiling and a whirlpool bath.
- Wider doorways and an alternate garage plan with a ramp instead of a storage area make this home adaptable to wheelchair use.

Plan AX-95367	
Bedrooms: 3	**Baths:** 2
Living Area:	
Main floor	1,595 sq. ft.
Total Living Area:	**1,595 sq. ft.**
Standard basement	1,595 sq. ft.
Garage and storage	548 sq. ft.
Exterior Wall Framing:	2x4
Foundation Options:	
Standard basement	
Crawlspace	
Slab	
(All plans can be built with your choice of foundation and framing. A generic conversion diagram is available. See order form.)	
BLUEPRINT PRICE CODE:	**B**

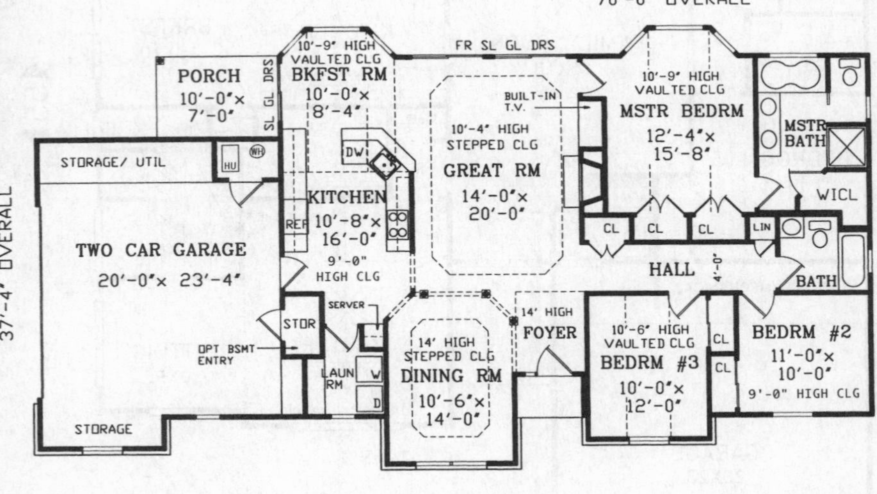

MAIN FLOOR

VIEW INTO GREAT ROOM FROM DINING ROOM

Mark Englund/Homestore™ Plans and Publications

Planned to Perfection

- This attractive and stylish home offers an interior design that is planned to perfection.
- The covered entry and vaulted foyer create an impressive welcome.
- The Great Room features a corner fireplace, a wet bar and lots of windows. The adjoining dining room offers a bay window and access to a covered patio.
- The gourmet kitchen includes an island cooktop, a garden window above the sink and a built-in desk. The attached nook is surrounded by windows that overlook a delightful planter.
- The master suite boasts a tray ceiling and a peaceful reading area that accesses a private patio. The superb master bath features a garden tub and a separate shower.
- Two secondary bedrooms share a compartmentalized bath.

Plan S-4789

Bedrooms: 3	**Baths:** 2
Living Area:	
Main floor	1,665 sq. ft.
Total Living Area:	**1,665 sq. ft.**
Standard basement	1,665 sq. ft.
Garage	400 sq. ft.
Exterior Wall Framing:	2x6
Foundation Options:	
Standard basement	
Crawlspace	
Slab	

(All plans can be built with your choice of foundation and framing. A generic conversion diagram is available. See order form.)

BLUEPRINT PRICE CODE: B

NOTE:
The photographed home may have been modified by the homeowner. Please refer to floor plan and/or drawn elevation shown for actual blueprint details.

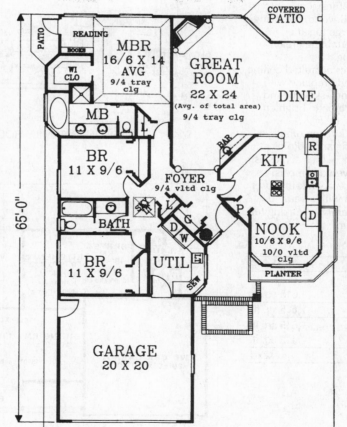

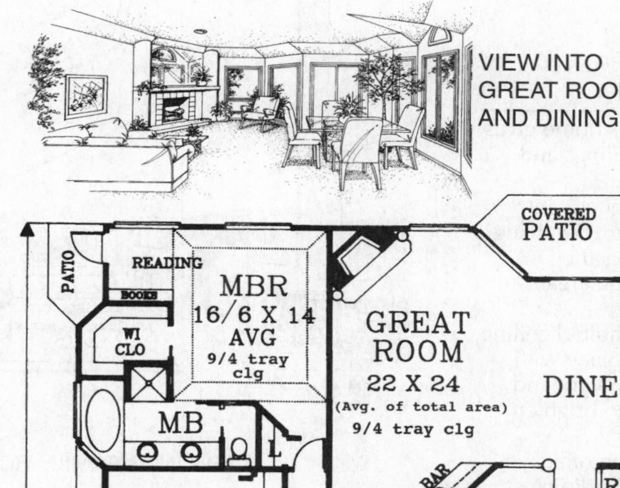

MAIN FLOOR

BASEMENT STAIRWAY LOCATION

Tradition Updated

- The nostalgic exterior of this home gives way to dramatic vaulted ceilings and illuminating skylights inside.
- The front porch welcomes guests into the stone-tiled foyer. Beyond, the living and dining rooms merge together, forming an open entertaining area under a vaulted ceiling.
- The family room shares a vaulted ceiling and a cozy three-sided fireplace with the living room. A sunny skylight and sliding glass doors to a patio brighten the room.
- The skylighted island kitchen offers yet another vaulted ceiling and adjoins a cheery breakfast nook, which serves as the perfect spot for everyday meals.
- The master suite boasts a walk-in closet and a skylighted bath with a vaulted ceiling, a dual-sink vanity, a soaking tub and a separate shower.

VIEW INTO FAMILY ROOM

NOTE: The above photographed home may have been modified by the homeowner. Please refer to floor plan and/or drawn elevation shown for actual blueprint details.

Plan AX-90303-A	
Bedrooms: 3	**Baths:** 2
Living Area:	
Main floor	1,615 sq. ft.
Total Living Area:	**1,615 sq. ft.**
Basement	1,615 sq. ft.
Garage	412 sq. ft.
Exterior Wall Framing:	2x4
Foundation Options:	
Daylight basement	
Standard basement	
Crawlspace	
Slab	

(All plans can be built with your choice of foundation and framing. A generic conversion diagram is available. See order form.)

BLUEPRINT PRICE CODE: B

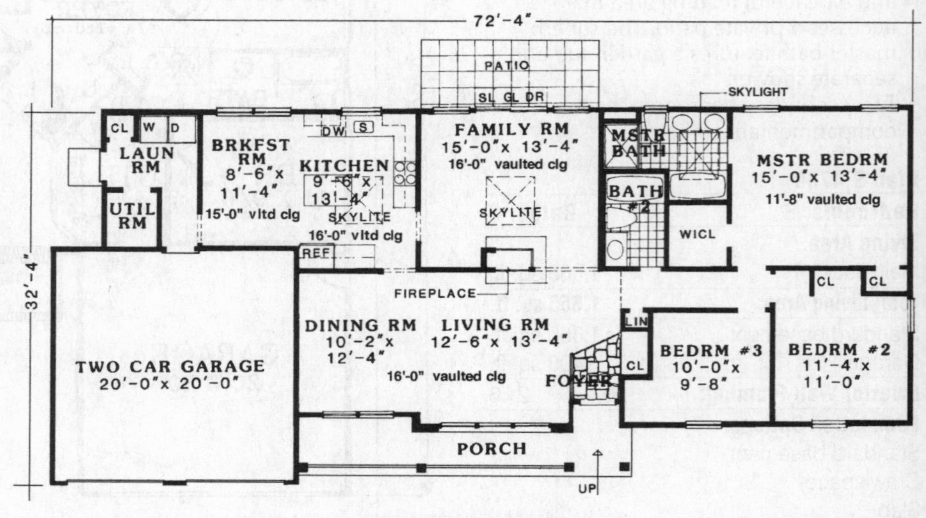

MAIN FLOOR

ORDER BLUEPRINTS ANYTIME! CALL TOLL-FREE 1-800-820-1296

Plan AX-90303-A

SEE ORDER INFO ON PAGES 12-15

familyhandyman.com/homeplans

Rustic Welcome

- This rustic design boasts an appealing exterior with a covered front porch that offers guests a friendly welcome.
- Inside, the centrally located Great Room features a cathedral ceiling with exposed wood beams. A massive fireplace separates the living area from the large dining room, which offers access to a nice backyard patio.
- The galley-style kitchen flows between the formal dining room and the bayed breakfast room, which offers a handy pantry and access to laundry facilities.
- The master suite features a walk-in closet and a compartmentalized bath.
- Across the Great Room, two additional bedrooms have extra closet space and share a second full bath.
- The side-entry garage gives the front of the home an extra-appealing and uncluttered look.
- The optional daylight basement offers expanded living space. The stairway (not shown) would be located along the wall between the dining room and the back bedroom.

Plan C-8460	
Bedrooms: 3	**Baths:** 2
Living Area:	
Main floor	1,670 sq. ft.
Total Living Area:	**1,670 sq. ft.**
Daylight basement	1,600 sq. ft.
Garage	427 sq. ft.
Storage	63 sq. ft.
Exterior Wall Framing:	2x4
Foundation Options:	
Daylight basement	
Crawlspace	
Slab	
(All plans can be built with your choice of foundation and framing. A generic conversion diagram is available. See order form.)	
BLUEPRINT PRICE CODE:	**B**

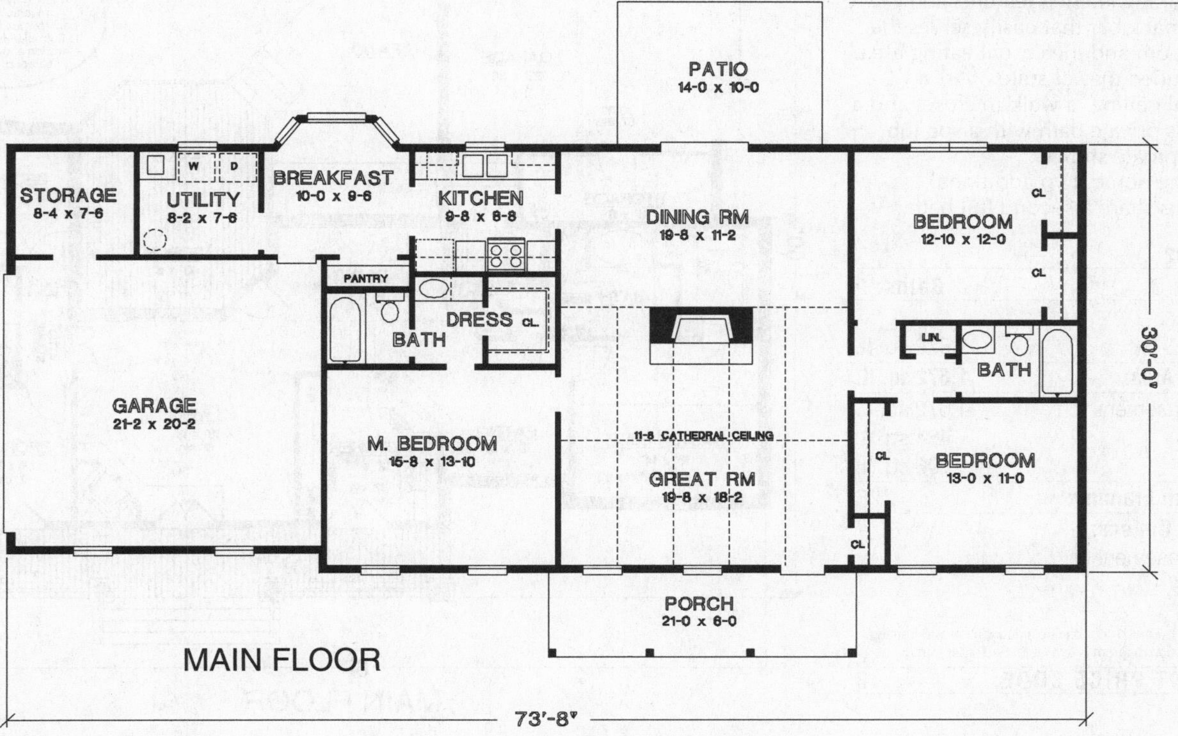

Plan C-8460

FOR MORE DETAILS, SEE PLAN AT
familyhandyman.com/homeplans

Mark Englund/Homestore™ Plans and Publications

Porch Offers Three Entries

- Showy window treatments, stately columns and three sets of French doors give this Plantation-style home an inviting exterior.
- High ceilings in the living room, dining room and kitchen add volume to the economically-sized home.
- A corner fireplace and a view to the back porch are found in the living room. The porch is accessed from a door in the dining room.
- The adjoining kitchen features an angled snack bar that easily serves the dining room and the casual eating area.
- The secluded master suite offers a cathedral ceiling, a walk-in closet and a luxurious private bath with a spa tub and a separate shower.
- Across the home, two additional bedrooms share a second full bath.

Plan E-1602	
Bedrooms: 3	**Baths:** 2
Living Area:	
Main floor	1,672 sq. ft.
Total Living Area:	**1,672 sq. ft.**
Standard basement	1,672 sq. ft.
Garage	484 sq. ft.
Storage	96 sq. ft.
Exterior Wall Framing:	2x6
Foundation Options:	
Standard basement	
Crawlspace	
Slab	

(All plans can be built with your choice of foundation and framing. A generic conversion diagram is available. See order form.)

BLUEPRINT PRICE CODE: B

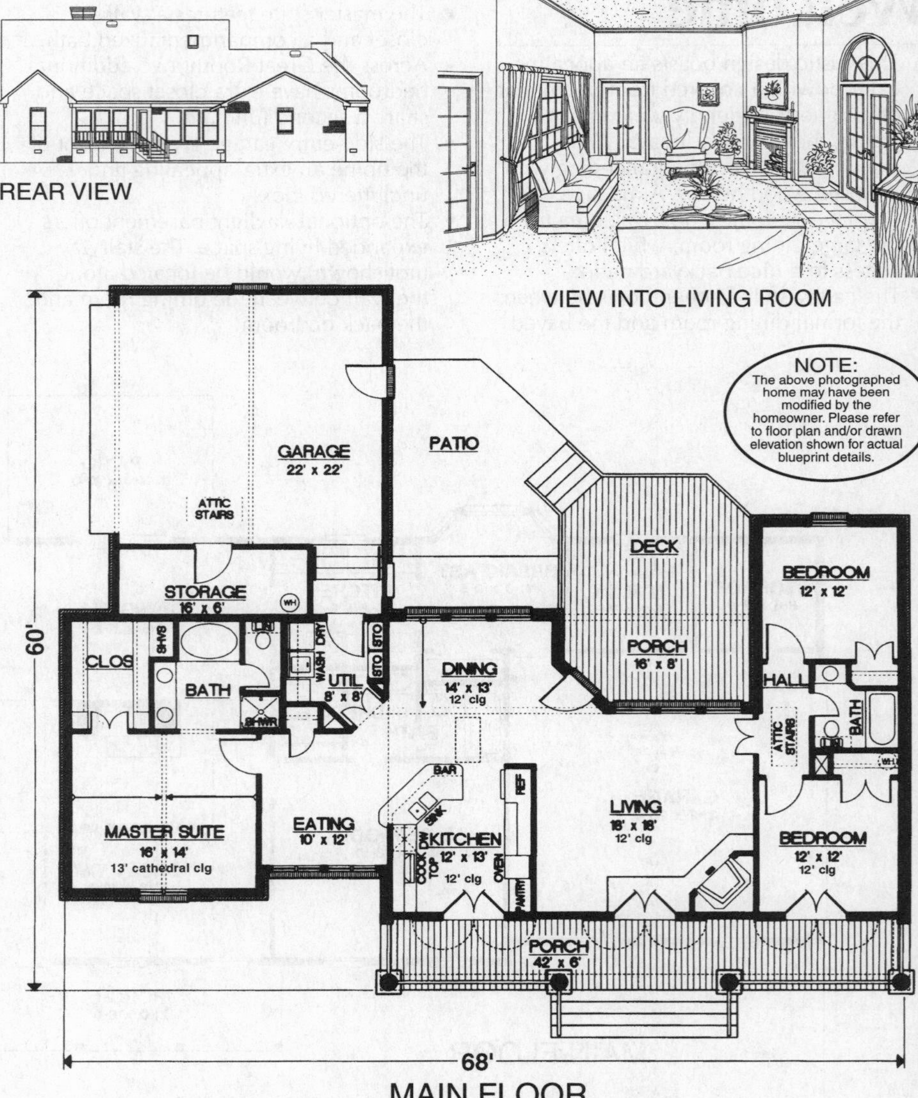

MAIN FLOOR

Sunny Disposition

- Natural light streams through the expansive windows lining the back of this sunny home, brightening your days—and even your disposition!
- The central Great Room benefits from a bayed wall of windows. A crackling two-way fireplace faces the windows, surrounding the space with warmth.
- Open to the Great Room, the bayed nook accesses an expansive deck, where the view exposed by all the windows really comes alive.
- Although kitchens have become important gathering areas in recent years, they're not the first thing you want people to see when they walk through the front door! Double doors hide this kitchen from immediate view, directing attention instead toward the columned formal dining room.
- Even more hidden is the master suite, which offers an unparalled private bath, plus French doors to the back deck.

Plan DW-1675

Bedrooms: 3	**Baths:** 2
Living Area:	
Main floor	1,675 sq. ft.
Total Living Area:	**1,675 sq. ft.**
Standard basement	1,675 sq. ft.
Garage and storage	618 sq. ft.
Exterior Wall Framing:	2x4
Foundation Options:	
Standard basement	
Crawlspace	
Slab	

(All plans can be built with your choice of foundation and framing. A generic conversion diagram is available. See order form.)

BLUEPRINT PRICE CODE: B

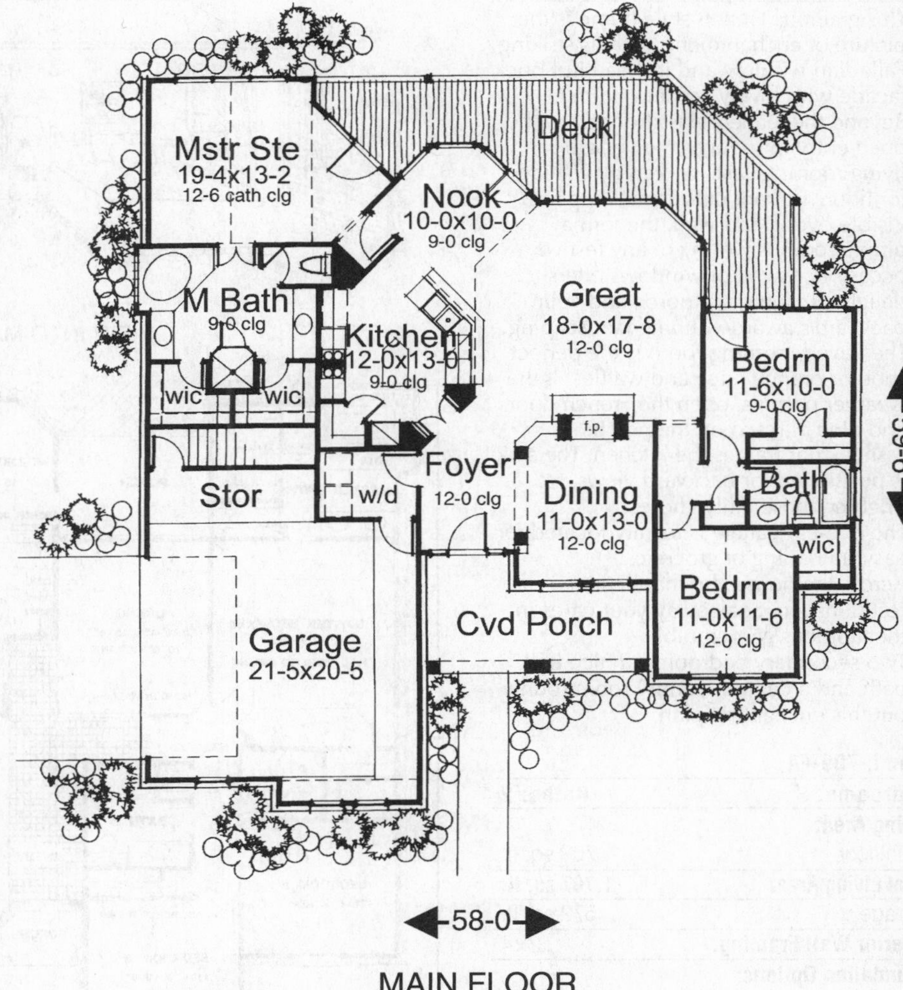

MAIN FLOOR

Enchanting!

- This gracious French-style home is the picture of enchantment, with its striking Palladian window and its beautiful brick facade with lovely corner quoins.
- Beyond the leaded-glass front door, the open entry introduces the versatile living room. Guests will enjoy visiting for hours in front of the crackling fire!
- Visible over a half-wall, the formal dining room is worthy of any festive occasion. A wall of windows offers delightful views to a porch and your backyard's award-winning landscaping.
- The bayed morning room is the perfect spot for orange juice and waffles. If the weather permits, open the French door and dine alfresco on the porch!
- A snack bar frames the kitchen. The sink is positioned for backyard views, to brighten those daily chores.
- The two-car garage is ideally located for easy unloading of groceries.
- Across the home, the master suite is a restful haven. Soak away your cares in the fabulous garden tub!
- Two secondary bedrooms, a nice hall bath and a central laundry room round out this enchanting plan.

Plan L-709-FA

Bedrooms: 3	**Baths:** 2
Living Area:	
Main floor	1,707 sq. ft.
Total Living Area:	**1,707 sq. ft.**
Garage	572 sq. ft.
Exterior Wall Framing:	2x4
Foundation Options:	
Slab	

(All plans can be built with your choice of foundation and framing. A generic conversion diagram is available. See order form.)

BLUEPRINT PRICE CODE: B

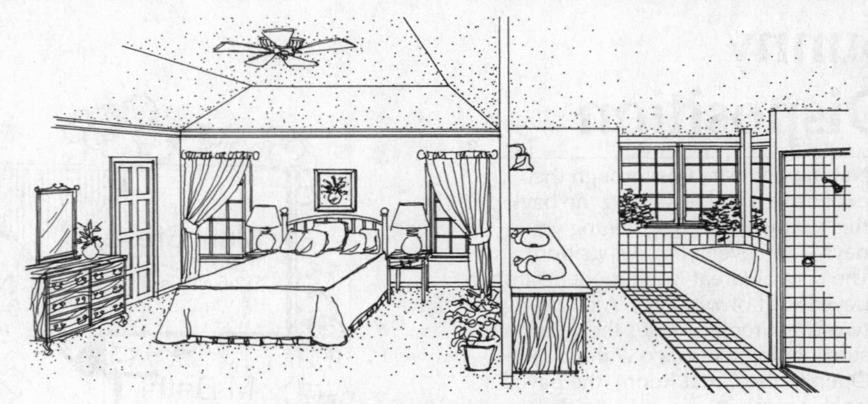

VIEW INTO MASTER SUITE

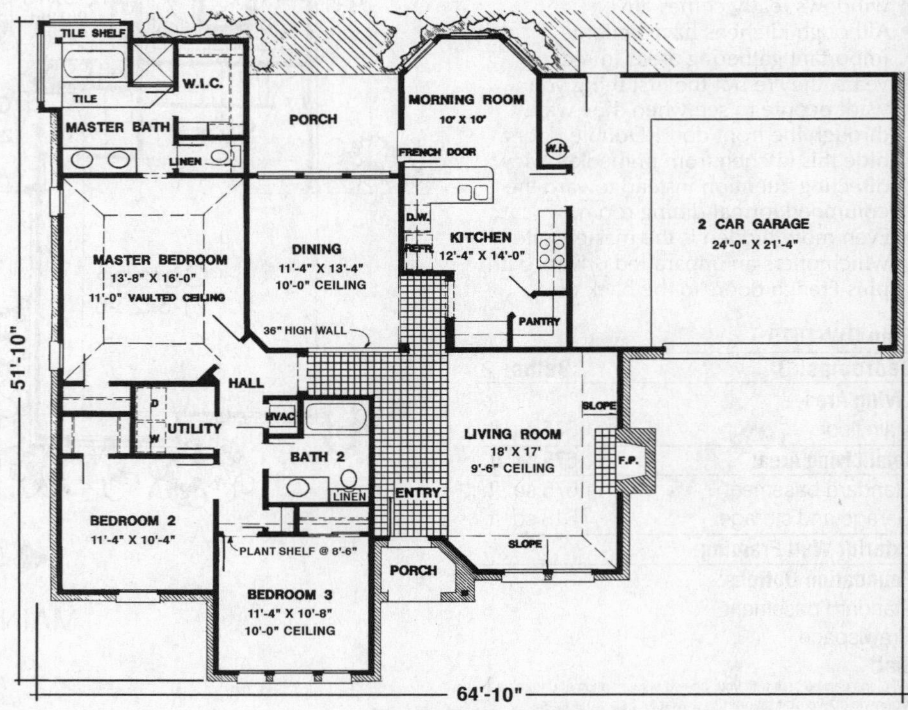

MAIN FLOOR

Plan L-709-FA

SEE ORDER INFO ON PAGES 12-15

Simply Beautiful

- This four-bedroom design offers simplistic beauty, economical construction and ample space for both family life and formal entertaining—all on one floor.
- The charming cottage-style exterior gives way to a spacious interior. A vaulted, beamed ceiling soars above the huge living room, which features a massive fireplace, built-in bookshelves and access to a backyard patio.
- The efficient galley-style kitchen flows between a sunny bayed eating area and the formal dining room.
- The deluxe master suite includes a dressing room, a large walk-in closet and a private bath.
- The three remaining bedrooms are larger than average and offer ample closet space.
- A nice-sized storage area and a deluxe utility room are accessible from the two-car garage.

Plan E-1702

Bedrooms: 4	**Baths:** 2
Living Area:	
Main floor	1,751 sq. ft.
Total Living Area:	**1,751 sq. ft.**
Garage	484 sq. ft.
Storage	105 sq. ft.
Exterior Wall Framing:	2x4

Foundation Options:

Crawlspace

Slab

(All plans can be built with your choice of foundation and framing. A generic conversion diagram is available. See order form.)

BLUEPRINT PRICE CODE: B

REAR VIEW

VIEW INTO LIVING ROOM

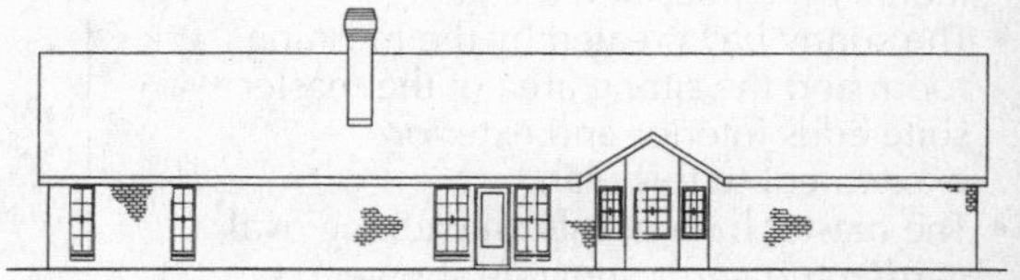

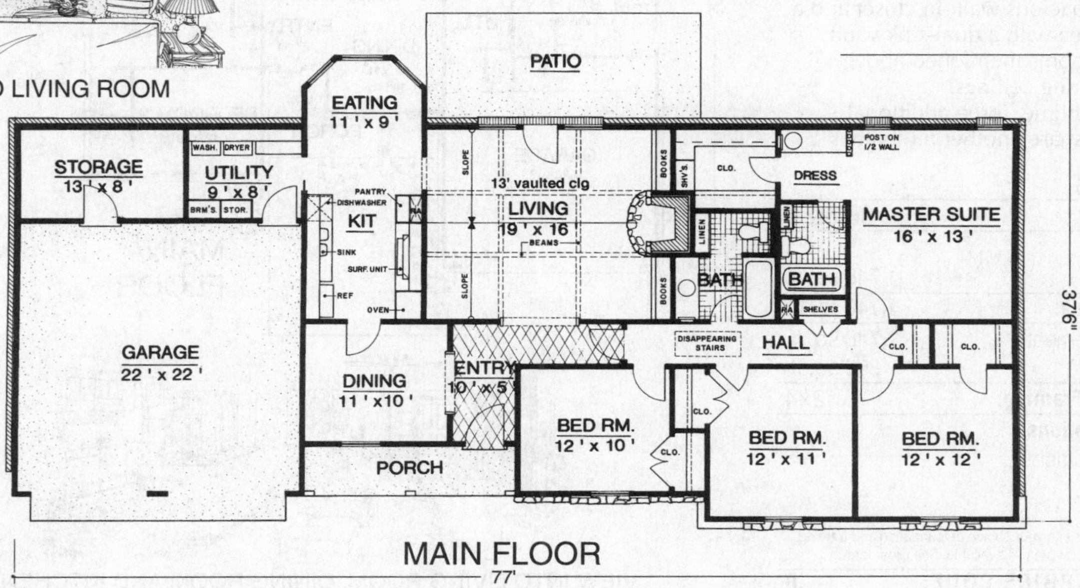

PATIO

EATING 11' x 9'

STORAGE 13' x 8'

UTILITY 9' x 8'

WASH DRYER

BRM'S STOR.

PANTRY DISHWASHER

KIT

SINK

SURF. UNIT

REF

OVEN

SLOPE

13' vaulted clg

LIVING 19' x 16'

BEAMS

BOOKS

SHV'S

CLO.

LINEN

BATH

POST ON 1/2 WALL

DRESS

MASTER SUITE 16' x 13'

BATH

SHELVES

DISAPPEARING STAIRS

HALL

GARAGE 22' x 22'

DINING 11' x 10'

ENTRY 10' x 5'

BED RM. 12' x 10'

BED RM. 12' x 11'

BED RM. 12' x 12'

PORCH

37'6"

77'

MAIN FLOOR

Designed for Livability

- With the separation of the master suite from the rest of the home, this design is ideal for the maturing family.
- Off the columned porch, the sidelighted front entry offers views through the bright living room to the backyard.
- An elegant column separates the formal dining room from the living room.
- The kitchen offers a sunny morning room, a pantry and handy access to the laundry facilities and the garage.
- The sunny bay created by the morning room and the sitting area of the master suite adds interior and exterior excitement to this plan.
- The master bath boasts an exciting oval garden tub and a separate shower, as well as a spacious walk-in closet and a dressing area with a dual-sink vanity.
- All of the rooms mentioned above feature soaring ceilings.
- Across the home, three additional bedrooms share another full bath.

Plan DD-1696

Bedrooms: 4	**Baths:** 2
Living Area:	
Main floor	1,748 sq. ft.
Total Living Area:	**1,748 sq. ft.**
Standard basement	1,748 sq. ft.
Garage	393 sq. ft.
Exterior Wall Framing:	2x4
Foundation Options:	
Standard basement	
Crawlspace	
Slab	

(All plans can be built with your choice of foundation and framing. A generic conversion diagram is available. See order form.)

BLUEPRINT PRICE CODE: B

REAR VIEW

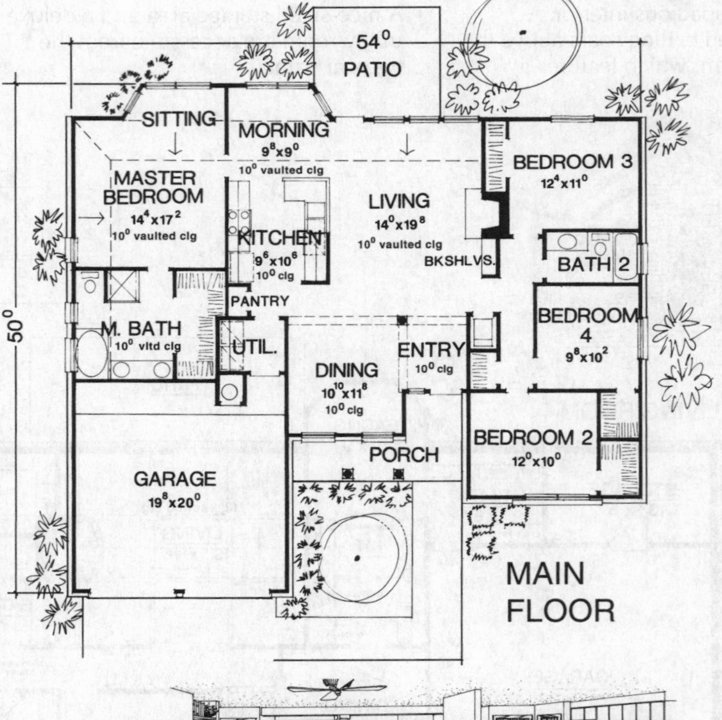

VIEW INTO LIVING ROOM, DINING ROOM AND KITCHEN

Plan DD-1696

SEE ORDER INFO ON PAGES 12-15

Free-Flowing Floor Plan

- A fluid floor plan with open indoor/outdoor living spaces characterizes this exciting luxury home.
- The stylish columned porch opens to a spacious living room and dining room expanse that overlooks the outdoor spaces. The breathtaking view also includes a dramatic corner fireplace.
- The dining area opens to a bright kitchen with an angled eating bar. The overall spaciousness of the living areas is increased with raised ceilings.
- A sunny, informal eating area adjoins the kitchen, and an angled set of doors opens to a convenient main-floor laundry room near the garage entrance.
- The vaulted master bedroom has a walk-in closet and a sumptuous bath with an oval tub.
- A separate wing houses two additional bedrooms and another full bath.
- Attic space is accessible from stairs in the garage and in the bedroom wing.

Plan E-1710

Bedrooms: 3	**Baths:** 2
Living Area:	
Main floor	1,792 sq. ft.
Total Living Area:	**1,792 sq. ft.**
Standard basement	1,792 sq. ft.
Garage	484 sq. ft.
Storage	96 sq. ft.
Exterior Wall Framing:	2x6

Foundation Options:

Standard basement
Crawlspace
Slab
(All plans can be built with your choice of foundation and framing. A generic conversion diagram is available. See order form.)

BLUEPRINT PRICE CODE: B

VIEW INTO LIVING ROOM

REAR VIEW

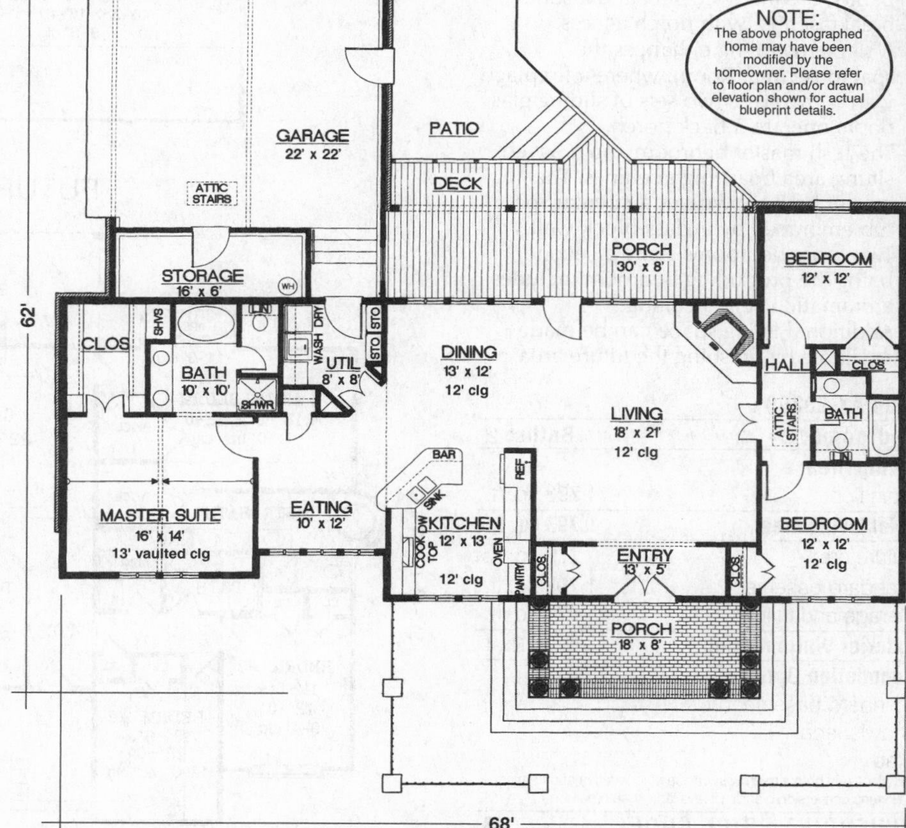

MAIN FLOOR

Plan E-1710

Fresh Air

VIEW INTO GREAT ROOM

- With its nostalgic look and country style, this lovely home brings a breath of fresh air into any neighborhood.
- Past the inviting wraparound porch, the foyer is brightened by an elliptical transom window above the front door.
- The adjoining formal dining room is defined by decorative columns and a stylish stepped ceiling.
- The bright and airy kitchen includes a pantry, a windowed sink and a sunny breakfast area with porch access.
- A stepped ceiling enhances the spacious Great Room, where a fireplace warms the area. Two sets of sliding glass doors open to a back porch.
- The lush master bedroom and a bayed sitting area boast high ceilings. The master bath showcases a circular spa tub embraced by a glass-block wall.
- Two more bedrooms share a second bath. The protruding bedroom includes a dramatic vaulted ceiling.
- Additional living space can be made available by finishing the future area.

Plan AX-93308

Bedrooms: 3+	**Baths:** 2
Living Area:	
Main floor	1,793 sq. ft.
Total Living Area:	**1,793 sq. ft.**
Future area	779 sq. ft.
Standard basement	1,793 sq. ft.
Garage and utility	471 sq. ft.
Exterior Wall Framing:	2x4

Foundation Options:

Standard basement

Crawlspace

Slab

(All plans can be built with your choice of foundation and framing. A generic conversion diagram is available. See order form.)

BLUEPRINT PRICE CODE: B

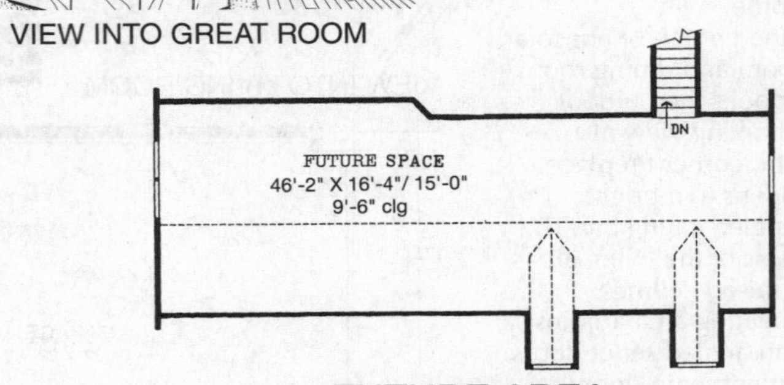

FUTURE AREA

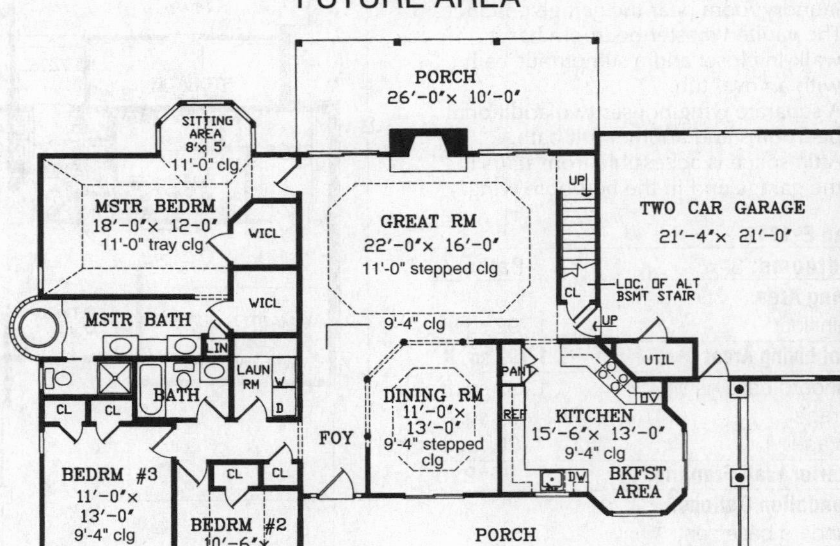

MAIN FLOOR

ORDER BLUEPRINTS ANYTIME!
CALL TOLL-FREE 1-800-820-1296

Plan AX-93308

Plan copyright held by home designer/architect

SEE ORDER INFO ON PAGES 12-15
familyhandyman.com/homeplans

Classic Country-Style

- At the center of this rustic country-style home is an enormous living room with a flat beamed ceiling, a massive stone fireplace and access to a patio and a covered rear porch.
- The adjoining eating area and kitchen provide plenty of room for casual dining and meal preparation. The eating area is visually enhanced by a sloped ceiling with false beams. The kitchen includes a snack bar, a pantry closet and a built-in spice cabinet.
- The formal dining room gets plenty of pizzazz from the stone-faced wall and arched planter facing the living room.
- The secluded master suite has it all, including a private bath, a separate dressing area and a large walk-in closet with built-in shelves.
- The two remaining bedrooms have big closets and easy access to a full bath.

Plan E-1808

Bedrooms: 3	**Baths:** 2
Living Area:	
Main floor	1,800 sq. ft.
Total Living Area:	**1,800 sq. ft.**
Garage	506 sq. ft.
Storage	99 sq. ft.
Exterior Wall Framing:	2x4

Foundation Options:
Crawlspace
Slab
(All plans can be built with your choice of foundation and framing. A generic conversion diagram is available. See order form.)

BLUEPRINT PRICE CODE: B

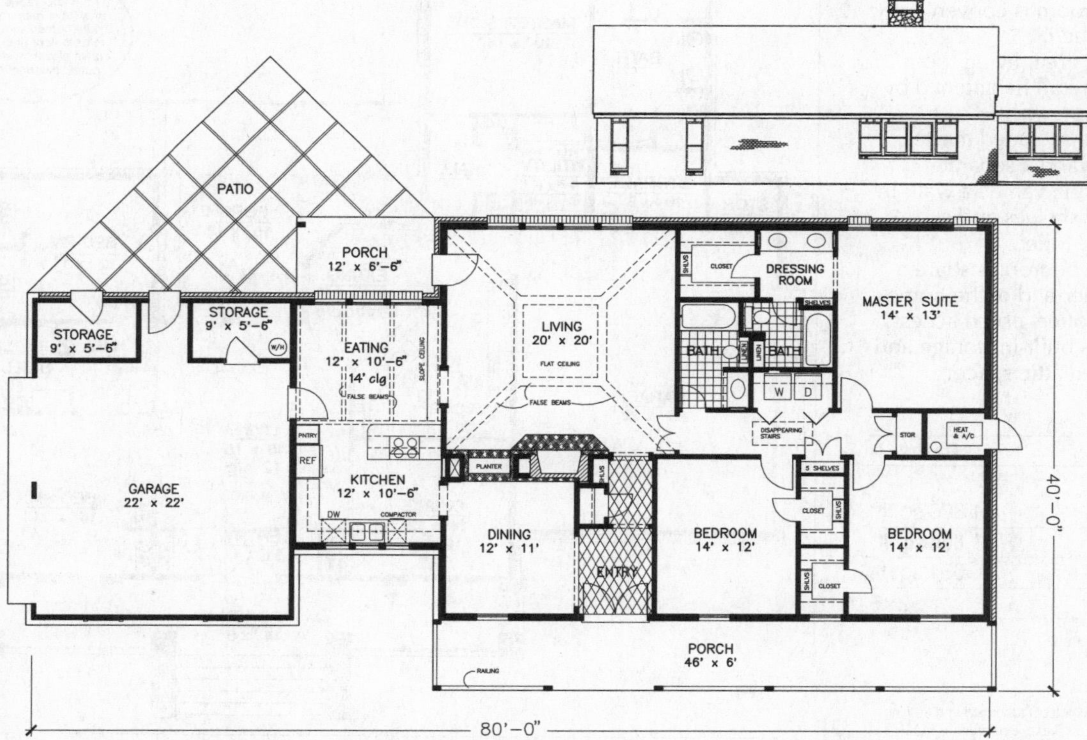

REAR VIEW

MAIN FLOOR

Plan E-1808

FOR MORE DETAILS, SEE PLAN AT
familyhandyman.com/homeplans

Photos by Mark Englund/Homestore™ Plans and Publications

Masterful Master Suite

- This gorgeous home features front and rear covered porches and a master suite so luxurious it deserves its own wing.
- The expansive entry welcomes visitors into a spacious, skylighted living room, which boasts a handsome fireplace. The adjacent formal dining room overlooks the front porch.
- Designed for efficiency, the kitchen features an angled snack bar, a bayed eating area and views of the porch. An all-purpose utility room is conveniently located off the kitchen.
- The kitchen, eating area, living room and dining room are all heightened by high ceilings.
- The sumptuous and secluded master suite features a tub and a separate shower, a double-sink vanity, a walk-in closet with built-in shelves and a compartmentalized toilet.
- The two secondary bedrooms share a hall bath at the other end of the home. The rear bedroom offers porch access.
- The garage features built-in storage and access to unfinished attic space.

Plan E-1811

Bedrooms: 3	**Baths:** 2
Living Area:	
Main floor	1,800 sq. ft.
Total Living Area:	**1,800 sq. ft.**
Garage and storage	634 sq. ft.
Exterior Wall Framing:	2x6
Foundation Options:	
Crawlspace	
Slab	

(All plans can be built with your choice of foundation and framing. A generic conversion diagram is available. See order form.)

BLUEPRINT PRICE CODE: B

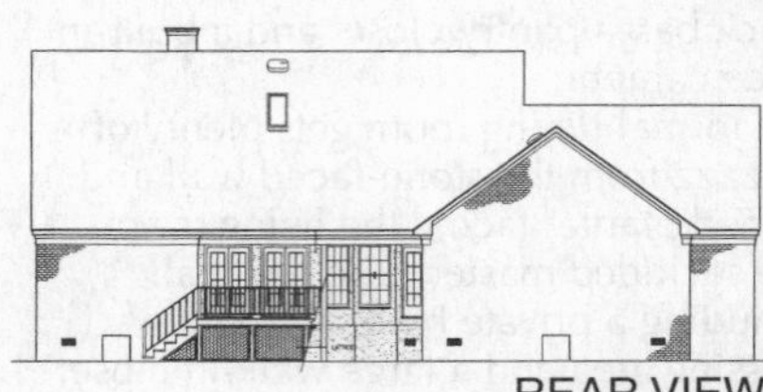

REAR VIEW

VIEW INTO LIVING ROOM

NOTE: The photographed home may have been modified by the homeowner. Please refer to floor plan and/or drawn elevation shown for actual blueprint details.

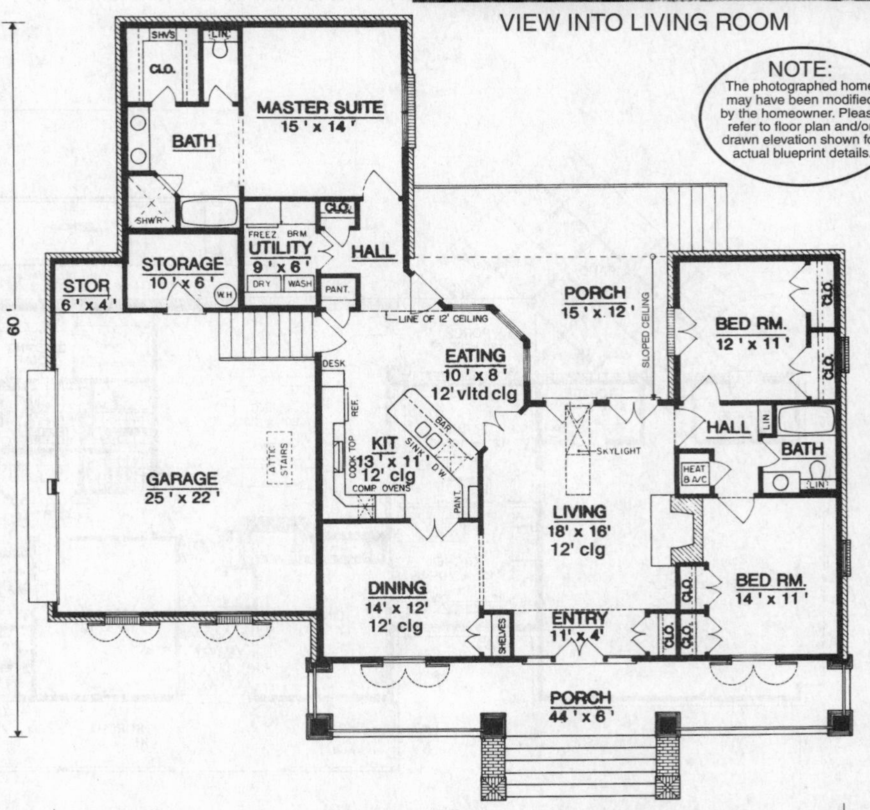

MAIN FLOOR

Mark Englund/Homestore™ Plans and Publications

Strength of Character

- The solid, permanent feel of brick and the intelligent, efficient floor plan of this stately one-story home give it an obvious strength of character.
- Guests are welcomed inside by an attractive raised foyer, from which virtually any room can be reached with just a few steps.
- With a high ceiling, a built-in bookcase, a gorgeous fireplace and French doors that lead to the backyard, the centrally located living room is well equipped to serve as a hub of activity.
- Smartly designed and positioned, the galley-style kitchen easily serves the cozy breakfast nook and the formal dining room.
- The beautiful master bedroom provides a nice blend of elegance and seclusion, and features a striking stepped ceiling, a large walk-in closet, a private bath and its own access to the backyard.
- Two additional bedrooms feature walk-in closets and share a full-sized bath.

Plan L-851-A

Bedrooms: 3	**Baths:** 2
Living Area:	
Main floor	1,849 sq. ft.
Total Living Area:	**1,849 sq. ft.**
Garage	437 sq. ft.
Exterior Wall Framing:	2x4
Foundation Options:	
Slab	

(All plans can be built with your choice of foundation and framing. A generic conversion diagram is available. See order form.)

BLUEPRINT PRICE CODE: B

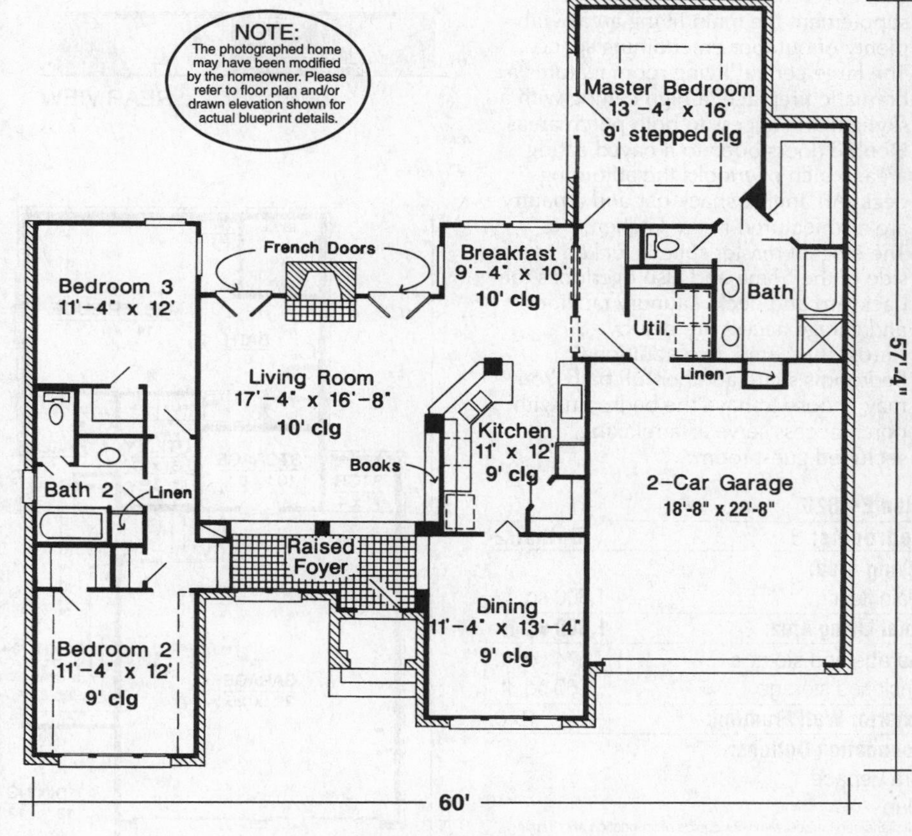

MAIN FLOOR

Builder: Conrad Martin Real Estate, Inc.

Mark Englund/Homestore™ Plans and Publications

Cozy Porches

- Twin dormers give this raised one-story design the appearance of a two-story. Two covered porches and a deck supplement the main living areas with plenty of outdoor entertaining space.
- The large central living room features a dramatic fireplace, a high ceiling with a skylight and access to both porch areas.
- Double doors open to a bayed eating area, which overlooks the adjoining deck. An angled snack bar and a pantry are also featured in the kitchen.
- The elegant master suite is tucked to one side of the home and also overlooks the backyard and deck. Laundry facilities and garage access are nearby.
- Across the home, two additional bedrooms share another full bath. You may choose to have the bedroom with porch access serve as a relaxing, secluded guest room.

Plan E-1826	
Bedrooms: 3	**Baths:** 2
Living Area:	
Main floor	1,800 sq. ft.
Total Living Area:	**1,800 sq. ft.**
Garage and storage	574 sq. ft.
Enclosed storage	60 sq. ft.
Exterior Wall Framing:	2x6
Foundation Options:	
Crawlspace	
Slab	
(All plans can be built with your choice of foundation and framing. A generic conversion diagram is available. See order form.)	
BLUEPRINT PRICE CODE:	**B**

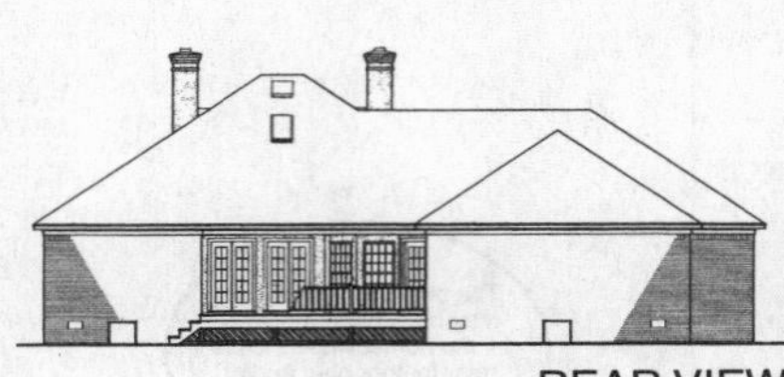

REAR VIEW

VIEW INTO LIVING ROOM

NOTE: The above photographed home may have been modified by the homeowner. Please refer to floor plan and/or drawn elevation shown for actual blueprint details.

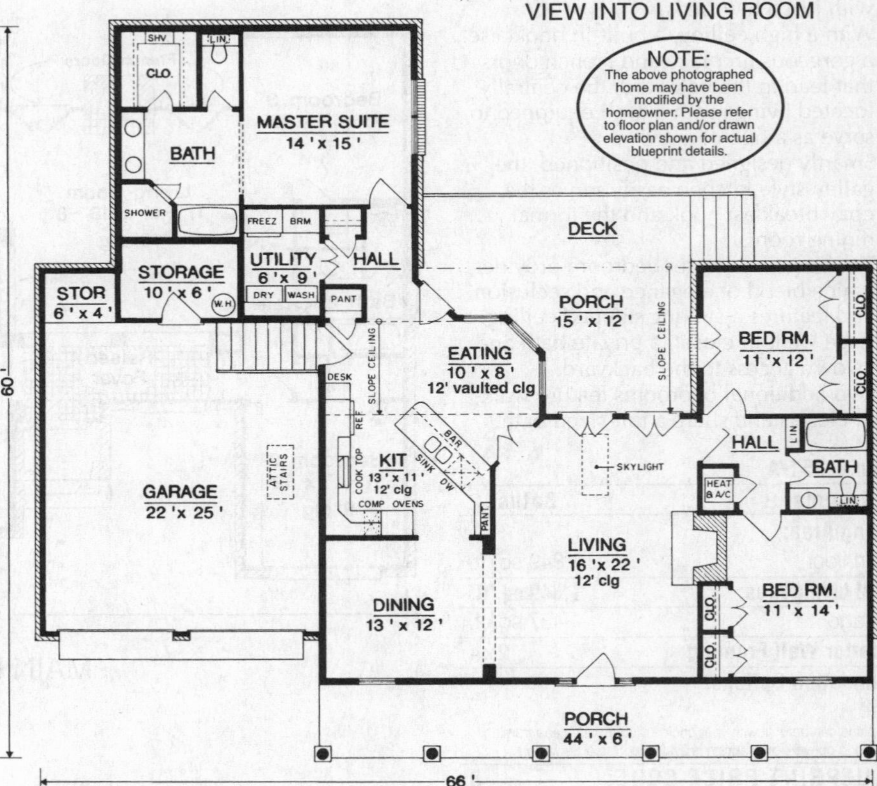

MAIN FLOOR

ORDER BLUEPRINTS ANYTIME!
CALL TOLL-FREE 1-800-820-1296

Plan E-1826

SEE ORDER INFO ON PAGES 12-15
familyhandyman.com/homeplans

Classic Ranch

- With decorative brick quoins, a columned porch and stylish dormers, the exterior of this classic one-story provides an interesting blend of Early American and European design.
- Just off the foyer, the bayed formal dining room is enhanced by a gorgeous stepped ceiling.
- The spacious Great Room, separated from the dining room by a columned arch, features a stepped ceiling, a handy built-in media center and a striking fireplace. Lovely French doors lead to a big backyard patio.
- The breakfast room, which shares an eating bar with the kitchen, boasts an airy ceiling. French doors access a sunny rear porch.
- The master bedroom has a tray ceiling, a bright bay window and a walk-in closet. The master bath features a whirlpool tub in a bayed nook and a separate shower.
- The front-facing bedroom is enhanced by a vaulted area over an arched transom window.

Plan AX-93304

Bedrooms: 3	**Baths:** 2
Living Area:	
Main floor	1,860 sq. ft.
Total Living Area:	**1,860 sq. ft.**
Standard basement	1,860 sq. ft.
Garage	404 sq. ft.
Utility	15 sq. ft.
Storage	15 sq. ft.
Exterior Wall Framing:	2x4

Foundation Options:

Standard basement
Crawlspace
Slab
(All plans can be built with your choice of foundation and framing. A generic conversion diagram is available. See order form.)

BLUEPRINT PRICE CODE: B

VIEW INTO GREAT ROOM

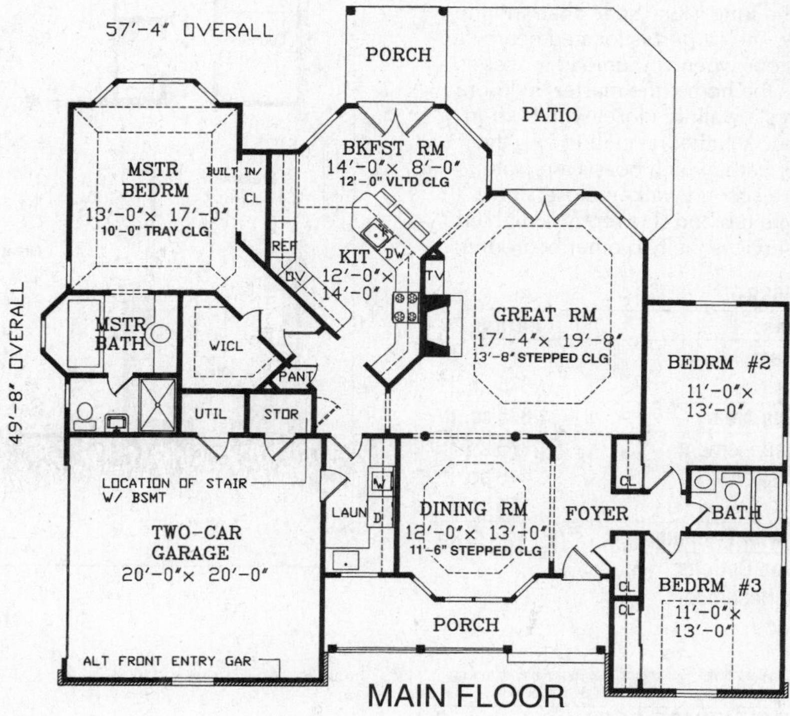

MAIN FLOOR

Plan AX-93304

FOR MORE DETAILS, SEE PLAN AT
familyhandyman.com/homeplans

Mark Englund/Homestore™ Plans and Publications

A Real Charmer

- A tranquil railed porch makes this country one-story a real charmer.
- The main entry opens directly into the Great Room, which serves as the home's focal point. A cathedral ceiling soars above, while a fireplace and a built-in cabinet for games make the space a fun gathering spot.
- Beautiful French doors expand the Great Room to a peaceful covered porch at the rear of the home. Open the doors and let in the fresh summer air!
- A bayed breakfast nook unfolds from the kitchen, where the family cook will love the long island snack bar and the pantry. The carport is located nearby to save steps when you unload groceries.
- Across the home, the master bedroom features a walk-in closet with built-in shelves. A cathedral ceiling tops the master bath, which boasts a private toilet, a second walk-in closet and a separate tub and shower. A skylighted bath services the two other bedrooms.

Plan J-9508	
Bedrooms: 3	**Baths:** 2½
Living Area:	
Main floor	1,875 sq. ft.
Total Living Area:	**1,875 sq. ft.**
Standard basement	1,875 sq. ft.
Carport	418 sq. ft.
Storage	114 sq. ft.
Exterior Wall Framing:	2x4
Foundation Options:	
Standard basement	
Crawlspace	
Slab	

(All plans can be built with your choice of foundation and framing. A generic conversion diagram is available. See order form.)

BLUEPRINT PRICE CODE: B

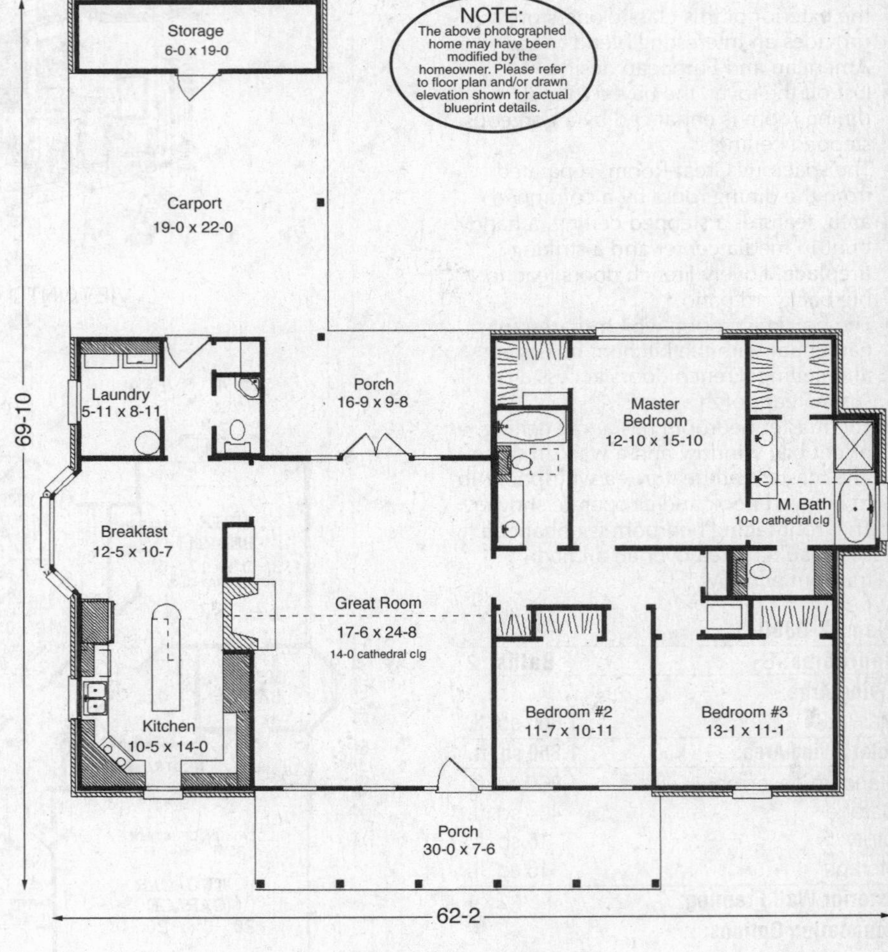

MAIN FLOOR

Plan J-9508

SEE ORDER INFO ON PAGES 12-15
familyhandyman.com/homeplans

Elegant Facade

- Eye-catching windows and columns add elegance to both the front and rear of this appealing one-story home.
- The columns of the front porch reflect those of the dazzling gallery inside, which basks in sunlight from a windowed dormer.
- The gorgeous Great Room features a cozy fireplace flanked by built-ins. Two sets of sliding glass doors with elliptical transoms open to a backyard terrace.
- The gourmet kitchen offers a handy snack bar, while the breakfast room expands to a columned rear porch.
- The stylish dining room boasts a stepped ceiling and a stunning front window.
- The secluded master suite provides a sitting area, porch access and a private bath with a whirlpool tub, dual sinks and twin walk-in closets.
- A unique combination of a vaulted ceiling and an arched window brightens the second bedroom.

VIEW INTO GREAT ROOM

Plan AX-4315

Bedrooms: 3	**Baths:** 2
Living Area:	
Main floor	2,018 sq. ft.
Total Living Area:	**2,018 sq. ft.**
Basement	2,018 sq. ft.
Garage and storage	456 sq. ft.
Utility room	18 sq. ft.
Exterior Wall Framing:	2x4

Foundation Options:

Daylight basement
Standard basement
Crawlspace
Slab
(All plans can be built with your choice of foundation and framing. A generic conversion diagram is available. See order form.)

BLUEPRINT PRICE CODE: C

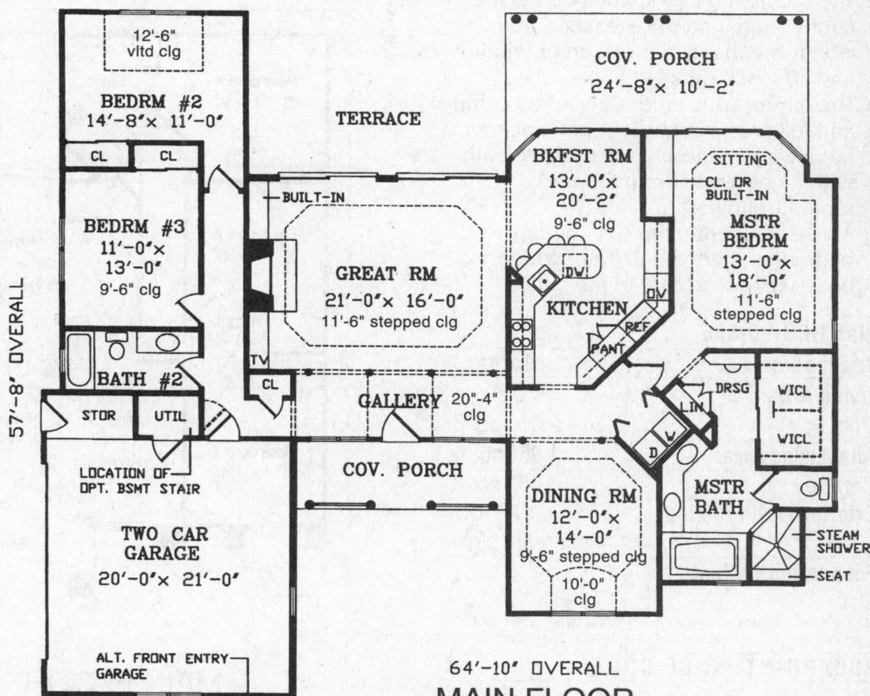

MAIN FLOOR

Plan AX-4315

FOR MORE DETAILS, SEE PLAN AT familyhandyman.com/homeplans

Mark Englund/Homestore™ Plans and Publications

Elaborate Entry

- This home's important-looking covered entry greets guests with heavy, banded support columns, sunburst transom windows and dual sidelights.
- Inside, the foyer is flanked by the formal living and dining rooms, which both have vaulted ceilings. Straight ahead and beyond five decorative columns lies the spacious family room.
- The family room features a vaulted ceiling that soars over its 8-ft.-high walls, plus a fireplace and sliding doors to a covered patio. A neat plant shelf above the fireplace adds style.
- The bright and airy kitchen serves the family room and the breakfast area, which is enhanced by a corner window and a French door.
- The master suite enjoys a vaulted ceiling and features French-door patio access, a large walk-in closet and a private bath with a corner platform tub and a separate shower.
- Across the home, three secondary bedrooms share a hall bath, which boasts private access to the patio.

Plan HDS-90-806	
Bedrooms: 4	**Baths:** 2
Living Area:	
Main floor	2,056 sq. ft.
Total Living Area:	**2,056 sq. ft.**
Garage	452 sq. ft.
Exterior Wall Framing:	2x4 or 8-in. concrete block
Foundation Options:	
Slab	

(All plans can be built with your choice of foundation and framing. A generic conversion diagram is available. See order form.)

BLUEPRINT PRICE CODE: C

NOTE: The above photographed home may have been modified by the homeowner. Please refer to floor plan and/or drawn elevation shown for actual blueprint details.

VIEW INTO DINING AND LIVING ROOMS AND FOYER

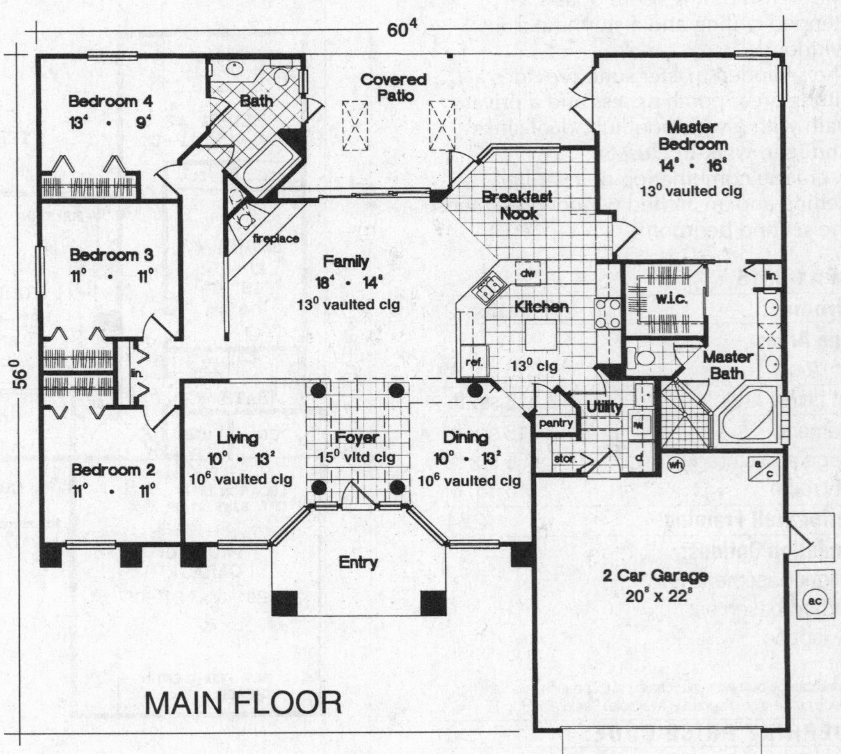

MAIN FLOOR

Une Belle Maison

- This charming French-style home will prompt exclamations of admiration and delight for such *une belle maison.*
- Inside, the formal living and dining rooms flank the foyer. Straight ahead, the spacious family room features sliding glass doors to a rear patio, sure to be the locale for many a barbecue or meal taken alfresco. Along the adjacent wall, media shelves flank a fireplace.
- The family room flows into the bayed breakfast nook, where a snack bar extends from the galley-style kitchen. The kitchen enjoys a walk-in pantry and easy access to the dining room.
- In its own private corner, the master suite is accessed through double doors. A large window overlooks the backyard, while dual sinks, a spa tub and a separate shower make the bath a luxurious haven.
- On the other side of the home, three secondary bedrooms boast plant shelves and share two full baths.

Plan HDS-99-301	
Bedrooms: 4	**Baths:** 3
Living Area:	
Main floor	2,104 sq. ft.
Total Living Area:	**2,104 sq. ft.**
Standard basement	2,160 sq. ft.
Garage	452 sq. ft.
Exterior Wall Framing:	2x4
Foundation Options:	
Standard basement (All plans can be built with your choice of foundation and framing. A generic conversion diagram is available. See order form.)	
BLUEPRINT PRICE CODE:	**C**

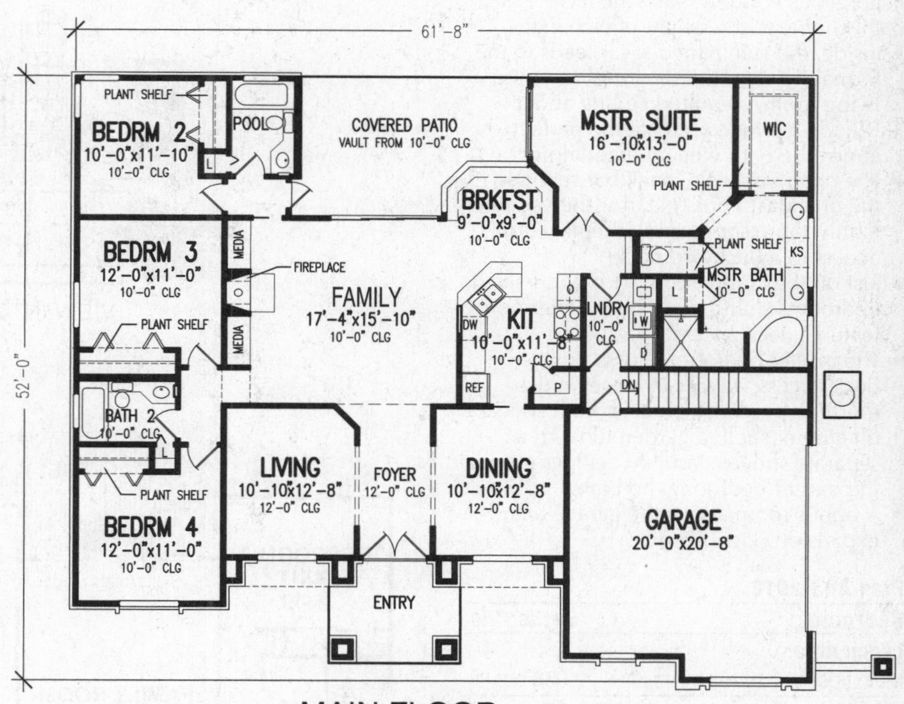

MAIN FLOOR

Plan HDS-99-301

FOR MORE DETAILS, SEE PLAN AT familyhandyman.com/homeplans

High Elegance

- Corner quoins, copper accents and gorgeous windows take the facade of this home to the height of elegance.
- Inside, the sidelighted foyer leads to the formal living and dining rooms. In the living room, a vaulted ceiling and a Palladian window create the perfect atmosphere for elegant entertaining.
- The open kitchen's snack bar services the breakfast nook. Nearby, the vaulted family room sports a big fireplace and access to a backyard deck.
- Just off the family room, two good-sized bedrooms share a split bath. One room features deck access.
- The master bedroom flaunts private deck access, a walk-in closet and a morning porch. The master bath shows off a plant shelf, a garden tub and a separate shower. Vaulted ceilings crown the master bedroom and bath.
- A bonus room above the garage offers expansion possibilities.

Plan APS-2018	
Bedrooms: 3+	**Baths:** 2½
Living Area:	
Main floor	2,088 sq. ft.
Total Living Area:	**2,088 sq. ft.**
Future area	282 sq. ft.
Daylight basement	2,088 sq. ft.
Garage	460 sq. ft.
Storage	35 sq. ft.
Exterior Wall Framing:	2x4

Foundation Options:
Daylight basement
Crawlspace
Slab
(All plans can be built with your choice of foundation and framing. A generic conversion diagram is available. See order form.)

BLUEPRINT PRICE CODE: C

VIEW INTO FAMILY ROOM

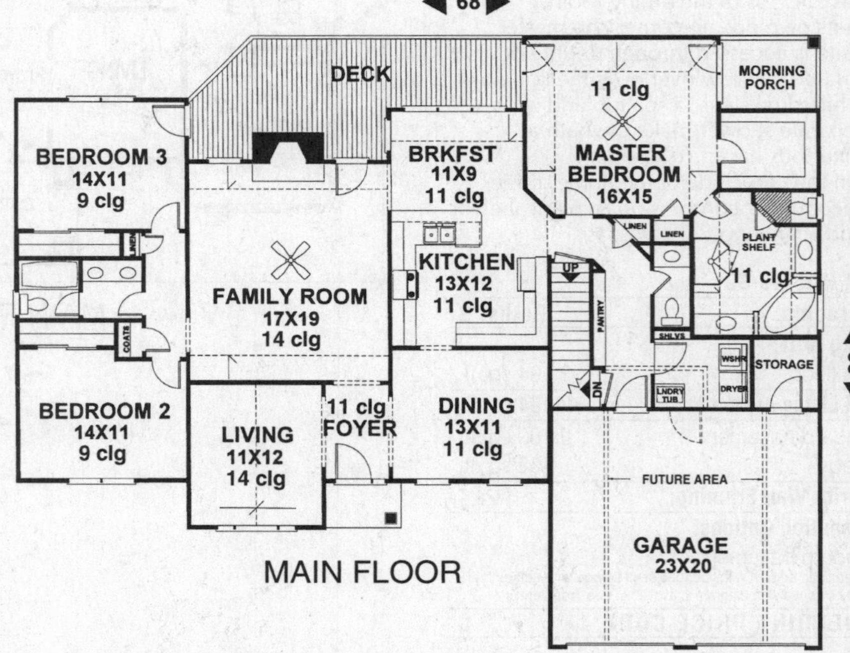

MAIN FLOOR

ORDER BLUEPRINTS ANYTIME!
CALL TOLL-FREE 1-800-820-1296

Plan APS-2018

SEE ORDER INFO ON PAGES 12-15
familyhandyman.com/homeplans

Arched Entry

- A beautiful arched entry introduces this grand Mediterranean-style home. High ceilings and lots of windows create an atmosphere of space and relaxation.
- Elegant double doors open into a tiled foyer, which is flanked by the formal living and dining rooms. Both rooms boast volume ceilings, and the dining room offers a tray ceiling.
- In the huge family room, sliding glass doors open to a covered patio. A fireplace flanked by built-in cabinets sets the stage for fun evenings at home.
- An 8-ft. wall separates the family room from the kitchen, which shares an angled serving counter with the sunny bayed breakfast nook. A built-in desk nearby is a great spot to pay the bills.
- The secluded master suite includes a sprawling overhead plant shelf and sliding glass doors to the patio. A dramatic arch introduces the private bath, which includes a garden tub, a separate shower and a dual-sink vanity.
- Across the home, two more bedrooms share a hall bath. A quiet rear bedroom is serviced by another full bath. Each room boasts a neat plant shelf.

Plan HDS-99-233

Bedrooms: 4	**Baths:** 3
Living Area:	
Main floor	2,140 sq. ft.
Total Living Area:	**2,140 sq. ft.**
Garage	430 sq. ft.
Exterior Wall Framing:	8-in. concrete block
Foundation Options:	
Slab	
(All plans can be built with your choice of foundation and framing. A generic conversion diagram is available. See order form.)	
BLUEPRINT PRICE CODE:	**C**

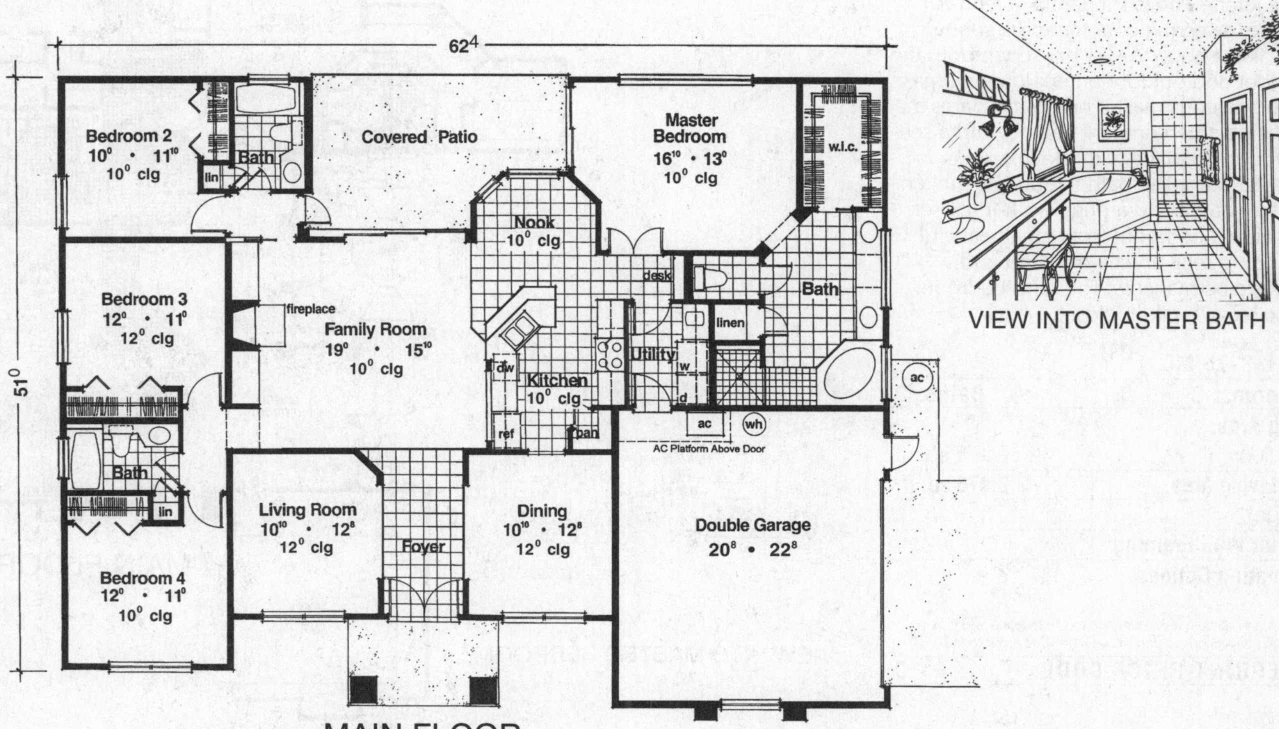

MAIN FLOOR

VIEW INTO MASTER BATH

LEFT VIEW

Mediterranean Splendor

- This splendid Mediterranean design has sunny living spaces both inside and out.
- Handsome double doors open to a huge covered porch/loggia. French doors beyond escort you into the tiled foyer. Windows along the left wall overlook a dramatic courtyard/arbor.
- Stately columns and overhead plant shelves accent the living and dining rooms, which are designed to view the courtyard. The living room features a built-in media center and a fireplace.
- The kitchen boasts a pantry, a Jenn-Air range, a serving counter and a sunny breakfast nook. A wet bar serves both the indoor and outdoor entertainment areas.
- The gorgeous master bedroom shares a rotating entertainment cabinet and a see-through fireplace with the luxurious master bath. The bath includes a sunken bathing area and a huge walk-in closet.
- A second bedroom features a peaceful window seat, a walk-in closet and private bath access. The third bedroom also has a walk-in closet.

Plan L-2176-MC	
Bedrooms: 3	**Baths:** 2
Living Area:	
Main floor	2,176 sq. ft.
Total Living Area:	**2,176 sq. ft.**
Garage	549 sq. ft.
Exterior Wall Framing:	2x4
Foundation Options:	
Slab	
(All plans can be built with your choice of foundation and framing. A generic conversion diagram is available. See order form.)	
BLUEPRINT PRICE CODE:	**C**

FRONT VIEW

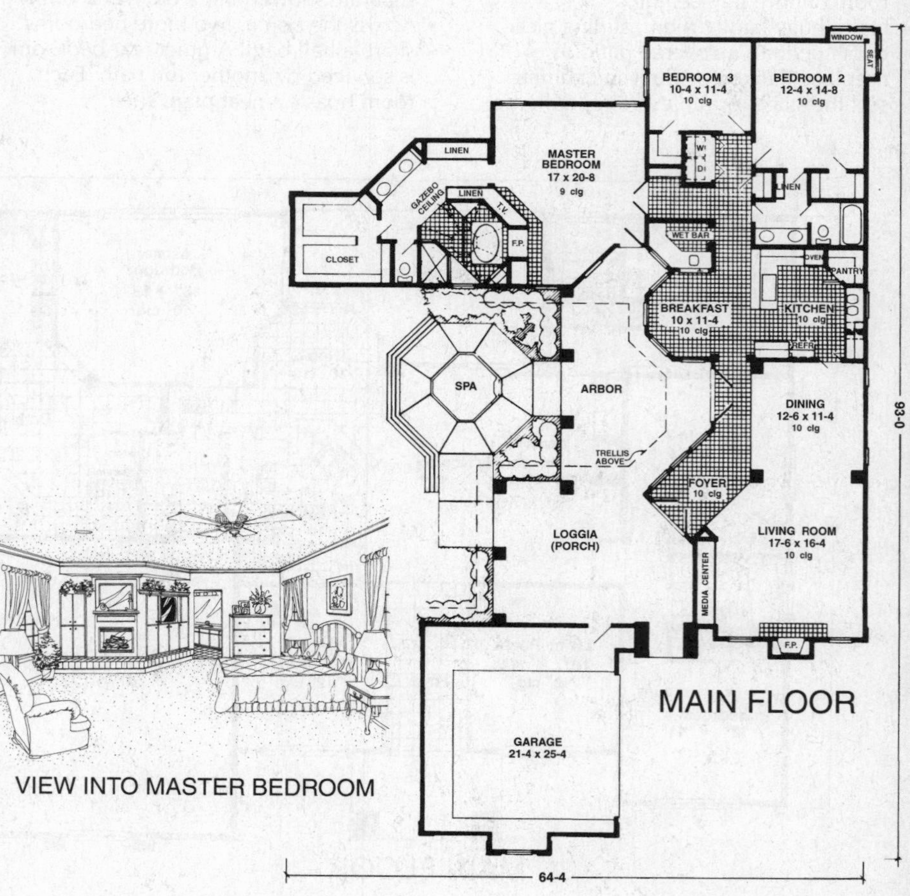

VIEW INTO MASTER BEDROOM

Plan L-2176-MC

SEE ORDER INFO ON PAGES 12-15

Mark Englund/Homestore™ Plans and Publications

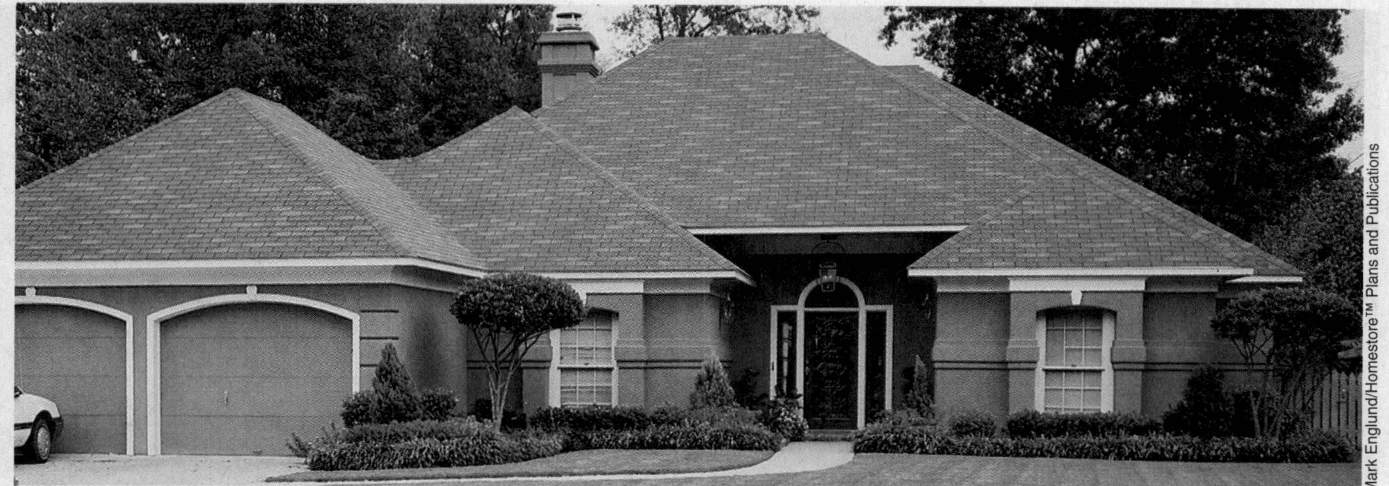

Luxurious Master Suite

- The inviting facade of this gorgeous one-story design boasts a sheltered porch, symmetrical architecture and elegant window treatments.
- Inside, beautiful arched openings frame the living room, which features a dramatic fireplace and a wet bar that is open to the deluxe kitchen.
- The roomy kitchen is highlighted by an island cooktop, a built-in desk and a snack bar that faces the bayed eating area and the covered back porch.
- Isolated to the rear of the home, the master suite is a romantic retreat, offering an intimate sitting area and a luxurious bath. Entered through elegant double doors, the private bath showcases a skylighted corner tub, a separate shower, his-and-hers vanities, and a huge walk-in closet.
- The two remaining bedrooms have walk-in closets and share a hall bath.

Plan E-2106	
Bedrooms: 3	**Baths:** 2
Living Area:	
Main floor	2,177 sq. ft.
Total Living Area:	**2,177 sq. ft.**
Standard basement	2,177 sq. ft.
Garage	484 sq. ft.
Storage	86 sq. ft.
Exterior Wall Framing:	2x4
Foundation Options:	
Standard basement	
Crawlspace	
Slab	

(All plans can be built with your choice of foundation and framing. A generic conversion diagram is available. See order form.)

BLUEPRINT PRICE CODE: **C**

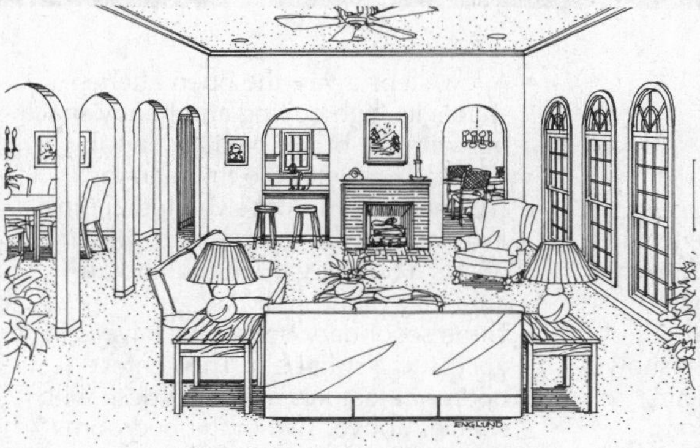

VIEW INTO LIVING ROOM

NOTE:
The above photographed home may have been modified by the homeowner. Please refer to floor plan and/or drawn elevation shown for actual blueprint details.

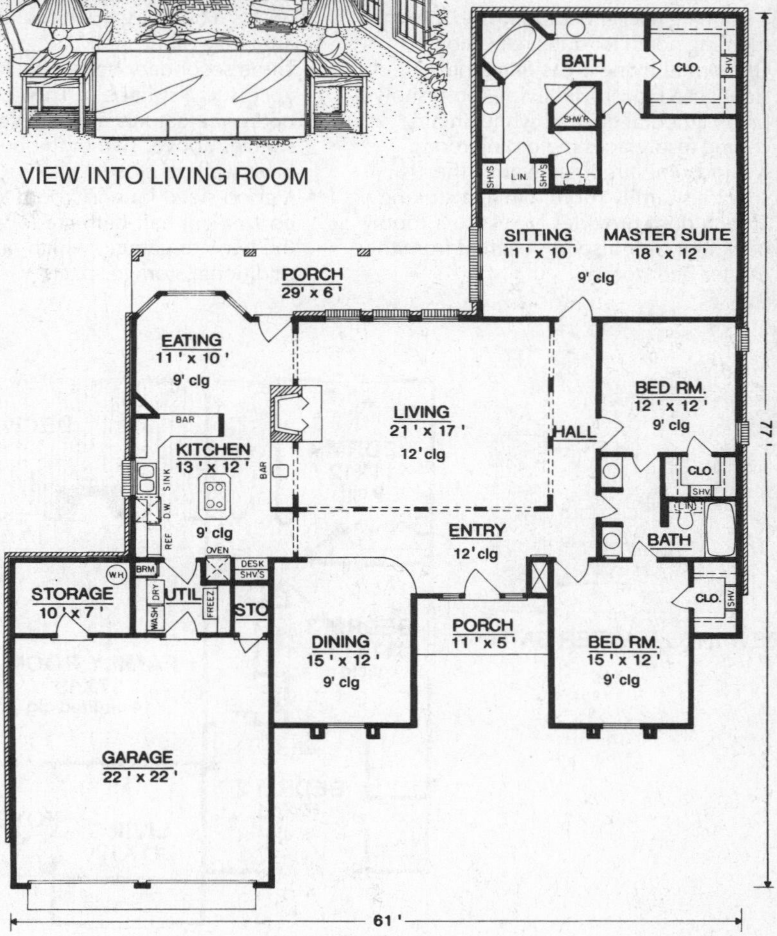

BATH
CLO.
SHVS
SHWR
LIN
SHVS
SITTING 11' x 10'
MASTER SUITE 18' x 12'
9' clg
PORCH 29' x 6'
EATING 11' x 10'
9' clg
BAR
KITCHEN 13' x 12'
SINK
D.W.
REF
BAR
9' clg
LIVING 21' x 17'
12' clg
HALL
BED RM. 12' x 12'
9' clg
CLO.
SHV
LIN
BATH
ENTRY 12' clg
OVEN
DESK SHVS
WH
BRM
STORAGE 10' x 7'
DRY
WASH
UTIL
FREEZ
STO
DINING 15' x 12'
9' clg
PORCH 11' x 5'
BED RM. 15' x 12'
9' clg
CLO.
SHV
GARAGE 22' x 22'
61'
77'

MAIN FLOOR

Plan E-2106

Plan copyright held by home designer/architect

Quiet Relaxation

- This elegant brick one-story home features a stunning master bedroom with a sunny morning porch for quiet relaxation.
- The formal living areas flank the sidelighted foyer. The living room shows off a cathedral ceiling, while an airy ceiling also graces the dining room.
- A handsome fireplace warms the spacious family room, while a striking French door provides access to a roomy deck that may also be reached from the master bedroom.
- A few steps away, the open kitchen shares its high ceiling and handy snack bar with the bright breakfast nook, which looks out onto the rear deck.
- The master bedroom's vaulted ceiling extends into the master bath, which boasts a corner garden tub and an attractive plant shelf.
- Three secondary bedrooms have easy access to a split bath. The center bedroom features a built-in desk with shelves above. Two of the bedrooms have walk-in closets.
- A good-sized laundry room and a convenient half-bath are located near the two-car garage, which offers additional storage space.

Plan APS-2117

Bedrooms: 4	**Baths:** 2½
Living Area:	
Main floor	2,187 sq. ft.
Total Living Area:	**2,187 sq. ft.**
Daylight basement	2,266 sq. ft.
Garage	469 sq. ft.
Storage/mechanical	23 sq. ft.
Exterior Wall Framing:	2x4

Foundation Options:

Daylight basement
Crawlspace
Slab

(All plans can be built with your choice of foundation and framing. A generic conversion diagram is available. See order form.)

BLUEPRINT PRICE CODE: C

VIEW INTO MASTER BATH

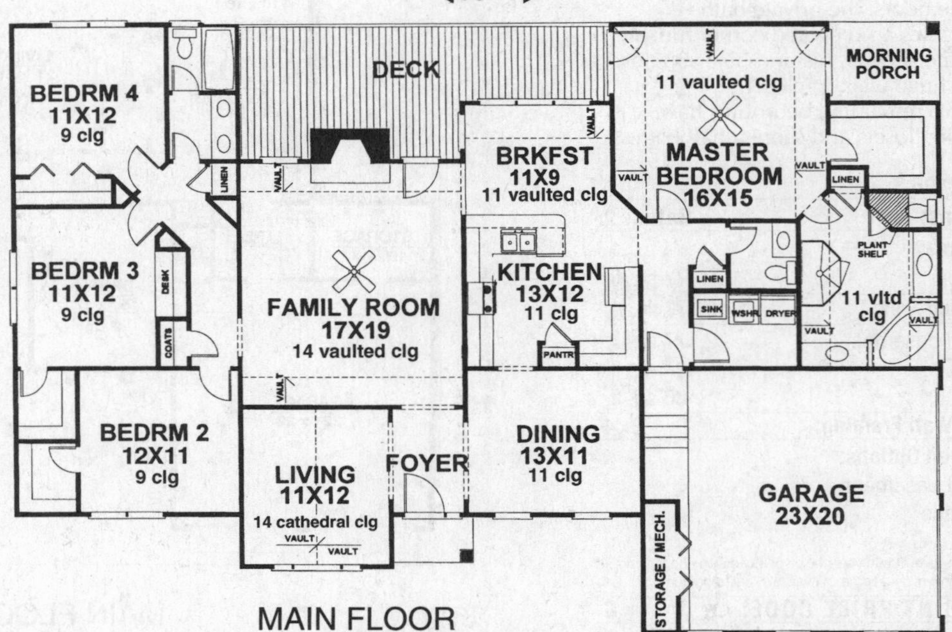

MAIN FLOOR

Plan APS-2117

SEE ORDER INFO ON PAGES 12-15

Nicely Done!

- An inviting window-covered exterior, coupled with an interior designed to give a sunny, open feel, will have you saying, "Nicely done!"
- Two eye-catching dormers, front-facing gables and two stately columns on the covered porch add a balanced sense of high style.
- The gallery, framed by columns, presents guests with a dramatic entrance, and offers a gorgeous view into the huge Great Room through three elegantly inviting openings.
- The island kitchen will lure any gourmet. Nestled between the formal dining room and the breakfast room, it stands ready for all types of meals. Just steps away, the mudroom lets you keep an eye on the laundry while you cook.
- The lovely master bedroom greets you with an abundance of charms: an enormous walk-in closet, a private bath with a dual-sink vanity and a garden tub, plus convenient access to the large covered patio in back.
- That patio, you'll find, is the stuff of dreams—allowing you to enjoy outdoor meals come rain or shine!

Plan DD-2228

Bedrooms: 3	**Baths:** 2
Living Area:	
Main floor	2,228 sq. ft.
Total Living Area:	**2,228 sq. ft.**
Standard basement	2,228 sq. ft.
Garage	431 sq. ft.
Exterior Wall Framing:	2x4
Foundation Options:	
Standard basement	
Crawlspace	
Slab	

(All plans can be built with your choice of foundation and framing. A generic conversion diagram is available. See order form.)

BLUEPRINT PRICE CODE: C

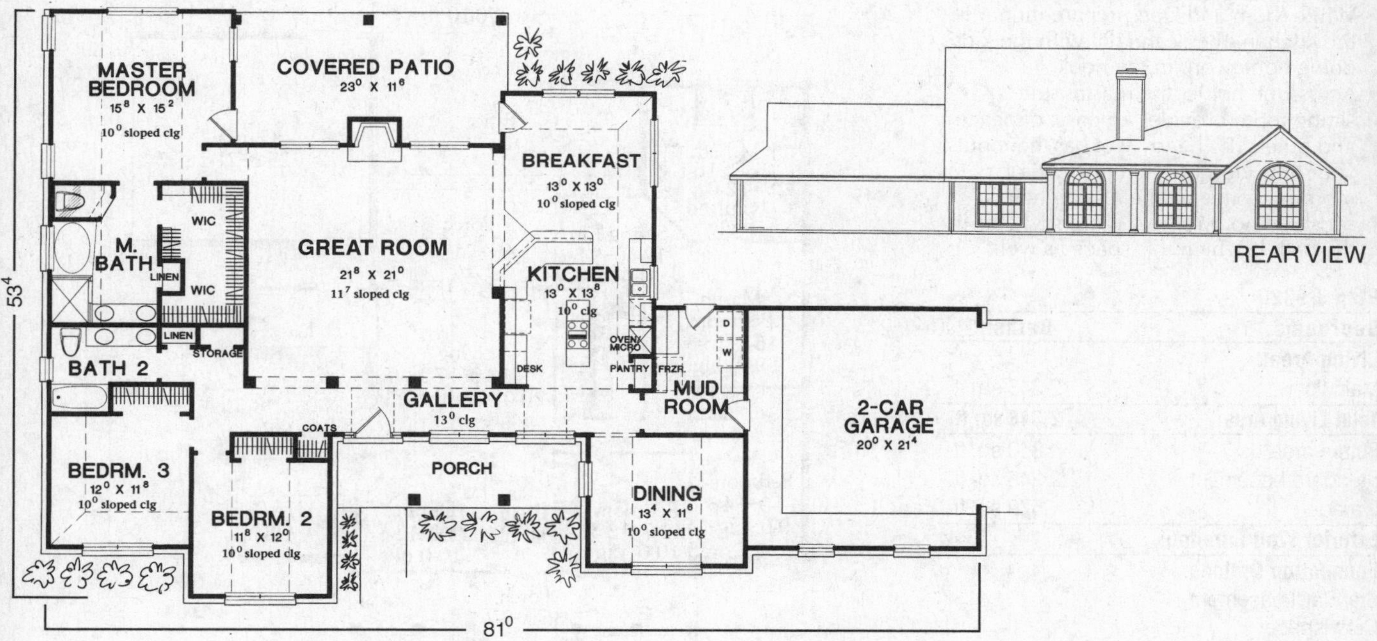

MAIN FLOOR

Mark Englund/Homestore™ Plans and Publications

Better by Design

- For the family that values an easygoing lifestyle, but also wants to impress friends with a beautiful home, this Southern-style design fits the bill.
- Hanging baskets dripping with vibrant flowers will dress up the front porch.
- Inside, handsome columns lend a look of distinction to the formal dining room, the ideal spot for classy meals. After dinner, guests can drift into the living room to continue their conversation. Plant shelves above display lush florals and greenery for all to admire.
- Casual meals have a place of their own in the kitchen and breakfast nook. While Mom and Dad prepare dinner in the kitchen, they can chat with the kids doing homework in the nook.
- Across the home, the master suite's sitting room provides an oasis of peace and quiet. The handy wet bar there puts you steps closer to that first cup of morning coffee, while a skylight lets sunshine pour in. Two more skylights in the bath brighten this space as well.

Plan J-9320

Bedrooms: 3+	**Baths:** 2½
Living Area:	
Main floor	2,348 sq. ft.
Total Living Area:	**2,348 sq. ft.**
Future area	860 sq. ft.
Standard basement	2,348 sq. ft.
Garage	579 sq. ft.
Exterior Wall Framing:	2x4
Foundation Options:	
Standard basement	
Crawlspace	
Slab	

(All plans can be built with your choice of foundation and framing. A generic conversion diagram is available. See order form.)

BLUEPRINT PRICE CODE: C

NOTE: The above photographed home may have been modified by the homeowner. Please refer to floor plan and/or drawn elevation shown for actual blueprint details.

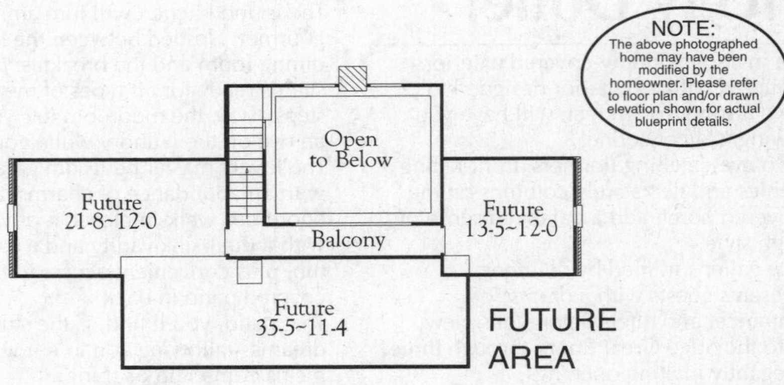

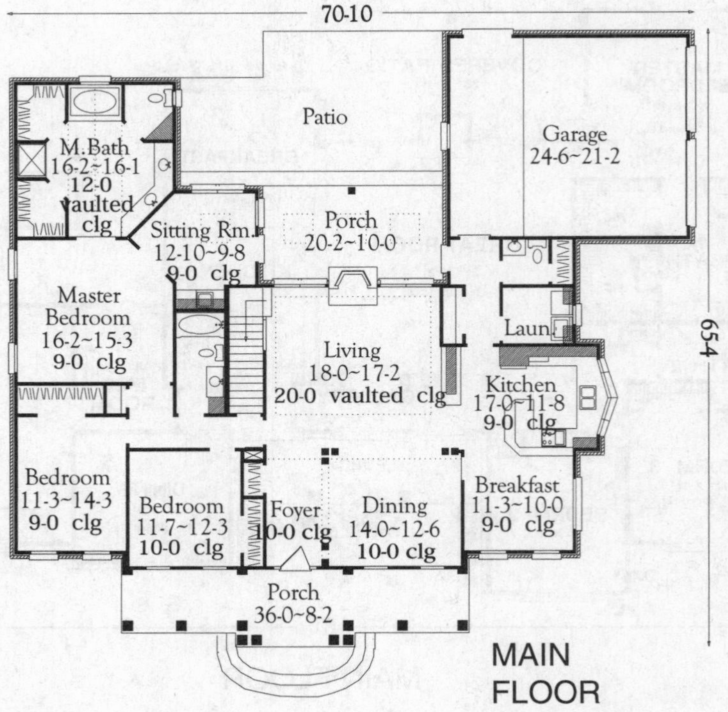

Plan J-9320

SEE ORDER INFO ON PAGES 12-15

Genteel Luxury

VIEW INTO KITCHEN

REAR VIEW

- This extraordinary home offers countless details and genteel luxury.
- In the foyer, an elegant marble floor and a high ceiling define the sunny space.
- A fireplace serves as the focal point of the living room, which extends to the dining room to isolate formal affairs. The dining room features a bay window and a French door to a lush courtyard.
- A columned serving counter separates the kitchen from the breakfast nook and the family room. A convenient built-in desk to the right is a great place to jot down a grocery list.
- A high ceiling soars over the versatile family room, where a corner fireplace and a French door to the backyard are great additions.
- A stepped ceiling, a romantic fireplace, a quiet desk and access to the backyard make the master bedroom an inviting retreat. A luxurious raised tub and a sit-down shower highlight the master bath, which also includes a neat dressing table between two sinks.
- Two more bedrooms, one with a high ceiling and a bay window, share a bath.

Plan L-483-HB

Bedrooms: 3	**Baths:** 2
Living Area:	
Main floor	2,481 sq. ft.
Total Living Area:	**2,481 sq. ft.**
Garage	706 sq. ft.
Exterior Wall Framing:	2x4
Foundation Options:	
Slab	
(All plans can be built with your choice of foundation and framing. A generic conversion diagram is available. See order form.)	
BLUEPRINT PRICE CODE:	**C**

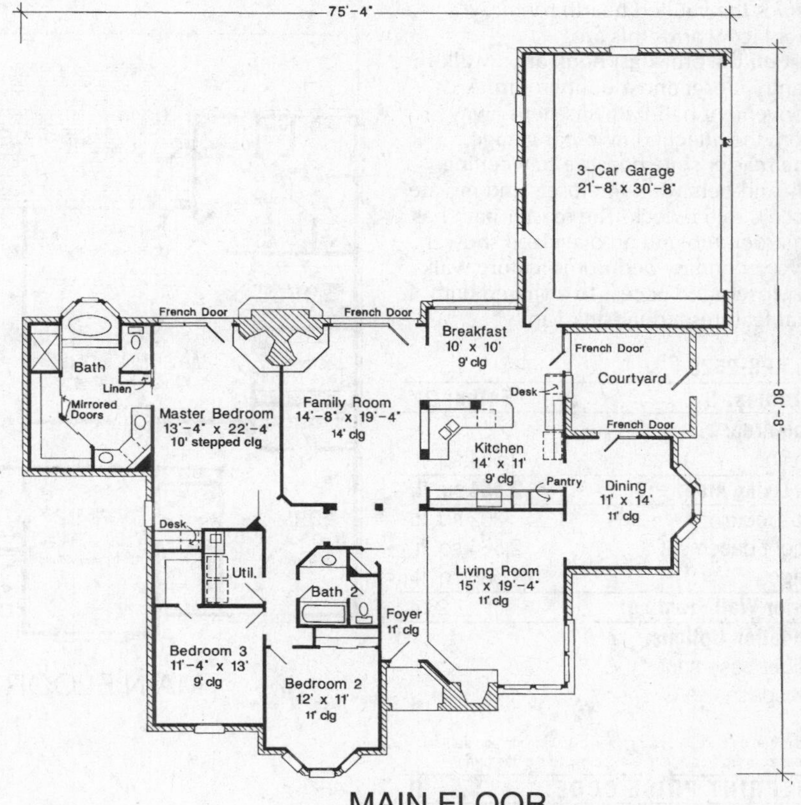

MAIN FLOOR

Sunny Spaces

- This spacious home offers plenty of large windows, sure to make every room a bright, sunny space. Vaulted ceilings add the finishing touch.
- The entry opens into the family room, which offers a high ceiling and access to a deck through French doors.
- Your choices are many when mealtime rolls around. The island kitchen serves the sunny vaulted dining room via a handy snack bar, while a second bar serves the vaulted hearth room. A fireplace warms this area.
- Just off the breakfast nook are a walk-in pantry closet and a utility room. A convenient half-bath sits steps away from the attached, two-car garage.
- The master suite boasts a tray ceiling, his-and-hers walk-in closets and private access to the deck. The master bath has a garden tub and an oversized shower.
- Two secondary bedrooms feature walk-in closets and access to a shared bath that features a dual-sink vanity.

Plan APS-2520	
Bedrooms: 3	**Baths:** 2½
Living Area:	
Main floor	2,564 sq. ft.
Total Living Area:	**2,564 sq. ft.**
Bonus room	302 sq. ft.
Daylight basement	2,564 sq. ft.
Garage	538 sq. ft.
Exterior Wall Framing:	2x4
Foundation Options:	
Daylight basement	
Crawlspace	
Slab	
(All plans can be built with your choice of foundation and framing. A generic conversion diagram is available. See order form.)	
BLUEPRINT PRICE CODE:	**D**

VIEW INTO FAMILY ROOM

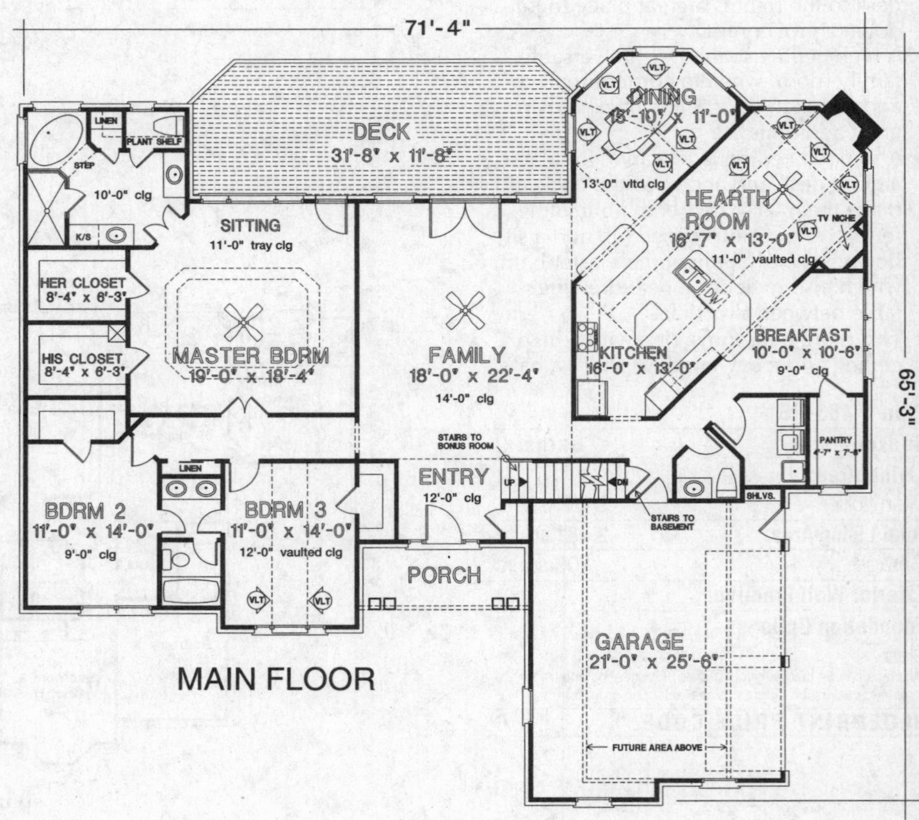

MAIN FLOOR

ORDER BLUEPRINTS ANYTIME!
CALL TOLL-FREE 1-800-820-1296

Plan APS-2520

SEE ORDER INFO ON PAGES 12-15
familyhandyman.com/homeplans

Mark Englund/Homestore™ Plans and Publications

Ornate French Provincial

- Brick and stucco adorn the exterior of this elegant French Provincial home, which also features quoins and keystones.
- At the center of the floor plan, the family room is framed by a ceramic tile floor that continues into the morning room and the airy kitchen. Bookshelves flank a tile-faced fireplace, and two sets of doors open to a back porch.
- Past a spectacular carousel atrium with a center planter and bright sky windows is an exciting game room with a refreshing wet bar.
- The formal spaces include a raised dining room and a living room that could also serve as a private sitting room for the master suite.
- Secluded from the rest, the master suite overlooks a courtyard and a side porch, and includes a private skylighted bath.
- The secondary bedrooms form a wing of their own. The third bedroom could also be used as a library.

Plan E-2704	
Bedrooms: 3+	**Baths:** 2
Living Area:	
Main floor	2,791 sq. ft.
Total Living Area:	**2,791 sq. ft.**
Garage	718 sq. ft.
Storage	70 sq. ft.
Exterior Wall Framing:	2x4
Foundation Options:	
Crawlspace	
Slab	

(All plans can be built with your choice of foundation and framing. A generic conversion diagram is available. See order form.)

BLUEPRINT PRICE CODE: **D**

NOTE:
The above photographed home may have been modified by the homeowner. Please refer to floor plan and/or drawn elevation shown for actual blueprint details.

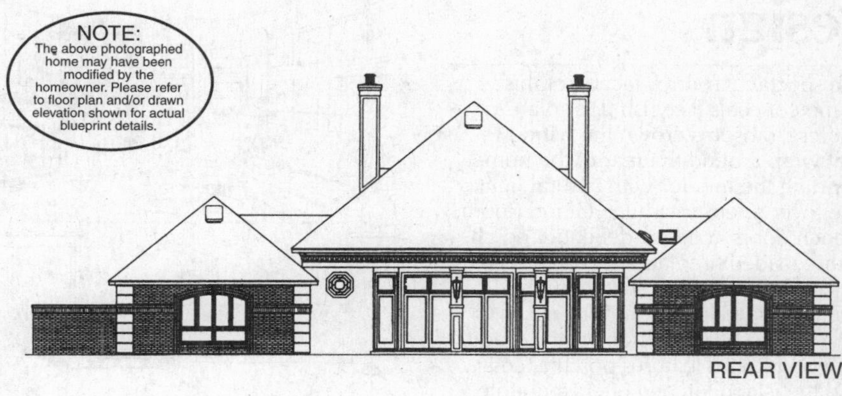

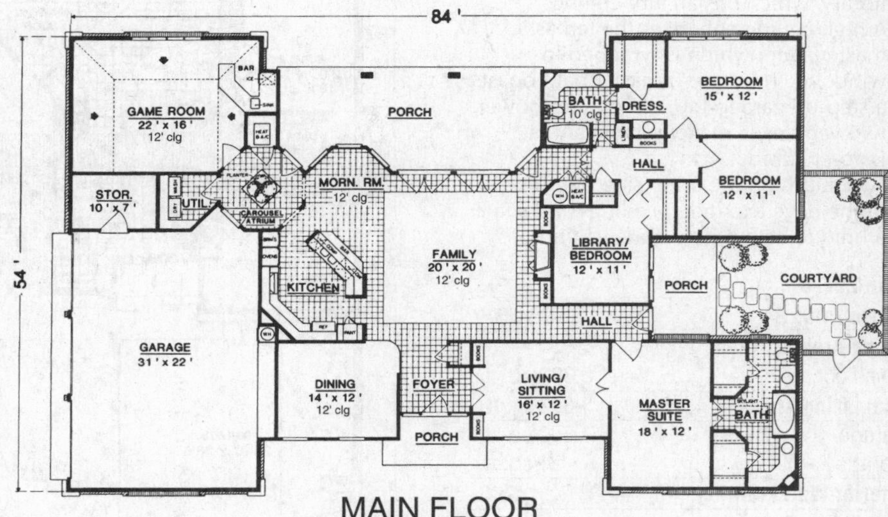

MAIN FLOOR

Spectacular Design

- The spectacular brick facade of this home conceals a stylish floor plan. Endless transoms crown the windows that wrap around the rear of the home, flooding the interior with natural light.
- The foyer opens to a huge Grand Room. French doors access a delightful porch.
- A three-sided fireplace warms the three casual rooms, which share a high ceiling. The Gathering Room is surrounded by tall windows; the Good Morning Room features porch access; and the island kitchen offers a double oven, a pantry and a snack bar.
- Guests will dine in style in the formal dining room, with its elegant tray ceiling and trio of tall, arched windows.
- Curl up with a good book in the quiet library, which has an airy ceiling.
- A high ceiling enhances the fantastic master suite, which is wrapped in windows. The superb master bath boasts a step-up garden tub, a separate shower, two vanities, a makeup table and a Euro-chic bidet.
- Two suites on the other side of the home have expanded ceilings and share a unique bath with private vanities.

Plan EOF-8

Bedrooms: 3+ **Baths:** 3½

Living Area:

Main floor	3,392 sq. ft.
Total Living Area:	**3,392 sq. ft.**
Garage	850 sq. ft.
Storage	21 sq. ft.
Exterior Wall Framing:	2x6

Foundation Options:

Slab

(All plans can be built with your choice of foundation and framing. A generic conversion diagram is available. See order form.)

BLUEPRINT PRICE CODE: **E**

VIEW INTO GATHERING ROOM, KITCHEN AND MORNING ROOM

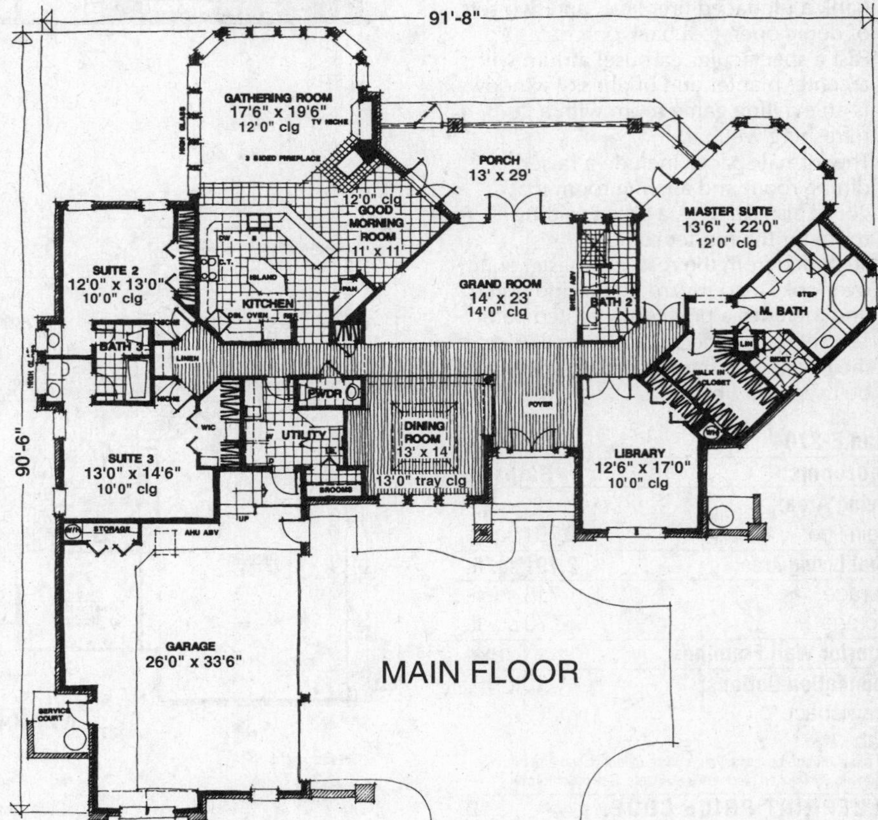

ORDER BLUEPRINTS ANYTIME!
CALL TOLL-FREE 1-800-820-1296

Plan EOF-8

Plan copyright held by home designer/architect

SEE ORDER INFO ON PAGES 12-15
familyhandyman.com/homeplans

Beautiful Bay Window!

- A beautiful bay window beneath a charming gable highlights the front of this single-level home.
- Just beyond the entry, the living room invites family members to gather around the warming fireplace. The windows draw in plenty of sunlight while a high ceiling soars above.
- An exit to the garage between the living room and the kitchen offers access to laundry facilities and makes it especially easy to unload groceries.
- The kitchen includes a vast expanse of counter space, as well as a raised bar that's perfect for buffet-style meals. A pantry maximizes storage space.
- On more formal occasions, guests will linger over after-dinner coffee in the bayed dining room.
- Across the home, the spacious master suite features a high sloped ceiling, two walk-in closets, a dressing area and a private bath.
- Two additional bedrooms share a compartmentalized bath.

Plan RD-1091

Bedrooms: 3	**Baths:** 2
Living Area:	
Main floor	1,091 sq. ft.
Total Living Area:	**1,091 sq. ft.**
Garage	528 sq. ft.
Exterior Wall Framing:	2x4
Foundation Options:	
Crawlspace	
Slab	

(All plans can be built with your choice of foundation and framing. A generic conversion diagram is available. See order form.)

BLUEPRINT PRICE CODE: **A**

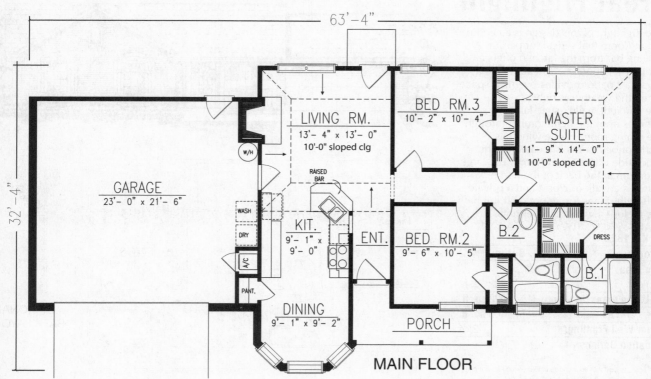

63'-4"
32'-4"
GARAGE
23'- 0" x 21'- 6"
W/H
WASH
DRY
A/C
PANT.
LIVING RM.
13'- 4" x 13'- 0"
10'-0" sloped clg
RAISED BAR
KIT.
9'- 1" x 9'- 0"
ENT.
DINING
9'- 1" x 9'- 2"
PORCH
BED RM.3
10'- 2" x 10'- 4"
BED RM.2
9'- 6" x 10'- 5"
MASTER SUITE
11'- 9" x 14'- 0"
10'-0" sloped clg
B.2
B.1
DRESS

MAIN FLOOR

Made for Fun

- Ready for an escape? This fun beach home is just what the doctor ordered.
- Two wide porches offer shade and ample opportunities for tropical vistas.
- The living room and the kitchen create the perfect spot for entertaining. With so much kitchen counter space, you'll have no trouble cooking up a storm.
- Speaking of storms, this home can weather the worst, thanks to its pole foundation with enclosed storage and high ceilings that help dissipate heat.
- Three bedrooms, including a roomy master suite, provide lots of quiet space for you, your kids and/or guests.

Plan CHP-1232-105A

Bedrooms: 3	**Baths:** 2
Living Area:	
Main floor	1,280 sq. ft.
Total Living Area:	**1,280 sq. ft.**
Lower-floor storage	223 sq. ft.
Exterior Wall Framing:	2x4
Foundation Options:	
Pole	

(All plans can be built with your choice of foundation and framing. A generic conversion diagram is available. See order form.)

BLUEPRINT PRICE CODE: **A**

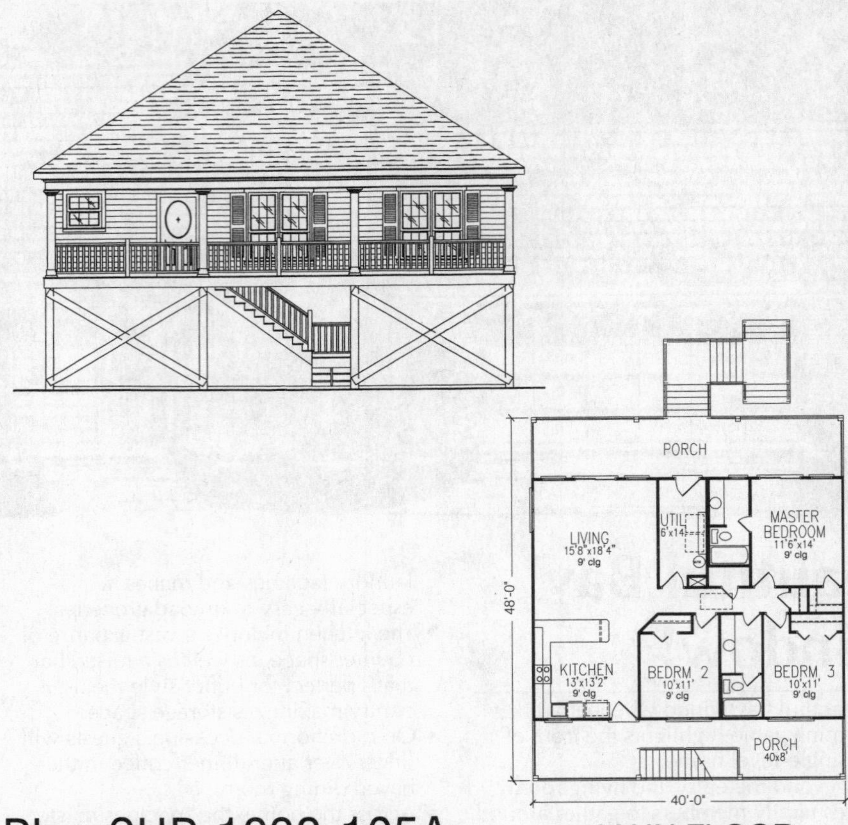

MAIN FLOOR

Plan CHP-1232-105A

Plan copyright held by home designer/architect

Great Highlight

- The highlight of this design is a central Great Room that's ideal for parties. A serving bar from the kitchen offers a spot for an appetizer spread, while a backyard patio provides overflow space when the weather is right.
- The efficient, galley-style kitchen benefits from the light coming through the dining room's large windows.
- A trio of bedrooms is located on the other side of the Great Room. The large bedroom at the back of the home features a walk-in closet and a private half-bath. Plans for an optional full bath are included with the blueprints.

Plan KD-1022

Bedrooms: 3	**Baths:** 1½–2
Living Area:	
Main floor	1,022 sq. ft.
Total Living Area:	**1,022 sq. ft.**
Garage and storage	460 sq. ft.
Exterior Wall Framing:	2x4
Foundation Options:	
Slab	

(All plans can be built with your choice of foundation and framing. A generic conversion diagram is available. See order form.)

BLUEPRINT PRICE CODE: **A**

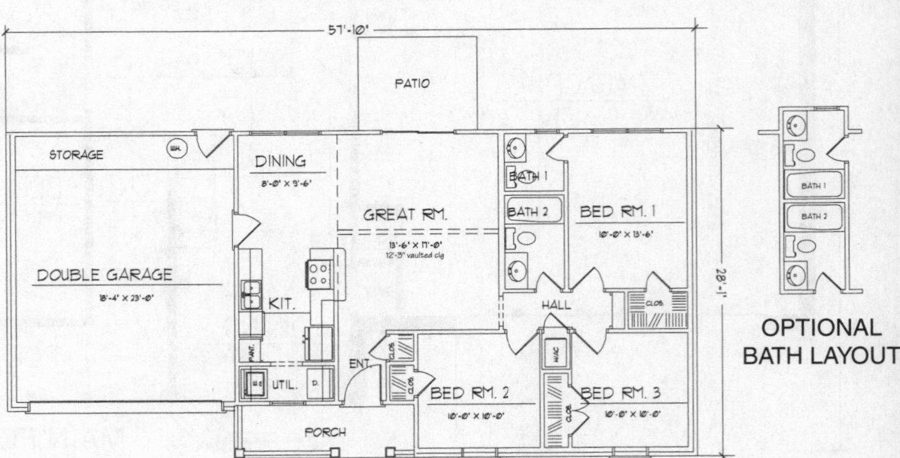

MAIN FLOOR

OPTIONAL BATH LAYOUT

Plan KD-1022

Plan copyright held by home designer/architect

SEE ORDER INFO ON PAGES 12-15

Welcoming Facade

- This home's welcoming facade features a cozy front porch, shuttered windows and an inviting bay window showcasing the dining room.
- The entry leads into the enchanting living room, which features a sloped ceiling, a warming fireplace and French-door access to the backyard.
- The kitchen offers a raised bar to the living room. Not only does this shelf hide kitchen clutter, it's a great place to spread appetizers or drinks when entertaining. For ease in unloading groceries, garage access is near the kitchen. A pantry near the bayed dining room augments storage space.
- Rest your weary bones in the master suite. The expansive bedroom boasts a luxurious sloped ceiling. A walk-in closet and a dressing area mark the entrance to the private bath.
- The home's two additional bedrooms feature ample closet space and bright windows. They share a linen closet in the hall, plus the compartmentalized hall bath, which provides a relaxing garden tub.

Plan RD-1094

Bedrooms: 3 **Baths:** 2

Living Area:

Main floor 1,094 sq. ft.

Total Living Area: 1,094 sq. ft.

Garage 528 sq. ft.

Exterior Wall Framing: 2x4

Foundation Options:

Crawlspace

Slab

(All plans can be built with your choice of foundation and framing. A generic conversion diagram is available. See order form.)

BLUEPRINT PRICE CODE: A

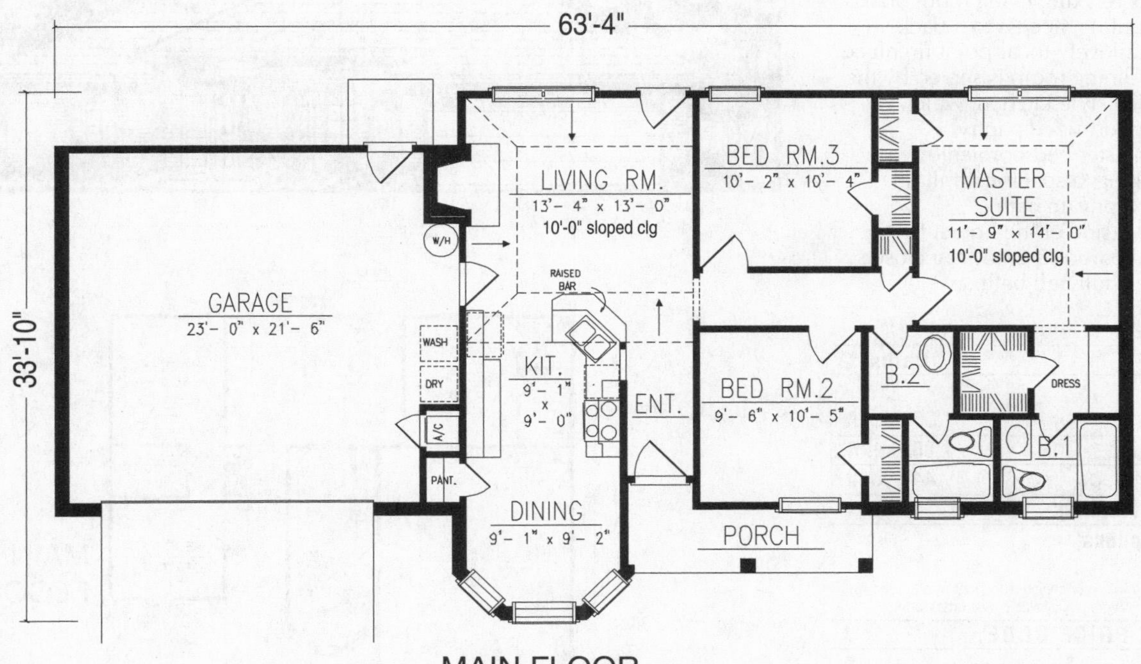

MAIN FLOOR

Perfect Starter

- Affordable and inviting, this country-style home is perfect for single owners or young families just starting out.
- The entry spills into the large central living room, which offers a nice view of a back patio.
- The kitchen provides a useful snack bar serving the living and dining rooms.
- At the end of the day, retreat to the alluring master bedroom, which boasts two large closets and adjoins a private bath with a garden tub.
- Two additional bedrooms share a full hall bath.

Plan DD-1050-C

Bedrooms: 2+	**Baths:** 2
Living Area:	
Main floor	1,038 sq. ft.
Total Living Area:	**1,038 sq. ft.**
Garage	248 sq. ft.
Exterior Wall Framing:	2x4
Foundation Options:	
Crawlspace	
Slab	

(All plans can be built with your choice of foundation and framing. A generic conversion diagram is available. See order form.)

BLUEPRINT PRICE CODE: A

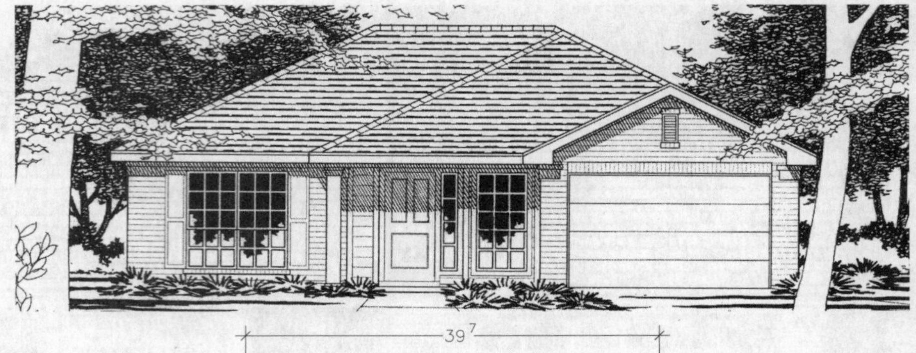

MAIN FLOOR

Plan DD-1050-C

Plan copyright held by home designer/architect

Fine Fireplace

- This home's relaxing living room boasts a vaulted ceiling, access to a back patio, and a lovely focal-point fireplace.
- The bayed dining room is served by the bright, galley-style kitchen, which features a good-sized pantry.
- The quiet master bedroom enjoys a vaulted ceiling, a spacious walk-in closet and a private bath.
- On the other side of the home, two additional bedrooms enjoy big closets. They share a full hall bath.

Plan KD-1052

Bedrooms: 3	**Baths:** 2
Living Area:	
Main floor	1,052 sq. ft.
Total Living Area:	**1,052 sq. ft.**
Garage and storage	447 sq. ft.
Exterior Wall Framing:	2x4
Foundation Options:	
Slab	

(All plans can be built with your choice of foundation and framing. A generic conversion diagram is available. See order form.)

BLUEPRINT PRICE CODE: A

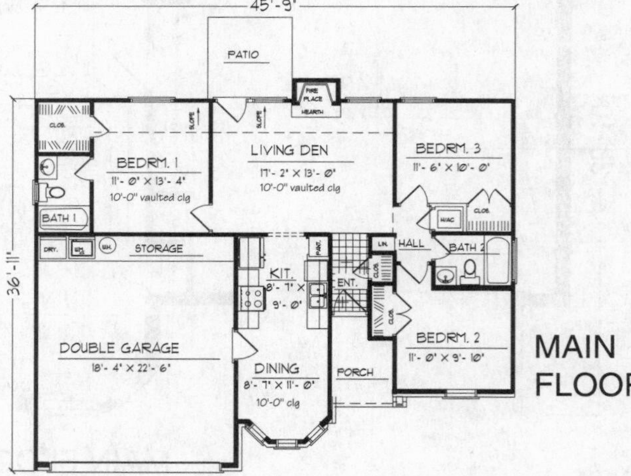

MAIN FLOOR

Plan KD-1052

Plan copyright held by home designer/architect

Narrow-Lot Dream

- Perfect for a narrow lot, this home will be a dream come true for a smaller family or empty nesters. The stucco facade has elegant keystones and a sidelighted entry with a nice transom.
- Inside, the vaulted living room features a corner window arrangement that lets light stream in from all directions. The adjoining dining room also enjoys a vaulted ceiling, as well as access to a back patio through sliding glass doors.
- Placed conveniently at the center of the home, the kitchen boasts an island with a snack bar serving the dining room.
- The spacious master suite features a vaulted ceiling and ample closet space. Its private bath provides a relaxing garden tub.
- Two secondary bedrooms share the well-placed hall bath.
- Access to the good-sized garage is granted just off the entry. You'll find room for your laundry, lawn tools—and maybe even a workbench!

Plan HDS-99-375	
Bedrooms: 3	**Baths:** 2
Living Area:	
Main floor	1,118 sq. ft.
Total Living Area:	**1,118 sq. ft.**
Garage	331 sq. ft.
Exterior Wall Framing:	8-in. concrete block
Foundation Options:	
Slab (All plans can be built with your choice of foundation and framing. A generic conversion diagram is available. See order form.)	
BLUEPRINT PRICE CODE:	**A**

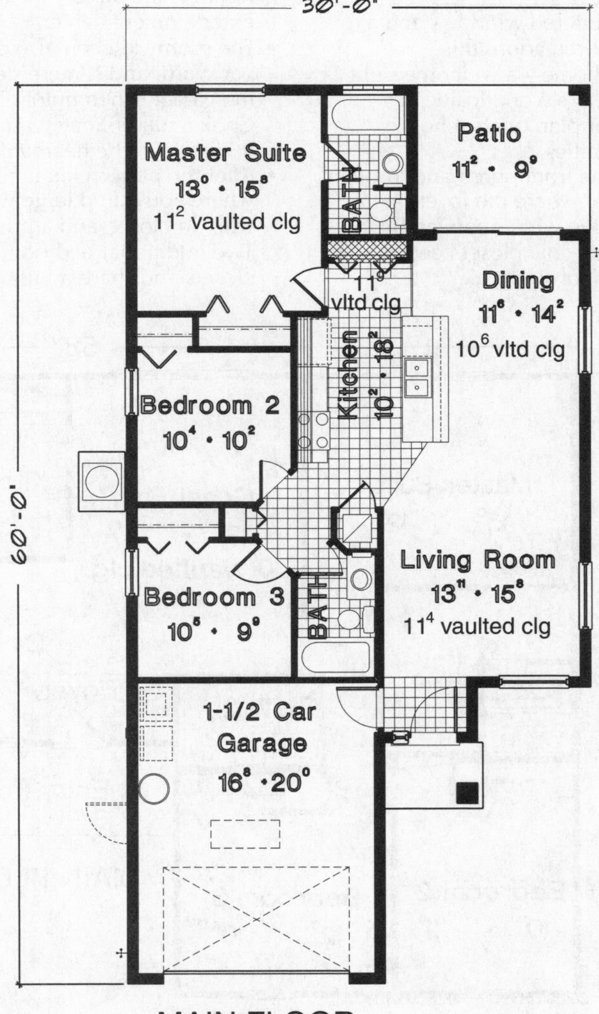

MAIN FLOOR

Plan HDS-99-375

FOR MORE DETAILS, SEE PLAN AT familyhandyman.com/homeplans

Comfy and Compact

- Charming shuttered windows and a railed front porch adorn this comfortable home—a welcome sight after a long day's work. Inside, a compact floor plan offers a host of modern amenities.
- Step across the front porch and through the front door, where the foyer opens directly into the wide-open family areas. A handy coat closet keeps outerwear out of sight.
- Casual and formal affairs are equally at home in the vaulted Great Room, which opens out to the backyard through sliding glass doors. The Great Room is the perfect location for your entertainment center.
- The roomy kitchen also overlooks the backyard, and is mere steps away from the garage when unloading groceries. Cook a full holiday feast and then serve it in style in the nearby dining room.
- After the party, relax in the master suite, where you'll find large windows, a vast walk-in closet, and a private, split bath. Two additional bedrooms hold sizable closets and share a full hall bath.

Plan HDS-99-338

Bedrooms: 3	**Baths:** 2
Living Area:	
Main floor	1,167 sq. ft.
Total Living Area:	**1,167 sq. ft.**
Garage	473 sq. ft.
Exterior Wall Framing:	2x4
Foundation Options:	
Slab	

(All plans can be built with your choice of foundation and framing. A generic conversion diagram is available. See order form.)

BLUEPRINT PRICE CODE: A

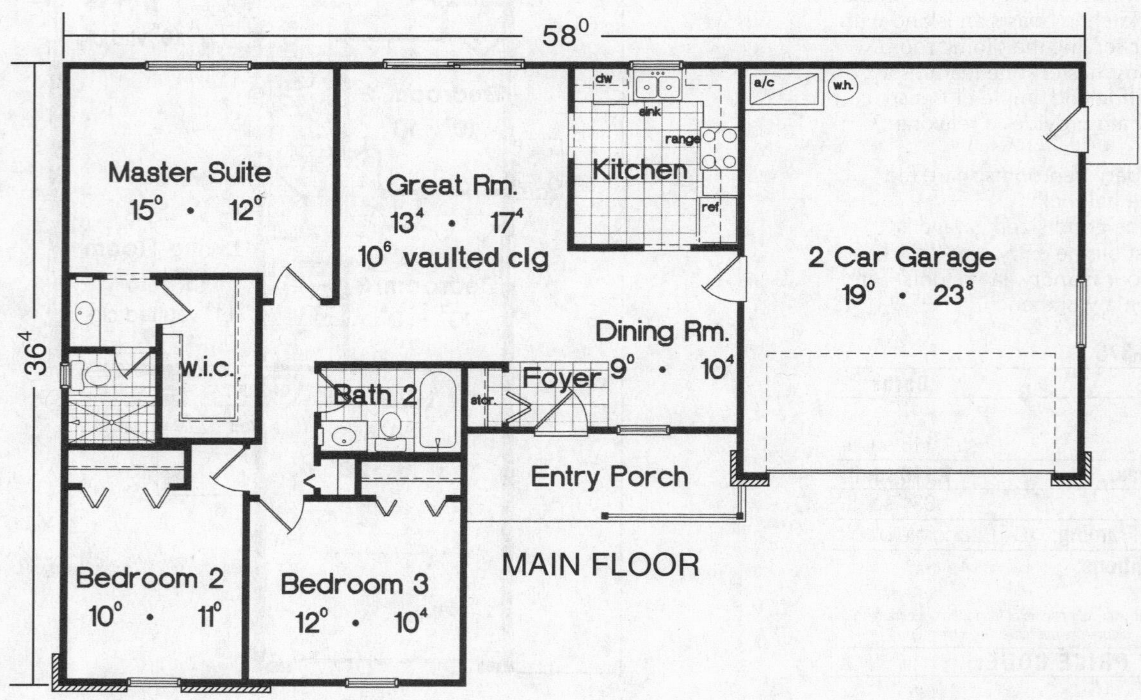

MAIN FLOOR

Plan HDS-99-338

SEE ORDER INFO ON PAGES 12-15

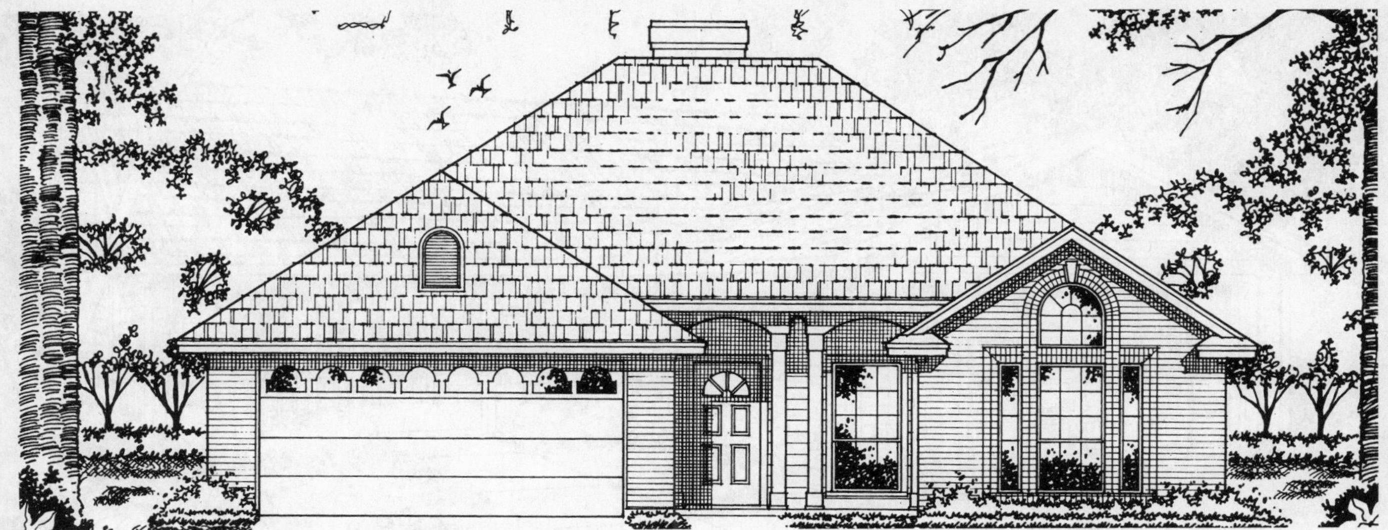

Fantastic Windows

- Fantastic windows light the main rooms of this cheerful, compact home, starting with the show-stopping Palladian window. Even the front door features a charming fanlight.
- Step across the columned front porch and into the tiled entry, which introduces the vaulted Great Room. Here, a wide fireplace adds ambience, and two windows overlook the backyard.
- Across a convenient breakfast bar, the U-shaped kitchen hosts plenty of counter space beneath the room's vaulted ceiling. The dining room enjoys another bright window.
- A short hallway leads to two front-facing secondary bedrooms, one flaunting the grand window arrangement. Both have ample closet space and share a hall bath and linen closet.
- Across the home, a short hall buffers the master suite from the busy family areas. Inside, you'll find a vaulted ceiling, two large windows, and a private bath with a walk-in closet and deluxe garden tub.

Plan KD-1225

Bedrooms: 3	**Baths:** 2
Living Area:	
Main floor	1,225 sq. ft.
Total Living Area:	**1,225 sq. ft.**
Garage and storage	485 sq. ft.
Exterior Wall Framing:	2x4
Foundation Options:	
Slab	

(All plans can be built with your choice of foundation and framing. A generic conversion diagram is available. See order form.)

BLUEPRINT PRICE CODE: A

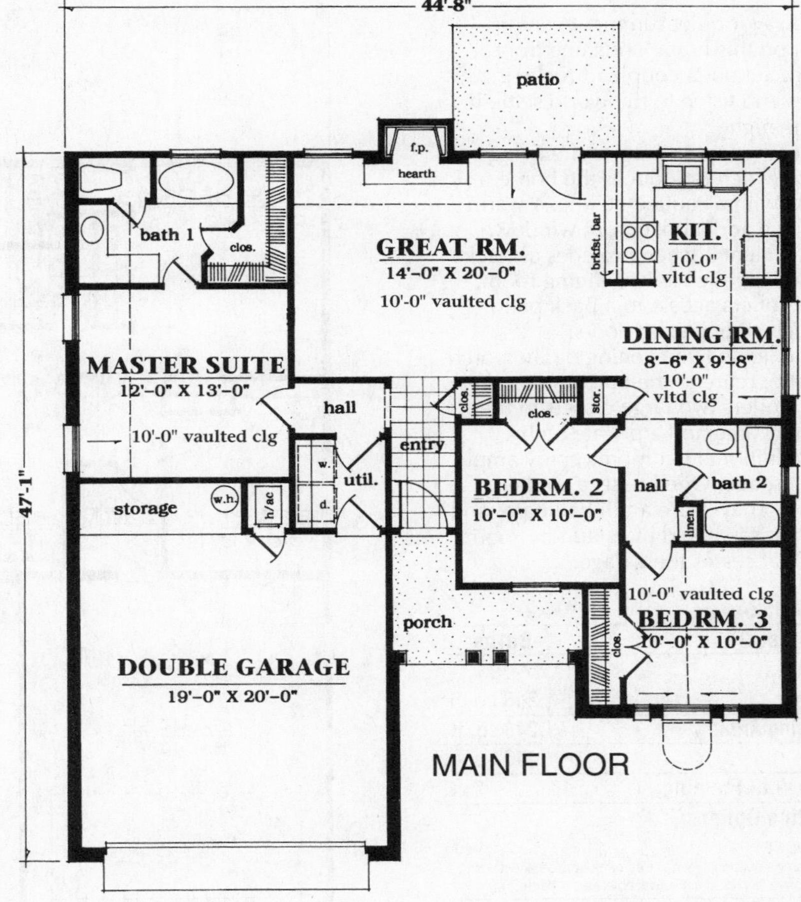

Plan KD-1225

FOR MORE DETAILS, SEE PLAN AT familyhandyman.com/homeplans

Quiet Summer Evenings

- You'll savor quiet summer evenings spent on this home's relaxing front porch. Set out a couple of rocking chairs and listen to the world settle in for the night.
- Inside, the foyer opens to the living room, which introduces the home nicely with a vaulted ceiling, a warm fireplace and a boxed-out window.
- The efficient kitchen provides a snack bar serving the vaulted dining room, which offers access to a back patio through sliding glass doors.
- After enjoying an evening on the porch or patio, retire to the quiet master suite, which offers two large closets in the sleeping area and a private bath.
- Two additional bedrooms enjoy ample closet space. One boasts a vaulted ceiling. They share a full hall bath, and they are separated by a laundry room, which accesses the garage.

Plan TS-9524

Bedrooms: 3	**Baths:** 2
Living Area:	
Main floor	1,248 sq. ft.
Total Living Area:	**1,248 sq. ft.**
Garage	440 sq. ft.
Exterior Wall Framing:	2x6
Foundation Options:	
Crawlspace	

(All plans can be built with your choice of foundation and framing. A generic conversion diagram is available. See order form.)

BLUEPRINT PRICE CODE: A

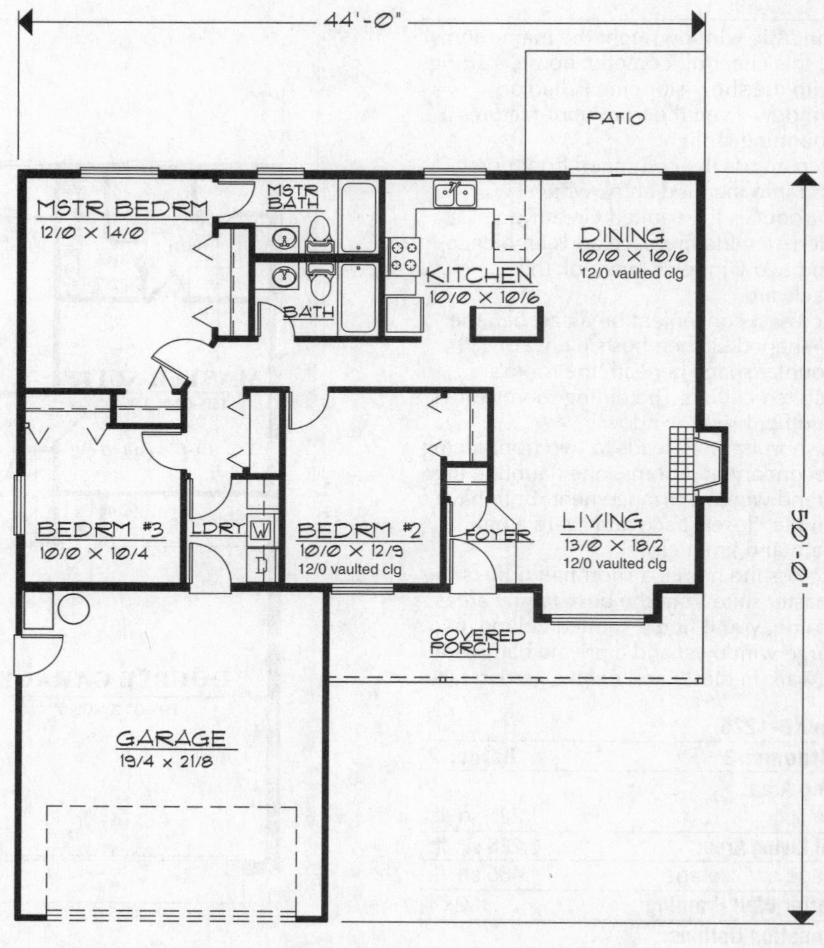

MAIN FLOOR

FRESH, NEW ONE-STORY DESIGNS

Plan TS-9524

SEE ORDER INFO ON PAGES 12-15

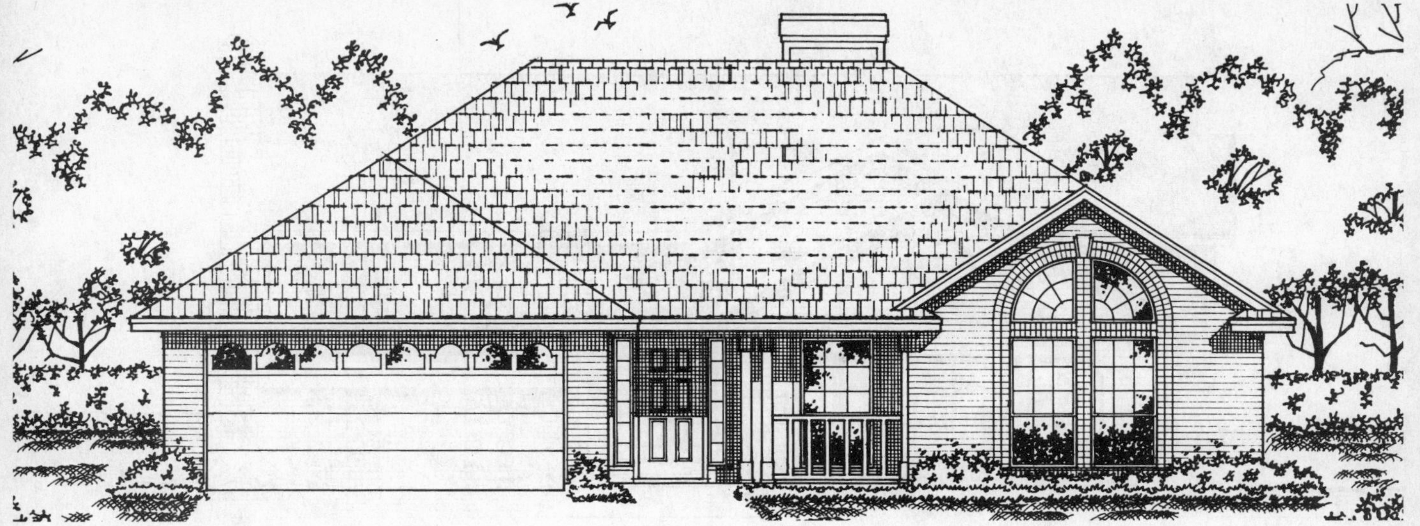

Detailed Facade

- This home's elegant facade features many attractive details, including a large arched window with a keystone, a cozy front porch with columns and rails, and a sidelighted entry.
- Inside, the entry opens to a spacious Great Room, which boasts a vaulted ceiling, access to the back patio, and a nice fireplace flanked by windows.
- Just over a handy breakfast bar lies the kitchen, which also enjoys a vaulted ceiling and a handy pantry. The bayed dining room is topped by another vaulted ceiling.
- One wing of the home is dominated by the master suite, which provides a vaulted ceiling, a large window in the sleeping area, and a private bath with two walk-in closets, a private toilet, a dual-sink vanity, a garden tub, and a separate shower with a seat.
- Down the hall, two additional bedrooms share a hall bath, which also flaunts a garden tub. One bedroom includes a vaulted ceiling, while the other boasts a big closet.

Plan KD-1278

Bedrooms: 3	**Baths:** 2
Living Area:	
Main floor	1,278 sq. ft.
Total Living Area:	**1,278 sq. ft.**
Garage and storage	419 sq. ft.
Exterior Wall Framing:	2x4

Foundation Options:

Slab

(All plans can be built with your choice of foundation and framing. A generic conversion diagram is available. See order form.)

BLUEPRINT PRICE CODE: A

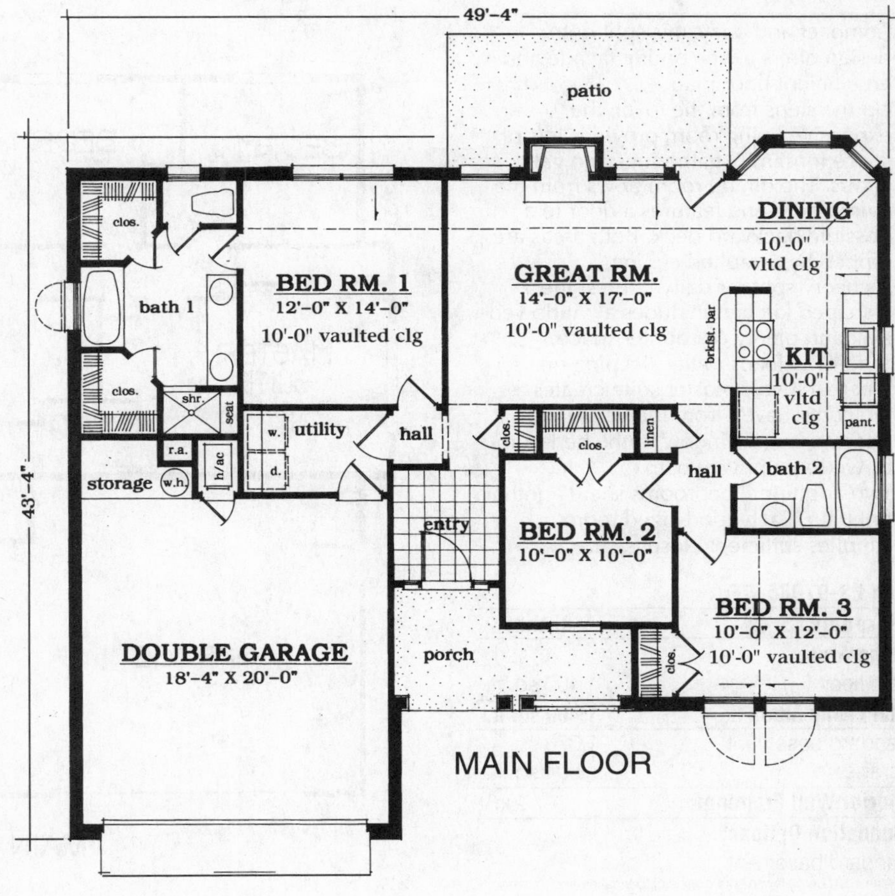

MAIN FLOOR

FRESH, NEW ONE-STORY DESIGNS

Plan KD-1278

Plan copyright held by home designer/architect

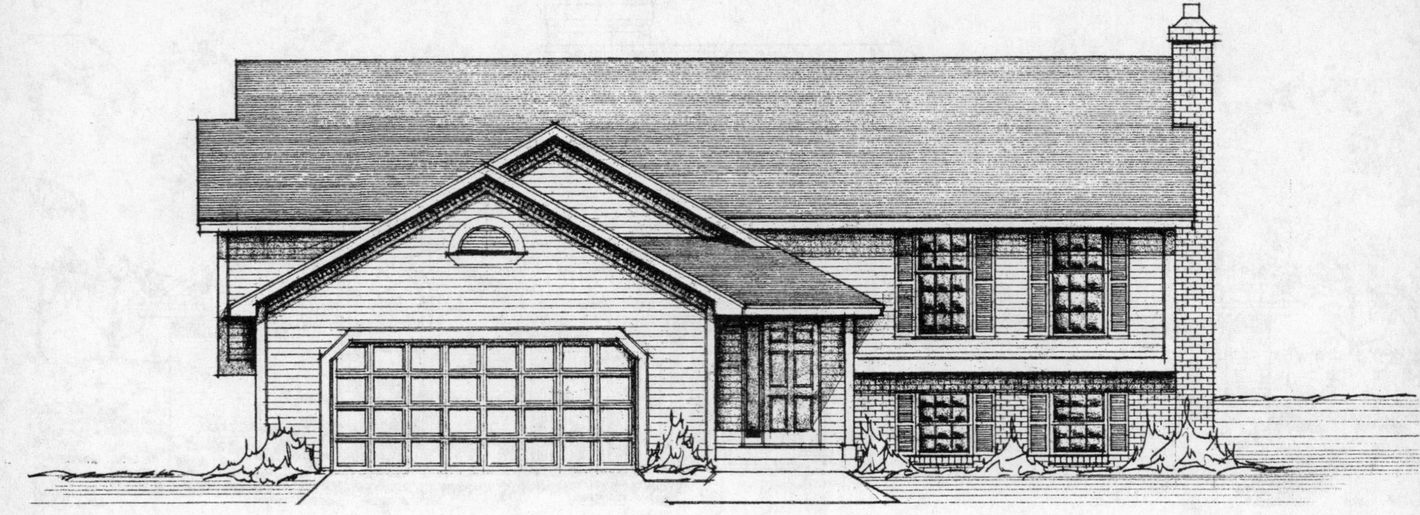

Compact and Cozy

- Compact and cozy, this split-entry design offers a welcoming facade and an efficient floor plan.
- Up the steps from the foyer, the expansive living room provides lots of space for family gatherings and gala affairs. The dining room flows from the living room and features a door to a possible backyard deck. Both areas are topped by a vaulted ceiling.
- A cheery spot for daily chores, the L-shaped kitchen includes a windowed sink and plenty of counter space.
- A hallway leads to the sleeping quarters, where a lovely master suite creates a welcome haven from the day's cares. It boasts a huge window in the bedroom, as well as a private bath.
- Two additional bedrooms share another full bath. Each good-sized room supplies sufficient closet space.

Plan LS-97985-RE

Bedrooms: 3	**Baths:** 2
Living Area:	
Main floor	1,400 sq. ft.
Total Living Area:	**1,400 sq. ft.**
Standard basement	1,376 sq. ft.
Garage	504 sq. ft.
Exterior Wall Framing:	2x6
Foundation Options:	
Standard basement	

(All plans can be built with your choice of foundation and framing. A generic conversion diagram is available. See order form.)

BLUEPRINT PRICE CODE: A

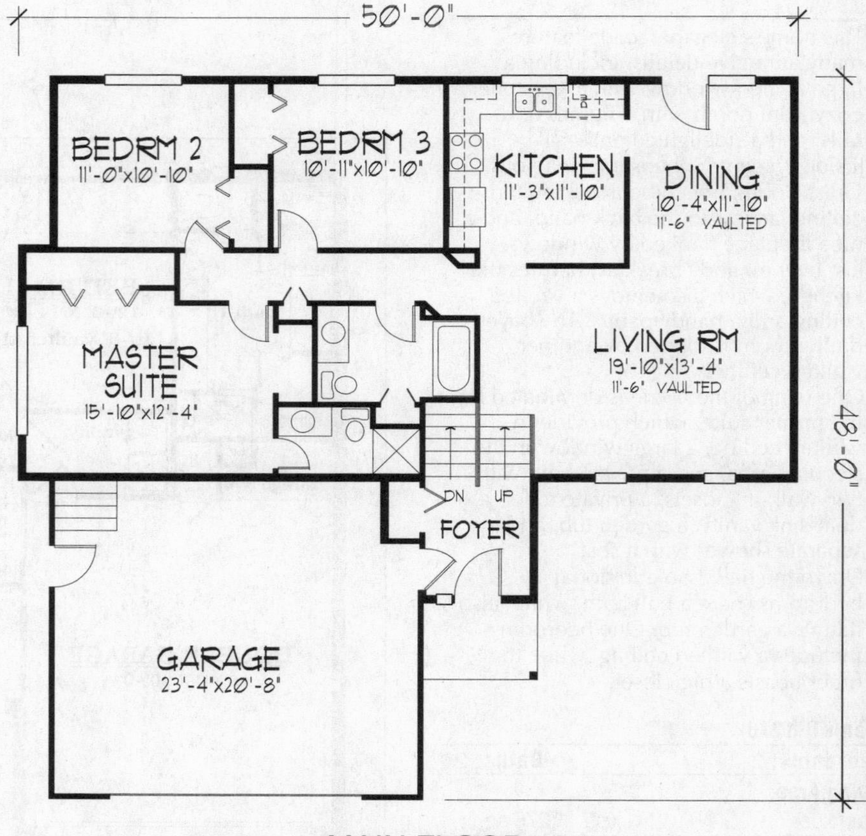

MAIN FLOOR

Plan LS-97985-RE

SEE ORDER INFO ON PAGES 12-15

Outdoor Spaces Galore!

- This home's great outdoor spaces include a lengthy side patio, accessed via the living room and the master suite, and a handy back porch, located just off the eating area.
- The bright, open feel continues in the living and dining rooms. Complete with a fireplace, this merged area is perfect for entertaining or just relaxing.
- The spacious kitchen offers ample counter space and a handy pantry, and includes a casual eating area.
- At the end of the day, retire to the elegant, spacious master suite. The bedroom offers a high ceiling and private access to the patio, while the master bath enjoys a large walk-in closet and a skylighted garden tub flanked by dual sinks.
- An additional bedroom at the front of the home features another high ceiling and private access to a full hall bath through the spacious walk-in closet.

Plan E-1401

Bedrooms: 2	**Baths:** 2
Living Area:	
Main floor	1,410 sq. ft.
Total Living Area:	**1,410 sq. ft.**
Garage	484 sq. ft.
Storage	40 sq. ft.
Exterior Wall Framing:	2x6

Foundation Options:

Slab

(All plans can be built with your choice of foundation and framing. A generic conversion diagram is available. See order form.)

BLUEPRINT PRICE CODE: A

78' – 0"
PATIO
M. BATH
9' clg
GARAGE
22' X 22'
DISAP. STAIRS
DINING ROOM & LIVING ROOM
26' X 13' – 9"
14' sloped clg
FIREPLACE
SLOPE
FLAT
SLOPE
MASTER SUITE
16' X 14'
9' clg
WIC
ENTRY
33' – 0"
FRONT OF HOME
STOR.
REFRIG.
PANTRY
AC
D
W
BEDROOM
14' X 13'
9' clg
EATING & KITCHEN
20' X10'
9' clg
RANGE
LINEN
PORCH
DW
SINK
BATH
WIC
MC

MAIN FLOOR

Well-Placed Porches

- Hearkening back to a simpler time, this home puts its best face forward with a handsome front porch. Shuttered windows and a sidelighted entry add to the curb appeal, while another porch in back completes the home's ample outdoor space.
- The foyer, serviced by a handy coat closet, is open to the dining room, which boasts a high ceiling and two nice columns.
- The open kitchen provides a good-sized pantry and a useful snack bar serving the bayed breakfast nook.
- Perfect for entertaining or spending time with your family, the central living room includes an elegant tray ceiling, a handsome corner fireplace and access to the back porch.
- Just down the skylighted hallway, the master bedroom offers private access to the porch, a spacious walk-in closet and a private bath featuring a garden tub, dual sinks and a separate shower.
- Two additional bedrooms each enjoy walk-in closets. They share a full hall bath, located nearby.

Plan CHP-1532-141A

Bedrooms: 3 — **Baths:** 2

Living Area:

Main floor	1,500 sq. ft.
Total Living Area:	**1,500 sq. ft.**
Garage	400 sq. ft.
Exterior Wall Framing:	2x4

Foundation Options:

Slab

(All plans can be built with your choice of foundation and framing. A generic conversion diagram is available. See order form.)

BLUEPRINT PRICE CODE: B

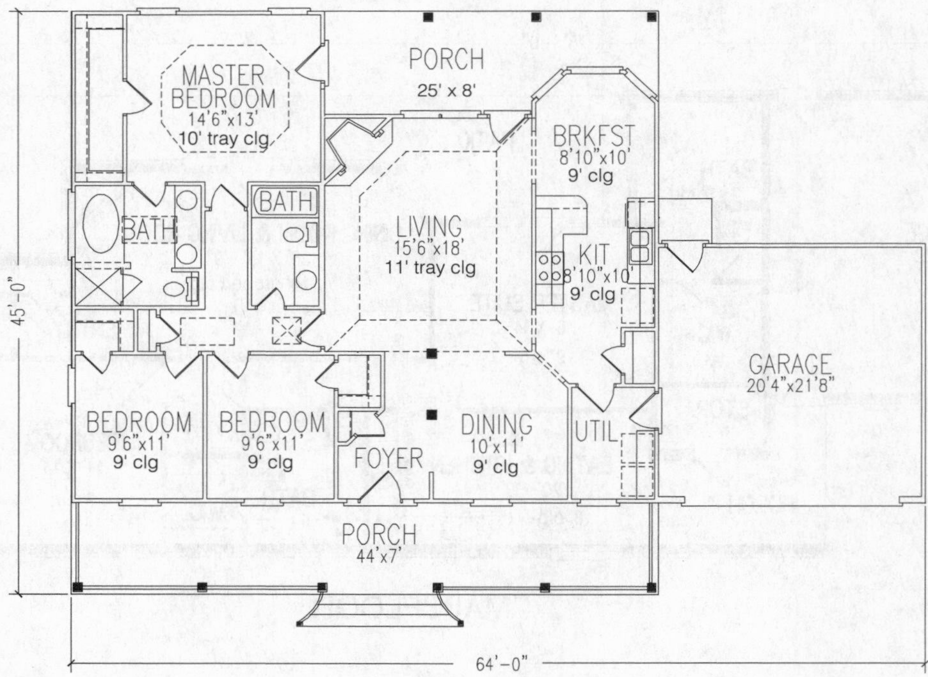

MAIN FLOOR

Plan CHP-1532-141A

SEE ORDER INFO ON PAGES 12-15

Spectacular Arched Entry

- In addition to lovely details such as keystones and arched windows, this home's facade features a spectacular entry, flanked by columns and sidelights and framed by an archway and a half-round transom window.
- Inside, the high ceilings begin in the foyer and continue throughout the shared spaces. The central Great Room features a vaulted ceiling, a toasty fireplace, built-in shelving and access to the backyard's outdoor spaces.
- The spacious kitchen features another vaulted ceiling, as well as a sun-drenched nook and a snack bar serving the Great Room and the adjoining dining room.
- Tucked away in a private wing, the master bedroom boasts private access to the porch, plus two closets, and a private bath with a large, oval garden tub, dual sinks and a separate shower.
- Two additional bedrooms on the other side of the home share a full hall bath.

Plan SDG-91099

Bedrooms: 3	**Baths:** 2
Living Area:	
Main floor	1,501 sq. ft.
Total Living Area:	**1,501 sq. ft.**
Garage	484 sq. ft.
Storage	14 sq. ft.
Exterior Wall Framing:	2x4

Foundation Options:

Slab

(All plans can be built with your choice of foundation and framing. A generic conversion diagram is available. See order form.)

BLUEPRINT PRICE CODE: B

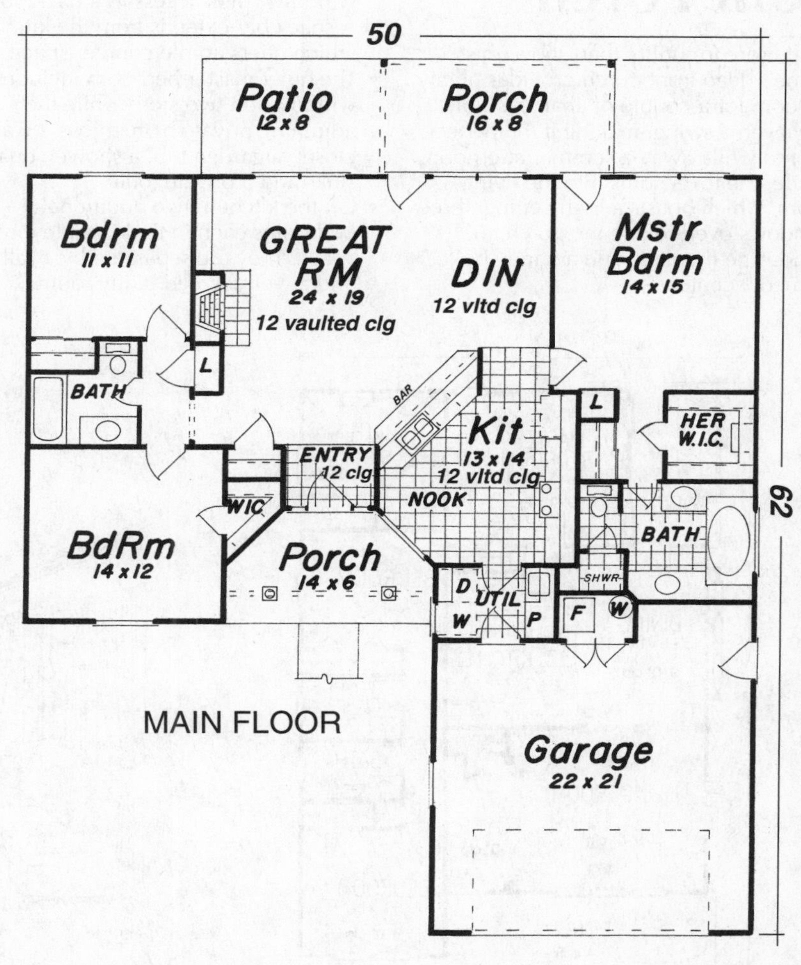

MAIN FLOOR

Livable Front Porch

- Built more for utility than show, this home's deep front porch provides plenty of room for a couple of chairs, a table and even a swing, making it the perfect spot to while away a summer afternoon.
- Inside, the foyer spills into the living room, which boasts a high ceiling, three windows overlooking the porch, a handsome fireplace and a handy built-in media center.
- The media center acts as a sideboard in the spacious dining room, which features a fantastic set of boxed-out windows, plus access to a back porch. A snack bar extends from the kitchen, which offers ample counter space.
- The quiet master bedroom includes windows on two sides while the adjoining private bath enjoys a walk-in closet, a garden tub, a shower, dual sinks and a private toilet.
- Off the kitchen, two additional bedrooms each include ample closet space. They are separated by a full bath and a well-located utility room.

Plan L-97123-UDA

Bedrooms: 3 **Baths:** 2

Living Area:

Main floor 1,581 sq. ft.

Total Living Area: 1,581 sq. ft.

Exterior Wall Framing: 2x4

Foundation Options:

Slab

(All plans can be built with your choice of foundation and framing. A generic conversion diagram is available. See order form.)

BLUEPRINT PRICE CODE: B

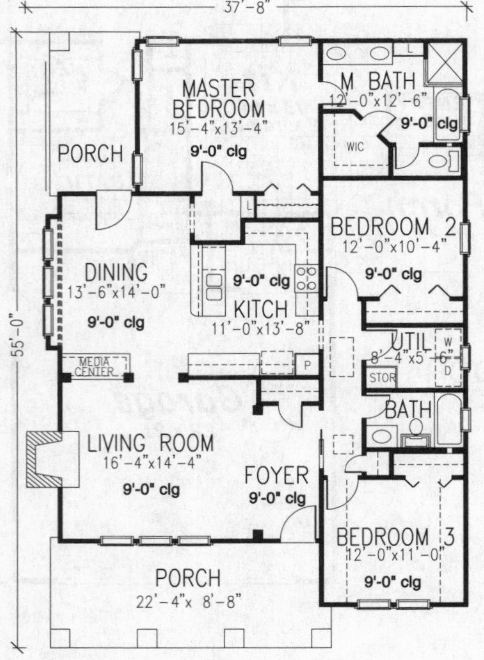

MAIN FLOOR

VIEW INTO LIVING ROOM

Plan L-97123-UDA

SEE ORDER INFO ON PAGES 12-15

Cozy Front Porch

- A cozy front porch greets you as you stroll up the sidewalk to this delightful home. Set out a rocking chair and enjoy an evening talking with the neighbors.
- Inside, the open kitchen includes a pantry closet and a snack bar. It serves a sunny breakfast nook and a handsome bayed dining room that looks onto the front porch.
- The spacious living room boasts a corner fireplace, a volume ceiling and access to a rear porch.
- This home's masterpiece, the master suite, offers a boxed-out window and a bath featuring two walk-in closets, a corner garden spa, a separate shower and two vanities.
- Two secondary bedrooms share a full bath and a dressing room that will make morning preparations a little bit easier for your children and guests.

Plan RD-1583

Bedrooms: 3 **Baths:** 2

Living Area:

Main floor 1,583 sq. ft.

Total Living Area: 1,583 sq. ft.

Garage 412 sq. ft.

Exterior Wall Framing: 2x4

Foundation Options:

Crawlspace

Slab

(All plans can be built with your choice of foundation and framing. A generic conversion diagram is available. See order form.)

BLUEPRINT PRICE CODE: B

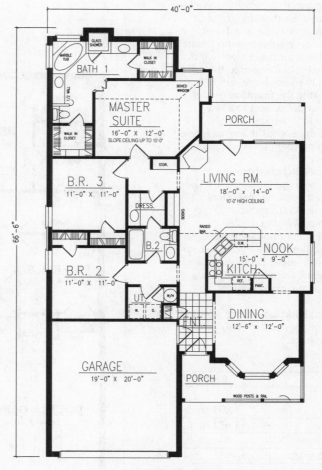

MAIN FLOOR

Great Expectations

- This charming and thoughtfully crafted home provides a great setting for your family's future. A cozy brick exterior and lovely window arrangements create high expectations for the design within.
- The high entry looks forward to the immense family room. Here, bright windows flanking the fireplace lend a view to the rear patio, and a raised ceiling adds a lofty feeling.
- To the side of the entry, the formal living room and dining room entertain guests comfortably.
- The galley-style kitchen shares a breakfast bar with the family room. The bayed breakfast nook nearby offers access to the backyard patio.
- The walk-in closet in the master bedroom will accommodate those who wonder where they'll store years' worth of belongings. A raised ceiling, and a private bath with a spa tub, a separate shower, and dual sinks complete the picture.
- Two additional bedrooms share another full bath. These rooms also supply ample closet space.

Plan KD-1604

Bedrooms: 3	**Baths:** 2
Living Area:	
Main floor	1,604 sq. ft.
Total Living Area:	**1,604 sq. ft.**
Garage and storage	445 sq. ft.
Exterior Wall Framing:	2x4

Foundation Options:

Slab

(All plans can be built with your choice of foundation and framing. A generic conversion diagram is available. See order form.)

BLUEPRINT PRICE CODE: **B**

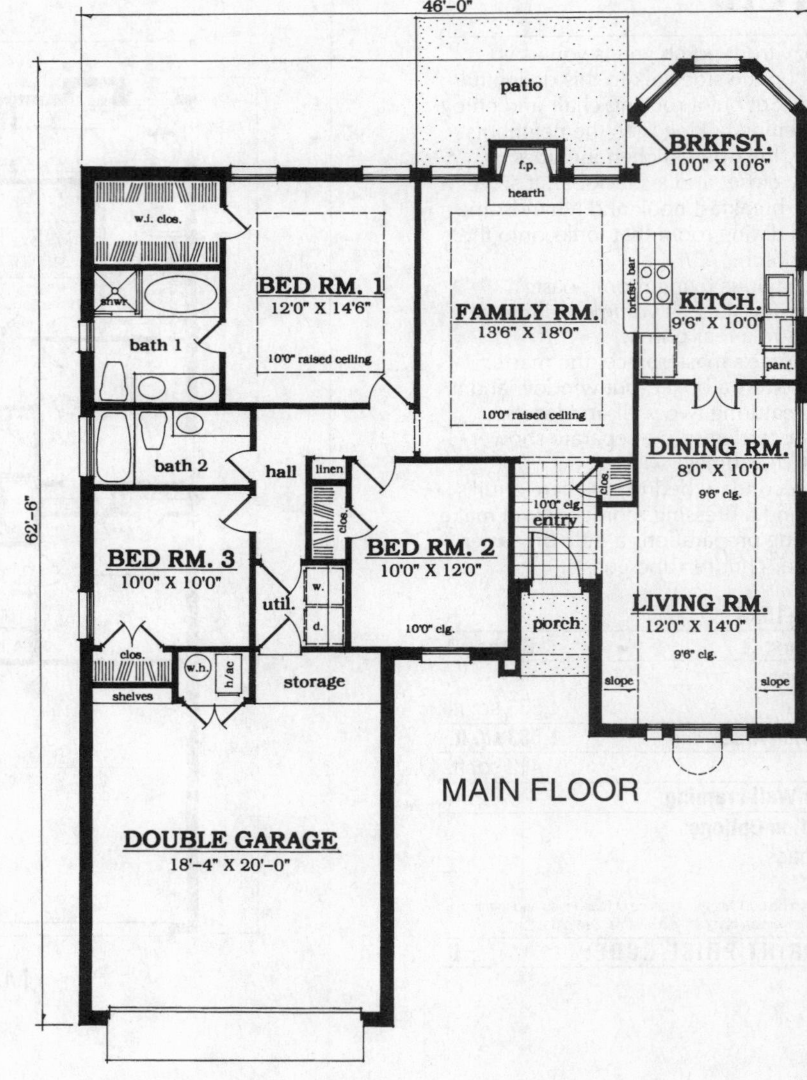

Plan KD-1604

SEE ORDER INFO ON PAGES 12-15

Slim Suburban

- Slim suburban lots require attractive, thoughtful homes like this one, which packs numerous amenities into a compact, economical size.
- Stately brick accents and a stylish bay window add value and visual interest to the facade, while classic gables lend the exterior a comforting, familiar feel.
- A brief entry allows guests to enter immediately into the living and dining rooms, making them feel welcome at once. The openness of these spaces enhances parties and gatherings, while a clever alcove provides just enough space for a china hutch or a buffet.
- The kitchen is not only a functional space, but an ideal gathering spot. An oversized island allows ample space for you to work or snack while chatting. Plus, it acts as the pivot point for all other meal preparations. A roomy nook and a bright sun room add to the appeal of this family-friendly area.
- The nearby master suite enjoys an extra-large sleeping area and a private, split bath. Two secondary bedrooms nicely accommodate children or guests. A full bath services these sizable rooms.

Plan LS-98817-GW	
Bedrooms: 3	**Baths:** 2
Living Area:	
Main floor	1,620 sq. ft.
Total Living Area:	**1,620 sq. ft.**
Standard basement	1,620 sq. ft.
Garage	361 sq. ft.
Exterior Wall Framing:	2x4
Foundation Options:	
Standard basement	

(All plans can be built with your choice of foundation and framing. A generic conversion diagram is available. See order form.)

BLUEPRINT PRICE CODE: B

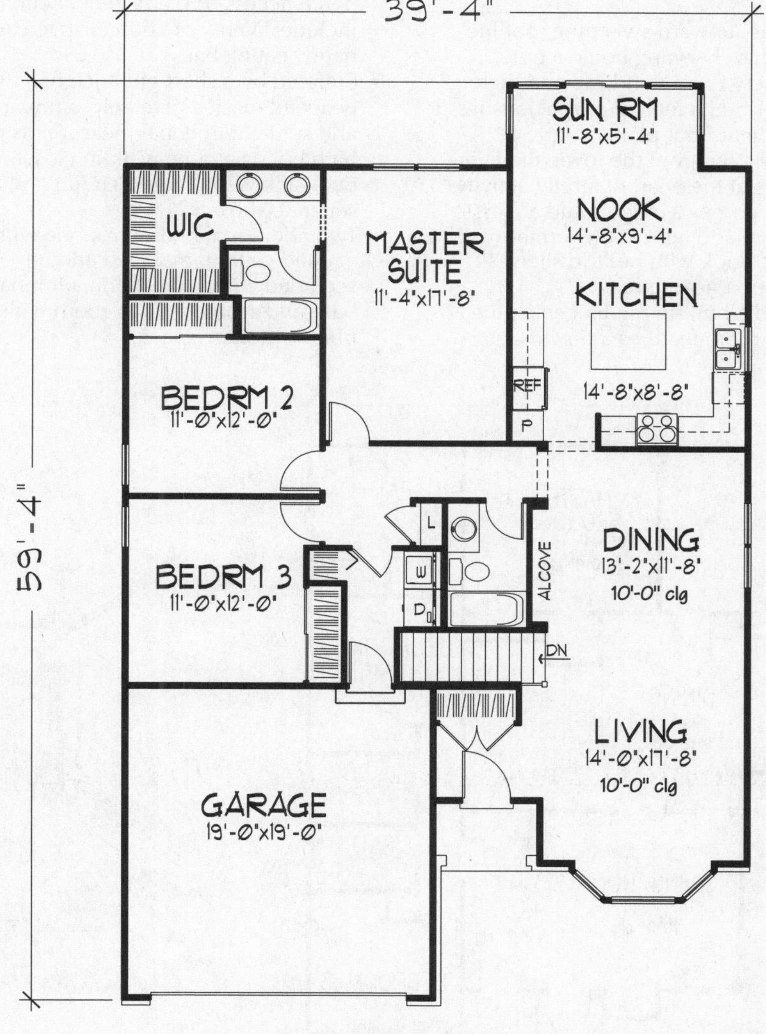

MAIN FLOOR

FRESH, NEW ONE-STORY DESIGNS

Plan LS-98817-GW

Quiet Charm

- A gentle, upward-sweeping roofline gives this charming home a quiet elegance. Large windows and high ceilings add a feeling of spaciousness to its efficient floor plan.
- Opening out from the foyer, the living room is at the heart of family activity. Lovely corner windows and a classic fireplace add light and warmth, while a unique nook with built-in shelves provides a neat retreat.
- Beyond a built-in media center, the dining room features a boxed-out window arrangement, as well as rear porch access. The adjacent kitchen includes plenty of counter space and a handy eating bar.
- Buffered by a short entrance hall, the peaceful master suite enjoys privacy and sunlight in equal measure. Its posh bath boasts a large walk-in closet, a dual-sink vanity, a garden tub and a separate shower.
- Two additional bedrooms, one with a vaulted ceiling, make up another secluded wing. They flank a full hall bath and a sunny utility room with built-in storage space.

Plan L-97122-UDA

Bedrooms: 3	**Baths:** 2
Living Area:	
Main floor	1,621 sq. ft.
Total Living Area:	**1,621 sq. ft.**
Exterior Wall Framing:	2x4
Foundation Options:	
Slab	

(All plans can be built with your choice of foundation and framing. A generic conversion diagram is available. See order form.)

BLUEPRINT PRICE CODE: B

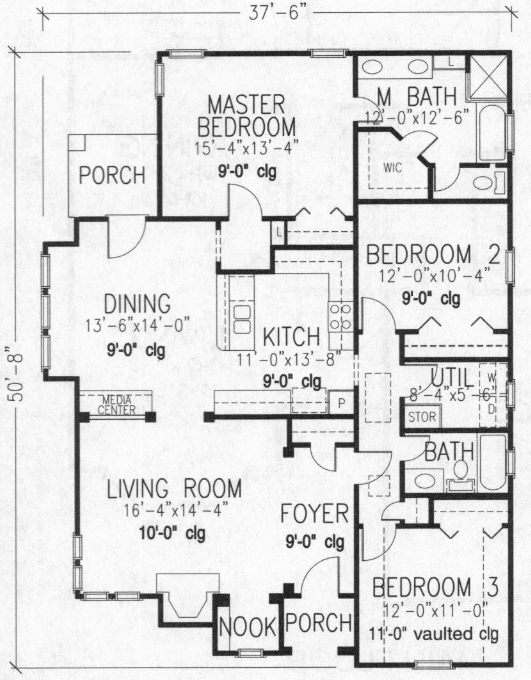

MAIN FLOOR

VIEW INTO LIVING ROOM

Beautiful Bay

- This home's facade showcases a beautiful bay window that illuminates the formal dining room. A sidelighted entry provides additional curb appeal to this well-designed gem.
- Inside, the bright entry spills into the vaulted dining room, which is served through a pocket door by the efficient kitchen. Ample counter space and a large pantry give way to a handy snack bar bordering the breakfast nook.
- Located near the breakfast nook, the skylighted Great Room enjoys a vaulted ceiling and access to a back patio.
- The relaxing master suite features a vaulted ceiling and a window facing the backyard, as well as a private bath with a dual-sink vanity, a roomy walk-in closet and lots of storage space.
- Two additional bedrooms share a full hall bath. One enjoys a vaulted ceiling, while the other offers a large closet.
- The nearby laundry room includes a sink and access to the two-car garage.

Plan TS-9525

Bedrooms: 3 **Baths:** 2

Living Area:

Main floor 1,630 sq. ft.

Total Living Area: **1,630 sq. ft.**

Garage 542 sq. ft.

Exterior Wall Framing: 2x6

Foundation Options:

Crawlspace

(All plans can be built with your choice of foundation and framing. A generic conversion diagram is available. See order form.)

BLUEPRINT PRICE CODE: **B**

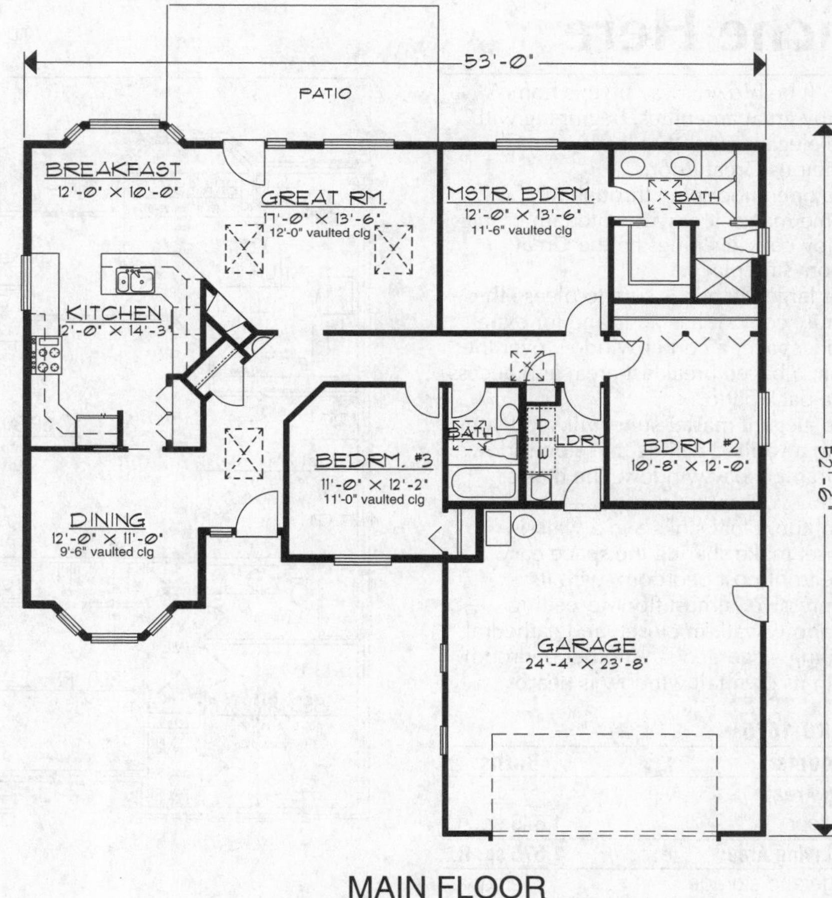

MAIN FLOOR

Plan TS-9525

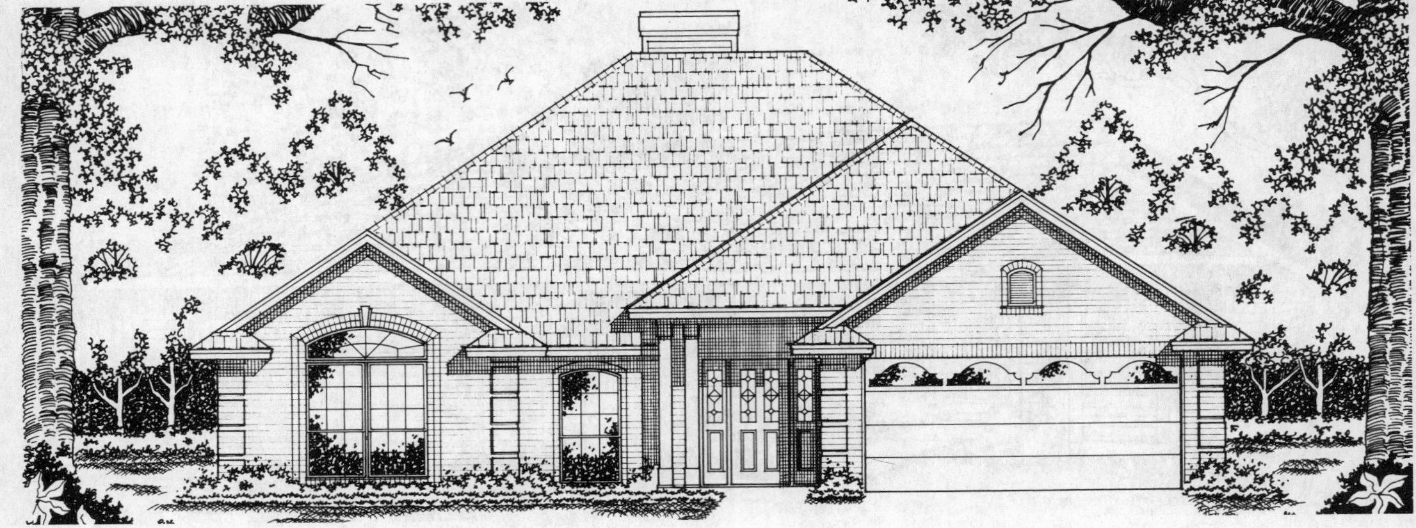

Find Your Niche Here

- You'll be blown away by this home's many great amenities, beginning with the elegant entry that leads into a spacious Great Room.
- The open floor plan throughout the home makes it easy to entertain or just enjoy cozy evenings by the Great Room's fireplace.
- The large kitchen is sure to please the family cook. It has an island for extra work space, a corner window over the sink, a bayed breakfast area, and access to a back patio.
- The elegant master suite will spoil you with a vaulted ceiling that slopes down to frame a bay window. The master bath—your own private spa—boasts an oval tub. Dual sinks and a walk-in closet make sharing the space easy.
- The frontmost bedroom, with its impressive, almost floor-to-ceiling window, walk-in closet, and cathedral ceiling, is gorgeous. Another bedroom with its own tall window is nearby.

Plan KD-1675

Bedrooms: 3	**Baths:** 2
Living Area:	
Main floor	1,675 sq. ft.
Total Living Area:	**1,675 sq. ft.**
Garage and storage	459 sq. ft.
Exterior Wall Framing:	2x4
Foundation Options:	
Slab	
(All plans can be built with your choice of foundation and framing. A generic conversion diagram is available. See order form.)	
BLUEPRINT PRICE CODE:	**B**

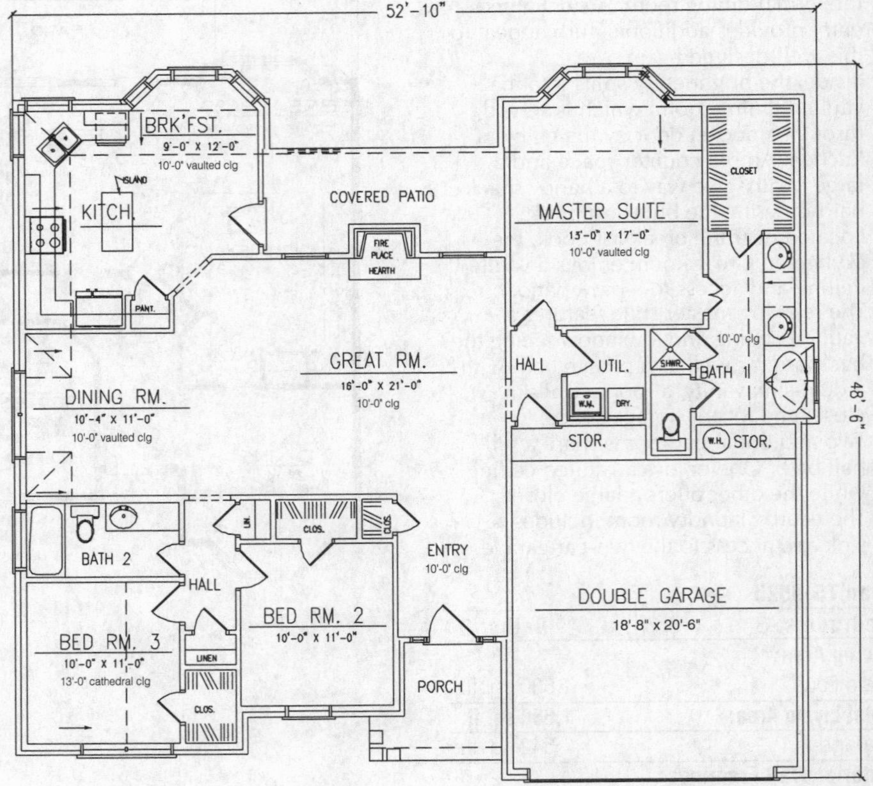

MAIN FLOOR

Plan KD-1675

SEE ORDER INFO ON PAGES 12-15
familyhandyman.com/homeplans

Fabulous, Flexible Home

- This compact, three-bedroom home will thrill you with its versatility. The adaptable option room would make a perfect formal dining room, a quiet den or even a fourth bedroom.
- With high ceilings throughout, this one-story home provides plenty of space, and its organized floor plan is adaptable to nearly any family's needs.
- The Great Room, sure to be a popular gathering place, has a fireplace, sliding doors leading out to a back patio, and a unique nook area that is perfect for casual meals as well as quiet reading, letter writing, or doing crafts while the rest of the family watches TV nearby.
- The master bedroom offers a private bath and a large walk-in closet. Enjoy a long soak in the master bath's oversized oval tub, which is tucked underneath a large window.
- Two additional bedrooms are close to the master suite and share a full hall bath. A convenient utility room with a washer and dryer lies nearby.

Plan S-3295-N

Bedrooms: 3+	**Baths:** 2
Living Area:	
Main floor	1,732 sq. ft.
Total Living Area:	**1,732 sq. ft.**
Garage	400 sq. ft.
Exterior Wall Framing:	2x6
Foundation Options:	
Crawlspace	

(All plans can be built with your choice of foundation and framing. A generic conversion diagram is available. See order form.)

BLUEPRINT PRICE CODE: B

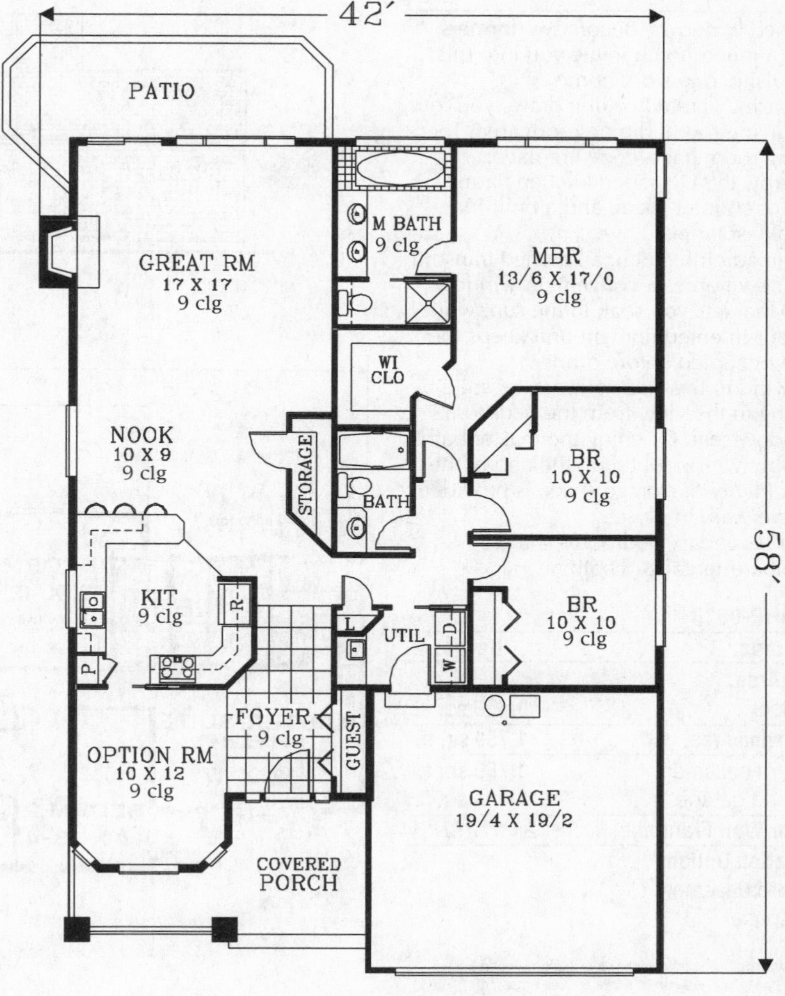

MAIN FLOOR

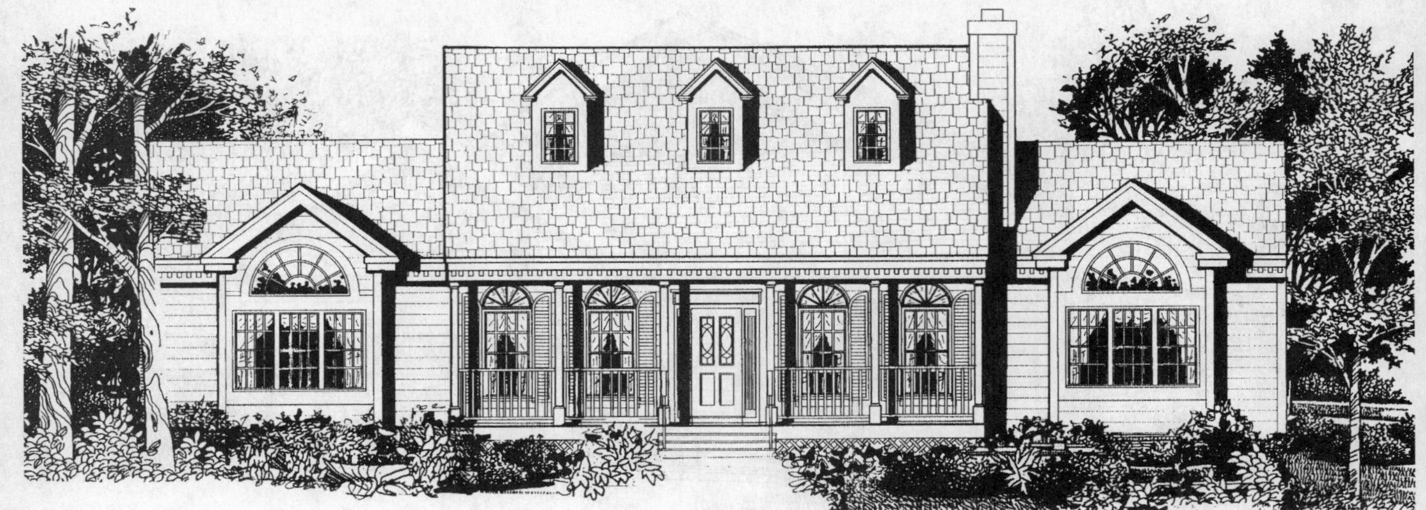

One Story, Many Comforts

- Arched windows, decorative dormers and a railed porch invite you into this exquisite, one-story home.
- A soaring vaulted ceiling draws you into the living room, dining room area. The living room has a cozy fireplace.
- Nearby, the U-shaped kitchen flaunts lots of counter space and a built-in breakfast table.
- In the adjoining den, an arched transom window frames a convenient window seat that lets you soak in the sun, while a built-in entertainment unit keeps the kids occupied before dinner.
- Unwind in the luxurious master suite by taking in the view from the bedroom's window seat. Or enjoy the master bath's bubbly whirlpool tub at the end of the day. Plenty of storage space is provided by the walk-in closet.
- Two secondary bedrooms share a compartmentalized bath.

Plan AHP-9810	
Bedrooms: 3	**Baths:** 2
Living Area:	
Main floor	1,759 sq. ft.
Total Living Area:	**1,759 sq. ft.**
Standard basement	1,759 sq. ft.
Detached garage	484 sq. ft.
Exterior Wall Framing:	2x4 or 2x6
Foundation Options:	
Standard basement	
Crawlspace	
Slab	

(All plans can be built with your choice of foundation and framing. A generic conversion diagram is available. See order form.)

BLUEPRINT PRICE CODE: B

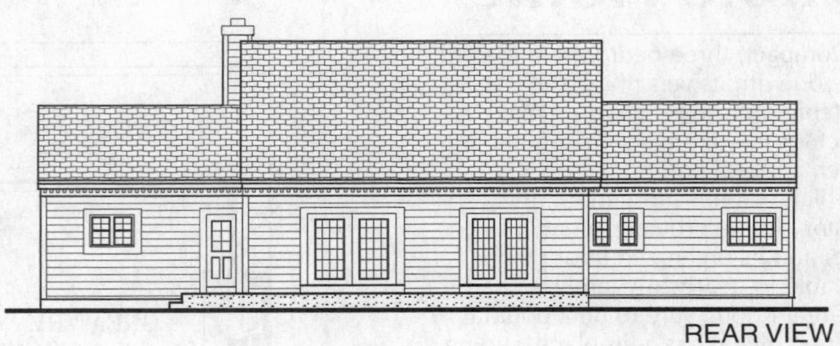

REAR VIEW

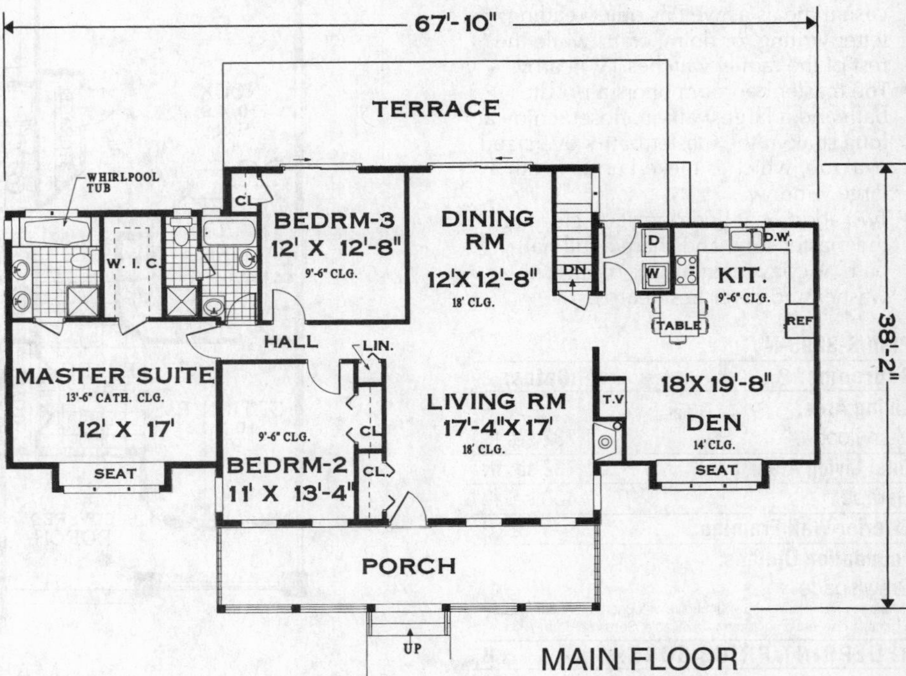

MAIN FLOOR

Plan AHP-9810

SEE ORDER INFO ON PAGES 12-15

For a Romantic getaway

- You'll fall in love with this one-story home's unique and convenient floor plan. The Great Room, with a high tray ceiling, a corner fireplace, and a handy serving bar that extends from the kitchen, will truly capture your heart.
- The kitchen's angles and ample counter space make preparing meals a breeze. A desk divides the kitchen, creating a nice area to write letters or pay bills.
- The master suite is secluded on one side of the home, making it a private getaway. The bedroom is topped off with a high tray ceiling and a large walk-in closet. The master bath has everything to pamper a tired body, including a whirlpool bath, a separate shower, and a dual-sink vanity.
- Two bedrooms on the opposite side of the home share a hall bath. Both have generous closets.
- Plenty of storage spaces are tucked away throughout the home.
- Outdoor living is easy with two big porches—a welcoming one in front and a relaxing one in back.

Plan VL-1765

Bedrooms: 3	**Baths:** 2
Living Area:	
Main floor	1,765 sq. ft.
Total Living Area:	**1,765 sq. ft.**
Garage	440 sq. ft.
Exterior Wall Framing:	2x4

Foundation Options:
Crawlspace
Slab
(All plans can be built with your choice of foundation and framing. A generic conversion diagram is available. See order form.)

BLUEPRINT PRICE CODE: B

68'
46'

GARAGE 20X21
PORCH 35X10
BEDRM # 3 12X12 9 clg
CLOSET
STOR
PANT
SINK
KITCHEN 10X16 9 clg
REFG
RANGE
DESK
FIREPLACE
LINEN
BATH 8X9
CLOSET 8X7
WASH
DRY
UTILITY 7X7
STOR
GREAT ROOM 15X23
BAR
CLOSET
STOR
MASTER SUITE 17X14
11 tray clg
SHWR
MASTER BATH 11X10
LINEN
WHIRLPOOL
DINING 13X11 9 clg
11 tray clg
BEDRM # 2 12X11 9 clg
PORCH 6X28

MAIN FLOOR

An Elegant Showplace

- You'll be surrounded with elegance in this wonderful one-story home, sure to be a neighborhood showplace. The open dining and living rooms will elicit gasps of approval when your guests gaze at the soaring ceiling.
- Their admiration will grow as they are ushered into the family room and they see an oversized fireplace flanked by a floor-to-ceiling window and sliding glass doors to a back terrace.
- What will surely impress, however, is the unique, curved wall of windows in the dinette area. The kitchen is open to the dinette and family room and has a skylight that further brightens this area.
- The master suite, with its private bath and large walk-in-closet, will delight the owner. The master bath features a dressing area with a vanity, plus a skylight to let in all the natural light.
- Nearby, two additional bedrooms share a full hall bath.

Plan K-819-V	
Bedrooms: 3	**Baths:** 2½
Living Area:	
Main floor	1,795 sq. ft.
Total Living Area:	**1,795 sq. ft.**
Standard basement	1,735 sq. ft.
Garage and storage	505 sq. ft.
Exterior Wall Framing:	2x4 or 2x6
Foundation Options:	
Standard basement	
Slab	

(All plans can be built with your choice of foundation and framing. A generic conversion diagram is available. See order form.)

BLUEPRINT PRICE CODE: B

VIEW INTO FAMILY ROOM

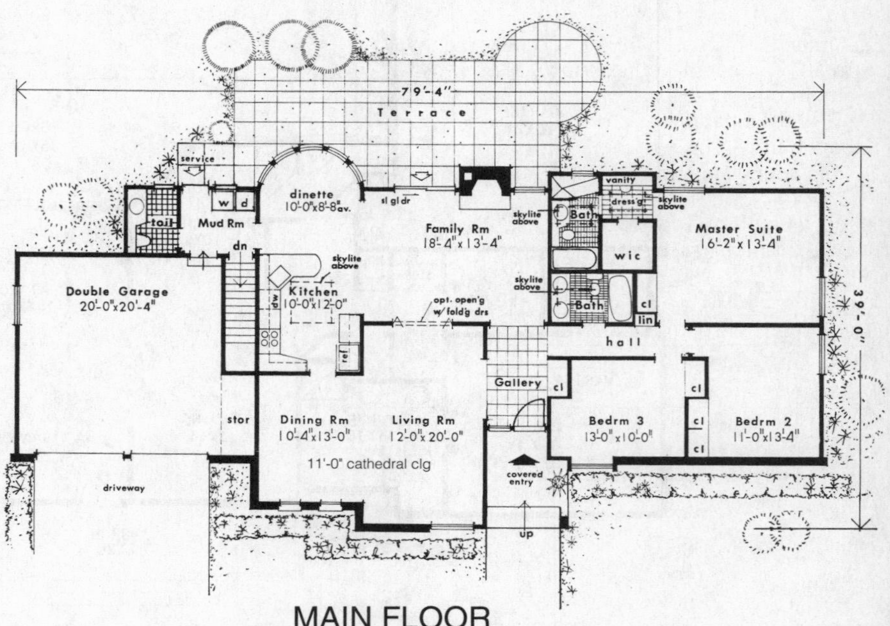

MAIN FLOOR

Plan K-819-V

SEE ORDER INFO ON PAGES 12-15

Bay Windows Make It Better

- This one-story home's brightest features are its three lovely bay windows. Two dress up the home's facade, while the third overlooks a back patio.
- The spacious floor plan is enhanced by a vaulted ceiling in each room, creating an air of spaciousness throughout the entire home.
- The family room is sure to attract much activity, with its built-in media shelves and sliding glass doors to the patio.
- The nearby nook is open to the kitchen and is a perfect place to enjoy informal dining. The formal dining room, on the other hand, lends an elegant touch to special occasions—or simply a nice dinner. Busy cooks will appreciate the smart, compact layout in the kitchen.
- The master suite is a secluded retreat. The bedroom adjoins a private master bath. Highlights here include a dual-sink vanity, a luxurious oval tub and a walk-in closet.
- A brief hallway separates the living areas from the secondary bedrooms.

Plan HDS-99-372

Bedrooms: 3	**Baths:** 2
Living Area:	
Main floor	1,806 sq. ft.
Total Living Area:	**1,806 sq. ft.**
Garage	491 sq. ft.
Exterior Wall Framing:	2x4 or 8-in. concrete block
Foundation Options:	
Slab	

(All plans can be built with your choice of foundation and framing. A generic conversion diagram is available. See order form.)

BLUEPRINT PRICE CODE: B

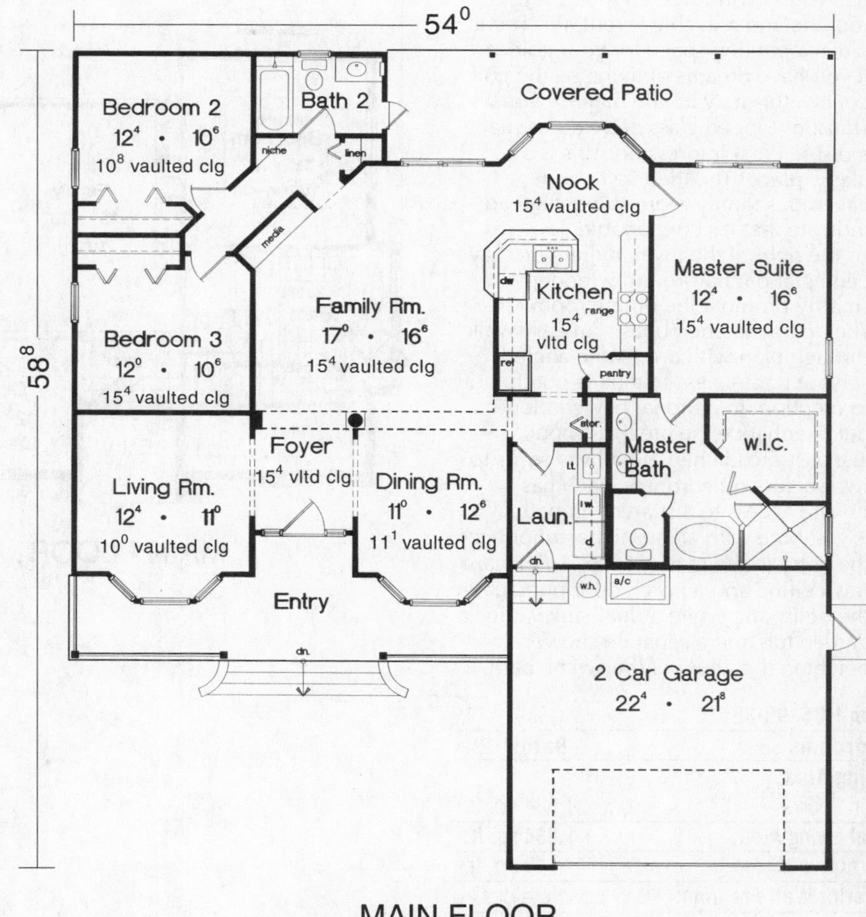

MAIN FLOOR

Plan HDS-99-372

FOR MORE DETAILS, SEE PLAN AT familyhandyman.com/homeplans

Golf, Anyone?

- Along with lovely arches that frame half-round windows, an interesting roofline and a livable layout, this home offers a parking space for your golf cart! If you have dreams of living by the golf course, this may be the plan for you.
- Transom-topped glass entry doors make a distinct first impression: This is a classy place! The tiled foyer and cavernous family room straight ahead indicate that it's comfortable, too.
- To the right of the foyer, a dramatic tray ceiling and a half-round window smartly promote the dining room.
- The nearby kitchen boasts an easy walk-through plan with a versatile angled serving bar. Access to a back porch, not to mention an optional bay window, deftly enhance the breakfast nook.
- Just past the kitchen, a hallway leads to two secluded bedrooms. Each has private access to a shared full bath.
- A vestibule with an art niche announces the entry to the master suite. An elegant tray ceiling and a porch door punctuate the bedroom, while a dual-sink vanity, a garden tub and a separate shower heighten the allure of the swank bath.

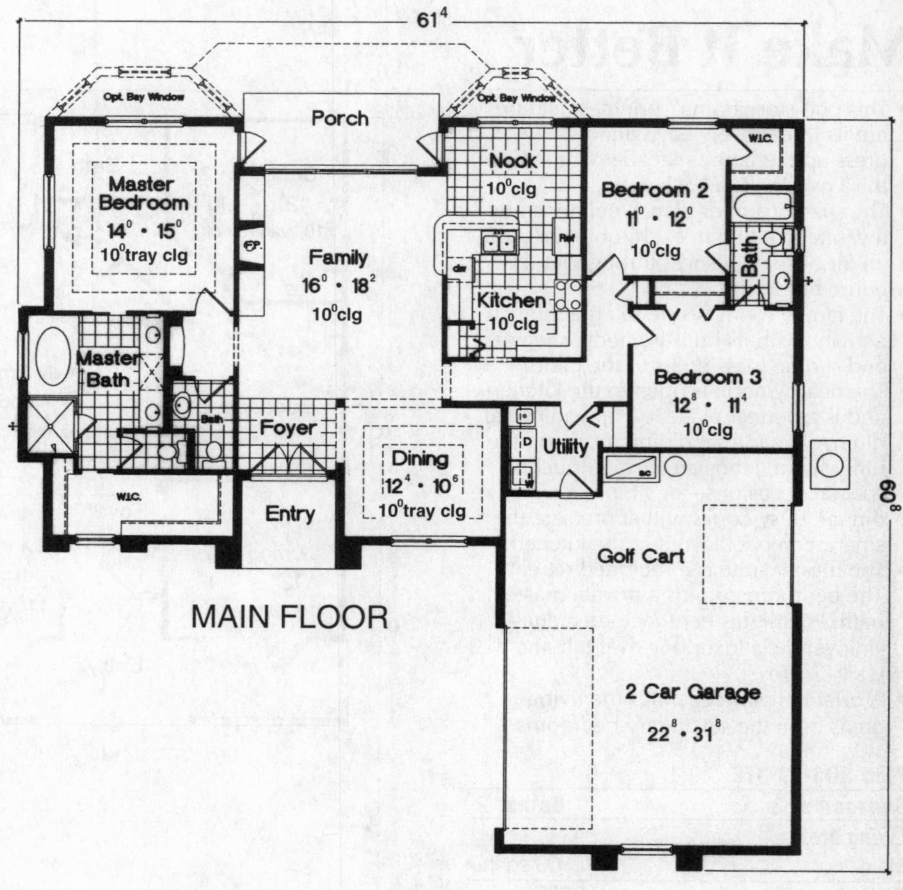

Plan HDS-99-355

Bedrooms: 3	**Baths:** 2½
Living Area:	
Main floor	1,834 sq. ft.
Total Living Area:	**1,834 sq. ft.**
Garage and storage	743 sq. ft.
Exterior Wall Framing:	8-in. concrete block
Foundation Options:	
Slab	

(All plans can be built with your choice of foundation and framing. A generic conversion diagram is available. See order form.)

BLUEPRINT PRICE CODE: B

Plan HDS-99-355

SEE ORDER INFO ON PAGES 12-15

Partake in Pleasure

- Your pleasure will double when you come home to this delightful one-story, four-bedroom home. Its curb appeal is undeniable, and inside it welcomes the family to enjoy the good things in life.
- From the entry, go into the heart of the home, the Great Room. Here, a warming fireplace is flanked by built-in cabinets. Access to a back patio is nice when the days grow warm.
- The up-to-date kitchen has a vaulted ceiling and a step-saving layout. The kitchen is convenient to the breakfast room and the formal dining room, which boasts a beautiful, tall window that will brighten any meal.
- The master bedroom is a picture of elegance with its high coffered ceiling and exquisite master bath. The bath features an oval tub and a separate shower, plus a dual-sink vanity and a large walk-in closet.
- Three additional bedrooms have high ceilings and are arranged for easy sharing of a full hall bath.

Plan KD-1839	
Bedrooms: 4	**Baths:** 2
Living Area:	
Main floor	1,839 sq. ft.
Total Living Area:	**1,839 sq. ft.**
Garage and storage	502 sq. ft.
Exterior Wall Framing:	2x4
Foundation Options:	
Slab (All plans can be built with your choice of foundation and framing. A generic conversion diagram is available. See order form.)	
BLUEPRINT PRICE CODE:	**B**

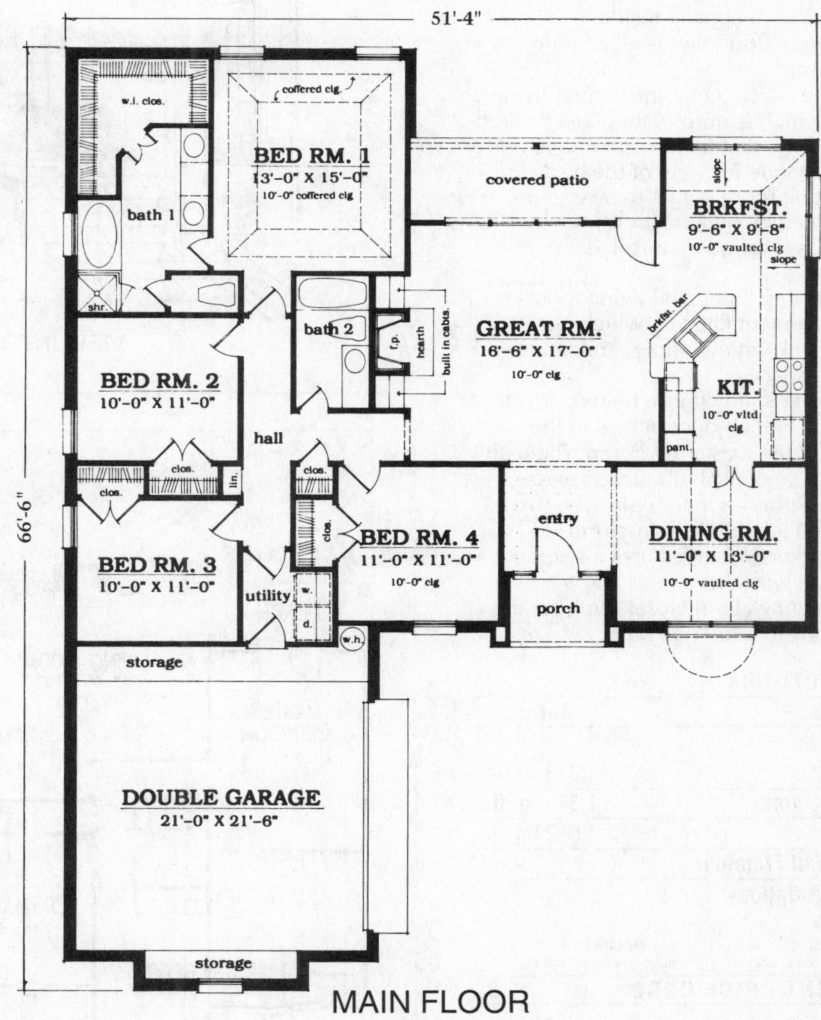

MAIN FLOOR

Near and Dear

- Roofline variations, an arched entry porch, and corner quoins give this home its curb appeal. Inside, a convenient floor plan is all a family could want.
- From the porch, enter the central living room, which features a fireplace flanked by windows that let in natural light and offer a wonderful view of the backyard.
- The dining room is sure to awe. Introduced by pillars, this room offers a gorgeous focal point: a Palladian window.
- Open to the dining and living rooms is the convenient kitchen, which boasts a corner sink with windows and ample counter space.
- The master suite offers a deluxe private bath and French-door access to the porch off the master bedroom. The bath enjoys a large oval tub tucked under a window, plus a separate shower, two sinks and a large walk-in-closet.
- A second bedroom features a second Palladian window; a third has a convenient walk-in closet. Both rooms are handy to a full hall bath.

Plan L-97071-UDA

Bedrooms: 3	**Baths:** 2
Living Area:	
Main floor	1,848 sq. ft.
Total Living Area:	**1,848 sq. ft.**
Garage	512 sq. ft.
Exterior Wall Framing:	2x4
Foundation Options:	
Slab	

(All plans can be built with your choice of foundation and framing. A generic conversion diagram is available. See order form.)

BLUEPRINT PRICE CODE: **B**

VIEW INTO DINING ROOM

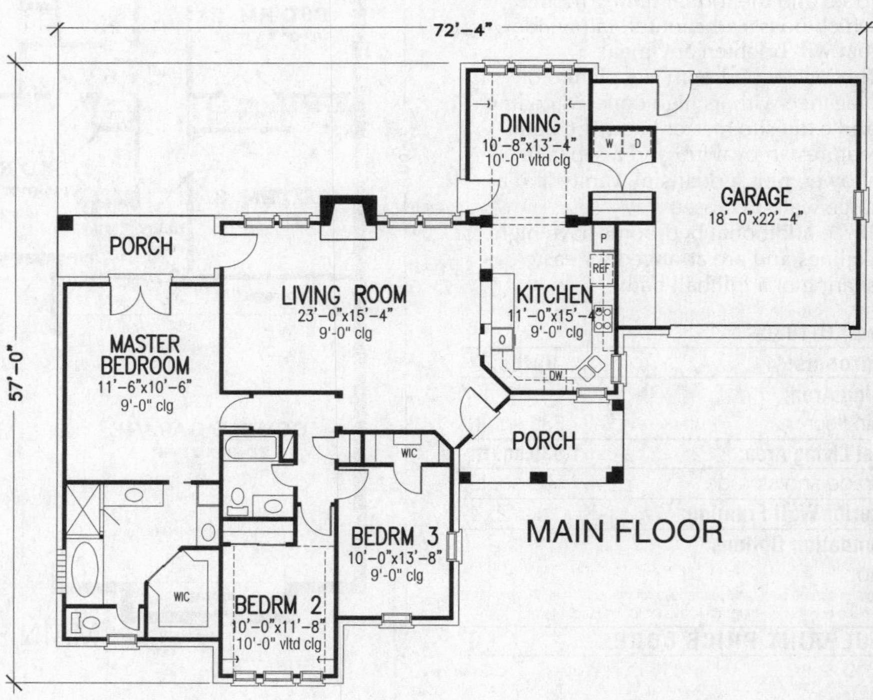

MAIN FLOOR

ORDER BLUEPRINTS ANYTIME!
CALL TOLL-FREE 1-800-820-1296

Plan L-97071-UDA

SEE ORDER INFO ON PAGES 12-15
familyhandyman.com/homeplans

High-Level Interaction

- With its high sloped ceilings and focus on interaction, this beautiful brick home fits the bill for luxurious and open family living.
- For greater adaptability, the blueprints include alternate plans that replace the living room with a fourth bedroom, and substitute a squared off nook for the breakfast bay.
- In the living room version, a dramatic two-way fireplace is the only separation between the intersecting living spaces, which slope to a peak at the center of the home.
- The spacious island kitchen offers a built-in desk and a functional serving bar. Sliding glass doors in the adjoining breakfast nook open to a splendid covered porch or patio.
- A French door from the master bedroom also accesses the porch. The master suite features an oversized sitting bay, and a private bath with a garden tub and dual sinks.
- Past the hallway laundry closet, the secondary bedrooms share a full bath.

Plan BRF-1851

Bedrooms: 3+	**Baths:** 2
Living Area:	
Main floor	1,851 sq. ft.
Total Living Area:	**1,851 sq. ft.**
Garage	426 sq. ft.
Exterior Wall Framing:	2x4
Foundation Options:	
Slab	

(All plans can be built with your choice of foundation and framing. A generic conversion diagram is available. See order form.)

BLUEPRINT PRICE CODE: B

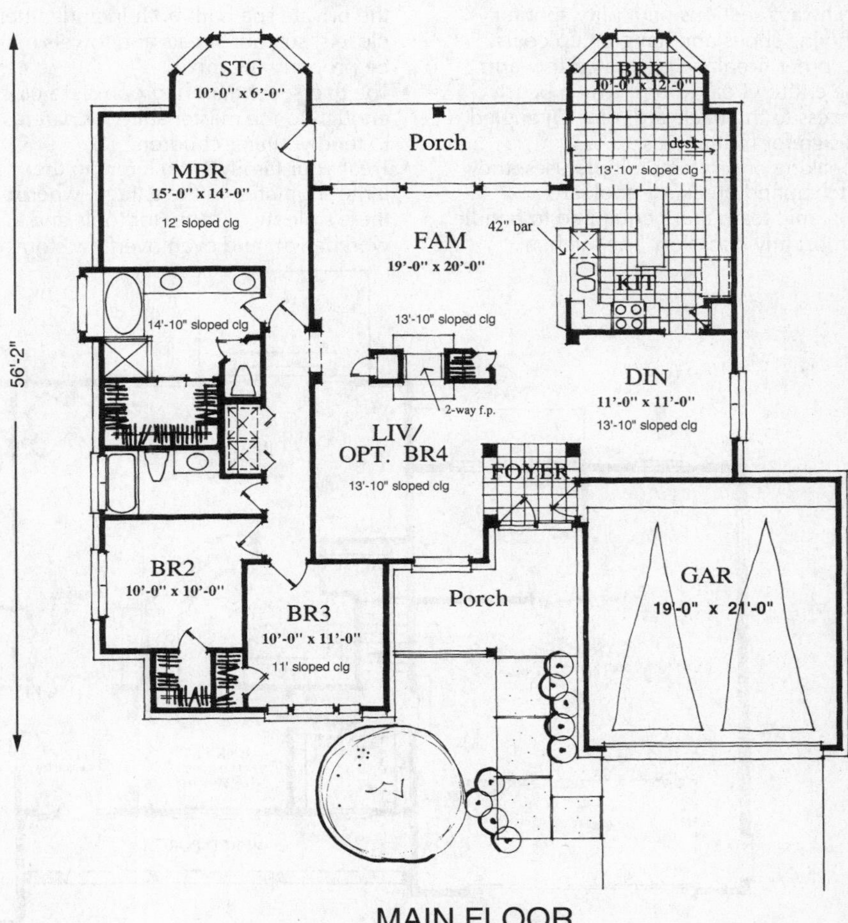

Plan BRF-1851

Plan copyright held by home designer/architect

FOR MORE DETAILS, SEE PLAN AT familyhandyman.com/homeplans

Come On In!

- Natural light from an arched clerestory window floods this home's stunning, vaulted entry. Nearby, a pair of archways sections off a nifty spot for untying shoes and hanging up coats.
- A corner fireplace is situated to warm the entire Great Room, which boasts access to the backyard, plus an angled design for multiple uses.
- Speaking of serving multiple uses, the kitchen and breakfast nook are a dynamic team that's equipped to handle almost any occasion. The kitchen features a pass-through into the Great Room, while the nook shares the entry's vaulted ceiling.
- Rest will come at last in the spacious master suite. The vaulted bedroom and the private spa bath both include linen closets, so your sheets and towels may be properly organized.
- The two secondary bedrooms are close enough to the master suite for parents to tend younger children.
- Treat your family's "tinkerer" to the large shop area in the garage, where there's plenty of room for tools and a workbench, and even overflow storage.

Plan SUN-1815

Bedrooms: 3	**Baths:** 2
Living Area:	
Main floor	1,856 sq. ft.
Total Living Area:	**1,856 sq. ft.**
Garage	638 sq. ft.
Shop	114 sq. ft.
Exterior Wall Framing:	2x6
Foundation Options:	
Crawlspace	
Slab	

(All plans can be built with your choice of foundation and framing. A generic conversion diagram is available. See order form.)

BLUEPRINT PRICE CODE: B

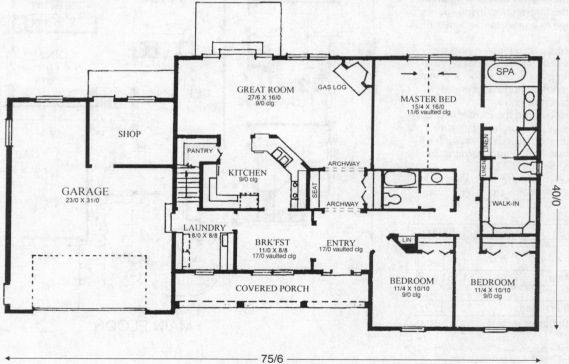

GREAT ROOM 27/6 X 16/0 9/0 clg
GAS LOG
MASTER BED 15/4 X 16/0 11/6 vaulted clg
SPA
LINEN
SHOP
PANTRY
KITCHEN 9/0 clg
ARCHWAY
SEAT
ARCHWAY
LINEN
WALK-IN
GARAGE 23/0 X 31/0
LAUNDRY 8/0 X 8/8
BRK'FST 11/0 X 8/8 17/0 vaulted clg
ENTRY 17/0 vaulted clg
LIN
COVERED PORCH
BEDROOM 11/4 X 10/10 9/0 clg
BEDROOM 11/4 X 10/10 9/0 clg
40/0
75/6

MAIN FLOOR

Plan SUN-1815

SEE ORDER INFO ON PAGES 12-15

Life Is Good

- The good life is possible in this cute, one-story, three-bedroom home. The home's exterior curb appeal is matched by its interior charm and livability.
- The leisure room is sure to become the center of family activity, with its large fireplace and unique corner-window view of the patio. A nook off the leisure room provides a quiet place to read, write or enjoy a hobby, yet remain close to family activities.
- The formal living room has a lovely bay window with a front-yard view.
- The central kitchen, as up-to-date as a demanding cook could desire, services both the formal dining room and the leisure room.
- The master suite has a bedroom with a stepped ceiling and a luxurious bath. The his-and-hers closets will accommodate extensive wardrobes, and the organized master bath is sure to get a couple off to a good start on a busy morning.
- Two additional bedrooms, both with ample closets, have convenient access to a full hall bath.

Plan LS-98814-GW

Bedrooms: 3	**Baths:** 2
Living Area:	
Main floor	1,933 sq. ft.
Total Living Area:	**1,933 sq. ft.**
Partial basement	690 sq. ft.
Garage	520 sq. ft.
Exterior Wall Framing:	2x4
Foundation Options:	
Partial basement	

(All plans can be built with your choice of foundation and framing. A generic conversion diagram is available. See order form.)

BLUEPRINT PRICE CODE: B

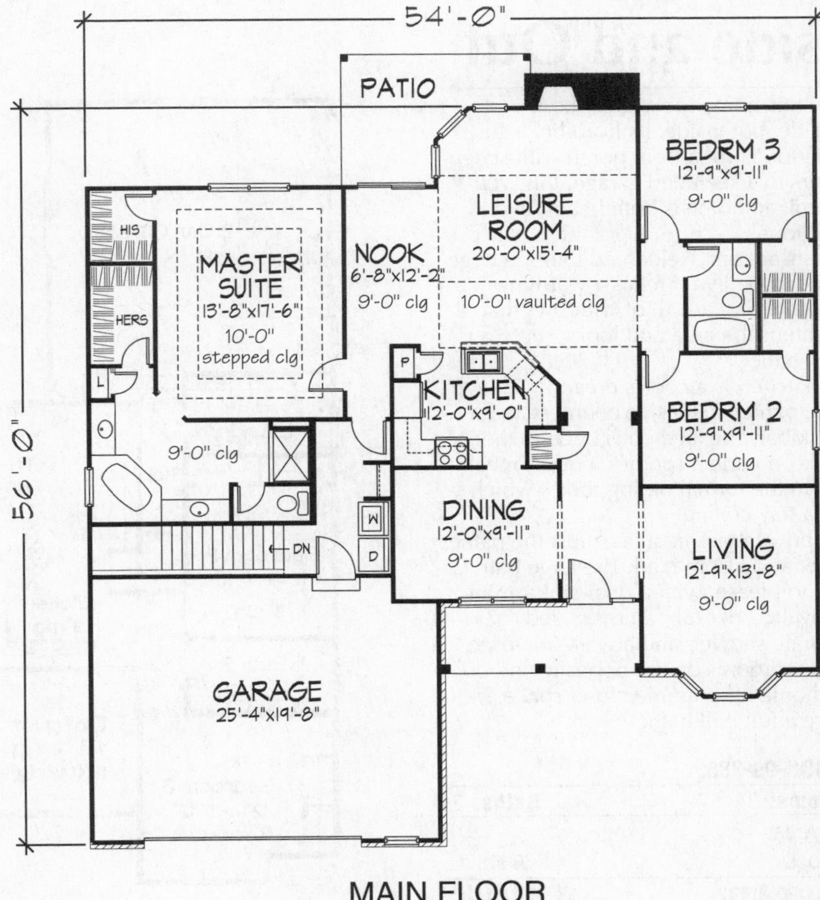

MAIN FLOOR

Plan LS-98814-GW

FOR MORE DETAILS, SEE PLAN AT familyhandyman.com/homeplans

Looks Great, Inside and Out

- Sure this home looks great on the outside, but inside, its livability is just superior. From a front porch with stately pillars to a secluded garage, this well-organized home is both beautiful and functional.
- Guests are first welcomed into the large family room, which has a warming fireplace and a wall of windows that brightens the area and looks out to a back patio.
- The kitchen is a cook's dream, with a large pantry, extensive counters and a snack bar. The kitchen is open to the nook—a perfect spot for a quick meal—and to the formal dining room, which has a tray ceiling.
- The private master suite is just the place to get away from it all. The large bath is sure to please, with a dual-sink vanity, an oval corner tub, an oversized separate shower, and a walk-in closet.
- Two bedrooms on the opposite end of the home have ample closet space and share a full hall bath.

Plan HDS-99-385	
Bedrooms: 3	**Baths:** 2
Living Area:	
Main floor	1,963 sq. ft.
Total Living Area:	**1,963 sq. ft.**
Garage	501 sq. ft.
Exterior Wall Framing:	2x4
Foundation Options:	
Crawlspace	
Slab	

(All plans can be built with your choice of foundation and framing. A generic conversion diagram is available. See order form.)

BLUEPRINT PRICE CODE:	**B**

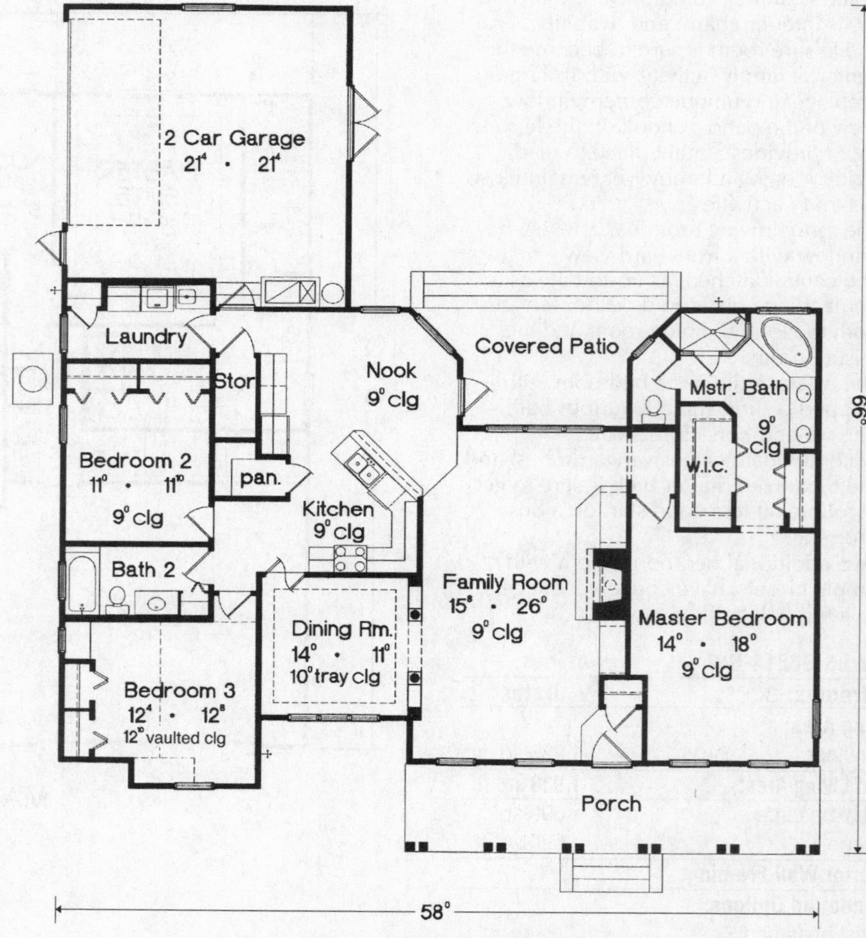

MAIN FLOOR

Plan HDS-99-385

SEE ORDER INFO ON PAGES 12-15
familyhandyman.com/homeplans

Outdoor Living at Its Best

- Porches at the front and back of this nice three-bedroom home, plus an open patio, provide terrific outdoor entertaining opportunities.
- Inside, the Great Room welcomes all, promising a wonderful place to gather around a cozy fireplace on a cold evening. The Great Room is open to the dining room.
- The kitchen has a center island and is convenient to the dining room, the Great Room, and the back porch.
- The secluded master bedroom features a luxurious private bath. The walk-in closet has built-in shelves. The nearby laundry room will save extra steps for a busy homemaker.
- On the opposite side of the home, two more bedrooms have ample closet space and share a full hall bath.

Plan J-9811	
Bedrooms: 3	**Baths:** 2
Living Area:	
Main floor	1,973 sq. ft.
Total Living Area:	**1,973 sq. ft.**
Standard basement	1,973 sq. ft.
Garage	555 sq. ft.
Storage	31 sq. ft.
Exterior Wall Framing:	2x4
Foundation Options:	
Standard basement	
Crawlspace	
Slab	
(All plans can be built with your choice of foundation and framing. A generic conversion diagram is available. See order form.)	
BLUEPRINT PRICE CODE:	**B**

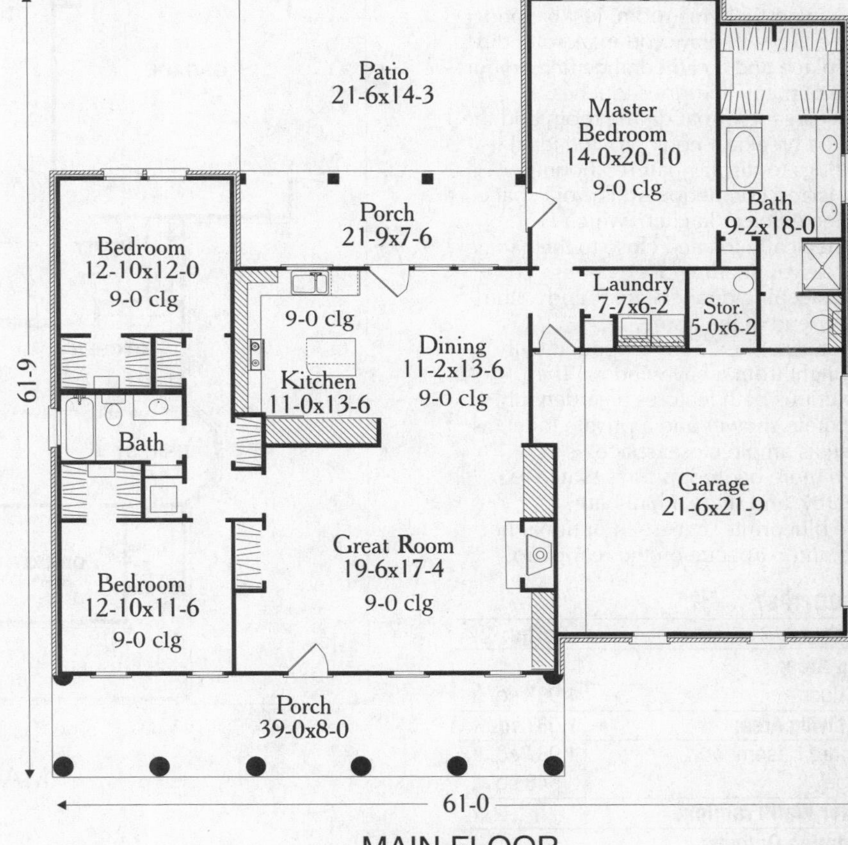

MAIN FLOOR

Plan J-9811

Easy Living

- You'll first notice the appealingly traditional exterior of this home; its modern comforts are hidden within.
- The majestic living room, just beyond the entry, will draw you in. A splendid fireplace and a cathedral ceiling are just two of many luxurious touches.
- The elegant formal dining room and the bayed breakfast nook provide ideal settings to display nature's bounty.
- An island countertop adds work space in the efficient kitchen, which is strategically located close to the garage for easy unloading of groceries.
- The sleeping quarters are found at the other end of the home.
- The master bedroom is flooded with sunlight from a bay window. The luxurious bath features a garden tub, a separate shower and a private toilet, as well as ample closet space.
- Two more bedrooms are situated nearby, and share a hall bath.
- The blueprints suggest an optional hot tub and barbecue on the rear patio.

Plan DD-1987

Bedrooms: 3	**Baths:** 2½
Living Area:	
Main floor	1,987 sq. ft.
Total Living Area:	**1,987 sq. ft.**
Standard basement	1,987 sq. ft.
Garage	548 sq. ft.
Exterior Wall Framing:	2x4

Foundation Options:
Standard basement
Crawlspace
Slab
(All plans can be built with your choice of foundation and framing. A generic conversion diagram is available. See order form.)

BLUEPRINT PRICE CODE: B

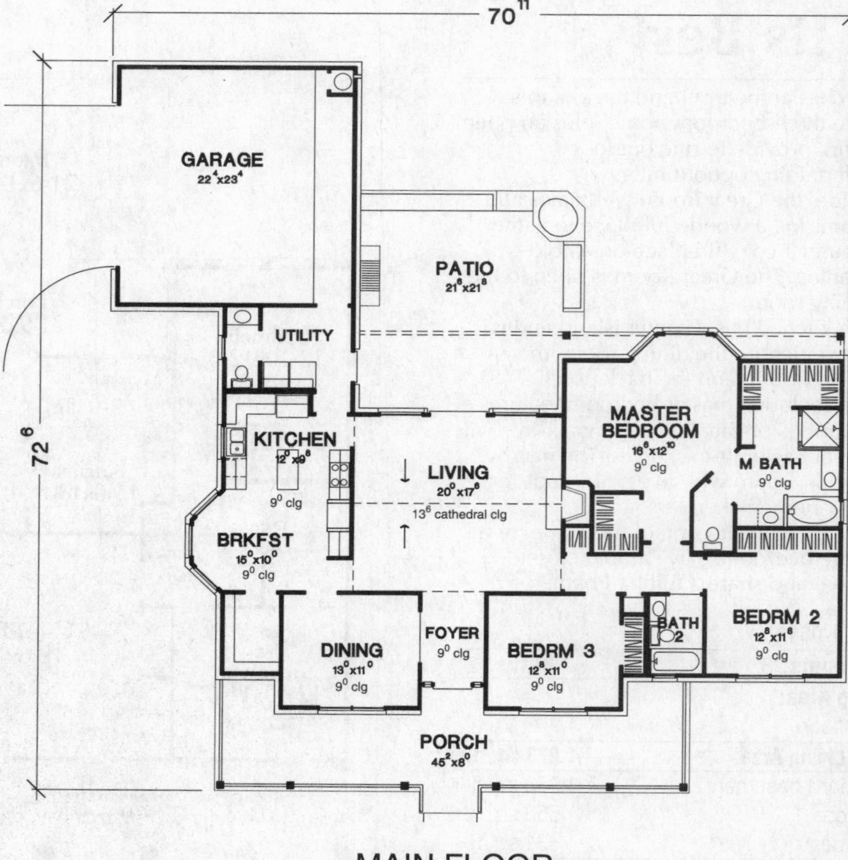

MAIN FLOOR

Plan DD-1987

SEE ORDER INFO ON PAGES 12-15

Magnificent Entry

- Magnificent pillars and a huge transom add stature to the double-door entry of this impressive home.
- Inside, the foyer enters into the open living and dining rooms. The living room features a corner fireplace and a high ceiling, while the formal dining room offers access to the back porch, deck and patio.
- A handy snack bar connects the dining room, eating nook and kitchen, which is brightened by an attractive window arrangement and a high ceiling.
- Tucked away in a private wing, the master bedroom enjoys an impressive cathedral ceiling, a walk-in closet, and a private bath with a dual-sink vanity, an oval tub, a private toilet, and a separate shower.
- Across the home, three additional bedrooms share a full hall bath with dual sinks. The front bedroom offers a high ceiling and a front-facing view.

Plan LS-98110-E	
Bedrooms: 4	**Baths:** 2
Living Area:	
Main floor	2,074 sq. ft.
Total Living Area:	**2,074 sq. ft.**
Garage	484 sq. ft.
Storage	132 sq. ft.
Exterior Wall Framing:	2x6
Foundation Options:	
Crawlspace	
Slab	

(All plans can be built with your choice of foundation and framing. A generic conversion diagram is available. See order form.)

BLUEPRINT PRICE CODE: C

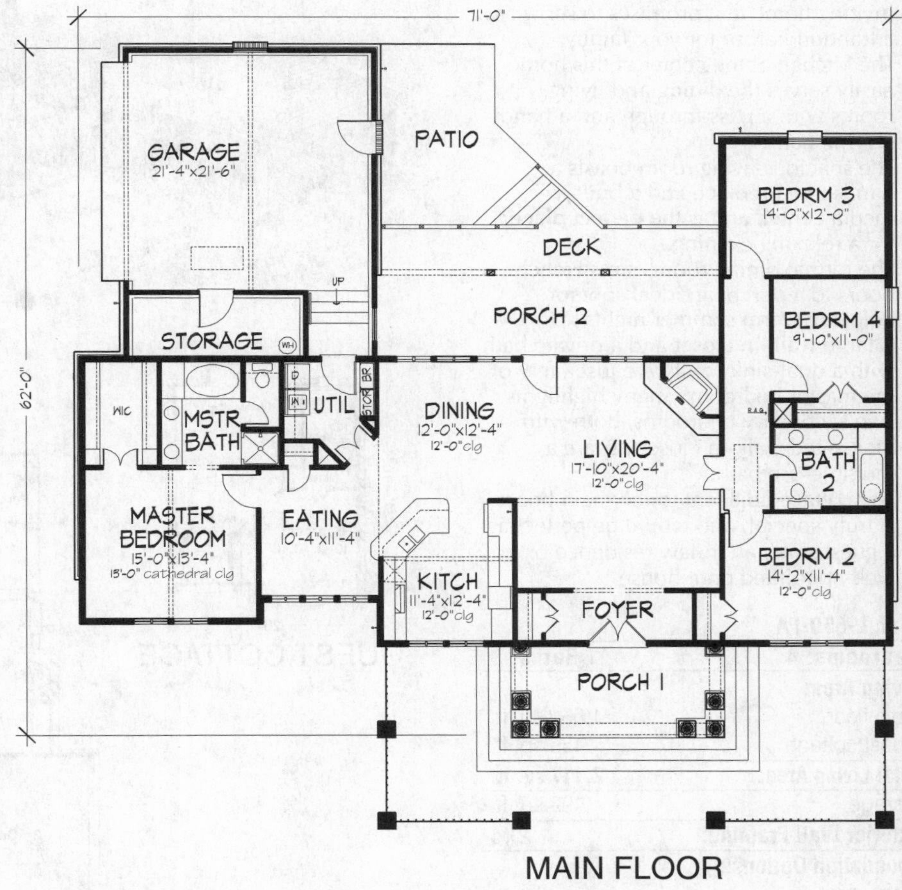

MAIN FLOOR

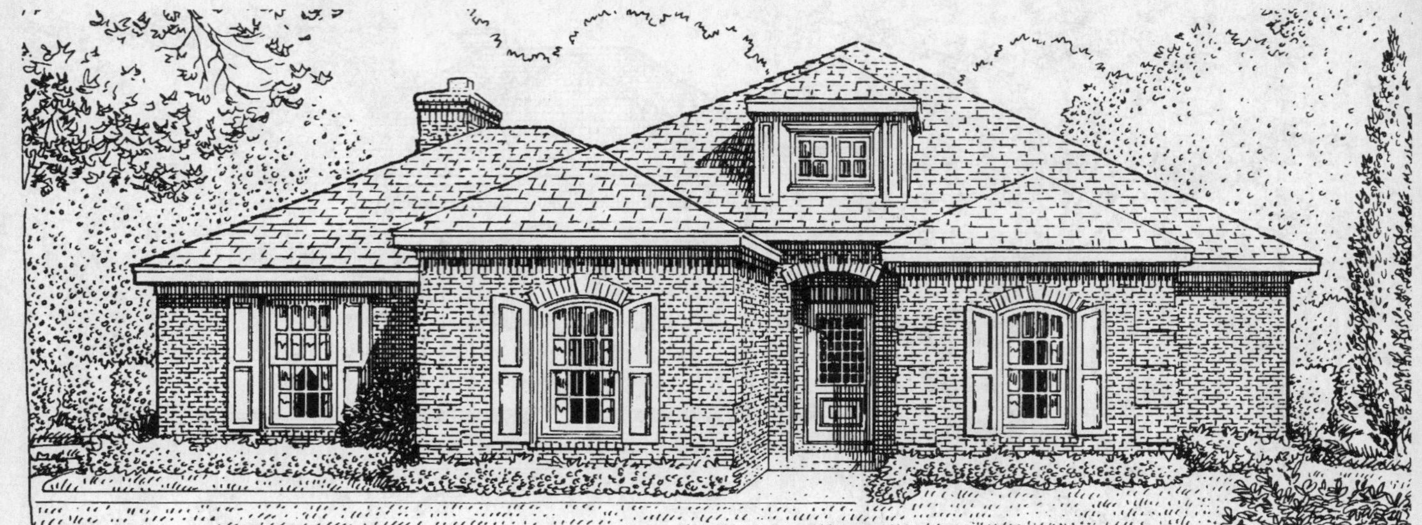

Tranquil Harbor

- Step past a lovely exterior, complete with shutters and keystones, into an inviting home that promises to serve as a tranquil harbor for your family.
- The kitchen at the center of this home easily serves the dining and living rooms with a pass-through and a handy serving bar.
- The spacious living room boasts a handsome fireplace and a built-in media center, and is the perfect place for a relaxing evening.
- The formal dining room offers French doors to a porch, an ideal spot for enjoying warm summer nights.
- A large walk-in closet and a private bath with a dual-sink vanity are just a few of the master bedroom's many highlights.
- Two secondary bedrooms, both with nice-sized walk-in closets, share a multiple-use bath.
- The cottage adjacent to the main home is truly special, and would be perfect as a guest suite, an in-law residence or a well-appointed pool house.

LEFT VIEW

Plan L-659-FA	
Bedrooms: 4	**Baths:** 3
Living Area:	
Main floor	1,661 sq. ft.
Guest cottage	456 sq. ft.
Total Living Area:	**2,117 sq. ft.**
Garage	499 sq. ft.
Exterior Wall Framing:	2x4
Foundation Options:	
Slab	

(All plans can be built with your choice of foundation and framing. A generic conversion diagram is available. See order form.)

BLUEPRINT PRICE CODE: **C**

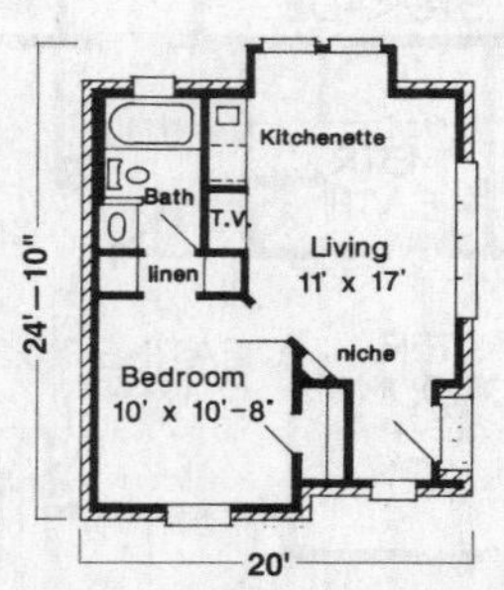

GUEST COTTAGE

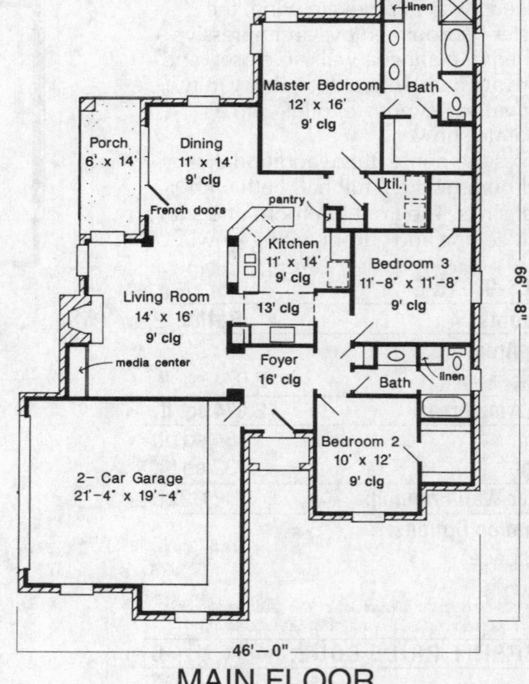

MAIN FLOOR

ORDER BLUEPRINTS ANYTIME!
CALL TOLL-FREE 1-800-820-1296

Plan L-659-FA

SEE ORDER INFO ON PAGES 12-15
familyhandyman.com/homeplans

Sunny Facade

- This home's elegant facade provides plenty of natural light for the rooms inside. Arched windows dominate, while a round window adds a lovely accent. The impressive double-door entry is framed nicely by columns and a half-round transom window.
- Inside, the foyer spills into an expansive gathering room, which boasts a vaulted ceiling, a huge window overlooking a back patio, and a warm fireplace flanked by built-ins.
- Formal areas surround the entry. The dining room features a high ceiling, while the den offers a closet, making it easy to convert into a bedroom.
- The modern kitchen features a large pantry and a handy snack bar that serves the bayed breakfast nook. In the summertime, head out to the patio to cook up your meals in the unique summer kitchen.
- A full wing of the home is dedicated to the master suite. The bedroom features a bayed sitting area and a walk-in closet. The private bath enjoys dual sinks, a corner garden tub, and a separate shower.

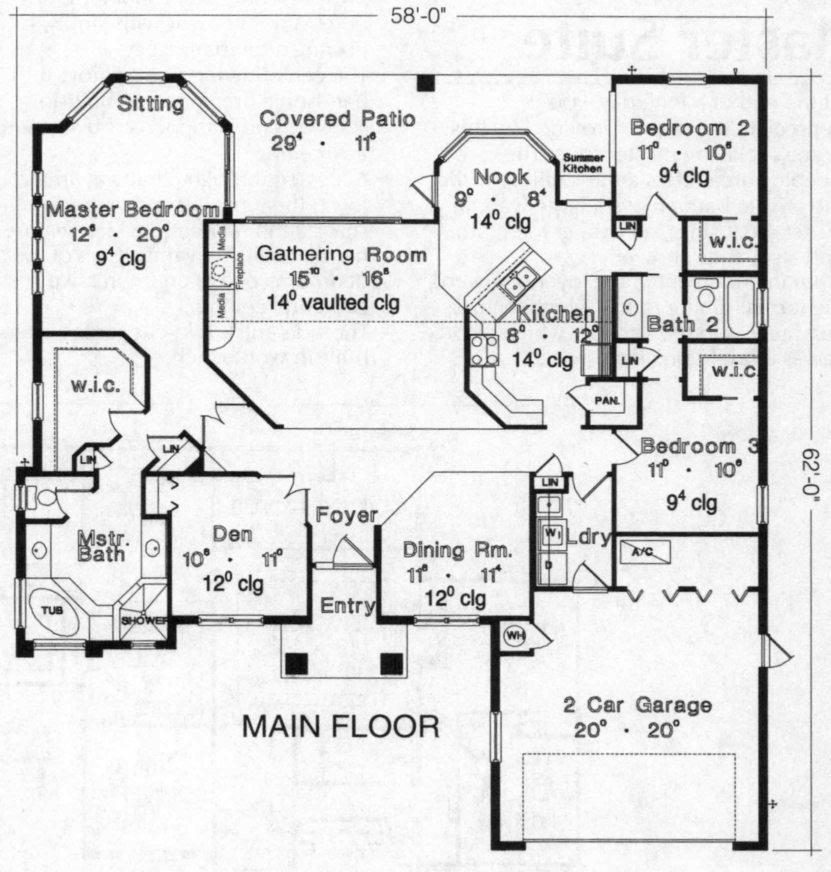

Plan HDS-99-394	
Bedrooms: 3+	**Baths:** 2
Living Area:	
Main floor	2,118 sq. ft.
Total Living Area:	**2,118 sq. ft.**
Garage	432 sq. ft.
Storage	51 sq. ft.
Exterior Wall Framing:	8-in. concrete block
Foundation Options:	
Slab	
(All plans can be built with your choice of foundation and framing. A generic conversion diagram is available. See order form.)	
BLUEPRINT PRICE CODE:	**C**

Relaxing Master Suite

- At the end of a long day, you'll appreciate the respite provided by this home's relaxing master suite. The sleeping area offers a tray ceiling, while the private bath enjoys a large walk-in closet, dual sinks, an oval garden tub, and a separate shower.
- From the main entry, the foyer opens to the formal dining room, which features easy access to the kitchen, which also serves a bright breakfast nook.
- Just off the nook, a screen porch provides the perfect spot for enjoying a quiet summer night with family, or for hosting a fun barbecue.
- The central living room enjoys a handsome fireplace and built-in shelves, and is topped off by a stunning tray ceiling.
- Accessed through a hallway in the foyer, the three secondary bedrooms share a full hall bath, which features a handy dual-sink vanity. One of the bedrooms boasts an impressive cathedral ceiling.
- The side-entry, two-car garage offers a built-in workbench.

Plan DHI-24

Bedrooms: 4	**Baths:** 2
Living Area:	
Main floor	2,178 sq. ft.
Total Living Area:	**2,178 sq. ft.**
Screen porch	200 sq. ft.
Garage and workbench	458 sq. ft.
Exterior Wall Framing:	2x4
Foundation Options:	
Slab	

(All plans can be built with your choice of foundation and framing. A generic conversion diagram is available. See order form.)

BLUEPRINT PRICE CODE: **C**

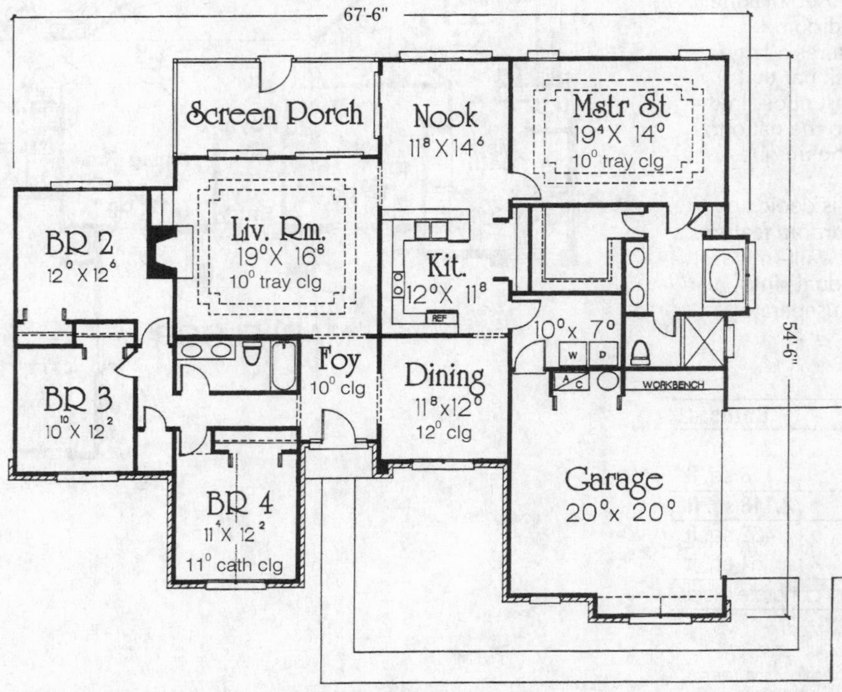

MAIN FLOOR

Plan DHI-24

SEE ORDER INFO ON PAGES 12-15

Double Dormers

- Two snappy dormers top off this home's attractive facade. The appealing look continues with ample windows, brick detailing and a sidelighted entry.
- Inside, the entry features a two-story, vaulted ceiling that is flanked by the formal areas. The living room boasts a columned entrance and a vaulted ceiling, while the formal dining room uses the same features to create a classic look.
- The family room also enjoys a vaulted ceiling, as well as a fireplace next to built-in shelves, and a wet bar, making this room perfect for entertaining.
- A handy snack bar unites the kitchen and the bright breakfast nook, which offers access to a backyard deck.
- The tucked-away master suite provides a vaulted ceiling in the sleeping area and a private bath with a walk-in closet, dual sinks, a garden tub and a separate shower.
- Two additional bedrooms on the other side of the home each enjoy ample closet space. They share a full hall bath, which offers an inviting tub.

Plan B-88092	
Bedrooms: 3	**Baths:** 2½
Living Area:	
Main floor	2,217 sq. ft.
Total Living Area:	**2,217 sq. ft.**
Standard basement	2,217 sq. ft.
Garage	427 sq. ft.
Exterior Wall Framing:	2x4
Foundation Options:	
Standard basement (All plans can be built with your choice of foundation and framing. A generic conversion diagram is available. See order form.)	
BLUEPRINT PRICE CODE:	**C**

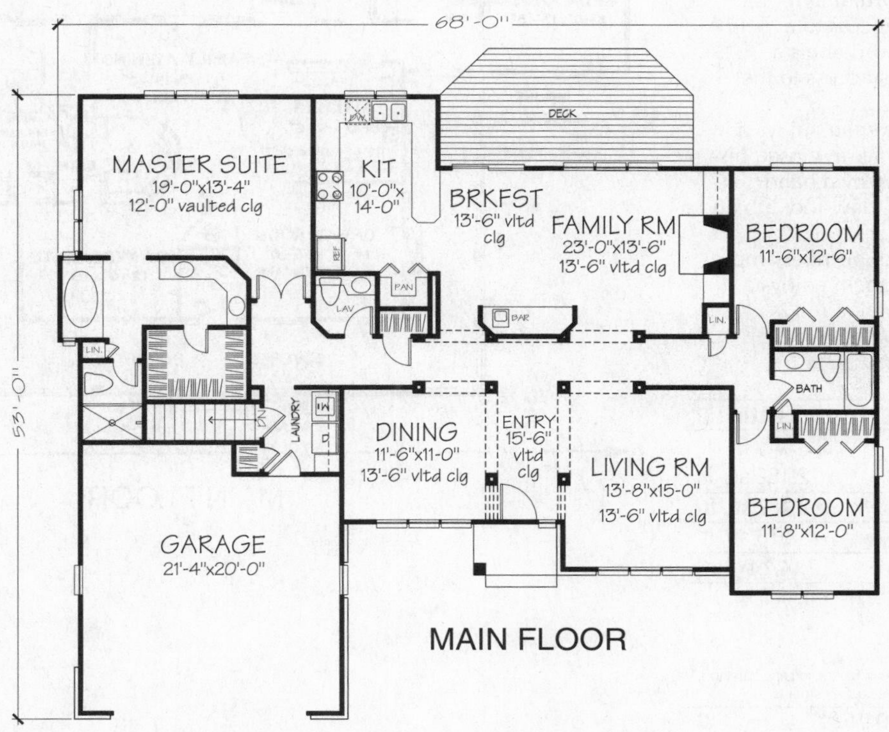

Wonderful Front Porch

- This home's impressive front porch just keeps on going, wrapping around both sides and providing plenty of room for your family and friends. The facade is made even more attractive with three dormers topping off the porch.
- Inside, the open floor plan promises easy living for all ages and abilities.
- The Great Room boasts a vaulted ceiling and a handsome fireplace.
- The sleek kitchen provides a large snack bar serving the family/dining room, which in turn offers access to a courtyard. The courtyard abuts a breezeway that grants access to the side-entry garage.
- The secluded owner's suite enjoys a private bath with a walk-in closet, his-and-hers sinks divided by a handy dressing table, plus a claw-foot tub and a private toilet.
- Both additional bedrooms offer ample closet space. One of them enjoys a built-in desk. They share a full, compartmentalized bath.

Plan PSC-2182	
Bedrooms: 3	**Baths:** 2
Living Area:	
Main floor	2,182 sq. ft.
Total Living Area:	**2,182 sq. ft.**
Garage	576 sq. ft.
Exterior Wall Framing:	2x4 or 2x6
Foundation Options:	
Crawlspace	
Slab	
(All plans can be built with your choice of foundation and framing. A generic conversion diagram is available. See order form.)	
BLUEPRINT PRICE CODE:	**C**

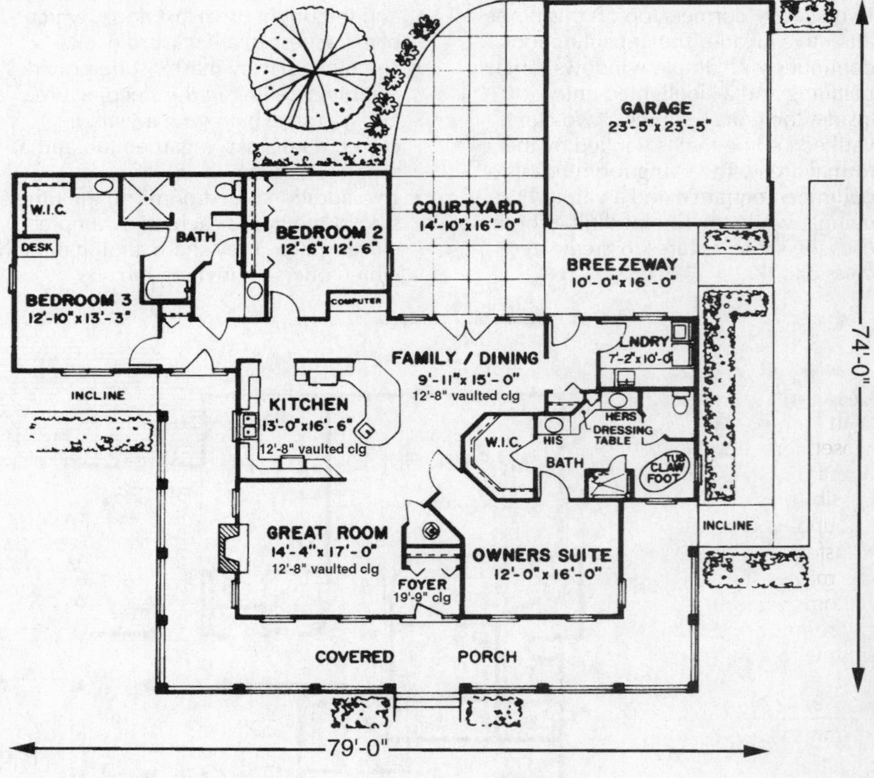

MAIN FLOOR

Plan PSC-2182

SEE ORDER INFO ON PAGES 12-15

Plenty of Space

- Plenty of space and an adaptable floor plan make this handsome design perfect for a growing family.
- Inside, the foyer unfolds into the living areas. Majestic archways introduce the family room, where a cozy fireplace is flanked by a built-in entertainment unit. Light the fire and enjoy a classic movie.
- The island kitchen boasts an adjoining breakfast nook with a built-in planning desk and a gorgeous view of the backyard through a wall of windows. Stroll out on the lanai for a dose of morning sunshine or for a casual, warm-weather meal.
- The spacious master suite includes a separate sitting area set off by a columned archway. The private master bath features an enormous walk-in closet, a garden tub, a separate shower and a dual-sink vanity.
- Possibilities for the growing family abound. The front-facing den is easily transformed into a third bedroom, and the master suite's sitting room could become a fourth. All secondary bedrooms are served by a shared full bath with dual sinks.

Plan B-92029

Bedrooms: 2+	**Baths:** 2
Living Area:	
Main floor	2,228 sq. ft.
Total Living Area:	**2,228 sq. ft.**
Garage	600 sq. ft.
Exterior Wall Framing:	2x6
Foundation Options:	
Slab	

(All plans can be built with your choice of foundation and framing. A generic conversion diagram is available. See order form.)

BLUEPRINT PRICE CODE: C

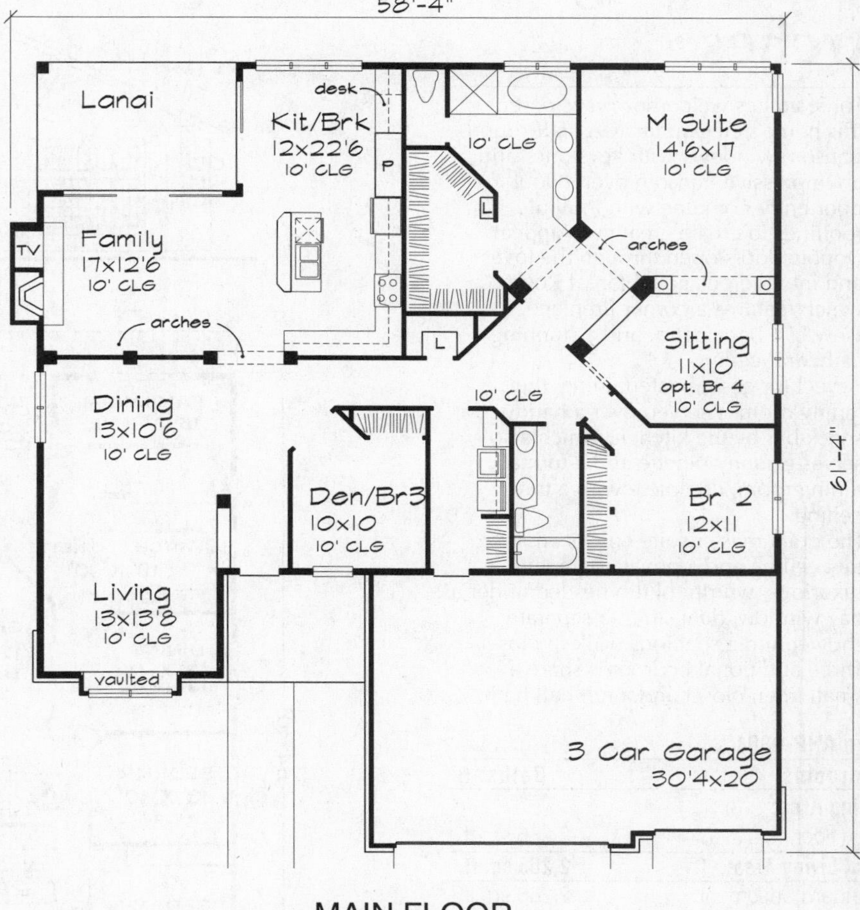

MAIN FLOOR

Plan B-92029

FOR MORE DETAILS, SEE PLAN AT familyhandyman.com/homeplans

Welcoming Arches

- Three arches welcome you as part of this home's elegant facade. Half-round transom windows with keystones and an impressive transom over a double-door entry combine with multiple rooflines to create great curb appeal.
- Double doors open through the foyer and into the octagonal Great Room, which features a corner fireplace, a view of a back patio, and a stunning cathedral ceiling.
- Perfect for casual entertaining, the family room is served over a handy snack bar by the kitchen, which also serves a sunny dinette and a formal dining room, complete with a tray ceiling.
- The quiet master suite enjoys another tray ceiling and a private bath with a luxurious, whirlpool tub nestled under a bay window, dual sinks, a separate shower and a spacious walk-in closet.
- Three additional bedrooms share a small linen closet and a full hall bath.

Plan AHP-9801

Bedrooms: 4	**Baths:** 3
Living Area:	
Main floor	2,266 sq. ft.
Total Living Area:	**2,266 sq. ft.**
Standard basement	2,266 sq. ft.
Garage	430 sq. ft.
Exterior Wall Framing:	2x4 or 2x6
Foundation Options:	
Standard basement	
Crawlspace	
Slab	

(All plans can be built with your choice of foundation and framing. A generic conversion diagram is available. See order form.)

BLUEPRINT PRICE CODE: C

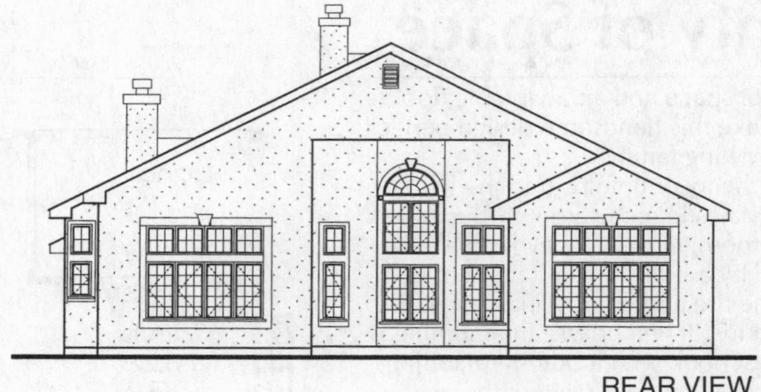

REAR VIEW

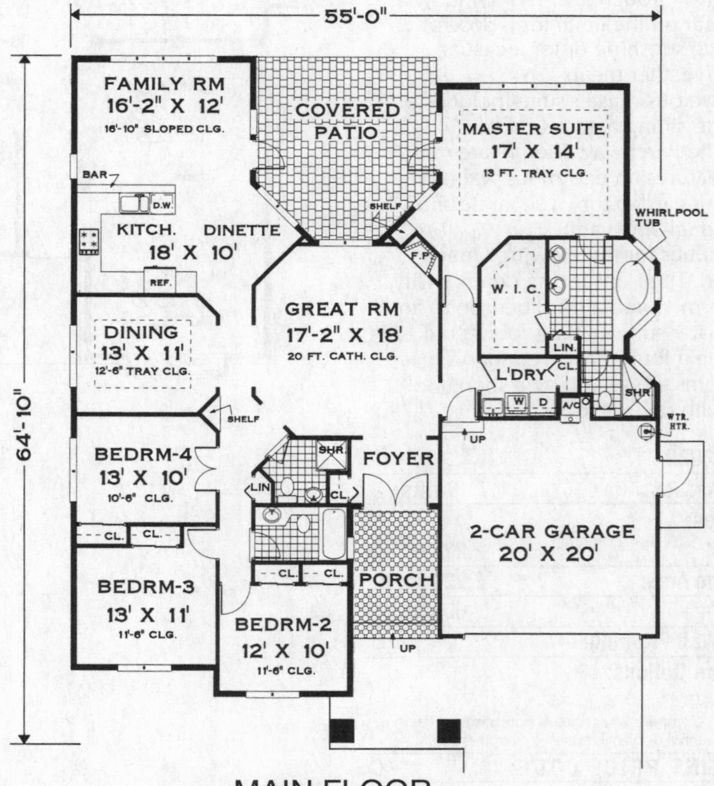

MAIN FLOOR

Plan AHP-9801

SEE ORDER INFO ON PAGES 12-15
familyhandyman.com/homeplans

Charmed Soul

- Its distinctive columned exterior offers a revealing glimpse into the charmed soul of this one-story home.
- Passersby get a view of the home's beautiful veranda, set off by those grand columns. Rambling and relaxing, the veranda is a great place for socializing on a pleasant summer evening.
- Inside, past the foyer and gallery, you'll arrive at the huge living room, complete with a cheery fireplace. A snack counter holds hors d'oeuvres from the kitchen during parties and family gatherings.
- The island kitchen is conveniently centered between the two eating areas. The casual dining room accesses a pretty covered patio in back.
- Luxury and efficiency meet in the master suite, which boasts two walk-in closets and a private bath whose tub features high glass block on three sides.
- Each of the three remaining bedrooms has a walk-in closet and is just steps from a full-size bath.

Plan L-9701-UDA

Bedrooms: 3+	**Baths:** 2
Living Area:	
Main floor	2,294 sq. ft.
Total Living Area:	**2,294 sq. ft.**
Garage and storage	606 sq. ft.
Exterior Wall Framing:	2x4
Foundation Options:	
Slab	

(All plans can be built with your choice of foundation and framing. A generic conversion diagram is available. See order form.)

BLUEPRINT PRICE CODE: C

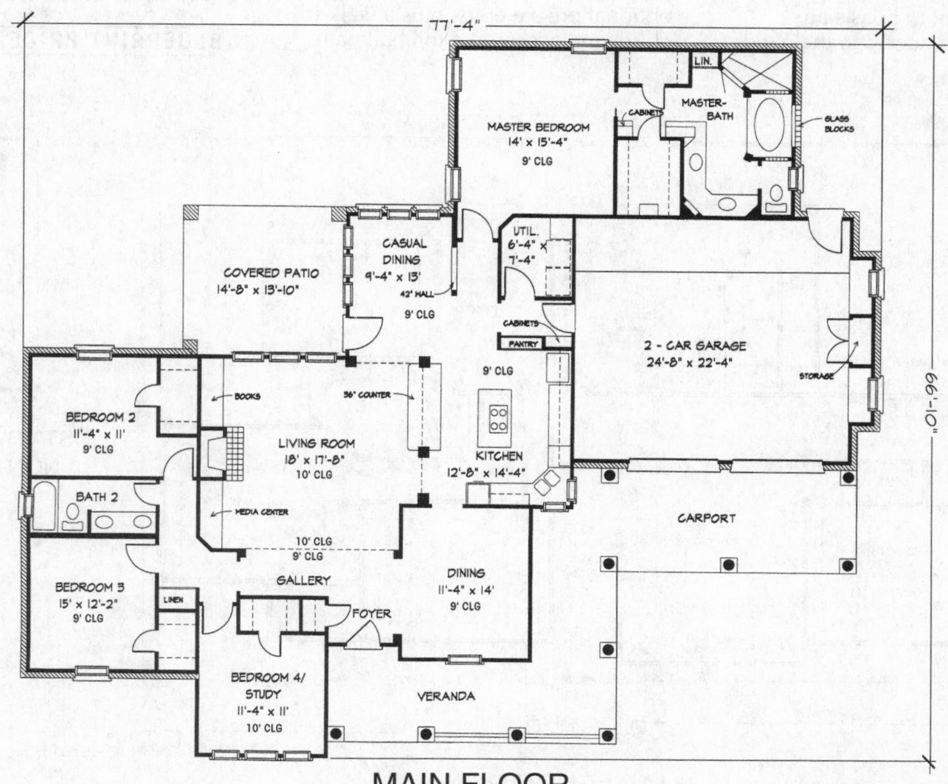

MAIN FLOOR

High Ceilings All Around

- In this home, everyone gets in on the space and beauty created by its high ceilings. Tray ceilings dominate this home, with a barrel vault thrown into the living room for spice.
- The entry opens through impressive arches to the living room, which enjoys a corner fireplace and a combination tray and barrel-vaulted ceiling.
- The formal dining room boasts an octagonal shape and access to the patio.
- You'll wonder how you ever lived without the splendid kitchen. Featuring an island workstation, a pantry and a handy snack bar serving the bright breakfast nook, the kitchen is rightfully at the center of this home.
- The enchanting master suite starts with a spacious sleeping room. The private bath boasts a walk-in closet, a dual-sink vanity, a relaxing Jacuzzi tub with a plant shelf, and a separate shower.
- The secondary bedroom offers a private bath and ample closet space.
- A unique guest room provides an optional private entry, plus a walk-in closet and access to a full hall bath.

Plan UD-120-D

Bedrooms: 3	**Baths:** 3½–4
Living Area:	
Main floor	2,532 sq. ft.
Total Living Area:	**2,532 sq. ft.**
Standard basement	2,532 sq. ft.
Garage and workbench	575 sq. ft.
Exterior Wall Framing:	2x4

Foundation Options:

Standard basement
Crawlspace
Slab

(All plans can be built with your choice of foundation and framing. A generic conversion diagram is available. See order form.)

BLUEPRINT PRICE CODE: D

83'-10"
55'-8"
GARAGE 22'-6"x23'-3"
WORKBENCH
CAB
WASH
DRY
LNDRY
CAB
BREAKFAST 15'-10"x10'-7"
PULL-DN STAIR
DN
COATS
BATH
FRIG
32"x60" TUB/SHWR
LS
EXTENDED COUNTER
KITCHEN 15'-6"x12'-8"
48"x24" ISLAND
DW
DBL OVEN
PANTRY
DINING ROOM 12'-0"x17'-8" (10' TRAY CLG)
COVERED PATIO 14'-0"x20'-4"
LIN
MASTER BATH
36"x72" JACC
PLANTS
LINEN
WALK-IN CLOSET
SHWR
32"x60" TUB/SHWR
LINEN
F.P.
GUEST BATH
WALK-IN CLOSET
LINEN
OPTIONAL DOOR & SIDEWALK
BEDROOM #3 (GUEST ROOM) 14'-8"x12'-10" (10' TRAY CLG)
LIVING ROOM 17'-0"x25'-0" (14' TRAY CLG)
ARCHES BETWEEN POSTS
BARREL VAULT OVER ARCH WINDOW
ENTRY (9' CLG)
COATS
CLOSET
CLOSET
BEDROOM #2 15'-0"x12'-9" (10' TRAY CLG)
MASTER BEDROOM 18'-0"x14'-3" (10' TRAY CLG)
LINEN
32"x60" TUB/SHWR
BATH
COVERED ENTRY

MAIN FLOOR

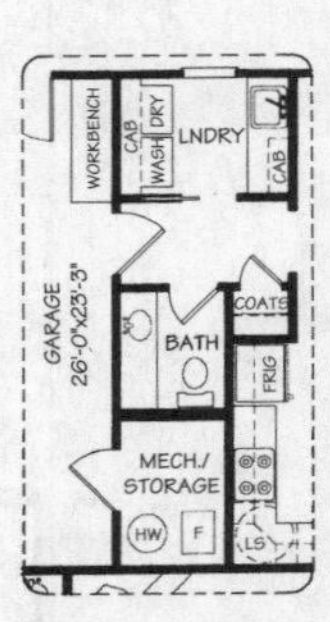

STAIRWAY AREA IN NON-BASEMENT VERSIONS

Plan UD-120-D

SEE ORDER INFO ON PAGES 12-15

Fantastic Front Porch

- This home's facade features exciting windows highlighted with keystones, a spectacular entry with a transom and sidelights, and a fantastic front porch with columns and plenty of room for sitting out on a summer night.
- Inside, the foyer opens to the expansive Great Room, which boasts a high, sloped ceiling, three double windows overlooking a backyard patio, and a handsome fireplace.
- The island kitchen includes a roomy pantry, a bayed breakfast nook with access to the patio, and across the hall, access to a formal dining room, which also offers a sloped ceiling.
- The utility room just off the breakfast nook enjoys outdoor access.
- Occupying its own wing, the master bedroom features large windows and adjoins a private bath with dual sinks, a garden tub, a separate shower, a private toilet and a large walk-in closet.
- Three additional bedrooms each offer walk-in closets and high ceilings. They share a full hall bath, which is compartmentalized for privacy.

Plan DD-2775-C

Bedrooms: 4+	**Baths:** 2½
Living Area:	
Main floor	2,783 sq. ft.
Total Living Area:	**2,783 sq. ft.**
Standard basement	2,783 sq. ft.
Exterior Wall Framing:	2x4
Foundation Options:	
Standard basement	
Crawlspace	
Slab	

(All plans can be built with your choice of foundation and framing. A generic conversion diagram is available. See order form.)

BLUEPRINT PRICE CODE: D

70'11"
51'6"
PATIO
BRKFST. 11'8" x 12'2" 10' clg
WIC
UTILITY
KITCHEN 13'11" x 13'2" 10' clg
PANTRY
GREAT ROOM 22'0" x 18'4" 10' sloped clg
MASTER BEDROOM 14'6" x 16'10" 10' sloped clg
BDRM 2 17'11" x 11'8" 9' clg
BATH 2
M. BATH 10' clg
PWD.
WIC
DINING 11'2" x 13'4" 10' sloped clg
FOYER 10' clg
WIC
BDRM 4 13'0" x 13'10" 9' clg
BDRM 3 14'11" x 12'10" 10' sloped clg
STUDY 10'7" x 11'6" 10' sloped clg
PORCH

MAIN FLOOR

Strong Symmetry

- The strong, smooth lines of this symmetrical one-story will bring forth years of joy and contentment.
- Escape to the wide front porch with a glass of lemonade and the latest best-seller in hand for a day of relaxation.
- An elegant tray ceiling and a fabulous built-in china cabinet are highlights of the formal dining room.
- Situated in the rear corner of the home, the spacious family room provides a warm, inviting space to entertain relatives and friends. It features a vaulted ceiling and a corner fireplace.
- With today's families always on the go, the U-shaped kitchen's handy eating bar makes serving meals at all hours of the day a snap. The attached breakfast room offers access to the large backyard patio.
- In search of a relaxing retreat? A soothing Jacuzzi in the master bedroom's private bath will help you to forget all the day's worries.
- Each remaining bedroom has a walk-in closet and shares a dual-sink full bath; one has French doors to the porch.

Plan UD-104-D

Bedrooms: 3	**Baths:** 2
Living Area:	
Main floor	2,651 sq. ft.
Total Living Area:	**2,651 sq. ft.**
Standard basement	2,651 sq. ft.
Garage	476 sq. ft.
Exterior Wall Framing:	2x4
Foundation Options:	
Standard basement	
Crawlspace	
Slab	

(All plans can be built with your choice of foundation and framing. A generic conversion diagram is available. See order form.)

BLUEPRINT PRICE CODE: D

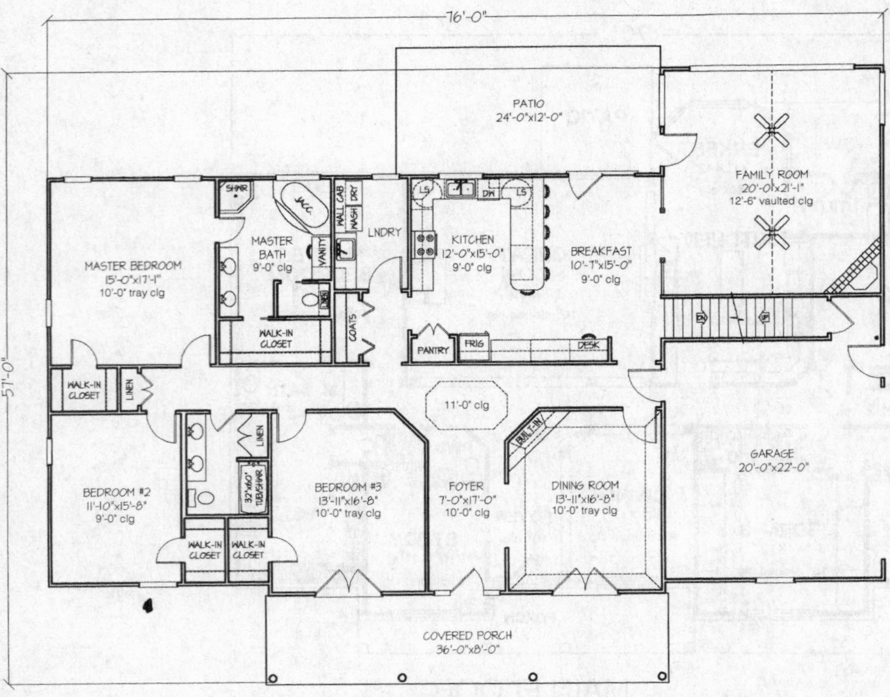

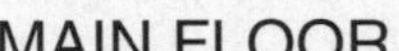
MAIN FLOOR

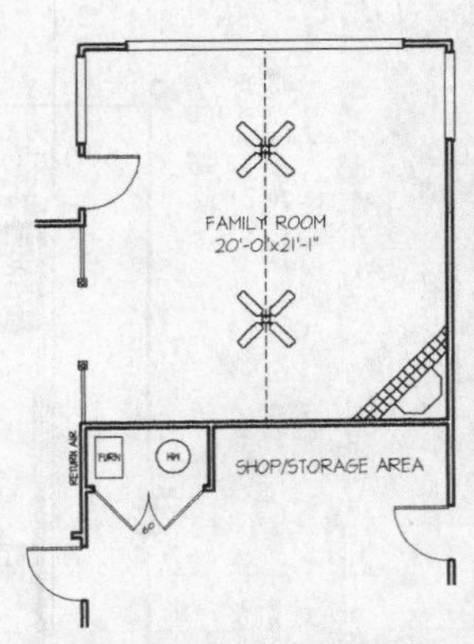

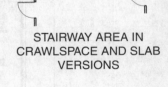

STAIRWAY AREA IN CRAWLSPACE AND SLAB VERSIONS

Plan UD-104-D

SEE ORDER INFO ON PAGES 12-15

Easy Living

- "Easy living" will become your mantra in this home, which includes sprawling shared spaces, luxurious sleeping quarters, and even a spot in the garage for a golf cart. This home has it all.
- The foyer opens to the central living room, which enjoys access to a backyard patio. Just down the hall, the corner family room offers a sloped ceiling, and a fireplace flanked by built-in shelves and a desk.
- The adjoining bayed breakfast nook is served over a snack bar by the island kitchen, which also serves the neighboring formal dining room.
- Opulence reigns in the master suite. The cavernous sleeping room is topped off with a sloped ceiling, while the private bath boasts a dual-sink vanity, a luxurious garden tub, a separate shower and two walk-in closets.
- Three additional bedrooms lie just down the hall. One bedroom enjoys a private bath, and another could be used as a study or home office.

Plan DD-3030	
Bedrooms: 3+	**Baths:** 3½
Living Area:	
Main floor	3,029 sq. ft.
Total Living Area:	**3,029 sq. ft.**
Standard basement	3,029 sq. ft.
Garage	698 sq. ft.
Exterior Wall Framing:	2x4
Foundation Options:	
Standard basement	
Crawlspace	
Slab	
(All plans can be built with your choice of foundation and framing. A generic conversion diagram is available. See order form.)	
BLUEPRINT PRICE CODE:	**E**

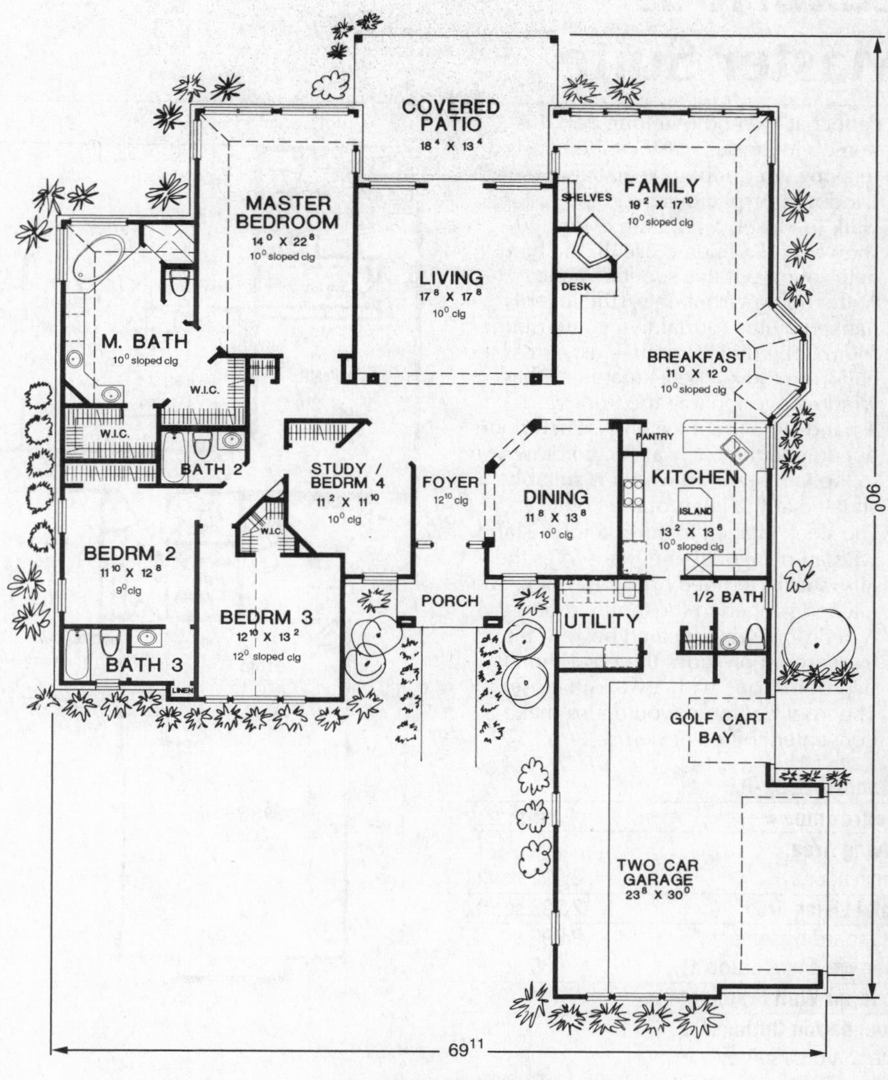

MAIN FLOOR

Luxurious Master Suite

- Perfect at the end of a long day, this home's luxurious master suite boasts a relaxing whirlpool tub surrounded by windows. A spacious bedroom, a long walk-in closet, a separate oversized shower and a linen closet in the bath help round out this superb space.
- At the home's front entry, the foyer is flanked by the formal living and dining rooms. The dining room—just across the hall from the kitchen—features a bay window overlooking the front yard.
- A handsome fireplace and French doors opening to the backyard patio draw you to the family room, which is suitably situated at the heart of the home.
- The sleek kitchen features a long island with an octagonal end that serves the airy, sunshine-filled breakfast nook. The kitchen is open to the family room.
- A bedroom wing located beyond the living room provides three additional bedrooms, one with a walk-in closet. The front bedroom would also make a convenient office or den.

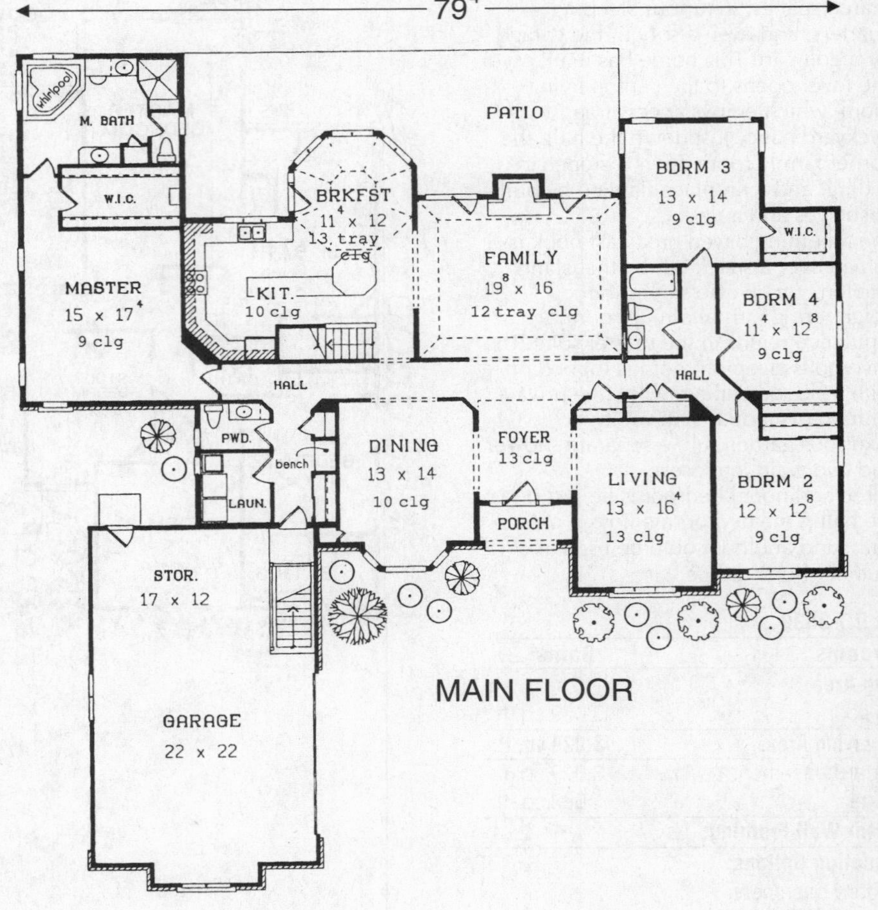

Plan GL-2992-R	
Bedrooms: 4	**Baths:** 2½
Living Area:	
Main floor	2,992 sq. ft.
Total Living Area:	**2,992 sq. ft.**
Standard basement	2,992 sq. ft.
Garage and storage	688 sq. ft.
Exterior Wall Framing:	2x6
Foundation Options:	
Standard basement (All plans can be built with your choice of foundation and framing. A generic conversion diagram is available. See order form.)	
BLUEPRINT PRICE CODE:	**D**

Plan GL-2992-R

SEE ORDER INFO ON PAGES 12-15
familyhandyman.com/homeplans